The Rise and Fall of Civilizations

Modern Archaeological Approaches to Ancient Cultures

selected readings

Jeremy A. Sabloff

C. C. Lamberg-Karlovsky

THE RISE AND FALL
OF CIVILIZATIONS

*Deep in the human unconsciousness is a
pervasive need for a logical universe that
makes sense. But the real universe is
always one step beyond logic.*

Frank Herbert, *Dune*

THE RISE AND FALL OF CIVILIZATIONS

Modern Archaeological Approaches to Ancient Cultures

Selected Readings

C. C. Lamberg-Karlovsky

Jeremy A. Sabloff

Harvard University

Cummings Publishing Company
Menlo Park, California

To Jack Ladd (1923-1971)

Cummings Publishing Company, Inc.
2727 Sand Hill Road
Menlo Park, California 94025

Preface

In 1970 we introduced at Harvard College a General Education course, "The Rise and Fall of Civilizations: An Archaeological Perspective." Increased student interest in the development of past civilizations and new anthropological approaches to study them had prompted us to pool our resources and our particular knowledge of Old World (Lamberg-Karlovsky) and New World (Sabloff) prehistory to conduct this course. We soon realized that there was neither an adequate text nor reader available to provide background for the lectures. This reader is an outgrowth of the need to fill this gap.

We believe that this book is of use on both an introductory level as well as on a more advanced level. It can be used as a basic text in introductory archaeology courses which include surveys of ancient civilizations. The reader can be a profitable aid for instructors of either New World or Old World archaeology courses by providing articles from their own areas of study as well as comparative material from a variety of other ancient civilizations. Moreover, it can be used in general archaeology or anthropology courses to illustrate approaches and new hypotheses archaeologists are currently using to help explain past civilizational developments. This reader will introduce students in history, classical archaeology, or art history courses to the anthropological/archaeological approach to ancient civilizations.

The articles have been selected to provide instructors with clear theoretical or substantive positions which can serve as a springboard for discussion and argument. For example, the evolutionary approach of the articles in Part I can either be supported or refuted in class lectures and discussions. Because the emphasis of this reader is generally theoretical or methodological rather than purely descriptive it can be a supplement to descriptive works such as Muriel Porter Weaver's *The Aztecs, Maya, and Their Predecessors,* Frankfort's *The Birth of Civilizations in the Near East,* or Kramer's *The Sumerians.*

Rather than attempting an encyclopedic coverage of all ancient civilizations, we have chosen certain papers which deal with a limited number of civilizations in detail, with a special emphasis on Mesoamerica and Mesopotamia and additional materials from Peru, Egypt, the Indus, China, and Europe. In particular, we have chosen ancient civilizations which have been the subject of recent archaeological work and which have been covered by clear, concise, and available articles, papers, or chapters. These papers have been reprinted in their original entirety (except in the few cases where noted) with the inclusion of full bibliographies and footnotes. Only a certain number of illustrations have been omitted. Included in the thirty-three readings are four original papers by Willey, Conrad, Day, and Tringham. Each reading is preceded by a short introduction identifying the author(s) and noting the importance of the paper. Our general theoretical point of view is presented in the "Introductory Remarks."

We wish to thank the Teaching Fellows at Harvard University, most particularly, Laurel Casjens and Philip Kohl who assisted us not only in the preparation of the course but also in the compilation of this reader. Mr. E. T. Wilcox, Director of General Education, and all the General Education staff have also been of great help to us. We are sincerely grateful for the cooperation of all the authors and publishers of these papers.

Lastly, we wish to dedicate this work to the memory of our friend and colleague, Dr. John Ladd. His interest in the processes of civilization stimulated our own and we feel that his premature death is an intellectual as well as a personal loss.

C. C. Lamberg-Karlovsky

Cambridge, Massachusetts   Jeremy A. Sabloff

Contents

Introductory Remarks

As archaeology developed into a recognized discipline over the last century, its practitioners joined the ranks of historians and philosophers in the search for answers to the question, why and how do civilizations develop and then collapse?

Recently, as anthropological archaeology has become explicitly interested in the formulation and testing of hypotheses concerning the 'whys' of culture change, concern with the nature of the development of civilization through time has intensified. However, basic problems, which have bothered archaeologists and other scholars throughout the years, relating to this interest still remain. One of the principal problems is definitional: what constitutes a civilization? Are there consistent criteria for distinguishing civilizations from other levels of cultural development? Are certain factors necessary for the evolution of civilization? Is the term 'civilization' synonymous with the state, and are the civilizational process and the urbanism process one and the same?

Archaeologists have experimented with several methodologies (or ways to formulate and solve a problem) in order to answer these questions. One of the earlier approaches which satisfied many scholars for decades was proposed by the British archaeologist V. Gordon Childe. In trying to answer the question, how do we define 'civilization,' Childe identified discrete elements of civilization. In his classic paper, "The Urban Revolution" (article 1), he listed ten criteria which he felt were necessary attributes for the rise of civilization.

Unfortunately, several of Childe's criteria do not appear to be related functionally, and others have proved not entirely satisfactory. For example, whereas Childe proposed that civilization and urbanism are synonymous, the ancient Maya and Egyptians apparently did not have true cities (only large ceremonial centers). Childe also stated that writing is a necessary criterion for civilization, but the Inca lacked writing. Most archaeologists would not wish to dismiss the Maya, Egyptians, and Inca from the roster of civilizations just because they lacked these criteria.

In order to rectify these mistakes, other archaeologists, who were stimulated by Childe's original ideas, proposed schemes which attempted to be more universal in their application. One good example can be found in Willey, Ekholm, and Millon's paper, "The Patterns of Farming Life and Civilization" which appeared in the *Handbook of Middle American Indians* and which offers seven criteria for defining civilization. Writing and cities are eliminated from their definition.

The Willey, Ekholm, and Millon scheme, like Childe's, emphasizes a limited number of discrete elements. To our mind, the major shortcoming of this approach to date has been that it often tends to emphasize disparate elements in a civilization rather than to treat a civilization as a functioning and evolving system. The approach, taken in

1

its extreme, can be seen in the sociologist Sorokin's view of civilization as a series of unconnected elements. He felt that civilizations cannot be seen as unified cultural systems, but only as "vast cultural dumps" (1950).

We reject this view in favor of a holistic and processual systems approach. It is our belief that this latter approach has the greatest promise for the elucidation of the evolution of particular civilizations and the revelation of possible cross-cultural regularities. When talking about systems, we start with Wagner's (1960: 6) simple definition: "The system is conceived as a set of interrelated variables, such that there are repercussions upon some or all of its member variables each time one of them is subjected to certain kinds of change."

We move on to a view of systems as developing and changing through time. That is to say, we should look at civilizations as evolutionary processes (cf. Ribiero 1968) and not as static entities. If we do adopt a systemic, processual analysis of the evolution of civilization, we then open up the possibility of testing the analogy between the evolution of civilization and 'ecological succession,' i.e. the succession of ecosystems in an ecological niche (cf. Boughey 1971). It should be noted that while the analysis of ecosystemic evolution has yielded general laws which, by definition, are universally applicable, we believe that the analysis of civilizational evolution can yield only probabilistic statements. This idea will be developed further below.

By treating civilization as a systemic process, archaeologists can focus their researches on the processes and interrelationships between particular subsystems such as technology, economics, politics, and religion. If hypotheses concerning these processes are proven to be successful explanations in one region, they should then be tested cross-culturally. In this sense, the study of urbanism, for example, can be viewed as the study of the processual development of one important subsystem, and a complicated one at that, of the whole civilizational system and process.

In other words, we would envision a working definition of civilization which would draw the line between civilization and noncivilization at those points in evolutionary processes when there is a systemic development involving related increases in stratification, population size and density, strength of ruling polity, trade, size and role of markets, technological advances, and so on. A cross-culturally valid definition like this, however, *still* has to be worked out by archaeologists.

When it is worked out, though, it will differ from the discrete element definition in that it will be a processual configuration. It will not consist of unrelated elements, but will consist of a complicated group of interrelated cultural processes which must be looked at through time and not at any one static point.

A systemic approach like the one too briefly sketched above eliminates a concern for such problems as 'is X a civilization even though it does not have large urban centers?' or 'is Y a civilization even though it lacks writing?' It is not the presence or absence of individual cultural traits or groups of traits which is important, but the interaction of a number of traits or trait groups. Some of these traits may often indicate that the level of civilization has been achieved but may not be causal factors to their rise, while others, such as social stratification, for example, may be necessary but not sufficient factors.

It is our belief that the systemic approach holds much promise for future civilizational studies. In relation to the time-honored and oft-debated question of the collapse of

Classic Maya civilization, it has brought us closer to an answer (or at least made us aware of the exact questions which must be answered) than have decades of single factor, catastrophic hypotheses (see Willey and Shimkin, article 9; also cf. Sabloff 1971, 1973). It also leads to the abandonment of once exciting but now out-of-date, single factor hypotheses, such as 'rich river-levee lands caused the rise of civilization,' and substitutes more sophisticated and generalizing hypotheses which link natural resources, technological exploitation of these resources, trade, and the rise of stratified societies (see, for example, Flannery, article 6).

This is not to say that the systemic approach to civilizational analysis is the 'be-all' and 'end-all' in archaeological explanation. It is a model which must be tested by its ability to produce useful and acceptable hypotheses about the rise, maintenance, and fall of specific civilizations. If possible, the approach should also yield strong cross-cultural probability statements about the nature of all civilizational change. Its practitioners must also take care not to create internally sophisticated and elegant schema which have little or no relation to reality. For example, what interrelationships can be shown archaeologically, and which ones must employ ethnographic analogies? How reliable, quantifiably speaking, are computer simulations of archaeologically unobtainable subsystems of past civilizations? Can these simulations be tested in a noncircular manner?

The above questions also relate directly to the goal of explaining the civilizational process. Will the archaeologist be able to arrive at general, absolute laws of culture change as some archaeologists would have us believe (cf. Fritz and Plog 1970; Watson, LeBlanc, and Redman 1971)? Or, as the archaeologist's systems model gets statistically further and further removed from reality with each additional analogical leap he is forced to make, will his ultimate goal become one of producing probabilistic statements about the nature of civilizational processes (cf. Meehan 1968; Tuggle et al. 1972; Willey and Sabloff 1973: Chapter 6)? We definitely believe that the systemic approach to the analysis of past civilizations leads to the latter conclusion and that general or covering laws regarding the rise and fall of civilizations are an unreachable goal for archaeologists. This is not to say, however, that they should not try to produce theories of as great as possible statistical strength, or that they should abandon the search for regularities in the civilizational trajectory through time and space. Nevertheless, the barrenness of absolutism can be just as confining as the narrowness of particularism. Some of our colleagues may look askance at our ready willingness to accept such a middle road, but we believe that the intellectual path we choose to follow is as valid as either extreme.

In brief, we believe that the archaeologist must stop at the level of probabilistic statement rather than general law while using the ecosystemic model. This is because the cultural factor in the evolution of specific civilizations is so complex and unique that the significant intervening variables in the systemic model would be lost when reducing the model to the level of general laws. Such a reduction would separate the model from reality to such a degree that it would be useless in explaining the evolution of civilization.

By using a processual model which is analogous to the ecosystemic one, archaeologists can attempt to study specific environmental parameters and levels of cultural development and look at specific adaptive changes. Furthermore, they can attempt to formulate hypotheses as to the systemic effects of changes within different kinds of parameters. That is, they can look for regularities in systemic change. Are some subsystems more important than others as regards the beginning or stimulation of change? Does a certain type of change in one subsystem lead to definite kinds of changes in others in most circumstances? For example, does an increase in population density usually lead to an increase in class stratification with many consequent ramifications, no matter what caused the population increase? These are the kinds of questions which archaeologists are and will be asking.

To conclude, the reader will see in the following essays that the archaeologist is still close to the early stages of explaining why and how civilizations rise, maintain themselves, and fall. There are a few hints of regularities, but no generally accepted laws of civilizational change. However, as can be seen in these essays, and in much recent archaeological research of civilizations, too, there are many important leads which were suggested in the past and remain to be tested. Furthermore, there are a vast number of exciting possibilities suggested by current research designs and studies with their explicit and sophisticated conceptual frameworks and strategies. For these reasons, we are quite optimistic and excited about the outlook for the future in civilizational studies and hope that the articles which follow will stimulate a similar excitement for the reader.

References

Boughey, A.S. 1971. *Man and the Environment.* MacMillan.

Fritz, J.M. and F. T. Plog. 1970. "The Nature of Archaeological Explanation." *American Antiquity*, Vol. 35, No. 4, pp. 405-12.

Meehan, E.J. 1968. *Explanation in Social Science.* Dorsey.

Ribiero, D. 1968. *The Civilizational Process.* Smithsonian Institution Press.

Sabloff, J.A. 1971. "The Collapse of Classic Maya Civilization." In: *The Patient Earth,* (edited by J. Harte and R. Socolow), pp. 16-27. Holt, Rinehart and Winston.

———— . 1973. "Major Themes in the Past Hypotheses of the Collapse." In: *The Classic Maya Collapse,* (edited by T. P. Culbert). University of New Mexico Press.

Sorokin, P.A. 1950. *Social Philosophies of an Age of Crises.* Beacon Press.

Tuggle, H.D.; A. H. Townsend, and T.J. Riley. 1972. "Laws, Systems, and Research Designs: A Discussion of Explanation in Archaeology." *American Antiquity*, Vol. 37, No. 1, pp. 3-12.

Wagner, P.L. 1960. *The Human Use of the Earth.* Free Press.

Watson, P.J.; S.A. LeBlanc, and C.L. Redman. 1971. *Explanation in Archaeology.* Columbia University Press.

Willey, G.R.; G. F. Ekholm, and R.F. Millon. 1965. "The Patterns of Farming Life and Civilization." In: *Handbook of Middle American Indians,* Vol. 1 (edited by R. Wauchope and G.R. Willey), pp. 446-498. University of Texas Press.

Willey, G.R. and J.A. Sabloff. 1973. *A History of American Archaeology.* Thames and Hudson.

Part I

Background

V. Gordon Childe (1892-1957) was director of the Institute of Archaeology in London from 1946 until his death. His many books on Old World archaeology and archaeological theory (including *The Dawn of European Civilization*, 1957; *Man Makes Himself*, 1951; *Social Evolution*, 1951; *What Happened in History*, 1954; and *A Short Introduction to Archaeology*, 1956) made him justly famous as a synthesizer and interpreter of prehistoric data. This article represents his classic definition of what is meant by *civilization*. The article met with trenchant criticisms and was later revised by Childe himself, but it still represents the basic starting point for any archaeological discussion of civilization.

The Urban Revolution

V. Gordon Childe

The concept of 'city' is notoriously hard to define. The aim of the present essay is to present the city historically—or rather prehistorically— as the resultant and symbol of a 'revolution' that initiated a new economic stage in the evolution of society. The word 'revolution' must not of course be taken as denoting a sudden violent catastrophe; it is here used for the culmination of a progressive change in the economic structure and social organisation of communities that caused, or was accompanied by, a dramatic increase in the population affected— an increase that would appear as an obvious bend in the population graph were vital statistics available. Just such a bend is observable at the time of the Industrial Revolution in England. Though not demonstrable statistically, comparable changes of direction must have occurred at two earlier points in the demographic history of Britain and other regions. Though perhaps less sharp and less durable, these too should indicate equally revolutionary changes in economy. They may then be regarded likewise as marking transitions between stages in economic and social development.

Sociologists and ethnographers last century classified existing pre-industrial societies in a hierarchy of three evolutionary stages, denominated respectively 'savagery,' 'barbarism' and 'civilisation.' If they be defined by suitably selected criteria, the logical hierarchy of stages can be transformed into a temporal sequence of ages, proved archaeologically to follow one another in the same order wherever they occur. Savagery and barbarism are conveniently recognized and appropriately defined by the methods adopted for procuring food. Savages live exclusively on wild food obtained by collecting, hunting or fishing. Barbarians on the contrary at least supplement these natural resources by cultivating edible plants and—in the Old World north of the Tropics— also by breeding

Reprinted from *Town Planning Review*, Vol. 21, No. 1, by permission of the Liverpool University Press. Copyright 1950 by the Liverpool University Press.

animals for food.

Throughout the Pleistocene Period—the Palaeolithic Age of archaeologists—all known human societies were savage in the foregoing sense, and a few savage tribes have survived in out of the way parts to the present day. In the archaeological record barbarism began less than ten thousand years ago with the Neolithic Age of archaeologists. It thus represents a later, as well as a higher stage, than savagery. Civilization cannot be defined in quite such simple terms. Etymologically the word is connected with 'city,' and sure enough life in cities begins with this stage. But 'city' is itself ambiguous so archaeologists like to use 'writing' as a criterion of civilization; it should be easily recognizable and proves to be a reliable index to more profound characters. Note, however, that, because a people is said to be civilized or literate, it does not follow that all its members can read and write, nor that they all lived in cities. Now there is no recorded instance of a community of savages civilizing themselves, adopting urban life or inventing a script. Wherever cities have been built, villages of preliterate farmers existed previously (save perhaps where an already civilized people have colonized uninhabited tracts). So civilization, wherever and whenever it arose, succeeded barbarism.

We have seen that a revolution as here defined should be reflected in the population statistics. In the case of the Urban Revolution the increase was mainly accounted for by the multiplication of the numbers of persons living together, i.e., in a single built-up area. The first cities represented settlement units of hitherto unprecedented size. Of course it was not just their size that constituted their distinctive character. We shall find that by modern standards they appeared ridiculously small and we might meet agglomerations of population today to which the name city would have to be refused. Yet a certain size of settlement and density of population, is an essential feature of civilization.

Now the density of population is determined by the food supply which in turn is limited by natural resources, the techniques for their exploitation and the means of transport and food-preservation available. The last factors have proved to be variables in the course of human history, and the technique of obtaining food has already been used to distinguish the consecutive stages termed savagery and barbarism. Under the gathering economy of savagery population was always exceedingly sparse. In aboriginal America the carrying capacity of normal unimproved land seems to have been from .05 to .10 per square mile. Only under exceptionally favourable conditions did the fishing tribes of the Northwest Pacific coast attain densities of over one human to the square mile. As far as we can guess from the extant remains, population densities in palaeolithic and pre-neolithic Europe were less than the normal American. Moreoever such hunters and collectors usually live in small roving bands. At best several bands may come together for quite brief periods on ceremonial occasions such as the Australian corroborrees. Only in exceptionally favoured regions can fishing tribes establish anything like villages. Some settlements on the Pacific coasts comprised thirty or so substantial and durable houses, accommodating groups of several hundred persons. But even these villages were only occupied during the winter; for the rest of the year their inhabitants dispersed in smaller groups. Nothing comparable has been found in pre-neolithic times in the Old World.

The Neolithic Revolution certainly allowed an expansion of population and enormously increased the carrying capacity of suitable land. On the Pacific Islands neolithic societies today attain a density of 30 or more persons to the square mile. In pre-Columbian North America, however, where the land is not obviously restricted by surrounding seas, the maximum density recorded is just under 2 to the square mile.

Neolithic farmers could of course, and certainly did, live together in permanent villages, though, owing to the extravagant rural economy generally practised, unless the crops were watered by irrigation, the villages had to be shifted at least every twenty years. But on the whole the growth of population was not reflected so much in the enlargement of the settlement unit as in a multiplication of settlements. In ethnography neolithic villages can boast only a few hundred inhabitants (a couple of 'pueblos' in New Mexico house over a thousand, but perhaps they cannot be regarded as neolithic). In prehistoric Europe the largest neolithic village yet known, Barkaer in Jutland, comprised 52 small, one-roomed dwellings, but 16 to 30 houses was a more normal figure; so the average local group in neolithic times would average 200 to 400 members.

These low figures are of course the result of technical limitations. In the absence of wheeled vehicles and roads for the transport of bulky crops men had to live within easy walking distance of their cultivations. At the same time the normal rural economy of the Neolithic Age, what is now termed slash-and-burnt or jhumming, condemns much more than half the arable land to lie fallow so that large areas were required. As soon as the population of a settlement rose above the numbers that could be supported from the accessible land, the excess had to hive off and found a new settlement.

The Neolithic Revolution had other consequences beside increasing the population, and their exploitation might in the end help to provide for the surplus increase. The new economy allowed, and indeed required, the farmer to produce every year more food than was needed to keep him and his family alive. In other words it made possible the regular production of a social surplus. Owing to the low efficiency of neolithic technique, the surplus produced was insignificant at first, but it could be increased till it demanded a reorganization of society.

Now in any Stone Age society, palaeolithic or neolithic, savage or barbarian, everybody can at least in theory make at home the few indispensable tools, the modest cloths and the simple ornaments everyone requires. But every member of the local community, not disqualified by age, must contribute actively to the communal food supply by personally collecting, hunting, fishing, gardening or herding. As long as this holds good, there can be no full-time specialists, no persons nor class of persons who depend for their livelihood on food produced by others and secured in exchange for material or immaterial goods or services.

We find indeed to day among Stone Age barbarians and even savages expert craftsmen (for instance flint-knappers among the Ona of Tierra del Fuego), men who claim to be experts in magic, and even chiefs. In palaeolithic Europe too there is some evidence for magicians and indications of chieftainship in pre-neolithic times. But on closer observation we discover that today these experts are not full-time specialists. The Ona flintworker must spend most of his time hunting; he only adds to his diet and his prestige by making arrowheads for clients who reward him with presents. Similarly a pre-Columbian chief, though entitled to customary gifts and services from his fellowers, must still personally lead hunting and fishing expeditions and indeed could only maintain his authority by his industry and prowess in these pursuits. The same holds good of barbarian societies that are still in the neolithic stage, like the Polynesians where industry in gardening takes the place of prowess in hunting. The reason is that there simply will not be enough food to go round unless every member of the group contributes to the supply. The social surplus is not big enough to feed idle mouths.

Social division of labour, save those rudiments imposed by age and sex, is thus impossible. On the contrary community of employment, the common absorbtion in obtaining food by similar devices guarantees a certain solidarity to the group. For co-operation is essential to secure food and shelter and for defence against foes, human and sub-human. This identity of economic interests and pursuits is echoed and magnified by identity of language, custom and belief; rigid conformity is enforced as effectively as industry in the common quest for food. But conformity and industrious co-operation need no State organization to maintain them. The local group usually consists either of a single clan (persons who believe themselves descended from a common ancestor or who have earned a mystical claim to such descent by ceremonial adoption) or a group of clans related by habitual intermarriage. And the sentiment of kinship is reinforced or supplemented by common rites focussed on some ancestral shrine or sacred place. Archaeology can provide no evidence for kinship organization, but shrines occupied the central place in preliterate villages in Mesopotamia, and the long barrow, a collective tomb that overlooks the presumed site of most neolithic villages in Britain, may well have been also the ancestral shrine on which converged the emotions and ceremonial activities of the villagers below. However, the solidarity thus idealized and concretely symbolized, is really based on the same principles as that of a pack of wolves or a herd of sheep; Durkheim has called it 'mechanical.'

Now among some advanced barbarians (for instance tattooers or woodcarvers among the Maori) still technologically neolithic we find expert craftsmen tending towards the status of full-time professionals, but only at the cost of breaking away from the local community. If no single village can produce a surplus large enough to feed a full-time specialist all the year round, each should produce enough to keep him a week or so. By going round from village to village an expert might thus live entirely from his craft. Such itinerants will lose their membership of the sedentary kinship group. They may in the end form an analogous organization of their own—a craft clan, which, if it remain hereditary, may become a caste, or, if it recruit its members mainly by adoption (apprenticeship throughout Antiquity and the Middle Age was just temporary adoption), may turn into a guild. But such specialists, by emancipation from kinship ties, have also forfeited the protection of the kinship organization which alone under barbarism, guaranteed to its members security of person and property. Society must be reorganized to accommodate and protect them.

In pre-history specialization of labour presumably began with similar itinerant experts. Archaeological proof is hardly to be expected, but in ethnography metal-workers are nearly always full time specialists. And in Europe at the beginning of the Bronze Age metal seems to have been worked and purveyed by perambulating smiths who seem to have functioned like tinkers and other itinerants of much more recent times. Though there is no such positive evidence, the same probably happened in Asia at the beginning of metallurgy. There must of course have been in addition other specialist craftsmen whom, as the Polynesian example warns us, archaeologists could not recognize because they worked in perishable materials. One result of the Urban Revolution will be to rescue such specialists from nomadism and to guarantee them security in a new social organization.

About 5,000 years ago irrigation cultivation (combined with stock-breeding and fishing) in the valleys of the Nile, the Tigris-Euphrates and the Indus had begun to yield a social surplus, large enough to support a number of resident specialists who were themselves released from food-production. Water-transport, supplemented in Mesopotamia and the Indus valley by wheeled vehicles and even in Egypt by pack animals, made it easy to gather food stuffs at a few centres. At the same time dependence on river water for the irrigation of the crops restricted the cultivable areas while the necessity of canalizing the waters and protecting habitations against annual floods encouraged the aggregation of population. Thus arose the first cities—units of settlement ten times as great as any known neolithic village. It can be argued that all cities in the old world are offshoots of those of Egypt, Mesopotamia and the Indus basin. So the latter need not be taken into account if a minimum definition of civilization is to be inferred from a comparison of its independent manifestations.

But some three millennia later cities arose in Central America, and it is impossible to prove that the Mayas owed anything directly to the urban civilizations of the Old World. Their achievements must therefore be taken into account in our comparison, and their inclusion seriously complicates the task of defining the essential preconditions for the Urban Revolution. In the Old World the rural economy which yielded the surplus was based on the cultivation of cereals combined with stock-breeding. But this economy had been made more efficient as a result of the adoption of irrigation (allowing cultivation without prolonged fallow periods) and of important inventions and discoveries—metallurgy, the plough, the sailing boat and the wheel. None of these devices was known to the Mayas; they bred no animals for milk or meat; though they cultivated the cereal maize, they used the same sort of slash-and-burn method as neolithic farmers in prehistoric Europe or in the Pacific Islands today. Hence the minimum definition of a city, the greatest factor common to the Old World and the New will be substantially reduced and impoverished by the inclusion of the Maya. Nevertheless ten rather abstract criteria, all deducible from archaeological data, serve to distinguish even the earliest cities from any older or contemporary village.

(1) In point of size the first cities must have been more extensive and more densely populated than any previous settlements, although considerably smaller than many villages today. It is indeed only in Mesopotamia and India that the first urban populations can be estimated with any confidence or precision. There excavation has been sufficiently extensive and intensive to reveal both the total area and the density of building in sample quarters and in both respects has disclosed significant agreement with less industrialized Oriental cities today. The population of Sumerian cities, thus calculated, ranged between 7,000 and 20,000; Harappa and Mohenjo-daro in the Indus valley must have approximated to the higher figure. We can only infer that Egyptian and Maya cities were of comparable magnitude from the scale of public works, presumably executed by urban populations.

(2) In composition and function the urban population already differed from that of any village. Very likely indeed most citizens were still also peasants, harvesting the lands and waters adjacent to the city. But all cities must have accommodated in addition classes who did not themselves procure their own food by agriculture, stock-breeding, fishing or collecting—full-time specialist craftsmen, transport workers, merchants, officials

and priests. All these were of course supported by the surplus produced by the peasants living in the city and in dependent villages, but they did not secure their share directly by exchanging their products or services for grains or fish with individual peasants.

(3) Each primary producer paid over the tiny surplus he could wring from the soil with his still very limited technical equipment as tithe or tax to an imaginary deity or a divine king who thus concentrated the surplus. Within this concentration, owing to the low productivity of the rural economy, no effective capital would have been available.

(4) Truly monumental public buildings not only distinguish each known city from any village but also symbolize the concentration of the social surplus. Every Sumerian city was from the first dominated by one or more stately temples, centrally situated on a brick platform raised above the surrounding dwellings and usually connected with an artificial mountain, the staged tower or ziggurat. But attached to the temples, were workshops and magazines, and an important appurtenance of each principal temple was a great granary. Harappa, in the Indus basin, was dominated by an artificial citadel, girt with a massive rampart of kiln-baked bricks, containing presumably a palace and immediately overlooking an enormous granary and the barracks of artizans. No early temples nor palaces have been excavated in Egypt, but the whole Nile valley was dominated by the gigantic tombs of the divine pharaohs while royal granaries are attested from the literary record. Finally the Maya cities are known almost exclusively from the temples and pyramids of sculptured stone round which they grew up.

Hence in Sumer the social surplus was first effectively concentrated in the hands of a god and stored in his granary. That was probably true in Central America while in Egypt the pharaoh (king) was himself a god. But of course the imaginary deities were served by quite real priests who, besides celebrating elaborate and often sanguinary rites in their honour, administered their divine masters' earthly estates. In Sumer indeed the god very soon, if not even before the revolution, shared his wealth and power with a mortal viceregent, the 'City-King,' who acted as civil ruler and leader in war. The divine pharaoh was naturally assisted by a whole hierarchy of officials.

(5) All those not engaged in food-production were of course supported in the first instance by the surplus accumulated in temple or royal granaries and were thus dependent on temple or court. But naturally priests, civil and military leaders and officials absorbed a major share of the concentrated surplus and thus formed a 'ruling class.' Unlike a palaeolithic magician or a neolithic chief, they were, as an Egyptian scribe actually put it, 'exempt from all manual tasks.' On the other hand, the lower classes were not only guaranteed peace and security, but were relieved from intellectual tasks which many find more irksome than any physical labour. Besides reassuring the masses that the sun was going to rise next day and the river would flood again next year (people who have not five thousand years of recorded experience of natural uniformities behind them are really worried about such matters!), the ruling classes did confer substantial benefits upon their subjects in the way of planning and organization.

(6) They were in fact compelled to invent systems of recording and exact, but practically useful, sciences. The mere administration of the vast revenues of a Sumerian temple or an Egyptian pharaoh by a perpetual corporation of priests or officials obliged its members to devise conventional methods of recording that should be intelligible to all their colleagues and successors, that is, to invent systems of writing and numeral

notation. Writing is thus a significant, as well as a convenient, mark of civilization. But while writing is a trait common to Egypt, Mesopotamia, the Indus valley and Central America, the characters themselves were different in each region and so were the normal writing materials—papyrus in Egypt, clay in Mesopotamia. The engraved seals or stelae that provide the sole extant evidence for early Indus and Maya writing, no more represent the normal vehicles for the scripts than do the comparable documents from Egypt and Sumer.

(7) The invention of writing—or shall we say the inventions of scripts—enabled the leisured clerks to proceed to the elaboration of exact and predictive sciences—arithmetic, geometry and astronomy. Obviously beneficial and explicitly attested by the Egyptian and Maya documents was the correct determination of the tropic year and the creation of a calendar. For it enabled the rulers to regulate successfully the cycle of agricultural operations. But once more the Egyptian, Maya and Babylonian calendars were as different as any systems based on a single natural unit could be. Calendrical and mathematical sciences are common features of the earliest civilizations and they too are corollaries of the archaeologists' criterion, writing.

(8) Other specialists, supported by the concentrated social surplus, gave a new direction to artistic expression. Savages even in palaeolithic times had tried, sometimes with astonishing success, to depict animals and even men as they saw them—concretely and naturalistically. Neolithic peasants never did that; they hardly ever tried to represent natural objects, but preferred to symbolize them by abstract geometrical patterns which at most may suggest by a few traits a fantastical man or beast or plant. But Egyptian, Sumerian, Indus and Maya artist-craftsmen—full-time sculptors, painters, or seal-engravers—began once more to carve, model or draw likenesses of persons or things, but no longer with the naive naturalism of the hunter, but according to conceptualized and sophisticated styles which differ in each of the four urban centres.

(9) A further part of the concentrated social surplus was used to pay for the importation of raw materials, needed for industry or cult and not available locally. Regular 'foreign' trade over quite long distances was a feature of all early civilizations and, though common enough among barbarians later, is not certainly attested in the Old World before 3,000 B.C. nor in the New before the Maya 'empire.' Thereafter regular trade extended from Egypt at least as far as Byblos on the Syrian coast while Mesopotamia was related by commerce with the Indus valley. While the objects of international trade were at first mainly 'luxuries,' they already included industrial materials, in the Old World notably metal the place of which in the New was perhaps taken by obsidian. To this extent the first cities were dependent for vital materials on long distance trade as no neolithic village ever was.

(10) So in the city, specialist craftsmen were both provided with raw materials needed for the employment of their skill and also guaranteed security in a State organization based now on residence rather than kinship. Itinerancy was no longer obligatory. The city was a community to which a craftsman could belong politically as well as economically.

Yet in return for security they became dependent on temple or court and were relegated to the lower classes. The peasant masses gained even less material advantages; in Egypt for instance metal did not replace the old stone and wood tools for agricultural work. Yet, however imperfectly, even the earliest urban communities must have been held together by a sort of solidarity missing from any neolithic village. Peasants, craftsmen, priests and rulers form a community, not only by reason of identity of language and belief, but also because each performs mutually complementary functions, needed for the well-being (as redefined under civilization) of the whole. In fact the earliest cities illustrate a first approximation to an organic solidarity based upon a functional complementarity and interdependence between all its members such as subsist between the constituent cells of an organism. Of course this was only a very distant approximation. However necessary the concentration of the surplus really were with the existing forces of production, there seemed a glaring conflict on economic interests between the tiny ruling class, who annexed the bulk of the social surplus, and the vast majority who were left with a bare subsistance and effectively excluded from the spiritual benefits of civilization. So solidarity had still to be maintained by the ideological devices appropriate to the mechanical solidarity of barbarism as expressed in the pre-eminence of the temple or the sepulchral shrine, and now supplemented by the force of the new State organization. There could be no room for sceptics or sectaries in the oldest cities.

These ten traits exhaust the factors common to the oldest cities that archaeology, at best helped out with fragmentary and often ambiguous written sources, can detect. No specific elements of town planning for example can be proved characteristic of all such cities; for on the one hand the Egyptian and Maya cities have not yet been excavated; on the other neolithic villages were often walled, an elaborate system of sewers drained the Orcadian hamlet of Skara Brae; two-storeyed houses were built in pre-Columbian *pueblos,* and so on.

The common factors are quite abstract. Concretely Egyptian, Sumerian, Indus and Maya civilizations were as different as the plans of their temples, the signs of their scripts and their artistic conventions. In view of this divergence and because there is so far no evidence for a temporal priority of one Old World centre (for instance, Egypt) over the rest nor yet for contact between Central America and any other urban centre, the four revolutions just considered may be regarded as mutually independent. On the contrary, all later civilizations in the Old World may in a sense be regarded as lineal descendants of those of Egypt, Mesopotamia or the Indus.

But this was not a case of like producing like. The maritime civilizations of Bronze Age Crete or classical Greece for example, to say nothing of our own, differ more from their reputed ancestors than these did among themselves. But the urban revolutions that gave them birth did not start from scratch. They could and probably did draw upon the capital accumulated in the three allegedly primary centres. That is most obvious in the case of cultural capital. Even today we use the Egyptians' calendar and the Sumerians' divisions of the day and the hour. Our European ancestors did not have to invent for themselves these divisions of time nor repeat the observations on which they are based; they took over—and very slightly improved systems elaborated 5,000 years ago! But the same is in a sense true of material capital as well. The Egyptians, the Sumerians and the Indus people had accumulated vast reserves of surplus food. At the same time they had to import from abroad necessary raw materials like metals and building timber as well as 'luxuries.' Communities controlling these natural resources could in exchange claim a slice of the urban surplus. They could use it as capital to support full-time specialists—

craftsmen or rulers—until the latters' achievement in technique and organization had so enriched barbarian economies that they too could produce a substantial surplus in their turn.

Karl A. Wittfogel, Adjunct Professor of Chinese History at Columbia University, is known to prehistorians through his study of irrigation and its influence on the nature of complex societies. This article contains a clear and concise statement of this theme, which Wittfogel later developed in a book, *Oriental Despotism* (1957). Though his view that irrigation was the single most important causative factor in the development of complex societies is thought by many archaeologists to be too simplistic and invalid (see, for example, Robert M. Adams' *The Evolution of Urban Society*, 1966), there are some strong defenders of Wittfogel's ideas (see Sanders and Price's *Mesoamerica: The Evolution of a Civilization*, 1968; Price's 1971 article, "Prehispanic Irrigation Agriculture in Nuclear America," *Latin American Research Review*, Vol. VI, No. 3, pp. 3-60, also presents an excellent discussion and restatement of the irrigation hypothesis).

Developmental Aspects
of Hydraulic Societies

Karl A. Wittfogel

1. The Great Challenge to a Unilineal Concept of Developments: Hydraulic ("Oriental") Society[1]

An awareness of the developmental peculiarity of irrigation-based "Oriental" society kept the classical economists from advocating simple schemes of unilineal evolution such as were the order of the day during and after the Industrial Revolution. The present efforts of anthropologists to establish multilineal patterns of development are methodologically subtler, and their roots are complex. But it is probably no accident that these new efforts are greatly concerned with the developmental history of "irrigation civilizations" in the New and in the Old World.

Through my work on Chinese history I have long been impressed with the developmental lessons to be learned from a study of agrarian societies based on large-scale and government-directed waterworks. These societies covered more territory, lasted for more years, and shaped more lives than any other stratified agrarian society. In contrast to the stratified agrarian societies of Medieval Europe, they failed, of their own inner forces, to evolve beyond their general pattern. Both their historical significance and their institutional peculiarity make them a productive starting point for a new inquiry into the nature of societal development.

Reprinted from *Irrigation Civilizations: A Comparative Study*, pp. 43-57, Social Science Monographs, Department of Cultural Affairs, Pan American Union, Washington, D.C. (1955), by courtesy of the General Secretariat of the Organization of American States and the author.

2. Two Basic Prerequisites and a Few Taxonomic Comments

Such an inquiry requires, first, the postulation of recognizable patterns of societal *structure* ("culture types") and second, the postulation of recognizable patterns of societal *change* ("development"). Both prerequisites have been successfully met by Julian Steward (Steward 1949, p. 2 ff.; *idem* 1953, p. 318 ff. and 321). Accepting the substance of his definitions, I shall, from the standpoint of the institutional historian, comment briefly on the morphology—and taxonomy—of societal types and changes.

a. Societal (culture) types

Societal types are operational units whose essential intellectual, technical, organizational, and social elements, although not necessarily specific in themselves, become specific through their dimension and the institutional setting in which they function. A substantially technological approach, as suggested by Leslie White (White 1949, p. 365, 375 ff., 377, 390), can be very productive in a study of the Industrial Revolution. But it fails to explain the beginnings of industrial capitalism, which at first reorganized rather than re-equipped industrial production. And, on the level of pre-industrial life, it prevents a clear understanding of the institutional processes that separated, not temporarily and accidentally, but structurally and over time, the hydraulic from the non-hydraulic part of the agrarian world.

In a recently published paper, Gordon Childe states that his definition of the Neolithic "stage" rests on economic and not on geologic or technologic criteria (Childe 1953, p. 193). Yet more than in the past, his discussion obscures the crucial socio-political differences behind similarities of material and technology; and also more than in the past, his use of the terms "neolithic revolution" and "urban revolution" obscures the peculiarities of the developmentally decisive hydraulic revolution.[2]

The men who accomplished this revolution often employed the same work tools (hoe, shovel, basket) and the same work materials (soil, stone, wood) as did the rainfall farmers. But by specific organizational means (large-scale cooperation, rigid subordination and centralized leadership) they established societies that differed structurally from societies based on rainfall farming.

The comprehensive use of metal contributed to the further growth of hydraulic societies and non-hydraulic agrarian societies, but it did not bring them into being. And the urban revolution that followed the hydraulic revolution was radically different in its socio-political content from the urban revolution that occurred in the non-hydraulic agrarian world.

Above the level of simple tribal life, and in most cases evolving directly from it, there obviously existed a number of higher pre-industrial civilizations whose diversities can be ascribed only to a limited extent to technological factors: stratified pastoral societies, hydraulic societies, the non-hydraulic and non-feudal agrarian societies of ancient Greece (with *metics* or free peasants as cultivators) and of republican Rome (increasingly employing slave labor in agriculture), the feudal societies of Europe (based on rainfall farming) and of Japan (based on small-scale irrigation); and perhaps some others that are less distinct typologically and less important historically.

b. Developmental patterns

Our reference to the multiple origins of higher agrarian societies indicates that societal development, like societal type, may show substantial and definable diversities. A comparative study of development has to recognize the possibility of single as well as multiple origin, and the possibility of multiple modes of development following upon both types of origin. It has to recognize societal stagnation and change, circular change (resulting in restoration) and permanent change (development proper). It has to recognize that in terms of values, development may be progressive or retrogressive, or ambivalent, its positive and negative values being determined (if not as easily as the 19th century evolutionists thought) by a judicious appraisal of technical, organizational, and social factors, and such basic human assets as freedom of opinion and opportunity for creative expression.

And then there is diversive change—societal transformation brought about, not developmentally, that is, not "spontaneously" and "from within" (cf. Kroeber 1948, p. 241), but by extraneous forces which compel the target society to move in a direction that it would not have taken without external interferences either at the moment of change or in a foreseeable future.

These developmental patterns occur in many combinations. All are pertinent, and some are crucial, for an understanding of the typological and developmental position of hydraulic society.

3. Hydraulic Society: The Over-all Conformation and Some Major Sub-types

a. Hydraulic ("oriental") society and "oriental despotism"

I suggest that the term "hydraulic agriculture" be applied to a system of farming which depends on large-scale and government-directed water control. I suggest that the term "hydraulic society" be applied to agrarian societies in which agro-hydraulic works and other large hydraulic and non-hydraulic constructions, that tend to develop with them, are managed by an inordinately strong government. I suggest that the term "state" be applied to a government that, on the basis of a sufficient surplus, is operated by a substantial number of full-time specialists: civil and military officials. I suggest that the term "hydraulic society" be used interchangeably with "Oriental society" in recognition of the geo-historical fact that the societal order under discussion appeared most significantly and lastingly to the east of those European countries, in which social scientists first tried to define these phenomena. To the best of my knowledge, John Stuart Mill was the first to use the formula "Oriental society" (Mill 1909, p. 20).

Although little effort has been made to clarify the underlying institutional facts, the term "Oriental despotism" has been widely accepted. Following Milukov, we may apply the designation "Oriental despotism" to a state that is stronger than all other forces of society (Milukov 1898, p. 111).

b. Basic institutional aspects of hydraulic society

The extraordinary power of the hydraulic state results from a number of institutional features that interlock and mutually support each other. Among them I consider outstanding the state's constructional, organizational, and acquisitive achievements; its success in keeping private property weak and in keeping the dominant religion attached to itself; and its specific type of ruling class—a monopoly bureaucracy.

The constructional achievements of Oriental despotism include the creation and maintenance of large waterworks for productive and protective purposes (irrigation and flood control) and, under certain conditions, the creation of navigation canals and extended aqueducts for conveying drinking water. Among the non-hydraulic installations that tend to grow with the growth of the various hydraulic installations we find monumental defense works (long walls and fortresses), far-flung roads, "big houses" (palaces, temples), and colossal tombs (pyramids, etc.).

The organizational achievements of Oriental despotism include certain operations inherent in large-scale and planned construction (counting, record-keeping, handling of large numbers of corviable persons), processes of using what has been constructed (management of hydraulic and non-hydraulic installations), and the application of the thus acquired organizational techniques to other operations: to quick communication and intelligence (the state post), and to the maintenance of coordinated and centrally directed armies. Tribal hydraulic communities are superior in food production to most of their non-agricultural neighbors; but the former are at a military disadvantage because of their fixed and, for the most part, small residences. They therefore excel in the defensive arts of war.[3] It is in the larger and state-centered hydraulic societies that integrated and relatively numerous armies provide the means for aggressive warfare and for regional and, eventually, super-regional expansion.

The acquisitive achievements of the hydraulic state include a variety of measures aimed at controlling the population's labor and/or the fruits of its labor. Under simpler conditions, agricultural corvee labor on "public fields" and government-assigned office land prevails; under more complex conditions, the government relies, in part or essentially, on raising taxes in kind and/or in cash. The acquisitive claim tends to affect the whole population; and being imposed from above, it tends to be heavy.

The hydraulic regime's power over the population's property manifests itself not only in its fiscal strength but also in acts of ruthless confiscation and in laws of inheritance which compel the more or less equal division of a deceased person's property among several heirs (usually his sons, but at times also his daughters or other relatives).

Still more consequential is the fact that the one-sided concentration of societal leadership in the government prevents the owners of private property, both mobile and immobile, from organizing independent and politically effective bodies, "corporations" or "estates." This was the case even for the non-office-holding members of the ruling class, the bureaucratic gentry. Only the executive activists were organized, and they were organized politically through the permanent operational centers (office, bureaus) that formed the administrative nuclei of the despotic ("apparatus") state. Jealously defending their monopoly of political organization, on occasion even at the expense of their proprietary interests, these men of the apparatus constituted a monopoly bureaucracy. In contrast to the representatives of so-called "monopoly capitalism", they were eminently successful in maintaining a monopoly of societal leadership (Wittfogel 1953a, p. 97, note 3).

Professional functionaries of the dominant religion often, and particularly under simpler conditions, acted also as government officials. But they never established independent churches that counterbalanced the power of the state, as did the *ecclesia militans* of the European Middle Ages. Throughout the Oriental world, and in a variety of ways, the dominant religion remained attached to the absolutist government which often appointed its priests and usually administered its property.

c. Major sub-types of hydraulic society

These are important aspects of the culture-type, hydraulic society. Their implication for the macro-morphology of development are apparent. They become still more apparent after we have examined the major sub-types of the over-all conformation.

The institutional tissue of hydraulic society differs structurally and definably with regard to hydraulic and managerial "density." It also differs with regard to proprietary "complexity": the quality and dimension of active (productive) private property and private-property-based enterprise.

In Inca society, ancient Egypt, and Mesopotamia the greater part of all arable land seems to have depended on irrigation water provided by government-controlled installations. Hydraulic agriculture prevailed absolutely; and the density of the bureaucratic-managerial apparatus was extreme. Under such conditions we are faced with a "compact" hydraulic society.

Where the hydraulic centers are spread out among large areas of small-scale irrigation and/or rainfall farming, we are faced with a "loose" hydraulic society. A number of territorial states of the Mexican highlands and of early China and India fall into this latter category.

Loose hydraulic societies include regions which lack agro-hydraulic works, but which are subject to the same organizational and acquisitive controls that the despotic state employs in its hydraulic core areas. When such regions, after gaining independence, still preserve Orientally despotic methods of statecraft, or when, under the influence of hydraulic societies, such methods emerge in adjacent countries that practice little or no hydraulic agriculture, then we are faced with a "marginal" hydraulic (Oriental) society.

In some instances, the government of a marginal hydraulic society undertook large non-hydraulic operations (Middle Byzantium, the Lowland Maya, the Liao empire). In other cases, such large non-hydraulic operations were practically lacking (Muscovite Russia). This divergence poses important questions of origin and structure. But it is imperative to realize that, in terms of political, social, and economic relations, all these civilizations definitely belonged to the hydraulic world, while other societies that preserved some elements of Oriental despotism, but represented different socio-cultural patterns, belonged to the "sub-marginal" part of the hydraulic world.

One of the most remarkable examples of a hydraulically sub-marginal civilization is Japan, which, on the basis of small-scale irrigation, evolved a system of social leadership and dependency that was as similar to that of feudal Europe as it was dissimilar to the great hydraulic society of the near-by mainland, China.

Varying density in the hydraulic and managerial spheres involves a varying administrative (bureaucratic) density among those who do the ruling. Varying complexity in the proprietary sphere involves a varying social differentiation among those who are ruled. In primitive (tribal) hydraulic societies, a higher degree of hydraulic density and/or a larger population seems to bring about stronger government control over both land and water. In hydraulic states, the bulk of all cultivable land is, for the most part, not privately owned but, on the village level, regulated by local officials or semi-officials.

As a rule, substantial private property-based social differences seem to have arisen first from differences in active mobile property—the material foundation of handicraft and trade. Simple hydraulic societies have few independent artisans and merchants. Pharaonic Egypt, until the New Kingdom, and Inca society are cases in point.

Semi-complex hydraulic societies have substantial groups of professional and independent artisans and merchants. Maya and Aztec society, and of course traditional India until the arrival of the British, exhibit this semi-complex pattern.

It seems certain that elements of private landownership were present in many simple and semi-complex hydraulic societies. But prior to the recent processes of disintegration, such ownership under Oriental despotism prevailed in relatively few civilizations (pre-eminent among them: imperial China). The developments of the 19th and 20th centuries, which in many parts of the Oriental world (India and the Near East) weakened the traditionally strong despotic state and favored the growth of absentee landlordism, must not obscure the fact that, in the long history of hydraulic society, complex conditions of property (that is, the prevalence of mobile *and* immobile private property) were more the exception than the rule.

4. Developmental Aspects of Hydraulic Society

Recently the development of hydraulic society has been analyzed particularly with regard to local origins, regional maturation, and empire-like expansion. And the terms "Formative", "Florescent" ("Classic") and "Empire" (or "Fusion") have been suggested for these phases. Formation, growth, and dimension are indeed vital phenomena. Their institutional meaning will become clearer, if they are examined in the light of our just-defined criteria: managerial density and proprietary complexity.

a. Origins (Formative I and II)

Irrigation societies, in the form of independent village communities, have existed for many centuries in the Pueblo area of North America. But students of the formative phase have neglected them for the study of Chavín-Cupisnique, Salinar, and other cultures which are assumed to have had an incipient ruling class and state. This approach ignores valuable socio-typological information; yet it implies a recognition of the fact that, in the major areas of hydraulic development, primitive hydraulic commonwealths expanded quickly beyond the single-village pattern that the Pueblos exemplify so strikingly (cf. Wittfogel and Goldfrank, 1943).

The radiocarbon data on the ancient Near East seems to indicate that "once food production came into being, the rate of technological (and cultural) acceleration was much more rapid than had been anticipated" (*Radiocarbon Dating,* p. 53). Obviously this thesis is not valid for regions in which limitations of water and soil caused the perpetuation of the single-village community. However, it may well explain why in the Andean zone, in Egypt, and Mesopotamia, the establishment of hydraulic society apparently occurred in two phases (Formative I and Formative II, if you wish), the second either quickly succeeding the first or being almost indistinguishable from it, and with groups larger than a single "local" unit combining for the initial communally-conducted hydraulic effort. Thus the criterion of dimension permits us to recognize, for the formative period of hydraulic society, a single-settlement type (Local I) and a multi-settlement and incipient city-state type (Local II).

In semi-arid settings, such as North China, early rainfall farmers probably practiced irrigation agriculture first along smaller water courses and later in the larger river plains and deltas, while they continued to cultivate and at times increase the extent of their non-hydraulic hinterland. Such a development would make for loose hydraulic societies. The agro-hydraulic conquest of arid regions, which often led to the establishment of compact hydraulic formations, may have been accomplished by representatives of loose hydraulic societies which had received their initial hydraulic experience in a semi-arid setting, or it may have been accomplished by rainfall farmers. The latter form of transition may have occurred in the main in areas in which innundation agriculture was possible. But circumstances permitting, it seems reasonable to assume that there was interaction between early, loose and compact hydraulic societies.

In terms of hydraulic density then, the formation of hydraulic societies probably occurred in several ways. And in all likelihood a variety of leaders (war chiefs, peace chiefs, priests) spear-headed, and benefited from, the hydraulic revolution.

On the eve of this revolution there may have existed various forms of property (clan, private, and communal). But the new development favored government control over specialized handicraft and exchange together with government control over the bulk of all cultivable land.

b. Regional and inter-regional (empire-like) developments

Viewing the hydraulic "region," as juxtaposed to the local "community," as a larger ecological unit that draws its water supply from a whole river system, or a self-contained part of such a system, we find the regional type of hydraulic development correlated with a maximum growth of compact hydraulic societies: witness the city or territorial states of coastal Peru, of ancient Mesopotamia, and pre-Thinite Egypt, and the "kingdom" of Dynastic Egypt. The territorial states of Chou China rarely outgrew their loose hydraulic origins:[4] but they often increased their hydraulic density. The northwestern state of Ch'in, which in 221 B.C. unified "all-under-heaven," eventually comprised two extremely compact and productive hydraulic areas: the Red Basin of Szechuan and central Shensi with its fabulous Chêng-Kuo irrigation system.

The fusion of several hydraulic regions into empire-like conformations occasionally stimulated the creation of interlinking navigation canals, such as the Chinese Grand Canal. But in the sphere of hydraulic agriculture a different trend became dominant. Since the old core areas usually reached the saturation point of their hydraulic growth in the period of regional development, the despotic state, while eager to develop hydraulic enterprises in new areas (where this was possible and rewarding), asserted its imperial power by acquiring, whenever recognized advantage suggested, a maximum of territories with a low hydraulic potential, small-scale irrigation and rainfall farming pure and simple. In consequence the great irrigation empires were usually loose hydraulic societies, and compared with the conditions of regional hydraulic development, the period of inter-regional fusion generally represented a lower coefficient of hydraulic density.

Proprietary complexity changed in a different way. With growing dimension and inter-regional communication, simple conditions of property tended to yield to semi-complex and eventually, but much more rarely, to complex conditions of property. For obvious reasons, managerially compact regions that disposed over a larger bureaucracy were more reluctant to allow professional handicraft and exchange to fall into the hands of private property and enterprise. In Inca society the hydraulic sponge was so effective that, even under conditions of empire, private-property-based enterprise in handicraft, and particularly in trade, was insignificant.

The Inca case, however, seems to be the exception rather than the rule. In most peacefully interrelated territorial states (cf. Buddhist India and later Chou China), and in the majority of all hydraulic empires, new and substantial industrial and commercial possibilities were opened up. And what may be called the *Law of Diminishing Administrative Returns* induced the rulers to permit a substantial increase in privately operating artisans and merchants. Thus in the period of fusion, semi-complex hydraulic societies replaced in many parts of the world the simple hydraulic societies of the period of regional development.

Semi-complex, not complex societies. The empires and quasi-empires of the Mexican highland, the Near East, and India, and also the marginally hydraulic world of Maya Yucatán favored non-governmental handicraft and commerce; but they did not convert the bulk of the land from regulated to private property. The establishment of private landownership in China (which greatly stimulated the intensity of agriculture) remained, until the recent time of transition, an exceptional case of complex proprietary development as, at the other end of the institutional scale, Inca society remained an exceptional case of simple proprietary development.

c. Institutional growth, stagnation, epigonal attitudes, and conspicuous retrogression

Thus progress from regional to inter-regional and empire like conditions increased man's freedom from government control (some scholars would say exaggeratedly: from "state slavery"). But this development rarely freed the villages from the bonds of official or semi-official regulation; nor was it paralleled by an expansion of hydraulic agriculture.

Worse, there was a tendency for hydraulic stagnation to give way to retrogression. The agro-managerial coefficient shrank *relatively* when Oriental despotism extended its non-hydraulic territory, while its hydraulically cultivated territory remained unchanged. The agro-managerial coefficient shrank *absolutely,* when the amount of hydraulically cultivated land decreased. This happened for internal reasons, when indigenous rulers paid less attention to maintaining agro-managerial standards than to invoking new methods of fiscal exploitation. This happened for external reasons, when hydraulically unconcerned "barbarians" placed themselves as conquerors over a hydraulic society. In the first case, retrogression might be combatted at intervals. In the second case, retrogression might lower the hydraulic effectiveness for long periods. This happened on a gigantic scale in the Old World, when, in the middle of the first millennium A.D. and in consequence of a great revolution in cavalry warfare (Wittfogel and Feng 1949, p. 505 ff.), a net of Orientally despotic conquest societies spread over the Near East, India, and China.

The relations between maturation, stagnation, and retrogression are not easily defined. But a few major trends may be tentatively suggested.[5] The growth in the magnitude of a socio-cultural unit does not necessarily involve a corresponding institutional and cultural growth. Loose interaction between numerous independent units proves more stimulating than island- or oasis-like isolation. It also proves more stimulating than imperial fusion, which tends to give the initiative for experiment and change to a single center. This probably accounts for the fact that the foremost representatives of Oriental civilization generally achieved the peak of their creativeness when they were part of a cluster of loosely related territorial states.

Practically all great Chinese ideas on the "way" *(tao)*, on society, government, human relations, warfare, and historiography crystallized during the classical period of the territorial states and at the beginning of the imperial period. The establishment of the examination system and the psychologically slanted reformulation of Confucianism followed the reunification of the empire, the transfer of the economic center of gravity to the Yangtze Valley, and the building of an artificial Nile, the Grand Canal. Other significant changes occurred during later periods of imperial China in the field of the drama and the popular novel; but they were largely due to a new influence, the complete subjugation of China by two "barbarian" conquest dynasties. And none of them shook the Confucian foundation of Chinese thought.

The climax of creative expression in India is similarly located. Hindu religion, statecraft, law, and family patterns originated and reached their "classical" maturity either when India was a network of independent states or during the early phase of imperial unification.

The Arab-dominated conquest societies of the Near East began on an empire-like level. But here again most of the great ideas concerned with law, statecraft, and man's fate were formulated, not at the close, but during the first and the early middle period of Islamic society.

Within a given framework, creative change does not continue indefinitely. When the possibilities for development and differentiation have in great part been realized, the creative process tends to slow down. Maturation becomes stagnation. And given time, stagnation results in stereotyped repetition (epigonism) or outright retrogression. Conquest and territorial expansion favor acculturation. But the ensuing changes do not seriously alter the existing pattern of society and culture. They will be of minor consequence; and eventually they also will yield to stagnation, epigonism, and retrogression.

The trend toward epigonism and retrogression may merge—and, in the Oriental conquest societies of the Old World it did merge—with a trend toward reduced hydraulic intensity and increased personal restriction. In terms of managerial action, personal freedom, and cultural creativeness, most hydraulic societies of the late "Empire" period probably operated on a level lower than that reached during the days of regional and early "Empire" florescense.

5. Hydraulic Societies that Lose their Institutional Identity

Under the shadow of the hydraulic state there arose no independent force strong enough to transform the agrarian order into an industrial society. Certain hydraulic societies evolved into non-hydraulic agrarian societies; but generally they did so in consequence of external aggression and conquest. They experienced a diversive rather than a developmental change. And recently many hydraulic societies have begun to lose their institutional balance, because they were shaken fundamentally by the imperialist, and non-imperialist, impact of modern industrial society. In a specific sense, they are hydraulic societies in transition.

a. Diversive changes

In the Mediterranean area diversive changes have expanded and reduced the hydraulic world since the time of Crete and Mycenae. This process was at work, when Greek influence in Western Asia rose and fell, when the Hellenistically despotic state of Western Rome collapsed under the attacks of non-Oriental barbarians, when the feudal kings of Castille and Aragon destroyed the Oriental despotism of Moorish Spain, and when the crusading representatives of feudal Europe paralyzed Byzantium.

b. Hydraulic society in transition

No comparative study of development in the hydraulic world may overlook the facts and patterns of these (and similarly structured) diversive changes. Nor may it overlook the developmental processes that recently have placed hydraulic society in its entirety in a state of transition. Marx, who, with significant inconsistencies (Wittfogel 1953, p. 351 ff.) maintained the Asiatic concept of the classical economists, was intrigued by the effect of British rule on "Asiatic society." Marx held no brief for British imperialism; he called its behavior in India "swinish." But he found that, by laying in India the foundations of a private-property-based modern society, the British accomplished "the only *social* revolution ever heard of in Asia" (Marx 1853).

Students of the developmental peculiarities of hydraulic society are uniquely prepared to explain why Japan, which was never hydraulic, evolved with relative ease into a modern industrial society. They are uniquely prepared to study the changes that, under direct or indirect Western influence, occurred during the 19th and early 20th centuries in India, Turkey, and Russia. They are uniquely prepared also to answer the question raised, in 1906, in a fateful discussion between the two top-ranking Russian Marxists, Plekhanov and Lenin, as to whether a new Russian revolution, irresponsibly handled might not lead to an "Asiatic restoration"—that is, to the restoration of Oriental despotism. The relevance of this question for the evaluation of contemporary Russia and China is evident.

By conscientiously and objectively studying the structure and the development of Oriental society, we may once again prove with new answers and new questions the scholarly (and the human) value of the social sciences which we serve.

Notes

[1] For a fuller presentation of the facts and problems discussed here, see my forthcoming book, *Oriental Society and Oriental Despotism*.

[2] In his earlier writings Childe stressed emphatically the ecological and organizational peculiarities in irrigation-based "Oriental" societies. He noted the pioneer position of these societies in the "second" neolithic revolution; and he took pains to distinguish the Oriental Bronze Age from the Bronze Age of temperate Europe (see Childe 1948, p. 105, 109, 128 ff., 140 ff.; *idem* 1946, p. 62 ff., 76, 161, 189, 198, 272). In his more recent

writings these distinctions become less meaningful(see Childe 1951 *passim* [based on lectures given in 1947/8]); and in his paper *Anthropology Today* (cf. Childe 1953, p. 208) they all but disappear.

[3]For a discussion of the elaborate defence measures taken by the Pueblo Indians and the Chagga, see Wittfogel, OS, chapter II.

[4]Renewed examination of the issue has convinced me that early historical (pre-Chou and Chou) China constituted not a hydraulically tainted feudal society, but a hydraulic society proper. The climate and the lay of the land made comprehensive hydraulic enterprises a basic prerequisite for permanent settlement and agricultural prosperity in the cradle of Chinese civilization, the river basins and plains of North China. Significantly, during the Chou period the rulers of the territorial states assigned land not to vassals who rendered limited and conditional services, but to officials who were expected to serve without limitation and unconditionally. Thus these lands were not fiefs, but office lands, a type of land-holding that is not at all infrequent under Oriental despotism.

[5]From this point to the end of this sub-section, see Wittfogel, OS, chapter X, D 1, a and b.

References

Childe, Gordon, 1946. *What happened in history*. Penguin Books, Inc., New York.

———— 1948. *Man makes himself*. Watts & Co., London.

————1951. *Social evolution*. Watts & Co., London.

————1953. Old World prehistory: Neolithic. *Anthropology today*, University of Chicago Press, Chicago.

Kroeber, Alfred, 1948. *Anthropology*. Harcourt, Brace & Co., New York.

Marx, Karl, 1853. The British rule in India. *New York Daily Tribune*, 25 de junio.

Mill, John Stuart, 1909. *Principles of political economy*. Longmans, Green and Co., London.

Milukow, Paul, 1898. *Skizzen Russischer Kulturgeschichte*. Vol. 1, Leipzig.

Radiocarbon dating, 1951. [Assembled by Frederick Johnson]. Memoirs of Society for American Archaeology, 8, Supplement to *American Antiquity*, 17, no. 1, part 2.

Steward, Julian, 1949. Cultural causality and law: A trial formulation of development of early civilizations. *American Anthropologist*, 51, no. 1.

———— 1953. Evolution and process. *Anthropology today*, University of Chicago Press, Chicago.

White, Leslie, 1949. *The science of culture*. Farrar, Strauss and Co., New York.

Wittfogel, Karl, 1953. The ruling bureaucracy of Oriental despotism: A phenomenon that paralyzed Marx. *Review of Politics*, 15, no. 3.

———— 1953a. Oriental despotism. *Sociologus*, 3, no. 2.

———— Ms. *Oriental society and Oriental despotism*.

Morton H. Fried received his Ph.D. from Columbia University in 1951 and is currently professor of anthropology at Columbia. He has been a leading evolutionary theorist for many years and is the author and editor of many books including *The Evolution of Political Society* (1967). In his important article reprinted here, he examines the evolutionary processes which led to the formation of the state from egalitarian, rank, and stratified societies. The reader may also wish to look at another important article which was recently published (1970) by Robert Carneiro, "A Theory of the Origin of the State" (*Science,* Vol. 169, pp. 733-8). While both authors hold similar evolutionary stances, they look to different prime movers in the evolution of the state. Carneiro's emphasis is essentially ecological and he focuses his attention on population crowding and land limitations, while Fried's emphasis is political. A social organization point of view can also be found in Elman Service's *The Evolution of Social Organization* (2nd edition, 1971). It is the editors' opinion that an evolutionary point of view, as expressed in Fried's article, is essential to any explanation of the civilizational process.

On the Evolution of Social Stratification and the State

Morton H. Fried

The evolutionists never discussed in detail—still less observed—what actually happened when a society in Stage A changed into a society at Stage B; it was merely argued that all Stage B societies must somehow have evolved out of the Stage A societies.

E. R. Leach, 1954, p. 283

To some extent E. R. Leach's charge, which relates to the evolution of political organization, is unfair. The climate in which pristine systems of state organization took shape no longer exists. The presence of numerous modern states and the efficiency of communications have converted all movements toward state level organization into acculturation phenomena of some degree. In fact, it seems likely that the only truly pristine states—those whose origin was *sui generis,* out of local conditions and not in response to pressures emanating from an already highly organized but separate political entity—are those which arose in the great river valleys of Asia and Africa and the one or two comparable developments in the Western Hemisphere. Elsewhere the development of the state seems to have been "secondary" and to have depended upon pressures, direct or indirect, from existing states. Where such pressures exist, the process of development

Reprinted from *Culture in History,* edited by Stanley Diamond, pp. 713-731, by permission of Columbia University Press and the author. Copyright 1960 by Columbia University Press.

is accelerated, condensed, and often warped, so that a study of contemporary state formation is a murky mirror in which to discern the stages in the development of the pristine states.

Further, the conditions of emergency of rank and stratification as pristine phenomena are similarly obscured when the impetus to change is the introduction of aspects of a market economy, money as a medium of exchange, rationalization of production, and the transformation of labor into a commodity. It would be extremely gratifying to actually observe societies in transition from a "Stage A" (egalitarian organization) to a "Stage B" (rank society) and from there to a "Stage C" (stratification society) and finally from that stage to a "Stage D" (state society). Indeed, some of these observations have been made, though no one has yet been able to follow a single society or even selected exemplars from a group of genetically related societies through all these stages. Instead a variety of unrelated societies are selected, each representing one or another of the several possible transitions. Mr. Leach himself has contributed one of the most valuable of the accounts dealing with this matter in his analysis of the movement from *gumlao* to *gumsa* organization among the Kachin of northern Buram.

Following leads supplied in the data of such accounts as that of Leach, just mentioned, of Douglas Oliver (1955), and others, it is our intention to discuss in detail the things which it seems to us must have occurred in order to make the previous transitions possible. Since the data are largely contemporary, the statements are to be viewed as hypotheses in their application to pristine situations beyond even archaeological recall.

Here then is what we seek to accomplish: (1) to suggest some specific institutional developments, the occurrences of which are normal and predictable in viable societies under certain conditions, and in the course of which the whole society perforce moves into a new level of socio-cultural organization; (2) to suggest some of the conditions under which these institutional developments occurred and came to florescence; (3) to indicate as a by-product, that the movement occurs without conscious human intervention, the alterations taking place slowly enough and with such inevitability that the society is revolutionized before the carriers of the culture are aware of major changes.

In approaching this task, it seems wise, if only to head off needless argument, to deny any intention of supplying a single master key to a lock that has defied the efforts of great talents from the time of the Classical civilizations to the present. It seems obvious that other sequences of events than those sketched here could, under proper circumstances, have had similar results. Indeed, the writer is eager to entertain other possibilities and hopes hereby to stimulate others to offer counter suggestions. It will also be obvious to the reader that substantial trains of thought herein stated are merely borrowed and not created by the writer. The recent strides in economic anthropology, and I refer primarily to the work of Polanyi, Arensberg, and Pearson (1957), the clarification of some basic concepts in the study of social organization, and the incentives provided by a seminal paper by Paul Kirchhoff (1935) have all been combined in the present effort.

The Non-Rank, Non-Stratified Society

Every human society differentiates among its members and assigns greater or less prestige to individuals according to certain of their attributes. The simplist and most universal criteria of differential status are those two potent axes of the basic division of labor, age and sex. Beyond are a host of others which are used singly or in combination to distinguish among the members of a category otherwise undifferentiated as to sex or age group. Most important of the characteristics used in this regard are those which have a visible relation to the maintenance of subsistence, such as strength, endurance, agility, and other factors which make one a good provider in a hunting and gathering setting. These characteristics are ephemeral; moreover, the systems of enculturation prevalent at this level, with their emphasis upon the development of subsistence skills, make it certain that such skills are well distributed among the members of society of the proper sex and age groups.

The major deviation from this system of subsistence-oriented statuses is associated with age. However, it makes no difference to the argument of this paper whether the status of the old is high or low since the basis of its ascription is universal. Anyone who is of the proper sex and manages to live long enough automatically enters into its benefits or disabilities.

Given the variation in individual endowment which makes a chimera of absolute equality, the primitive societies which we are considering are sufficiently undifferentiated in this respect to permit us to refer to them as "egalitarian societies." An egalitarian society can be defined more precisely: it is one in which there are as many positions of prestige in any given age-sex grade as there are persons capable of filling them. If within a certain kin group or territory there are four big men, strong, alert, keen hunters, then there will be four "strong men"; if there are six, or three, or one, so it is. Eskimo society fits this general picture. So do many others. Almost all of these societies are founded upon hunting and gathering and lack significant harvest periods when large reserves of food are stored.

There is one further point I wish to emphasize about egalitarian society. It accords quite remarkably with what Karl Polanyi has called a reciprocal economy.[1]

Production in egalitarian society is characteristically a household matter. There is no specialization; each family group repeats essentially similar tasks. There may be individuals who make certain things better than do others, and these individuals are often given recognition for their skills, but no favored economic role is established, no regular division of labor emerges at this point, and no political power can reside in the status (Leacock, 1958). Exchange in such a society takes place between individuals who belong to different small-scale kin groups; it tends to be casual and is not bound by systems of monetary value based upon scarcity. Such exchanges predominate between individuals who recognize each other as relatives or friends, and may be cemented by such procedures as the provision of hospitality and the granting of sexual access to wives.

Within the local group or band the economy is also reciprocal, but less obviously so. Unlike the exchanges between members of different local groups which, over the period of several years, tend to balance, the exchanges within a group may be quite asymmetrical over time. The skilled and lucky hunter may be continually supplying others with meat; while his family also receives shares from the catch of others, income never catches up with the amounts dispensed. However, the difference between the two quantities is made up in the form of prestige, though, as previously mentioned, it conveys no privileged economic or political role. There frequently is a feeling of transience as it is understood that the greatest hunter can lose his luck or his life, thereby making his family dependent on the largesse of others.

In all egalitarian economies, however, there is also a germ of redistribution. It receives its simplest expression in the family but can grow no more complex than the pooling and redisbursing of stored food for an extended family. In such an embryonic redistributive system the key role is frequently played by the oldest female in the active generation, since it is she who commonly coordinates the household and runs the kitchen.

The Rank Society

Since a truly egalitarian human society does not exist, it is evident that we are using the word "rank" in a somewhat special sense. The crux of the matter, as far as we are concerned, is the structural way in which differential prestige is handled in the rank society as contrasted with the way in which egalitarian societies handle similar materials. If the latter have as many positions of valued status as they have individuals capable of handling them, the rank society places additional limitations on access to valued status. The limitations which are added have nothing to do with sex, age group, or personal attributes. Thus, the rank society is characterized by having fewer positions of valued status than individuals capable of handling them. Furthermore, most rank societies have a fixed number of such positions, neither expanding them nor diminishing them with fluctuations in the populations, save as totally new segmented units originate with fission or disappear as the result of catastrophe or sterility.

The simplest technique of limiting status, beyond those already discussed, is to make succession to status dependent upon birth order. This principle, which is found in kinship-organized societies, persists in many more complexly organized societies. At its simplest, it takes the form of primogeniture or ultimogeniture on the level of the family, extended family, or lineage. In more complex forms it may be projected through time so that only the first son of a first son of a first son enjoys the rights of succession, all others having been excluded by virtue of ultimate descent from a positionless ancestor. There are still other variants based on the theme: the accession to high status may be by election, but the candidates may come only from certain lineages which already represent selection by birth order.

The effects of rules of selection based on birth can be set aside by conscious action. Incompetence can be the basis for a decision to by-pass the customary heir, though it would seem more usual for the nominal office to remain vested in the proper heir while a more energetic person performed the functions of the status. A strategic murder could also accomplish the temporary voiding of the rule, but such a solution is much too dangerous and extreme to be practical on the level which we are considering. It is only in rather advanced cultures that the rewards associated with such statuses are sufficient to motivate patricide and fratricide.

Whether accomplished by a rule of succession or some other narrowing device, the rank society as a framework of statuses resembles a triangle, the point of which represents the leading status hierarchically exalted above the others. The hierarchy thus represented has very definite economic significance, going hand in hand with the emergence of a superfamiliar redistributive network. The key status is that of the central collector of allotments who also tends to the redistribution of these supplies either in the form of feasts or as emergency seed and provender in time of need. Depending on the extent and maturity of the redistributive system, there will be greater or lesser development of the hierarchy. Obviously, small-scale networks in which the members have a face-to-face relationship with the person in the central status will have less need of a bureaucracy.

In the typical ranked society there is neither exploitative economic power nor genuine political power. As a matter of fact, the central status closely resembles its counterpart in the embryonic redistributive network that may be found even in the simplest societies. This is not surprising, for the system in typical rank societies is actually based upon a physical expansion of the kin group and the continuation of previously known kinship rights and obligations. The kingpin of a redistributive network in an advanced hunting and gathering society or a simple agricultural one is as much the victim of his role as its manipulator. His special function is to collect, not to expropriate; to distribute, not to consume. In a conflict between personal accumulation and the demands of distribution it is the former which suffers. Anything else leads to accusations of hoarding and selfishness and undercuts the prestige of the central status; the whole network then stands in jeopardy, a situation which cannot be tolerated. This, by the way, helps to explain that "anomaly" that has so frequently puzzled students of societies of this grade: why are their "chiefs" so often poor, perhaps poorer than any of their neighbors? The preceding analysis makes such a question rhetorical.

It is a further characteristic of the persons filling these high status positions in typical rank societies that they must carry out their functions in the absence of political authority. Two kinds of authority they have: familial, in the extended sense, and sacred, as the redistributive feasts commonly are associated with the ritual life of the community. They do not, however, have access to the privileged use of force, and they can use only diffuse and supernatural sanctions to achieve their ends. Indeed, the two major methods by which they operate are by setting personal examples, as of industriousness, and by utilizing the principles of reciprocity to bolster the emergent redistributive economy.[2]

Despite strong egalitarian features in its economic and political sectors, the developing rank society has strong status differentials which are marked by sumptuary specialization and ceremonial function. While it is a fact that the literature abounds in references to "chiefs" who can issue no positive commands and "ruling classes" whose members are among the paupers of the realm, it must be stated in fairness that the central redistributive statuses *are* associated with fuss, feathers, and other trappings of office. These people sit on stools, have big houses, and are consulted by their neighbors. Their redistributive roles place them automatically to the fore in the religious life of the community, but they are also in that position because of their central kinship status as lineage, clan,[3] or kindred heads.

From Egalitarian to Rank Society

The move from egalitarian to rank society is essentially the shift from an economy dominated by reciprocity to one having redistribution as a major device. That being the case, one must look for the causes of ranking (the limitation of statuses such that they are fewer than the persons capable of handling them) in the conditions which enable the redistributive economy to emerge from its position of latency in the universal household economy, to dominate a network of kin groups which extend beyond the boundaries of anything known on the reciprocal level.

Though we shall make a few suggestions relating to this problem, it should be noted that the focus of this paper does not necessitate immediate disposition of this highly complicated question. In view of the history of our topic, certain negative conclusions are quite significant. Most important of all is the deduction that the roots of ranking do not lie in features of human personality. The structural approach obviates, in this case, psychological explanations. To be precise, we need assume no universal human drive for power[4] in comprehending the evolution of ranking.

It is unthinkable that we should lead a reader this far without indicating certain avenues whereby the pursuit of the problem may be continued. We ask, therefore, what are the circumstances under which fissioning kin or local groups retain active economic interdigitation, the method of interaction being participation in the redistributive network?

In a broad sense, the problem may be seen as an ecological one. Given the tendency of a population to breed up to the limit of its resources and given the probably universal budding of kin and local groups which have reached cultural maxima of unit size, we look into different techno-geographical situations for clues as to whether more recently formed units will continue to interact significantly with their parent units, thereby extending the physical and institutional range of the economy. Such a situation clearly arises when the newer group moves into a somewhat different environment while remaining close enough to the parent group to permit relatively frequent interaction among the members of the two groups. Given such a condition, the maintenance of a redistributive network would have the effect of diversifying subsistence in both units and also providing insurance against food failures in one or the other. This is clearly something of a special case; one of its attractions is the amount of work that has been done upon it by another student of the problem (Sahlins, 1957, 1958).

It is possible to bring to bear upon this problem an argument similar to that employed by Tylor in the question of the incest taboo (Tylor, 1888, p. 267; White, 1948), to wit: the redistributive network might appear as a kind of random social mutation arising out of nonspecific factors difficult to generalize, such as a great personal dependence of the members of the offspring unit upon those they have left behind. Whatever the immediate reason for its appearance, it would quickly show a superiority over simple reciprocal systems in (a) productivity, (b) timeliness of distribution, (c) diversity of diet, and (d) coordination of mundane and ceremonial calendars (in a loose cyclical sense). It is not suggested that the success of the institution depends upon the rational cognition of these virtues by the culture carriers; rather the advantages of these institutions would have positive survival value over a long period of time.

We should not overlook one other possibility that seems less special than the first one given above. Wittfogel has drawn our attention on numerous occasions to the social effects of irrigation (see Wittfogel, 1957, for a summation of his latest thinking). The emergence of the superfamilial redistributive network and the rank society seem to go well with the developments he has discussed under the rubric "hydro-agriculture," in which some supervision is needed in order to control simple irrigation and drainage projects yet these projects are not large enough to call into existence a truly professional bureaucracy.

It may be wondered that one of the prime explanations for the emergence of ranking, one much favored by notable sociologists of the past, has not appeared in this argument. Reference is to the effects of war upon a society. I would like in this article to take a deliberately extreme stand and assert that military considerations serve to institutionalize rank differences only when these are already implicit or manifest in the economy. I do not believe that pristine developments in the formalization of rank can be attributed to even grave military necessity.

The Stratified Society

The differences between rank society and stratified society are very great, yet it is rare that the two are distinguished in descriptive accounts or even in the theoretical literature. Briefly put, the essential difference is this: the rank society operates on the principle of differential status for members with similar abilities, but these statuses are devoid of privileged economic or political power, the former point being the essential one for the present analysis. Meanwhile, the stratified society is distinguished by the differential relationships between the members of the society and its subsistence means —some of the members of the society have unimpeded access to its strategic resources[5] while others have various impediments in their access to the same fundamental resources.

With the passage to stratified society man enters a completely new area of social life. Whereas the related systems of redistribution and ranking rest upon embryonic institutions that are as universal as family organization (*any* family, elementary or extended, conjugal or consanguineal, will do equally well), the principles of stratification have no real foreshadowing on the lower level.

Furthermore, the movement to stratification precipitated many things which were destined to change society even further, and at an increasingly accelerated pace. Former systems of social control which rested heavily on enculturation, internalized sanctions, and ridicule now required formal statement of their legal principles, a machinery of adjudication, and a formally constituted police authority. The emergence of these and other control institutions were associated with the final shift of prime authority from kinship means to territorial means and describes the evolution of complex forms of government associated with the state. It was the passage to stratified society which laid the basis for the complex division of labor which underlies modern society. It also gave rise to various arrangements of socio-economic classes and led directly to both classical and modern forms of colonialism and imperialism.

The Transition to Stratified Society

The decisive significance of stratification is not that it sees differential amounts of wealth in different hands but that it sees two kinds of access to strategic resources. One of these is privileged and unimpeded; the other is impaired, depending on complexes of permission which frequently require the payment of dues, rents, or taxes in labor or in kind. The existence of such a distinction enables the growth of exploitation, whether of a relatively simple kind based upon drudge slavery or of a more complex type associated with involved divisions of labor and intricate class systems. The development of stratification also encourages the emergence of communities composed of kin parts and non-kin parts which, as wholes, operate on the basis of non-kin mechanisms.

So enormous is the significance of the shift to stratification that previous commentators have found it essential that the movement be associated with the most powerful people in the society. Landtman, for example, says: "It is in conjunction with the dissimilarity of individual endowments that inequality of wealth has conduced to the rise of social differentiation. As a matter of course the difference as regards property in many cases goes hand in hand with difference in personal qualities. A skilful hunter or fisher, or a victorious warrrier, has naturally a better prospect of acquiring a fortune than one who is inferior to him in these respects" (Landtman 1938, p. 68).

If our analysis is correct, however, such is definitely not the case. The statuses mentioned by Landtman are not those which stand to make great accumulations but rather stand to make great give-aways. Furthermore, the leap from distribution to power is unwarranted by the ethnographic evidence.

There are unquestionably a number of ways in which secondary conditions of stratification can emerge. That is, once the development of stratification proceeds from contact with and tutelage by cultures which are at the least already stratified and which may be the possesors of mature state organization, there are many specific ways in which simpler cultures can be transformed into stratified societies. The ways which come quickest to mind include the extension of the complex society's legal definitions of property to the simpler society, the introduction of all-purpose money and wage labor, and the creation of an administrative system for the operation of the simpler society on a basis which is acceptable to the superordinate state. Often the external provenance of these elements is obvious in their misfit appearance. A sharper look may reveal, indeed, that the stratified system is a mere facade operated for and often by persons who have no genuine local identities, while the local system continues to maintain informally, and sometimes in secrecy, the older organization of the society. Put more concretely, this means that "government" appointed chiefs are respected only in certain limited situations and that the main weight of social control continues to rest upon traditional authorities and institutions which may not even be recognized by the ruling power.

An excellent climate for the development of stratification in a simple society can be supplied in a relatively indirect way by a society of advanced organization. Let us take the situation in which a culture has no concept of nuclear family rights to land. The economy is based upon hunting, trapping, and fishing, with the streams and forests being associated in a general way with weakly organized bands which have a decided tendency to fragment and reconstitute, each time with potentially different membership.

Subvert this setup with an external market for furs and a substantial basis for stratification has been laid. This system, like the direct intervention of a superordinate state,
also seems to have certain limitations for there is ample evidence that the development
of private property in such a system as that just mentioned is confined to trapping lines
and does not extend to general subsistence hunting and fishing in the area (see Leacock,
1958).

Another situation that bears study is one in which important trade routes linking
two or more advanced societies traverse marginal areas in which simple societies are
located. Certain geographical conditions make it possible for the relatively primitive folk
to enhance their economies with fruits derived from the plunder of this trade or, in a more
mature system, by extorting tribute from the merchants who must pass by. The remote-
ness of these areas, the difficulty of the terrain and the extreme difficulties and costs of
sending a punitive force to pacify the area often enables the simpler people to harass
populations whose cultural means for organized violence far exceeds their own. Be this
as it may, the combination of the examples of organization presented by the outposts
of complexly organized societies and the availability of commodities which could not be
produced in the simple culture may combine to lay the basis for an emergence of stratification. Precisely such conditions seem partially responsible for the political developments
described for the Kachin (Leach, 1954, esp. pp. 235, 247 ff.).

None of this seems to apply to the pristine emergence of stratification. As a matter
of fact, it is not even particularly suggestive. There is, however, one particular ecological
condition that appears in highland Burma which also has been noted elsewhere, each time
in association with rather basic shifts in social organization paralleling those already
sketched in the previous section of this paper. We refer to the shift from rainfall to
irrigation farming, particularly to the construction of terraced fields. This is admittedly
a restricted ethnographic phenomenon and as such it cannot bear the weight of any
general theory. It is the suggestive character of these developments and the possibility of
extrapolating from them to hypothetical pristine conditions that makes them so interesting.

In brief, the shift to irrigation and terracing is from swiddens or impermanent fields
to plots which will remain in permanent cultivation for decades and generations. Whereas
we have previously stressed the possible role of hydro-agriculture in the transition from
egalitarian to rank society, we now note its possible role in the transition to stratification.
This it could accomplish by creating conditions under which access to strategic resources,
in this case land and water, would be made the specific prerogative of small-scale kin
groups such as minimal lineages or even stem families. Through the emergence of hydro-
agriculture a community which previously acknowledged no *permanent* association between
particular component units and particular stretches of land now begins to recognize such
permanent and exclusive rights. Incidentally, the evidence seems to indicate that the
rank-forming tendencies of hydro-agriculture need not occur prior to the tendencies
toward stratification: both can occur concomitantly. This in turn suggests that we must
be cautious in constructing our theory not to make stratification emerge from ranking,
though under particular circumstances this is certainly possible.

A point of considerable interest about hydro-agriculture is that it seems to present
the possibility of an emergence of stratification in the absence of a problem of over-popu-

lation of resource limitation. We need a great deal of further thought on the matter. Studies of the last two decades, in which a considerably higher degree of agricultural expertise on the part of the fieldworkers has been mainifested than was formerly the case, have increasingly tended to show that hydro-agriculture does not invariably out-produce slash and burn and that, other things being equal, a population does not automatically prefer hydro-agriculture as a more rationalized approach to agricultural subsistence. Here we can introduce a factor previously excluded. The hydro-agricultural system invariably has a higher degree of settlement concentration than swiddens. Accordingly, it would seem to have considerable value in the maintenance of systems of defense, given the presence of extensive warfare. Here then, is a point at which military considerations would seem to play an important if essentially reinforcing role in the broad evolutionary developments which we are considering.

The writer is intrigued with another possibility for the emergence of stratification. Once again, the conditions involved seem a little too specific to serve the purpose of a single unified theory. It requires the postulation of a society with a fixed rule of residence, preferably one of the simpler ones such as patrilocality/virilocality or matrilocality/uxorilocality[6] and a fixed rule of descent, preferably one parallel to the residence rule. It further postulates a condition of population expansion such that, given slash and burn agriculture, the society is very near the limits of the carrying capacity of the system. Such conditions are very likely to develop at varying speeds within an area of several hundred miles due to obvious imbalances in reproductive rates and to microecological variation. Now, as long as there is no notable pressure of people on the land, deviation in residence and even in descent will be expectable though quite unusual and lacking in motivation. As the situation grows grave in one area but remains relatively open in another, there may be a tendency for a slight readjustment in residence rules to occur. For example, in a normally virilocal society, the woman who brings her husband back to her natal group transgresses a few customary rules in doing so but presents her agnates with no basic problems in resource allocation since she, as a member of the agnatic group, has her own rights of access which may be shared by the spouse during her lifetime. The complication arises at her death when her husband and all of her children discover themselves to be in an anomalous position since they are not members of the kin community. Where local land problems are not severe and where such breaches of the residence pattern are yet uncommon, it is not unlikely that the aliens will be accepted as *de facto* members of the community with the expectation that future generations will revert to custom, the unorthodox switch of residence fading in memory with the passage of time. Here we have a crude and informal *ambil-anak*. But as the local community enters worsening ecological circumstances and as the exceptional residence becomes more frequent, the residence and descent rules, particularly the latter, assume greater and greater importance. As the situation continues, the community is slowly altered, though the members of the community may be unable to state exactly what the changes are. The result, however, is clear. There are now two kinds of people in the village where formerly there was only one. Now there are kernel villagers, those who have unimpaired access to land, and those whose tenure rests upon other conditions, such as loyalty to a patron, or tribute, or even a precarious squatter's right.

The State Society

> The word should be abandoned entirely . . . after this chapter the word
> will be avoided scrupulously and no severe hardship in expression will
> result. In fact, clarity of expression demands this abstinence.
>
> (Easton, 1953, p. 108)

The word was "state" and the writer, a political scientist, was reacting to some of
the problems in his own field in making this judgment, but it does look as if he was
pushed to drastic action by the work of some anthropologists in whose hands the
concept of state lost all character and utility, finally ending as a cultural universal.
E. Adamson Hoebel, one of the few United States anthropologists to make a serious
specialization in the field of law and the state, formerly introduced students to this
question by remarking that

> where there is political organization there is a state. If political organization
> is universal, so then is the state. One is the group, the other an institutional-
> ized complex of behavior.
>
> (Hoebel, 1949, p. 376)

In a revision of the same book after a few years, Hoebel's treatment of the subject seems to indicate that he is in the process of rethinking the matter. His summary
words, however, repeat the same conclusion:

> Political organization is characteristic of every society. . . . That part of
> culture that is recognized as political organization is what constitutes the
> state.
>
> (Hoebel, 1958, p. 506)

This is a far cry from the approach of evolutionists to the state as exemplified in
Sumner and Keller (1927, I, 700):

> The term state is properly reserved for a somewhat highly developed regu-
> lative organization. . . . It is an organization with authority and discipline
> essential to large-scale achievements, as compared with the family, for
> example, which is an organization on the same lines but simpler and less
> potent.

Without making a special issue of the definition of the state (which would easily
consume the entire space of this article, if not the volume) let me note one used by
the jurist Léon Duguit which conveyes the sense most useful to the point of view of
this paper:

> En prenant le mot dans son sens le plus général, on peut dire qu'il y a un Etat
> toutes les fois qu'il existe dans une société donnée une différenciation politique,
> quelque rudimentaire ou quelque compliquée et developée qu'elle soit. Le mot
> Etat designe soit les gouvernants où le pouvoir politique, soit la société elle-
> même, où existe cette différenciation entre gouvernants et gouvernés et où
> existe par là même une puissance politique.
>
> (Duguit, 1921, p. 395)

The difference between Hoebel and Duguit seems to be in the clear statement of power. Reviewing our own paper in the light of this difference we note our previous emphasis on the absence of coercive economic or political power in the egalitarian and rank societies. It is only in the stratified society that such power emerges from embryonic and universal foreshadowings in familial organization.

The maturation of social stratification has manifold implications depending on the precise circumstances in which the developments take place. All subsequent courses, however, have a certain area of overlap; the new social order, with its differential allocation of access to strategic resources, must be maintained and strengthened. In a simple stratified society in which class differentials are more implicit than explicit the network of kin relations covers a sufficient portion of the total fabric of social relations so that areas not specifically governed by genuine kinship relations can be covered by their sociological extensions. The dynamic of stratification is such that this situation cannot endure. The stratified kin group emphasises its exclusiveness: it erodes the corporate economic functions formerly associated with stipulated kinship and at every turn it amputates extensions of the demonstrated kin unit. The result of this pruning is that the network of kin relations fails more and more to coincide with the network of personal relations. Sooner or later the discrepancy is of such magnitude that, were non-kin sanctions and non-kin agencies absent or structured along customary lines only, the society would dissolve in uncomposable conflict.

The emergent state, then, is the organization of the power of the society on a supra-kin basis. Among its earliest tasks is the maintenance of general order but scarcely discernible from this is its need to support the order of stratification. The defense of a complete system of individual statuses is impossible so the early state concentrates on a few key statuses (helping to explain the tendency to convert any crime into either sacrilege or lèse majesté) and on the basic principles of organization, e.g., the idea of hierarchy, property, and the power of the law.

The implementation of these primary functions of the state gives rise to a number of specific and characteristic secondary functions, each of which is associated with one or more particular institutions of its own. These secondary functions include population control in the most general sense (the fixing of boundaries and the definition of the unit; establishment of categories of membership; census). Also a secondary function is the disposal of trouble cases (civil and criminal laws moving toward the status of codes; regular legal procedure; regular officers of adjudication). The protection of sovereignty is also included (maintenance of military forces; police forces and power; eminent domain). Finally, all of the preceding require fiscal support, and this is achieved in the main through taxation and conscription.

In treating of this bare but essential list of state functions and institutions the idea of the state as a universal aspect of culture dissolves as a fantasy. The institutions just itemized may be made to appear in ones or twos in certain primitive societies by exaggeration and by the neglect of known history. In no egalitarian society and in no rank society do a majority of the functions enumerated appear regardless of their guise. Furthermore there is no indication of their appearance as a unified functional response to basic sociocultural needs except in those stratified societies which are verging upon statehood.

The Transition to State

Just as stratified society grew out of antecedent forms of society without the conscious awareness of the culture carriers, so it would seem that the state emerged from the stratified society in a similar, inexorable way. If this hypothesis is correct, then such an explanation as the so-called "conquest theory" can be accepted only as a special case of "secondary-state" formation. The conquests discussed by such a theorist as Franz Oppenheimer (1914) established not stratification but super-stratification, either the conqueror or the conquered, or perhaps even both, already being internally stratified.

The problem of the transition to state is so huge and requires such painstaking application to the available archaeological and historical evidence that it would be foolish to pursue it seriously here. Let us conclude, therefore, by harking back to statements made at the outset of this paper, and noting again the distinction between pristine and secondary states. By the former term is meant a state that has developed *sui generis* out of purely local conditions. No previous state, with its acculturative pressures, can be discerned in the background of a pristine state. The secondary state, on the other hand, is pushed by one means or another toward a higher form of organization by an external power which has already been raised to statehood.

The number of pristine states is strictly limited; several centuries, possibly two millennia, have elapsed since the last one emerged in Meso-America, and there seems to be no possibility that any further states of the pristine type will evolve, though further research may bring to light some of the distant past of which we yet have no positive information. In all, there seems to have been some six centers at which pristine states emerged, four in the Old World and two in the New: the Tigris-Euphrates area, the region of the lower Nile, the country drained by the Indus and the middle course of the Huang Ho where it is joined by the Han, Wei, and Fen. The separate areas of Peru-Bolivia and Meso-America complete the roster.

If there is utility in the concept of the pristine state and if history has been read correctly in limiting the designation to the six areas just enumerated, then we discover a remarkable correlation between areas demanding irrigation or flood control and the pristine state. Certainly this is no discovery of the author. It is one of the central ideas of Wittfogel's theory and has received extensive treatment from Julian Steward and others (see Steward, 1955, pp. 178-209; Steward *et al.,* 1955). The implication of the "hydraulic theory" for this paper, however, is that the development of the state as an internal phenomenon is associated with major tasks of drainage and irrigation. The emergence of a control system to ensure the operation of the economy is closely tied to the appearance of a distinctive class system and certain constellations of power in the hands of a managerial bureaucracy which frequently operates below a ruler who commands theoretically unlimited power.

It is an interesting commentary on nineteenth-century political philosophy that the starting point of so many theories was, of necessity, the Classical world of Greece and Rome. According to the present hypothesis, however, both of these great political developments of antiquity were not pristine but secondary formations which built on cultural foundations laid two thousand years and more before the rise of Greece. Furthermore, it would seem that the active commercial and military influences of the truly ancient pristine states, mediated through the earliest of the secondary states to appear in Asia Minor and the eastern Mediterranean littoral, were catalysts in the events of the northern and western Mediterranean.

Conclusion

The close of a paper like this, which moves like a gadfly from time to time, place to place, and subject matter to subject matter, and which never pauses long enough to make a truly detailed inquiry or supply the needed documentation, the close of such a paper requires an apology perhaps more than a conclusion.

I have been led to write this paper by my ignorance of any modern attempt to link up the contributions which have been made in many sub-disciplines into a single unified theory of the emergence of social stratification and the state. That the theory offered here is crude, often too special, and by no means documented seems less important than that it may be used as a sitting duck to attract the fire and better aim of others.

Notes

[1] The reader may object to crediting Polanyi with the concept of a reciprocal economy. While it is true that Thurnwald and Malinowski earlier expressed similar concepts, and Durkheim, with his distinction between segmental and organic societies, also foreshadows this development, it awaited Polanyi's analysis to place reciprocal economies into systematic harmony with other, more complex types of economy, such as the redistributive type discussed later on, and the market kind as well. For Polanyi's definitions of each of these types see Polanyi, Arensberg, and Pearson, 1957, pp. 250-56.

[2] For an ethnographic illustration of this point see Oliver, 1955, pp. 422 ff.

[3] These, of course, would be ranked lineages or ranked clans. Cf. Fried, 1957, pp. 23-26.

[4] As does Leach 1954, p. 10.

[5] Strategic resources are those things which, given the technological base and environmental setting of the culture, maintain subsistence. See Fried, 1957, p. 24.

[6] Our residence terms follow usage suggested by J. L. Fischer (1958).

References

Duguit, Léon. 1921. Traité de droit constitutionnel. 2d ed. Vol. 1. Paris.

Easton, David. 1953. The Political System. New York.

Fischer, J.L. 1958. "The Classification of Residence in Censuses," *American Anthropologist,* 60:508-17.

Fried, Morton H. 1957. "The Classification of Corporate Unilineal Descent Groups," *Journal of the Royal Anthropological Institute,* 87:1-29.

Hoebel, E. Adamson. 1949. Man in the Primitive World. 1st ed. New York.

———— 1958. Man in the Primitive World. 2d ed. New York.

Kirchhoff, Paul. 1935. "The Principles of Clanship in Human Society." (Ms; cf. *Davidson Journal of Anthropology* 1 [1955]).

Landtman, Gunnar. 1938. The Origin of the Inequality of the Social Classes. London.

Leach, E.R. 1954. Political Systems of Highland Burma. Cambridge, Mass.

Leacock, Eleanor. 1958. "Status among the Montagnais-Naskapi of Labrador," *Ethnohistory*, 5: Part 3:200-209.

Oliver, Douglas. 1955. A Solomon Island Society. Cambridge, Mass.

Oppenheimer, Franz. 1914. The State: Its History and Development Viewed Sociologically. New York.

Polanyi, Karl, Conrad M. Arensberg, and Harry W. Pearson, eds. 1957. Trade and Market in the Early Empires. Glencoe, Ill.

Sahlins, Marshall. 1958. Social Stratification in Polynesia. Seattle.

———— 1957. "Differentiation by Adaptation in Polynesian Societies," *Journal of the Polynesian Society*, 66:291-300.

Steward, Julian H. 1955. Theory of Culture Change. Urbana, Ill.

Steward, Julian H., *et al.* 1955. Irrigation Civilizations: A Comparative Study. Social Science Monographs #1, Washington, D.C.

Sumner, W.G., and A.G. Keller. 1927. The Science of Society. New Haven, Conn.

Tylor, Edward B. 1888. "On a Method of Investigating the Development of Institutions; Applied to Laws of Marriage and Descent," *Journal of the Royal Anthropological Institute*, 18:245-69.

White, Leslie. 1948. "The Definition and Prohibition of Incest," *American Anthropologist*, 50:416-35.

Wittfogel, Karl A. 1957. Oriental Despotism. New Haven, Conn.

Part II

The New World

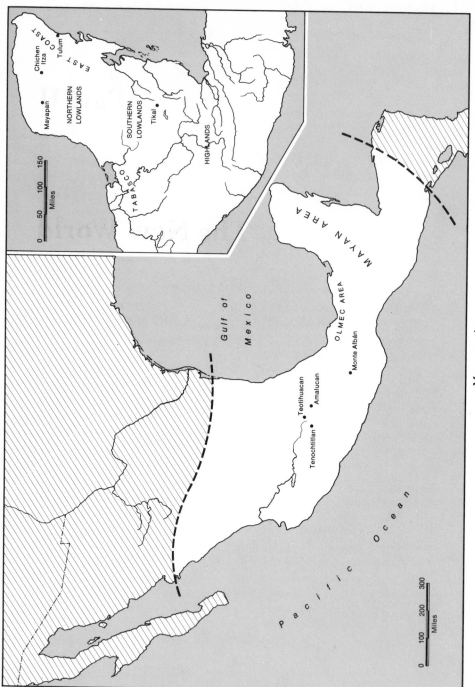

Mesoamerica.

Richard S. MacNeish is director of the R. S. Peabody Foundation, Andover
Academy, in Andover, Massachusetts. Since receiving his Ph.D. from the
University of Chicago in 1949, he has worked from the farthest reaches
of North America, in the Arctic, to the southern highlands of Peru in South
America. In his classic study of the arid Tehuacan Valley in Mexico, which
drew on several natural sciences as well as archaeology, he traced the development of culture and economy from 10,000 B.C. to the time of the Spanish
Conquest. Four volumes of the final report of this monumental project,
The Prehistory of the Tehuacan Valley (1967-1971) have recently been
published. In this article and the succeeding one, two different hypotheses
concerning the reasons for the rise of settled village life in Mesoamerica
are presented. MacNeish supports a highland argument, while Coe and
Flannery argue for the primacy, or at least the importance of, the lowlands.
These two articles provide a foundation for the articles on the rise and fall
of civilization which follow.

Speculation about How and Why Food Production and Village Life Developed in the Tehuacan Valley, Mexico

Richard Stockton MacNeish

The main purpose of the Robert S. Peabody Foundation's archaeological endeavors
in the Tehuacan Valley of central Mexico was to try to understand the beginnings of food
production (mainly corn agriculture) and the rise of village life. To accomplish this,
archaeological reconnaissance was undertaken in this small ecological zone with its four
micro-environs, and thus 454 sites were found. Later, twelve stratified sites with 138
superimposed floors were excavated. Study of the 10,000 artifacts, 500,000 sherds and
50,000 ecofacts (remnants of the environment) from these floors, plus 120 radiocarbon
determinations, together with many interdisciplinary studies, resulted in our defining a
long cultural sequence from about 10,000 B.C. to A.D. 1520. The first six of our nine
culture phases, roughly from 10,000 to 850 B.C., have given us considerable new information in understanding how and why agriculture and village life began in this small region.
In the following pages, I shall summarize these earlier culture phases and attempt to explain why the major culture changes occurred.

The earliest components from 10,000 to 6700 B.C. have been classified into the
Ajuereado phase, so called from the site. The sustenance of these earliest peoples seems
to have been mainly meat (perhaps over 70%) with a lesser amount gained from vegetal

Reprinted from *Archaeology*, Vol. 24, No. 4, pp. 307-315, by permission of the Archaeological Institute
of America and author. Copyright 1971 by Archaeological Institute of America.

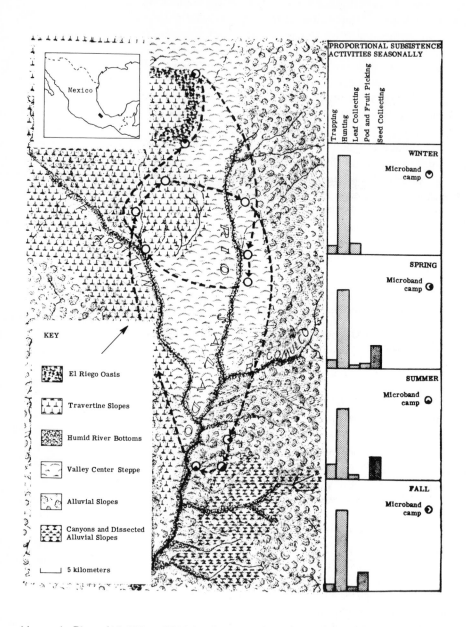

Ajuereado Phase (10,000 to 7000 B.C.) with estimates of proportions of subsistence activities by season (right column) and the distribution of seasonal microband camps with their hypothetical wanderings that form Nomadic microband communities in the micro-environments of the Tehuacan Valley, Mexico (left column).

foods. In terms of subsistence activities, hunting was of prime importance: drives, ambushing with lance and dart-stalking were techniques utilized in all seasons. In the winter, hunting was probably the only means of subsistence. In other periods of the year, meat was supplemented by collecting pods in the spring, seeds in the spring and summer, fruits in the fall, and by cutting opuntia and agave leaves in all of these seasons.

Stone tools give evidence of industrial activity. These were usually hard stone percussion chipped flakes derived from blocky cores, usually without prepared striking platforms. Some of these flakes were finished by pressure retouching. Diagnostic tool types include Lerma and Abasolo points, flake and slab choppers, crude blades, well-made end scrapers, gravers and side scraper knives. These latter tools hint that there probably was a hide-working industry. Chipped spokeshaves, possibly indicate a woodworking industry.

All components uncovered came from site areas of less than one hundred square meters, and most excavated components had only one or two fireplaces. In this way, I consider all components to have been occupied by less than three families, and I have classified all such sites as microband camps. When looking at the site distribution over the valley, no clustering can be discerned, so there is no evidence of territoriality, nor is there any correlation between seasonal occupations and any particular micro-environment. On the basis of this data I have classified the community pattern of Ajuereado as *Nomadic Microbands*, that is, groups of families who hunted game in all seasons without regard to any well-regulated subsistence scheduling or well-defined territories.

In my opinion the change from *Nomadic Microbands* to *Seasonal Macro-Microbands* (the community type characteristic of our next two phases) was a slow process which began about a thousand years before the transition actually took place—roughly during the late Ajuereado phase, say, about 9600 B.C. Previous to this time our evidence reveals that the Valley people had specialized in various kinds of hunting activities, but in the long period of the development of these techniques, they also acquired, as a by-product, a tremendous knowledge of the other food potential of their micro-environments at various seasons. As a supplement to their meat diet they had experimented with seed collection, pod and fruit picking, and leaf cutting. This gradual accumulation of subsistence and ecological knowledge coincided with the waning of the Pleistocene with its changes in weather and rainfall which resulted in a greater diversity in seasons, a drier and warmer climate, a diminution of grassland steppes and water holes, as well as an expansion of the thorn forests on the alluvial slopes, and an expansion of the cactus forests on to the travertine slopes. In part, these changes brought about the extinction of the various "herd" animals, such as horse and antelope, as well as the disappearance of other Pleistocene fauna ranging from the jack rabbit to the mammoth and mastodon. In this way, changes in the ecosystem became interconnected with changes in subsistence; with changes in subsistence patterns, there were alterations to the ecosystem. An interstimulating feedback cycle was in process. Although climactic changes and changes in the ecosystem had probably occurred previously in the Tehuacan Valley, apparently never before had they coincided at a time when men were ready with exactly the right variety of eco-subsistence knowledge crucial to cause a major culture change.

We may speculate, in terms of seasonal cycles, that in the spring, the Ajuereado people, as was their wont, hunted for herd animals on the grasslands in most of the center of the valley, but as the waning Pleistocene caused this grassland to shrink in size, causing some herd animals to die off, other animals disappeared because man could more easily kill off the remainder in this more limited area. This meant that through time, in the spring, groups began to subsist more and more on the seed and pod foods from the steppe rather than from the meat. They collected these seeds and pods from spots they already knew and by techniques they had already developed.

The summer wet season that formerly had always been the time when food was plentiful now saw man move out of the grasslands since seeds had already been picked and game had already been hunted out. The people turned to exploit any of the other available micro-environs. But, again, game was disappearing, so more and more of man's summer food also came from leaves, fruits and seeds, again from places they knew well and by techniques they had earlier developed but previously used little.

Fall, which formerly would have yielded game in any ecological niche, now had little game. Pod, seed and leaf foods had also been collected from most areas, so many moved on into the few areas he knew about where there were still fruits and plants to pick.

The winter season which, even in Pleistocene times, had never been productive as far as plant food was concerned had allowed for hunting in a number of areas. Winter hunting now became even worse because of the increased dryness and smaller grassland area. Both man and animal were forced instead to cluster around the few well-watered areas, which again meant man further diminished the supply of game. Thus, the Tehuacanos shifted gradually from hunting over a wide area, in all seasons, to a system of well-scheduled subsistence activities in terms of particular seasons and micro-environments.

Life style changes such as these may have later led to new developments in technology, for instance, perhaps paintstones developed into mortar and milling stones to grind the increasing quantity of plant-derived foods. Certainly, by the end of Ajuereado times, Valley people were moving about in well-regulated regional cycles so that bands became tied to territories and, gradually, as they found abundant foodstuffs at particular places in the wet seasons, small groups coalesced into larger groups (macrobands) for brief periods. Changes in the social system may also have taken place in response to the new way of life and the slightly greater population. These changes in technology, territoriality, settlement patterns, population growth and social structure, however, came after the changes in environment, and after the necessary accumulation of ecological and subsistence knowledge. I am, therefore, suggesting that environmental and subsistence changes are the causative factors, resulting in changed settlement patterns, technology, etc.

What I am leading up to is this. Is the above described process not similar to that which occurred in the Zagros Mountains of the Near East between the cultural phases of Baradostian and Zarzi, after the climatic change of 14,000 B.C. as indicated in the pollen profile? And, aren't these two instances of cultural change similar to what happened in the Andes of Peru in the change from the cultural phase of Huanta to Puente, just after the final extinction of the Pleistocene fauna at about 7400 B.C.? I am suggesting these three illustrations are comparable.

But to return to the Tehuacan Valley. The El Riego phase, 6700-5000 B.C., brought certain new changes in subsistence patterns although at this time period 54% of their food was still from meat, 40% came from vegetal stuffs and 0-6% was from agricultural produce. The major difference as formerly, however, was in the particular scheduling of their subsistence activities. The picture for the El Riego phase, as I see it, seemed to be as follows: in the winter, these people obtained most of their food by hunting (mostly by lance-ambushing or dart-stalking) and they supplemented this activity with leaf cutting and trapping. In the spring, their predominant activity was seed collecting and pod picking which was also supplemented by hunting and leaf cutting. The summer season continued these spring practices, except that activities were now augmented by barranca horticulture of mixta squash, amaranth and chile. Fall saw fruit picking becoming the predominant activity which in turn was supplemented by hunting, leaf cutting and avocado cultivation which required a system of hydro-horticulture.

Industrial activities had also changed although our most substantial evidence still comes from chipped stone tools. Flakes and crude blades are now struck from cores usually with prepared platforms by hard and soft (antler) hammers, and then retouched. Tools so made include such point types as Flacco, El Riego, Trinidad and Hidalgo. There were gouges and crude blades, too. Many tools, however, are at this time made from the cores themselves, such as, bifacial choppers and scraper planes turned out by percussion chipping with soft hammers. A new ground stone industry occurs, and we now find mortar, pestle, milling stones and mullers. We also find wooden tools, the weaving of non-interlocking stitch baskets and knotted and knotless nets. There is mat twining, string making and bone awl and antler hammer manufacturing as well as bead making.

We also found a few group burials and there is some evidence of cremation, and possibly of human sacrifice and infanticide. These latter ritual activities which became so prevalent in later Mesoamerica evidently were developing at these earlier times.

A study of the twenty-four microband and eleven macroband occupations of the El Riego phase is the basis for the belief that the community pattern here represented might be classified as *Seasonal Micro-Macrobands* having territoriality and a scheduled subsistence system. Here, a number of family groups or microbands staying within their own designated territory would usually gather together into macrobands in various places in the river bottoms, or at lusher niches on the alluvial slopes in the summer when food was plentiful. Then, with the coming of fall they would break up into microbands to hunt and collect fruits on the alluvial slopes, or in the dissected canyons, or on the steppes of the various parts of their band territory. In the drier winter months, the microband would move again to hunt in the oasis area, the travertine canyons, the humid river bottoms, the alluvial slopes or the dissected canyons, or anywhere else where they could find game. As spring came on and as pods and seeds became available, the small family groups would move into any of the various zones of their territories where these foods were available, and then the cycle would start over again with the coming of the wet summer.

The Coxcatlan phase, from 5000 to 3400 B.C., sees some changes from El Riego times in the proportion of foodstuffs consumed, with wild plants composing 52% of their diet, meat 34% and agricultural produce 14%, but the subsistence activities and their scheduling is much the same. The fall and winter activities were also similar to the El Riego phase and in the spring seed collection is still predominant, but it is now supplemented by leaf cutting, pod picking, hunting, root digging and barranca horticulture involving the growth of amaranth. The summer season during Coxcatlan times is different

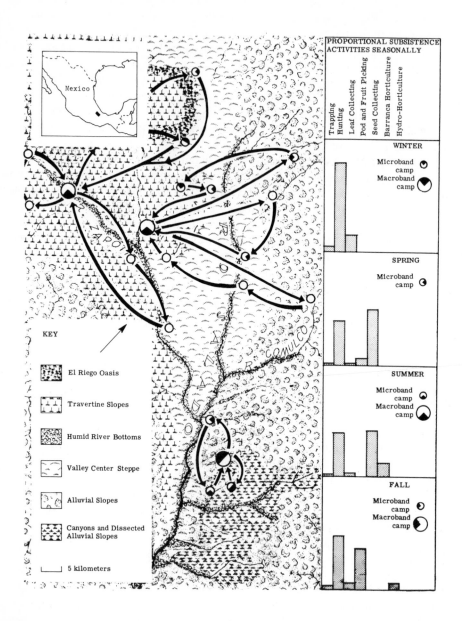

El Riego Phase (7000 to 5000 B.C.) with estimates of proportions of seasonally scheduled subsistence activities (right column) and the distribution of seasonal microband-macroband camps with their possible cyclical movements that form communities of seasonal micro-macrobands in territories within the micro-environments of the Tehuacan Valley (left column).

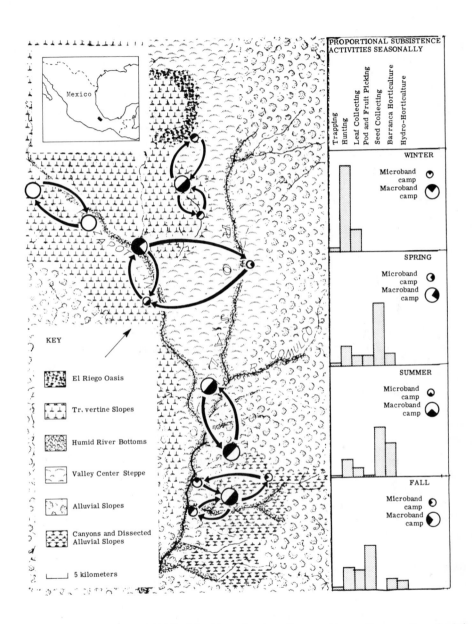

Coxcatlan Phase (7000 to 3400 B.C.) with estimates of proportions of seasonally scheduled subsistence activities (right column) and the distribution of seasonal macroband and microband camps with their possible cyclical movements that form communities of seasonal macro-microbands in territories within the micro-environments of the Tehuacan Valley, Mexico (left column).

with the emphasis being on seed collection and barranca horticulture of a wide variety of plants, such as corn, beans, zapotes, gourds, etc. with only minor supplemental hunting subsistence activities.

Techniques of chipping flint are little different from previously but there is more fine pressure retouching and some blades are struck from cylindrical cores by indirect percussion. There are, however, a host of new chipped stone types such as Tilapa, Coxcatlan, Almagre and Garyito points, fine blades, end of blade scrapers, etc. The ground stone industry continues with manos, metates and anvil stones being new types. More wooden tools include digging sticks and atlatl (a throwing stick) dart parts. Bone needles are added to the bone tool complex. The weaving and string making industry is little changed but interlocking and split stitch baskets appeared for the first time. Complex burials continue to occur. Our study of sites and occupational floors indicated that the Coxcatlan phase had a settlement and community pattern like that of El Riego, Seasonal Macro-Microbands, with territoriality and with a scheduled subsistence including horticulture.

Now to speculate about the change from Seasonal *Macro-Microbands* to *Central-Based Bands,* our next community pattern type: it would appear that the use of a scheduled subsistence system in the ecosystem of the Tehuacan Valley led at first to the development of more and more specialization in various kinds of collection techniques, such as, seed collection and fruit picking.

One might guess that at an early stage it was merely a matter of returning to the same seed or fruit area each year. This in turn led to some clearing (weeding), some enrichment and general improvement of the area which then provided a new artificial environment for the seeds or fruits. This in turn would have led to various genetic changes in the seed or fruit population. Eventually, this may have led to actual cultivation (perhaps at first merely taking seeds or leaves from one environs and dropping them in another) then to purposeful planting, and finally to seed selection and horticulture. This process coupled with the introduction of other domesticates from other regions must have led to longer residence at the halting places and to rescheduling of macroband activities. Perhaps, macrobands came to collect some seeds in the spring along the barrancas, as well as planting some seeds and fruits. These latter plants reached fruition in the summer rainy seasons, thereby allowing the bands to be in the same spot for two seasons, and this then became a base for hunting and collecting camps in other regions in the leaner seasons. This process again would gradually result in some technological advances, greater populations and new changes in their social system. In this way, the basic causative factors were again changes in subsistence techniques, for the Coxcatlan phase, the two principal factors were an intensified scheduled subsistence system and the diffusion of many domesticated plants into this region. Obviously, there are environmental limitations to these changes.

In the Ayacucho region of highland Peru, there is a similar life zone with great micro-environmental diversity and with some wild plants (and animals) susceptible to domestication, and a similar development seems to have occurred during Jaywa and Piki times from 6700 to 9300 B.C. Did such a process occur during Zarzi times, 15,000 to 9000 B.C. in the Zagros Mountains in the Near East?

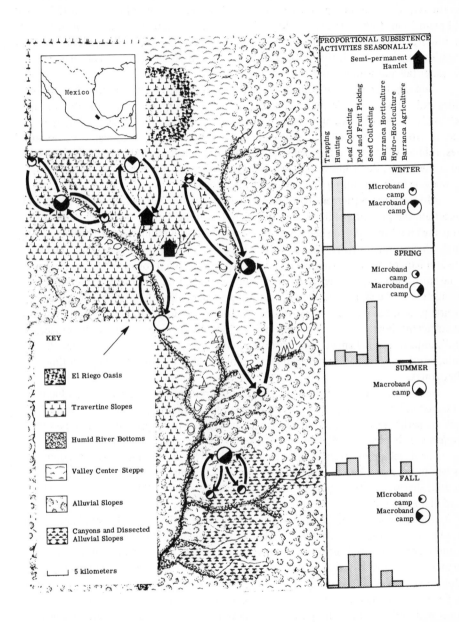

Abejas Phase (3400 to 2300 B.C.) with estimates of proportions of seasonally scheduled subsistence activities (right column) and the distribution of their hamlets and macroband camps that were the bases for the seasonal microband and macroband camps, forming communities of Central based bands within the micro-environments (left column).

But back to Mexico, and the following Abejas phase from 3400 to 2300 B.C. which sees the rise of agricultural produce (at least 25%) at the expense of both meat (25%) and wild plant foods (50%). The scheduling of the subsistence activities is like that of Coxcatlan, but again in the summer and spring the barranca horticulture increases. These increased activities may have at this time produced surpluses that could be stored and then eaten in the leaner fall and winter months.

Chipping techniques are much the same as those of Coxcatlan, although more fine blades and cores appear. Again, of course, new types of chipped stone artifacts turn up such as Catan and Pelona points, fine rectangular blades and bifacial disks. More new types of ground stone tools also appear such as discoidal beads, ovoid plano-convex metates, rubbed pebbles, paint palettes, cuboid pestles, polishing pebbles, spherical manos and stone bowls. Bone and wood tools and types of cordage are about the same, as was the weaving industry. Burial practices are little known.

Although the settlement pattern information has similarities to both El Riego and Coxcatlan, the presence of linear waterway hamlets along with an increased number of camp sites tend to make me believe that a new type of community pattern was emerging which I have termed *Central Based Bands*. Here, I believe, most bands had a permanent base at a hamlet or macroband camp, and that groups banded together as macrobands in the spring and stayed together through summer and/or fall. Probably, they collected and planted in the spring and then later in the summer and/or fall are their limited agricultural produce as well as wild stuffs. Their agricultural production in the main was still not sufficient, however, for all macrobands to live all year round either in their macroband camps or in the hamlets. So, with the coming of the leaner months, in the fall and winter some of them had to move and to exploit (mainly by collecting and hunting) other zones.

Nevertheless, with the coming of spring they returned once again to their hamlets or macroband base camps. Obviously, this type of community pattern is transitional from the earlier seasonal macro-microband type and the next type called *Semi-permanent Hamlets* which existed in Ajalpan times but may have commenced in Purron.

The development from Central-Based Bands to Semi-permanent Hamlet communities was in large part due to three factors. One was a change in the mode of food production, that is, a shift from horticulture with a wide variety of domesticated or cultivated plants, to intensively growing a few plants (corn, chile, beans and squash) in/or just before the rainy seasons in the barrancas, i.e., barranca agriculture. This subsistence activity, plus the fact that a number of the plants they grew were now vigorous hybrids, a second factor, produced sufficient food to allow them to live in hamlets all year round. Further, this relatively stable subsistence allowed them to make improvements in technology, and as well to borrow a number of cultural improvements, such as, pottery-making, wattle-and-daub house making, the figurine cult, etc. It follows that a stimulating interaction with other slightly different cultural developments in other environs became a third crucial factor in cultural change. Needless to say, the population increased and new mechanisms of social control developed which again changed their social system.

Isn't the process of change in the Zagros of Iraq from the time of Zawi Chemi or Karim Shahir to Jarmo, so succinctly described by Braidwood, similar to what I have just speculated for Tehuacan? There are also hints that in periods from Piki to Chihua and/or Cachi in highland Peru a similar process may have evolved.

The next phase in Tehuacan, Purron, 2300 to 1500 B.C., is extremely poorly known, but barranca agriculture probably increased in the summer and spring to give surpluses that could be eaten in the fall and winter. The only discernible new aspect of their technology was the introduction of pottery. Only two cave floors were uncovered so there is little we can say about settlement patterns.

The next cultural phase, Ajalpan, 1500 to 850 B.C., is better known. Foodstuffs from excavation reveal that about 40% of their diet came from agricultural produce, 31% from wild plants and 29% from meat. In terms of subsistence activities the year was now divided into two parts—the "wet" spring-summer season when they still did hunting and collecting but with the hamlets as their base camps. In other words, they were growing sufficient food in one season to last all year and for this reason I refer to this system as *Subsistence Agricultural* production rather than effective food production.

Their technology also saw a shift with the ceramic industry now of major importance with ten monochrome pottery types and six or seven figurine types being manufactured. The weaving industry also changed with cotton string now being made by use of a spindle whorl and cloth woven on a loom, while baskets and mats were twilled. As well, various kinds of beads and pendants were made. New utilitarian types of ground stone tools come to the fore. The chipped stone, woodworking, leather and bone working industries changed but little, even though new types occurred.

Burials now were placed in deep bell-shaped pits and there is evidence of "cult" object ceremonies.

Settlement pattern studies of Ajalpan reveal that there were now twelve hamlets, a single macroband spring-summer occupation and a single microband summer occupation in caves. And this pattern made up three or four separate communities aligned along the edge of waterways. Thanks to intensive agriculture in the spring and summer wet seasons in the barrancas or river bottoms which gave a whole year's supply of food, the residents were now sedentary, although occasional trips were still made out from their homes for planting, harvesting, plant collection and hunting. This community pattern which I have classified as the Semi-permanent Hamlet type represents the time when village life based on subsistence food production began in the Tehuacan Valley. It also represents the first time that population increased markedly, a major causative factor for cultural change in later periods.

The next phase, Santa Maria, 850 to 150 B.C., sees the rise of templed villages, a figurine cult, the beginning of irrigation agriculture, truly effective food production and many other cultural innovations, but this is outside our present realm of discourse and after the period under discussion. Also later is the later Palo Blanco phase, 150 B.C. to A.D. 700, with its great population increases, hilltop towns and classic Monte Alban-like features, and in addition our final Venta Salada phase, A.D. 700 to 1500, with its city-states and Mixteca-Puebla type of culture is beyond the scope of this essay.

Therefore, as far as the Tehuacan Valley is concerned, the Ajalpan phase sees the first establishment of village life, and sees the end of the story about the beginnings of food production. This whole picture is, of course, far from complete, but I believe we now have at least some inklings about how and why it happened, at least in one valley, in one culture area, in one world—the New World. Was not the process analogous to processes in other similar areas where pristine civilization occurred?

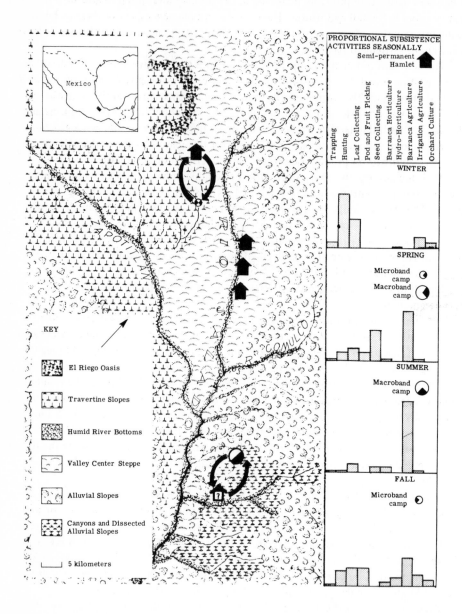

Ajalpan Phase (1500 to 850 B.C.) with estimates of proportions of subsistence activities that were basically food producing at all seasons (right column) and distribution of semi-permanent sedentary hamlets or villages and their seasonal microband and macroband camps for planting and harvesting in the micro-environments of the Tehuacan Valley, Mexico (left column).

Michael D. Coe (Ph.D., Harvard, 1959) is professor of anthropology at
Yale University and has worked widely in Mesoamerica. He is the author
of two very popular books on Mesoamerican archaeology, *The Maya*
(1966) and *Mexico* (1962). He also is responsible for some of the most
important discoveries and significant ideas concerning the rise of Olmec
civilization in the mid-second millenium B.C. in Mexico (see *America's
First Civilization*, 1968).

Kent V. Flannery is professor of anthropology at the University
of Michigan and a curator of the Museum of Anthropology there. He
received his Ph.D. from the University of Chicago in 1964. His interests
lie particularly in environmental archaeology and cultural ecology, and
he has done field work in both Mesoamerica and the Near East. He is the
co-author of *Prehistory and Human Ecology of the Deh Luran Plain* (1969)
and is currently directing a major project in the Valley of Oaxaca, Mexico.

The change from nomadic hunting-gathering to settled village agriculture was a giant step forward on the pathway to civilization. In this
article, Coe and Flannery explore the reasons why man chose to make
such a change in his life-ways, and the effects of such economic change
on the rest of his culture.

Microenvironments and Mesoamerican Prehistory

Michael D. Coe
Kent V. Flannery

A crucial period in the story of the pre-Columbian cultures of the New World is the
transition from a hunting-and-collecting way of life to effective village farming. We are
now fairly certain that Mesoamerica[1] is the area in which this took place, and that the
time span involved is from approximately 6500 to 1000 B.C., a period during which a
kind of "incipient cultivation" based on a few domesticated plants, mainly maize, gradually supplemented and eventually replaced wild foods.[2] Beginning probably about 1500
B.C., and definitely by 1000 B.C., villages with all of the signs of the settled arts, such as
pottery and loom-weaving, appear throughout Mesoamerica, and the foundations of pre-
Columbian civilization may be said to have been established.

Much has been written about food-producing "revolutions" in both hemispheres.
There is now good evidence both in the Near East and in Mesoamerica that food produc-

Reprinted from *Science*, Vol. 143, pp. 650-654, by permission of the publisher and authors. Copyright
1964 by the American Association for the Advancement of Science.

tion was part of a relatively slow *evolution,* but there still remain several problems related to the process of settling down. For the New World, there are three questions which we would like to answer.

(1) What factors favored the early development of food production in Mesoamerica as compared with other regions of this hemisphere?

(2) What was the mode of life of the earlier hunting-and-collecting peoples in Mesoamerica, and in exactly what ways was it changed by the addition of cultivated plants?

(3) When, where, and how did food production make it possible for the first truly sedentary villages to be established in Mesoamerica?

The first of these questions cannot be answered until botanists determine the habits and preferred habitats of the wild ancestors of maize, beans, and the various cucurbits which were domesticated. To answer the other questions, we must reconstruct the human-ecological situations which prevailed.

Some remarkably sophisticated, multidisciplinary projects have been and still are being carried out elsewhere in the world, aimed at reconstructing prehistoric human ecology. However, for the most part they have been concerned with the adaptations of past human communities to large-scale changes in the environment over very long periods—that is, to alterations in the *macroenvironment,* generally caused by climatic fluctuations. Such alterations include the shift from tundra to boreal conditions in northern Europe. Nevertheless, there has been a growing suspicion among prehistorians that macroenvironmental changes are insufficient as an explanation of the possible causes of food production and its effects,[3] regardless of what has been written to the contrary.

Ethnography and Microenvironments

We have been impressed, in reading anthropologists' accounts of simple societies, with the fact that human communities, while in some senses limited by the macroenvironment—for instance, by deserts or by tropical forests[4]—usually exploit several or even a whole series of well-defined *microenvironments* in their quest for food.[5] These microenvironments might be defined as smaller subdivisions of large ecological zones; examples are the immediate surroundings of the ancient archaeological site itself, the bank of a nearby stream, or a distant patch of forest.

An interesting case is provided by the Shoshonean bands which, until the mid-19th century, occupied territories within the Great Basin of the American West.[6] These extremely primitive peoples had a mode of life quite similar to that of the peoples of Mesoamerica of the 5th millennium B.C., who were the first to domesticate maize. The broadly limiting effects of the Great Basin (which, generally speaking, is a desert) and the lack of knowledge of irrigation precluded any effective form of agriculture, even though some bands actually sowed wild grasses and one group tried an ineffective watering of wild crops. Consequently, the Great Basin aborigines remained on a hunting and plant-collecting level, with extremely low population densities and a very simple social organization. However, Steward's study[6] shows that each band was not inhabiting a mere desert but moved on a strictly followed seasonal round among a vertically and horizontally differentiated set of microenvironments, from the lowest salt flats up to piñon forest, which were "niches" in a human-ecological sense.

The Great Basin environment supplied the potential for cultural development or lack of it, but the men who lived there selected this or that microenvironment. Steward clearly shows that *how* and *to what* they adapted influenced many other aspects of their culture, from their technology to their settlement pattern, which was necessarily one of restricted wandering from one seasonally occupied camp to another.

Seasonal wandering would appear to be about the only possible response of a people without animal or plant husbandry to the problem of getting enough food throughout the year. Even the relatively rich salmon-fishing cultures of the Northwest Coast (British Columbia and southern Alaska) were without permanently occupied villages. Contrariwise, it has seemed to us that only a drastic reduction of the number of niches to be exploited, and a concentration of these in space, would have permitted the establishment of full-time village life. The ethnographic data suggest that an analysis of microenvironments or niches would throw much light on the processes by which the Mesoamerican peoples settled down.

Methodology

If the environment in which an ancient people lived was radically different from any known today, and especially if it included animal and plant species which are now extinct and whose behavior is consequently unknown, then any reconstruction of the subsistence activities of the people is going to be difficult. All one could hope for would be a more-or-less sound reconstruction of general ecological conditions, while a breakdown of the environment into smaller ecological niches would be impossible. However, much if not most archaeological research concerns periods so recent in comparison with the million or so years of human prehistory that in most instances local conditions have not changed greatly in the interval between the periods investigated and the present.

If we assume that there is a continuity between the ancient and the modern macroenvironment in the area of interest, there are three steps which we must take in tracing the role of microenvironments.

(1) Analysis of the present-day microecology (from the human point of view) of the archaeological zone. Archaeological research is often carried out in remote and little known parts of the earth, which have not been studied from the point of view of natural history. Hence, the active participation of botanists, zoologists, and other natural scientists is highly recommended.

The modern ethnology of the region should never be neglected, for all kinds of highly relevant data on the use of surrounding niches by local people often lie immediately at hand. We have found in Mesoamerica that the workmen on the "dig" are a mine of such information. There may be little need to thumb through weighty reports on the Australian aborigines or South African Bushmen when the analogous custom can be found right under one's nose.[7] The end result of the analysis should be a map of the microenvironments defined (here aerial photographs are of great use), with detailed data on the seasonal possibilities each offers human communities on certain technological levels of development.

(2) Quantitative analysis of food remains in the archaeological sites, and of the

technical equipment (arrow or spear points, grinding stones for seeds, baskets and other containers, and so on) related to food-getting. It is a rare site report that treats of bones and plant remains in any but the most perfunctory way. It might seem a simple thing to ship animal bones from a site to a specialist for identification, but most archaeologists know that many zoologists consider identification of recent faunal remains a waste of time.[8] Because of this, and because many museum collections do not include postcranial skeletons that could be used for identification, the archaeologist must arrange to secure his own comparative collection. If this collection is assembled by a zoologist on the project, a by-product of the investigation would be a faunal study of microenvironments. Similarly, identification of floral and other specimens from the site would lead to other specialized studies.

(3) Correlation of the archaeological with the microenvironmental study in an overall analysis of the ancient human ecology.

The Tehuacán Valley

An archaeological project undertaken by R. S. MacNeish, with such a strategy in mind, has been located since 1961 in the dry Tehuacán Valley of southern Puebla, Mexico.[2, 9] The valley is fringed with bone-dry caves in which the food remains of early peoples have been preserved to a remarkable degree in stratified deposits. For a number of reasons, including the results of his past archaeological work in Mesoamerica, MacNeish believed that he would find here the origins of maize agriculture in the New World, and he has been proved right. It now seems certain that the wild ancestor of maize was domesticated in the Tehuacán area some time around the beginning of the 5th millennium B.C.

While the Tehuacán environment is in general a desert, the natural scientists of the project have defined within it four microenvironments.

(1) *Alluvial valley floor,* a level plain sparsely covered with mesquite, grasses, and cacti, offering fairly good possibilities, especially along the Rio Salado, for primitive maize agriculture dependent on rainfall.

(2) *Travertine slopes,* on the west side of the valley. This would have been a niche useful for growing maize and tomatoes and for trapping cottontail rabbits.

(3) *Coxcatlán thorn forest,* with abundant seasonal crops of wild fruits, such as various species of *Opuntia,* pitahaya, and so on. There is also a seasonal abundance of whitetail deer, cottontail rabbits, and skunks, and there are some peccaries.

(4) *Eroded canyons,* unsuitable for exploitation except for limited hunting of deer and as routes up to maguey fields for those peoples who chewed the leaves of that plant.

The correlation of this study with the analysis, by specialists, of the plant and animal remains (these include bones, maize cobs, chewed quids, and even feces) found in cave deposits has shown that the way of life of the New World's first farmers was not very different from that of the Great Basin aborigines in the 19th century. Even the earliest inhabitants of the valley, prior to 6500 B.C., were more collectors of seasonally gathered wild plant foods than they were "big game hunters," and they traveled in microbands in an annual, wet-season-dry-season cycle.[10] While slightly more sedentary macrobands appeared with the adoption of simple maize cultivation after 5000 B.C., these people nevertheless still followed the old pattern of moving from microenvironment to microenvironment, separating into microbands during the dry season.

The invention and gradual improvement of agriculture seem to have made few profound alterations in the settlement pattern of the valley for many millennia. Significantly, by the Formative period (from about 1500 B.C. to A.D. 200), when agriculture based on a hybridized maize was far more important than it had been in earlier periods as a source of food energy, the pattern was still one of part-time nomadism.[11] In this part of the dry Mexican highlands, until the Classic period (about A.D. 200 to 900), when irrigation appears to have been introduced into Tehuacán, food production had still to be supplemented with extensive plant collecting and hunting.

Most of the peoples of the Formative period apparently lived in large villages on the alluvial valley floor during the wet season, from May through October of each year, for planting had to be done in May and June, and harvesting, in September and October. In the dry season, from November through February, when the trees and bushes had lost their leaves and the deer were easy to see and track, some of the population must have moved to hunting camps, principally in the Coxcatlán thorn forest. By February, hunting had become less rewarding as the now-wary deer moved as far as possible from human habitation; however, in April and May the thorn forest was still ripe for exploitation, as many kinds of wild fruit matured. In May it was again time to return to the villages on the valley floor for spring planting.

Now, in some other regions of Mesoamerica there were already, during the Formative period, fully sedentary village cultures in existence. It is clear that while the Tehuacán valley was the locus of the first domestication of maize, the origins of full-blown village life lie elsewhere. Because of the constraining effects of the macroenvironment, the Tehuacán people were exploiting, until relatively late in Mesoamerican prehistory, as widely spaced and as large a number of microenvironments as the Great Basin aborigines were exploiting in the 19th century.

Coastal Guatemala

Near the modern fishing port of Ocós, only a few kilometers from the Mexican border on the alluvial plain of the Pacific coast of Guatemala, we have found evidence for some of the oldest permanently occupied villages in Mesoamerica.[12] We have also made an intensive study of the ecology and ethnology of the Ocós area.

From this study[13] we have defined no less than eight distinct microenvironments within an area of only about 90 square kilometers. These are as follows:

(1) *Beach sand and low scrub.* A narrow, infertile strip from which the present-day villagers collect occasional mollusks, a beach crab called *chichimeco* and one known as *nazareño,* and the sea turtle and its eggs.

(2) *The marine estuary-and-lagoon system,* in places extending considerably inland and ultimately connecting with streams or rivers coming down from the Sierra Madre. The estuaries, with their mangrove-lined banks, make up the microenvironment richest in wild foods in the entire area. The brackish waters abound in catfish *(Arius* sp. and *Galeichthys* sp.), red snapper *(Lutjanus colorado),* several species of snook *(Centropomus* sp.), and many other kinds of fish. Within living memory, crocodiles *(Crocodylus astutus)* were common, but they have by now been hunted almost to extinction. The muddy banks of the

estuaries are the habitat of many kinds of mollusks, including marsh clams *(Polymesoda radiata)*, mussels *(Mytella falcata)*, and oysters *(Ostrea columbiensis)*, and they also support an extensive population of fiddler and mud crabs.

(3) *Mangrove forest*, consisting mainly of stilt-rooted red mangrove, which slowly gives way to white mangrove as one moves away from the estuary. We noted high populations of collared anteater *(Tamandua tetradactyla)* and arboreal porcupine *(Coendu mexicanus)*. A large number of crabs (we did not determine the species) inhabit this microenvironment; these include, especially, one known locally as the *azul* (blue) crab, on which a large population of raccoons feeds.

(4) *Riverine,* comprising the channels and banks of the sluggish Suchiate and Naranjo rivers, which connect with the lagoon-estuary system not far from their mouths. Freshwater turtles, catfish, snook, red snapper, and mojarra *(Cichlasoma* sp.) are found in these waters; the most common animal along the banks is the green iguana *(Iguana iguana).*

(5) *Salt playas*, the dried remnants of ancient lagoon-and-estuary systems which are still subject to inundation during the wet season, with localized stands of a tree known as *madresal* ("mother of salt"). Here there is an abundance of game, including whitetail deer and the black iguana *(Ctenosaura similis),* as well as a rich supply of salt.

(6) *Mixed tropical forest*, found a few kilometers inland, in slightly higher and better drained situations than the salt *playas*. This forest includes mostly tropical evergreens like the ceiba, as well as various zapóte and fan palms, on the fruit of which a great variety of mammals thrive—the kinkajou, the spotted cavy, the coatimundi, the raccoon, and even the gray fox. The soils here are highly suitable for maize agriculture.

(7) *Tropical savannah*, occupying poorly drained patches along the upper stream and estuary systems of the area. This is the major habitat in the area for cottontail rabbits and gray foxes. Other common mammals are the coatimundi and armadillo.

(8) *Cleared fields and second growth*, habitats which have been created by agriculturists, and which are generally confined to areas that were formerly mixed tropical forest.

Among the earliest Formative cultures known thus far for the Ocós area is the Cuadros phase, dated by radiocarbon analysis at about 1000 to 850 B.C. and well represented in the site of Salinas La Blanca, which we excavated in 1962.[14] The site is on the banks of the Naranjo River among a variety of microenvironments; it consists of two flattish mounds built up from deeply stratified refuse layers representing house foundations of a succession of hamlets or small villages.

From our analysis of this refuse we have a good idea of the way in which the Cuadros people lived. Much of the refuse consists of potsherds from large, neckless jars, but very few of the clay figurines that abound in other Formative cultures of Mesoamerica were found. We discovered many plant remains; luckily these had been preserved or "fossilized" through replacement of the tissues by carbonates. From these we know that the people grew and ate a nonhybridized maize considerably more advanced than the maize which was then being grown in Tehuacán.[15] The many impressions of leaves in clay floors in the site will, we hope, eventually make it possible to reconstruct the flora that immediately surrounded the village.

The identification of animal remains (Fig. 1), together with our ecological study and with the knowledge that the people had a well-developed maize agriculture, gives a

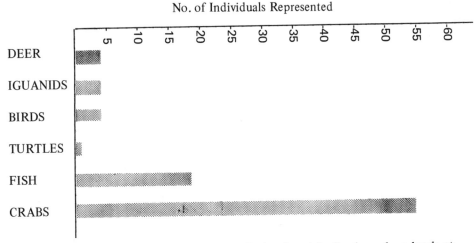

Fig. 1. Animal remains, exclusive of mollusks, found in Cuadros phase levels at Salinas La Blanca.

great deal of information on the subsistence activities of these early coastal villagers. First of all, we believe they had no interest whatever in hunting, a conclusion reinforced by our failure to find a single projectile point in the site. The few deer bones that have been re-covered are all from immature individuals that could have been encountered by chance and clubbed to death. Most of the other remains are of animals that could have been col-lected in the environs of the village, specifically in the lagoon-estuary system and the flanking mangrove forest, where the people fished, dug for marsh clams, and, above all, caught crabs (primarily the *azul* crab, which is trapped at night). Entirely missing are many edible species found in other microenvironments, such as raccoon, cottontail rab-bit, peccary, spotted cavy, and nine-banded armadillo.

There is no evidence at all that occupation of Salinas La Blanca was seasonal. An effective food production carried out on the rich, deep soils of the mixed tropical forest zone, together with the food resources of the lagoon-estuary system, made a permanently settled life possible. Looked at another way, developed maize agriculture had so reduced the number and spacing of the niches which had to be exploited that villages could be occupied the year round.[16]

Conditions similar to those of the Ocós area are found all along the Pacific Coast of Guatemala and along the Gulf Coast of southern Veracruz and Tabasco in Mexico, and we suggest that the real transition to village life took place there and not in the dry Mexi-can highlands, where maize was domesticated initially.[17]

Conclusion

The interpretation of archaeological remains through a fine-scale analysis of small ecological zones throws new light on the move toward sedentary life in Mesoamerican pre-history. In our terms, the basic difference between peoples who subsist on wild foods and those who dwell in permanent villages is that the former must exploit a wide variety of small ecological niches in a seasonal pattern—niches which are usually scattered over a wide range of territory—while the latter may, because of an effective food production, concentrate on one or on only a few microenvironments which lie relatively close at hand.

Fine-scale ecological analysis indicates that there never was any such thing as an "agricultural revolution" in Mesoamerica, suddenly and almost miraculously resulting in village life. The gradual addition of domesticates such as maize, beans, and squash to the diet of wild plant and animal foods hardly changed the way of life of the Tehucán people for many thousands of years, owing to a general paucity of the environment, and seasonal nomadism persisted until the introduction of irrigation. It probably was not until maize was taken to the alluvial, lowland littoral of Mesoamerica, perhaps around 1500 B.C., that permanently occupied villages became possible, through reduction of the number of microenvironments to which men had to adapt themselves.

References and Notes

[1] Mesoamerica is the name given to that part of Mexico and Central America which was civilized in pre-Columbian times. For an excellent summary of its prehistory, see G. R. Willey, *Science* 131, 73 (1960).

[2] R. S. MacNeish, *Science* 143, 531 (1964).

[3] See C. A. Reed and R. J. Braidwood, "Toward the reconstruction of the environmental sequence of Northeastern Iraq," in R. J. Braidwood and B. Howe, "Prehistoric Investigations in Iraqi Kurdistan," *Oriental Institute, University of Chicago, Studies in Ancient Oriental Civilization No. 31* (1960), p. 163. Reed and Braidwood also convincingly reject the technological-deterministic approach of V. G. Childe and his followers.

[4] See B. J. Meggers, *Am. Anthropologist* 56, 801 (1954), for an environmental-deterministic view of the constraining effects of tropical forests on human cultures.

[5] See F. Barth, *ibid.* 58, 1079 (1956), for a microenvironmental approach by an ethnologist to the exceedingly complex interrelationships between sedentary agriculturists, agriculturists practicing transhumant herding, and nomadic herders in the state of Swat, Pakistan.

[6] J. H. Steward, "Basin-Plateau Aboriginal Sociopolitical Groups," *Smithsonian Inst. Bur. Am. Ethnol. Bull 120* (1938).

[7] The pitfalls of searching for ethnological data relevant to archaeological problems among cultures far-flung in time and space are stressed by J. G. D. Clark, *Prehistoric Europe, The Economic Basis* (Philosophical Library, New York, 1952), p. 3.

[8] See W. W. Taylor, Ed., "The identification of non-artifactual archaeological materials," *Natl. Acad. Sci.-Natl. Res. Council Publ. 565* (1957). For a general article on the analysis of food remains in archaeological deposits see R. F. Heizer in "Application of quantitative methods in archaeology." *Viking Fund Publications in Anthropology No. 28* (1960), pp. 93-157.

[9] P. C. Mangelsdorf, R. S. MacNeish, W. C. Gallinat, *Science* 143, 538 (1964). We thank Dr. MacNeish for permission to use unpublished data of the Tehuacán Archaeological-Botanical Project in this article.

[10] R. S. MacNeish, *Second Annual Report of the Tehuacán Archaeological-Botanical Project* (Robert S. Peabody Foundation for Archaeology, Andover, Mass.,1962).

11The research discussed in this and the following paragraph was carried out by Flannery as staff zoologist for the Tehuacán project during the field seasons of 1962 and 1963; see K. V. Flannery, "Vertebrate Fauna and Prehistoric Hunting Patterns in the Tehuacán Valley" (Robert S. Peabody Foundation for Archaeology, Andover, Mass., in press); ——, thesis, Univ. of Chicago, in preparation.

12M. D. Coe, "La Victoria, an early site on the Pacific Coast of Guatemala," *Peabody Museum, Harvard, Papers No. 53* (1961).

13The study was carried out largely by Flannery.

14The final report on Salinas La Blanca by Coe and Flannery is in preparation. The research was supported by the National Science Foundation under a grant to the Institute of Andean Research, as part of the program, "Interrelationships of New World Cultures." The oldest culture in the area is the Ocós phase, which has complex ceramics and figurines; the paleoecology of Ocós is less well known than that of Cuadros, which directly follows it in time.

15P. C. Mangelsdorf, who has very kindly examined these maize specimens, informs us that they are uncontaminated with *Tripsacum,* and that probably all belong to the primitive lowland race, Nal-Tel.

16To paraphrase the concept of "primary forest efficiency," developed by J. R. Caldwell ["Trend and Tradition in the Eastern United States," *Am. Anthropol. Assoc. Mem. No. 88* (1958)], we might think of the Cuadros phase as leaning to a "primary lagoon-estuary efficiency." We might think the same of the Ocós phase of the same region, which may date back to 1500 B.C.

17An additional factor which may in part account for the priority of coastal Guatemala over Tehuacán in the achievement of a sedentary mode of life is the presence of an extensive system of waterways in the former region, which might have made it less necessary for local communities to move to productive sources of food. By means of canoes, a few persons could have brought the products of other niches to the village. However, our evidence indicates that the Cuadros people largely ignored the possibilities of exploiting distant niches.

In this article, Kent V. Flannery proposes an intellectually exciting and plausible hypothesis to explain the interrelated rise of civilization on the Gulf Coast and in the Oaxaca highlands of Mexico towards the latter part of the second millenium B.C. He uses general ethnographic analogies to good advantage in formulating a testable hypothesis to account for the related highland and lowland events. The article also clearly shows the necessity for tight archaeological chronologies in the testing of processual hypotheses.

The Olmec and the Valley of Oaxaca:
A Model for Inter-regional Interaction
in Formative Times

Kent V. Flannery

Introduction

In recent years it has become increasingly apparent that the zenith of Olmec art and mound-building took place earlier in the Formative period than anyone had previously suspected, and that the advanced and sophisticated Olmec had an unmistakable impact on their less advanced and less sophisticated highland neighbors. Michael Coe (1963:33) has suggested that "it would be as meaningless to ignore this as it would be to attempt an understanding of the European Neolithic without taking into account the coeval civilizations of Bronze Age Mesopotamia." With the new rush of attention to the Olmec area, however, there is a real danger that the pendulum may swing too far the other way: that anything and everything elaborate in the Formative will be called "Olmecoid," and that all or much of the progress of the highland Formative will be hurriedly attributed to "Olmec influence." In this paper I will attempt to define what "Olmec influence" means in the case of the Valley of Oaxaca. I suspect that if I had more data at my disposal, I would find that the same definition would apply to the Río Balsas headwaters, the Valley of Morelos and Izúcar de Matamoros, and several other highland areas where "Olmec influence" has been detected.

In an age in which we are accustomed to read of Formative voyages across the whole of the Pacific from Japan to Ecuador, and of migration or "diffusion" from Ecuador to the Caribbean coast, from there to Mesoamerica, and then up the Gulf to Florida and the eastern woodlands, my paper will perhaps come as a disappointment: I cannot

Reprinted from *Dumbarton Oaks Conference on the Olmec,* edited by E. P. Benson, pp. 79-110, Dumbarton Oaks Research Library and Collection, by permission of the publisher and author. Copyright 1967 by Dumbarton Oaks Research Library and Collection.

even propose a migration from the Olmec area to the Valley of Oaxaca, a distance of only a hundred miles or so. Nor will I be able to offer (as a consolation) even so much as a small invasion, or a proselytizing expedition by Olmec "missionaries." Having examined Formative sites now for two seasons in only one small part of the Valley of Oaxaca, I have gradually come to the conclusion that an Olmec raiding party, armed with "knuckle dusters" (see, for example, Coe 1965b: 764), would probably have encountered quite a sizable resistance force in that area. It also occurs to me, looking around at the size of the Valleys of Mexico, Puebla, Toluca, Morelos, and the upper Balsas, that there probably were not quite enough Olmec to colonize the whole of the Mesoamerican highlands. I will therefore be forced to propose a model for inter-regional interaction which does not necessitate invasions, missionaries, or colonization by an "Olmec elite."

"Olmec influence" in the Valley of Oaxaca has been a topic of discussion for about thirty years. In the past, such discussion centered mainly on the Monte Albán I period, which has produced incense burners with clear representations of the "were-jaguar," a deity with a human face and a feline mouth (Paddock 1966: Fig. 3), and a number of reputedly "Olmecoid" carved stones, the *danzantes* of Monte Albán. Basic to these discussions was the assumption that Monte Albán I was contemporary with La Venta.

Today, the tendency to see direct Olmec characteristics in the *danzantes* has dwindled; as Ignacio Bernal expressed it in a recent publication, "though the Danzantes and the Olmec sites of the coast of Veracruz and Tabasco have some fundamental similarities, it is just as evident that they have fundamental differences" (1967: 3). And, perhaps most importantly, recent stratigraphic work and new radiocarbon dates from the Olmec area (Coe, Diehl, and Stuiver 1967) have indicated that San Lorenzo Tenochtitlán and Complex A La Venta are not contemporary with Monte Albán I, but earlier—overlapping in time only slightly, if at all, with the latter phase. This throws the relationship of the Gulf Coast and the Valley of Oaxaca still further open to question.

The task of this paper will be to cover three related aspects of the problem.[1] First, I will briefly describe two recently-discovered Formative phases in the Valley of Oaxaca, which preceded Monte Albán I and which were certainly contemporary with San Lorenzo and La Venta. Second, I will assess the similarities and differences between the Formative of the Valley of Oaxaca and the Gulf Coast. Finally, I will present a model,

[1] In the course of preparing this paper I have profited from discussions with Jane C. Wheeler, Susan H. Lees, and Richard I. Ford, all of the University of Michigan. Miss Wheeler's study of the magnetite sources of the Valley of Oaxaca will provide a far more detailed picture of this aspect of the Formative than can be given here. Miss Lees' studies of ritual exchange in the New Guinea highlands, summarized in a paper given at the Michigan Academy of Sciences in 1967, contributed useful data on the extent to which pre-industrial peoples may convert their surplus into exotic raw materials rather than storing it. Ford's work among the Tewa pueblos has yielded important data, still largely unpublished, on the movement of raw materials and the ways in which they may be taken out of circulation. Obviously, however, none of the aforementioned should be blamed for any of my errors of interpretation, nor will they necessarily agree with my conclusions.

The 1966 field season of the Oaxaca Project was supported by the Smithsonian Institution. The 1967 field season was supported by National Science Foundation Grant GS-1616 to the University of Maryland.

based on ethnographic data, which I feel constitutes at least one reasonable explanation for the interaction between the two regions.

The Early and Middle Formative of the Valley of Oaxaca

The sub-area of the Valley of Oaxaca which we have so far been able to survey and test most extensively for Formative sites is the region drained by the uppermost twenty miles of the Atoyac River, northwest of Oaxaca City. This sub-area, known as the Valley of Etla, has three main physiographic provinces: a zone of steep mountains, a region of gentle piedmont slopes, and a flat, narrow alluvial plain left by the Atoyac and its tributaries. Our attention was first directed to the Etla region by the dense pattern of Monte Alban I sites discovered there by Bernal.

Two principal types of situations seem to have attracted Formative farmers in the Etla Valley. The first is a strip of land to either side of the Atoyac where water is always available at a depth of no more than 3 meters below the surface of the alluvium. Two crops a year can be obtained in this zone either by irrigating from shallow wells, or by diverting water from the river itself, which flows almost at the surface of the plain. The second situation is in the upper piedmont, at the point where permanent (or nearly permanent) tributary streams emerge from the mountains. Two crops a year can be obtained in this zone by diverting stream water and bringing it to the fields by gravity flow in small canals. Early Formative sites so far located occur exclusively in the high-water-table zone along the main Atoyac River. Middle Formative sites occur either in that same zone, or in the upper piedmont on reasonably permanent streams. Late Formative sites occur primarily in these same situations, but a few occur elsewhere.

The Valley of Etla is temperate; frosts occasionally occur, and may inhibit a crop planted too early or harvested too late. Farther down the Atoyac, south of Oaxaca City, lie areas which are virtually frost-free, where today sugar cane can be grown. We have not yet surveyed these areas extensively enough to be sure of the settlement pattern, but it appears that there—as in the Valley of Etla—Formative sites are located principally with regard to surface and subsurface water resources, rather than soil type or precipitation gradient. This suggests that irrigation played an important role in Formative agriculture in the Valley of Oaxaca, a suggestion which is strengthened by the fact that we have already located at least one Middle Formative well and several fossil Late Formative irrigation canals (Flannery, A. Kirkby, M. Kirkby, and Williams 1967).

We have investigated three Formative periods which are relevant to the Olmec problem. The first of these is the San José Phase, which falls near the end of the Early Formative; the second is the Guadalupe Phase, which marks the beginning of the Middle Formative; the third is sub-Phase A of Monte Alban I, which brings the Middle Formative to a close.

The San José Phase

The San José Phase dates, on the basis of ceramic cross-ties, to between 1200 and 900 B.C. Two samples of radiocarbon from the terminal part of the phase have so far been analyzed, yielding dates of 930 and 975 B.C.

Pottery of the San José Phase shows strong resemblances to material from the looted cemetery at Las Bocas (Coe 1965c), near Izúcar de Matamoros in the Balsas headwater region of southern Puebla. Ties are also strong with the Grijalva Depression (Chiapa I Phase), Guatemalan coast (Cuadros Phase), southern Veracruz (San Lorenzo Phase), and Tlatilco. What the San José Phase shares with Early Formative cultures of the highlands is a high proportion of bowls and necked jars, with *tecomates* or "neckless jars" less abundant than at contemporary sites in the lowlands. The difference is simply one of proportion, and probably has something to do with differences of food preparation, serving, and meal scheduling between the highlands and the coast.

Unslipped pottery in the San José Phase most commonly is brownish or brick red, and occurs frequently in the form of necked jars *(ollas)* for cooking or storage. Slipped pottery may be monochrome white, bichrome red-on-white, polished black, white-rim black, polished cloudy gray, or polished specular hematite red. Flat-based bowls with out-slanted sides, and flat-based cylinders are common shapes. Some bowls have super-thick rims, as in Chiapa I (Dixon 1959: Fig. 3); others, with simple direct rims, may be slipped white with a red band at the rim, as in the Cuadros Phase (Coe and Flannery 1967: Pl. 13). Bowl interiors or cylinder exteriors in white, black, or gray may be decorated with excised *(raspada)* designs, which are often filled with red pigment. Some of the designs cut into these vessels are the St. Andrew's cross, the U-motif, and the "paw-wing" motif, all of which Coe (1965b) has described as common "Olmec" themes.

Tecomates often are rocker-stamped, usually in zones. One type of *tecomate* is white with a red band at the rim, and with further red bands separating the body of the vessel into large triangular or diamond-shaped zones; these zones will have horizontal, vertical, or diagonal strings of plain rocker stamping. Interesting local variations include a kind of "interrupted" rocker stamping (which looks as if the rocker instrument had a purposeful notch cut out of it).

Figurines are abundant in the San José Phase, and include both the small solid kind and the large hollow type found by Richard MacNeish (1964) at Ajalpan in the Tehuacán Valley. The small solid figurines typically have eyes made by two plowing strokes, with no pupil indicated. Some show similarity to Types C and D from the Valley of Mexico, especially those from Tlatilco; others are vaguely "Olmecoid," with helmets or with mouths that turn down at both corners.

Type locality for the San José Phase is the site of San José Mogote, which covers the tip of a piedmont spur that projects out, like a low peninsula, into the high-water-table zone of the Atoyac in the central Valley of Etla. Like Chiapa de Corzo, San José Mogote is a very large site (covering more than 100 hectares) with a long sequence spanning the period from Early Formative to Late Classic. The alluvium which flanks it on three sides is today irrigated by means of canals, pumps, and shallow wells.

Materials of the San José Phase can be picked up over an area roughly 450 meters on a side, giving us a village of an estimated 20 hectares (45 acres) in extent. Within this area, surface materials reflect at least three different kinds of residential patterns: (1) an area of wattle-and-daub houses with relatively fancy pottery and a low percentage of chipping debris and utilitarian ground stone; (2) an area of wattle-and-daub houses with less fancy pottery and higher frequencies of chipping debris and utilitarian ground stone; and (3) an area of some 5 acres or more, near the eastern limits of the Early Formative settlement, with abundant fancy pottery and a disproportionately high surface yield of worked and unworked magnetite, ilmenite, hematite, white and black mica, green quartz of various qualities, Gulf Coast mussel shell, and fragments of marine mollusk shells including *Spondylus*, pearl oyster, marsh snails *(Cerithidium)*, and *Anomalocardia subrugosa*. On one corn field in this area, which we surface-collected still more intensively once we had realized the pattern, more than five hundred fragments of magnetite and related iron ores were present. At the present writing, this is the only area of San José Mogote which we have been able to test-excavate adequately.

Stratigraphic tests in this part of the site in 1966 revealed a whole series of wattle-and-daub hourses which had evidently been occupied by artisans. Posthole patterns (and occasional burned house corners) indicate that these structures were rectangular, with square rather than rounded corners; because of the limited area excavated, no complete house plans were recovered, but floor areas were larger than 3 by 5 meters. Walls were of finger-sized poles, plastered with mud, then whitewashed with the same kind of white-to-buff clay used on the pottery of that period. On the floors there were no projectile points and almost nothing in the way of *metates* and *manos;* the most common stone tool recovered was a small type of chert drill used for drilling shell. Other common tools were burins for cutting shell, polishers of quartz and iron ore for working magnetite, and so on. Accompanying these tools were abundant fragments of unworked and partially worked magnetite; cut fragments of mica; discarded parts of marine shell; unused, unmodified shells; fragments of shell ornaments which had broken in the process of manufacture; and small, flat mirrors of magnetite and ilmenite, about the size of a thumbnail. Finished products were rare; what we found mainly appeared to be workshop debris from the manufacture of ornaments.

In 1967 we opened up a much larger area in this part of the site, hoping to get an idea of whole house plans and the placement of houses relative to one another. Immediately to the south of the area we had tested in 1966, we came across the buried foundations of a rectangular, stepped platform faced with stone. The platform, which rose in two stages to a height of about 2 meters, was contoured to the slope of the piedmont spur, but oriented roughly north-south like the structures at Complex A La Venta. The construction technique, however, was quite different from the La Venta mounds and platforms: the natural piedmont slope was terraced with a facing of volcanic tuff and *tepetate,* arranged in alternating stages of cobbles and flat slabs. This facing was not verticle, but lay at an inclined angle like a *talud,* and it in turn had been set in (and covered with) a layer of hard, puddled adobe clay. Associated pottery dated this platform to the late San José Phase; and among the associated figurines were fragments of several large, hollow, white-slipped "dolls" of the Gualupita-Las Bocas type, and two small, solid, white-slipped figurine heads representing the "were-jaguar." On at least two sides, the platform supported the plastered and whitewashed houses of craft specialists, and surface indications are that such houses, in fact, surrounded it.

Sixteen kilometers upstream, in the village of San Pablo Huitzo, we investigated another, smaller site of the San José Phase. The prehistoric deposits underlie the modern Barrio del Rosario, from which the site derives its name; early settlement seems to have taken place at the point of transition from the piedmont to the valley floor, and the western portion of the site is partially covered by recent alluvium. Because modern houses cover much of the deposit it was not possible to determine the extent of the village in San José times, but it evidently covered several hectares.

Founded almost on virgin soil at Barrio del Rosario was a structure 2 meters high and more than 15 meters wide, built of earth and faced with stone much in the same manner as the platform at San José Mogote. The structure at Huitzo also rose in tiers, with a sloping outer wall, and was oriented 8° west of true north. Although the outside presents a boulder or cobble facing set in hard clay, the interior is of earthen fill containing San José Phase sherds. Retaining the earthen fill are walls made of plano-convex or "bun-shaped" adobes, about 25-30 centimeters in diameter, with some walls rising to a height of 2 meters. Included in the structure were two carbonized posts 30 centimeters in diameter, which evidently supported a substantial building. Judging by the burned remains we found, the building was of wattle-and-daub, with a very thick coating of clay but no slip or whitewash. The entire construction was designated Platform 4, and it appears to have been built at the end of the San José Phase and enlarged early in the subsequent Guadalupe Phase. Unfortunately, because it underlay modern houses, Platform 4 could not be fully investigated, and we do not know its precise shape or dimensions.

Not a single fragment of magnetite was found at Barrio del Rosario; shell and mica were much rarer than at San José Mogote. Availability is not the question here, for Jane Wheeler of the Oaxaca project, who is surveying the valley for mineral resources, reports magnetite sources even closer to Huitzo (personal communication); in fact, there are numerous sources within ten miles of both sites. The implication is that access to magnetite was not universal; ninety per cent of the fragments we found occurred in one small area of households in one very large village. Almost the same was true of *Spondylus* and pearl oyster. Clearly, social rather than geographic factors determined who got magnetite and how much.

There is one other interesting consideration: magnetite mirrors identical to those being turned out by the artisans at San José Mogote occur in contemporary deposits at San Lorenzo Tenochtitlán, more than one hundred kilometers from the nearest possible source (Coe, personal communication; Curtis 1959: Fig. 80). Garniss Curtis (1959: 287) in his identification of the magnetite from La Venta, places its probable point of origin in "the metamorphic and granitic province to the south"; his map indicates that the Oaxaca highlands and Pacific coast are the heartland of that province. Although there are scattered finds of small magnetite mirrors throughout Formative Mesoamerica, I know of no site outside the Valley of Oaxaca that has shown evidence of the extensive magnetite *accumulation and working* that is seen at San José Mogote. Oaxaca must therefore be considered a tentative source for the Olmec magnetite, pending technical analyses. It is this possibility that will be explored further in this paper.

The Guadalupe Phase

So far we have identified three villages of the San José Phase (one of which is very large) from the Etla arm of the valley alone, and more are beginning to show up as our survey moves downstream. By the succeeding Guadalupe Phase there were five or six villages in the Etla Valley (or one about every three miles along the river), ranging in size from 5 to 90 acres. Middens of the Guadalupe Phase, whose carbonized plant remains and animal bones are just now undergoing study, have given us a good look at subsistence along the Atoyac at this time period. Domesticates included corn, beans, squash, avocados, chile peppers, and dogs, and wild foods utilized included deer, cottontails, prickly pear fruits, pitahayas, and other local plants. The site of Mitla was first founded during this phase, and it was in the Guadalupe deposits at Mitla in 1966 that we recovered a 4-meter deep well (Flannery, A. Kirkby, M. Kirkby, and Williams 1967).

We have no radiocarbon dates yet for the Guadalupe Phase, but on the basis of ceramic cross-ties it must date between 900 and 600 B.C. Its relationships are with Chiapa de Corzo II, Conchas I on the Guatemalan coast. Complex A at La Venta, and the Early Santa María Phase in the Tehuacán Valley. The early Guadalupe Phase is easy to define; the late Guadalupe Phase gradually turns into the sub-phase which Bernal has called "Monte Albán I-A," and the boundary between the two is still very hard to draw.

Most typical of the Guadalupe Phase is a yellowish, or white-to-buff slipped pottery, in which the dominant vessel is a flat-based bowl with outslanting sides. The rims of these bowls are often decorated with parallel incised lines, with one line turning up at intervals to meet the other—the so-called "double-line-break" motif. This type of pottery is the Oaxaca homologue of Canoas White in the Tehuacán Valley, Conchas White-to-buff on the Guatemala coast, La Venta Coarse Paste Buff Ware, Burrero Cream in the Grijalva Depression, and some of the incised white wares of El Trapiche and early Zacatenco.

Another common pottery type of the Guadalupe Phase is a sandy brown or brick-red ware with a coarse red wash, which appears in the form of *tecomates* and necked jars. This is the Oaxaca Valley equivalent of Tehuacán's Rio Salado Coarse and the Guatemalan coast's Conchas Red Unburnished. One characteristic which seems to be peculiar to Oaxaca, however, is decoration by means of zoned areas of punctation or herringbone-spaced slashes or stepped jabs, separated by bands of red wash; this is most typical on early Guadalupe Phase necked jars.

Coarse pot stands, some of them impressed with a *petate* or woven mat while still wet, are also typical of the Guadalupe Phase, and carry through into Monte Albán I. None appear to be *incensarios;* and I would like to add that, unless the Guadalupe Phase villagers were shaped quite differently from most human beings, these objects were true pot rests and not pottery stools, as has sometimes been suggested in the literature (cf. Coe 1965a: 690).

Late in the Guadalupe Phase appear bowls with composite silhouettes, mostly in gray monochrome ware which clearly foreshadows later Monte Albán I pottery. The trend during the phase is for bowl walls to change from outslanted to outcurved, and for rims to become increasingly flaring, eventually truly everted. Polished, waxy gray monochrome gradually replaces white-to-buff pottery, and "double-line-breaks" give way to wavy lines, sine curves, and cross-hatching in panels or in triangular areas on the rim. Scalloped rims or rims with eccentric tabs or nodes appear during the late Guadalupe Phase, and apparently are ancestral to the "fish plates" and scalloped rim vessels of Monte Albán I. Still rare or absent in the Guadalupe Phase are vessel supports, lugs, or handles of any kind.

Small solid figurines in the Guadalupe Phase are mainly of the type called "A" in the Valley of Mexico, "realistic projecting eyeball" by MacNeish (1954), and "double-triangle-and-punch eye" by Coe (1961). Eyes have a clearly-defined pupil which is perforated as in Mamom, Conchas I, and the Santa María Phase. Turbans are particularly large and ornate on Guadalupe Phase females, who also wear ear spools, necklaces, pectorals, and sandals, and have red pigment in their navels. Males are often as bald as Yul Brynner and sit cross-legged, like paunchy executives pondering some crucial decision. We also found fragments of a few large, hollow, cream or white-slipped "dolls" of the Gualupita-Las Bocas type.

During the Guadalupe Phase, San José Mogote grew to cover more than 40 hectares (90 acres), but we have not yet been able to determine the extent of monumental construction from that phase. The platform previously mentioned was covered over and surrounded by literally tons of rubble and black clay during early Guadalupe times, either to enlarge it or to level the area for future constructions.

At Barrio del Rosario Huitzo, a number of structures were built stratigraphically above Platform 4. One of these, called Platform 3, dated to the Guadalupe Phase. This was a platform nearly 1.5 meters high and roughly 12 meters wide, which faced onto a patio of equal width. Traces of other structures nearby suggested to us that possibly we were dealing with a rectangular patio oriented 8° west of true north, with four large house platforms arranged around it, but we were only able to expose the corners of what we believe to have been two other platforms. Platform 3, which would have been on the south side of the patio if our suppositions are correct, had a stairway 8 meters wide which led down to patio level, and where its upper surface was preserved we found a line of postholes from the house it had supported.

Not only was this platform oriented like the platforms at La Venta Complex A; its construction technique was also suggestive of the latter site, and its associated pottery reasonably similar. There were, however, some regional differences. Like La Venta, the platform had adobe retaining walls, but they were constructed of plano-convex, "bun-shaped" adobes rather than rectangular ones. Between these retaining walls were layers of black clay and gritty yellow loam. The steps of the stairway were built of rows of adobes, capped with hard clay. However, over the whole front face of the platform and stairway was a layer of white plaster, a trait common in Valley of Oaxaca sites but not at La Venta. The patio also appears to have had a layer of white plaster, but it is much more poorly preserved. The collapsed remains of the house above the platform indicate that it was a very large structure of wattle-and-daub, rectangular, with a thick coating of adobe clay, and that it had also been surfaced with white plaster. The midden layers in the patio and around the edges of the platform contained only household debris, ash, carbonized seeds, and animal bones, suggesting that Platform 3 had supported an elite residence rather than a "ceremonial" structure. In fact, no objects of "ceremonial" nature were found anywhere in the area.

This same stratigraphic zone yielded remnants of six or eight wattle-and-daub houses of a much humbler type. None had platforms, plaster, or even whitewash. All were roughly 4 by 6 meters in size and rectangular, with walls of finger-sized poles packed with mud. Floors had a coating of fine sand over them, usually ashy, and postholes were only about 7 centimeters in diameter. These houses were not located away from the patio, with its much larger and fancier house platforms, but lay immediately adjacent to it. Between them were small midden areas with what appeared to be household trash, little different from that found around the large platforms. I conclude that either (1) elite residences were not spatially separated from those of the common farmers at Huitzo, or else (2) elite residences were accompanied by the houses of retainers, servants, extra wives, poor relations, or the like.

The Monte Albán I-A Sub-Phase

It is clear from our excavations at Huitzo, as well as from previous work by Bernal, that Monte Albán I is a long period which it may someday be possible to subdivide. Its initial stage still belongs, I feel, to the Middle Formative period, although it admittedly falls near the end of that period. Ceramic cross-ties are with the Conchas II sub-Phase on the Guatemalan coast, Chiapa de Corzo III and IV, post-Complex A La Venta, early Tres Zapotes, and the middle part of the Santa María Phase in the Tehuacán Valley. Pending the analysis of our radiocarbon samples, my guess is that Monte Albán I-A must fall somewhere in the neighborhood of 500 B.C.

Monte Albán I-A is characterized by gray ware which has a polished, waxy slip. Common shapes are flat-based bowls with flaring walls which may be incised on the interior of the rim. "Double-line breaks" still occur among these designs, but are less frequent than panels of hatching, sinuous lines like clouds or waves, and strings of short diagonal strokes. Composite silhouettes become increasingly frequent; there is an obvious trend toward experimentation with wide "rim tabs" and wide-everted rims which are incised on top. However, this sub-Phase A of Monte Albán I still lacks a number of characteristics of the Late Formative. Rim flanges, basal flanges, swollen mammiform supports, bridge spouts, and wide-everted grooved rims are rare or absent. On the other hand, small solid feet and low annular bases begin in period I-A.

Two platforms of this sub-phase were found at Huitzo, stratigraphically above Platform 3. Platform 2 was of earth, with rough stone and adobe retaining walls, oriented 8° west of north; under one retaining wall was an extended burial which seemed to have been included in the construction either as a dedication or a sacrifice. Platform I was a structure in true Monte Albán style, of roughly-cut stones set in adobe mortar, complete with stone-lined drain and associated plaster floors. Like some of the earlier structures at Barrio del Rosario, it appears to have been residential in nature. By this period, rectangular adobes had joined the earlier "bun-shaped" type, and seem to have been used in wall foundations. Houses of adobe and wattle-and-daub occur also in Monte Albán I-A levels at San José Mogote, where they lie stratigraphically above the rubble covering the pyramid we investigated.

Even when Monte Albán I was the oldest Formative culture known in the Valley of Oaxaca, it was, as pointed out repeatedly by Bernal, a culture already advanced, already far from primitive. The period features calendrics, hieroglyphic writing, a distinct regional art style involving both bas-relief stone carving and pottery sculpture, massive stone masonry architecture, and the concept of the rectangular patio with four buildings around it, oriented to the cardinal points by presumably astronomical means. Monte Albán itself was founded during sub-Phase I-A, but it is not yet known how many of the characteristics mentioned above were present at the very start of the phase. Nor is it yet known how many of the other Monte Albán I mound groups date to sub-Phase I-A; by the end of

Monte Albán I, there were at least fifteen in the Etla region and forty in the Valley of Oaxaca as a whole. Not a few of these exceed 100 acres; some reach 200 acres, and include some of the most immense Middle and Late Formative sites the writer has ever seen. The settlement pattern includes hilltop elite centers, densely occupied valley floor sites which could almost be classified as "semiurban," and piedmont villages and towns on key tributary streams. At one site in the mountains, called Hierve el Agua, James Neely of the Oaxaca Project investigated a number of agricultural terraces with irrigation canals fossilized in travertine, which date back to Monte Albán I times (Neely 1967; Flannery, A. Kirkby, M. Kirkby, and Williams 1967).

Oaxaca and the Olmec

What, then, are some of the similarities and differences between the Valley of Oaxaca Formative cultures and those of the Olmec?

First of all, both areas seem to have been very successful agriculturally at an early time period; yet their agricultural technologies were probably very different. Our excavations in 1966 in caves in the Valley of Oaxaca produced dried remains of beans and squash (Flannery, A. Kirkby, M. Kirkby, and Williams 1967) and pollen grains of maize and *Tripsacum* (James Schoenwetter, personal communication) which suggested local use of those plants already between 7000 and 6000 B.C. By 900 B.C., the Valley of Oaxaca contained some of the largest Early Formative sites known in the highlands. Settlement patterns, fossil canals, and a well from later stages of the Formative indicate that this development was based on water-control systems which were worked out as an adaptation to local conditions. Such systems are not yet known from the Olmec area, where the higher annual precipitation makes dry-farming more reliable than in the Valley of Oaxaca. The continual population explosion, massive construction, and technology of the Valley of Oaxaca Formative cannot be explained as the result of "influence" from the Gulf Coast; they are understandable only as the products of successful irrigation systems specifically designed to exploit the peculiar natural resources of the Valley of Oaxaca.

Secondly, both the Formative Valley of Oaxaca and the Olmec area show a pattern of large, nucleated villages (or towns) rather than scattered small hamlets. Ronald Spores (1965) and Oscar Schmieder (1930) point out that this was still true of the Valley Zapotec at the time of the Conquest, and that it set them apart from their neighbors in the Mixe sierra. While the Mixe occupied small scattered farmsteads near their fields, the Zapotec lived in nucleated communities even if they owned land in several different zones, such as the alluvium, piedmont, and mountains. According to Schmieder, this was because the Zapotec cooperated in clearing large tracts of land, then divided it between the participants. This resulted in dispersal of a family's land holdings over a wide area, which made it no advantage to live on any one parcel. I suggest that, in fact, this system may have been a good adaptation, since it spread land-holdings over several environmental zones; in the Valley of Oaxaca, this is good insurance against the erratic yearly rainfall, which may be unpredictably weaker than average in one zone or another in any given year. Whatever the case, as Schmieder argues (1930: 77), "field dispersion resulted in the growth of larger, more compact settlements, in which a differentiation of activities became possible. Crafts, art, and science developed and were maintained by the mass of the population which nevertheless remained agricultural." Much the same contrast may be seen between the Formative peoples of the Guatemalan coastal estuary system, who lived in numerous but small villages, evidently near their fields (Coe and Flannery 1967), and the Olmec of the San Lorenzo Tenochtitlán area, who left behind fewer sites, but much larger and more nucleated ones (Coe, personal communication). I think Schmieder's observation applies to both the Valley of Oaxaca and the Olmec: large, nucleated settlements, for whatever reason they may arise, provide a better matrix for the development of science and craft specialization among primitive agriculturalists than do small scattered hamlets. It is probably for this reason, rather than because of "Olmec influence," that communities such as San José Mogite, Tlatilco, and Las Bocas achieved higher standards of craftsmanship than many of their neighbors.

A third similarity between Oaxaca and the Olmec area is that both regions, quite early in their development, already give evidence of considerable disparities in wealth and status between communities and between members of the same community. Some people lived in small, rude, wattle-and-daub houses; others lived in large, plastered houses on platforms with stairways and patios. Some people had considerable access to luxury items like pearl oyster, jade, and magnetite; other people did not. Some communities had only products that could have come from within a radius of twenty kilometers; other communities had products that had to have been imported over two hundred kilometers. I suggest that this movement of exotic raw materials was functionally related to the developing social stratification of the southern Mesoamerican Formative, and that ornaments and implements of these exotic materials functioned as the insignia of status.

The kind of status to which I am referring is not the kind that can be acquired by an individual during the course of his lifetime, through his own accomplishment—the difference, let us say, between a good farmer and a bad one, between a good artisan and a bad one, or between the head of a Pueblo community and the other members of the community, who are his equals at birth. I am referring to a kind of status that is ascribed at birth, such as characterized the chiefs of the Natchez, or the Indians of the Pacific Northwest Coast. Among the Mixtec and Zapotec at the time of Conquest, for example, a man was born a *cacique,* a *principal* or noble, a *macehual* or commoner, or a slave; men came into the world already unequal, with a rank determined by their genealogies (Spores 1965: 969). Only the hereditary Zapotec nobility could wear decorated cotton mantles, lip-plugs, earrings, gold and stone beads, and so on. That is what is meant by "insignia of status."

Such status distinctions begin to appear in Mesoamerica toward the end of the Early Formative. At Zacatenco, for example, most adult burials had no offerings or ornaments at all, while at nearby El Arbolillo there were infants buried in slab-lined graves, or with jade earspools (Vaillant 1930, 1935). At La Venta, one basalt column tomb in Mound A-2 contained two juvenile burials accompanied by "figurines, beads, a pendant in the form of a clam shell, and a sting-ray spine, all of jade" (Coe 1965a: 690). It is doubtful that these infants and juveniles could have *acquired* sufficient status (through accomplishment during their lifetimes) to warrant such elaborate burials, at a time when most contemporary adults were simply wrapped in a *petate* and thrown in a hole; a more likely explanation is that their status was inherited. It also seems likely that such status was often expressed, as among many ethnographically-documented pre-industrial societies, by restricting access to certain luxury materials to the elite. This is fortunate for the archaeologist, since many of these luxury materials are nearly indestructible and can be traced to definite source areas.

To return to the comparison between the two cultures, a fourth point is that the elite and "ceremonial" architecture of the Formative Valley of Oaxaca shows some similarity of tradition with the Gulf Coast. The use of adobe walls and colored clay in the construction of platforms, and the orienting of those platforms 8° west of north, are all shared characteristics. Yet even our earliest structures from the Valley of Oaxaca have architectural features, such as the use of white plaster and building stone, which set them apart from the Olmec and suggest that they are not just highland imitations of the San Lorenzo or La Venta platforms. They are, as Bernal put it, fundamentally related, but already fundamentally different; and the aspects in which they differ are aspects shared by later structures in the Valley of Oaxaca.

Finally, it is in symbolism and iconography that Oaxaca seems most closely related to the Gulf Coast, and the relationship appears stronger the farther back one goes in time. The representation of the "were-jaguar," the use of the St. Andrew's cross, U-motif, "paw-wing" design, and the other symbols of the "Olmec art style" as defined by Coe (1965b) are clearest in the San José Phase. At that point, as Coe indicates, they are already so stereotyped as to suggest that they may be actual glyphs, although their meaning is not yet clear. Such symbolism is already beginning to fade in the Guadalupe Phase, and by Monte Albán I it is virtually gone; it has been replaced by a different system, one which is distinctly Oaxacan, and which characterizes not only the Valley of Oaxaca but also an area in excess of 25,000 square kilometers, from the Tehuacán Valley in the north to the Pacific Coast of Oaxaca (Flannery, A. Kirkby, M. Kirkby, and Williams 1967). By that time, La Venta had ceased to be important as a nucleus of political power, and Monte Albán was on its way to becoming the major nuclear center of the southern highlands.

Let us sum up the similarities and differences in this way. Both Oaxaca and the Gulf Coast had, by Early Formative times, achieved a measure of agricultural success which supported large nucleated communities with a hereditary elite and craft specialization. There is reason to believe that the two areas achieved this success through independently-derived agricultural technologies. It is the Gulf Coast, however, which had the largest communities and the most sophisticated level of art and craftsmanship, judged by our standards. Also, if degree of status may be fairly measured by quantity and quality of mortuary offerings, the Olmec had achieved a level of social stratification barely approached by the highlands.

The Olmec and the Valley of Oaxaca interacted most strongly on a level of shared concepts about religion, symbolism, and status paraphernalia. Olmec motifs are commonly and skillfully executed in Oaxacan ceramics, and the principal Olmec deity is represented by Oaxacan figurines and sculptured pottery. Important Oaxacan buildings are oriented in the same way as the structures at Complex A La Venta. The Olmec imported foreign magnetite and ilmenite, which appear at San Lorenzo Tenochtitlán in the form of beads and small flat mirrors; the Oaxacan craftsmen accumulated local magnetite and ilmenite, which they also worked into small flat mirrors, many of which were probably exported. One might tentatively suggest, therefore, that one of the main mechanisms of communication between the two regions was through the exchange of exotic raw materials. I find this interesting, in view of the fact that Coe (1965c) has already pointed out that the upper Balsas River region, where so many so-called "highland Olmec" objects have been found, is also a possible source for some of the Olmec serpentine and jadeite.

There exist, in the ethnographic literature, many examples of developing societies which used imported and exotic raw materials to reinforce their status systems. I will draw on two examples in this paper, on the basis of which I feel one might present a hypothesis about the relation between the Olmec and the Valley of Oaxaca—or, for that matter, the Río Balsas area, Las Bocas, the Valley of Morelos, and so on. This hypothesis requires only two propositions: first, that it was important for the Olmec status system (and the reinforcement of certain of their religious commitments) to establish and maintain a flow of jade, magnetite, ilmenite, and other luxury goods into their nuclear centers; second, that the highland peoples who supplied the Olmec with these luxury goods were as interested as the Olmec in maintaining the exchange network.

The Tlingit and the Fur Trade

The first example I would like to cite is drawn from Catherine McClellan's work (1953) on the Indians of the Pacific Northwest, with special reference to the Tlingit-speakers of the southeastern Alaskan coast. The Tlingit, as every student of ethnography knows, had a stratified society with nobility, commoners, and slaves; their economy, keyed to the salmon runs and the pursuit of other marine and terrestrial game, operated at a surplus, much of which went into reinforcing status. Their nobility consumed, gave away, and destroyed wooden canoes, slaves, copper, furs, blankets, and hundreds of other objects in the process of demonstrating its wealth and prestige.

Inland from the Tlingit lived the Athabascan-speaking groups of interior British Columbia and the southern Yukon. The Athabascan groups lived a somewhat humbler and more nomadic existence, based on the hunting of caribou, moose, small game, and fresh-water fish. Their territory centered around a series of small lakes in the dry plateau area fifty to one hundred miles from the Pacific Coast. The principal exportable resource of this area, at least so far as the Tlingit were concerned, was fur.

Furs were important in the prestige systems of the coastal Tlingit, and with the beginning of trade with the white man they took on even greater value. Consequently the Tlingit blockaded the interior, allowing no inland natives to come to the coast, and effectively monopolizing fur trade with the whites. Destruction of sea otter populations late in the eighteenth century removed one great fur source and increased the demand for land-animal furs of the kind the inland Athabascans could supply (McClellan 1953: 49).

McClellan describes the way in which Tlingit-speaking groups like the Chilkat formed fur-procurement alliances with inland groups like the Tagish and Teslin. Chilkat "trade partners" came into the territory of the Tagish, some taking wives from the interior group, others sending their daughters to marry Tagish men. She says:

Actual social alliance had a distinct commercial advantage for the coastal Tlingit. It was no trick for them to manipulate Tlingit reciprocal kin obligations and trading partner patterns to their advantage. Even daughters might well be married to the interior. The furs which a good son-in-law gave to his wife's family had a value that only the strategically located Chilkat could fully exploit. (49)

Everyone profited from the arrangement. White traders got the furs they wanted; the Tlingit nobility, who were already rich and prestigious, got richer and more prestigious, gave bigger potlatches, burned more canoes, and sacrificed more slaves than before. What happened to the Tagish and their Athabascan neighbors?

McClellan suggests that they were gradually "Tlingitized." During the course of the nineteenth century, while some retained their Athabascan dialect, most Tagish and Teslin began to speak a kind of "inland Tlingit." Having married into Tlingit families, the Teslin began to speak of themselves in Tlingit kin terms. All Teslin came to belong either to a Wolf or Crow moiety, which were "matrilineal exogamous divisions which correspond to the Wolf and Raven moieties of the Alaskan Tlingit and are called by the identical names. Everybody belongs also to a matrilineal clan of which other segments are localized on the coast" (47). The Tlingitized Athabascans became more conscious of social rank; the concept of nobility was well-ingrained, and slaves were kept. They practiced funeral potlatching, and adopted many songs and myths which featured coastal animals never even glimpsed by the Tagish or Teslin. In spite of this, patterns of subsistence and everyday material culture remained "overwhelmingly *more* typical of . . . northern Athabascan groups . . ." (48). The inland Athabascans took seriously their marriage ties to Tlingit clans, emulated the esoteric and prestigious aspects of Tlingit culture to the best of their ability, but continued to earn a living in the manner of Athabascans. And the Tlingit, for their part, continued to regard the inlanders simply as "foreigners" from whom they obtained furs.

Highland Burma and the Jade Trade

The second example comes from farther afield. It is abstracted from Edmund R. Leach's (1954) classic description of highland Burma, with special reference to the valley-dwelling Shan and the Kachin hill tribes who supply them with jade.

The Shan are sedentary wet-rice cultivators with a stratified society consisting of nobility, farmers, and lower-class persons or slaves. Buddhism is their official religion, and (with a few exceptions) they speak mainly Tai. Their culture resembles that of the Burmese.

The Kachins are slash-and-burn cultivators who occupy the hill lands above the Shan. They speak a variety of dialects, some of which are mutually unintelligible. Their sociopolitical organization ranges from an egalitarian system called *gumlao*, in which all lineages are considered of equal rank, to a system called *gumsa*, in which lineages are ranked: there is a chiefly lineage, several lineages of aristocrats, and other lineages of commoners, or of slaves.

The history of the area, as reconstructed by Leach, has involved constant sparring and competition between Kachin groups, and between Kachin and Shan. During the course of the centuries, while the organization of the sophisticated feudal states of the Shan has remained relatively stable, Kachin tribes have oscillated from egalitarian to stratified, and back again. This oscillation is understandable only in the light of the relationship between the hill peoples and the Shan states.

While Shan states are reasonably self-sufficient, Kachin villages may not be—they may, in fact, be dependent on the Shan for much of their rice (Leach 235). On the other hand, the Kachin mountaineers have access to, and control of, a number of sources of exotic raw materials which the Shan desire and can make better use of: among these are jade, amber, tortoise shell, gold, and silver (Leach 238). The value of these commodities fluctuates through time, and is directly determined by the economic and political environment (Leach 25). The Kachin need food; the Shan need exotica so that they can either use them in their own prestige systems or trade them on to the Chinese.

The way in which the Shan and Kachin form alliances is not unlike that of the Tlingit and the Athabascans: they intermarry at the upper echelon. Most commonly, a Shan prince will send a daughter to marry a Kachin chief—perhaps including a dowry of rice land—and gain access to some desired mountain resources. For example:

> The Kansi chiefs who are Kachin overlords of the jade-producing area west of Kamaing have for several generations married Shan as well as Kachin wives. The Shan women are members of the family of the former *saohpa* [prince] of Mŏng Hkawm. . . . (220)

What is the effect of alliances between the Shan and their less sophisticated mountain neighbors? The effect is that, when Kachin communities are in the process of going from egalitarian *(gumlao)* to stratified *(gumsa)* society, the form taken by the stratification is an imitation of Shan stratification. "Kachin chiefs, when they have the opportunity, model their behaviour on that of Shan princes" (Leach 213); thereby "their chiefly status as Kachins is enhanced" (222). The Kachin chief may learn to speak Tai, he may adopt the Buddhist religion, he may dress like a Shan, and use Shan ritual and symbolism to support his position. Leach gives examples of whole Kachin communities whose aristocracies have become "Hill Shan"—he suggests, in fact, that all Kachin villages were once egalitarian, and that the stratified version is an unstable and artificial emulation of the Shan way of life. It is part of a process in which ". . . individuals faced with a choice of action will commonly use such choice as to gain power . . . or, to use a different language, they will seek to gain access to office or the esteem of their fellows which may lead them to office" (10).

Kachins and Shans are mutually contemptuous of each other. They compete for food and resources in a rugged and ecologically-varied region. In spite of their mutual contempt, the Shan and Kachin establish exchange relations through intermarriage, with the Kachins receiving subsistence products and the Shan exotic raw materials. Let me emphasize that this exchange, or "trade" if you will, does not cause the Kachin to become stratified, nor does it maintain stratification when the unstable *gumsa* begins to break down and revert to egalitarian organization. The point is this: when the Kachin do achieve stratification, the form it takes is an imitation of the language, religion, behavior, and symbolism of the more sophisticated Shan who consume their jade and amber. In much the same way, the Tagish who become stratified adopt the language, behavior, and symbolism of the Tlingit who consume their furs.

I suggest that such exchange systems are not without adaptive value. In ecological terms, they make possible the more nearly total exploitation of a very diversified environment, many of whose sub-areas could not otherwise sustain a self-sufficient population. In isolation, the Shan would survive with a surplus, but many areas of the Kachin hills would not be suitable for permanent communities. Intermarriage and the jade trade, bringing the Shan rice surplus up into the hill country, leads to one big economic system rather than several small ones, and makes more "niches" potentially usable. And the *gumsa* system, with all its strutting provincial imitation of Shan society, would probably be of great value in reinforcing the symbiotic network if only it could be stabilized.

A Model for Oaxaca and the Olmec

I am confident that many more examples of this kind could be found in the ethnographic literature. To sum up: data from several parts of the world suggest that a special relationship exists between consumers of exotic raw materials and their suppliers, especially when the suppliers belong to a society which is only slightly less stratified than that of the consumers. First, it seems that the upper echelon of each society often provides the entrepreneurs who facilitate the exchange. Second, the exchange is not "trade" in the sense that we use the term, but rather is set up through mechanisms of ritual visits, exchange of wives, "adoption" of members of one group by the other, and so on. Third, there may be an attempt on the part of the elite of the less sophisticated society to adopt the behavior, status trappings, religion, symbolism, or even language of the more sophisticated group—in short, to absorb some of their charisma. Fourth, although the exchange system does not alter the basic subsistence pattern of either group, it may not be totally unrelated to subsistence. It may, for example, be a way of establishing reciprocal obligations between a group with an insecure food supply and one with a perennial surplus.

Here, then, is one possible model for what happened in our case.

By the start of the first millennium B.C., the Valley of Oaxaca had reached the point where an emerging Formative elite sought to express its differential status through ornaments of magnetite, pearl oyster, and mica. Marine shells were imported from the Pacific Coast, and local sources of iron and mica had been found and were being exploited. At least one barrio of the largest-known San José Phase site in the Etla valley was occupied by craftsmen who accumulated and worked the above-mentioned materials.

The Oaxaca peoples were aware of, and in contact with, a more sophisticated and more highly stratified group of people occupying the southern Gulf Coast, from whom they obtained pearly fresh-water mussel shell. Judging by Curtis' mineralogical map, the Olmec probably first became aware of the possibilities of polishing iron ores when they came in contact with highland Oaxacan peoples who had access to the sources. The flow of magnetite and ilmenite may have begun on a small scale, involving tiny flat mirrors of the type seen at San Lorenzo Tenochtitlán, and expanded later to include nodules large enough for the parabolic mirrors recovered at La Venta. If our ethnographic data is in any way analogous, the mechanism which facilitated this inter-regional flow of goods should have been one which linked the highest-ranking lineages of the Oaxaca peoples to one or more of the higher-ranking Olmec lineages. One would also predict that the highland Oaxaca elite would begin to emulate the religion, symbolism, dress, and behavior of the Olmec elite, insofar as it would enhance their own status among their own people. We might predict, for example, that while their patterns of settlement and subsistence remained unchanged, they might adopt the St. Andrew's cross, the U-motif, the "paw-wing" motif, and the deity who was part man and part jaguar. Certainly there is some evidence of the ceramics of the San José Phase that the latter steps were taken in the Valley of Oaxaca.

Our model suggests one further point: the areas most likely to form exchange systems with, and truly emulate the behavior and symbolism of, the Olmec were not the least developed regions of the highlands, but the most developed—areas of high agricultural and demographic potential like the Valleys of Oaxaca, Mexico, Morelos, and Puebla, for example. Many of these regions already are known to have large nucleated communities in the Early Formative, and some already had patterns of monumental architecture which were too regionally distinct to be considered Olmec-derived. On the basis of the ethnographic data presented above, I suggest that it was precisely because these areas were on the verge of stratified society themselves that they were so fascinated by the Olmec and so predisposed to adopt their status paraphernalia. All the valleys of highland Mexico contain some exotic raw material which could be used for the manufacture of status items, but many such materials were rarely or never used in the Early Formative: native copper, amethyst, plate chalcedony, and galena are only a few of the overlooked possibilities. I suspect that, for the most part, the materials used were those occurring in areas where relatively large, stratified highland communities were already present. I make this point because I feel that, as more and more "Olmec-influenced" communities are discovered in the *tierra templada,* it may become tempting to view the highlands of Mesoamerica as a vast underdeveloped backwater into which Olmec messiahs spread. I would argue the reverse: Olmec influence will appear most strong in those areas which were already most developed and already had status systems into which Olmec concepts could be most profitably fitted.

In other words, I suspect that the peoples who have been called "Highland Olmec" were not really Olmec, any more than the "Inland Tlingit" were really Tlingit or the "Hill Shan" were really Shan. They were indigenous mountain peoples, successfully pursuing multi-crop agriculture, competing for good land and water, and using their surplus to support a hierarchy, craft specialists, and community-sponsored construction projects. Had they not been, they would probably not have gained as much from contact with the Olmec as they did.

Some Speculations on Function

Finally, we come to the last question: why did it happen at all? Here the available archaeological data are so inadequate that they make a conclusive answer impossible; I can only offer suggestions for future research.

Let us assume, for the moment, that the systems of inter-regional interaction did not spring up by accident during the Formative: there was a reason for them. Let us assume that systems of exchange profited both the Olmec and the peoples of the highlands, and that that is why the exchange was so striking and extensive. As in the case of any system, the behavior of the participants should (perhaps in some nearly-concealed way) have served to maintain the exchange pattern. In studying such a system, therefore, we must be careful to distinguish between the *purpose* of the participants' behavior, which may be quite easy to figure out, and the *function* of that behavior in an adaptive sense, about which we can only hypothesize.

For example, we have suggested that the *purpose* of the accumulation of magnetite or jade by highland peoples, its working by craft specialists, and its export to the Olmec, was to enhance and reinforce previously-existing systems of status, in which access to certain exotic raw materials was restricted to an elite. Its *function,* however, may have been to convert some of their agricultural surplus into a kind of imperishable "wealth" which could be used to set up reciprocal obligations with neighboring people whose food supply was even more secure. (This seems, for example, to have been the case among the Kachin tribesmen who depend on the Shan for part of their rice.)

Similarly, as Drucker, Heizer, and Squier (1959: Footnote 33) have already suggested, the *purpose* of the massive offerings of serpentine, jade, and magnetite made at La Venta may have been to restate and reinforce commitment to the Olmec social and religious systems. The buried pavements, they point out, were not made to be admired; the act of creating and burying such offerings, made valuable by the difficulty of their acquisition, was the important point. But the underlying *function* of burying such offerings may have been to take the materials themselves out of circulation. It was a way of consuming, or destroying in a sense, a whole series of otherwise imperishable materials, thereby necessitating the acquisition of more of the same. As Leach points out, the value of jade depends directly on the current economic situation; had such exotic materials continued to pile up at La Venta they would soon have lost whatever value derived from their rarity and foreignness, and the flow would have slowed down.

Two aspects of the system, therefore, may have been this: the highland people converting their occasional surplus into exotic items for export to the Olmec; the Olmec maintaining the flow by taking it out of circulation as soon as it arrived. And the overall function of the whole system may have been to create one big economic sphere where previously many small ones had existed—to set the stage, in a way, for the great inter-regional symbiotic networks which Sanders (1956) describes for later periods of Meso-american prehistory. In the process, the elite of a number of key highland regions came to emulate the behavior of the Olmec elite, to borrow their symbolism, and adopt those aspects of Olmec religion which lent further prestige to their own position. Perhaps one superficial effect of this process was the spread of the Olmec art style throughout the highlands. I say "superficial" because I am confident that the spread of that style was not a primary *cause* of Formative Mesoamerica's unity, but one reflection of the fact that it was already united, in an economic sense.

Bibliography

Bernal, Ignacio 1967. La Presencia Olmeca en Oaxaca. *Culturas de Oaxaca, Pub. 1.* Museo Nacional de Antropología, Mexico.

Coe, Michael D. 1961. La Victoria, an Early Site on the Pacific Coast of Guatemala. *Papers of the Peabody Museum of Archaeology and Ethnology, Harvard University,* vol. 53. Cambridge, Massachusetts.

————1963. Cultural Development in Southeastern Mesoamerica. *In* Aboriginal Cultural Development in Latin America: an Interpretative Review (Betty J. Meggers and Clifford Evans, eds.). *Smithsonian Miscellaneous Collections,* vol. 146, no. 1, pp. 27-44. Washington.

————1965a. Archaeological Synthesis of Southern Veracruz and Tabasco. *In* Handbook of Middle American Indians, vol. 3, part 2, pp. 679-715. University of Texas Press, Austin.

————1965b. The Jaguar's Children: Pre-Classic Central Mexico. The Museum of Primitive Art, New York.

————1965c. The Olmec Style and its Distributions. *In* Handbook of Middle American Indians, vol. 3, part 2, pp. 739-775. University of Texas Press, Austin.

Coe, Michael D., R. A. Diehl, and M. Stuiver 1967. Olmec Civilization, Veracruz, Mexico: Dating of the San Lorenzo Phase. *Science,* vol. 155, no. 3768, pp. 1399-1401. Washington.

Coe, Michael D. and Kent V. Flannery 1967. Early Cultures and Human Ecology in South Coastal Guatemala. *Smithsonian Contributions to Anthropology,* vol. 3. Washington.

Curtis, Garniss H. 1959. The Petrology of Artifacts and Architectural Stone at La Venta. *In* Excavations at La Venta, Tabasco, 1955. *Bureau of American Ethnology, Bulletin 170,* Appendix 4, pp. 284-289. Washington.

Dixon, Keith A. 1959. Ceramics from Two Preclassic Periods at Chiapa de Corzo, Chiapas, Mexico. *Papers of the New World Archaeological Foundation,* no. 5. Orinda, California.

Drucker, Philip, R. F. Heizer, and R. J. Squier 1959. Excavations at La Venta, Tabasco, 1955. *Bureau of American Ethnology, Bulletin 170.* Washington.

Flannery, Kent V., A. V. Kirkby, M. J. Kirkby, and A. W. Williams, Jr. 1967. Farming Systems and Political Growth in Ancient Oaxaca. *Science,* vol. 158, no. 3800, pp. 445-454. Washington.

Leach, Edmund R. 1954. Political Systems of Highland Burma. (1965 ed.) Boston.

MacNeish, Richard S. 1954. An Early Archaeological Site near Panuco, Veracruz. *Transactions of the American Philosophical Society,* New Series, vol. 44, part 5, pp. 539-641. Philadelphia.

———— 1964. The Origins of New World Civilization. *Scientific American,* vol. 211, no. 5, pp. 29-37. Washington.

McClellan, Catharine 1953. The Inland Tlingit. *In* Asia and North America: Transpacific Contacts. *Memoirs of the Society for American Archaeology,* no. 9, pp. 47-52. Salt Lake City.

Neely, James A. 1967. Organización hidráulica y sistemas de irrigación prehistóricos en el Valle de Oaxaca. *Boletín del Instituto Nacional de Antropología e Historia,* no. 27, pp. 15-17. Mexico.

Paddock, John 1966. Oaxaca in Ancient Mesoamerica. *In* Ancient Oaxaca (John Paddock, ed.), pp. 83-242. Stanford University Press, Stanford.

Sanders, William T. 1956. The Central Mexican Symbiotic Region; a Study in Prehistoric Settlement Patterns. *In* Prehistoric Settlement Patterns in the New World (Gordon R. Willey, ed.). *Viking Fund Publications in Anthropology,* no. 23, pp. 115-127. New York.

Schmieder, Oscar 1939. The Settlements of the Tzapotec and Mije Indians, State of Oaxaca, Mexico. *University of California Publications in Geography,* vol. 4, pp. 1-184. Berkeley.

William L. Rathje received his Ph.D. from Harvard in 1971 and is now an assistant professor at the University of Arizona. He has worked in the southwestern United States and Mesoamerica and has recently co-directed a project with J. A. Sabloff which has explored the ancient port-of-trade at Cozumel, Mexico.

There is no agreement among archaeologists on the reasons for the rise of Classic Maya civilization. In any case, the answer is certain to be a complex one. In this stimulating article, Rathje suggests that a climate and topography that on first glance appear to be a detriment to the development of a civilization were, in fact, instrumental in its rise.

The Origin and Development of Lowland Classic Maya Civilization

William L. Rathje

The southern Maya lowlands present a largely redundant environment which does not possess the potential for major internal symbiotic regions or for irrigation. In fact, the interior of this region is uniformly deficient in resources essential to the efficiency of every individual household engaged in the Mesoamerican agricultural subsistence economy: mineral salt, obsidian for blades, and hard stone for grinding. Yet, in the core of this rain forest region, the basic elements of Classic Maya civilization first coalesced. A model involving methods of procuring and distributing the resources necessary to the efficiency of an agricultural subsistence economy explains the loci of lowland Classic Maya development and the order in which these loci developed. This model can also be applied to the Olmec civilization.

A major archaeological problem today seems to be—why did the lowland Maya civilization evolve in its ecological setting? This paper will develop a hypothesis to explain the evolution of lowland Classic Maya civilization.

Since I subscribe to cultural ecology, the environmental configuration of the Petén rain forest is an obvious beginning. This expansive ecological zone has been characterized as lacking developmental potential because: (1) the environment is redundant in access to resources; (2) transportation of goods is difficult; and (3) slash-and-burn agriculture is the main subsistence technique. As a result, it is thought that there was little stimulus toward trade and redistribution; nucleated centers were rarely maintained and a scattered light settlement was typical; and there were no obvious changes in the subsistence system through time which would have required community efforts and caused increasing ceremonialism (Meggers 1954; Palerm and Wolf 1957; M. Coe 1961; Sanders 1964;

Reproduced by permission of the Society for American Archaeology and the author, from *American Antiquity,* Vol. 36, No. 3, pp. 275-285, 1971.

Webb 1964).

Sanders (1964:236) concludes that there were few integrative factors operating in ancient Maya society and many disruptive ones. Accepting this characterization of the rain forest environment, how can the inception of lowland Maya civilization be explained?

The stress of Meggers (1954:817), Sanders (1964:238), and Sanders and Price (1968: 142-145) upon a diffusion of civilization into the lowland rain forest raises a major issue. Since acceptance usually occurs only where the diffusing complex is useful, what was the function of that complex? By Sanders' own admission, there would have been little advantage to sustain a well integrated organization in the Maya lowlands.

Most other hypotheses propose that the Maya cult developed, not out of economic need, but merely to glorify itself (Webb 1964:420-422). I find this an ineffective hypothesis. Therefore, the function of socio-political integration in lowland rain forest environments is a crucial question.

In solving this problem, an understanding of the conjunction of environment and technology is significant. Every household (the minimum production-consumption unit, i.e., extended family, nuclear family, etc.) needs basic resources to efficiently exploit a given eco-zone. I define basic resources as those which are present archaeologically, ethnohistorically, and ethnographically, in every household participating in a specific subsistence configuration, in this case the maize agriculture complex. I will discuss three resources here: igneous or hard-stone metates, razor-sharp obsidian tools, and salt.

The metate is found in every household in Mexico. Because stones wear and leave grit in ground corn, the harder the stone the more efficient the metate. Data on excavated metates in the Maya area indicate that subcrystalline limestone metates are rarely found, as natural limestone is too soft to be efficient. Limestone metates occur abundantly only in areas close to major sources of semi-crystalline limestone, such as on the upper Usumacinta and near the Sierra de Yucatan. In environment and geographic position of the core, thus, also select for the elaboration of services and products that reinforce community integration. Such services and commodities are the only scarce resources the core area can tap; its exports will therefore be the by-products of community stratification—a specific ceremonial configuration producing access to the supernatural in terms of temples, altars, ritual and astronomical knowledge, polychrome pottery, ceremonial paraphernalia, and other items of status reinforcement (see Figs. 1 and 2).

Several factors are obvious: There is a limit on socio-political development in rain forest environments; the only scarce resources that lowland core areas have to market for strategic goods are the by-products of superior socio-political organization. Therefore, if the buffer zone is socio-politically developed, the best a core area can do is compete on an equal organizational base. Because of spatial proximity the buffer zone will obviously maintain control over strategic resources. Thus, the core area's advantage cannot develop if, at the time of settlement, competing and resource areas are already developed to or beyond the potential of the rain forest.

I hypothesize that given the preconditions of environment, subsistence base, technology, and the existence of basic resources not located in the lowlands, complex socio-political organization in the rain forests of Mesoamerica developed originally in response to the need for consistent procurement, importation, and distribution of non-local basic

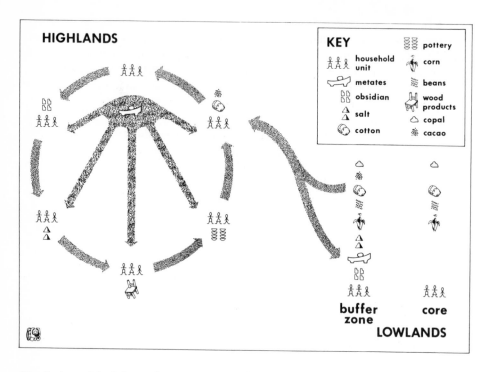

Fig. 1. A model of the exchange potential of natural resources between highland, buffer zone, and core areas.

resources useful to every household. This is a specific formulation of a more general explanatory statement previously proposed by Sahlins (1958), Fried (1967), Hill (personal communication), and others: complex socio-political organization rises in response to the need for procurement and allocation of critical resources or services.

This hypothesis must be tested with available archaeological data. The data utilized in this paper are from the Maya area, although data from the Olmec area provide an equally valid test (Rathje, n.d.). Using the hypothesis, I predict the earliest evidence of complex socio-political organization will occur in the resource deficient core area of the Maya lowlands. No sites of equal complexity will be found in the buffer zone.

Here is a good opportunity to compare hypotheses. Sanders and Price (1968), predict socio-political development where zones of differing production are closely spaced, especially in alluviated floodplains. Thus, the first cult developments should, according to Sanders and Price (especially as interpreted by Adams 1969), occur in the buffer zone.

Granted, the first known heavily populated settlements of the Maya lowlands are located along rivers, but Sanders and Price (especially as interpreted by Adams 1969) are not predicting the location of settlements however early. They are predicting the location of the first development of the Maya cult, for which I do not feel Xe or any other buffer zone Early Preclassic settlements qualify. In fact, most of the buffer zone did not develop complex organization until the late Classic. These data do not deny the importance of economic symbiosis in stimulating socio-political development, especially in the highlands; they do show that additional factors have effected lowland cultural

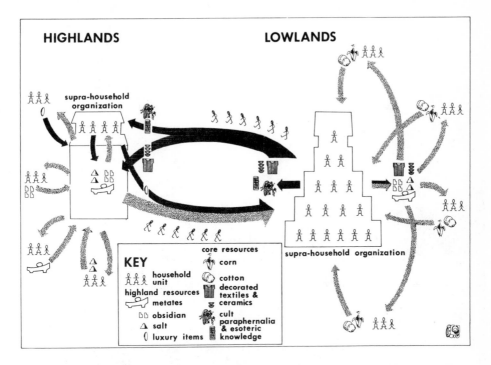

Fig. 2. A model of the exchange functions of the core's cult organization.

development.

If the chiefdoms and cult of the lowland Maya did not develop in the buffer zone, did they develop in the core as I predict? First, the core area of least resource exchange potential must be defined. Because of the ethnohistoric record, it is possible to plot post-conquest Yucatán population distributions (Fig. 3). The only area that can be confirmed as largely vacant by the records is the center of the northeast Petén (Thompson 1951: 390, 1966:29; Scholes and Roys 1968:463-464; MacNutt 1908:2:29; Means 1917:124-129). This pattern is supported archaeologically (Bullard 1960, 1970). The northeast Petén is one of the areas most distant from salt, obsidian, and igneous stone resources. Obviously, it was not an area with any special tradeable environmental resource not found abundantly in the rest of the Maya lowlands (Sanders and Price 1968:169). This then I define as the lowland core area, the area hardest to reach, with the least economic potential; the one area that was too much trouble to settle and supply with basic resources in the sixteenth century (Fig. 4).

Most Mayanists today believe that the Maya cult complex, in a recognizable constellation, crystallized first within the lowland core area, the northeast Petén (Willey 1966: 117; Thompson 1967:35; W. Coe 1965). The 2 largest sites of the Maya cult, Mirador (Figs. 3, 4, site 28) and Tikal (Figs. 3, 4, site 6), are within this core area. One confirmation of the prediction is provided by stela inscriptions, the earliest of which occur within

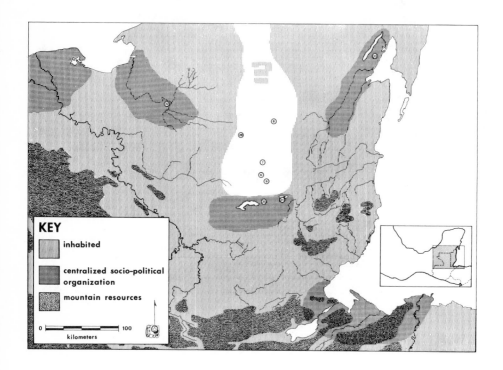

Fig. 3. Sixteenth century population distributions in central Yucatán (after Scholes and Roys 1968; Thompson 1967). The numbered sites are: Tikal, 6; Uaxactun, 7; Balakbal, 8; Uolantun, 9; Mirador, 28; Tapoxte, 31; Itzamkanac, 32; Chetumal, 33; El Zapote, 35.

the core area (Morley 1937-38; I. Graham, personal communication).

A second prediction is that: (1) core area influence will spread into areas vital to the procurement of basic resources—into buffer zones, along trade routes, and into resource areas; and (2) this influence will take the form of wholesale importation of the by-products of complex socio-political organization—cult ideology, cult technology, and manu-factured cult commodities from the core area.

After the original appearance of the cult in the northeast Petén, it spread into the buffer zone (see Fig. 5). The Usumacinta-Pasíon drainage, which was a major sixteenth century trade route, produced Piedras Negras (Fig. 5, site 13), Yaxchilan (Fig. 5, site 12), and Altar de Sacrificios (Fig. 5, site 11) as cult members. Altar's river junction location stands in a special relationship to the Guatemalan highlands. The only salt sources near the lowlands are located up the Chixoy River from Altar. During the Early Classic, strong influences from the Petén spread over the highlands. Most interesting is the fact that later, when much of the highlands became isolated from core area influences, the salt producing Chixoy area remained within the Peten diffusion sphere and in the Chama district (Fig. 5, no. 30) one of the great polychrome styles of Mesoamerica emerged (Rands and Smith 1965:131, 144). All of these influences from the Peten passed through strategically located Altar into important highland resource areas. Altar was the only one of the major tested Usumacinta-Pascion sites with an Early Classic cult development of consequence.

Another important buffer zone cult center developed at Copan (Fig. 5, site 10), an area geographically in the highland resource zone near obsidian sources and on a Postclassic trade route. During the Copan archaic, a minimal population of farmers and gatherers had only sporadic contact with the outside. Suddenly, in the Early Classic, the Maya cult arrived. Trade with outside regions increased including the wholesale importation of ceremonial items from the central Peten (Longyear 1952:32, 68, 70).

Another possible cult member was Tulum (Fig. 5, site 14), located directly across from Cozumel, the island stopping point in the Postclassic salt trade between northern Yucatan, Belize, and Honduras. Also of note is the seemingly one-way trade between the Peten core area and Dzibilchaltun (Fig. 5, site 15), where according to Andrews (1965: 305) literally thousands of Peten trade pieces pepper the Early period deposits. The Yucatec were enthusiastic customers for the decorated polychromes of Guatemala. Perhaps these data form part of the early development of a Peten-Yucatan salt trade.

Obviously, from its complexity, the spread of the cult required importation of specialists and skilled craftsmen or training of buffer zone individuals at centers in the Peten. Socio-technic and ideo-technic cult products were subject to wholesale importation. The following are typical assessments of the distribution of core area ceramics during the cult's early development:

1. Beginning with the Protoclassic and continuing into the Early Classic. . . is a trend toward massive production and extensive distribution of Peten Gloss Ware (Rands and Smith 1965:533).
2. Decorated and monochrome black ware types from the environs of the Peten ceremonial centers reached Barton Ramie in abundance or were imitated by craftsmen who must either have been schooled in the Peten or instructed by persons directly emanating from Peten sources (Willey and others 1965:350).

The ideology and technology of temple architecture, glyphic writing, astronomical knowledge, stela erection, carved eccentrics, and jades diffused similarly. Morley and Brainard conclude:

The area of Classic Maya culture constituted nearly 100,000 square miles, a major segment of Mesoamerica. Over this region there is evidence of a rapid spread of calendric innovations and an identity of religious symbolism as well as a series of concurrent changes in pottery . . . . This remarkably widespread homogeneity occurred in an area notable nowadays for its nearly impassible terrain [1946:46].

Thus, the disadvantages of dispersed settlement, great distance from resources, poor transportation, and central location in an area whose redundancy mitigated against

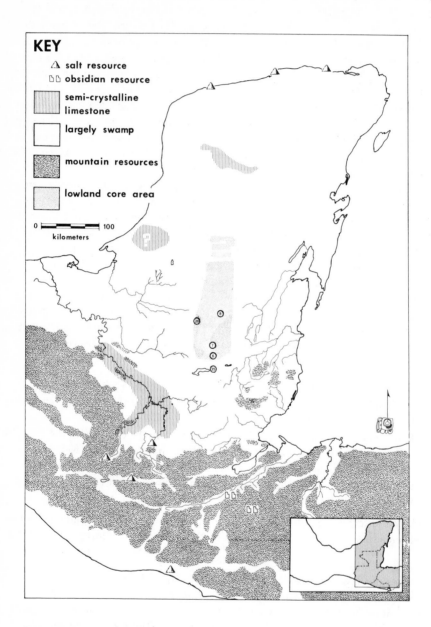

Fig. 4. The central Yucatán core area and surrounding resource zones (after Thompson 1964; Dirreccion General de Cartografis 1964; Blom 1932; Graham 1967). The numbered sites are: Tikal, 6; Uaxactun, 7; Balakbal, 8; Mirador, 28; El Zapote, 35.

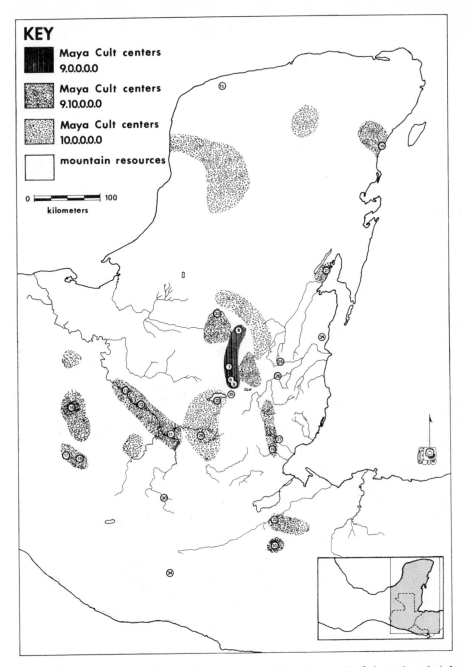

Fig. 5. The spread of the Maya cult as represented by the spread of the stela cult (after Morley 1937-38). The numbered sites are: Tikal, 6; Uaxactun, 7; Balakbal, 8; Uolantun, 9; Copan, 10; Altar de Sacrificios, 11; Yaxchilan, 12; Piedras Negras, 13; Tulum, 14; Dzibilchaltun, 15; Tonina, 16; Comitan, 17; Chinkultic, 18; Pusilha, 19; Calakmul, 20; Ichpaatun, 21; Quirigua, 22; Tayasal, 23; Altun Ha, 24; San Jose, 25; Barton Ramie, 26; Lubaantun, 27; Seibal, 29; Chama Valley, 30; Kaminaljuyu, 34; El Zapote, 35.

local exchange all worked toward integrating communities; and complex socio-political organization in the lowland Maya rain forest developed originally in response to the need for consistent procurement, importation, and distribution of basic resources useful to every household.

Acknowledgements

Special thanks to Gordon R. Willey who made this paper possible; to Michael D. Coe and Robert Fry for generous assistance; to C. C. Lamberg-Karlovsky for detailed constructive criticisms; to Kent Day, William Fitzhugh, James Humphries, John Ladd, Mark Leone, Renato Rosaldo, Jeremy Sabloff, Edward Sisson, and Gair Tourtellot for willing ears and considered opinions. This paper was prepared through the aid of the Wenner-Gren Foundation for Anthropological Research and read at the 35th annual meeting of the Society for American Archaeology in Mexico City, May, 1970.

References

Adams, R. E. W. 1969. Maya archaeology 1958-1968, a review. *Latin American Research Review* 4(2):3-45.

Andrews, E. W. 1965. Archaeology and prehistory in the northern Maya lowlands: an introduction. In *Handbook of Middle American Indians*, Vol. 2, edited by Gordon R. Willey, pp. 288-330. University of Texas Press, Austin.

Binford, L. R. 1962. Archaeology as anthropology. *American Antiquity* 28:217-225.

Bloch, M. R. 1963. The social influences of salt. *Scientific American* 209:88-98.

Blom, F. 1932. Commerce, trade and monetary units of the Maya. *Tulane University Middle American Research Series, Publication 4.*

Bullard, W. R., Jr. 1960. Maya settlement pattern in northeastern Petén, Guatemala. *American Antiquity* 25:355-372.

———— 1970. The status of postclassic archaeology in Petén, Guatemala. Paper read at the 35th Annual Meeting of the Society for American Archaeology, May, 1970. Mexico City.

Chapman, A. C. 1957. Port of trade enclaves in Aztec and Maya civilization. In *Trade and market in the early empires*, edited by K. Polanyi, C. M. Arensberg, H. W. Pearson, pp. 114-153. Free Press, New York.

Coe, M. D. 1961. Social typology and the tropical forest civilizations. *Comparative Studies in Society and History* 4:65-85.

Coe, W. R. 1965. Tikal, Guatemala, and the emergent Maya civilization. *Science* 147:1401-1419.

Culbert, T.P. 1970. Sociocultural integration and the classic Maya. Paper read at the 35th Annual Meeting of the Society for American Archaeology, May, 1970, Mexico City.

Dirreccion General de Cartografia de Guatemala. 1964. *Atlas preliminar de Guatemala: segunda edicion.*

Flannery, K. V. 1968. The Olmec and the valley of Oaxaca: a model for inter-regional interaction in formative times. In *Dumbarton Oaks Conference on the Olmec*, edited by Elizabeth P. Benson, pp. 79-117. Dumbarton Oaks, Washington, D. C.

Fried, M. H. 1967. *The evolution of political society: an essay in political anthropology.* Random House, New York.

Fry, R. 1969. Ceramics and settlement in the periphery of Tikal, Guatemala. Unpublished Ph.D. dissertation. Department of Anthropology, University of Arizona.

Graham, I. 1967. Archaeological explorations in El Peten, Guatemala. *Tulane University Middle American Research Series, Publication 33.*

Leone, M. P. 1968. Economic autonomy and social distance: archaeological evidence. Unpublished Ph.D. dissertation. Department of Anthropology, University of Arizona.

Longyear, J. M. III. 1952. Copan ceramics: a study of southeastern Maya pottery. *Carnegie Institution of Washington, Publication 597.*

MacNutt, F. A. (Editor and Translator). 1908. *Letters of Cortes: the five letters of relation from Fernando Cortes to the emperor Charles V.* G. P. Putnam's Sons, New York.

McBryde, F. W. 1945. Cultural and historical geography of southwest Guatemala. *Smithsonian Institution, Institute of Social Anthropology, Publication 4.*

Means, P. A. 1917. History of the Spanish conquest of Yucatan and the Itza. *Peabody Museum of American Archaeology and Ethnology, Papers 7.*

Meggers, B. J. 1954. Environmental limitations on the development of culture. *American Anthropologist* 56:801-824.

Morley, S. G. 1937-38. The inscriptions of Peten. *Carnegie Institution of Washington, Publication 437.*

Morley, S. G., and G. W. Brainard. 1946. *The ancient Maya.* Stanford University Press, Stanford, California.

Nash, M. 1967. Indian economies. In *Handbook of Middle American Indians,* Vol. 6, edited by Manning Nash, pp. 87-102. University of Texas Press, Austin.

Palerm, A., and E. R. Wolf. 1957. Ecological potential and cultural development. In *Pan American Union Social Science Monograph* 3:39-69.

Rands, R. A., and R. E. Smith. 1965. Pottery of the Guatemalan highlands. In *Handbook of Middle American Indians,* Vol. 2, edited by Gordon R. Willey, pp. 95-145. University of Texas Press, Austin.

Rappaport, R. 1967. *Pigs for the ancestors: Ritual in the ecology of a New Guinea people.* Yale University Press, New Haven.

Rathje, William L. n.d. Praise the gods and pass the metates: a hypothesis of the development of lowland rainforest civilizations in Mesoamerica. In *Contemporary archaeology: an introduction to theory and contributions,* edited by Mark P. Leone. (In Press).

Redfield, R. 1941. *The folk culture of Yucatan,* University of Chicago Press, Chicago.

Sabloff, J. A., and G. Tourtellot. 1969. Exchange systems and the ancient Maya. Paper read at the 68th Annual Meeting of the American Anthropological Association, November 1969, New Orleans.

Sahlins, M. D. 1958. Social stratification in Polynesia. *The American Ethnological Society.* University of Washington Press, Seattle.

———— 1963. Poor man, rich man, big-man, chief: political types in Melanesia and Polynesia. *Comparative Studies in Society and History,* 5:285-303.

Sanders, W. T. 1964. Cultural ecology of the Maya lowlands. *Estudios de Cultura Maya* 4:203-241.

Sanders, W. T., and B. H. Price. 1968. *Mesoamerica: the evolution of a civilization.* Random House, New York.

Scholes, F. V., and R. L. Roys. 1968. *The Maya Chontal Indians of Acalan-Tixchel: a contribution to the history and ethnography of the Yucatan Peninsula.* 2nd edition. University of Oklahoma Press, Norman.

Tax, S., and R. Hinshaw. 1969. The Maya of the midwestern highlands. In *Handbook of Middle American Indians,* Vol. 7, edited by Evon Z. Vogt, pp. 69-100. University of Texas Press, Austin.

Thompson, J. E. S. 1951. The Itza of Tayasal, Peten. In *Homenaje Caso.* Mexico.

———— 1964. Trade relations between the Maya highlands and lowlands. *Estudios de Cultura Maya* 4:13-49.

———— 1967. The Maya central area at the Spanish conquest and later: a problem in demography. *Royal Anthropological Institute of Great Britain and Ireland, Proceedings 23-37.*

Webb, M. C. 1964. The post-classic decline of the Peten Maya: an interpretation in the light of a general theory of state society. Unpublished Ph.D. dissertation. Department of Anthropology, University of Michigan.

Willey, G. R. 1966. *An introduction to American Archaeology*, Vol. 1: *North and Middle America*. Prentice-Hall, New York.

Willey, G. R., W, R. Bullard, Jr., J. B. Glass, J. C. Gifford, and others. 1955. Prehistoric Maya settlements in the Belize Valley. *Peabody Museum of American Archaeology and Ethnology, Papers 54.*

Wolf, E. R. 1967. Levels of communal relations. In *Handbook of Middle American Indians*, Vol. 6, edited by Evon Z. Vogt, pp. 299-316. University of Texas Press, Austin.

Gordon R. Willey (Ph.D., Columbia University, 1942) is the Bowditch
Professor of Mexican and Central American Archaeology and Ethnology
at Harvard University, and has been recognized as one of the most eminent American archaeologists for more than two decades. He has undertaken archaeological field studies throughout the Americas (in Peru,
Panama, Nicaragua, British Honduras, Honduras, Guatemala, and the
southeastern United States) and has written numerous books and
articles including the landmark work *Method and Theory in American
Archaeology* (1958, with Philip Phillips) and the monumental two volume *Introduction to American Archaeology* (1966-1971). One of
Willey's major areas of interest has been the nature of civilization. At a
recent Wenner-Gren Symposium on the Emergence of Civilization in
Mesoamerica, he was asked to write a commentary on the papers by
E. W. Andrews IV and by L. Parsons and B. Price (the reader is referred
to the *Contributions of the University of California Archaeological
Research Facility*, No. 11, 1971 for their papers). We have excerpted
part of Willey's commentary which we feel will be of general interest
to the readers of our collection.

Commentary on the Emergence of
Civilization in the Maya Lowlands

Gordon R. Willey

. . . I conceive of civilization as having three essential dimensions: (1) large population size and density; (2) marked social complexity; and (3) a complex network of
intercommunication among its social components. More specifically, I submit that a
civilization integrates the lives of more than 5000 persons. This integration may be
achieved in either a concentrated, or urban, settlement or in a dispersed, or non-urban,
settlement. The crucial factor is that the energies and abilities of a population of this
size are drawn upon and integrated to a common purpose. As to social complexity,
a civilization is characterized by marked divisions of labor, by a complex ranking system or by social classes, and by an hierarchial governmental structure. These circumstances and institutions may be reflected in various ways in the archaeological record:
in differentiation in the size and elegance of living quarters; in the presence of construct-

Reprinted from *Contributions of the University of California Archaeological Research Facility,* No. 11,
pp. 97-111, Department of Anthropology, University of California, Berkeley (1971), by permission of
the publisher and author.

ions dedicated to public purposes or personages—temples and palaces; in evidences for the specialized manufacture of various goods; in evidences for the differential distribution and use of these goods as seen in dwellings or in burials. As to the nature of the governmental structure, I would say that this could be either that of a chiefdom or a state, as these terms have been used recently by anthropologists (Service, 1962). That is, I would not restrict the condition of civilization to the political form of the state. I accept the chiefdom-state distinction and the evolutionary implications of this distinction, however; and I would see the sanctions of a large scale force, as these can be manipulated by the state, as the essential differentiation between the two.

As to the network of intercommunications, the key points in such a network are either cities or ceremonial centers. It is from these that government, religion, and trade are controlled. Media of communication are obviously of great importance. Language is the foremost of these in any human communication, but in the context of a civilization it is important that the word be recorded, and so writing has become, deservedly, a classic hallmark of the status of civilization. But this is not the only way, in a broader sense, that the "word" is recorded. Art is another communicative form. As Proskouriakoff (1970, Ms.) notes, "Monumental . . . arts provided validation for hierarchial society and maintained communication between administration and the populace." The communication network of a civilization binds not only the present with the traditions of the past, but it ties hamlet to village and village to city or major center. The construction and enlargement of such a network may be effected through political or military power, but it may also be effected through trade.

I make no claim here to great originality in the formulation of these criteria of civilization. Gordon Childe (1950) and others have offered similar ones. My attempt here has been to place them in systemic context; but they can be summarized as traits as follows:

(1)   Communities of more than 5000 people or the clear evidence of the integration of such numbers in a close-knit cultural system.
(2)   Marked divisions of labor.
(3)   A complex ranking system or social classes.
(4)   An hierarchial governmental structure.
(5)   Monumentality in architecture.
(6)   A codified symbolic system (such as writing or a pervasive art style.)
(7)   Interregional trade.

Before turning to the status of civilization in the Maya lowlands, we should consider one other matter: the different kinds of civilizations. In their symposium paper Parsons and Price (1970, Ms.) define two basic kinds of civilization for Mesoamerica. In referring to what they have said, I beg indulgence for anticipating the formal discussion of their paper, but their thoughts on the matter are very pertinent both to the symposium theme as a whole and to the Maya lowlands in particular. They refer to "urban" and "non-urban" civilizations. These have, respectively, the diagnostic feature of the presence or the absence of the trait of true urban settlement. They also have other associated traits. The urban civilization is associated with a market economy and a merchandising middle class, with a greater social class complexity than the non-urban civilization, with a landed aristocracy, and with a militaristic leadership. It is the setting for the state. The non-urban civilization is linked to a redistributive economy in the hands of an aristocracy, to a social ranking system, to corporate or kin ownership of land, and to a theocratically oriented leadership. It is the setting of the chiefdom.

The extent to which these two trait clusters are functionally associated with their respective urban and non-urban settlement types is yet to be fully demonstrated. Sanders and Price (1968), and again, Parsons and Price (1970, Ms.), have argued for functional interrelationships. They see the urban type civilization as developing in regions of diversified natural resources. In Mesoamerica, these are the upland valleys, with deep soils suitable for intensive cultivation techniques and a variety of items for exchange—obsidian, jadeite, basalt. This micro-environmental diversity was best served by a local market economy, and such an economy, and the positive feedback from it, flourished best in a true urban setting. The lowlands, on the other hand, lacked environmental differentiation of resources and the symbiosis between micro-environmental niches. For them, the most important trade was long-distance trade which was mediated by the nobility or by the lineage heads whose ceremonial centers were the redistributive points for a dispersed peasantry. These are instructive models; I am inclined to agree with them; whether they are correct or not in all details will be revealed, we hope, by further archaeological testing. The two models carry with them an implication of evolutionary sequence, with the stage of non-urban civilization preceding the urban. Parsons and Price (1970, Ms.) caution, however, that this need not be the case and cite Morton Fried's (1960) model of the "secondary state." The Mesoamerican non-urban civilization of the lowlands could be such a "secondary state"—that is, one which developed in response to, and from contact with, the primary state of an urban civilization, in this case one from the Mesoamerican highlands. Although this point is not pressed in the Parsons-Price paper, it is favored in the earlier Sanders-Price argument where Maya Classic Tikal is seen in such a "secondary state" relationship to Teotihuacan. In this particular instance, I am inclined to doubt the "secondary state" model as being fully applicable to what happened in the Maya lowlands; but, as a way of going into that, let us get back now to my specific theme, the rise of civilization in the Maya lowlands.

The Status of Civilization in the Maya Lowlands

The greater part of our Maya lowland evidence for population size, settlement distribution, clues to social classes, and trade comes from the Late Classic Period, and, especially in the south for what is designated as the Tepeu 2 sub-phase (ca. A.D. 700-800). We will take a look at these Late Classic data first—in the light of our foregoing criteria of the condition of civilization—and then consider how far back in time we may project these patterns.

That there were Late Classic Maya lowland communities that integrated the lives and efforts of more than 5000 people is now fully demonstrated. Earlier versions of Tikal population estimates give figures of 10,000 to 11,000 persons for the 16 square kilometer mapped central zone, and this was supplemented by another 10,000 persons in a surrounding peripheral belt (Carr and Hazard, 1961; Haviland, 1965). Now more recent estimates following strip-sample surveys radiating out from the center of the site have increased these figures to a total of 49,000 people within a zone of 163 square kilometers (Haviland, 1969). As far as we know, this was the largest Classic Maya community of the south, and it seems to be unique in its great size; however, other ceremonial centers, although smaller than Tikal, are estimated to have controlled sustaining areas of more than 5000 people. Seibal is one example (Gair Tourtellot, personal communication 1970); Benque Viejo, in the Belize Valley, another (Willey and others, 1965); and in the north, Dzibilchaltan was the major center in a very large population zone (Andrews, 1961). It has been argued, indeed, that some of these Maya lowland centers were true urban communities, not just ceremonial centers with dispersed sustaining populations. Haviland (1969), especially, has made this point with regard to Tikal. To settle such an argument requires a more exact definition of what we mean by urban than I have given so far in this discussion. To me, there is a significant difference between Tikal's 49,000 persons scattered over an area of 163 square kilometers and the 100,000 persons that are estimated as having been grouped within the 19 square kilometers of Teotihuacan (Sanders and Price, 1968; Millon, 1967, 1968). Still, I admit there is room for discussion and further examination of this urban question. For our immediate consideration, though, whether urban or non-urban, we can affirm without doubt that the Maya Classic Period culture of the lowlands had integrated communities of over 5000 people.

Marked division of labor seems well attested for the Maya Classic. It is unlikely that the fine craft goods, the monumental sculptures, Maya writing, and calendrics were made or manipulated by part-time farmers. Maya society must have had certain persons whose lives were devoted to such tasks and activities. Certainly there was an aristocratic leadership. We see this depicted in Maya art; we see it in Maya tombs and burials; we see it in the esoteric knowledge that was part of Maya religion. As to the size and composition of what might have been a "middle class", we are more in the dark. As mentioned, professional artisanry is implied by the nature of some of the luxury products that we find in graves and caches. Other proofs of full-time craft specialists are more equivocal. Culbert (1958, Ms.) stated that he saw no evidence at Tikal for craft barrios, such as are identified for Tenochtitlan and Teotihuacan; Haviland (Haviland and others, 1968) contrariwise, insists that there are indications that certain sections of the site had been the residences of flint or obsidian workers. Coe's (W. R. Coe, 1967) tentative identification of a Tikal marketplace is another datum that can be taken to support both economic differentiation and social differentiation within Classic Maya society.

An hierarchial governmental structure, monumentality in architecture, and a codified symbolic system (or systems) are all so heavily and obviously documented from Maya archaeology that they need no further discussion. The same now is true for interregional trade.

The Maya Late Classic, then, meets all of the traits or criteria that I have set down as diagnostics of the condition of civilization. How far back in time can we push this civilizational threshold for the lowland Maya? I do not think there can be any question about extending it back to the Early Classic. Although settlement data are less secure for this earlier period, we know that Tikal had a very large population by this time (W. R. Coe, 1965; Haviland, 1969). Social class differentiation was probably less marked than later (Rathje, 1970); nevertheless, it was in the Early Classic that Tikal enjoyed a trade in luxury goods with Teotihuacan, and the nature of this trade implies that a non-egalitarian society had already taken form in the Maya lowlands. Other traits—great architecture, sculpture, and hieroglyphic writing—are all present at the beginning of the Early Classic.

The Teotihuacan relations with Tikal, and the southern Maya lowlands as a whole, raise the question of the role of that highland site in the development of Maya civilization. Can the Maya achievement be explained as a response to these contacts? Or, as we have asked earlier, was Maya lowland civilization a "secondary" formation made possible by Teotihuacan trade and political influence? I would answer this in the negative. We know that those unusually sophisticated Maya forms—its architecture, its art, its hieroglyphics, and its calendar—were all present before Teotihuacan influence is registered in the Maya lowland sequences; and I think it is highly probable that those other traits which I have listed here as marking the threshold of civilization were present then as well. Without question, Teotihuacan had a very important effect on Maya culture, but I do not see these Teotihuacan influences as the levers which raised Maya society and culture from the level of simple village agriculture to the status of civilization. Rather, the impact of Teotihuacan had the effect of moving a non-urban Maya civilization in the direction of full urbanism and the state; but, as I have said in a previous paper (Willey, 1968, Ms.), I do not believe that this transformation to the developed state was ever complete.

If we hold to the above arguments, and see Maya lowland culture as being on the level of a civilization at the beginning of the Early Classic, can we push this back to the Pre-Classic? Quite probably we can, although here we are handicapped by our relatively slight knowledge of the lowland Maya Proto-Classic and Late Preclassic Periods. For the moment, I think the best that we can do is to say that the Maya cultural continuum of the lowlands attained the status of civilization—as I have defined it here—in the span of the Late Preclassic-to-Proto-Classic or between about 400 B.C. and A.D. 200.

Comments on Process and Cause

Of all of the symposium papers, the one most concerned with process and cause is that of Parsons and Price on "Mesoamerican Trade." They see this trade as an important factor, perhaps the key factor, in the systemic relationships that led to civilization. It is their position that the generation of a non-egalitarian society is the first important step-up to the threshold of civilization; and they ask the question: under what circumstances will a society produce a surplus of goods and voluntarily cede it to others? The answer to the first part of the question is essentially an ecological one; in Mesoamerica it was man as an agricultural exploiter of his natural environment. Their answer to the second part of the question is that a society will voluntarily cede a surplus to others if there is some advantage to everyone in doing so. Such advantages accrue from trade, from the opportunity to obtain items that are not immediately at hand. These items may be either basic necessities or exotic luxuries. With the increase of Early Formative Period populations egalitarian mechanisms for inter-regional trade would be inadequate to supply the increasing demands for non-local products. Trade would come to be administrated by an elite who would, thereby, become an aristocratic leadership through their control of the distribution of wealth.

This hypothesis deserves very serious consideration and should prompt further archaeological testing. At the moment, I am inclined to accept it and to go even further and add another "twist" to it, one developed by William Rathje (1970, Ms.) in a recent but still unpublished paper. This additional aspect of the interpretation impresses me as the first fully satisfactory explanation for the primacy of Olmec civilization in Meso-america. The early rise of the great lowland Tabasco-Veracruz ceremonial centers at La Venta and San Lorenzo, dating back before the first millennium B. C. (see Bernal, 1970, Ms.) has always been a puzzle, especially if one followed the Sanders-Price (1968) reasoning that Mesoamerican civilization must necessarily have arisen first in a subarea of diversified natural resources and with a potentiality for irrigation farming. In their present symposium paper Parsons and Price seem to shift away from this view, at least to the extent of explaining early Olmec leadership in the march toward civilization to the advantages in river levee soils for high crop yields. Undoubtedly, these local riverine conditions gave the early Olmec an initial boost and provided them with a surplus that they could invest in trade for needed items; but, to apply Rathje's hypothesis[1], the crucial transformation of an egalitarian to a non-egalitarian society resulted from this trade in the desired upland products—stone for corn-grinding implements and obsidian for cutting tools. This trade was mediated by early entrepreneurs who eventuated into a class of aristocratic priest-chiefs, and with this change Olmec society was on its way toward the civilization whose monuments and evidences we see not only at San Lorenzo and La Venta but elsewhere in the Mesoamerican Middle Formative world.

Once trade was established by the lowland Olmec leadership with the highland regions the peoples of the latter, in a rapid accommodative adaptation, converted to non-egalitarian social modes. With their basic advantages in resources and demographic potential, they outstripped the Olmec by the end of the Middle Formative. Quite proba-bly, they passed rapidly through the stage of non-urban civilization; certainly, by Teotihuacan II times they had become fully urbanized. The lowlands, on the other hand, never really accomplished this final step-up to full urban civilization although the Late Classic Maya, in places such as Tikal, were moving toward it.

As a final word, I'd like to enter one caution about these hypotheses concerning the rise to civilization. Parsons and Price (1970, Ms.) state:

> Archaeologically, the distribution of elite goods is merely the indication that we are dealing with a ranked society based economically on a system of redistributive exchanges. Such an indication cannot be analytically regarded as in any sense the cause of that system.

I would accept that the goods, *per se,* are not the cause of the system—if this is what the statement is intended to mean. In fact, I would insist that they are not. A few years ago I published a paper (Willey, 1962) about the Olmec art style and its horizontal pervasiveness in Mesoamerica. I postulated that this style was the symbolic system of an ideology that had an important part in synthesizing the first Mesoamerican co-tradition, the first areal oikoumene of shared beliefs. I did not state that I believed the distribution of this style to have been carried by proselytizing force, nor do I think so now. In the light of the ideas which Sanders, Parsons, Price, Flannery (1968), Rathje, and others have advanced, I think it very likely that trade was the mechanism which carried the style. At the same time, I think that more was carried than the elite goods or the physical properties of the style. There was also transmission of ideas, of a religious ideology; and this ideology was an important force in the formation of all Mesoamerican civilizations—or, if you like, of Mesoamerican civilization. It helped make and perpetuate it. The continuity of this ideology—undoubtedly modified—is seen persisting down to the Aztec empire—as Bernal has pointed out to us in his present paper. In fact, I think we have here a fourth dimension of civilization to add to our other three—the dimension of ideology. Intercommunication among discrete social segments is a necessity for the rise of civilization, as I have argued at the beginning of this commentary, and, undoubtedly, McLuhan's concept that the medium is the message has much to recommend it; nevertheless, I would argue that the idea content of the message is the most important of all. For if we do not accept this then we are saying that there are no differences in ideas whatsoever, that ideology can be held as a constant as we seek for the causes of civilizational growth only among the variables of ecology, demography, and technology. With what I know of the world around me and what I know of the past through history and archaeology, this seems highly unlikely, and I cannot accept this view. I offer this as no cry of reaction, no retreat from the attack on the ecological-demographic-technological front. Archaeology has made great advances along this line in the last two decades, and there is still much ground to be won; but this approach will not tell us everything worth knowing about past human affairs. What I am saying is that I am certain that some ideas, some ideologies were "better" than others or were more successful adaptations that prepared the road to civilization. Whether we will ever be able to reveal the nature of these Precolumbian Mesoamerican ideologies in any meaningful way, to appreciate them as adaptive mechanisms of greater or lesser social and political success, remains to be seen. Obviously, it is archaeology's most difficult task, but I don't think we should pretend that such a task, such a challenge, does not exist.[2]

Notes

[1] Rathje's (1970, Ms.) hypothesis was applied to the lowland Maya; however, as he acknowledges (personal communication), it also seems to apply to the rise of the earlier Olmec.

[2] This commentary is published essentially as it was written in June of 1970, prior to the symposium sessions at Burg Wartenstein in early July. Some minor changes have been made in the body of the text, and the final paragraph has been expanded somewhat over the original version.

Bibliography

Andrews, E. W. IV. 1961. Preliminary Report on the 1959-60 Field Season, National Geographic Society-Tulane University, Dzibilchaltun Program, Miscellaneous Series, No. 11, Middle American Research Institute, Tulane University, New Orleans.

———— 1970 Ms. The Emergence of Civilization in the Maya Lowlands. Paper prepared in advance for Burg Wartenstein Symposium No. 47, Wenner Gren Foundation, New York.

Bernal, Ignacio. 1970 Ms. The Olmec Region—Oaxaca. Paper prepared in advance for Burg Wartenstein Symposium No. 47, Wenner Gren Foundation, N. Y.

Carr, R.F. and J.E. Hazard. 1961. Map of the Ruins of Tikal, El Peten, Guatemala. Tikal Reports, No. 11, University of Pennsylvania, Museum Monographs. Philadelphia.

Childe, V.G. 1950. The Urban Revolution. Town Planning Review, Vol. 21, No. 1, pp. 3-17, University of Liverpool.

Coe, W.R. 1965. Ten Years of Study of a Maya Ruin in the Lowlands of Guatemala. Expedition, Vol. 8, No. 1, pp. 5-56, University of Pennsylvania Museum, Philadelphia.

————— 1967. Tikal: A Handbook of the Ancient Maya Ruins. University Museum, Philadelphia.

Culbert, T.P. 1968 Ms. Specialization in Classic Maya Society. Paper presented at 33rd Annual Meeting, Society for American Archaeology, Santa Fe, N. M.

Flannery, K. V. 1968. The Olmec and the Valley of Oaxaca: A Model for Interregional Interaction in Formative Times. Dumbarton Oaks Conference on the Olmec, E. P. Benson, ed., pp. 79-117, Dumbarton Oaks, Washington, D.C.

Fried, M. H. 1960. On the Evolution of Social Stratification and the State. Culture History: Essays in Honor of Paul Radin, Stanley Diamond, ed., pp. 713-731. Columbia University Press, N. Y.

Haviland, W. A. 1965. Prehistoric Settlement at Tikal, Guatemala. Expedition, Vol. 7, No. 3, pp. 14-23, University of Pennsylvania Museum, Philadelphia.

————— 1969. A New Population Estimate for Tikal, Guatemala. American Antiquity, Vol. 34, No. 4, pp. 429-433, Salt Lake City, Utah.

Millon, R. F. 1967. Estensión y Población de La Ciudad de Teotihuacán en Sus Diferentes Períodos: Un Calculo Provisional, 11th Mesa Redonda, pp. 57-58, Sociedad Mexicana de Antropología, Mexico, D. F.

Parson, L. A. 1969. Bilbao, Guatemala (Vol. 2) Publications in Anthropology, No. 12, Milwaukee Public Museum.

Parsons, L. A. and B. J. Price. 1970 Ms. Mesoamerican Trade and Its Role in the Emergence of Civilization. Paper prepared in advance for Burg Wartenstein Symposium No. 47, Wenner Gren Foundation, New York.

Proskouriakoff, Tatiana. 1970 Ms. Early Architecture and Sculpture in Mesoamerica. Paper prepared in advance for Burg Wartenstein Symposium No. 47, Wenner Gren Foundation, New York.

Rathje, W.L. 1970. Socio-Political Implications of Lowland Maya Burials: Methodology and Tentative Hypotheses. World Archaeology, Vol. 1, No. 3, pp. 359-374, Routledge and Kegan Paul, London.

————— 1970 Ms. The Daily Grind. Paper presented at 35th Annual Meeting, Society for American Archaeology, Mexico City.

Sanders, W. T. and B. J. Price. 1968. Mesoamerica: The Evolution of a Civilization. Random House, N. Y.

Service, E. R. 1962. Primitive Social Organization: An Evolutionary Perspective, Random House, New York.

Smith, A. L. 1950. Uaxactun, Guatemala: Excavations of 1931-37. Publication 588, Carnegie Institution of Washington, Washington, D.C.

Smith, A. L. and G. R. Willey. 1969. Seibal, Guatemala in 1968: A Brief Summary of Archaeological Results. 38th International Congress of Americanists, Vol. 1, pp. 151-158, Munich.

Willey, G. R. 1962. The Early Great Styles and the Rise of the Pre-Columbian Civilizations. American Anthropologist, Vol. 64, Pt. 1, pp. 1-14, Menasha, Wisconsin.

————— 1968 Ms. Urban Trends of the Lowland Maya and the Mexican Highland Model. Paper presented to the 33rd Annual Meeting, Society for American Archaeology, Santa Fe, New Mexico.

Willey, G. R., T. P. Culbert and R. E. W. Adams, eds. 1967. Maya Lowland Ceramics, A Report from the 1965 Guatemala City Conference. American Antiquity, Vol. 32, No. 3, pp. 289-315, Salt Lake City.

Willey, G. R. and A. L. Smith. 1969. The Ruins of Altar de Sacrificios, Department of Peten, Guatemala, an Introduction. Papers, Peabody Museum, Harvard University, Vol. 62, No. 1, Cambridge, Mass.

Willey, G. R. and others. 1965. Prehistoric Maya Settlements in the Belize Valley. Papers, Peabody Museum, Harvard University, Vol. 54, Cambridge, Mass.

Demitri B. Shimkin (Ph.D., University of California at Berkeley, 1939), professor of anthropology and geography at the University of Illinois, has had a long-term interest in ecology and evolution and is one of the few anthropologists who truly can be called a generalist. In their article, Shimkin and Gordon R. Willey write on the fall of Classic Maya civilization. Among archaeologists, there is no more agreement on why this civilization fell than on why it arose (see article 7). In this paper, a number of possible causes are discussed, the systemic complexity of the situation is revealed, and a plausible new approach for studying the fall is offered. For a full treatment of this fascinating problem, the reader is referred to the papers in *The Classic Maya Collapse* (1973), edited by T. Patrick Culbert.

The Collapse of Classic Maya Civilization in the Southern Lowlands: A Symposium Summary Statement

Gordon R. Willey
Demitri B. Shimkin

A review of evidence on the cultural, economic, and demographic collapses in the Maya southern lowlands after 790 A.D. has led to new theories of the history and causes of these events. Intense population growth, rising socio-political competition between centers, sharpening class divisions, and nascent militarism generated difficult problems for the conservative theocracies of the Maya polity. These problems were intensified by military and economic pressures ultimately originating from the more dynamic Mexican societies. Ensuing breakdowns in trade and agriculture led to an intensifying cycle of disbalances and, finally, collapses. Maya recovery was later inhibited by the rise of new competing centers with stronger resource bases than those of the Maya southern lowlands.

Ever since the translation of the Maya Long Count dates and their correlation with the Christian calendar, archaeologists studying the Maya have been aware that a radical change took place in Maya Lowland culture several centuries before the Spanish Conquest. The writings on this subject are extensive, but even a sampling will indicate the variety of opinion that has been expressed as to the probable nature and causes of this change (Ricketson and Ricketson 1937; Morley 1946; Meggers 1954; Jimenez Moreno 1959; Thompson 1966, 1970; G. L. Cowgill 1964; Sabloff and Willey 1967; Erasmus 1968). In order to examine this question of the collapse more thoroughly, a group of archaeologists and anthropologists organized and held a symposium on the subject. This paper is a summary

Reproduced by permission of the publisher and the authors from *Southwestern Journal of Anthropology,* Vol. 27, No. 1, pp. 1-18, 1971.

presentation of their symposium deliberations and tentative conclusions.[1] It is organized under six sub-heads that approximate, in substance and in order, the nature and course of the symposium discussions: 1) the problem; 2) the archaeological data structure; 3) the Maya climax; 4) inferred internal stress factors; 5) the collapse; and 6) the inhibition of recovery.

The Problem

Very briefly—and from the standpoint of archaeological description—the drastic change in Maya Classic culture that has been referred to as the collapse is seen in the cessation of elaborate architectural construction, monumental art, and the carving and erecting of dated stelae. In addition, although this was not altogether clear to the earlier workers in the field, most of the ancient Maya cities or centers were abandoned at about the same time. These changes in prehistoric Maya culture and society can be observed most strikingly in the southern half of the Maya Lowlands—in what is the Guatemalan Peten, adjacent Chiapas, Tabasco, and Campeche to the west, and British Honduras and the edge of Honduras to the east. In the northern half of the lowlands—in the Yucatan Peninsula—what appeared to be related changes in Maya culture also occurred, although here, perhaps, the changes were less marked than, and possibly not fully synchronous with, those of the south.[2]

The research problem is two-fold: to reconstruct the history of events that are associated with the southern lowland Classic Maya cultural failure and to explain the causes that brought it about.

In the last 20 years, much of Maya archaeological research has been carried out with the question of the Maya civilizational collapse in mind; we now know somewhat more about the circumstances of the cultural changes in the Maya Lowlands than we did previously. The development of ceramic sequences in a number of regions, their cross-dating, and their integration with the Maya dated-monument calendar have provided us with better chronological control than was available when the collapse phenomena were first observed. Settlement pattern studies, which have embraced domestic dwellings as well as ceremonial center constructions, have given us a more realistic conception of prehistoric population sizes and their changes through time and have indicated, within reasonable limits, the degree to which we are talking about true abandonments of entire regions or, instead, only the dwindling or cessation of monumental architectural activities. Some progress has been made with ecological conerns as well. We have a clearer picture of just what could have been grown and harvested in the rainforest jungles, and under what conditions, than we did. Finally, archaeological research has progressed rapidly in other parts of the Mesoamerican sphere, of which the Maya Lowlands is and was an integral part; and this has resulted in a number of insights that were impossible before for lack of more precise and systematic archaeological knowledge.

Specifically, we must reject the ingenious iconoclastic view of Erasmus (1968) that there was in fact no collapse of Maya civilization in the southern lowlands but rather a mere re-orientation to a more secular, pragmatic, and warlike society. Erasmus is correct in emphasizing that labor-saving architectural techniques are signs of progress via more efficient use of resources rather than of decay. He has also anticipated an emphasis in our findings that the Maya must be considered not as isolates but within a larger Middle American context. Nevertheless, these qualifications should not obscure the great preponderance of evidence for cultural, economic, and demographic collapses in the Maya southern lowlands after A.D. 790.

There remain many shortcomings—in the data and, no doubt, in the way the data have been put to use. These will be exposed in the following discussion and need not be listed here. It goes without saying that all of us who are represented by this summary preliminary presentation of the Santa Fe (School of American Research) symposium on the Maya collapse are dedicated to finding out whatever we can about the problem and, at least, are hopeful (although in varying degrees) of determining process and cause, from the archaeological evidence available to us, behind the events of the Maya Classic collapse.

The Archaeological Data Structure

The archaeological regions and sites with which we were particularly concerned are: (1) those of the northeastern Peten, especially Uaxactun and Tikal, where there has been intensive investigation and where there are long archaeological sequences; (2) the Belize Valley of British Honduras, with Barton Ramie and Benque Viejo; (3) the Pasion drainage, with Altar de Sacrificios and Seibal; and (4) the western edges of the southern lowlands and the sites of Piedras Negras, Palenque, and Trinidad. At its widest, the chronological range with which we are concerned spans from about A.D. 600 until the Spanish Entradas of 1520-1540, in other words, the Late Classic and Postclassic Periods. But within this we can narrow dates down considerably more when we come to the events of the collapse. The beginning of the cultural decline is first noticed at the Maya *katun* ending 9.18.0.0.0 (A.D. 790).[3] In the terms of ceramic chronologies this is the latter half of the Tepeu 2 sphere. By 10.0.0.0.0 (A.D. 830), which may be considered as the beginning of Tepeu 3, there had been a notable decline in architectural and sculptural activities in most of the southern lowland centers. The *katun* ending 10.3.0.0.0 (A.D. 889) sees the last of dated monuments in the south; and very shortly after this—certainly by 10,6.0.0.0 or about A.D. 950—the Maya southern Classic centers were to all purposes abandoned. The Tepeu 3 ceramic sphere probably had died out before this; certainly it lasted no longer.

Subsequently, although this takes us beyond the essential events of the collapse, the Postclassic occupation of the southern lowlands relates to other pottery traditions. One of these is known as the Central Peten tradition (consisting of the Augustine, Paxcaman, and Topoxte ceramic groups);[4] the other is that of the Fine Paste pottery wares and is best known from sites on the Usumacinta-Pasion drainage in the western and southern Peten. These pottery traditions—which are notably different from the old Classic ones—characterized the Maya populations who continued to live in, or who moved into, the southern lowlands after the events of the collapse. All our archaeological data indicate that these Postclassic populations were of notably smaller size than those who had occupied the area prior to the collapse. One of the few known clusterings of these late populations was around the Peten lakes—including Lake Peten Itza and Lake Yaxha. All during the Early and Middle Postclassic their style of life appears to have been that of simple villagers. However, in the Last Postclassic, small ceremonial centers were built on the lake islands in the kind of cultural "revival" which may relate to the Late Postclassic cultures of the northern lowlands but which has little in common with the old southern Classic culture.

The Maya Climax

The period immediately before the century of the collapse marks the climax of Maya Lowland civilization. For most of the southern lowlands this period can be narrowed to the earlier part of the Tepeu 2 horizon or from about 9.14.0.0.0 (A.D. 711) to 9.18.0.0.0 (A.D. 790). Included in the horizon would be Tepeu proper at Uaxactun and related phases at many other sites, including the Tepejilote at Seibal, the Pasion at Altar de Sacrificios, the Chacalhaaz at Piedras Negras, Naab at Trinidad, and Early Spanish Lookout and Benque Viejo IIIB in the Belize Valley. In other sites there are indications that this period of the climax or "peak" was of somewhat longer duration, beginning a century or so earlier, as at Palenque and Tikal (Haviland 1970). Everywhere, though, it was a Late Classic Period phenomenon of 100 to 200 years duration.

This climax of the Maya Classic is seen in a number of ways. Demographically, it marked a population peak in the south. More ceremonial centers are known from this period than ever before. Virtually all of those which had been occupied in Preclassic and Early Classic times were now built over; and, in addition to these, many new centers were founded. House mound or domestic dwelling surveys show Tepeu 2 as the peak period of construction and occupation. Absolute population figures for the entire southern lowlands or any sizable part of it must still be highly speculative. Such estimates have been approached in two ways: through settlement studies and domestic structure counts and through computations on the carrying power of the available agricultural land. The first approach offers a more promising beginning; but we still do not have enough settlement samplings for large-scale population reckonings. Some centers, such as Seibal, appear to have been supported by sustaining area populations of as few as 3000 persons (Tourtellot 1970). In contrast to this, the great center of Tikal is estimated to have drawn upon the services of about 50,000 (Haviland 1969). Reckonings from agricultural production estimates per unit of land are hampered because we cannot be certain of the degree to which more intensive agricultural methods supplemented swidden farming of maize. Recent studies and observations suggest that there were intensifying and supplementing techniques. Agricultural terraces in some regions and reliance upon root crops and breadnut harvests are possibilities; it is highly likely that all of these techniques were employed in Late Classic times.

The Maya climax can also be measured in sheer architectural volume in the ceremonial centers. Regional authorities state that the estimated differences in construction volume between the Tepeu 2 horizon (8th century A.D.) and the Tepeu 3 horizon (9th century A.D.) range from an order of 10 to 1 to as much as 100 to 1. One of the few exceptions is Seibal, but it presents a special case, to which we will return later. The authorities are also agreed that the Tepeu 2 building volume was probably substantially greater than that of the periods leading up to it, although here the contrast was not so marked.

Art, ceremonialism, and calendrics also peak in Tepeu 2 times. There are more dated monuments from the 8th century A.D. than from any time previous or later. There are more hieroglyphic inscriptions. There are more temple and palace buildings, especially the latter. Even allowing for the fact that the Tepeu 2 horizon constructions are the latest ones at most sites, and that therefore they are more visible and more frequently hide or cover earlier constructions and decorative adornments, it still seems reasonably certain that the Tepeu 2 time horizon marks the major elaborations of politico-religious buildings. The same florescence can be seen in Tepeu 2 polychrome pottery and in contemporaneous craft luxury goods of all kinds.

Finally, there are many indications, as these can be inferred from the archaeological evidence, that Maya socio-political structure also attained its most complex development in Tepeu 2 times. Maya society, from at least Late Preclassic times forward, had been a ranked one. This is reflected in burial differences and in artistic representations of elaborately costumed high dignitaries interviewing petitioners or persons of lesser status, but as we move to Late Classic times there are many clues to the rise of a truly stratified or class society. The locations and accoutrements of burials provide one line of evidence for this (Rathje 1970). Another is the proliferation of multi-roomed palace-type buildings in the ceremonial centers (Adams 1956). Substantial numbers of people of both sexes and all ages were now living in and being buried in the ceremonial precincts. Moreover, the physical remains of these ceremonial-center dwellers show a greater stature than those of fellow Maya buried in the outlying domestic-quarter districts (Haviland 1967). Hieroglyphic inscriptions, insofar as they can be translated, tell us of royal lineages (Proskouriakoff 1963, 1964). In sum, the interpretations lead easily to that of an emerging hereditary aristocracy as the guiding force of Late Classic Maya civilization.

Just how far along the road to the development of the "state" the Maya had actually marched, in addition to the development of a class society, is not yet clear from the archaeological record—or from the way different authorities interpret it. There was some warfare or fighting, we know; but there are no signs, other than the Piedras Negras lintel with its suggestions of uniform and rank, of a professional military body or class like the Central Mexican Eagle or Jaguar "Knights." Nor are there any sure signs of the large open markets such as existed in Tenochtitlan and Teotihuacan. There is evidence for trade, to be sure, but a redistributive system, controlled by the aristocracy, seems a more likely mechanism for the circulation of trade goods. There were obviously some craft specialists in Ancient Maya society, but how many were full-time is uncertain. So far, even at Tikal, which was the largest Classic center and the one most closely resembling an urban metropolis that Maya civilization produced, there are only slight indications of craft barrios (Haviland 1970), such as are reported for Teotihuacan and Tenochtitlan. To sum up, Maya socio-political structure of Tepeu 2 times had moved farther along the way toward a state society than at any previous point in its history. It still, however, had not advanced as far on this course as some of its contemporaries in the Mesoamerican world (Willey MS).

Inferred Internal Stress Factors

As noted, we can date the decline of Maya Classic civilization of the southern lowlands to the 9th century A.D., at the end of which period this unique and spectacular way of life disappeared forever. The archaeological record also shows us that this civilization had reached its zenith—in the size and complexity of its society and in its material creations—in the century just prior to decline. If we assume that it is at least a reasonable possibility that the nature and condition of Maya Lowland civilization in some way contributed to its decline and collapse, we may then properly ask: what were the internal stress factors operating within the society during its heyday? And how might they have contributed to its downfall?

First, in the ecological-demographic realm, it is possible that the expansion and intensification of agriculture, which necessarily supported the population increases of the Late Classic Period, made the Maya more vulnerable to short-term agricultural disasters. If agricultural terracing, the exploitation of marginal agricultural lands such as savannas or *bajos,* the growing of root crops (Bronson 1966), and a partial dependency upon breadnut harvests (Puleston 1968) were all being carried out to maintain the Tepeu 2 population levels—and if these various facets of agriculture were carefully scheduled to allow for maximum man-power to be diverted to other, non-agricultural activities—then farming or food-production failures, if only of a short-term nature, could have brought about imbalances and crises and thus easily triggered long-term trouble.

Second, intensive land clearance and the more intensive agricultural use of lands and bogs would have reduced animal, fish, and mollusk populations and, hence, the supplies of animal protein. In the areas of densest occupation, such as Tikal, even cooking fuel for the commoner might have become scarce. Pressures on the forests and bogs, and denser and more stable human populations would have increased the hazards of disease by way of insect vectors shifting to new hosts. In particular, Chagas' disease is likely to have contributed heavily to infant mortality and to adult debilitation (Gonzalez-Angulo and Ryckman 1967; Köberle 1968). Periodic epidemics of jungle yellow fever would have been increasing threats as forest clearance disturbed monkey populations and other wild-animal reservoirs of this disease (National Research Council 1962).

Moreover, new land clearance and other attempts to expand marginal food-producing resources would have decreased overall labor productivity in agriculture at a time of sustained and probably growing demand for man-power for ceremonial construction, transportation, and social control.

Third, there was undoubtedly considerable competition between ceremonial centers. Overt signs of it are seen in pictures of captives, who are obviously other Maya, not foreigners. This competition is probably to be seen more covertly in the magnificence of the centers themselves. They represent great numbers of man-hours of skilled craftsmanship and, on the highest social level, of priestly-aristocratic scholarship. In efforts to outdo each other, to draw more wealth and prestige to themselves, to bring more worshippers and taxpayers into their particular orbits, the priest-leaders of these Maya "cities" must have diverted all possible labor and capital to their aggrandizement. New emerging centers and ruling lineages needed particularly to consolidate their statuses through ceremonial splendor. And this competition, too, would have involved more mundane and crucial matters such as foodstuffs, a point at which this stress relates to the previous one.

A fourth stress factor has often been mentioned as one which might have led to a "peasant revolt" or perhaps a "peasant collapse." This was the fruit of the growing gulf, the increasing social distance between the aristocratic leadership and the sustaining farming populations. We have discussed this in our observations about Maya socio-political structure and the transformation from a ranked, and probably kin-based, society to a class-structured one (Rathje 1970). Such a process need not have led to a "peasant revolt" to have had deleterious effects on the Maya system. A growing upper class (Haviland 1966), together with its various retainers, would have increased the economic strain on the society (Willey *et al.* 1965:580-581), particularly in conjunction with both the first and second stress factors. The skeletal evidence to date, although still sparse, indicates that by Late Classic times the skeletons of commoners were appreciably smaller and less robust than those of the elite (Haviland 1967).[5] A concurrent increase in maternal and infant mortality from disease and malnutrition is also probable (Saul MS). In some areas, in fact, it is possible that by the end of the Classic period the numbers of commoners were being maintained only by recruitment and capture from other sites. Yet the upper class continued to grow and to expand its demands for luxury and funerary splendor. This required the allocation of considerable resources for the conduct of long distance trade and the production of the fine manufactures for export. This leads us to our fifth stress factor.

Long-distance trade was probably always of importance to the Lowland Maya. In fact, it may well be that the demand for obsidian and salt and, in some places, for suitable stone for metates and manos was the lever that started the Maya on the way toward the organization of a complex society (Rathje 1969). Trading expeditions had to be organized. Entrepreneurs in trade were thus able to elevate themselves to positions of power by their control and distribution of trade goods. Later, with the rise of chiefdoms, luxury products were imported as status symbols, and this trade flourished and increased with the consolidation of social classes. Trade fed into and was an important part of the Maya cultural system. It demanded time, wealth, and administrators or managerial personnel. It was both a benefit and a source of hazards.

Foreign trade put Lowland Maya society into juxtaposition with the more dynamic and aggressive societies then emerging in Mexico. Better craft organization and, often, access to superior resources made these societies formidable competitors. Their representatives were shrewd professional merchants, probably often backed up by military force and eager to profit from Maya wealth and disunity.

This takes us to the threshold of the collapse.

The Collapse

Up to this point in our deliberations, the symposium group had displayed an amazing concord of opinion. Arguments on the archaeological structure of events for the southern lowlands were minor and easily reconciled. The 9.18.0.0.0 to 10.3.0.0.0 bracketing of the swift decline of the civilization is as solid as is the joint opinion on the mounting Maya climax of the preceding century. The slowdown and stoppage of Maya ceremonial center architecture and great art, the abandonment or partial abandonment of these centers, and the population decline and evacuation of village and hamlet settlements were also agreed upon. Nor was there any real disagreement about the probable stress factors operating within the Maya Late Classic system. But when we came to the actual events of the collapse or, more properly, the mechanisms and causes of these events, we hit some rough ground. Without reporting in detail on the division in this preliminary summary, let us say that some of us were "internally" oriented while others were "externally" oriented. After a few hours of argument two areas of agreement in this field of debate did emerge. One was that we must admit that Maya society and culture—and its eventual fate— cannot be properly understood except in the larger context of Precolumbian Mesoamerica. The other was that the Maya collapse was a complex phenomenon combining a variety of internal and external events, still imperfectly understood, into an intensifying disaster.

To place the Maya in Mesoamerican-wide perspective, let us start by noting that Maya beginnings were intimately involved with other Late Preclassic cultures of southern Mexico-Guatemala. Then, in its Early Classic Period, the Maya culture had important contacts with Central Mexican Teotihuacan. Finally, we know that the eventual history of the Postclassic Maya was bound up with Central Mexican cultures. Now, this last does not mean that the southern Lowland Maya were brought down by invaders from some other part of Mesoamerica—especially Mexican or Mexican-influenced groups.[6] But there was agreement that the Lowland Maya were very much a part of a larger diffusion sphere, that there had been an intensification of regional inter-influencing toward the end of the Late Classic Period, and, further, that the kind of culture which the Lowland Maya possessed at that time would have been particularly vulnerable to the main currents of influence running through Mesoamerica in the 8th and 9th centuries A.D.

For Maya Classic society, let us remember, was the old kind of Mesoamerican society, the kind that was born with the Olmec. We could call it a "high chiefdom," based on sanctified rank, on hereditary leadership, and on the beginnings of an upper-class bureaucracy (Fried 1960, 1967; Sanders and Price 1968). The remainder of the society was largely that of a peasant class, with only an emerging group of specialists and retainers. Hierarchies of ceremonial centers and their sustaining areas developed and were to a degree consolidated by warfare and perhaps the control of resources such as obsidian. Yet the society was neither fully stratified nor authoritatively administered. Within each area, treasure items such as polychrome pottery long continued to flow to all social levels; distinct strata and taxation without fair returns emerge only in Late Classic times. The competitions of the elite were long moderated and regulated by participation in common esoteric knowledge, by ceremonial visits, and by dynastic inter-marriage and alliances.

This kind of society began to be replaced toward the end of the Preclassic Period, at Teotihuacan and probably at places like Monte Alban and Kaminaljuyu. In the Maya Lowlands this old form of society persisted later than it did in most other parts of the Mesoamerican area; but in so doing it came into contact with the new society, the state structure of the Central Mexican highlands. These contacts first came from Teotihuacan back in Early Classic times. They definitely involved trade, and in some places, as at Tikal, these contacts influenced the high ceremonial life of the Maya. Thus, it seems quite probable that Lowland Maya economics and politics underwent some changes as the result of these Early Classic Period relationships with Central Mexico. This supposition is reinforced by the fact that it is in the Late Classic, following the Teotihuacan contacts, that we see the changes indicative of a developing class structure. These changes were obviously related to population growth in the lowlands, but they also could have been responsive adaptations to Mayan participation in the wider Mesoamerican economic and political scene.

After the disappearance of Teotihuacan influence there are no signs of comparable Mexican impingements on the Maya Lowland realm for at least 200 years. There are, to be sure, some evidences of Mexican contacts. *Tlalocs* are a minor but widespread motif in Late Classic Maya sculpture and also occur on Late Classic pottery (Smith 1955:72). There are also other elements in the art of some of the western lowland centers (Proskouriakoff 1950, 1951) which reflect contacts with cultures to the north and east. But in all of these instances the foreign elements have been thoroughly integrated with those of the resident Maya. For the most part, the Maya of Tepeu 1 and 2 times appear culturally quite self-contained, although there were trade contacts for raw materials with outside areas. This brings us to the brink of the collapse.

As we have noted, the cultural decline leading to the collapse started in the latter part of the Tepeu 2 horizon (ca. A.D. 790), just 20 years after the peak of big building construction and stelae dedication had been reached throughout the Maya southern lowlands. This decline is seen in a number of ways. The earliest effective abandonments of big ceremonial centers, such as Piedras Negras and Palenque, come at this time. In other sites where stelae continued to be carved and erected there are losses of lunar information and full calendrical terminology in the dates and inscriptions of this *katun* ending. The iconography of the remaining monuments stresses war and political ceremonialism to a high degree. A ceramic regionalism sets in, indicating a breakdown in inter-site trade in fine polychromes and also a general decay of ceramic decoration. The Piedras Negras and Palenque abandonments are either coincident with the appearance of a new pottery tradition—that of Fine Gray wares—at those sites or occur just before the appearance of these wares. A little later, at the Maya date of 10.0.0.0.0 (A.D. 830), Fine Orange of the Balancan ("Z") and Altar ("Y") groups appear as intrusives in the west, at Palenque, and on up the Usumacinta-Pasion drainage at Altar de Sacrificios and Seibal. They appear in the contexts of local Classic Maya ceramic traditions; they are clearly exotics in these Pasion site contexts; and it seems likely that these Fine Paste wares were made in the Chiapas-Tabasco lowlands.

After A.D. 830 we move into the Tepeu 3 horizon, which brought the acceleration of the Maya Classic decline. During this period Fine Orange wares are found farther to the east, as at Uaxactun and Tikal. At the latter site they are a part of the Eznab complex. By this time, however, Tikal had been declining culturally for at least 60 to 80 years; and it was to die almost completely in another 20 to 40 years.

The picture then, as succinctly as we can sum it up, shows a first cessation of Maya ceremonial center activity on the western edge of the southern lowlands. This begins as early as A.D. 790 and progresses rapidly in the west over the next 40 years. The first signs of decline—as evidenced in major site abandonment, reduction in glyphic and calendric information in inscriptions, and artistic and craft reduction—seem to be more or less simultaneous with the appearance of the first Fine Paste wares in the west.[7] However, farther to the east and south the cultural decline in the ceremonial centers was already well in progress by some 40 to 80 years before the Fine Paste wares occur. When they do appear, the decline usually continues or possibly accelerates.

How do we interpret all this? Does the collapse occur first and thereby allow the admission of the foreigner? Is the collapse a direct and simple result of invasion? Or does foreign pressure on the western frontier exacerbate stresses within Maya society, setting in motion a rapid decline, during which time foreign elements move more deeply into the southern lowlands proper? There was symposium debate on this point, as may be imagined. Clearly, there is no ready solution, and we can only hope that our deliberations up to this juncture provide an understanding of the available data and suggest courses for future research to the imaginative. The hypothesis favored by the symposium group at the present time is based upon the latter of the above alternatives. This is the proposition which holds that Classic Maya exposure to, contacts with, and pressures from non-Classic Maya groups at its western frontier set in motion a series of events that resulted in the collapse and eventual extinction of the old Maya way of life.

Particularly telling for this hypothesis are the west-to-east sequence of the collapse, the advent of cultural changes and declines in the central area prior to massive declines in population, the general absence of evidence of massive destruction or other evidences of violent conquest, and the signs of late and pitiful attempts (as in the Eznab phase at Tikal) to reinstitute customs of stelae dedication and old elite burial practices. All of these manifestations speak against theories of large-scale military conquests or of violent and general "peasant revolts." Nor do they fit well with the idea of a major agricultural failure which, it seems more likely, would have begun in the drier eastern regions than in the west. They are, however, consistent with the disruptions that a delicately balanced socio-economic system might undergo from small bands of intruders expert in violence yet ignorant of management or indigenous values. Even small numbers of such intruders could easily intensify conflicts within Maya society which hitherto had been self-limiting. The ensuing breakdowns in trade and agricultural activity would lead to population movements promoting the spread of disease, local overloading of agricultural resources, and hunger. Such disturbances if continued through a century of decline would be sufficient to deplete heavily both the labor force and the reservoirs of skilled economic leaders, even without catastrophic droughts, hurricanes, or wars.

Three mechanisms may well have been important. One would have been the cumulative effect of disbalances. Thus, excessive infant mortality and female infanticide would have delayed consequences in later manpower shortages under circumstances requiring much effort for the rehabilitation of neglected fields, pathways, waterworks, and other productive capital. Another is that Maya responses to calamity may often have been maladaptive, such as those aimed at greater ceremonial splendor or more raids for sacrificial victims to appease the gods. The third is that, under conditions of acute manpower shortage, the competition—including feuds and warfare (Vayda 1961)—for secondary milpa (needing less work to clear than primary forest) would have become ever more severe. As a result, social units and trade would be fragmented, while losses in fighting would intensify the labor shortage and the competition for easily worked land even more.

Any outside intruders need not have been limited to a single expedition or occasion. Actually, the Fine Paste ware influxes are multiple. The first Fine Grays found at Piedras Negras are not the same as the later Fine Oranges and Fine Grays of the Usumacinta-Pasion sites, and at Altar de Sacrificios there are indications of at least two waves of foreign

Fine Paste Wares. If these multiple ceramic phenomena can be correlated with foreign invaders, then we would expect continued and increased disorganization that would have accelerated the breakdown.

The Inhibition of Recovery

To understand fully the nature of the collapse of Classic Maya culture and population, some consideration must be given to the failure of recovery in the centuries following. The Maya had had a previous setback, as indicated by the hiatus in stelae dedication following 9.5.0.0.0 (A.D. 534); yet they arose from this to the heights of the Late Classic. But after 10.3.0.0.0 (A.D. 889) they made no significant comeback in the southern lowlands. It is true that the area was not entirely abandoned and some Postclassic centers were established, especially in those territories peripheral to the old northeastern Peten heartland. With reference to these, it is probably significant that some of these Postclassic centers were on the northwestern frontier, as at Potonchan and Itzamkanac (Thompson 1967). This is Chontal Maya country, and the Chontal were strongly influenced by the Central Mexicans and their ruling families intermarried with them.

Other Postclassic Maya centers were established on the east coast of the Yucatan Peninsula, around Chetumal, and in the southeast near the mouth of the Chamalecon River. Even in the central Peten we know of two small Postclassic centers, Topoxte and Tayasal. The former, which is better known archaeologically (Bullard 1970), seems to be allied in its architectural styles to Yucatan rather than to be a continuation of the old local Classic traditions. Both its ceramics and those of the Tayasal are of the new Central Peten tradition. The latter site is assumed to have been a settlement of the Itza after their flight from northern Yucatan. According to the early Spanish accounts (Thompson 1967), Tayasal and the Lake Peten Itza were important politically and militarily, at least on a small local scale. They also controlled local trade, but they no longer participated in the long-distance trading networks.

This change of trade patterns may be a key to the failure of recovery in the southern lowlands. As we have already argued, long-distance trade would have been a sphere of natural conflict between the Classic Mayans and their Mexican or Mexicanized (Chontal) rivals on their northwestern border. Once control of this trade had been wrested from the Classic Maya by these rivals, it would have been extremely difficult to regain, especially in the wake of the disorders and disruptions that we have postulated. The new centers of power would have held the trade, and they would have been the ones which attracted the merchants, craftsmen, and population support to the continued disadvantage of older Peten centers. Some of these new centers—those of modest size—were in the Chontal country; others, larger and more important, were probably in Yucatan; but still others, those which held the ultimate power on the Mesoamerican scene, were distant from the Maya Lowlands altogether. In effect, these lowlands, and especially their southern regions, had been bypassed during the progress of Mesoamerican civilization, for they lacked the resources necessary in the formation of a state of the new type.

With reference to Postclassic population numbers, we have noted that there are indications that at some sites reduced populations lived in or near major ceremonial centers after the collapse; however, they remained only until about the mid-10th century

A.D. This seems to have been the case at Tikal, Altar de Sacrificios, and Seibal—three southern lowland centers where extensive house mound surveys have been carried out. It is also true that there was a Postclassic house mound occupation at Barton Ramie, on the Belize River in British Honduras (Willey *et al.* 1965). This occupancy is referred to as the New Town phase. It appears to post-date the abandonment of the nearest major ceremonial center, that at Benque Viejo or Xunantunich, but the principal question concerning the New Town occupation is just how long it lasted. We have been uncertain of this, but Bullard's recent definition of the Central Peten ceramic tradition has helped in this regard. New Town pottery belongs to this tradition, and the great bulk of it belongs to the earliest ceramic group within the tradition, the Augustine. The somewhat later, probably Middle Postclassic, pottery group of the tradition, the Paxcaman, is present at Barton Ramie but is restricted to a very few house mounds and probably is to be attributed to occasional later re-occupation of house sites by relatively small numbers of people. In sum, from what we know now—admittedly, the data are still few and more are needed—there was a truly massive population loss in the Maya southern lowlands, and this occurred not long after the close of the Classic Period and was not followed by a substantial recovery.

In final summary, we believe that the problem of the Maya collapse involves a major cultural, social, and demographic failure. This failure occurred in what are designated as the southern lowlands over a period lasting something over a century—from A.D. 790 to A.D. 950. Afterwards, there was no recovery to any manifestations resembling the old levels or old standards in cultural, socio-political, or demographic dimensions. We think that the problem of this collapse must be viewed systemically, with an eye to the interactions of natural environmental, ecological, demographic, economic, social, and political factors. In our further opinion, ecology and demography provide critically important limits and sources of stress, but they do not appear to have been immediately determinative. More pertinent in this regard are the capacities and interactions of different socio-political systems, as they can be reconstructed in their immediate operations in the Maya Lowlands, and also as they can be seen in the broader developmental spectrum of ancient Mesoamerican civilizations. Obviously, much work remains to be done to test these views—in the quantification of prehistoric population data and agricultural output, in the search for evidences of disease and malnutrition, in clues to migrations, in a better understanding of the workings of social and political systems, and, very basically, in the finer determination of chronologies and inter-site relationships that make up the skeletal structure of archaeology. The development of reliable data on climatic fluctuations in the Maya Lowlands is an urgent need. Comparative studies, particularly on the rise and decline of Angkor (Hall 1968), promise insights which may be of value to cultural anthropology generally.

For these reasons, it is hoped that the present summary yields a useful model of current understanding and a working basis for future research.

Notes

[1] The symposium was held under the aegis of the School of American Research, Santa Fe, New Mexico, on October 19-24, 1970. The symposium was partially supported

by a grant from the National Science Foundation (GS-3182). Participants included: R. E. W. Adams, E. W. Andrews IV, W. R. Bullard, Jr., T. P. Culbert, J. A. Graham, Robert Rands, J. A. Sabloff, W. T. Sanders, D. B. Shimkin, Malcolm Webb, and G. R. Willey. A monograph on the results of the symposium, including background data papers by all participants and a lengthy summary of the discussions, will be published by the School of American Research. The present paper is a revised version of one presented at the annual meetings of the American Anthropological Association in San Diego, California, in November 1970.

[2]There is a sharp difference of opinion between Andrews (1965), who believes that the Maya Late Classic (Tepeu) culture of the southern lowlands was extinct before the rise of the Florescent (Puuc, Chenes, Rio Bec) cultures of the northern lowlands, and most other Maya archaeologists, who feel that the southern Late Classic and the northern Florescent were essentially contemporaneous. This complex question cannot be explored here but will be treated in the longer monographic presentation of the symposium proceedings. While not immediately germane to the cultural collapse of the south, it has an obvious tangential bearing upon it.

[3]Here and elsewhere, Maya Long Count dates are rendered in the 11.16.0.0.0 (GMT) Correlation.

[4]This Central Peten ceramic tradition is discussed by Bullard in his symposium data paper. Similarly, other new data and new formulations to which we will refer have come from the symposium background data papers. These will not be cited specifically.

[5]Haviland writes more recently (personal communication, 8 January 1971) that revised Tikal stature data now indicate the situation to have been much the same for both Early and Late Classic. That is, the physical anthropological evidence for an aristocracy-peasant split suggests that this came about at the close of the Late Preclassic rather than later. It should also be noted here that in his most recent interpretation of all Tikal data Haviland finds fewer differences between Early and Late Classic conditions than did the members of the symposium in their interpretations of the southern Maya lowlands as a whole.

[6]The Sabloff and Willey (1967) formulation sought to emphasize the evidence for external invasions. These authors now view the postulated invasions as parts of a wide historical and developmental (or evolutionary) perspective.

[7]Palenque is something of an exception to this statement in that some Fine Paste wares (although not Fine Orange) occur well prior to the cessation of ceremonial center activity.

Bibliography

Adams, R. M. 1956. Some Hypotheses on the Development of Early Civilizations. *American Antiquity* 21:227-232.

Andrews, E. W., IV. 1965. Progress Report on the 1960-64 Field Seasons: National Geographic Society–Tulane University Dzibilchaltun Program. *Middle American Research Institute*, publication 31, pp. 23-67.

Bronson, Bennet. 1966. Roots and the Subsistence of the Ancient Maya. *Southwestern Journal of Anthropology* 22:251-280.

Bullard, W. R., Jr. 1970. "Topoxte, a Postclassic Site in Peten, Guatemala," in *Monographs and Papers in Maya Archaeology* (ed. by W. R. Bullard, Jr.), pp. 247-307. Papers of the Peabody Museum, vol. 61.

Cowgill, G. L. 1964. The End of Classic Maya Culture: a Review of Recent Evidence. *Southwestern Journal of Anthropology* 20:145-159.

Erasmus, C. J. 1968. Thoughts on Upward Collapse; an Essay on Explanation in Anthropology. *Southwestern Journal of Anthropology* 24:170-194.

Fried, M. H. 1960. "On the Evolution of Social Stratification and the State," in *Culture in History: Essays in Honor of Paul Radin* (ed. by Stanley Diamond) pp. 713-731. New York: Columbia University Press.

———— 1967. *The Evolution of Political Society*. New York: Random House.

Gonzales-Angulo, W., and R. E. Ryckman. 1967. Epizootiology of *Trypanosoma cruzi* in Southwestern North America. Part IX: An Investigation to Determine the Incidence of *Trypanosoma cruzi* Infections in Triatominae and Man on the Yucatan Peninsula of Mexico. *Journal of Medical Entomology* 4:44-47.

Hall, D. G. E. 1968. *A History of South-East Asia*. 3d ed. London: Macmillan

Haviland, W. A. 1966. Social Integration and the Classic Maya. *American Antiquity* 31: 625-632.

———— 1967. Stature at Tikal, Guatemala: Implications for Ancient Maya Demography and Social Organization. *American Antiquity* 32:316-326.

———— 1969. A New Population Estimate for Tikal, Guatemala. *American Antiquity* 34:429-433.

———— 1970. Tikal, Guatemala and Mesoamerican Urbanism. *World Archaeology* 2: 186-199.

Jimenez Moreno, Wigberto. 1959. "Sintesis de la Historia Pretolteca de Mesoamerica," in *Esplendor del Mexico Antiguo* (C. Cook de Leonard, Coordinator), vol. 2, pp. 1019-1108. Mexico, D. F.: Centro de Investigaciones Antropológicas de Mexico.

Köberle, F. 1968. Chagas' Disease and Chagas' Syndromes: the Pathology of American Trypanosomiasis. *Advances in Parasitology* 6:63-116.

Meggers, B. J. 1954. Environmental Limitation on the Development of Culture. *American Anthropologist* 56:801-824.

Morley, S. G. 1946. *The Ancient Maya*. Palo Alto: Stanford University Press.

National Research Council. 1962. *Tropical Health. A Report on a Study of Needs and Resources*. National Academy of Sciences-National Research Council, publication 996.

Proskouriakoff, Tatiana. 1960. *A Study of Classic Maya Sculpture*. Carnegie Institution of Washington, publication 593.

———— 1951. "Some Non-Classic Traits in the Sculpture of Yucatan," in *The Civilization of Ancient America: Selected Papers of the 29th International Congress of Americanists* (ed. by S. Tax), vol. 1, pp. 108-118, Chicago: University of Chicago Press.

———— 1963. Historical Data in the Inscriptions of Yaxchilan (Part I). *Estudios Cultura Maya* 3:149-167.

———— 1964. Historical Data in the Inscriptions of Yaxchilan (Part II). *Estudios Cultura Maya* 4:177-203.

Puleston, D. E. 1968. New Data from Tikal on Classic Maya Subsistence. Paper delivered at the Annual Meeting of the Society for American Archaeology, Santa Fe, New Mexico, May 11.

Rathje, W. L. 1969. The Daily Grind. Paper delivered at Annual Meeting, Society for American Archaeology, Mexico City.

———— 1970. Socio-political Implications of Lowland Maya Burials: Methodology and Tentative Hypotheses. *World Archaeology* 1:359-375.

Ricketson, O. G., Jr., and E. B. Ricketson. 1937. *Uaxactun, Guatemala Group E-1926-1931*. Carnegie Institution of Washington, publication 477.

Sabloff, J. A., and G. R. Willey. 1967. The Collapse of Maya Civilization in the Southern Lowland: a Consideration of History and Process, *Southwestern Journal of Anthropology* 23: 311-336.

Sanders, W. T., and B. J. Price. 1968. *Mesoamerica, the Evolution of a Civilization.* New York: Random House.

Saul, Frank.Ms. Observations on Human Skeletal Material from Altar de Sacrificios. In preparation for Altar de Sacrificios series, Papers of the Peabody Museum.

Smith, R. E. 1955. *Ceramic Sequence at Uaxactun, Guatemala.* 2 vols. Middle American Research Institute, publication 20.

Thompson, J. E. S. 1966. *The Rise and Fall of Maya Civilization.* 2nd ed. Norman: University of Oklahoma Press.

———— 1967. The Maya Central Area at the Spanish Conquest and Later: a Problem in Demography. *Proceedings of the Royal Anthropological Institute for 1966,* pp. 23-37.

———— 1970. *Maya History and Religion.* Norman: University of Oklahoma Press.

Tourtellot, Gair. 1970. "The Peripheries of Seibal: an Interim Report," in *Monographs and Papers in Maya Archaeology* (ed. by W. R. Bullard, Jr.), pp. 405-421. Papers of the Peabody Museum, vol. 61.

Vayda, A. P. 1961. Expansion and Warfare among Swidden Agriculturists. *American Anthropologist* 63:346-358.

Willey, G. R. Ms. Urban Trends of the Lowland Maya and the Mexican Highland Model. Paper delivered at the 38th International Congress of Americanists, Stuttgart, Germany, 1968.

Willey, G. R., W. R. Bullard, Jr., J. B. Glass, and J. C. Gifford. 1965. *Prehistoric Maya Settlements in the Belize Valley.* Papers of the Peabody Museum, vol. 54.

William T. Sanders received his Ph.D. from Harvard University in 1957 and
is currently professor of anthropology at Pennsylvania State University.
He has worked extensively throughout Mesoamerica with special attention
to Central Mexico and the Teotihuacan Valley. Sanders has been one of
the major pioneers in combining ecological, evolutionary, and systemic
thinking in his archaeological research. The book *Mesoamerica: The
Evolution of a Civilization* (1968), which he wrote with Barbara Price, is
considered by many a pathbreaking study in Mesoamerican archaeology.
He is also coauthor of *New World Prehistory* (1970). His important article below indicates clearly the benefits of combining these approaches in
the study of the civilizational process.

Hydraulic Agriculture, Economic Symbiosis, and the Evolution of States in Central Mexico

William T. Sanders

Environment and Culture

Perhaps the central concept of 20th Century anthropology has been the view that
each of man's cultures is an integrated organized system. Anthropologists have argued
that a given culture should be analyzed in terms of its own organizational principles, and
not be judged on the basis of values derived from other cultures. This approach has, of
course, been an extraordinarily productive one, but has certain weaknesses and limitations.
In my own case, my research interests concern the origin and development of a basic
pattern or type of cultural behavior archeologists call "civilization". This pattern evolved
in a number of diverse, distinct cultural systems. A detailed analysis of the values, ethos
and postulates (in other words, the organizing principles of each of the various cultural
systems) leads us nowhere in an understanding of the developmental processes that are
involved. Such studies tell us how each system works; they do not answer the fundamental question as to why and how such systems evolved.

I believe that the relatively new and rapidly developing ecological approach in
anthropology is a way out of this impasse. Briefly, the cultural ecologist sees the culture
of a given people as a subsystem in interaction with other subsystems. He argues that the
key to an understanding of the developmental process of the cultural subsystem lies in
this interactive relationship. This larger total system I will call the ecological system. It

Reproduced by permission of the American Anthropological Association and the author from *Anthropological Archaeology in the Americas,* edited by B. G. Meggars, pp. 88-107, 1968.

includes the cultural, biological and physical environments.

By way of warning, I wish to emphasize that I hold no brief for 19th and 20th Century concepts of environmental determinism. Neither, however, shall I reject the powerful influence of the biological and physical environments on the development of man's diverse cultural systems. The cultural, biological and physical are all components in an overall system. This means that all three subsystems interact mutually in a three-way process. Cultural systems modify the biological and physical environment and vice versa. Perhaps Toynbee (1947) in his Challenge and Response Theory comes closest to a formal presentation of this ecological approach. I will state the ecologist's position as I see it by way of the following postulates:

1. Each biological and physical environment offers certain problems to human utilization.

2. Diverse environments offer different problems; therefore, the response (i.e., the development of a cultural subsystem) will be different.

3. To a given environment, there are a variety of responses possible but not an unlimited number (e.g., the cultural systems of Bronze Age Egypt and Mesopotamia evolved in similar environments, but they were quite distinct).

4. Responses to environmental challenges may be technological, social or ideational.

5. In a broad sense, men living in similar environments solve the problems of adjustment in similar ways, in different environments in different ways. This is essentially what Steward (1949) demonstrates in his concept of multilineal evolution. Furthermore, although a number of alternative solutions are possible, certain kinds of responses are more likely to occur than others and to be repeated throughout the culture history of a given area.

6. There is some overlapping of responses and solutions even in cases of strikingly dissimilar environments; i.e., the Mesoamerican cultural system occurred in arid mountain valleys and lush tropical lowlands.

7. Cultures, like all of the components that make up an ecological system, are dynamic and the degree of integration of a cultural subsystem to the total ecological system will vary. In part this is a function of time, in part of external disturbances that temporarily disrupt the integrative process (the Mongol invasion of Mesopotamia is an extreme example of the latter), and in part because the initial trend of development itself may not have been one leading to the most efficient adjustment. As a simple measure of "efficiency of adjustment" I would utilize population density.

With this preliminary statement of principles, we will now apply them to one of the major cultural historical problems in American archaeology, the origin and development of Mesoamerican civilization.

Civilization is a special type of cultural growth that occurred only in a few regions of the world. Archaeologists define civilizations in terms of excellence of technology, and especially by the presence of monumental architecture. More significant, however, are the social and economic implications of these technological achievements. They are always the product of a *large organized human society with marked occupational specialization and social stratification.* Furthermore, in pre-Iron Age technologies, with relatively primitive basic tools and transportation techniques, the base of the system is intensive agriculture and a high population density. Civilization is thus one kind of solution to the problem of adjustment to a physical and biological environment.

The major question to consider is why civilizations were evolved so rarely, and what factors were involved in their development. Here, we will confine our application of ecological theory to one of these centers, Mesoamerica.

Environment and Culture in Mesoamerica: General Considerations

Excluding Mesoamerica, all of the centers of pre-Iron Age civilization occurred in areas with bio-physical environments falling into two basic types: (1) Rainless deserts with extensive alluvial plains, fertile soils and major rivers usable for irrigation and transportation; or (2) Areas of light seasonal rainfall (topographically, occurring in riverine or coastal plains or mountain plateaus and valleys), sparse vegetation, fertile but friable soils. The geographical characteristics of Mesoamerica, however, are much more complex—over distances of 40 to 50 miles, we may encounter nearly all of the world's environments.

Elevations vary from sea level to nearly 5500 m., temperatures from tropical to arctic, rainfall from near desert conditions to 6000 mm. (240 inches) of average annual precipitation, soils from laterites to chernozems, topography from steep canyon valleys to flat riverine flood plains. Vegetation ranges through xerophytic, steppe, mixed forest, boreal forest, tundra, tropical grassland, jungle and tropical rainforest. Mesoamerican civilization was found wherever maize could be grown, and it is perhaps the adaptability of the Mesoamerican maize farmer to the fantastically diverse landscape that is the most impressive achievement of this civilization.

Although hundreds of environmental types could be established based on combinations of the geographical characteristics noted above, six broad ecological types may be defined on the basis of human utilization of the area.

1. Tierra Caliente (Hot Country) 0 to 1000 m. above sea level.
   a. Humid, excess of 1200 mm. average annual precipitation.
   b. Sub-humid, average annual precipitation below 1200 m.m.
2. Tierra Templada (Temperate Country) 1000 to 2000 m.
   a. Humid, average annual precipitation in excess of 1000 mm.
   b. Sub-humid, average annual precipitation below 1000 mm.
3. Tierra Fria (Cold Country) 2000 to 2800 m.
   a. Humid, average annual precipitation in excess of 1000 mm.
   b. Sub-humid, average annual precipitation below 1000 mm.

Within Mesoamerica is a band of territory that includes the Mesa Central (Central Plateau) and the Southern Highlands, which have identical bio-physical environments to type (2), and fit into our Mesoamerican ecologial types (2) and (3b). With this in mind, several researchers, among them Armillas (1949), Palerm (1954, 1961), Wolf (1959), Millon (1954, 1957) and the present author (1956, 1962, 1965), have attempted to apply the concept of the "Irrigation State" to Mesoamerica. This concept, expressed here very summarily, states that successful manipulation of an arid environment by a farming population requires organization of people of a large scale, to dig and maintain main canal and dike systems. Furthermore, some type of supra-community organization is necessary to police and regulate the distribution of water.

Although Millon (1962) and Adams (1960) have demonstrated that several kinds of arrangements are possible, the most effective social organization is the state with its hierarchy of formal status positions and their delegated powers and centralized authority. This is essentially what I meant in my postulate number (5), which stated that certain solutions are more efficient than others and, therefore, tend to be repeated in similar environments or in one area several times during the course of human adjustment. It is argued that the investment of control of water in the hands of a small group of directors was one of the factors that resulted in the evolution of the highly stratified society characteristic of all of the pre-Iron Age civilizations.

Irrigation farming, furthermore, is extraordinarily productive and permits very dense populations and large communities even with a partly or predominantly rural base. There are *chinampa* communities in the Southern Basin of Mexico with populations ranging from 3000 to 6000 that are completely rural in subsistence, and one partly-rural-partly-urban community (Xochimilco) has a population of 30,000. Even in 1910, before Mexico City became industrialized in a modern sense, Xochimilco had 15,000 inhabitants. The resultant social system is precisely the type we have defined as an essential characteristic of all civilizations. Generalizing to another level of abstraction, one might say that in the "Irrigation State" hypothesis the factors that produce civilizations rest in a community of interests, needs and activities.

This argument, however, does not explain the diffusion of civilization into other environmental zones in Mesoamerica, nor does it entirely explain the development of certain characteristics of Highland Mesoamerican civilizations. For this reason, I feel that other interactive processes in the ecological system must be considered. In the brief survey of Mesoamerican bio-physical environments just presented, the most striking characteristic of the area is its extraordinary diversity. This diversity may have been as important a factor in the evolution of Mesoamerican civilization as irrigation agriculture.

The tight microgeographical zoning creates an extraordinary diversity and highly localized distribution of raw materials, even involving basic food crops and raw materials for peasant technology. Herein lies the ecological problem: how can a small community situated in one area achieve the raw materials or finished products necessary for the maintenance of a peasant economy? One alternative is incessant warfare, by which each community procures such materials by raiding periodically the territory of other communities. Another is, of course, organized trade combined with part-time or full time community specialization. McBryde's (1954) superb analysis of patterns of trade and specialization in the Southwest Highlands of Guatemala is a good example of this type of response. Community specialization and supra-community socio-political systems are obviously a more efficient solution to the bio-physical challenge than intercommunity warfare. Wholly aside from the need of a peaceful and stable political climate for the successful establishment of such economic patterns, the traditional repetitive market encounters of people from different communities would tend to produce a feeling of community of interests and social identification that should act as a subtle integrative factor.

The development of large social systems, therefore, can be seen as the product of two integrative forces in Highland Mexico: irrigation and regional trade. Or, phrased another way, the forces for integration are based on two sets of factors: communality of interests, needs and activities; and diversity of interests, needs and activities.

Up to this point I have discussed in a theoretical way how the ecological approach may be applied to the analysis of the evolution of Mesoamerican civilization. This approach will now be applied directly to a body of factual data derived from recent archeological studies in the Central Mexican Plateau.

The Teotihuacan Valley as a Test Case

The diversity that we emphasized is both macro- and micro-geographical in nature. The Teotihuacan Valley is a small sub-valley within the Basin of Mexico. Oriented roughly northeast-southwest, it is approximately 35 km. long and covers approximately 600 km^2. To the south the valley is bordered by a solid phalanx of hills called the Patlachique range, with a maximum elevation of 2650 m. above sea level. This range is a spur of the Sierra Nevada, the main range that delimits the Basin of Mexico to the east. To the north is a series of isolated volcanic zones separated by broad passes and tributary valleys. The highest cone (Cerro Gordo) is 2950 m. above sea level. The valley floor varies in elevation from 2250 m. on the southwest to 2450 m. on the northeast.

The valley is a hydrographic unit. All drainage collects in ravines or *barrancas* that flow only for short periods following the rains and finally drain into a single river system. At San Juan, situated midpoint in the long dimension of the valley, there are approximately eighty springs with a permanent flow averaging approximately 600 liters per second. They also feed into the system, so that below San Juan the river is a permanent stream. The drainage ultimately reaches Lake Texcoco, a huge saline lake situated in the center of the Basin of Mexico.

On the basis of the geographical characteristics of the valley, a number of problems involved in its occupation by a Neolithic peasantry can be recognized, and the responses actually made by the Mesoamerican farmers observed.

1. *Problem*—The annual rainfall averages approximately 500 mm., nearly all of which falls between May 1 and September 30. This rainfall varies considerably from year to year, and month to month, and frequent prolonged droughts occur even during the rainy season. Rains are highly localized even within this small valley, and tend to be torrential in nature. Rainfall is heavier in the nearby hills. These characteristics make agriculture without humidity conservation techniques precarious, although some crops may be grown. Over a ten-year period, it is doubtful that the average yield of maize on unirrigated land would exceed 500 kg. a hectare (10 bushels of grain per acre). On slopes where soil cover is less than 50 c.m., the average yield would be much lower.

Response—Use of *barranca* water from the hills for flood water irrigation, use of the springs at San Juan for permanent irrigation, terracing of hillsides to build up the soil depth.

2. *Problem*—Winter frosts, usually beginning in October and ending by March 1, are severe enough to prohibit planting of Mesoamerican crops during the winter months. Furthermore, early and late frosts are frequent. Although generally speaking, increased elevation correlates with increased severity of frosts and shorter growing season, in the Teotihuacan Valley the surrounding hills are only a few hundred meters higher than the valley floor and are frost free. The presence of winter frosts limits the growing season, therefore, to 8 months in *normal* years. The higher yielding varieties of maize, the staple food, require a six month growing season.

Response—Intensive utilization of all land resources with little land in rest, development of other exploitive activities and exchange of surpluses for agricultural surpluses from the southern and central Basin of Mexico. In the early occupation of the valley before humidity conservation techniques were developed, the frost free hills were selected for cultivation.

3. Problem—The timing of frosts and rains is a crucial matter on the valley floor. In ideal years, when the rainy season begins in May and severe frosts start in November, annual rainfall is usually sufficient for crops on the deep soil plains. The inception and cessation of frosts and rains is quite erratic, however, and a combination of a late rainy season with early frosts produces agricultural disasters.

Response—Use of springs at San Juan for pre-rainy season irrigation to give crops a head start. Intensive cultivation of frost-free slopes. Planting of lower yield, quicker maturing, varieties of maize. In areas of flood water irrigation, a complex of practices including deep flooding of fields in the previous autumn (fields are surrounded with earth dikes up to a meter high); deep hoeing to facilitate downward drainage and storage of water; and early planting, using a technique called "a cajete" (excavating pits to the humid subsoil).

4. Problem—The vegetation is xerophytic and has probably never been luxuriant except near the springs, along the river or near the lake shore. Scrub forest probably characterized the slope areas. Soils are mostly loamy in texture. The feeble vegetation, texture of the soils and torrential character of rainfall make erosion a serious problem. (Today many slopes are denuded by sheet erosion and many of the *barrancas* are deeply cut, but archaeological evidence demonstrates that much of the erosion is post-hispanic.)

Response—Canalization of all drainage with stone retaining walls, construction of stone and maguey terraces on the slopes.

5. Problem—A high percentage of the 600 km² is generally classifiable as marginal land for agriculture today and is characterized by extreme erosion and thin soil cover, which cannot adequately store the generally sparse rainfall. Even before the 16th century, deterioration of the hillsides as agricultural land, this undoubtedly was a problem.

Response—Extensive cultivation of two cacti, maguey and nopal, which are drought resistant and will grow in thin soils. The maguey is a producer of a staple food, *pulque* (a mildly alcoholic drink), and the nopal of a fruit called *tuna*.

6. Problem—Soils fall generally into the category called "chestnut", and over most of the valley vary in texture from sandy to clay with loams predominating. They are characterized by a high concentration of such minerals as calcium and phosphate, but have low to moderate nitrogen and humus content. Below the top soil is a hard, nearly impervious layer of compacted earth called *tepetate*. Soil depth varies enormously from exposed *tepetate* on heavily eroded slopes to seven meters of alluvial accumulation below San Juan. Where soil depth exceeds 50 cm., soils are generally fertile and capable of sustained continuous cultivation with only moderate soil restorative techniques. They have excellent water retention capacity due to their loose texture and the presence of the relatively impermeable *tepetate* below.

Response—Intensive cultivation of all deep soil areas. Irrigation, especially flood water with its fresh soil and minerals in solution, used as a technique of soil restoration. Application of human and domestic animal fertilizer (dogs, turkeys). Crop rotation involving legumes, maize, and amaranth. Rebuilding of thin soil slopes by terracing.

7. *Problem*–There is great variation in soil humidity. Around springs the water table is less than a meter below the surface, and drainage is a severe problem. In the alluvial plain below the springs, the water table is too low for the plant roots to reach.

Response–Conversion of the swampy spring area into *chinampas* (land formed by excavating canals around long rectangular plots) and use of run-off water to irrigate 3600 hectares of fertile alluvial plain.

8. *Problem*–Highly localized distribution of key resources, such as salt, volcanic debris for construction materials, obsidian, and clay.

Response–Local community specializations to exploit and export these resources.

On the basis of the above considerations, the valley might be divided into four human occupational zones as follows:

Upper Valley. The Valley here fans out into a large oval depression perhaps 15 km. in diameter. In the center is a small deep-soil plain covering perhaps 25 km^2, where the present town of Otumba is located. Surrounding this is a broad belt of gradually sloping, badly eroded, thin soil terrain, which in turn is bordered by the Patlachique range to the south and a series of very small isolated volcanoes to the north. Absence of permanent water resources makes this the most unfavorable segment of the valley for grain cultivation today. There are, however, abundant obsidian deposits.

Middle Valley. This is the area between San Juan and a point just west of Otumba. Two huge volcanoes, Cerros Malinalco and Gordo, to the north and the Patlachique range to the south, both with extensive runoff *barranca* systems, combine with a relatively narrow (5 km.) piedmont and deep soil flood plain to make this section ideal for flood water irrigation. At least three ecological strips should be defined: steep slopes and intermontane plains, gradual slopes and piedmonts, and the alluvial plain. This section of the valley is especially rich in volcanic debris for construction materials and there are excellent clay deposits near the archeological zone.

Lower Valley. This is an oval alluvial plain covering 2500 hectares, with soils often reaching a depth of five to six meters, crossed by the San Juan River. In the center, the plain is approximately three kilometers wide; between Tepexpan and Cuanalan, it narrows to one and a half kilometers. To the south it is bordered by a gently sloping piedmont, in turn delimited by the solid rampart of the Patlachique range. To the north is a broad area of gently sloping piedmont, and beyond it the great volcanic cone of Cerro Chiconauhtla. The combination of deep soil, level plain and permanent water makes this the prize agricultural area of the valley. Sixteen villages and six haciendas utilize the water from the springs for permanent irrigation.

Delta. Below the Cuanalan-Tepexpan constriction, the alluvial plain fans out into an extensive deltaic plain coterminous with the great Texcoco plain to the south. It was delimited by Lake Texcoco to the west, to the north by the Chiconauhtla slope, and includes approximately 1000 hectares of deep fertile soil. Several considerations govern my decisions to separate this area from the Lower Valley: The distance from the springs and their present lowered output results in a greater water deficiency here than in the Lower Valley. Other distinctive characteristics are lack of nearby steep slopes to provide runoff of floodwater irrigation, the predominance of clay-textured soils excellent for adobe manufacture, and the presence of the saline lake, which provided a key resource, salt.

On the basis of the above description and what we know about human settlement of the area from 1519 (the date of the Spanish Conquest) until recent times, several patterns of local specialization may be emphasized. In each of our transverse ecological divisions there are deep soil alluvial plains, ideal for maize cultivation. In 1519, amaranth was also a staple and apparently cultivated in the same area. Today it has been replaced by winter wheat and summer barley or alfalfa. Bordering the plains are strips of gentle slope or piedmont with shallow soils that are terraced by planting rows of maguey contoured to the slope, or by construction of stone terraces. Between these *bancals* are planted beans and the faster maturing varieties of maize. Maguey furnished a basis for a variety of specialized activities such as manufacture of sugar, vinegar, honey, pulque, textiles, cordage, roofing material, and awls. Steep slopes today provide communal pastures for goats and sheep, and are used for maguey cultivation. In pre-hispanic times, they were probably used for maguey, nopal, hunting and wild plant collecting. Nopal today, and probably in pre-hispanic times as well, is generally a house-lot orchard crop of hillside or Middle Valley villages.

Aside from this transverse patterning of specialization, the Upper Valley as a whole, with its shallower soils and paucity of irrigation resources, is generally a bean-maguey-nopal rather than a maize producing zone; the Lower Valley is a much more productive area for basic grains because of its deep soil and permanent water resources. In the immediate area of the springs, where the water table is exceptionally high, *chinampas* occur and this area is a center of truck gardening today; in pre-hispanic times it was probably a center of chile pepper, tomato and squash production. Today, and also at the time of the Conquest, several villages on the lake shore specialized in salt making and adobe manufacture, and several in the Middle Valley in pottery making. The localized distribution of obsidian, *tezontle* gravel and basalt, plus good archaeological evidence for exploitation of the first two, also imply highly developed patterns of specialization.

If we apply our two basic principles to the Teotihuacan Valley, the growth of civilization in that area would seem to be a natural process of solution to problems of human adjustment to the environment. The socio-economic patterns characteristic of the valley in 1519 would seem to validate our principles. At that time all the Basin of Mexico, including the Teotihuacan Valley, was tributary to the great superstate headed by the confederation of the three states of Tenochtitlan, Texcoco, and Tlacopan. Generally, however, local states maintained a political semi-autonomy and were required to pay annual taxes in goods and services to the three centers. The Teotihuacan Valley was divided into six semi-autonomous states, each ruled by a hereditary despot whose capital was a large town with a population varying from three to six thousand people, situated at the edge of the alluvial plain. Dependent on each town were a large number of villages and hamlets. Three of the city-state territories took the form of a transverse strip crossing the valley from range to range so as to include the three basic segments of the environment. Three others were located in the delta and their territories included a portion of alluvial plain and adjacent hill and piedmont strips. Each city-state held a strip of territory averaging 200 km² (portions of which lay outside the Teotihuacan Valley area) and had a range in population of 5-40,000 people. At least three (and probably all) of the towns had regional markets held on different days of the five-day Mesoamerican week.

The socio-economic system of each town consisted of a centralized political organization with a hereditary ruler, and a social system stratified into at least five levels (nobility; priests and professional warriors; elite craftsmen; lay craftsmen; peasant farmers and serfs), and was characterized by close economic interdependence between villages and between villages and the town via the town market and the tribute systems (taxes in labor, goods, military services).

The settlement patterns reflect very convincingly the significance of the springs, the dominance of the Lower Valley alluvial plain, and local specialization in the culture history of the valley. Four of the six towns were located on the Delta and Lower Valley plain. The largest town, with the biggest regional market, was located in the center of the valley at the springs, which were apparently owned in 1519 by the ruler, to whom the towns below paid an annual water tax. All six towns were located within or on the edge of an alluvial plain, as were all of the larger, more tightly nucleated rural communities. A series of smaller or more dispersed settlements occupied the point where piedmont and steep slope join. In areas where hills were continuous, such settlements formed an almost unbroken strip of varying density (as in the case of the Patlachique range bordering the valley to the south); where the valley was delimited by separate hills, the strips extended around the periphery of each hill. In the hills and intermontane valleys of the Patlachique range, there were other hamlets.

The significance of towns in the evolution of civilization should be evident from our description of their characteristics. The town was the focus of the large sociopolitical system and economic specialization that characterizes civilization. The growth of such communities may be a simple matter of competitive dominance, and relate to richer agriculture resources. We have previously noted that irrigation agriculture greatly facilitates the growth of large rural communities. Such communities enjoy a demographic advantage in military competition with hillside rural settlement in the same area. Furthermore, it is my belief that the incipient traits of urban communities; i.e., occupational specialization, social stratification, formal government, may be the direct product of population growth. That is, when a community reaches a population of 5000 people or more, its very size necessitates the evolution of these urban characteristics.

The emergence of small states may, therefore, be considered as the outcome of the natural population growth of a few rural communities situated in exceptionally favorable segments of the landscapes. The development of occupational specialization in the town may also be considered as rooted in the community specialization of pre-urban periods. That this pattern of community interdependence was not a local phenomenon in the Teotihuacan Valley is evident from the analysis of Palerm and Wolf (1961) of the ecological zoning and specialization within the Texcoco area just to the south, from McBryde's (1945) study in Guatemala and that of West (1948) in Michoacan.

We are calling this pattern of intense local specialization and socio-economic interdependence of human communities *symbiosis*. In a general sense, symbiotic relationships between human communities are found the world over in all cultural systems, but they are especially highly developed in tropical mountain areas where environmental zoning is intense and closely spaced. The symbiosis can be a significant force in patterning interaction between communities only if the volume of goods moved from market to market is great, and the more primitive the transportation the greater the need for close spacing of contrasting environmental strips. It is only in such areas, therefore, that one can emphasize the role of symbiotic relationships as operative forces in the integration of communities into large socio-economic systems.

In the Teotihuacan Valley, the development of both irrigation and symbiotic patterns were apparently the primary factors in the evolution of civilization. The settlement pattern data demonstrate conclusively that the symbiotic patterns described for the Aztec Period (A.D. 1200 to 1519) were fully developed at least by the preceding Toltec Period (A.D. 800 to 1200), and were incipiently developed by Late Ticoman times (500 to 300 B.C.). During the intervening periods, and particularly in the later phases of Teotihuacan, a special kind of symbiotic pattern evolved to replace the simple town-village-hamlet symbiosis. This was the growth of a gigantic city, which at its peak covered possibly 19 km^2 (Millon, 1964, 1966). The city represents a hypertrophy of mutual interdependence on a scale and intensity far in excess of the small town-rural community symbiosis of the Aztec Period. At least three-fourths of the population of the Teotihuacan Valley in the final phase of the growth of the city was living in the metropolitan center. The extraordinary influence of the center on all other Mesoamerican regional cultures is closely related to its huge size and to the extraordinary level of socio-economic integration that may be inferred from its size.

The Basin of Mexico, the Central Plateau, and Mesoamerica as Symbiotic Regions

The Teotihuacan Valley was only a small part of a larger hydrographic unit, the Basin of Mexico, and the latter belonged to still larger regional configurations. The cultural geography and history of each of these territorial levels can be explored in terms of the theoretical arguments presented previously.

The Basin of Mexico is a large hydrographic basin covering 8000 km^2, surrounded by high ranges on the east, south and west, and low hills on the north. The floor is approximately 2240 m. above sea level and the surrounding mountains reach a maximum height of slightly below 5500 m. (in the southeast). In 1519, approximately one-sixth of the Basin was occupied by a chain of lakes. Zumpango-Xaltocan to the north was slightly saline and drained into the highly saline Lake Texcoco in the lowest part of the Basin. Also draining into the latter from the south was the fresh-water Lake Chalco-Xochimilco. The lake system provided efficient water transportation that must have acted as a further stimulus to trade and, therefore, the growth of cities and large states.

In the northern part of the Basin of Mexico, maize can be grown only with great difficulty because of thin soils, lower rainfall (400 to 600 mm.), lack of permanent water resources for irrigation and high mountains as a source of floodwater irrigation. In the 16th Century, villages in this area specialized in the manufacture of lime, maguey products, and nopal. In the Pachuca mountain range, obsidian mining on a grand scale was carried out as a local specialization. Villages within and on the shores of Lake Xaltocan-Zumpango, specialized in fishing, mat and basket making.

In the central part of the Basin of Mexico are large alluvial plains with deep soils, and high mountains provide water for floodwater irrigation. The rainfall in this area is (with the exception of the Teotihuacan subvalley) heavier than in the north, ranging from 600 to 800 mm. per year, and a series of local springs provided water for permanent irrigation. Besides the Teotihuacan system, springs were located at Cuauhtitlan, on the piedmont of Texcoco, and at Coyoacan. A number of lakeside communities specialized in salt making and pottery manufacture.

In the southern Basin of Mexico, rainfall is considerably higher than elsewhere, with stations on the lake shore recording averages of 800 to 1000 mm. annually, and increasing to 1200 to 1400 mm. on the slopes. Maize may be grown effectively everywhere at elevations below 2800 m. *Huauhtli* cultivation was also a specialty, along with tomato and chili peppers. For growing the latter, bat guano was imported from caves situated on the other side of the Ajusco mountains in the state of Morelos. The upper slopes, along with those in the central part of the basin, were heavily forested and strings of villages in this area specialized in lumbering and the manufacture of wooden objects, along with gathering of wild plants and hunting.

The southern lakes were much richer in water products than those in the north, and fishing and fowling were major activities. The richest resource of Lake Chalco-Xochimilco, however, was the *chinampas*. Much of the lake surface was converted by an extraordinary display of human energy into a network of canals and artificial islands, which were the most productive and intensively cultivated lands in Mesoamerica. The growth of Tenochtitlan was linked intimately with the expansion of *chinampa* agriculture. The *chinampa* area had the added convenience of canoe transportation to all the lake shore towns and cities. As late as 1910, *chinamperos* paddled their truck garden produce to the markets in Mexico City. Along with maize, avocados, chayotes, tomatoes, chili peppers, quilites (a green vegetable), squash, and string beans were grown.

All over the Basin of Mexico, then, there were patterns of local trade and specialization similar to, but of much greater variety and intensity than those noted for the Teotihuacan Valley, with the lake, alluvial plain, piedmont, and mountains as the major ecological components, but the entire basin being a symbiotic region tied together by the lake system. The patterns of local-state ecology described for the Teotihuacan Valley also apply to the larger unit. Most local states in the Basin were comparable in size and population to those in the Teotihuacan Valley. In most cases, they occupied a territory that transversed the various ecological niches: lake shore, plain, piedmont, lower slopes and upper slopes. The same basic patterns of land use and agricultural technology prevailed in the larger unit. Nearly all of the centers were located within the alluvial plain and within easy access of the lake shores. Examples include the core states of Texcoco, Huexotla, Coatlichan, Chimalhuacan, and Cuauhtitlan.

Syntheses on a higher level were achieved in the provinces of Chalco and Xochimilco. Chalco was originally composed of four separate small states, two of which (Atenco, Chimalhuacan) occupied the alluvial plain, one the lower piedmont (Tlalmanalco) and a fourth (Amecameca) most of the upper piedmont. If our analysis of the ecological significance of transverse zoning is correct, this pattern should be unstable; as a matter of fact, in the final phase of independent political development (that is prior to the conquest of the area by Tenochtitlan), the four states confederated into a superstate, in which each maintained its territorial integrity. Xochimilco occupied a territory comparable in size to Chalco, but was a centralized political or economic entity with its capital at the huge lake shore town of Xochimilco. Perhaps the enormously greater productivity of *chinampa* agriculture produced a pattern of niche dominance of greater intensity than in the province of Chalco, where hydraulic agriculture was absent.

To the south of the Basin of Mexico and the geographically similar Valley of Puebla is a strip of escarpment. The densest population in the area is clustered in a band ranging from 800 to 1600 m. above sea level. This zone is low enough so that tropical fruits such as pineapple, papaya, zapotes, mameys, guayabas, guanabanas, and tropical roots such as sweet potatoes, peanuts, manioc and jicama may be grown. Even cacao can be produced at the lowest elevations. Its close proximity to the northern, higher mountain basins made it an ideal source for such products. Furthermore, most of the area is frost free so that such Mesoamerican staples as maize may be produced all year, making up for a serious deficiency in the agricultural systems to the north, especially in bad years. This winter cropping, which was based on the irrigation, gave the southerners a definite market advantage. At lower elevations, cotton and the paper fig tree, so important in Aztec religion, were grown. Here, a system of hydraulic agriculture comparable to that described for the Teotihuacan Valley developed in pre-hispanic times, providing the unique combination of a highland and a lowland environment in close proximity, both with intensive agriculture. Although the higher northern strip played the dominant role from Late Pre-classic times onward, archeological evidence suggests that the more tropical escarpment was the area where agriculture and the first steps toward the evolution of civilization were initiated.

This brings us to a major problem in Mesoamerican archeology: explanation of the growth of huge cities with tens of thousands of inhabitants, and large states involving millions of people and thousands of square miles of territory. All of them were centered in the Central Plateau. Classic Teotihuacan was only one of the many such socio-economic systems, and during the Aztec Period the Teotihuacan Valley as whole was a small part of the huge tripartite empire of Tenochtitlan, Texcoco, and Tlacopan; the former city with a population as great as Teotihuacan itself.

The Teotihuacan Valley irrigation system is one of the largest in the Central Plateau. It is difficult to see the functional relationship between the harnessing of small irrigation systems and the growth of such huge centers and tributary states. Their *initial* growth, I feel, was closely related to the establishment of such systems. For example, the Teotihuacan system provides water for land that could not supply more than twenty to twenty-five thousand people with basic grains. There is some evidence that the city of Teotihuacan reached this population during its first phase of growth. The 600 km^2 of the valley, with effective terracing of hillsides and use of flood water irrigation, could support seventy to one hundred thousand people, the population during the final Aztec Period.

Why then should a city of at least 50,000 possibly 100,000 develop in such a location? Clearly its growth relates to an expansion of the dependent territory far beyond the Teotihuacan Valley. The final growth of these large plateau cities and the huge territories that they ruled clearly cannot be linked to the development of irrigation agriculture except in an indirect way; i.e., the demographic advantage held by small irrigation states in military competition with their neighbours. One possible exception was Tenochtitlan, where Palerm (1961) has convincingly demonstrated the interrelationship between the construction of huge dikes for the conversion of parts of saline Lake Texcoco into fresh water lakes for *chinampa* cultivation and the growth of the Aztec city and state.

I feel that the concept of expansion of symbiotic patterns goes far towards an explanation of the growth of these super-social systems, and that the geographical diversity of the Central Plateau provided the major stimulus to this expansion. A careful examination of the history of the Aztecs and the study of the "Matricula de los Tributos" (a 16th Century copy of Montezuma's tax lists) reveals definitely that the primary purpose of

Aztec wars was to secure tribute from areas with specialized resources and to protect trade routes. The Teotihuacan Valley and all areas of comparable size within this Central Plateau region either are deficient in or lack entirely certain fundamental resources, so that small city-state political systems could never fully resolve the problems fostered by the extraordinary diversity of the geography of the region. The larger super-states might be viewed therefore as a cultural solution to a major ecological problem.

Documentary data for Aztec Tenochtitlan and inferential archeological data for the preceding periods, makes it evident that as these colossal communities and states reached their peak even the symbiotic patterns of the Central Plateau were insufficient to fulfill certain needs. As the system of social stratification and the religious cult became more elaborate, and more central to the maintenance of the social systems in the Central Plateau region, the supply of certain products could not meet the demands of larger ruling classes and expanded urban populations. Such products included cocoa, turquoise, copal (for incense), jade, honey, liquid amber, rubber, and dyes, all restricted in use to the upper levels of the society or for the religious cult. Many occur only in the lowlands or southern highlands, others were found in the Morelos escarpment but in quantity insufficient to meet the expanded demand. As a consequence, during the florescence of Tenochtitlan and Teotihuacan, there was an expansion of trade and political control into those areas.

With respect to the spread of Mesoamerican civilization into all of the available ecological zones, I do not believe that the only mechanism was the evolution of super-states of the plateau type. All of the archeological data suggest that Mesoamerican civilization was already widely dispersed at least a thousand years before the evolution of the first super-states. The major vehicle may have been organized trade stimulated by the variations in natural resources. Even in later times, when states did play a powerful role in the diffusion of cultural patterns, organized trade was still a major force. The extraordinary diversity of Mesoamerican environment, instead of acting as an obstacle to the diffusion of civilization, was one of the most important factors in its rapid spread and elaboration.

Summary and Conclusions

One of the major problems being investigated by archeologists today is the origin and development of the special type of culture known as "civilization". Since the evidence is primarily technological, civilization is defined by the presence of exceptionally skilled craftsmanship and monumental architecture. The socio-economic implications of these technological achievements, however, are more significant to the understanding of the process of civilizational growth. They are the product of large socially stratified societies with a great deal of economic specialization. It is the origin and development of this type of socio-economic system, then, that is the major problem.

It is argued here that the key to an understanding of the process of development of civilization lies in the interaction between culture and the biophysical environment. Each culture is a sub-system in interaction with other sub-systems making up the "Ecological System". There is nothing absolute about this interactive relationship and various responses of a culture to an environment are possible. Civilization is one of these responses.

In the history of Mesoamerican civilizations, two basic interactive patterns between environment and culture were intimately related to its growth. One was the evolution of irrigation agriculture in the arid highlands and of a social system involving supra-community monarchial states, developed as a response to the problem of excavation and maintenance of canal and dike systems and policing of water distribution. The other pattern was community economic specialization and regional markets that tended to integrate communities into larger socio-economic groupings. This, I have called "Economic System Symbiosis." The sharply contrasting microgeographic patterns characteristic of the natural environment of Mesoamerica tended to intensify symbiotic relationships.

Both irrigation and economic symbiosis in their most exaggerated development are characteristic of the Central Plateau region of Mesoamerica, and I feel that the main current of Mesoamerican civilization developed there. The spread of civilization into other ecological zones, I see as the extension of symbiotic patterns as the Central Plateau civilization evolved.

Literature Cited

Adams, Robert M. 1960. Early Civilizations, Subsistence and Environment. In *City Invincible*, Oriental Institute Special Publication, pp. 269-295. University of Chicago Press.

Armillas, Pedro. 1949. Notas Sobre Systemas de Cultivo en Mesoamerica: Cultivo de Riego de Humedad en la Cuenca del Rio de Las Balsas. Anales del Instituto Nacional de Antropología e Historia, vol. 3, pp. 86-113.

McBryde, F. W. 1945. The Cultural and Historical Geography of Southwestern Guatemala. Institute of Social Anthropology Publ. no. 4, Smithsonian Institution.

Millon, Rene. 1954. Irrigation at Teotihuacán. American Antiquity, vol. 20, pp. 177-180.

———— 1957. Irrigation Systems in the Valley of Teotihuacán. American Antiquity, vol. 23, pp. 160-166.

———— 1962. Variations in Social Responses to the Practice of Irrigation Agriculture. Utah Anthropological Papers.

———— 1964. The Teotihuacán Mapping Project. American Antiquity, vol. 29, pp. 345-352.

———— 1966. Latest Conclusions on America's Earliest City. International Congress of Americanists, Buenos Aires.

Palerm, Angel. 1954. La Distribución del Regadio en el Area Central de Mesoamérica. Ciencia Sociales, vol. 5, pp. 2-15, 64-74.

———— 1961. La Base Agrícola de la Civilización Urbana en Mesoamerica. Revista Interamericana de Ciencias Sociales, Segunda Epoca, vol. 1, pp. 269-280.

Palerm, Angel and Eric Wolf. 1961. Agricultura de Riego en el Viejo Señorio del Acolhuacan. Revista Interamericana de Ciencias Sociales, Segunda Epoca, vol. 1, pp. 288-296.

Sanders, William T. 1956. The Central Mexican Symbiotic Region. Viking Fund Publications in Anthropology, no. 23, pp. 115-127.

———— 1962. Cultural Ecology of Nuclear Mesoamerica. American Anthropologist, vol. 64, pp. 34-44.

———— 1965. Cultural Ecology of the Teotihuacan Valley, A Preliminary Report. University Park, Pa.

Steward, Julian H. 1949. Cultural Causality and Law: A Trial Formulation of the Development of Early Civilizations. American Anthropologist, vol. 51, pp. 1-27.

Toynbee, Arnold. 1947. A Study of History. Oxford University Press.

West, R. C. 1948. Cultural Geography of the Modern Tarascan Area. Institute of Social Anthropology Publ. no. 7. Smithsonian Institution.

Wolf, Eric. 1959. Sons of the Shaking Earth. University of Chicago Press.

In this paper, written specially for this reader, Gordon R. Willey examines a basic and much disputed problem in Mesoamerican archaeology (and in civilizational studies in general) which was mentioned previously in the introduction to R. S. MacNeish's article (4). This problem concerns the ecological potential of the highlands versus the lowlands in relation to the process of cultural evolution: In the MacNeish and in the Coe and Flannery articles (5), we saw this problem discussed as regards the rise of agriculture and settled village life. Flannery (article 6) comments also on the question in discussing the rise of civilization in the Gulf Coast lowlands and the Oaxacan highlands of Mexico. Willey, in the paper below, compares the rise of the city in Central Mexico and the Maya Lowlands. Specifically, he focuses his attention upon the two great centers of Teotihuacan and Tikal in order to see if he can perceive any similarities or regularities in their growth. Extremely important studies by Professor Rene Millon and his colleagues and the Instituto Nacional de Antropología e Historia at the former site and by Prof. William R. Coe and his associates at the latter have provided much new data which have aided Willey in his comparative study.

Precolumbian Urbanism:
The Central Mexican Highlands
and the Lowland Maya[1]

Gordon R. Willey

    This is an appraisal and brief analysis of what we know, to date, about the origins and nature of Precolumbian urbanism in the Central Mexican Highlands and the Maya Lowlands. The procedure will be to construct first a diachronic model of the development of the urban phenomenon in Central Mexico, drawing upon archaeological data from the site of Teotihuacan and supplementing this with archaeological and ethno-historical information from the later sixteenth century Aztec city of Tenochtitlan. This model will then be used as a device by which to view, and against which to measure, the Lowland Maya data.

    In the Central Mexican Highlands, and particularly in the Valley of Mexico, the earliest farming populations for which we have sound archaeological evidence date from the Middle Preclassic Period (1200-400 B.C.). At this time Central Mexico was a somewhat backward province of Mesoamerica. The general level of cultural development had not gone beyond that of sedentary village agricultural organization despite signs of contact with the more advanced Olmec culture of the Mexican Gulf Coast (Tolstoy and

Paradis, 1971). Beginning at this village agricultural baseline, W. T. Sanders and B. J. Price (1968) see three separate but interrelated processes as leading from this condition to the urban threshold. These processes were population growth, population nucleation, and socio-economic differentiation within the society. Let us consider these processes as they pertain to the rise of the earliest Central Mexican city, Teotihuacan.

First, the basic population growth that made Teotihuacan possible was the result of a sudden and dramatic increase in agricultural production. This increase was, in turn, linked to the introduction of irrigation cultivation. The evidence for such irrigation is indirect. While there are no traces of early canal systems associated with Teotihuacan, the arguments that such systems existed are very good. For instance, we know that the Teotihuacan Valley, a branch of the larger Valley of Mexico, was very thinly populated in Middle Preclassic times and that this early population was found on the slopes of the hills bordering the valley flats. As these hillslopes constitute a micro-environmental zone which enjoys seasonally earlier and generally heavier rainfalls than the valley floor (and did so in the past), it is reasoned that such a setting was better adapted to the needs of early, pre-irrigation farmers than the drier, lower terrain. Then, in Late Preclassic times (400 B.C.-A.D. 100) there was a settlement shift from the hillslopes to the valley flats. This shift was accompanied by a rapid regional population increase, reflected in more sites and in the first appearances of some relatively large sites. Such a population upswing must be correlated with an important change in food production. Given the agricultural bases of the Precolumbian Mexican cultures, and the semiarid environment of the Teotihuacan Valley flats (where today profitable agriculture is carried on only with irrigation), it is difficult to see how this change could have been anything other than the introduction of canal irrigation (see Armillas, 1951; Sanders, 1965; Price, 1971; Parsons, 1971).

The evidence for the second process, that of population nucleation, comes from archaeological settlement pattern studies. At about the beginning of the Christian era the largest of the large sites of the Teotihuacan Valley flats was Teotihuacan proper. At that time it covered only two square kilometers. But in the next few centuries it became a metropolis of nineteen square kilometers of closely packed dwelling units plus numerous larger constructions. In the Classic Period, at about A.D. 400, this city is estimated to have had a population of from 85,000 to 200,000 persons (Millon, 1966a, b, 1967; Sanders and Price, 1968). While this amazing urban concentration reflects an overall population increase for the Teotihuacan Valley, it is also a function of settlement shifting and nucleation. Thus, settlement pattern studies in the Teotihuacan Valley at large, as well as in the adjoining Texcoco region, show a corresponding decrease in the number and size of other sites during this time of the city's growth (Sanders, 1965; Parsons, 1971). Teotihuacan's enlargement was at the expense of outlying hamlets, villages, and towns, so that just before the fall of Teotihuacan (ca. A.D. 700), it is estimated that ninety percent of the population of the Teotihuacan Valley and Texcoco region lived within the city proper. For whatever purposes and by whatever means, people were being drawn from the smaller settlements to live within the urban zone.

This brings us to the third process in the Sanders-Price explanation of Teotihuacan urbanism: socio-economic differentiation. Quite obviously, the urban nucleation was in response to social and economic functions. At the same time, these functions enjoyed

a further development from the phenomenon of nucleation. Such systemic interrelationships and "positive feedbacks" are far from being fully understood in terms of "prime"
or "triggering" causes; still, there can be little doubt that social and economic differentiations were important processes in the transformation from an egalitarian village farming
society to a nonegalitarian urban one. Much of the evidence for these differentiations is
in the physical nature of the city of Teotihuacan itself. Let us consider it.

The basic plan of Teotihuacan follows that of two giant streets or concourses laid
out like a huge cross oriented to the cardinal directions. Apparently, this formal conception
of the city was laid down early in its history. The main public or politico-religious buildings are located on the northern arm of this cross, the "Pyramid of the Moon" being at
the northernmost end of the arm while the even larger "Pyramid of the Sun" lies on the
eastern side of the concourse. A great many smaller (but still sizable) terraced platforms
line both sides of this northern concourse or street. At the main intersection of the cross
is a mammoth rectangular enclosure with another major pyramid (the "Temple of Quetzalcoatl") in its center. It has been surmised that this enclosure was the principal palace
complex or administrative headquarters of the city. Just across the concourse intersection
from this "Temple of Quetzalcoatl" enclosure was another enclosure (now destroyed)
which has been interpreted as the central marketplace of ancient Teotihuacan. Lying
back away from the major concourses, but immediately surrounding the "downtown"
zone of public buildings and facilities, are hundreds of elaborate palace-type structures.
These are all built on a similar plan: a central courtyard surrounded on four sides by
rooms. Many are distinguished by columned porticos and wall paintings. Then, still farther away from the "core" of the city are even greater numbers of less elaborate multi-
roomed structures. Both the palace-type units and the less elaborate compartmented
buildings give archaeological evidences of cooking and living functions. The overall aspect of Teotihuacan is, thus, that of a great urban agglomeration, with a center of public
or politico-religious structures, an adjacent zone of palatial residences, and a larger outer
zone of tightly packed humbler dwellings (see Bernal, 1963; Millon, 1967; Sanders and
Price, 1968).

To return to our questions about process, what were the social and economic
components of such a city? If we accept the estimate that ninety percent of the total
population of the entire Teotihuacan-Texcoco regions were living within the confines
of the city of Teotihuacan proper, then it must be recognized that some of these people,
in spite of their urban residence, were farmers. While the small, scattered ten percent of
the Teotihuacan-Texcoco rival population was probably primarily engaged in agriculture,
it seems unlikely that their efforts would have been sufficient to have sustained the
masses of the city. With this in mind, Millon (1966a, b, 1967) has estimated that three-
quarters of the city-dwellers worked as agricultural laborers. This in itself is another
argument in favor of irrigation cultivation, for only such an intensive farming technology
could have given adequate crop yields within the small area serviced by workers walking
daily to and from the fields.

The remaining twenty-five percent of the city's population are believed to have
been engaged in craft manufactures, trade, or politico-religious functions. Of these, it
would seem most likely that the greatest number were artisans, and archaeological evidences of craft specializations are seen in sectional concentrations of artifacts and in-

dustrial refuse within the city. Thus, abundant obsidian scrap and obsidian tools are found in certain building complexes or parts of the ruin, while other sections of the urban zone give evidences of ceramic or of figurine manufacture. Such industrial precincts suggest craft or guild *barrios* not unlike those of later Tenochtitlan, and an organization of this type is an aspect of full-time specialization.

The importance of trade to the Teotihuacan economy and to the socio-economic differentiation of the city is attested to by both internal Teotihuacan evidences and by more widely diffused Mesoamerican ones. We have mentioned the great market enclosure at the center of the planned urban zone. Both local and exotic goods were probably dispensed here. Archaeologists have also found concentrations of foreign goods in some zones of the city which suggest foreign "trading missions" or "colonies." As examples, both Classic Maya Lowland and Classic Monte Alban (Oaxacan) enclaves have been so identified. Outside Teotihuacan such long distance trade—documenting the commercial power and cultural prestige of Teotihuacan—is also reflected in Teotihuacan trade goods (especially pottery) found as far away as the Maya Lowlands or the Mexican Gulf Coast.

That a sizable number of persons within the city were in the service of the "state," in matters of governance and religion, is very directly implied by the large number of public-type structures and by the very great size and complexity of the city itself. The great temples and palaces would have been attended or lived in by priests and administrators, as well as serviced by lesser functionaries. The urban masses of 85,000 or more persons, living in close approximation to each other, could not have been kept in order through simple tribal sanctions; cadres of bureaucrats and police would have been necessary.

These inferences about the nature of the Teotihuacan state inevitably raise further questions about the powers and geographical extent of such a state. How far did these reach beyond the Teotihuacan-Texcoco regions? The far-flung trading network and the examples of Teotihuacan-type architecture in distant contemporaneous centers (such as Kaminaljuyu in Guatemala) suggest a state of imperial dimensions. At the same time, there is no hint of militarism in Teotihuacan art, nor are there good instances of fortified sites or fortifications associated with Teotihuacan culture. Thus, for the present, we cannot answer this question about political empire. We would speculate, though, that imperial institutions were probably less developed than in the later Aztec state.

The very nature of Teotihuacan strongly suggests that there were social class differences. It can hardly be questioned that there was an upper class leadership. Certainly the architectural variations and the distributions of fine craft goods support the thesis of a ruling class. It also seems quite likely that between an aristocratic leadership at one end of the social scale and an agricultural if urbanized peasantry at the other there were "middle class" components in Teotihuacan society, composed of craftsmen, traders, and bureaucrats. This latter inference receives support from our direct historical knowledge of the later Aztecs.

To offer a brief historical perspective on the Aztecs, or Tenochcas, they were one of the warring tribes who competed for political dominance in Central Mexico in the fourteenth and fifteenth centuries. Immigrants from the northwestern frontier of Mesoamerica, and barbarians at first, they assimilated rapidly to Central Mexican culture of the

Postclassic Period. This culture, sometimes referred to as "Mixteca-Puebla" culture, was in a direct line of descent from Teotihuacan, through such intermediary developments as those of Cholula, Xochicalco, and Tula; and we can be reasonably certain that it retained the urban living patterns of Teotihuacan.

Aztec Tenochtitlan was described by the early Spaniards as covering twelve square kilometers on its lake island location, plus additional concentrations of settlement on the adjacent mainland. Thus, while not quite as large as Teotihuacan, it approaches the dimensions of the earlier city. Like Teotihuacan, it had a central core of temples and palaces, including an imperial administrative enclosure which was the residence of Moctezuma and his bureaucratic entourage. There was also a great market center. The more elaborate residences, as in the case of Teotihuacan, were found at the center of Tenochtitlan, with the humbler dwellings nearer the outskirts. Occupational differentiation was well-documented by the Spaniards who noted the presence of craft guilds in certain sections or *barrios* of the city. Law-enforcement officers and government bureaucrats are described, as are merchants. These various groups were clearly on their way to being consolidated as a part of a "middle class." At the top of the social scale was an aristocracy. The lower social orders were represented by an agricultural peasantry and, below them, a landless urban poor.

An interesting feature of these early accounts of Tenochtitlan is their reference to *calpulli* or kin groups within the city. These kin units were, to some degree, both residential and occupational. That is, they coincided, in some instances, with the above-mentioned guild or *barrio* divisions of the city. While there has been debate over their significance, it is probable that the Aztec calpulli represent the vestiges of an earlier form of social organization that was being eroded by the emergence of a class system within an urban setting for Tenochtitlan (see Bernal, 1959; Monzon, 1949; Calnek, 1967).

These brief glimpses of Tenochtitlan in 1519-21, together with our archaeological knowledge of Teotihuacan, have allowed archaeologists to draw still more detailed inferences about the social organizational changes that took place in Central Mexican societies. Robert M. Adams (1966) has done this in a recent comparative study of ancient Mesopotamian and Precolumbian Mexican societies. In this, Adams relied largely upon Aztec data although he was also concerned with Teotihuacan and the Central Mexican upland cultural tradition as a whole. Eric Wolf (1967, p. 453), quoting in part from Adams, sums up the Adams analysis of the changeover that occurred at the urban threshold:

> [The transformation] . . . comprises two closely related determinate processes: first, the course of development 'in which corporate kin groups, originally preponderating in control of the land, were gradually supplemented by the growth of private estates in the hands of urban elites'; second, the replacement of priests as chief decision-makers in the society by 'militaristic groups,' a process 'closely accompanied by the transformation of a solidary social organization composed of ascriptive segments into a hierarchial increasingly autocratic one.'

Certainly, sixteenth-century Tenochtitlan appears to have been undergoing this transformation. There was both private and corporate ownership of land, but the former seems to have been increasing at the expense of the latter. The duality of leadership and "decision-making" in Aztec society is seen in the division between priestly and secular-militaristic roles; but it is probably significant that the emperor, Moctezuma, "wore both hats," depending upon the occasion. He was, in his primary functions and in his great powers, a civil and military leader. That he was also "head of the church" was another fact of the all-powerful emergent state.

In my opinion, it is likely that the processes of social organizational changes that Adams and Wolf see as operating within the Aztec capital had been set in motion in the earlier city of Teotihuacan. However, it is probable that these processual trends had advanced further with the Aztecs. If we summarize the Sanders-Price and Adams-Wolf processes in a serried development we come up with the following steps: (1) population increase; (2) population nucleation; (3) social and economic differentiation of these populations, as closely inter-linked with this nucleation; (4) the shift from a kin-based social order to a class-stratified one, also closely linked to socio-economic differentiation; and (5) the replacement of kin and sacred sanctions by those of force and the emergence of military leadership. I would see the first four of these processes as having taken place in Teotihuacan times, and, perhaps, the fifth was partially accomplished then. I would doubt, however, the supremacy of the military in the Teotihuacan state and would also question its full imperial development. These were features that probably were not achieved until later—possibly not until Toltec times and maybe not until we come to the Aztecs.

With this dynamic model of urban development in the Mexican Highlands in mind let us consider the data of the Lowland Maya. How well does the model approximate what happened there in the Late Preclassic and Classic Periods? To take up first the matter of population increase, a steady climb of Maya Lowland population from the Middle Preclassic to a maximum in Late Classic times is documented by a proliferation of ceremonial centers in the Late Classic (Willey and Shimkin, 1971, 1972) and by the swelling trend in domestic structure counts throughout the Preclassic-to-Late Classic time span. This last has been noted at Barton Ramie (Willey et al., 1965; Haviland, 1965; Tourtellot, 1970). At the same time, in making our comparative examination, it should be noted that there are no indications that absolute population numbers for the Maya Lowlands as a whole were ever as great as those for the Mexican Highlands. The agricultural potential for the rainforest jungle was simply not comparable to that for the uplands, especially the uplands under hydraulic methods of cultivation (Sanders 1962-63, 1972.[2] This factor of overall regional population density, and its causal correlates, undoubtedly bear on the next urbanization process, that of population nucleation.

We have noted that Teotihuacan had an estimated 85,000 to 200,000 people in an area of nineteen square kilometers. By contrast, Tikal, the largest Maya center of the southern lowlands in the Classic Period, had an estimated population of 39,000 persons for an area of sixty-three square kilometers including and immediately surrounding the major politico-religious buildings of the site. By adding another surrounding 100 square kilometers to this zone, the estimate is boosted to about 45,000 people for the 163 square kilometers of what might be called a "greater Tikal" (Haviland, 1969, 1970).[3] This is a sizable population concentration, but, as is obvious, the densities of dwellings and of persons per square kilometer are not of the same order as those of Teotihuacan. While the term "city" may be applied to Tikal,[4] it was not the same kind of nucleation, at least in its physical form, that we have observed at Teotihuacan and Tenochtitlan. That this difference in the urban physical form, as seen in the more dispersed settlement at Tikal, might reflect differences in function is certainly a possibility.

What can we say about social and economic differentiation within such a city as Tikal and within Classic Maya society? To what extent were these differentiations comparable to those of the Mexican Highland cities and to what degree were the same processes of social change operating? That the Lowland Maya were led by an elite class is certain. Such a class dominated the ceremonial centers, as is evidenced in their monumental art and in the hieroglyphic texts which are dedicated to the validation of an hereditary aristocracy (Proskouriakoff, 1960, 1963). Furthermore, there is good reason to believe that class stratification was solidifying during the Maya Classic Period (A.D. 300-900). Rathje's (1970) analysis of burial practices shows that in Late Preclassic and Early Classic times the lavish burials of the ceremonial centers are primarily those of elderly males while wealthy burials in outlying house sites or hamlets include both young and old males. This suggests a society of some social mobility and one in which high leadership was, at least to a degree, achieved with age and accumulating prestige. But by Late Classic times (after A.D. 600) rich burials are found only in the ceremonial centers, and, what is more, they contain the remains not only of senior males but of persons of all ages and both sexes. An hereditary aristocracy is implied, with its residence in the ceremonial precincts.

A peasant or farming population undoubtedly sustained the ceremonial center aristocracy, and some of these farmers probably lived in or near the center. But to what extent was there a "middle class" on the order of that of Teotihuacan or Tenochtitlan? To begin with, the lesser residential density of the great Maya Lowland centers, such as Tikal, suggests that this "middle class" was not as well developed as in the Central Mexican Highlands. Obviously, there were government functionaries or bureaucrats. The elaborate rituals and ceremonies depicted in the high art portray such persons, priestly or administrative assistants; and it is logical that the highly complicated calendrics and astronomy of the Maya demanded full-time clerical and scholarly devotees. I would question, however, that Maya society was "policed" to the same degree as Tenochtitlan or Teotihuacan. As to traders, it is doubtful if the Maya had an "open" market of the same kind as that known in the Central Mexican Highlands. In fact, it has been surmised by some that Maya Lowland trade was largely of a "distributive" sort, with rulers or lineage heads controlling foreign imports—such as obsidian and salt—and doling these out to their retainers for services rendered rather than allowing them to be obtained through market exchange.[5] To turn to artisanry and crafts, it is difficult to conceive of some of the high quality Maya goods—the exquisite lapidary work or the polychrome pottery—as being produced by other than full-time craftsmen. There is, though, some difference of opinion among authorities as to whether or not such full-time artisans were numerous enough to have formed guilds or craft *barrios,* like those historically observed at Tenochtitlan or adduced from the archaeological evidence at Teotihuacan.[6]

To conclude, the urban trends of the Lowland Maya appear to approximate but not equal those outlined in the model we have drawn for the Mexican Highlands. Demographic pressures on the Maya were less than those of the Mexican uplands. While there was a definite Maya trend toward urban nucleation this never resulted in the city-like densities of population that we see in Teotihuacan and Tenochtitlan. Nevertheless, social and economic divisions must have been forming in Maya society, and it is likely that this was accompanied by a shift away from a kin-based social order to a class-stratified one. At the same time, there is, in my opinion, less evidence for a large Maya "middle class" than at either Teotihuacan or Tenochtitlan. Signs of "open" market trade, of institutionalized craft guilds, and certainly "military decision-making" are less than they are in Central Mexico. In political institutional terminology, I would estimate that the Lowland Maya of the Classic Period were in process of changing from a "chiefdom" to a "state" (Service, 1962). In contrast, Classic Teotihuacan had gone much further on this course of development.

It has been argued by some that urban development in the Maya Lowlands and state formation there were "imports" from Teotihuacan (Sanders and Price, 1968). I would not go quite this far. There are indications that the same fundamental demographic and social processes were already under way in the Maya Lowlands prior to their first contacts with Teotihuacan. At the same time, Maya social evolution did not take place in a vacuum. Its trade and contacts with the Central Mexican uplands were always important. This became especially so when, toward the end of the Classic Period, the great Maya Lowland centers found themselves unable to compete successfully with the rising forces of the more fully developed states of Central Mexico. The full story of the Maya decline has not yet been told (see Sabloff and Willey, 1967; Willey and Shimkin, 1971, 1972); but, in one sense, it might be considered as a failure in adaptation to the full urban order.

Footnotes

[1] This paper has gone through several revisions, occasioned by shifts of emphasis and by factural updating. It was originally presented under the title, "Inferences About Classic Maya Society and a Consideration of a Model for Social Change," at the annual meeting of the Society for American Archaeology, Santa Fe, New Mexico, May 1968. A second version, "Urban Trends of the Lowland Maya and the Mexican Highland Model," was read at the International Congress of Americanist Sessions, held in Stuttgart, August 1968. A considerably expanded, and illustrated presentation, "Precolumbian Urbanism: The Lowland Maya and the Mexican Highland Model," was given as a lecture at the Latin American History Center, University of London, February 1969. The present version was prepared in early 1972.

[2] The agricultural potential of the Maya Lowlands has been much debated (Dumond, 1961; Cowgill, 1962; Sanders, 1962-63). I am inclined to side with Sanders in seeing this potential as considerably less than that of the irrigated Mesoamerican uplands. The probability of more intensive agricultural techniques in the lowlands has been considered by some writers (see Puleston and Puleston, 1971; Willey and Shimkin, 1971; Wilken, 1971) as has also that of additional food resources of a cultivated (Bronson, 1966), semi-cultivated (Puleston, 1968, ms.), or wild (Wilken, 1971) nature. While not denying these probabilities or possibilities, I think it still safe to say that the combined productivity of all of these food sources would not have equaled that of Mesoamerican upland irrigated fields.

[3] Sanders (1972) feels that these estimates are much exaggerated and would be inclined to halve them.

[4] Contrary to an earlier opinion in which I shared (Willey and Bullard, 1965).

[5]The nature of Maya Lowland trade has been considered in detail by Rathje (1971, 1972) and Webb (1964, ms., 1972). W. R. Coe (1965) feels that there was a marketplace or market area at Tikal.

[6]Haviland (1968) has argued for the presence of such craft *barrios* at Tikal (see also Haviland, et al., 1968) while Culbert (1968, ms.) is less convinced.

References Cited

Adams, Robert McC. 1966. *The Evolution of Urban Society, Early Mesopotamia and Prehispanic Mexico.* Aldine Publishing Co., Chicago.

Armillas, Pedro. 1951. "Tecnología, Formaciones Socio-Económicas y Religion en Mesoamerica," *Civilizations of Ancient America*, pp. 19-30, *Selected Papers, 29th International Congress of Americanists*, S. Tax, ed., Vol. 1, University of Chicago Press.

Bernal, Ignacio. 1959. *Tenochtitlan en Una Isla*, Serie Historia II, Instituto Nacional de Antropología e Historia, Mexico, D.F.

———— 1963. *Teotihuacan.* Instituto Nacional de Antropología e Historia, Mexico, D. F.

Bronson, Bennett. 1966. "Roots and the Subsistence of the Ancient Maya," *Southwestern Journal of Anthropology*, Vol. 22, pp. 251-280, Albuquerque, New Mexico.

Calnek, E. E. 1967. "Land Tenure Systems and Social Change in Preconquest Mexico," National Science Foundation Proposal, Mimeographed, Rochester, N. Y.

Coe, W. R. 1965. "Tikal: Ten Years of Study of a Maya Ruin in the Lowlands of Guatemala," *Expedition*, Vol. 8, No. 1, pp. 5-56, University of Pennsylvania Museum, Philadelphia.

Cowgill, U. M. 1962. "An Agricultural Study of the Southern Maya Lowlands," *American Antiquity*, Vol. 64, pp. 273-286, Menasha, Wisconsin.

Culbert, T. P. 1968 Ms. "Specialization in Classic Maya Society." Paper presented at the 33rd Annual Meeting, Society for American Archaeology, May 11, 1968, Santa Fe, New Mexico.

Dumond, D. E. 1961. "Swidden Agriculture and the Rise of Maya Civilization," *Southwestern Journal of Anthropology*, Vol. 17, pp. 301-316, Albuquerque, New Mexico.

Haviland, W. A. 1965. "Prehistoric Settlement at Tikal, Guatemala," Expedition, Vol. 7, No. 3, pp. 14-23, University Museum, Philadelphia.

———— 1968. "Ancient Lowland Maya Social Organization," *Middle American Research Institute*, Publication 26, pp. 93-117, Tulane University, New Orleans.

———— 1969. "A New Population Estimate for Tikal, Guatemala," *American Antiquity*, Vol. 34, pp. 429-433, Salt Lake City.

———— 1970. "Tikal, Guatemala and Mesoamerican Urbanism," *World Archaeology*, Vol. 2, pp. 186-198, London.

Haviland, W. A., D. E. Puleston, R. E. Fry, and Ernestene Green. "The Tikal Sustaining Area: Preliminary Report on the 1967 Season," Mimeographed, University of Vermont, Burlington, Vt. Supported by National Science Foundation Grant, GS-1409.

Millon, R. F. 1966a. "Urbanization at Teotihuacan." Paper presented at the 37th International Congress of Americanists, Mar del Plata, Argentina.

———— 1966b. "Extensión y Población de La Ciudad de Teotihuacan en Sus Diferentes Periodos: Un Calculo Provisional." Paper presented at the 11th Mesa Redonda de la Sociedad Mexicana de Antropología, Mexico, D. F.

———— 1967. "Teotihuacan," *Scientific American*, Vol. 216. No. 6, pp. 38-63, New York.

Monzon, A. 1949. *El Calpulli en la Organizacion Social de Los Tenochca,* Publicaciones del Instituto de Historia, No. 14, Mexico, D. F.

Parsons, J. R. 1971. *Prehistoric Settlement Patterns in the Texcoco Region, Mexico,* Memoirs, Museum of Anthropology, No. 3, University of Michigan, Ann Arbor.

Price, B. J. 1971. "Prehispanic Irrigation Agriculture in Nuclear America," *Latin American Research Review,* Vol. 6, No. 3, University of Texas, Austin.

Proskouriakoff, Tatiana. 1960. "Historical Implications of a Pattern of Dates at Piedras Negras, Guatemala," *American Antiquity,* Vol. 25, No. 4, pp. 454-475. Salt Lake City.

———— 1963. "Historical Data in the Inscriptions of Yaxchilan," *Estudios Cultura Maya,* Univ. Nacional de Mexico, Vol. 3, pp. 149-167, Mexico, D. F.

Puleston, D. E. 1968 Ms. "New Data From Tikal on Classic Maya Subsistence." Paper presented at the 33rd Annual Meeting of the Society for American Archaeology, May 11, 1968, Santa Fe, New Mexico.

Puleston, D. E. and O. S. Puleston. 1971. "An Ecological Approach to the Origins of Maya Civilization," *Archaeolcgy,* Vol. 24, No. 4, pp. 330-337, New Brunswick, New Jersey.

Rathje, W. L. 1970. "Socio-Political Implications of Lowland Maya Burials," *World Archaeology,* Vol. 1, pp. 359-374, London.

———— 1971. "The Origin and Development of Lowland Classic Maya Civilization," *American Antiquity,* Vol. 36, pp. 275-286, Salt Lake City.

———— 1972. "Classic Maya Development and Denouement," *Symposium on the Collapse of the Classic Maya,* T. P. Culbert, ed., to be published by the School of American Research, Santa Fe.

Sabloff, Jeremy A. and Gordon R. Willey. 1967. "The Collapse of Maya Civilization in the Southern Lowlands: A Consideration of History and Process," *Southwestern Journal of Anthropology,* Vol. 23, No. 4, pp. 311-336, University of New Mexico, Albuquerque.

Sanders, W. T. 1962-63. "Cultural Ecology of the Maya Lowlands," Parts I and II, *Estudios de Cultura Maya,* Vols. 2 and 3, pp. 79-122 and 203-241, Universidad Nacional de Mexico, Mexico, D. F.

———— 1965. *Cultural Ecology of the Teotihuacan Valley.* Department of Sociology and Anthropology, Pennsylvania State University.

———— 1972. "Cultural Ecology of the Lowland Maya: A Re-evaluation," *Symposium on the Collapse of the Classic Maya,* T. P. Culbert, ed., to be published by the School of American Research, Santa Fe, New Mexico.

Sanders, W. T. and B. J. Price. 1968. *Mesoamerica, the Evolution of a Civilization.* Random House Studies in Anthropology, Random House, New York.

Service, E. R. 1962. *Primitive Social Organization: An Evolutionary Perspective.* Random House, New York.

Tolstoy, Paul and L. I. Paradis. 1971. "Early and Middle Preclassic Culture in the Basin of Mexico, *Observations on the Emergence of Civilization in Mesoamerica,* R. F. Heizer and J. A. Graham, eds., pp. 7-29, Contribution of the University of California Archaeological Research Facility, No. 11, Berkeley.

Tourtellot, Gair, III. 1970. "The Peripheries of Seibal: an Interim Report," Peabody Museum Papers, Vol. 61, No. 4, pp. 405-420, Harvard University, Cambridge, Mass.

Webb, M. C. 1964 Ms. "The Post-Classic Decline of the Peten Maya: An Interpretation in the Light of a General Theory of State Society," Ph.D. Thesis, Department of Anthropology, University of Michigan, Ann Arbor.

———— 1972. "The Peten Maya Decline Viewed in the Perspective of State Formation," *Symposium on the Collapse of the Classic Maya,* T. P. Culbert, ed., to be published by School of American Research, Santa Fe, N. M.

Wilken, G. C. 1971. "Food-Producing Systems Available to the Ancient Maya," *American Antiquity,* Vol. 36, No. 4., pp. 432-449, Salt Lake City.

Willey, Gordon R. and William R. Bullard, Jr. 1965. "Prehistoric Settlement Patterns in the Maya Lowlands," *Handbook of Middle American Indians,* Archaeology of Southern Mesoamerica, Part I, Robert Wauchope and G. R. Willey, eds., Vol. 2, pp. 360-378, University of Texas Press, Austin.

Willey, G. R., W. R. Bullard, Jr., J. B. Glass, and J. C. Gifford. 1965. *Prehistoric Maya Settlements in the Belize Valley.* Peabody Museum Papers, Vol. 54, Harvard University, Cambridge, Mass.

Willey, G. R. and D. B. Shimkin. 1971. "The Collapse of Classic Maya Civilization in the Southern Lowlands: A Symposium Summary Statement," *Southwestern Journal of Anthropology,* Vol. 27, pp. 1-18, Albuquerque, New Mexico.

Willey, G. R. and D. B. Shimkin. 1972. "The Maya Collapse: A Summary View," *Symposium on the Collapse of the Classic Maya,* T. P. Culbert, ed., to be published by the School of American Research, Santa Fe, N. M.

Wolf, Eric R. 1967. "Understanding Civilizations: A Review Article," *Comparative Studies in Society and History,* Vol. 9, No. 4., The Hague, Netherlands.

Geoffrey Conrad is an advanced graduate student in archaeology at Harvard University and has done archaeological fieldwork in Peru and Canada. In his paper, which appears here for the first time, he emphasizes the continuities in Mesoamerican prehistory and views its civilizational developments from the Olmec to the Aztec as one great Mesoamerican civilization. He offers an hypothesis of how the Mesoamerican civilizational system grew stronger and expanded through time. Following the lead of many other archaeologists, the systemic 'prime mover' is generally seen as technological, although the rationale is seen as economic and political. Even though Conrad's model may be somewhat premature in relation to the state of our knowledge of Mesoamerican archaeology, it still can stimulate future lines of research as well as provide archaeologists with a framework to organize newly obtained data and generate new hypotheses.

Toward a Systemic View of Mesoamerican Prehistory: Inter-Site Sociopolitical Organization

Geoffrey W. Conrad

Introduction

It has long been recognized that trade was one of the major mechanisms of inter-site sociopolitical organization in prehistoric Mesoamerica and thus had a vital role in the rise of civilization in that area. Among the key questions involved in the investigation of this role are those relating to major control of long-distance trade—who had it, and how did they obtain it? This paper is an attempt to answer these questions from the standpoint of systems theory. That is, viewing inter-site sociopolitical organization as a cultural subsystem, we shall endeavor to show that through the medium of trade it was articulated with certain other subsystems—subsistence, craft production, intra-site sociopolitical organization, and religion—and to demonstrate the part played by these articulations in the development of Mesoamerican civilization.

The integrative framework of this effort is provided by the concept of an interaction sphere (Caldwell 1964), a set of cultural groups linked by specific, recurring contacts. The view taken is that participants in an interaction sphere progress by continually presenting to one another new cultural forms and recombinations of old forms, and that hence an inquiry into the nature of their contacts can yield considerable information concerning the process of their development.

In this paper we shall consider Mesoamerica in terms of three interaction spheres: a Mexican one corresponding to present-day Mexico and the Pacific coast of Guatemala, a Mayan one which includes the Maya Highlands and Lowlands, and a Mesoamerican one which is a combination of the former and the latter. Although the first two always overlapped to some degree, it was not really until Postclassic times that major control of trade in nearly all of Mesoamerica came into the hands of a single group—first the Toltec and then the Aztec—and we can speak of a true Mesoamerican Interaction Sphere.

The history of the spheres is marked by shifts in control which expanded and intensified them. A crucial point to note here (and which will be elaborated upon later) is the fact that in every case of such a shift, the new dominant group had been an active participant in the interaction sphere under the previous power. From this follows the basic assumption of the paper: the ruling class of a society involved in one of the spheres knew of its existence and extent and, recognizing the advantages of control (more power for their people with respect to other peoples, more power for themselves within their own group, better access to basic resources and exotic raw materials for the production of status-related and ceremonial items, etc.), would attempt to obtain control, given the opportunity.

The purpose of this paper, then, is to present systemic models to account for two phenomena: the formation and first control of the two original interaction spheres, and the opportunities obtained and utilized by other cultures to dominate them and the succeeding Mesoamerican sphere. Let us begin with a review of the data from which these models have been derived. Unfortunately, the data are not equally good for every sub-area involved. In general, the present state of our knowledge allows for more detailed statements about the Mexican and Mesoamerican Interaction Spheres than about the Mayan.

The Mexican and Mesoamerican Interaction Spheres

Although there were a number of smaller Early Preclassic interaction spheres, such as that of the people of the Ajálpan phase of the Tehuacán Valley—which included the southern Veracruz-Tabasco sub-area (MacNeish 1967: 12)—it was the Middle Preclassic Olmec, inhabitants of the last-named region, who first consolidated them into the Mexican Interaction Sphere, of which they were the original controllers from about 1200 to 600 B.C. In a series of recent papers William Rathje (1972; this volume) has argued that the complex sociopolitical organization which appeared first among the Olmec was the result of the need for the importation and distribution of strategic resources. Actually, Rathje has applied this model to both the Olmec and Lowland Maya. Since the article included in this volume refers specifically to the Maya, a brief consideration of the Olmec data is perhaps in order.

The Olmec heartland is a lowland rainforest with good agricultural potential for river levee farming (Coe 1968a: 107; Sanders and Price 1968: 134), but lacking in other items necessary for supporting a large though scattered population—particularly salt for dietary requirements, obsidian for cutting tools, and igneous rock for metates, all of which are primarily highland resources (Rathje 1972: 7-8). In order to obtain these materials, the Olmec established a trade network which included the highland sub-areas of Oaxaca, central Mexico, and possibly Kaminaljuyú in the Maya Highlands, as well as Central Veracruz and the Pacific coast (Coe 1969: 11; Borhegyi 1965: 16-18; Miles 1965: 248).

Once a constant supply of all subsistence necessities in the homeland had thus been assured, the Olmec population could expand. However, a larger population necessitated more complicated organization, since greater quantities of goods had to be procured from dispersed sources, imported, and distributed to scattered localities (Rathje 1972: 17). Increasing power came into the hands of the relatively few men who gained primary access to these goods by subsidizing trade (Rathje 1972: 5, 11, 13), since they maintained economic control over every household (Rathje 1972: 6-7). In this way there developed the integrative devices of a complex sociopolitical organization involving greater status differentiation (Rathje 1972: 18) and a unifying religious cult whose ceremonial centers served also as distributional centers (Rathje 1972: 12). The nature of the ceremonial constructions attests to the power of the ruling class.

With the development of complex organization non-utilitarian items—those relating to status differentiation and religion—became essential for maintaining sociocultural integration (Rathje 1972: 7-8). In other words, there was an increasing need for what Lewis Binford (1962: 219) has termed sociotechnic and ideotechnic artifacts. We can see reflections of this in the Olmec hollow white-ware figurines, stone heads, earspools, carved jade, and magnetite mirrors (Coe 1968b: 46). Many of these items probably functioned in more than one way. For example, the jaguar mask, while depicting a cult symbol, might also have served to assert the rank and power of its wearer; in short, it may have been a sociotechnic as well as an ideotechnic artifact (Joyce P. Marcus, personal communication).

Some of these objects were made of local raw materials, while the materials necessary for manufacturing others had to be imported. The production of these items thus involved a further elaboration of trade and most likely craft specialization (Flannery 1968: 85).

Although the Olmec heartland lacked certain resources, it now possessed one which other sub-areas did not have: the features associated with complex organization. These features—the sociotechnic and ideotechnic items and the rationalizations for their use— were highly exportable to other cultural groups, and by exchanging them for necessary materials the Olmec gained control of the Mexican Interaction Sphere (Rathje 1972: 16, 20). Thus the Olmec religion spread with trade.

Key points in Rathje's hypothesis are the predictions that complex organization will develop first in a core region which is the most deficient in resources and that, since complex organization is all that the core group has to offer, power will pass into the hands of societies in the distant resource regions or intermediate buffer zones once they have reached a similar or higher level of organization (Rathje 1972: 20). This is exactly the picture we see with the Olmec—their civilization seems to have developed first at San Lorenzo and La Venta, but in the late Middle Preclassic (ca. 600-500 B.C.) major control of·long-distance trade shifted to Monte Albán in the Valley of Oaxaca (Flannery 1968: 90-97).

Prior to this time Oaxaca had been an important member of the interaction sphere under the Olmec, supplying the latter with volcanic stone for metates (Rathje 1972: 36) and probably jade, magnetite, and ilmenite (Flannery 1968: 89). Oaxaca was also a region of early experimentation with agricultural water-control techniques (Flannery et al. 1967: 453). The success of dry farming and pot irrigation in the alluvial zone of the valley floor had created a population pressure which forced expansion into the higher piedmont zone. In Monte Albán I times (600-300 B.C.) the agricultural pattern seems to have been one of an intensively cultivated, irrigated central zone and a surrounding hillside zone less intensively cultivated by dry farming (Flannery *et al.* 1967: 451). Such a pattern represented a marked improvement over its Olmec counterpart.

This improved subsistence technology led to continued population growth (Flannery *et al.* 1967: 452; Flannery 1968: 98; Paddock 1966: 99), which in turn created new integrative requirements. These needs, coupled with the lessons learned from the Olmec, produced a more complex sociopolitical organization in which the ruling class was able to make the gains in strength and centralization which are apparent during the late Middle Preclassic Monte Alban I and Late Preclassic Monte Alban II (ca. 300 B.C. to A.D. 300) times (Bernal 1965: 800; Paddock 1966: 119; Flannery 1968: 99-100). I suggest that this ruling class desired to gain the advantages brought by domination of the interaction sphere and, with their own greater, more centralized power and the more productive Oaxacan economy, were able to do so by having more capital than anyone else to invest in long-distance trade through the subsidization of merchants.

During the Monte Alban I phase the site maintained contacts with southern Veracruz-Tabasco, the Tehuacán Valley, Chiapas, and the Pacific coast (Flannery 1968: 97). In the succeeding Monte Alban II phase trade connections extended to Teotihuacán, Chiapas, Kaminaljuyu, Guatemala, Honduras, and British Honduras, the first being the most important (Caso and Bernal 1965: 880-881).

The latter half of Monte Alban II was coeval with Teotihuacán II. During this period the two sites were competing for the control of the Mexican Interaction Sphere. Teotihuacán influences appeared in Oaxaca, Guererro, southern Veracruz, and at Kaminaljuyu at this time (Sanders 1965: 179). By the beginning of the Classic period control had shifted to Teotihuacán, and during phases III and IV of its occupation (A.D. 300-700) the city maintained trade relations with much of Mesoamerica.

The process by which Teotihuacán gained economic power was similar to that already seen at Monte Alban. The former, like the latter, participated in the interaction sphere before controlling it, and an improvement in subsistence technology seems to have been involved in Teotihuacán ascendancy, as it was in that of Monte Alban.

During the Teotihuacán I phase changes in agricultural and settlement patterns began to occur, with settlement shifting to the valley floor and concentrating largely in a single community. It is thought that irrigation agriculture appeared in the Valley of Mexico at this time. Although there is at present no direct evidence, undated abandoned ditches and climatic evidence of a dryer period tend to support this theory. Terraces may also have been used, although concrete evidence is again unavailable (Millon 1954: 179; Sanders 1965: 151-153).

Tremendous population increases are evident from the later part of Teotihuacán I through Teotihuacán IV (Sanders 1965: 156, 168-172; Parsons 1968: 873-876). Faced with new integrative requirements, the site became a true urban center with a strong, most likely theocratic, government presiding over a stratified society (Millon *et al.* 1965: 35-36; Sanders and Price 1968: 141). By Teotihuacan II the ruling class possessed enough authority to undertake construction of the Pyramids of the Sun and the Moon (Willey 1966: 176).

I think that here again we see a case of the ruling class of a group participating in the interaction sphere, desirous of control, who were provided with an improved subsistence base. This had two results. First, it enlarged the population, thereby creating new integrative requirements which increased the power of the rulers. Second, it provided the ruling class with more capital to invest in long-distance trade, and they were able to "buy" control. In this instance investing capital meant primarily subsidizing mercantile activities. However, the existence of the eagle and jaguar orders indicates that the government of Teotihuacán may have been more militaristic than that of other contemporary sites—perhaps due to the near-frontier location of the city (Adams 1966: 132; Thompson 1966: 304). Some of the investment may then have been in the form of sponsorship of military orders, and Teotihuacán may not have maintained its control in an entirely peaceful manner.

In the Late Classic (ca. A. D. 700) Teotihuacán was destroyed by the Toltecs, who then assumed leadership in the Mexican Interaction Sphere. During the Early Postclassic (beginning ca. A. D. 900) they extended their influence throughout nearly all of Mesoamerica, creating a true Mesoamerican Interaction Sphere (whose precursors can be seen in the southern trade connections of the Olmec, Monte Albán, and Teotihuacán) and establishing the structure of the later Aztec tribute empire.

This is the first instance of a shift in domination which cannot be linked to an improvement in subsistence technology. Actually, we know very little about Toltec agriculture, although the possibility of irrigation works in the region around Tula, the Toltec capital, should be noted (Sanders 1965: 186). At any rate, it seems unlikely that their agricultural practices represented any advance over those of Teotihuacán.

In other respects, however, the manner in which the Toltec took over trade may not have been as different as it might seem. Tula was founded perhaps as early as A. D. 510 as a provincial center tributary to Teotihuacán (Sanders 1965: 182). Thus the Toltec too took part in the interaction sphere before they dominated it. (In fact, the Toltec present one of the best arguments in support of the assumption that participation in an interaction sphere brought knowledge of its existence and extent: their well-known sudden appearance at Chichén Itzá in the Maya Lowlands is difficult to explain if we postulate that they did not know the location of that site beforehand.) Secondly, Tula was located in a frontier area, and the power of its secular forces grew with the need for defense. The military societies became more important, and, although they were still associated with religion, their main function was probably that of creating a tribute "empire" (Adams 1966: 135-136; Wolf 1959: 122). In short, the rulers of Tula may simply have invested more capital than anyone else in subsidies to the military, spending less on the merchants, until they had built up a force capable of taking over the interaction sphere by conquest.

Tula itself was destroyed in A. D. 1168. There followed a period of wars between city-states, most of which claimed descent from the Toltec state through their ruling families (Wolf 1959: 123; Coe 1962: 138) and had thus been members of the Toltec-dominated interaction sphere. The eventual winner was Tenochtitlán, the Aztec capital.

Unsurprisingly, an improvement in subsistence economy seems to have been involved in the Aztec victory. The Aztecs employed a system of highly intensive agriculture, including *chinampas,* irrigation works, canals, dams, and terraces, which enabled the Valley of Mexico to attain its maximum Pre-Columbian population (Soustelle 1961: 9;

Gibson 1964: 5; Sanders 1965: 191). Secular and religious forces integrated this large, stratified society headed by a semi-divine despot and his high officials. A sizable bureaucracy administered their authority (Coe 1962: 166). Wealth was measured in possessions, and the Aztec lords were unbelievably wealthy. Many of the materials used in the manufacture of goods were collected as tribute from the "outlying provinces" (Chapman 1957: 126), which included most of Mesoamerica. The market was controlled by the state, and all commerce had to pass through it (Wolf 1959: 140).

It is not difficult to see how the Aztecs defeated their contemporaries and came to control the Mesoamerican Interaction Sphere. Given the fantastically productive Aztec subsistence economy and the power of their rulers, their warrior societies and merchant *(pochteca)* class were extremely well-supported. Any potential commercial rival would have had to outstrip both groups. Since no other people had the Aztec subsistence base or population, none were able to do it. In fact, what actually happened was that the *pochteca* only traded in a region until it was subdued. Once it had been conquered by the military and made a tributary state, the merchants ceased to operate there (Chapman 1957: 122).

The Mayan Interaction Sphere

The origins of Maya civilization and the formation of the Mayan Interaction Sphere have already been discussed in detail by Rathje (this volume), and there is no point in repeating the argument here. Suffice it to note that the development began during the Middle Preclassic (ca. 700-300 B.C.) in the center of the northeast Petén in the Maya Lowlands, a rainforest sub-area which, like the southern Veracruz-Tabasco Olmec heartland, is capable of supporting a large though scattered population practicing slash-and-burn agriculture once certain basic items have been imported. The process seems to have been exactly the same as in the Olmec case.

Control of the interaction sphere remained in the Petén for a long time. It was not until the Late Classic Tepeu phase (ca. A. D. 600-900) that a shift away from the core area began. During this period there was a greater trend toward local diversity, and sites in the buffer zone began to monopolize strategic resources (Rathje 1972: 31). This accords well with the predictions that the core area has only complex sociopolitical organization and its trappings to offer and that once the buffer and resource zones attain a similar or higher level of development, the core will lose sway over them. It was during the Late Classic that most of the buffer zone developed complex organization (Rathje 1972: 23).

After the termination of the Petén domination of trade within the Mayan Interaction Sphere, no other group in the Maya Lowlands or Highlands gained major control. This may be explained by two factors. Firstly, no group in the lowlands developed an improved agricultural technique of the type necessary to provide the greater amount of capital which had to be invested in trade if power was to be obtained—slash-and-burn continued as the principal technique (Rathje 1972: 1). Secondly, at the beginning of the Postclassic the Maya Highlands, the logical place to look for the next controller, were drawn into the interaction sphere of the Toltec, and regularized trade relations with central

Mexico were established. (Toltec influences also appeared in the Maya Lowlands, as is evident from Chichén Itzá.) Thus the expanding Mexican Interaction Sphere cut short the history of its Mayan counterpart by absorbing it into a true Mesoamerican Interaction Sphere.

The Models

The data that have been presented allow for the formulation of two tentative models: the first for the origin and primary control of the Mexican and Mayan Interaction Spheres and the second for the emergence of a new controller of either the Mexican or the combined Mesoamerican Sphere. These models employ systems theory insofar as they attempt to articulate various cultural subsystems in explanations of these phenomena.

A Tentative Model for the Origin and First Control of the Mexican and Mayan Interaction Spheres

This model, which is summarized in Figure 1, is based on the data pertaining to the Olmec and the Petén Maya and is essentially that derived by Rathje (this volume; 1972). These two groups inhabited lowland rainforest environmental zones which had the agricultural potential to support a large though scattered population but which lacked other subsistence necessities. Each group established its interaction sphere by consolidating pre-existing smaller trade networks in order to obtain, import, and distribute the missing basic resources.

The sub-areas, now well-supplied with all subsistence necessities, were able to support a larger population. Such an increase, however, required two things: new devices for integrating the larger population and an intensification of trade to provide a greater volume of goods. The new internal integrative requirements and the need for maintaining the intensified network of trade and distribution led to the development of complex sociopolitical organization involving increased status differentiation and a unifying religious cult, with power concentrated in the hands of those who sponsored long-distance trade.

Status differentiation and religion, with their now-greater cultural emphasis, required more artifacts which could serve as their visible adjuncts—in other words, a larger supply of sociotechnic and ideotechnic items. Some were produced from local raw materials; trade was elaborated to provide the raw materials for the production of others. Craft specialization became important in the manufacture of these goods.

These sociotechnic and ideotechnic artifacts and the rationalizations for their use—more complex sociopolitical organization and the new religious cults—were exportable to those peoples who did not possess them, and the lowland rainforest groups who did were able to gain control of the interaction spheres by trading their inventions for subsistence necessities. They maintained their power until other societies reached a similar or higher level of organizational complexity.

Figure 1: A Tentative Model for the Origin and First
Control of the Mexican and Mayan Interaction Spheres

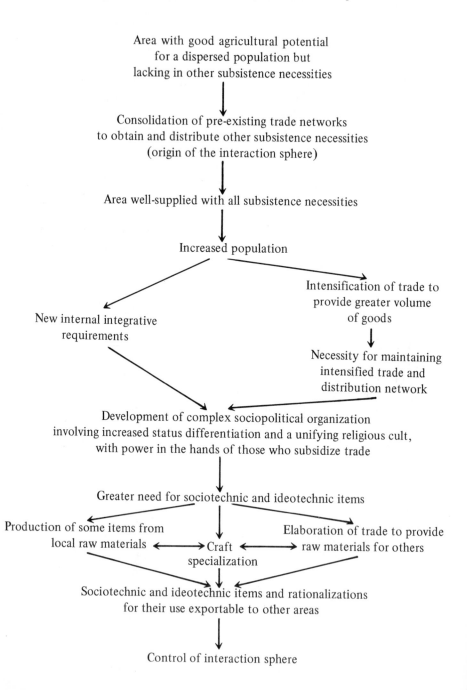

A Tentative Model for the Emergence of a New Controller of the Mexican or Mesoamerican Interaction Sphere

This model, which is summarized in Figure 2, is based on the data pertaining to Monte Albán, Teotihuacán, the Toltec, and the Aztec. Since each new dominant group had been an active member of the interaction sphere under the previous director, we have assumed that the ruling class of any participant knew of the existence and extent of the sphere and would have been eager to obtain the advantages conferred by control: greater economic power for their people with respect to other peoples, greater economic power for themselves within their own society, and better access to exotic raw materials for the manufacture of status symbols and religious items.

Temporarily excluding the Toltec, every new controller seems to have been given its initial impetus by the development of an improved agricultural technique which resulted in a more productive subsistence economy. This led to an increased population and new integrative requirements and consequently to a greater complexity of sociopolitical organization with more power in the hands of the ruling class. Thus each group in turn had more powerful leaders eager to dominate the interaction sphere. As a result of the more productive economy these leaders possessed greater amounts of capital to invest in long-distance trade by subsidizing merchant classes, military orders, or both. This ability to invest more capital than any other competitor enabled them to become dominant by paying higher prices, sponsoring more merchants, subduing recalcitrant neighbors, or any combination of the three. Control brought the desired advantages and was maintained until another participant developed a still more effective agricultural technique and was able to invest even more heavily in long-distance trade.

The Toltec really represent only a special case which can be accommodated by this model. It has been suggested that, given a subsistence economy that was probably as effective as that of Teotihuacán (and thus more productive than those of most other contemporary peoples), the Toltec leaders simply utilized a greater percentage of their capital for sponsoring their warrior societies, thereby creating a more efficient military arm which allowed them to take over the interaction sphere by direct conquest.

Summary and Conclusion

In attempting to arrive at a systemic view of intersite sociopolitical organization in prehistoric Mesoamerica, we have treated the area in terms of three interaction spheres: the original Mexican and Mayan ones and a later Mesoamerican one which represents the merging of the two. The data pertaining to their origin and first domination and to subsequent shifts in control have been reviewed, and tentative models have been presented to explain these facts. Obviously, all the crucial data are not available, and more work will be necessary to prove or disprove these hypotheses. However, it is hoped that they may be of some use in further studies.

One final note: little has been said here of the highland/lowland dichotomy which has often been stressed in studies of Mesoamerican prehistory. If any such dichotomy has become apparent in the preparation of this paper, it is this: the original interaction spheres were formed and first dominated by lowland peoples, but once a highland group h⁻¹

Figure 2: A Tentative Model for the Emergence
of a New Controller of the Mexican or Mesoamerican Interaction Spheres

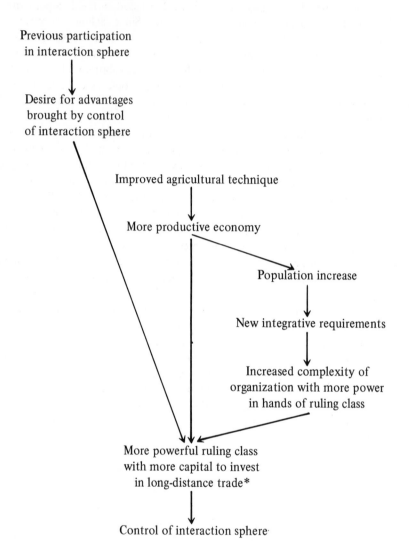

*Capital may be invested by subsidizing merchant classes or military societies or both.

wrested control away from them, it never again reverted to the lowlands. The lowland environment did not permit the development of the more productive agricultural techniques which would have been necessary for regaining preeminence.

Acknowledgments

I wish to express my gratitude to Drs. Gordon R. Willey, Jeremy A. Sabloff, and William L. Rathje for their advice in the preparation of this paper.

Bibliography

Adams, R. McC. 1966. *The Evolution of Urban Society: Early Mesopotamia and Pre-hispanic Mexico*. Aldine, Chicago.

Bernal, I. 1965. Archaeological Synthesis of Oaxaca. In *Handbook of Middle American Indians*, Vol. 3, edited by R. Wauchope and G. R. Willey, pp. 788-814. University of Texas Press, Austin.

Binford, L. R. 1962. Archaeology as Anthropology. *American Antiquity*, Vol. 28, pp. 215-225.

Borhegyi, S. F. de. 1965. Archaeological Synthesis of the Guatemala Highlands. In *Handbook of Middle American Indians*, Vol. 2, edited by R. Wauchope and G. R. Willey, pp. 3-59. University of Texas Press, Austin.

Caldwell, J. R. 1964. Interaction Spheres in Prehistory. *Illinois State Museum Scientific Papers*, Vol. 12, no. 6, pp. 133-143. Springfield.

Caso, A., and I. Bernal. 1965. Ceramics of Oaxaca. In *Handbook of Middle American Indians*, Vol. 3, edited by R. Wauchope and G. R. Willey, pp. 871-896. University of Texas Press, Austin.

Chapman, A. M. 1957. Port of Trade Enclaves in Aztec and Maya Civilizations. In *Trade and Market in the Early Empires*, edited by K. Polanyi, C. M. Arensberg, and H. W. Pearson, pp. 114-153. Free Press, New York.

Coe, M. D. 1962. *Mexico*. Praeger, New York.

———— 1968a. *America's First Civilization*. American Heritage, New York.

———— 1968b. San Lorenzo and the Olmec Civilization. In *Dumbarton Oaks Conference on the Olmec*. edited by E. P. Benson, pp. 41-72. Dumbarton Oaks, Washington.

———— 1969. The Archaeological Sequence at San Lorenzo, Tenochtitlán, Veracruz, Mexico. Paper read at the 34th Annual Meeting of the Society for American Archaeology, 1969, Milwaukee.

Flannery, K. V. 1968. The Olmec and the Valley of Oaxaca: A Model for Inter-Regional Interaction in Formative Times. In *Dumbarton Oaks Conference on the Olmec*, edited by E. P. Benson, pp. 79-111. Dumbarton Oaks, Washington.

Flannery, K. V., A. V. T. Kirkby, M. J. Kirkby, and A. W. Williams, Jr. 1967. Farming Systems and Political Growth in Ancient Oaxaca. *Science*, Vol. 158, pp. 445-454.

Gibson, C. 1964. *The Aztecs Under Spanish Rule: A History of the Indians of the Valley of Mexico, 1519-1810*. Stanford University Press, Stanford.

MacNeish, R. S. 1967. *The Prehistory of the Tehuacán Valley*, Vol. 2. University of Texas Press, Austin.

Marcus, Joyce P. 1970. Personal communication.

Miles, S. W. 1965. Sculpture of the Guatemala-Chiapas Highlands and Pacific Slope, and Associated Hieroglyphs. In *Handbook of Middle American Indians*, Vol. 2, edited by R. Wauchope and G. R. Willey. University of Texas Press, Austin.

Millon, R. F. 1954. Irrigation at Teotihuacan. *American Antiquity,* Vol. 20, pp. 177-180.

Millon, R. F., B. Drewitt, and J. A. Bennyhoff. 1965. The Pyramid of the Sun at Teotihuacan: 1959 Investigations. *Transactions of the American Philosophical Society,* n.s., Vol. 55, part 6.

Paddock, J. 1966. Oaxaca in Ancient Mesoamerica. In *Ancient Oaxaca: Discoveries in Mexican Archaeology and History,* edited by J. Paddock, pp. 83-242. Stanford University Press, Stanford.

Parsons, J. R. 1968. Teotihuacan, Mexico, and the Impact on Regional Demography. *Science,* Vol. 162, pp. 872-877.

Rathje, W. L. 1972. Praise the Gods and Pass the Metates: A Hypothesis of the Development of Lowland Rainforest Civilization in Mesoamerica. In *Contemporary Archaeology: An Introduction to Theory and Contributions,* edited by M. P. Leone. (In Press).

Sanders, W. T. 1965. *The Cultural Ecology of the Teotihuacan Valley: A Preliminary Report of the Results of the Teotihuacan Valley Project.* Pennsylvania State University.

Sanders, W. T., and B. J. Price. 1968. *Mesoamerica: The Evolution of a Civilization.* Random House, New York.

Soustelle, J. 1961. *The Daily Life of the Aztecs on the Eve of the Spanish Conquest,* translated by P. O'Brian. Weidenfeld and Nicolson, London.

Thompson, J. E. S. 1966. *The Rise and Fall of Maya Civilization,* 2nd edition. University of Oklahoma Press, Norman.

Willey, G. R. 1966. *An Introduction to American Archaeology,* Vol. 1: *North and Middle America.* Prentice-Hall, Englewood Cliffs.

Wolf, E. R. 1959. *Sons of the Shaking Earth.* University of Chicago Press, Chicago.

Gordon R. Willey's classic article on the "Early Great Styles" serves as a link between our Mesoamerican and Andean articles. Willey discusses the stylistic similarities between the basal civilizations of the two areas, the Olmec and the Chavin. Contrary to the path which most archaeologists have followed, Willey looks to religion as one possible fundamental cause for the similarities between the two. A recent and provocative paper by Donald Lathrap takes this idea much further and should be consulted by all interested readers (see "Complex Iconographic Features Shared by Olmec and Chavin and Some Speculations on Their Possible Significance" in press in the *Primer Simposio de Correlaciones Antopologicos Andino-Mesoamericana,* Salinas, Ecuador).

The Early Great Styles and the
Rise of Pre-Columbian Civilizations[1]

Gordon R. Willey

Experience has shown that it is hopeless to storm, by a frontal attack, the great citadels of the causality underlying highly complex groups of facts. —A. L. Kroeber

In native America, not a great many centuries after the establishment of a village agricultural way of life, two major art styles of the first rank appear, more or less contemporaneously, in southern Mesoamerica and in northern Peru. These are known as the Olmec and the Chavín. I purpose to consider these two art styles, first, and briefly, as to their content and form and, secondly, but in more detail, in their cultural settings and from the general perspective of New World culture history. For what engages our attention is that both styles occur at that point in time which might be said to mark the very first stirrings of civilization in the Mesoamerican and Peruvian areas. What role did these art styles, or the motivations of which they are the symbols, play in the rise and development of pre-Columbian civilizations? Are they, the styles themselves, the touchstones of that condition we refer to as civilization? What do we know of their origins or, if not their origins, their pre-conditions?

Like most anthropologists who are interested in culture history I am interested in origins and causes, but I am not sanguine about the possibilities of easy or early victories. Certainly the answers to the ultimate causal questions as to why the ancient American civilizations began and flourished where they did and when they did still elude us, and what I can offer here will do little more, at best, than describe and compare certain situations and series of events.

Reproduced by permission of the American Anthropological Association and the author, from *American Anthropologist,* Vol. 64, No. 1, 1962.

My use of the term "great styles" is a special and intentional one. I refer to art styles and to manifestations of these generally considered as "fine arts" (Kroeber 1957: 24-26). Their greatness is judged in their historical contexts, but it is none the less real. These great pre-Columbian art styles of Mesoamerica and Peru are expressed monumentally; they occur in settings that were obviously sacred or important in the cultures which produced them; they are also pervasive, being reproduced in a variety of media and contexts; the products are rendered with the consummate skill of the specially and long-trained artist; they conform to strict stylistic canons; their subject matter tends to be thematic; and finally, the finest monuments or creations in these styles are truly powerful and awe-inspiring. These last criteria are subjective, but I do not think we can ignore them. We see ancient art—the word "primitive" is here most inappropriate—across the millennia and with the eyes of an alien culture; yet we are not unmoved. Man speaks to man through art, and the screen of cultural difference and relativism does not strain out all emotional effect. Olmec and Chavín art measure fully to standards of greatness.

Olmec and Chavín

The Olmec style of Mesoamerica has been known for 30 years as such. Stirling (1943) and his associates (Weiant 1943; Drucker 1943, 1952) fully revealed the style in their discoveries in southern Veracruz and Tabasco. They and Caso (1942) and Covarrubias (1942, 1946, 1957) made it widely known and also opened the question of its cultural and chronological position in Mesoamerican culture history (see also Greengo 1952; Coe 1957). Olmec art is rendered in life-size, or greater than life-size, full-round, and bas-relief stone monuments. These include free-standing heads, human and anthropomorphic figures, stelae, and altars. Carvings are also found on natural boulders after the manner of pictographs, but most of these are done with such skill and are so much a part of the deliberate style, that "bas-relief," rather than "pictograph," is the fitting term to describe them. Olmec sculptures also occur as small pieces: jade and serpentine figurines, celts, ornamental effigy axes, plaques, and other small ornaments. Ceramic objects in the Olmec style are less common but include figurines, pottery stamps, and vessels.

The central theme of Olmec art is a jaguar-human or were-jaguar being. The concept is nearly always expressed as more human, in total characteristics, than jaguar. The face is frequently infantile as well as jaguar-like, and in many instances actual human infant bodies are portrayed. But subtle shades of this infantile jaguarism infect almost all human or anthropomorphic representations, ranging all the way from only slightly snubbed, feline noses and down-turned dropping mouths to toothed and snarling countenances. Some stelae and monuments bear another concept, elderly men with aquiline noses and beards who are sometimes depicted with portrait realism; but there is also a fusion of the jaguar-like anthropomorph with the bearded man in Olmec iconography (Coe 1960 Ms). Other motifs are rarer: fully animalized jaguars, bird and duck monsters, serpents, and fish.

The formal properties of the Olmec style are highly distinctive. Although the subject matter is to a large extent in the mythological realm the portrayals are carried out with a "realistic" intent. It is thoroughly nongeometric and nonabstract; lines have a slow curvilinear rhythm, and free space balances figures. There is little fine detail (Coe

1960 ms). As a style it is the equivalent of any of the later great styles of Mesoamerica, and in the full-round treatment of the human body it is the superior of all.

The climax region of the Olmec style was southern Veracruz and Tabasco in such ceremonial center sites as La Venta, Tres Zapotes, and San Lorenzo. Insofar as the style is expressed monumentally there is little doubt but that this is its homeland. Elsewhere, Olmec monuments are widely scattered and occasional. Most are bas-relief figures carved on boulder outcrops, as in Morelos (Piña Chan 1955), Chiapas (Ferdon 1953), Guerrero (Jimenez Moreno 1959: fig. 4, Pl. I-a), Guatemala (Thompson 1948: fig. 111a), and Salvador (Boggs 1950). Aside from these monuments, portable objects of the Olmec style, such as jade figurines, ornaments, and small manufactures, are found throughout much of southern Mesoamerica, from the Valley of Mexico and Guerrero on the northwest down through Chiapas and Pacific Guatemala. Covarrubias (1957) held the opinion that Guerrero was the ancestral home of the Olmec style, in its pre-monumental era, but it has yet to be demonstrated that the numerous Olmec figurines found in that region are earlier manifestations of the style than the great sculptures of Veracruz-Tabasco. In any event, for our present discussion, it is sufficient to note that the climax of the "great" aspects of the style are in this latter zone but that the style as a whole is spread over much of southern Mesoamerica. Wherever it can be dated, Olmec art appears in the Middle pre-Classic Period of Mesoamerican history, with an outer dating range of 1000 to 300 B.C., and a probable more specific bracketing by radiocarbon determinations of between 800 and 400 B.C. (Drucker, Heizer, and Squier 1959:248-67).

Chavín style art is named for Chavín de Huántar, an imposing archaeological site in the Marañon drainage of the north highlands of Peru. Tello, more than any other archeologist, called attention to Chavín art (Tello 1942, 1943, 1960); subsequently, Bennett (1943, 1944), Larco Hoyle (1941), Kroeber (1944:81-93), and Carrion Cachot (1948) made significant contributions (see also Willey 1951; Coe 1954). Like Olmec, the Chavín style is one closely adapted to sculptural forms, both monumental and small. The heroic-sized sculptures are mostly free-standing monoliths or stelae, lintels, cornices, and decorative features of buildings. These are executed with a relief-incision and champlévé technique in stone or are modelled in clay. Some full-round carving and modelling is also attempted in heads or figures tenoned or affixed to walls or buildings. Chavín small carving produced stone and bone plaques, stone and gourd vessels, ceremonial stone mortars and pestles, and ornaments. The style also appears in finely modelled and incised pottery vessels, in repoussé goldwork, and even in textile designs. In sum, it enters into more varied media than the Olmec style, but both styles are most at home in carving, particularly in large sculptures and in the work of the lapidary.

The content of Chavín art, like that of Olmec, deals with a few powerful central themes. With Chavín the dominant motif is either the feline or the fusion of feline elements, such as fangs and claws, with other beings, including humans, condors, the cayman, and the serpent. The fantastic beings of Chavín art emphasize somewhat more the animal attributes than the human, in contradistinction to Olmec. Strictly human representations are rare, and none of these have the qualities of portraiture observed in some of the Olmec sculptures. Although firmly set in a unified style, the monster or composite beings, show great variations in the combination of jaguar or puma and other animal elements.

The formal properties of the Chavín style, which are its essence, are decidedly different from those of Olmec. No one would mistake the two styles in juxtaposition. Chavín is intricate with detail in a way that Olmec is not. It does not employ free space, but seeks to fill it with such things as small secondary heads and eyes disposed over the body of the central monster figure of the sculpture. There is little mastery of realism or naturalism. It has more features that are stiff and "archaic." As styles the two have common ground only in that they rely upon slow heavy curves rather than straight lines, and both have a quality of the esoteric about them rather than the obvious.

The heartland of the Chavín style, insofar as it is monumental and in stone or sculptured adobe, is in the north highlands of Peru, at such sites as Chavín de Huántar, Yauya, and Kuntur Wasi, and in the coastal valleys of Nepeña and Casma. This is but one sector of the larger Peruvian culture area, and as such this focal concentration is comparable to the distribution of Olmec art in the Veracruz-Tabasco region within the larger sphere of Mesoamerica. The wider compass of Chavín art, as expressed in small manufactures, takes in much of the Peruvian culture area. Formerly thought to embrace only the northern part of Peru, its definite influence is now traced as far south on the coast as the Cerrillos phase of the Ica and Nazca Valleys (Lanning 1959). Thus, in its total geographic extent Chavín outstrips Olmec, the latter being confined to the southern half, or less, of its culture area setting. Chronologically, Chavín art belongs to the Formative Period of Peruvian prehistory and to either the Early or Middle subdivision of that period, depending upon one's terminology. The gross estimated dates for the Peruvian Formative Period are approximately the First Millennium B.C. Within this range, and with the aid of radiocarbon determinations, the horizon of the Chavín art style is narrowed to between 800 and 400 B.C. (Collier 1959, 1960 Ms; Lanning 1959). As will be noted, this is identical to the dates for the time span estimated for the Olmec style in Mesoamerica. These two sets of dates, incidentally, were arrived at quite independently by different sets of archaeologists.

Olmec and Chavín in Culture Historical Perspective

As we have already observed, Olmec and Chavín styles make their first appearance on an underlying base of village agriculture. In Mesoamerica, village agriculture, defined as sedentary life based primarily upon maize cultivation, became established by about 1500 B.C., following a long epoch of incipient plant domestication (Willey 1960). The presence of ceremonial architecture, in the form of platform mounds for temples or other buildings, in the early centuries of Mesoamerican agricultural life is probable, although not well documented. But by 800 B.C., some 700 years or so after the village agricultural threshold, the great Olmec ceremonial center of La Venta was founded in Tabasco. At the same time that these events were taking place in Mesoamerica, similar and related ones were going on in Peru. At about 1500 B.C. a well-developed variety of Mesoamerican maize appeared in coastal Peru and was rapidly assimilated into the local root-crop agricultural economies of the Peruvian coastal communities (Lanning quoted from Collier 1960; Mangelsdorf, MacNeish, and Willey 1960 Ms). Soon after this the Peruvians were making pottery and building ceremonial mounds, and to clinch the relationships between Peru and the north at this time, a distinctly Mesoamerican figurine has been found in one of these early Peruvian ceremonial sites known as Las Aldas (Ishida and others 1960, 97 ff.) The Chavín style appears shortly after this. During its period, contact between Mesoamerica and Peru continued. For example, among the best known traits that have often been pointed to as linking the Olmec phase of Tlatilco and the Chavín Cupisnique phase are figurines, rocker-stamped pottery, incised and color-zoned wares, flat-bottomed open-bowl forms, and the stirrup-mouth jar (Engel 1956; Porter 1953; Willey 1955; Coe 1960).

In this setting of an almost exact equation in time, and with further evidences of contact in specific ceramic items, can we go further and argue that Olmec and Chavín are definitely related? Drucker (1952:231), Wauchope (1954), and I (Willey 1959) have all called attention to this possibility, and Della Santa (1959) has argued the case in earnest; but on reflection I do not think that the two styles show a close relationship. At least they do not exhibit a relationship which, in the realm of art, is a counterpart to the Mesoamerican maize in Peru or the Tlatilco-Cupisnique ceramic ties. What they possess in common, except for an addiction to sculptural and lapidaristic modes of expression, is largely for the concept of the feline being, most probably the jaguar.[2] Therefore, their relationship, if it existed, must have been on a level of concept and mythology, either an ancient undercurrent of belief on which both Peruvian and Mesoamerican societies could have drawn to develop quite different art styles or by a stimulus diffusion in which the source idea was drastically reworked in the recipient setting. In this last connection the example of Mesopotamian stimuli to the rise of early Egyptian civilization comes to mind. If this interpretation of the relationship between Olmec and Chavín is the correct one, I would, all things considered, see Mesoamerica as the source and Peru as in the role of the receiving culture.

An argument against a close, continuous Olmec-Chavín relationship on the level of style is, of course, the absence of either style, or any style definitely related to either, in the Intermediate area of Lower Central America, Columbia, and Ecuador. The San Agustín sculptures of southern Colombia are, perhaps, the only candidates (Preuss 1931; Bennett 1946:848—49); but they are remarkably unlike either Olmec or Chavín, sharing with them only the attribute of feline-fanged beings, and they are only dubiously dated on the same time level as Olmec and Chavín. Further, as a style, San Agustín is considerably below the quality or sophistication of these great styles (Kroeber 1951). This absence of stylistic linkages in the Intermediate area stands in contrast, however, to many of the significant traits of the village agricultural base out of which Olmec and Chavín seem to have developed. Evidence is rapidly accumulating from Ecuador (Evans and Meggers 1957, 1958; Estrada 1958), Colombia (Reichel-Dolmatoff 1959), and Lower Central America (Coe and Baudez 1961) which shows the Intermediate area to be a common participant in early ceramic and other traits held also by Mesoamerica and Peru. A notable example of this is the striking similarity between Guatemalan Ocos pottery and that of the Ecuadorean Chorrera phase (Coe 1960). Thus, in spite of this background of apparent intercommunication and interchange down and up the axis of Nuclear America, the entities of style which we recognize as Olmec and Chavín remain bound to their respective areas. They did not spread to the Intermediate area, nor can they reasonably be derived from there.

The Early Great Styles as Precursors to Civilization

We have placed Olmec and Chavín at that point in the developmental history of the Mesoamerican and Peruvian cultures where village farming societies undergo a transformation to become temple center-and-village societies. This event is another major threshold in pre-Columbian life. It is a different kind of threshold than that of village agriculture which precedes it by a few hundred years, but it signals important changes. It is, in effect, the threshold of complex society that leads on to civilization. The economy appears much the same as earlier; it is based on maize, or maize and root crops, supplemented with other American food plants. The technology includes pottery-making, weaving, stone carving—in brief, the village agricultural neolithic arts. Houses were permanent to semi-permanent affairs disposed in small hamlets or villages. The most noticeable difference on the cultural landscape is the ceremonial center. These centers were not urban zones. Heizer (1960) has made quite explicit the nonurban nature of La Venta, and he estimates that the constructions there could have been built and sustained only by the cooperative efforts of villagers from a surrounding radius of several kilometers. Although Chavín de Huántar is situated in a radically different natural environment from La Venta, it, too, appears to have been a complex of ceremonial buildings and chambers without a large resident population in close proximity (Bennett 1944; Tello 1960).

It is in such ceremonial centers that the outstanding monuments of the Olmec and Chavín styles are found. In Mesoamerica it is assumed that this ceremonial center-with-outlying hamlets type of settlement pattern is allied with a theocratic political structure. The assumption derives partly from the nature of the settlement and the feeling that such dispersed societies could only have been bound together by strong religious beliefs, but it derives mostly from our knowledge of the late pre- and early post-Columbian periods in Mesoamerica when lowland ceremonial centered societies were known to have a strong theocratic bias. In Peru this kind of theocratic orientation was not a feature of the Inca state; but there the archeological record shows a definite trend, from early to late times, that can best be interpreted as a movement away from religion as a dominant force and the gradual ascendance of secular power (Willey 1951). In the light of such trends it is likely that priest leadership was more important in Chavín times than later. Thus, archaeological inference is on the side of identifying the nonurban ceremonial center as primarily a sacred or religious establishment whatever other functions may have been served there. Olmec and Chavín works of art must surely, then, have been religious expressions. This concatenation of circumstances, the shift from simple village agricultural societies to complex temple-centered ones and the appearance of the two great styles, suggests that Olmec and Chavín are the symbols of two ecumenical religions. These religions lie at the base of the subsequent growth of pre-Columbian Mesoamerican and Peruvian civilizations (see Bernal 1960).

This fundamental underlying nature of Olmec and Chavín art is revealed in the later cultures and styles in the two areas. For Mesoamerica, Michael D. Coe (1960 Ms) suggests that all known major art styles of the southern part of the area have an origin in the Olmec style. Most directly related among these would be the styles of the slightly later "danzante" monuments at Monte Alban and the Monte Alban I phase effigy incensarios (Caso 1938), the Olmec-derived sculptures from the later pre-Classic Period levels at Tres Zapotes, the Izapa style stelae in Chiapas, and the closely similar Late pre-Classic monuments found recently in Kaminaljuyu. More remotely, but nevertheless showing affiliations with Olmec art, especially through the link of the Izapa style, would be the Classic Maya and Classic Veracruz styles (Proskouriakoff 1950:177, Covarrubias 1957:166). Further afield, the derivative influences are dimmed or uncertain. Classic Teotihuacan art stands most apart in showing little Olmec influence, and perhaps this may be correlated with the relatively slight impress of Olmec art on an earlier level in the Valley of Mexico where it is known mainly in the occasional Tlatilco ceramic objects. But that some connections, however indirect, did exist between Olmec and Teotihuacan iconography is shown by Covarrubias (1957: fig. 22) in his diagram of the stylistic evolution of the Teotihuacan and other rain gods from the prototype of the Olmec baby-jaguar face.

For Peru, the story is much the same. There, the distribution of the Chavín style was more nearly area-wide. Perhaps as a consequence, nearly all post-Chavín styles show some Chavín feline elements (Willey 1951). Mochica art, of the north coast, depicts a feline or anthropomorphic feline as an apparent deity. Feline symbolism has an important part in Recuay, Pucara, and Nazca cultures. It is present in Tiahuanaco art, although not as the dominant motif.

Considerations of Causality

We see Olmec and Chavín styles at the root of civilization in Mesoamerica and Peru. We also note, in the wider perspective of Nuclear America, that contemporaneous and related societies of the geographically intervening Intermediate area do not possess comparable great styles. Neither do they go on to civilization. From these facts I think we may reasonably conclude that Olmec and Chavín art are in some way involved with the rise to the status of civilization in their respective areas. But these are observations of history, or pre-history, and like all such observations it is difficult and perilous to attempt to read causality into them. In pointing to what I think is a special relationship between the early great styles and civilization, am I not merely defining civilization in terms of itself? In a partial sense I am; great art styles are one of the criteria by which the condition of civilization may be judged (Childe 1950). But it is not, however, altogether true in that many of the criteria of civilization are not yet present in either Mesoamerica or Peru at the time of Olmec and Chavín art florescence. Certainly one of the most significant of these, urbanization, is not; writing and metallurgy, if present, are only in their infancy; and the institution of the state, in any extensive territorial sense, is highly unlikely. The appearance of the first great styles, then, comes early in the growth of these American civilizations. By the time a full civilizational status has been achieved in either Mesoamerica or Peru these styles, as organized entities, have vanished, leaving only their residue in later styles. Nevertheless, styles themselves cannot be reified into civilization builders. They are, as I have said, symbols of institutions, attitudes, beliefs. Is, then, a belief system, a religion, a prime causal force as Toynbee has stated? I would think so, or at least I consider it near enough to a causal core to speculate on the processes whereby fundamental beliefs and their representative art may promote the growth of civilization.

In making these speculations let us consider a hypothesis about culture development in native America and particularly in the Nuclear American areas. Casting back to earlier chronological ranges than I have been talking about, it is now becoming evident that man changed from a collecting-hunting mode of existence to one of food plant cultivation by a process of introgression. The term is a botanical one, and it applies to what happened to plants over the several millennia leading up to village agriculture in Mesoamerica; but I also think it applicable to the culture change that went along with the gradual domestication of plants. The studies of Mangelsdorf and MacNeish (Mangelsdorf, MacNeish, and Willey 1960 Ms; MacNeish 1958 and personal communication 1961) have shown that original wild plants were found in a great many small locales where they were gathered and used and where seeds were eventually sown and plants tended by small, local populations. With contact between two such small communities, of plants and people, plant introgression and hybridization ensued with a genetically improved result. This process continued among enclaves with both hybridization and with the interchange of different species as well. Present investigations indicate that primitive maize, beans, and squashes do not follow the same sequence of occurrence in incipient agricultural stratigraphies in all parts of Mesoamerica but that the order varies from region to region (MacNeish, personal communication 1961). This diversity in development led, eventually, to the New World complex of food plants and to village agriculture. I would suggest that culture, too, evolved along with plants in much the same way, by introgression or interchange and by hybridization or fusion. This, I believe, is an aspect of what Lesser (1961) is saying in his concept of social fields. To follow the analogy, I think that this is what continued to happen in the development of cultures and societies after the attainment of village agriculture. Regional interchange or regional symbiosis provided an important impetus for change and growth. Sanders (1956, 1957; Braidwood and Willey 1960 Ms) has detailed this process for parts of ancient Mesoamerica. It led to civilization.

In this hypothesis an obviously crucial factor is natural environmental setting and a multiplicity of varied settings in relatively close juxtaposition to one another. As has been pointed out by various authors (eg., Wolf 1959: 17–18), Mesoamerica is well suited in this regard. It is a land of climatic, altitudinal, and vegetational variety; it is rich in natural resources. Further, the archaeological record shows trade and contact among distinct natural environmental and cultural regions from early times. Peru, as well, although not quite so varied, has dramatic regional differentiation, particularly between coast and highland; and the prehistory of that area may be read as a kind of counterpoint between the regional cultures of these natural zones (Kroeber 1927). Contrast the potentialities of these two areas with others of the New World which also had a basis of village agriculture. The natural environmental and cultural contours of differentiation within the Amazon basin or the Eastern Woodlands of North America are low in comparison. Products from region to region were the same or similar. Perhaps this homogeneity discouraged exchange (Coe 1961 Ms).

Are we, now, at the nexus of causality in the rise of pre-Columbian civilizations in certain areas but not in others? Although conceding the importance of intra-areal cultural heterogeneity, and realizing that such heterogeneity must be to a large extent based in natural environment, I am not convinced. What of the Intermediate area which lies between and close to both of our areas of high civilization and which did not match them in these conditions of civilization? It is an area of spectacular regional environmental differentiation, tropical and semi-arid coasts, tropical lowlands, semi-tropical and temperate valleys, cool-temperate uplands. It has them all, and it is not an area poor in resources. We also know that the communities of this area were in possession of agriculture about as early as those of either Mesoamerica and Peru. These village agriculturists were similarly skilled in pottery making and, probably, the other neolithic crafts. In fact, they participated in the same technical traditions as their Mesoamerican or Peruvian contemporaries. Where then is the lack? What are the essential differences between the Intermediate area and its native cultures and those of the Mesoamerican and Peruvian areas?

I return, again, to the great styles, to Olmec and Chavín, for which there is no counterpart from Honduras to southern Ecuador. I have suggested that they, in themselves, are but the symbols for the religious ideologies of the early farming societies of Mesoamerica and Peru. I would further suggest that in these ideologies these early societies had developed a mechanism of intercommunication, a way of knitting together the smaller parts of the social universe of their day into a more unified whole than it had heretofore been or would otherwise be. In a way similar to that of the interchange of objects, plants, and techniques which had previously prepared the village agricultural threshold, the sharing of common ideologies led to the threshold of civilization by enlarging the effective social field. By this enlargement more individuals, more social segments, more local societies combined and coordinated their energies and efforts than at any time before. Regional differentiation in culture is an important precondition to cultural development insofar as differences contribute to the richness of the larger order, but without union the different parts remain isolated and in danger of stagnation. There are various ways by which man has promoted such union, but mutually and deeply held beliefs seem paramount. Such belief systems were, I think, the distinguishing features of the Mesoamerican and Peruvian societies of the first half of the First Millennium B.C., and the great Olmec and Chavín art styles are our clues to them.

Yet, even if my thesis is accepted thus far, have we done more than follow the chimaera of causality into one more disguise? Why did Mesoamerica and Peru develop early great religions and art styles and other areas not? What was the reason for their genius? I do not know. I do not think that it sprang from a seed planted by Chinese voyagers—or from two seeds brought by two such sets of voyagers—despite the facts that the Chou dynasty is replete with prowling tigers and that the time element is right for such a transference (Heine-Geldern 1959). It does us no good to deny the sudden mutation of creative change to the aborigines of America. It is no easier to explain elsewhere than it is here. What we are seeking is probably in New World soil, but genius must arise from preconditions which to our eyes do not foreshadow it. Local prototypes of Chavín and Olmec may eventually be found, although these will only carry the story back a little in time and leave the startling florescences unexplained.

I do not reject in their entirety any of the factors or forces we have been discussing as having had possible important influence in the growth of New World civilization. Climate, soil, agricultural potential, natural regional variety, all undoubtedly were significant. I am hesitant, however, to pinpoint any one of them as *the cause*. I am equally hesitant to advance my thesis of any early, prevailing, multi-regional ecumenical religion in either Mesoamerica or Peru as a *sole cause* of later civilizational greatness. I ask, rather, that such phenomena as I have directed attention to be considered as a step in the process of cultural development— a step which almost certainly was taken in these two areas of native America. For it may be that we phrase the problem wrong, that the search for the very well-springs of origin and cause is meaningless, and that the limits of anthropology are to appraise and understand the continuum of process as it is disclosed to us rather than to fix its ultimate beginnings.

Notes

[1] The author gratefully acknowledges the critical reading of the manuscript and the suggestions made by M. D. Coe and D. W. Lathrap in July 1961.

[2] M. D. Coe has called my attention to a small but specific design element found in Olmec sculptures and also present on Chavinoid incised pottery from Kotosh, Peru, recently excavated by the University of Tokyo Expedition to Peru but not yet published. This element is a U-shaped figure with what may be a stylized ear of maize emerging from the opening.

References Cited

Bennett, W. C. 1943. The position of Chavín in Andean sequences. Proceedings of the American Philosophical Society 86:323—27.

———— 1944. The north highlands of Peru. Excavations in the Callejón de Huaylas and at Chavín de Huántar. Anthropological Papers of the American Museum of Natural History, Vol. 39, Pt. 1.

———— 1946. The archaeology of Colombia. In Handbook of South American Indians, Vol. 2, J. H. Steward, ed. Bureau of American Ethnology Bulletin 143.

Bernal, Ignacio. 1960. Toynbee y Mesoamérica. Estudios de Cultura Nahuatl 2:43—58. Mexico, Universidad Nacional Autónoma de Mexico.

Boggs, S. H. 1950. "Olmec" pictographs in the Las Victorias group, Chalchuapa archaeological zone, El Salvador. Notes, Vol. 4, No. 99, Carnegie Institution of Washington.

Braidwood, R. J. and G. R. Willey. 1960 Ms Conclusions. In Courses toward urban life. Symposium to be published by the Wenner-Gren Foundation for Anthropological Research, New York. Quoted by permission of the authors.

Carrión Cachot, Rebecca. 1948. La cultura Chavín. Dos nuevas colonias: Kuntur Wasi y Ancon. Revista del Museo Nacional de Antropología y Arqueología 2:(1:)99—172. Lima.

Caso, Alfonso. 1938. Exploraciones en Oaxaca; quinta y sexta temporadas, 1936—37. Instituto Panamericano de Geografía e Historia, Publicacion 34. Mexico, D. F.

———— 1942. Definicion y extension del complejo "Olmeca." In Mayas y Olmecas, segunda reunion de Mesa Redonda sobre problemas antropologicas de Mexico y Centro America, Sociedad Mexicana de Antropologia. Chiapas, Tuxtla Gutierrez.

Childe, V. G. 1950. The urban revolution. Town Planning Review 21:(1:)3—17. University of Liverpool.

Coe, M. D. 1954. Chavín: its nature and space-time position. Seminar Paper, Peabody Museum Library, Harvard University.

————— 1957. Cycle 7 monuments in Middle America: a reconsideration. American Anthropologist 59:597—611.

————— 1960. Archaeological linkages with North and South America at La Victoria, Guatemala. American Anthropologist 62:363—93.

————— 1960 Ms. The Olmec style and its distributions. Ms prepared for the Handbook of Middle American Indians. Quoted by permission of the author.

————— 1961 Ms. Social typology and the tropical forest civilizations. To be published in Comparative studies in society and history.

Coe, M. D. and C. F. Baudez. 1961. The zoned bichrome period in northwestern Costa Rica. American Antiquity 26:505—15.

Collier, Donald. 1959. Agriculture and civilization on the coast of Peru. Paper presented at the meeting of the American Anthropological Association, December 1959, Mexico, D. F.

————— 1960 Ms. The central Andes. In Courses toward urban life. Symposium to be published by the Wenner-Gren Foundation for Anthropological Research, New York. Quoted by permission of the author.

Covarrubias, Miguel. 1942. Origen y desarollo del estilo artistico "Olmeca." In Mayas y Olmecas, segunda reunion de Mesa Redonda sobre problemas antropologicas de Mexico y Centro America, Sociedad Mexicana de Antropologia. Chiapas. Tuxtla Gutierrez.

————— 1946. El arte "Olmea" o de La Venta. Cuadernos Americanos, 5:(4:)153—79. Mexico, D. F.

————— 1957. Indian art of Mexico and Central America. New York, Alfred A. Knopf.

Della Santa, Elizabeth. 1959. Les Cupisniques et l'origine des Olméques. Revue de l'Université de Bruxelles 5:340—63. Bruxelles.

Drucker, Philip. 1943. Ceramic sequences at Tres Zapotes, Veracruz, Mexico. Bureau of American Ethnology Bulletin 140.

————— 1952. La Venta, Tabasco, a study of Olmec ceramics and art. Bureau of American Ethnology Bulletin 153.

Drucker, Philip, R. F. Heizer, and R. J. Squier. 1959. Excavations at La Venta, Tabasco, 1955. Bureau of American Ethnology Bulletin 170.

Engel, Frederic. 1956. Curayacu—a Chavinoid site. Archaeology 9:(2:)98—105. Cambridge, Mass.

Estrada, Emilio. 1958. Las culturas pre-Clasicas, Formativas, o Arcaicas del Ecuador. Publicacion No. 5, Museo Victor Emilio Estrada, Guayaquil.

Evans, Clifford and B. J. Meggers. 1957. Formative period cultures in the Guayas Basin, Coastal Ecuador. American Antiquity 22:235—46.

————— 1958. Valdivia—an early Formative culture on the Coast of Ecuador. Archaeology 11:175—82.

Ferdon, E. N. 1953. Tonala, Mexico, an archaeological survey. School of American Research Monograph 16, Santa Fe.

Greengo, R. E. 1952. The Olmec Phase of eastern Mexico. Bulletin of the Texas Archaeological and Paleontological Society 23:260—92.

Heine-Geldern, Robert. 1959. Representation of the Asiatic tiger in the art of the Chavin culture: a proof of early contacts between China and Peru. In Actas del 33 Congreso Internacional de Americanistas, Vol. 1, San Jose, Costa Rica.

Heizer, R. F. 1960. Agriculture and the theocratic state in lowland southeastern Mexico. American Antiquity 26:215—22.

Ishida, Ehchiro and others. 1960. Andes, the report of the University of Tokyo Scientific Expedition to the Andes in 1958. University of Tokyo.

Jiménez Moreno, Wigberto. 1959. Sintesis de la historia Pretolteca de Mesoamerica. *In* Esplendor del Mexico Antiguo, Vol. 2. Mexico, D. F., Centro de Investigaciones Antropológicas de México.

Kroeber, A. L. 1927. Coast and highland in prehistoric Peru. American Anthropologist 29:625–53.

————— 1944. Peruvian archaeology in 1942. Viking Fund Publications in Anthropology No. 4. New York, The Viking Fund, Inc.

————— 1951. Great art styles of ancient South America. *In* The civilizations of ancient America, S. Tax, ed. Selected Papers of the 29th International Congress of Americanists, Vol. 1. University of Chicago Press.

————— 1957. Style and civilizations. Ithaca, Cornell University Press.

Lanning, E. P. 1959. Early ceramic chronologies of the Peruvian coast. Mimeographed. Berkeley, California.

Larco Hoyle, Rafael. 1941. Los Cupisniques, Lima, "La Crónica" y "Variedades."

Lesser, Alexander. 1961. Social fields and the evolution of society. Southwestern Journal of Anthropology 17:40–48.

MacNeish, R. S. 1958. Preliminary archaeological investigations in the Sierra de Tamaulipas, Mexico. Transactions of the American Philosophical Society, Vol. 48, Pt. 6.

Mangelsdorf, P. C., R. S. MacNeish, and G. R. Willey. 1960 Ms. Origins of agriculture in Mesoamerica. Ms prepared for the Handbook of Middle American Indians. Quoted by permission of the authors.

Piña Chan, Roman. 1955. Chalcatzingo, Morelos. Informes No. 4 Direccion de Monumentos Pre-Hispanicos, Instituto Nacional de Antropologia e Historia, Mexico, D.F.

Porter, M. N. 1953. Tlatilco and the pre-Classic cultures of the New World. Viking Fund Publications in Anthropology No. 19. New York, Wenner-Gren Foundation for Anthropological Research, Inc.

Preuss, K. Th. 1931. Arte monumental prehistorico 2 vols. 2nd ed. Bogotá, Colombia, Escuelas Salesianas.

Proskouriakoff, Tatiana. 1950. A study of classic Maya sculpture. Carnegie Institution of Washington Publication 593.

Reichel-Dolmatoff, Gerardo. 1959. The Formative Stage, an appraisal from the Colombian perspective. *In* Actas del 33 Congreso Internacional de Americanistas, Vol. 1. San Jose, Costa Rica.

Sanders, W. T. 1956. The Central Mexican symbiotic region: a study in prehistoric settlement patterns. *In* Prehistoric Settlement patterns in the New World, G. R. Willey, ed. Viking Fund Publications in Anthropology No. 23. New York, Wenner-Gren Foundation for Anthropological Research, Inc.

————— 1957. Tierra y agua (Soil and water). A study of the ecological factors in the development of Meso-American civilizations. Doctoral dissertation, Harvard University.

Stirling, M. W. 1943. Stone monuments of southern Mexico. Bureau of American Ethnology Bulletin 138.

Tello, J. C. 1942. Origin y desarrollo de las civilizaciones prehistoricas andinas. Actas y Trabajos Cientificos del XXVII Congreso Internacional de Americanistas, Lima, 1939. Tomo 1, pp. 589-720.

————— 1943. Discovery of the Chavin culture in Peru. American Antiquity 9:135–60.

————— 1960. Chavin, cultura matriz de la civilizacion Andina. Primera Parte. Revised by T. Mejia Xesspe. Publicacion Antropologica del Archivo "Julio C. Tello," Vol. 2. Lima, Universidad Nacional Mayor de San Marcos.

Thompson, J. E. S. 1948. An archaeological reconnaissance in the Cotzumalhuapa region, Escuintla, Guatemala. Contributions to American Anthropology and History, Vol. 9, No. 44. Carnegie Institution of Washington.

Wauchope, Robert. 1954. Implications of radiocarbon dates from Middle and South America. Middle American Research Records, Vol. 2, No. 2. Middle American Research Institute, Tulane University, New Orleans.

Weiant, C. W. 1943. An introduction to the ceramics of Tres Zapotes. Bureau of American Ethnology Bulletin 139.

Willey, G. R. 1951. The Chavín problem, a review and critique. Southwestern Journal of Anthropology 7:103–144.

———— 1955. The prehistoric civilizations of Nuclear America. American Anthropologist 57:571–93.

———— 1959. The "Intermediate" area of Nuclear America: its prehistoric relationships to Middle America and Peru In Actas del 33 Congresco Internacional de Americanistas, Vol. 1. San Jose, Costa Rica.

———— 1960. New World prehistory. Science 131:73–83.

Wolf, E. R. 1959. Sons of the shaking earth. Chicago, University of Chicago Press.

Donald Collier received his Ph.D. from the University of Chicago in 1955
and currently is Curator of Middle and South American Archaeology and
Ethnology at the Field Museum of Natural History in Chicago. His major
field work has been in Peru, where he was a member of the important
Viru Valley Project. In this article, he provides a concise background to
Central Andean prehistory and then proceeds to examine the factors which
led to the rise of urbanism in this area.

The Central Andes

Donald Collier

Introduction

The area under consideration includes the coast and highland of Peru and the adjoining Titicaca basin in Bolivia (Fig. 1). This stretch of the Andes contained a major native
areal culture with time depth, which Bennett has called the "Peruvian Co-tradition"
(Kroeber, 1944, p. 111; Bennett, 1948).

The narrow coastal region is an extremely arid but temperate desert cut transversely
at intervals by mountain-fed rivers that form oasis valleys. The highland consists of intermontane valleys and basins separated by lofty plateaus and high mountain passes. In the
coastal valleys intensive agriculture is dependent on irrigation, although small-scale cultivation is possible without irrigation in the moist areas at valley mouths close to the sea.
In the mountain valleys irrigation is less vital, but everywhere it increases crop yields. In
spite of differences between coast and highland, there are certain major uniformities.
Both regions have large cultivable areas with rich soils not covered with resistant grasses
or forest and with water available for irrigation. Temperature and other contrasts due to
differences in altitude are minimized by the cold Peru current and proximity to the
equator. The Peru current also accounts for an exceptionally rich marine fauna, which
amply compensates for the barrenness of the coastal desert. Both coastal and highland
valleys are geographically isolated but close enough to other valleys for trade and cultural
interchange.

Native history in the Central Andes may be divided into three major stages of subsistence. These are a largely inferred early hunting stage (about 8000 B.C. until an unknown date), a stage of food-collecting and incipient cultivation (2500–750 B.C.), and
a stage of agriculture (750 B.C.–A.D. 1532). The incipient cultivation stage includes two
major periods: the earlier Preceramic, which lacked both ceramics and maize, and the

Reprinted from Robert J. Braidwood and Gordon R. Willey, editors, *Courses Toward Urban Life,*
(Chicago: Aldine Publishing Company, 1962); copyright © 1962 by Wenner-Gren Foundation for
Anthropological Research, Inc. Reprinted by permission of Aldine·Atherton, Inc.

Figure 1. The Central Andes

Subsistence Stages	Periods	North Coast	North Highland	Central Coast	Central Highland	South Coast	South Highland
INTENSIVE AGRICULTURE	POSTCLASSIC	Inca	Inca	Inca	Inca	Inca	Inca
		Chimu	Late Huamachuco	Late Chancay Late Ancón	Early Inca	Late Poroma Ica	Callao
		B.W.R. Geom Coast Tiahuanaco	Middle Huamachuco Wilcawaín	B.W.R. Geom Coast Tiahuanaco	Huari Lucre	Middle Ica Huari Pacheco	Decadent Tiahuanaco
ESTABLISHED AGRICULTURE	CLASSIC	Mochica Galli nazo ← ←	Recuay B	Nievería	Waru Derived Chanapata	Nazca ←	Pucara Classic Tiahuanaco
			Recuay A	Maranga			
	FORMATIVE	Gallinazo Salinar	Huaraz W-on-R	Playa Grande Baños de Boza	Classic Chanapata	Paracas Paracas	Early Pucara Tiahuanaco Chiripa
		Cupisnique Cupisnique	Kuntur Wasi Chavín de Huantar	Colinas Curayacu 2 (Early Ancón)	Marcavalle	Paracas Cerillos	
INCIPIENT CULTIVATION	INITIAL	Middle Guañape Early Aldas Guañape		Curayacu 1 Aldas			
	PRE-CERAMIC / CERAMIC	Huaca Cerro Prieta Prieto		Aspero Río Seco		Asic Atuma	

A.D. / B.C.

1532 — 800 — A.D. / B.C. — 400 — 750 — 1200 — 2500

Figure 2. Cultural periods in the Central Andes

later Initial Ceramic, which included pottery-making and the cultivation of maize (Fig. 2). The agricultural stage is divisible into an earlier substage of established agriculture[1] (Formative period) and a later substage of intensive agriculture (Classic and Postclassic periods).

In a previous paper on the development of agriculture in Peru (Collier, n.d.) the Initial Ceramic was included as the first subperiod of the Formative, but I pointed out that in terms of subsistence patterns it should be grouped with the Preceramic in a stage of incipient agriculture. The Initial Ceramic could well be set apart as a transitional stage between the stages of incipient cultivation and established agriculture.

Early Hunters

As yet, evidence of the early hunting stage in the Central Andes is minimal. Heavy, pressure-flaked, stemmed and/or lanceolate projectile points have been found on the coast in Chicama Valley, at San Nicolás south of Nazca, in the highland in caves near Huancayo, and in a surface deposit at Viscachani south of La Paz, Bolivia (Bird, 1948, p. 27; Larco Hoyle, 1948, pp. 11–12; Strong, 1957, pp. 8–11, Tschopik, 1946; Menghin, 1953–54). Although typológically these finds appear early, there is no evidence linking them with extinct Pleistocene mammals, and both geological and absolute dates are lacking. But the presence of early hunting cultures at the southern tip of the continent shortly after 7000 B.C. (Bird, 1938; 1946; 1951, pp. 44–46), and the recent discovery of an apparently early lithic assemblage near Quito, Ecuador (Bell and Mayer-Oakes, 1960), strengthen the probability that the Central Andean finds pertain to the early hunters. Until additional geological and archeological investigations are made, nothing reliable can be said about the environment and the ecological adaptations of these post-Pleistocene hunters.[2]

Collectors and Incipient Cultivators

At present there is a hiatus between the inferential early hunting stage in the Central Andes and the beginning of incipient cultivation about 2500 B.C. This gap may have been occupied by a food-collecting stage, during which a culture similar to the shell fishhook culture of northern Chile (Bird, 1943) existed along the Peruvian coast, but as yet no remains of this hypothetical fishing culture have been recognized.

More than forty habitation sites of the incipient cultivation stage, called the Preceramic in Peruvian archeology, are known from the Peruvian coast (Bird, 1948; Engel, 1957a, b, 1958). The earliest of these seems not to have been occupied before 2500 B.C. These sites are located near the sea at the mouths of rivers or on the shores of coastal lagoons. Subsistence of these people, as revealed by plant and animal remains recovered from refuse deposits, was based on collecting wild fruits and tubers, gathering shellfish, catching fish by net and line, taking sea lion and porpoise by unknown methods, and cultivating squash, chili peppers, jack beans *(Canavalia)*, lima beans,[3] and achira tubers. They also cultivated gourds, which were used for containers and net floats, and cotton, which they made into cordage, nets, twined and looped textiles, and, rarely, woven textiles. This first cultivation was carried out without irrigation in the moist areas at the mouths of valleys, which were the natural habitat of some of the wild plants gathered for food.

The surprisingly crude stone tools of these people were roughly chipped flakes, cores, and hammerstones. Pressure flaking was absent on the north coast but seems to have been practiced by the Preceramic peoples on the central and south coasts. Fish-hooks were of shell. Stone projectile points were not made except on the south coast. Cooking was done with heated stones, thousands of burned fragments of which are found mixed with the shells in the refuse deposits. Houses were small rectangular or oval structures of beach cobbles, rough stone, adobe, or wattle-and-daub construction, with roofs supported by beams of wood or whalebone. Settlements consisted of a few to a dozen houses scattered at random on the refuse deposits. At two of the sites there are specialized structures that may be the first shrines or community buildings.

Toward the end of the Preceramic, woven textiles appear at most sites, and at the very end of the period, probably between 1400 and 1200 B.C., the first maize is found. The evidence consists of a few maize cobs in the upper levels of four Preceramic sites (Lanning, 1959, p. 48; personal communication, 1959). The first pottery appears about 1200 B.C., marking the beginning of the Initial Ceramic period (Bird, 1948; Strong and Evans, 1952; Lanning, 1959). The first pottery was simple in form and undecorated; color was variable because of lack of control in firing. Later, burnishing and incising were added. These early pottery-makers cultivated peanuts and maize in addition to the plants of the Preceramic period. In spite of the use of these new food plants, there was no immediate shift in subsistence pattern, and settlements were still close to the sea. Probably there was a progressive increase in dependence on cultivated plants, but evidence for this is lacking. There was a gradual shift from twined to woven textiles, and jet mirrors, which may have had ritual uses, were made for the first time. Some of the Initial Ceramic settlements were larger than those of the Preceramic and contained small temple centers. The most impressive of these is the terrace-pyramid-sunken-court complex built of rough basalt blocks at the Aldas site on the north-central coast (Engel, 1957b; Lanning, 1959).

In contrast to the coastal region, there is no evidence bearing on the presence and nature of human occupation of the highland during the Preceramic and Initial Ceramic periods.

Agriculturalists

Formative period

During the Formative period full-time agriculture was achieved and many of the basic traditions or trends were established in Central Andean technology, religion, and art.

The Formative began with the appearance of loom weaving,[4] the Chavín style of ceramics and stone carving, the use of gold for ornaments, and at least three new plants—warty squash, sweet manioc, and avocados. Although there is no direct evidence of canal irrigation at this time, the shift from seaside to inland settlements, the size of some settlements, and the magnitude of some of the ceremonial centers they supported suggest that water control had advanced beyond simple flood-water irrigation.

The community consisted of several villages of stone or adobe houses clustered about a ceremonial nucleus. In some valleys the ceremonial centers were small, simple platform structures of stone or adobe. In others they were large stepped platforms of stone or adobe with sculptured, incised, or painted decorations. The most elaborate center, at Chavín de Huantar in the north highland, was composed of a sunken court flanked by stone-faced platforms and a terrace surmounted by a massive temple of dressed stone containing a honeycomb of interior galleries. The temple and other buildings were ornamented with stone sculpture and low-relief carving on stelae and flat slabs.

The Chavín style and associated religious cult, which was centered around jaguar and serpent deities, spread widely and rapidly over much but not all of the Central Andes. But there is no evidence of wide political control or organized warfare. Probably the villages supporting a ceremonial center were integrated by priestly leadership.

The later Formative was a time of regional development and experimentation. It was characterized by the following important new traits and developments: expanding canal irrigation; agricultural terracing; kidney beans, pepino fruits, and quinoa; domesticated llama,[5] alpaca, and guinea pig; coca-chewing; positive and negative painting on pottery; and ornaments of copper and copper-gold alloy. Wool was used in textiles, and weaving techniques were elaborated. Weavers produced turbans, headbands, shirts, shawls, breechcloths, and girdles, which together comprised the basic Peruvian clothing pattern from this time onward.

The number of villages greatly increased, but they remained small. Groups of villages were clustered around pyramid mounds of stone or adobe. Elaborate hilltop fortifications of stone were constructed, probably for defense against intervalley raids. Variations in the richness of burial offerings suggest differences in wealth and social status.

Classic period

The full utilization in the Classic period of the Formative technologies emphasized the geographical differences of size and fertility of regions, and these differences played a part in the development of marked regional specialization. Of particular significance are the following Classic traits and complexes: intensive agriculture based on transvalley irrigation systems and use of fertilizer; marked population increase; craft specialization and production of luxury goods; the construction of enormous temple mounds of adobe bricks; ornaments of gold, copper, silver, and their alloys; copper tools and weapons; class-structured societies; state control under the leadership of priest kings; and organized warfare. Villages became larger, and a few towns, clustered around the temple pyramids, grew by accretion until they contained a thousand or more closely packed dwellings.

Postclassic period

The Postclassic period is characterized by increased warfare, progressive urbanization, mass production of goods, and final political unification of the Central Andes under the Inca empire. Planned urban centers laid out on a rectangular grid and enclosed by defense walls appeared at the beginning of the period and reached a climax in Chanchan, the Chimu capital, which had a population estimated at 50,000. The growth of cities coincided with the development of inter-valley irrigation systems. Mold-made domestic pottery was mass produced, and bronze was used for the first time.

Discussion

Owing to a gap in our knowledge of Andean prehistory, it is not possible to assess the degree and nature of the intensification of food-collecting prior to the emergence of incipient cultivation in the area. When initially observable, about 2500 B.C., the first cultivated plants, playing together a minor subsistence role, fitted neatly into a well-diversified system of exploitation of wild food plants and marine fauna. The moist areas at valley mouths that were most favorable for initial cultivation were also the habitat of the most useful wild food plants, and these places were convenient to the marine food supply. This congruence of the loci of food resources accounts for the concentration of settlements in such locations throughout the stage of incipient cultivation in the coastal zone. It is noteworthy that two of the cultivated plants, the gourd and cotton, were of no immediate food value but were important in net fishing.

The first maize, which probably appeared about 1400 B.C., one or two centuries before pottery, was a primitive and not very productive variety. It seems to have been of minor importance in subsistence throughout the Initial Ceramic period. Only in the early Formative (Chavín) subperiod, five or six hundred years after the first maize, did this plant assume a major role. At this time an improved form of maize was introduced, and warty squash, sweet manioc, and avocados were added to the earlier cultivated plants. Effective food production (established agriculture) can be said to have begun (Fig. 2). But even before this, in the Initial Ceramic period, plant cultivation seems to have had a cumulative effect, for it was already possible for small ceremonial centers to develop. Thus, in the Central Andes, in contrast with Mesoamerica, the ceremonial center had its beginning before full food production.

It is not at present possible to identify the effects of expanded cultivation in terms of changes in the tools of food production and preparation, but the inventory of food remains in refuse, and the location and size of settlements do reflect the new pattern. There was a progressive shift of settlements away from the sea, marine foods diminished in importance, and villages became larger. These shifts seem to have resulted from the increasing productivity of plant cultivation and the inadequacy of the valley mouths for the expanding agriculture. The ability to build and maintain large ceremonial centers at this time and the development of elaborate stone architecture and sculpture also suggest the effectiveness of food production. The extent of canal irrigation, which was well developed in the following subperiod (late Formative), is still uncertain.

The problem of the origin of the patterns of incipient cultivation and of effective food production in the Central Andes is extremely complex, and it is not possible to review here the relevant botanical and cultural evidence. It is probable that both patterns were stimulated at least in part by diffusion of plants and ideas from Mesoamerica. Specimens of maize in both the Preceramic and the Chavín period include varieties that are related to Mexican races that have greater antiquity in the north (Mangelsdorf, 1959; personal communication, 1960). Effective agriculture, including improved varieties of maize, began spreading southward from Mesoamerica shortly before 1000 B.C. (Mangelsdorf, MacNeish, and Willey, n.d.), and the beginning of established agriculture in Peru about 750 B.C. at the start of the Chavín period appears to be a reflection of this diffusion. This conclusion is strengthened by other cultural evidence. For example, a number of ceramic traits of Chavín are found in various pottery complexes of the middle Formative period in Mesoamerica (Porter, 1953; Coe, 1960), and a connecting link is found in the ceramics of the Chorrera period on the coast of Ecuador (Meggers and Evans, 1957). There seems little doubt that these traits diffused from north to south.

On the other hand, the presence in Peru of non-Mesoamerican maize and bean varieties of considerable antiquity suggests the possibility that there were primary or secondary centers of plant domestication in the Central Andes (or neighboring areas), as well as in Mesoamerica. Furthermore, the highland complex of Central Andean root crops, which appears to be very old and to have been largely independent of maize cultivation until the Postclassic period (Sauer, 1950, pp. 513–19; Murra, 1956, pp. 13–31), may well have developed quite independently of Mesoamerican influence. The connection between this complex and Sauer's suggested center of root-crop domestication in northeastern South America (Sauer, 1953, pp. 40–73) is an important but, at the moment, completely speculative question.

In the Central Andes the establishment of effective food production had a markedly explosive effect. In the brief span of 750 years, which comprised the Formative period as used in this paper, the culture of the coast of Peru developed from a simple, relatively uniform level to the complexity of the regionally differentiated Classic cultures, which were on the threshold of civilization. This rapid evolution contrasts sharply with the slow development in the preceding stage of incipient cultivation, during which culture changed relatively little, in spite of the introduction of maize and ceramics. If, as it appears, Formative development was more rapid in the Central Andes than in Mesoamerica, the explanation probably lies in the fact that Peruvian village-farming culture was initially established at a more complex level than in Mesoamerica as a result of strong cultural influence from the latter area.

I have shown in Figure 3 the general time of appearance in the Central Andes of various aspects of urban life. The first ten characteristics are Childe's criteria of the city (Childe, 1950), arranged in the order of their appearance. Two of these—large settlements and writing—have been subdivided to bring out the special situation in Peru. Highways have been added as an additional important characteristic of urbanization.

It is seen that half these urban characteristics were developed during the Formative period and that by the early part of the Classic the only essential traits lacking were really large settlements and some form of notation. In the Postclassic, large, planned cities were built, state control was vastly extended, a highway system was developed, and there was a system of numerical notation (the quipu); but writing was completely absent. There was a notable lack of development in mathematics, astronomy, and calendrics; undoubtedly these lacks were related to the absence of writing. And yet the Incas were able to maintain a governmental bureaucracy, to construct elaborate public works (roads, bridges, canals, and terrace systems), and to carry out social and economic planning (city planning, "valley authorities," and resettlement projects). The quipu was evidently adequate for keeping track of statistical and fiscal matters—census figures, army statistics, stocks in government storehouses, the size of llama herds, and the like. But it could not be extended beyond these functions, and the valuable economic and demographic data recorded on the Inca quipus were lost to us with the passing of their professional keepers, the *quipu-camayoc,* after the Spanish conquest.[6]

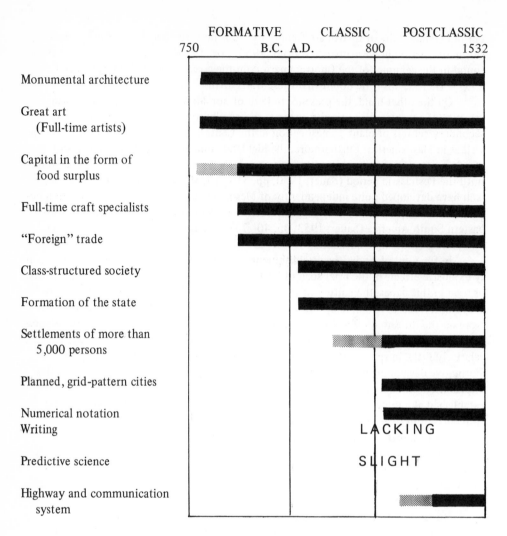

Figure 3. The time of appearance of aspects of urbanism in the Central Andes.

In terms of Central Andean data the most essential preconditions of urbanization appear to be (*a*) an intensified food production capable of producing substantial surpluses, (*b*) a high population density, and (*c*) an economically and socially differentiated society. All these were found in Peru by the end of the Formative. Of the three, a dense population seems to be the most essential. On the Peruvian coast maximum density was on the order of twenty-five times that of the density during the Chavín (early Formative).[7] This maximum was achieved by the Middle Classic in some valleys (e.g., Virú, Chicama) but not until the Postclassic in others (Lambayeque, Casma, Rimac).[8] The situation in these coastal valleys suggests a correlation, which needs much more substantiation, between the first really large settlements and near-maximum population density.

In the Central Andes, as apparently in other areas that developed cities, urbanization tended to intensify further the characteristics mentioned above as preconditions. For this reason it is extremely difficult to distinguish cause from effect in the process of urbanization. The more precise determination, both qualitative and quantitative, of these preconditions and investigation of the varieties of urbanization itself appear to be the two more fruitful approaches to an understanding of the urbanization process.

Notes

[1] The term "established agriculture" was introduced by Willey (1960).

[2] Since this was written, Kardich (1960, pp. 107–14) has published a brief description of an early lithic sequence in caves at Lauricocha, Department of Huánuco, Peru. The earliest of three preceramic horizons (Lauricocha I) contained crude flake tools (scrapers and perforators but no projectile points), animal bones, and human skeletons. Carbon samples from this horizon have yielded a date of 7566 $\pm$ 250 B.C.

[3] Lima beans (*Phaseolus lunatus*) occurred in the earliest levels at Huaca Prieta (M.A. Towle, personal communication, 1960).

[4] It is not clear whether the loom was already in use in the initial ceramic period.

[5] The llama may have been domesticated in the early Formative or toward the end of the Initial Ceramic.

[6] It was asserted by a few chroniclers that the quipu was used to record history, but there is no evidence to confirm this and it seems improbable.

[7] This estimate is based on Virú valley data (Willey, 1953).

[8] Available data (Collier, n.d.; Kosok, 1959; Schaedel, 1951; Stumer, 1954; Willey, 1953) point to this conclusion, but much more supporting evidence is needed.

Bibliography

Bell, Robert E., and W. J. Mayer-Oakes. 1960. "An Early Lithic Site near Quito, Ecuador." (Paper delivered at the 25th Ann. Meeting, Soc. Amer. Archaeol., New Haven, May 5, 1960.)

Bennett, Wendell C. 1948. "The Peruvian Co-tradition." In W. C. Bennett (ed.), *A Reappraisal of Peruvian Archaeology*, pp. 1–7. ("Mem. Soc. Amer. Archaeol.," No. 4.) Menasha, Wis.

Bird, Junius B. 1938. "Antiquity and Migrations of the Early Inhabitants of Patagonia," *Geo. Rev.*, 28:250–75.

――― 1943. *Excavations in Northern Chile.* ("Amer. Mus. Nat. Hist. Anthrop. Papers," Vol. 38, Part 4.) New York.

――― 1946. "The Archeology of Patagonia." In J. H. Steward (ed.), *Handbook of South American Indians*, pp. 17–24. (Smithsonian Inst., Bur. Amer. Ethnol., Bull. 143, Vol. 1.) Washington, D.C.

――― 1948. "Preceramic Cultures in Chicama and Viru." In W. C. Bennett (ed.), *A Reappraisal of Peruvian Archaeology*, pp. 21–28. ("Mem. Soc. Amer. Archaeol.," No. 4.) Menasha. Wis.

――― 1951. "South American Radiocarbon Dates." In F. Johnson (ed.), *Radiocarbon Dating*, pp. 37–49. ("Mem. Soc. Amer. Archaeol.," No. 8) Salt Lake City.

Childe, V. Gordon. 1950. "The Urban Revolution," *Town Planning Review* (Liverpool), 21:3–17.

Coe, Michael D. 1960. "Archeological Linkages with North and South America at La Victoria, Guatemala," *Amer. Anthrop.* 62:363–93.

Collier, Donald. 1955a. *Cultural Chronology and Change as Reflected in the Ceramics of the Virú Valley, Peru.* (Chicago Nat. Hist. Mus., Fieldiana: "Anthropology," Vol. 43.) Chicago.

———— 1955b. "Development of Civilization on the Coast of Peru." In J. H. Steward (ed.), *Irrigation Civilizations: A Comparative Study.* (Pan American Union Soc. Sci. Monogs., 1:19–27). Washington, D.C.

———— 1958. "El Desarollo de la Civilización Peruana," *Revista Colombiana de Anthropología*, 7:271–87. Bogotá.

———— n.d. "Agriculture and Civilization on the Coast of Peru." (Paper given in the Symposium on the Evolution of Native Horticultural Systems in South America, Ann. Meeting A.A.A., Mexico, December 28, 1959.) (In press.)

———— n.d. "Archaeological Investigations in the Casma Valley, Peru." (Paper presented at the 34th Internat. Cong. of Americanists, Vienna, July 20, 1960.) (In press.)

Engel, Frederic. 1957a. "Early Sites on the Peruvian Coast," *Southwestern J. Anthrop.*, 13:54–68.

———— 1957b. "Sites et Établissments sans Céramique dans le Côte Peruvienne," *J. Soc. des Américanistes* (Paris), 46:67–155.

———— 1958. "Algunos Datos con Referencia a los Sitios Precerámicos de la Costa Peruana," *Arqueológicas.* (Museo Nacional de Antropolgía y Arqueología, Lima), Vol. 1, No. 3.

Kardich, Augusto. 1960. Investigaciones Prehistóricas en los Andes Peruanas. In *Antiguo Peru: Espacio y Tiempo* (Trabajos Presentados a la Semana de Arqueología Peruana, 9–14 Noviembre de 1959), pp. 89–118. Lima.

Kosok, Paul. 1959. "El Valle de Lambayeque." In *Actas del II Congreso Nacional de Historia del Peru, 1958,* pp. 49–67. Lima.

Kroeber, A. L. 1944. *Peruvian Archeology in 1942.* ("Viking Fund Publs. in Anthrop.," No. 4.) New York.

Lanning, Edward P. 1959. "Early Ceramic Chronologies of the Peruvian Coast." Berkeley. (Mimeographed.)

Larco Hoyle, Rafael. 1948.*Cronología Arqueológica del Norte del Perú.* Buenos Aires.

Mangelsdorf, Paul C., Richard S. MacNeish, and Gordon R. Willey. n.d. "Origins of Agriculture in Mesoamerica." In Robert Wauchope (ed.), *Handbook of Middle American Indians,* Vol. 1. (In preparation.)

Mangelsdorf, Paul C., and Robert C. Reeves. 1959. "The Origin of Corn IV: Place and Time of Origin." *Bot. Mus. Leaflets*(Harvard Univ.), 18:413–27.

Meggers, Betty J., and Clifford Evans. 1957. "Formative Period Cultures in the Guayas Basin, Coastal Ecuador."*Amer. Antiq.,* 22:235–47.

Menghin, O. F. A. 1953–54. "Culturas Precerámicas en Bolivia," *Runa* (Buenos Aires), 6:125–32.

Murra, John V. 1956. "The Economic Organization of the Inca State." (Unpubl. Ph.D. diss., Univ. Chicago.)

Porter, Muriel N. 1953. *Tlatilco and the Pre-Classic Cultures of the New World.* ("Viking Fund Publs. in Anthrop.," No. 19.) New York.

Rowe, John H. 1956. "Archaeological Explorations in Southern Peru," *Amer. Antiq.,* 22:135–50.

Sauer, Carl O. 1950. "Cultivated Plants of South and Central America." In J. H. Steward (ed.), *Handbook of South American Indians,* pp. 487–543. (Smithsonian Inst., Amer. Ethnol., Bull. 143, Vol. 6.) Washington, D.C.

————— 1952. *Agricultural Origins and Dispersals.* New York: American Geographical Society.

Schaedel, Richard P. 1951. "Major Ceremonial and Population Centers in Northern Peru." In Sol Tax (ed.), *The Civilizations of Ancient America,* pp. 232–43. *Sel.Papers 29th Internat. Cong. Americanists.* Chicago.

Strong, William Duncan. 1957. *Paracas, Nazca, and Tiahuanacoid Cultural Relationships in South Coastal Peru.* ("Mem. Soc. Amer. Archaeol.," No. 13.) Salt Lake City.

Strong, William Duncan, and Clifford Evans, Jr. 1952. *Cultural Stratigraphy in the Viru Valley, Peru: The Formative and Florescent Epochs.* ("Columbia Studies in Archael. and Ethnol.," Vol. 4.) New York.

Stumer, Louis M. 1954. "Population Centers of the Rimac Valley, Peru," *Amer. Antiq.,* 20:130–48.

Tschopik, Harry, Jr. 1946. "Some Notes on Rock Shelter Sites near Huancayo, Peru," *Amer. Antiq.,* 12:73–80.

Willey, Gordon R. 1953. *Prehistoric Settlement Patterns in the Viru Valley, Peru* (Smithsonian Inst., Bur. Amer. Ethnol., Bull. 155.) Washington, D.C.

————— 1960. "Historical Patterns and Evolution in Native New World Cultures." In Sol Tax (ed.), *Evolution after Darwin,* Vol. 2: *The Evolution of Man,* pp. 89–118. Chicago.

Willey, Gordon R., and John M. Corbett. 1954. *Early Ancon and Early Supe Culture.* ("Columbia Studies in Archaeol. and Ethnol.," Vol. 3.) New York.

Kent C. Day is completing his Ph.D. at Harvard University and currently
is affiliated with both the Royal Ontario Museum and Trent University
in Canada. He has had extensive field experience throughout the New
World, including excavations in the Great Basin and the Southwestern
United States, the Guatemalan highlands and lowlands, and the northern
coast of Peru. In this paper, which appears here for the first time, Day
examines the fall of the great city of Chanchan, which along with
Teotihuacan and Tenochtitlan, ranks as one of the biggest and most
important Precolumbian urban centers in the New World. A vast research
program at Chanchan under the direction of Dr. M. E. Moseley and
Dr. Carol MacKey is now nearing completion. The appearance in the
near future of the final publications of this important project should
greatly augment our knowledge of the processes of Precolumbian urbanism. Day's short paper is a good indication of the value which these new
data will have.

Walk-in-Wells and Water
Management at Chanchan, Peru

Kent C. Day

One of the problems faced by any population in a city is to provide themselves an
adequate and continuous supply of potable water. At Chanchan, where the climate was
arid and there was no available surface water nearby, the problem of water supply was
acute. The solution was relatively simple: wells were dug. These wells were important in
themselves but were only one aspect of a system of relationships that included physical
setting, community settlement pattern and socioeconomic organization of the site. The
intent of this paper is to examine the content of the water supply at Chanchan and suggest the following systemic relationships.

1. The various groups who made up the social matrix of Chanchan depended
upon a steady water supply from numerous, elaborate walk-in-wells. Such wells were
dug and in use according to the population size and density of the site with no apparent concern for diminishing the ground water supply.

2. This supply remained more than adequate as long as an extensive irrigation system was maintained in the formerly desolate area upslope from the site.

3. Responsibilities and rights to construct, maintain, and expand the major hydraulic works rested in the hands of those who had the status and power to make and
enforce public decisions. Such capacity was a prerogative and duty of the Chimu leaders resident in the great ciudadelas. Their position was probably sanctioned by socio-
economic status relevant to land tenure, water rights, and a religious or ceremonial aura.

4. Capitulation of the Chimu leaders to the Inca was partially due to the disruption of the irrigation system by the Inca or lack of maintenance of the system during the Inca seige.

5. Since the city was probably also a symbol of centralized Chimu authority, the change in leadership and shift in power base from Chanchan to Cuzco effectively destroyed the former exploitation pattern of the Moche valley.

In order to understand how these factors are related, it is necessary to describe the physical setting and the community settlement pattern of Chanchan. Socioeconomic inferences drawn from these data provide a background for the systemic interpretation of water management and use of wells by the Chimu.

Physical Setting

Chanchan was built near the foot of a low ridge that separates the main, perennial course of the Moche River from the dry bed of Rio Seco. The NNW-SSE long axis of the ridge slopes downward from Cerro Cabras toward the site and the sea. In common with much of the coast, the ridge consists of Quaternary sands and gravels that act as a natural aquifer (Cossio and Jaen 1967: 56—7). Aerial photographs (Shippee-Johnson series, 1932) and ground survey show that many large fields existed north of Chanchan on the seaward slope of Cerro Cabras. These fields were irrigated from a complex system of canals and feeder ditches that had their source in both the Chicama and Moche valleys. The largest and highest canals from the two valleys converge on the lower slope of Cerro Cabras nearly due north of Chanchan. Recently, this major hydraulic network has been partially mapped and a few sections of it intensively investigated (Kus 1971). Based on this preliminary work, it appears certain that the large canals were in operation between AD 1000 and 1400 when Chanchan was occupied. The borders of irrigated fields that run north from Chanchan to the canals align along the same axis as the site and are additional evidence for the temporal relationship. Another factor that indicates contemporaneity of the canals and their subsidiary ditches and fields with Chanchan is a long road that reaches in nearly a direct line from the west side of the site to the junction of the Chicama-Moche canal. If nothing else existed, this road linking the site with the canal junction demonstrates the relationship of the largest Chimu site in the valley to a critical point in the ancient water distribution system.

As a supplement to the natural ground water, subsoil filtration from the large canals, ditches and irrigated fields above Chanchan would have charged the aquifer and raised the water table. If this assumption is correct, it follows that, as long as the canals remained in operation and the fields under more or less continuous cultivation, the flow of ground water beneath Chanchan would have been augmented. Conversely, if the canals were not kept in operation and the fields left fallow or abandoned, the water table would drop in volume and depth to its natural level.

Community Settlement

Assuming that density of settlement, formality of layout, quality of architecture, residence proximity, conspicuous utilization of space, separateness, and amount of storage facilities are indicative of corporate unity and socioeconomic standing, four resident groups at Chanchan can be postulated.

Ciudadela Group: High status, small groups appear to have been resident in part of the spacious, formally organized ciudadelas. These great rectangles are divided into three parts, two of which contain large courtyards, colonnades, several U-shaped buildings, scores of storerooms and a few specialized structures. The third part, the *canchone,* is separated from the other two sectors by a transverse wall. This area, discussed below, lacks the massive architecture characteristic of the rest of the ciudadela.

Access to the ciudadela is frequently limited to one or two entries. Corridors off the main entries lead to large entry courts, beyond which are tortuous corridors leading to smaller open courts or courts containing U-shaped buildings. Additional corridors interconnect the U-shaped buildings or lead to storage areas.

The storage areas consist of isolated courts containing contiguous or closely set rows of gable ended structures. These structures are 2.5 to 4.5 meters square and have single entries, frequently with thresholds a meter high. Since no remains of domestic activities have been found in or near any of these structures, it is doubtful they were used as living quarters. Although there is little evidence for what was stored in these buildings, their size, high entries, compact arrangement, and semi-isolation suggest they were storage facilities.

It is evident that, in order to reach the storage facilities in the ciudadelas, it was necessary to pass by or through a court containing a U-shaped building. Therefore, the group that possessed the right to occupy U-shaped buildings had control over the passage of people and goods to or from the storerooms. Thus, by their location, the residents in the U-shaped buildings would have had the power to direct the economy, amass wealth, and maintain their high status.

As noted above, since the field borders and road from the site to the canal junction are orderly, massive and integrated into the layout of the ciudadelas, the high status ciudadela groups probably extended their influence beyond the city as administrators of water distribution, land utilization, and production.

Small Enclosure Group: Another group of high status residents at Chanchan is represented by the inhabitants of the small enclosures described by West (1970). Similar to the great ciudadelas, many of the small enclosures contain architectural elements and share certain aspects of the formalized arrangement of the ciudadelas. Although none has been cleared, entry courts, corridors, U-shaped buildings, and storerooms are common features in many of the small enclosures. The lesser socioeconomic status of the residents here is indicated by the lack of tripartite divisions of the enclosures, smaller amounts of open space, fewer storerooms, and no specialized structures. Thus, the residents in the small enclosure groups seem to have shared some of the status of the ciudadela residents but on a lesser scale of complexity and grandeur. Rather than leaders, these people may have been functionaries closely associated with the high status administrators at Chanchan.

Canchone/Annex Group: The third sector of each ciudadela is an open area called a *canchone.* At the other north end of several ciudadelas there is an annex surrounded by high walls. Both of these areas contain ruins of low structures and large amounts of domestic debris. The most distinctive architectural features of the canchone/annexes, however, are cobble-based platforms and sunken passages. The platforms vary somewhat in size and shape but are usually 5 to 10 meters to a side and are square or rectangular in plan. The surface of the platforms is generously covered with food remains, sherds, and charcoal. In addition, a few pieces of reed impressed wall or ceiling plaster have been found there. This evidence suggests that perishable dwellings once stood on the platforms.

Sunken passages occur around and among the platforms. Those passages located nearest entries to corridors or the main entry in the north ends of the ciudadelas are about 3 meters wide. Corridors about the house platforms are smaller the farther they are from the principal entries of the ciudadelas. A few small colonnades and gable storerooms occur in the annexes but not in the canchones. It is probable that the canchone/annex groups could, with further excavation, be subdivided into two groups. For the moment, however, they are designated as a single social unit because of the similarity of house platforms and sunken passages found in both localities.

When compared to the other sectors of the ciudadelas and the small enclosures, the canchone/annex area is more crowded, lacks large open spaces, monumental buildings, tortuous corridors and extensive storage facilities. The people who lived here were probably lower on the social scale than the ciudadela and small enclosure groups. Due to their presence within or adjacent to the ciudadelas the canchone/annex groups were possibly craftsmen or specialists directly dependent upon the economic life of the city for survival and identity.

Small Residence District: A fourth social group lived along the southern and western sides of the site and at scattered locations adjacent to ciudadelas and small enclosures. Cobble, pebble and adobe brick foundations of small agglutinated rooms, middle piles and countless sherds are characteristic of these areas. Most of the room outlines are adjacent or contiguous with one another. The middens are scattered among the rooms or partially cover abandoned rooms. Sherds and other domestic debris appear everywhere upon or just beneath the present surface in this district. The rooms in this area are about 2 to 4 meters to a side and seem to have had compact earth or garbage filled floors. Walls and ceilings were probably built of canes and plaited reeds. Storage pits, firepits, and postmolds are found inside the rooms, frequently filled with garbage. Food remains and other domestic equipment have been found in the middens and in the floor fill of the rooms. In a few cases, bin-like structures have been found adjacent to rooms. It is likely that these bins were household storerooms.

In contrast to the other parts of the site, the layout, architecture, use of space, and storage facilities in the small residence district are the least sophisticated or elaborate at the site. Wherever they appear, the small residences consist of structures that are crowded together and appear to lack any overall plan except in those localities where they are bounded by other, larger structures. Furthermore, the homogeneity of the small residences is an indication that their inhabitants lived in a similar way and probably shared a uniformly lower socioeconomic status than the rest of the occupants of Chanchan. The people who lived in this district may have been a landless population that formed a ready labor pool involved in manual work in fields, canals, or the city. A steady source of potable water from the walk-in-wells probably tended to hold the residents of this district to their settlement.

The Walk-in-Wells

There are many subsurface excavations at Chanchan that were dug to reach the
water table. Near the coast there are three huge, rectangular cuts that are man-made en-
largements of natural erosion channels (Aerial Photographs of the Servicio Aereofoto-
grafico Nacional, Peru). These cuts are relatively well known (most recently Parsons
1969; Rowe 1969; Moseley 1969; West 1970) and are variously called *pukios, mahamaes,*
or *wachakes.* At Chanchan the *pukios* are presently under cultivation and some of the
crops in them are irrigated with water drawn from shallow, hand-dug wells. Inland, among
the ruins of the site there are at least 125 large pits that probably served as walk-in-wells
for the population of Chanchan. Although wells have hardly been mentioned in the
twentieth century literature about Chanchan, Martinez de Compagnon (Kosock 1965),
Bandelier (Kosock 1965), and Squier (1877) all note how common they are at the site.

The walk-in-wells that have been found in the past year are square or rectangular
in plan and are usually about 10 to 15 meters to a side and 2 to 6 meters deep. One exceptionally large walk-in-well in ciudadela Tschudi is about 60 meters wide, 140 meters
long and 8 meters deep. Here, the difference between the water table surface in a hand-
dug well and the ancient water mark on the walls clearly shows that the water table
has dropped as much as 3 meters since Chimu times. The present water surface in a
test pit in a walk-in-well east of ciudadela Tschudi is slightly more than a meter below
undisturbed sediments in the bottom of the well.[1]

Remnants of cobble and adobe brick faced walls, terraces, and ramps still exist in
some of the wells. The ramps were built along walls of the wells and usually slope downward from one corner to another. Some wells are furnished with two ramps that descend
in opposing angles on facing walls. In addition, a few of the others have a single or a pair
of spiral ramps that descend from the mouth downward to opposite corners before reaching the bottom. In several instances there is a slot cut into one corner of the mouth of a
well to accommodate the entry of a ramp. Occasionally adobe brick or cobble faced wall
remnants are found around the mouths of wells. The walls around the perimeter of the
wells indicates that access was limited, perhaps to a single entry. Although a deep test pit
was excavated in one of the walk-in-wells, no finished floor was found upon the natural
deposits at the bottom. If any floors exist, they may well be found around the edges of
the wells or at the foot of the ramps.

[1] The present water table level is probably affected by recent irrigation near Chanchan and does not necessarily indicate the depth of the water table at the time the site
was abandoned. Other recent changes that certainly affect the present water table level
include water use and disposal by the population around Trujillo and the use of pumps
to draw ground water for irrigation in the valley.

Interpretation

The best preserved walk-in-wells are located within and between the ciudadelas and along the western side of the site. Each of the ten ciudadelas and their annexes at the site has at least one walk-in-well within its confines and some have as many as 15 (Rivero 2; Tschudi 2; Chaihuac 8 (?); Laberinto 6; Tello 1; Uhle 15; Bandelier 5; Velarde 12; Squier 4; Gran Chimu 14; Total 69). Two wells near the center of the site are surrounded by high walls, completely isolated from the ciudadelas or other structures. The remaining wells are located around the ciudadelas and are particularly numerous on the western and southern edges of the site.

Fifty-four walk-in-wells occur in association with the small residence district and small enclosure units, although they are more common among the small residences. Even though it is unlikely that the entire area of the small residences was covered with dwellings at the same moment, it is clear this district was the most densely populated part of the site. In contrast, the small enclosure units contain less domestic debris than the small residence district and, therefore, probably held fewer residents.

The ciudadelas probably had at least two kinds of permanent residents, one group living in the ciudadela itself and another living in the canchone/annex. The two sectors of each ciudadela that are devoted to large, open courts, U-shaped buildings, storerooms, and other specialized structures usually are furnished with a single "kitchen court." Packed deposits containing food remains, firepits, charcoal and culinary pottery occur only in these kitchen courts. Considering how relatively little space is devoted to domestic activities and how much to open space or storage within the ciudadelas, it seems likely that few people lived there as permanent residents.

Domestic debris and evidence of dwellings occur in abundance in the canchones at the seaward ends and in the annexes attached to the landward ends of the ciudadelas. The house platforms and amount of domestic debris in these areas indicates that this group—who were furnished with walk-in-wells—were also more numerous than the exclusive ciudadela group.

It is obvious from the distribution of walk-in-wells, therefore, that they occur most frequently where the greatest number of people lived. Although, at present, it is impossible to determine exactly the population of Chanchan, the community settlement pattern noted above, plus the number and distribution of walk-in-wells (assuming they are all roughly contemporary), are factors indicative of a dense population, perhaps as great or greater than the 69,000 suggested by West (1970).

Although the Chimu may not have been aware that their canals and irrigation system were charging an aquifer beneath Chanchan, their discovery of ground water and its utilization from wells was probably an important consideration in the establishment of the city and certainly one of the determining factors in the continued occupation of the site. An event that is said to have occurred about 1470 points out the importance of water distribution to the Chimu and the residents at Chanchan. The seventeenth century chronicle of Fernando de Montesino (1930:117) states that Inca Tupac Yupanqui subjugated the Chimu with a notable stratagem:

Después de muchas consultas se arbitró en una, que supuesto que los valles se

regaban con agua y ríos de la sierra, y que sin ellos no podían pasar los
Chimo, que se cortasen las madres y se dividiesen por diferentes parajes,
para que no se pudiesen aprovechar los Chimos de las acequias, y que con
esto se rendirían para siempre. Fué uno de los majores arbitrios que se
dieron, porque al punto envió muchos gastadores el Inga, acompañados
con cuatro mil soldados, y en breves días divirtieron el río de Chimo por
unos arenales que lo bebían todo.

He goes on to say that, once informed of this event, the Chimu capitulated to the
Inca and became tribute-paying vassals. Kosok (1965:82) mentions that, according to
local tradition, the Inca cut off the water supply to Chan Chan but the inhabitants there
survived with water drawn from hidden canals. It was not until the hidden canals were
revealed to the Inca that the water supply was destroyed and the city capitulated. There
is no evidence for any hidden canals, and I doubt if they existed at Chan Chan. On the
other hand, the Inca tactic of canal destruction was probably remembered correctly.
Hence, it is possible that one or more of the breaks far up valley in the Chicama and
Moche branches of the canal which led to the vicinity of Chanchan were made by Inca
invaders. If such disruption of the hydraulic system were laid to the Inca seige and water
was diverted back to the river channels high in the valleys, much of the irrigation system
near Chanchan would have been in disarray and the canals dry. Were this the case, Chanchan could survive for some time upon water from the aquifer (the hidden canal?) beneath the city. However, if the canals were cut near their source and the irrigated fields
above the site abandoned for long, the water table would drop and the wells run dry,
eventually forcing the abandonment of the city. And, it is clear that the massive irrigation system above the city has lain abandoned, but almost intact to this day.

Another related event of great importance seems to have occurred when the
Chimu capitulated to the Inca. Kosok (1965) relates that, under Inca rule, the last independent king of Chanchan was replaced by one of his sons, and the new puppet king's
residence was established at Mansiche, a few kilometers from Chanchan. It is reported,
too, that when the king was replaced Chimu craftsmen and specialists from Chanchan
were relocated to Cuzco in service to the Inca. Similar to the abandoned canals and
fields, the ciudadelas, small enclosures, and canchones/annexes that the resettled leaders,
functionaries, and draftsmen once occupied now lie in ruins. Since both the hydraulic
system and the elaborate parts of Chanchan were linked together during the occupation
of the site and both were apparently abandoned at the same time, it is clear that the high
status residents of the site were probably responsible for the construction, maintenance,
and control of the major hydraulic system.

It is evident then that the Inca conquest—attendant with the resettlement and diminished authority of the Chimu leaders—sundered the administrative system associated
with the large scale waterworks. Although the canals could have been repaired and it
would have been a relatively simple matter to deepen the wells at Chanchan until the
water table was restored to its former height, such tasks were not undertaken. There is
some archaeological evidence, however, that Chanchan was occupied between the time
of the abandonment of the city and the arrival of the Spanish. Although no Inca materials
have yet been found in the city, remains of small, crude dwellings have been found in the

entry courts of some of the ciudadelas. The lateness of these buildings is attested by their pebble and adobe brick foundations having been built upon blowsand and dirt that had accumulated upon the original court floors subsequent to the abandonment of the ciudadelas. Furthermore, these late structures were not built in accordance with the architectural canons characteristic of the ciudadelas, small enclosures, or even the house platform groups in the canchones and annexes. Since the late structures are most similar to dwellings found in the small residence district, they probably represent the homes of people from there who moved into the courts vacated by higher status residents. It is not known when these last squatters left the city. Apparently they stayed long enough to plant gardens in abandoned courts but did not attempt to reactivate the massive canals or irrigation system on the slope north of the site. It is likely, though, that they deepened some of the walk-in-wells in the city and used others as sumps to catch drain water from their gardens.

Of the four postulated groups, the high status residents in the ciudadelas probably had the most far reaching power and authority to manage the exploitation of natural and human resources. Their socioeconomic advantages are reflected in their relatively small numbers, disproportionately large amount of storage space at their residences, and their isolation. Indeed, the great walls of ciudadelas may symbolize the socioeconomic separateness of their residents from the rest of the populace.

If, as seems to be the case, the various high status residents held sway over land utilization, water distribution, public works, economic activities, political life, and ceremonial standards of Chanchan, the city could exist only as long as they were present. Moreover, continued occupation of the city naturally depended upon water, and the water supply was directly related to the hydraulic system and land tenure. The walk-in-wells were one aspect of such a closed system of leadership, land use, and water distribution. Once this system was disrupted and the administration displaced, it was never restored to its former pattern. Subsequent changes in population, administration, settlement, and technology have resulted in different systems and patterns of utilization of some of the same land and water resources exploited by the Chimu.

References

Cossio, Aurelio y Hugo Jaen. 1967. Geologia de los cuadrangulos de Puemape, Chocope, Otuzco, Trujillo, Salaverry y Santa. *Boletin No. 17,* Servicio de Geologia y Mineria, Ministerio de Fomento y Obras Publicas, Republica del Peru. Lima

Kosok, Paul. 1965. *Life, Land and Water in Ancient Peru.* New York

Kus, James S. 1971. *An Archeogeographic Investigation of the Chicama-Moche Canal, Peru.* PhD Dissertation, University of California, Los Angeles.

Montesinos, Fernando. 1930. Memorias antiguas, historiales y politicas del Peru. *Coleccion de Libros y Documentos referentes a la Historia del Peru,*Tomo 6. Lima

Moseley, M. Edward. 1969. Assessing the Archaeological Significance of Mahamaes. *American Antiquity,* Vol. 34, No. 4. Salt Lake City

Parsons, Jeffrey R. 1969. The Archaeological Significance of Mahamaes Cultivation on the Coast of Peru.*American Antiquity,* Vol. 33, No. 1, pp. 80-5. Salt Lake City

Rowe, John H. 1969. The Sunken Gardens of the Peruvian Coast. *American Antiquity,* Vol. 34, No. 3, pp. 320-5. Salt Lake City

Squier, Ephraim G. 1877. *Incidents of Travel and Exploration in the Land of the Inca.*

New York

West, Michael. 1970. Community Settlement Patterns at Chan Chan, Peru. *American Antiquity*, Vol. 35, No. 1, pp. 74-86. Salt Lake City

Craig Morris (Ph.D., University of Chicago, 1967) is an assistant professor
of anthropology at Brandeis University, and Donald E. Thompson (Ph.D.,
Harvard University, 1962) is a professor of anthropology at the University
of Wisconsin. They both have had extensive field experience in Peruvian
archaeology and have written a number of articles on their excavations.
In this paper, they use their data from the well-preserved Inca center of
Huánuco Viejo in the Peruvian highlands in order to test some basic
general assumptions about the rise of cities.

Huanuco Viejo:
An Inca Administrative Center

Craig Morris
Donald E. Thompson

Abstract
*Survey and excavations carried out at the Inca administrative center of Huánuco
Viejo revealed a large city with a ceremonial and palatial section, large residential zones,
and huge storage facilities. Well-cut Cuzco style masonry was limited to the ceremonial
areas, which included platforms, gateways, a bath and an elaborate apartment, probably
intended to house royalty or important officials. The residential districts were Inca
derived in architecture and planning, and the pottery was virtually limited to Inca inspired wares, thus demonstrating a lack of influence in either architecture or ceramics
of the local peasants who served at the site. The huge storage areas housed mostly local
highland produce which was used to sustain the city, mita laborers, and transients, and
was probably not used for extensive redistribution to the local villages in the surrounding area. The city, then, must be described as an artificial device imposed by the Inca
for administrative and political purposes, rather than as a city which arose because of
local conditions or needs.*

Introduction

This discussion of the former Inca administrative center of Huánuco Viejo, now an
extensive ruin located in the North Central Highlands of Peru, is based on part of the results
of a broader project conceived by John V. Murra (1962a) for a study of provincial Inca
life (Fig. 1). Drawing upon the fields of ethnology, botany, ethnohistory, and archaeology,
the project was built around a detailed 16th century *visita* to Huánuco (Ortiz de Zúñiga

Reproduced by permission of the Society for American Archaeology and the authors from *American
Antiquity*, Volume 35, No. 3, 1970.

1920-25, 1955-61, 1967), and had as one of its major objectives the study of provincial villages and the peasant populations under Inca rule (Thompson 1967, 1968a, 1968b, 1968c; Thompson and Murra 1966). The *visita* contained detailed census data and much testimony regarding economic organizations, political structure, and religion during the period of Inca domination, and it was felt that archaeological data would substantially augment the information provided in the *visita*.

In addition to the location and study of local peasant communities which fell under Inca rule, it would obviously also be important to know something about the local Imperial Inca administrative center at which the surrounding population served and to which they carried goods and produce, as the *visita* indicates.

Since the work done at Huánuco Viejo was part of a larger project, its character was determined by the part it played in a broader research design rather than by a program of research which was aimed specifically at the city as an entity. This in part accounts for the incomplete nature of our results; certain aspects of the city received far greater attention than others.

Central to the study of the site was the search for evidence of relationships, particularly economic relationships, between the administrative center and its subject villages. These relationships were investigated through the hundreds of storehouses in which goods brought by village residents were stored in Huánuco Viejo and by comparison of the architecture and ceramics of the city's residential zones to those of the villages. Peripheral to this interest in city-village relationships, some general documentation of the local manifestations of Imperial Inca culture was made to provide comparative data and suggest the degree to which Cuzco derived traits became modified in distant provinces of the empire. The general documentation sought to provide basic information about the site's architecture and planning and how this architecture and planning related to activities in the city and to its overall functions. Our conclusions in this regard are both limited and tentative, but they hopefully form the basis from which worthwhile questions can be raised for further work and for comparison with data from other Inca centers as these become available.

The plans for collecting architectural and ceramic data in the city for comparison with village architecture and ceramics were based on the hope that it would give us concrete and roughly quantitative information of the extent to which the people of the local ethnic groups were involved in the city's activities. Since the city was presumably built by *mita* labor service, it was thought that the architecture might reflect the varying local peasant traditions of its builders, giving us an idea of the contributions various groups had made. It was also thought that the domestic pottery used by the builders and subsequent inhabitants of the residences could have been in the local, rather than in the Cuzco Incaic, traditions. This could have provided for the archaeological definition of several ethnic "neighborhoods." Due to the relatively good state of the site's preservation, it seemed likely that such a study could be based almost entirely on surface remains.

In an initial test of the feasibility of these plans, large surface collections were made from the site's various zones, a rapid and superficial, but fairly complete, survey of the architecture was made, and several test pits were placed in various parts of the site to determine if any significant stratigraphy was present. The analysis of that material suggested that most of the significant variation lay in the realm of function; the stratigraphic tests showed only a shallow Inca occupation over sterile earth, and essentially no evidence linking the city with the villages of the surrounding countryside was obtained. While this last conclusion was in itself important to an understanding of the nature of Huánuco Viejo, it indicated that even a very large and systematic sampling of the city's surface architecture and ceramics would not produce data relevant to the original questions. Further work was thus confined to the storage zone and to increasing the above mentioned general documentation, particularly in the ceremonial sections.

The plans for the study of storage had also envisioned the possibility of varying ceramic traditions as indicators of the origins of stored goods, but from the outset they also included a functional study dealing with the kinds and quantities of goods stored. Toward these ends systematic excavations were necessary, as described in a later section.

Huánuco Viejo is one of a number of administrative centers built along the highland Inca highway between Cuzco and Quito. Along the road between the administrative centers are smaller *tampu* or way stations a day's journey apart. Although they vary in

Fig. 1. Outline map of modern Peru. The location of Huánuco Viejo is shown in relation to the ancient Inca capital of Cuzco and the modern capital of Lima.

Fig. 2. Plan of Huánuco Viejo. The map is partially based on aerial photographs and is incomplete since many buildings are not shown and the dimensions of many of those that are shown may not be precise. The dotted lines indicate the approximate boundaries of the ruins in sections which are badly destroyed. The dashed lines running from the Central Plaza indicate the position of the Inca Highway. The *qollqa* to the southwest follow the curvature of the hill on which they are built, the highest and most distant row being 192 meters above the Central Plaza.

detail, the administrative centers have much in common in overall plan. Usually present is a large plaza flanked by buildings, some of which may be quite long. A small platform or *ushnu* is usually in the center of the plaza. Present also are storage facilities, usually on a hillside above the site. Residential zones vary in organization and placement, but it is usually possible to distinguish at least one zone of elite residence. The *tampu* between the administrative centers are in some ways like miniature versions of the larger sites. A plaza flanked by some long buildings, a few warehouses, and housing including an elite section is usually present.

A comparison of the ceramics from several administrative centers and *tampu* indicates that while almost all such pottery is Cuzco Inca inspired, minor variations in shape and paste would suggest local manufacture to Inca specifications rather than importation from Cuzco for the majority of the vessels used at the sites. As will be brought out in greater detail below, this situation fits well with what we know of the economic and political organization worked out by the Inca for conquered territories.

Previous research at Huánuco Viejo has been neither very frequent nor very detailed. Since Sobreviela and Sierra's (1786) map of Huánuco Viejo, various travellers have visited and commented briefly on the site, outstanding among whom were Reginald Enock (1905, 1907), who described and illustrated sections of the site, and Antonio Raimondi (Raimondi 1874; Squier 1877), who drew one of the most accurate maps ever published of the ceremonial sections of the site. In more recent years, Huánuco Viejo has been visited by Donald Collier of the Field Museum and by the Japanese expedition of 1958, in the report of which is published a fuller bibliography than we are providing here (Ishida and others 1960). Huánuco Viejo also figures in the broader *Historia de Huánuco* published by José Varallanos (1959), but the fullest recent treatment is that of Emilio Harth-Terré (1964), which includes a number of plans and photographs.

Our own work at Huánuco Viejo began in 1964 and continued through 1966. All full time members of the project participated in the work there to some degree, but we were aided periodically by many others, amongst whom we should especially mention Manuel Chávez Ballón, Luis Barreda Murillo, John Cotter, and Peter Jenson. Some preliminary results of the work have appeared in essays by Shea, Murra, and Hadden in *Cuadernos de Investigación* (1966) and in papers by Shea (1968), Morris (1967), and Thompson (1968a, 1968b, 1968c, 1969). In the paragraphs that follow, we plan to describe some of the lesser known details of this huge and fascinating site (Fig. 2), and to discuss some of the conclusions we have reached concerning the ways in which it functioned.

The Ceremonial Sections

Those parts of Huánuco Viejo which make use of the rare, finely cut and fitted, Imperial Inca style masonry, and which appear by the presence of unusual building types to have served special functions, have been designated as ceremonial sections. There are two main areas so classified; the so-called *Casa del Inca,* which occupies a large part of the eastern section of the city, and the main central plaza itself, especially the central platform, called the *Castillo* or *Ushnu.* Other areas within Huánuco Viejo undoubtedly served ceremonial functions, but it is very difficult to identify such zones though some attempts have been made to do so. Harth-Terré (1964), for example, claims to have identified the *aqllawasi* (house of the chosen women) among other things.

The *Casa del Inca* and the central plaza really form one continuous complex, and the breakdown used here is merely for convenience. The *Casa del Inca* is approached from the plaza by passing eastward between the ends of two long buildings, called *kallanka,* that face on the plaza, and then continuing through a series of three sets of gates separated by courtyards. The gates themselves are constructed of high quality Imperial Inca style masonry, but the adjoining walls are of *pirka* (fieldstone set in mud). Maps of the whole section have been sketched by Raimondi (Squier 1877:216) and Harth-Terré (1964), among others.

The *kallanka,* which form the eastern side of the plaza, are large buildings which contain no cut and fitted stones but are built of high quality *pirka* masonry. The northern and larger of the two *kallanka* measures over 11 by 71 meters and has 9 doorways opening westward onto the plaza, 10 windows on the east side, a pair of windows high up in the gable on the north end wall, and a doorway in addition to a pair of similar windows in the south end wall. Excavations revealed that there were probably at least 7 necessary central posts helping to support the roof. The presence of horse and cow teeth confirms the later use, quoted below, of the building as a corral after it had burned. The scarcity of sherds in the excavations suggests that pottery was not important in the original functioning of the structure. The *kallanka* to the south is slightly smaller and has 5 windows and 4 doors, rather than 9 doors, facing the plaza. The function of these structures remains uncertain, although they are a common type of building in Inca sites, turning up in small *tampu* such as Tunsucancha (Morris 1966) as well as in other large sites. They could have served as barracks, as counting houses, or any one of a number of other purposes. They are almost certainly the buildings to which Vásquez de Espinoza (1942: 486) was referring when he wrote in 1616:

> . . . all around were many outbuildings, beginning with two galpones or halls, each large enough to contain a racecourse, and with many doors; this must have been where the Indian chiefs and lords were lodged, when visiting the kings; at present they are used for stabling cattle. Between these two large halls one enters a square plaza, fenced in; opposite these two gates there were and still are two other gates, well built of hewn stone, with the insignia of the kings, and a slab on top over 3 varas long and well carved, serving as an arch for the gates; these gates stood opposite each other and 10 feet apart; Farther on is another enclosed plaza, very well laid out, with two other gates, one in front of the other; then another plaza like the preceding, with two other gates beyond, of the same hewn stone. From outside, all the gates could be seen, and many apartments and private rooms, all in hewn stone, and some baths; doubtless this was where the king lived; and there were other large buildings, with a wall encircling all the settlement.

The hewn stone gates referred to by Vásquez de Espinoza are, of course, the ones of Imperial Inca masonry; the "insignia" are the crudely carved figures, perhaps pumas, adorning either side of the tops of some of the gates.

The inner section of the *Casa del Inca* is made up of some 15 structures of various types and functions. The masonry ranges from the well-dressed Imperial Inca style to crude *pirka*. Today, as one passes eastward through the last of the gates, one immediately sees the fine masonry fo the two best-preserved houses. A closer examination reveals that this pair of houses forms the eastern end of a group of six structures which surround a central courtyard. The four others, however, are badly fallen and only foundations and bits of low wall remain; indeed, the exact positions of doorways and corners are not always completely certain. All the structures open onto the central courtyard, however. A ditch may once have crossed the courtyard, but if so it was probably covered.

The two easternmost structures of Imperial Inca style masonry have typical trapezoidal niches in those walls that remain high enough to preserve these features. The buildings are also divided lengthwise by a central wall. Since the ground slopes down toward the east at this point, these central dividing walls also served a retaining function, and the rooms to the west had higher floor levels than those to the east. Whether communication between these rooms was possible is uncertain, given the buildings' state of preservation. These two buildings also form a single structural unit in the sense that their facing end walls form a passageway with a good trapezoidal gateway at the eastern end. This passage links the courtyard just described to another open space to the east, an area to be discussed shortly.

To the south of this main house group is a second group of three houses opening onto a common courtyard, the fourth side of which is formed by a freestanding wall. These houses are of *pirka* masonry.

To the east of this small group is a covered ditch which enters the complex from the south. To the east and below the ditch lies a large walled sunken area which was probably a pool fed by the ditch. Within the pool are two squarish mounds, rather like small artifical islands.

Below the pool is a sunken bath of good, Imperial Inca style masonry. The bath contains a pair of trapezoidal niches and, on the western side, a pair of channels cut into the stone provided ducts for the water. A wall, now badly fallen, once surrounded the bath. To the north of the bath is an open space—a kind of courtyard—bounded on the south by the bath, on the west by the lower western rooms of the pair of well-built houses, on the north by two squarish buildings, and on the east by the retaining wall of a large terrace. The two structures to the north have interior dividing walls, but they are difficult to discuss without excavation for it is likely that they have been modified in historic times, probably to serve as animal pens.

The large terrace to the east of the whole complex appears to be a flat-topped structure with two slightly higher platforms on top. The ground slopes here and, as a result, the eastern retaining wall is much higher than the western one. Today the terrace is referred to as the *kusipata,* but relationships to the *kusipata* in Cuzco are uncertain. To the east the terrace overlooks a very large, trapezoidally-shaped, walled enclosure, within which there is a large depression, perhaps once another pool or a sunken garden.

Just to the north of the high terrace and within the great walled enclosure lies an interesting structure which may possibly have served as a temple. The building is rectangular and is constructed of high quality Imperial Inca style masonry. Unlike most ordinary houses, it appears to have been entered from one end, the south, rather than from the side. At the north end, opposite the door, there appears to have been a large recessed niche. Four recessed niches also adorn the exterior of the east wall. Three plain niches occur on the interior of the west wall and could have occurred on the interior of the east wall as well. Reconstruction of the exact ground plan was made difficult partly because of destruction, but partly also, we feel, because the building was never completed before Huánuco Viejo was abandoned (Murra and Hadden 1966:137).

The most likely interpretation of this section of the site is that it served as a royal apartment and/or a ceremonial zone. No contradiction need be involved in a dual function, of course, for the Inca himself was a descendant of the sun and was divine. Whether the houses of superior masonry served as dwellings for the elite or as a temple or as both simultaneously thus remains uncertain, though the authors favor the royal apartment idea, with the other nearby domestic-type structures of inferior masonry housing servants. In this connection, it is interesting that all the pottery excavated from pits in the *Casa del Inca* area was utilitarian, again suggesting a domiciliary function, but such evidence should be used with great care since the whole *Casa del Inca* area has been heavily pothunted.

The main central plaza at Huánuco Viejo, as was observed earlier in this discussion, is connected with the *Casa del Inca* by a series of gateways. The fact that the carved stone animals or insignia on the sides of the gateway's lintels are found only on the side facing the *Casa del Inca* suggests that the passage or view toward the plaza was more highly regarded or more important than the reverse.

The plaza and some of the buildings within it have been discussed in some detail by Shea (1966, 1968). The plaza is huge, measuring about 350 by 550 meters, and in its center lies the *Ushnu,* a solid platform of good Imperial Inca style masonry. The *Ushnu,* which measures about 32 by 48 meters at the base and about 3.5 meters high, appears to be set upon two low terraces, the outer, lower one, about 12 meters wide and the inner, upper one, about 1.5 meters wide. Two small buildings on the east side of the lower terrace may have functioned in connection with ceremonies performed on the *Ushnu* itself (Shea 1968:19-21).

The top of the *Ushnu* is reached by a staircase on the south side, now in ruins but estimated by Shea (1968:17) to have had 32 steps. The top itself is enclosed by a bifacial wall well over a meter thick and 1.5 meters high. A small exterior horizontal projection on the top of the wall produces a cornice around the top of the *Ushnu.* Two gates, each just under 3 meters wide, give access to the top of the structure from the staircase. The gates are flanked by small, poorly executed pieces of stone sculpture, probably representing pairs of pumas back to back. A similar piece of low relief sculpture depicted in situ in the side of the *Ushnu* by Enock (1905:159) had since fallen but was replaced again in 1966. The wall around the top of the *Ushnu* also contained 10 niches, 6 of which are still clearly visible. These niches had no tops and could possibly have served as seats.

The *Ushnu* is not unique to Huánuco Viejo, for very similar structures have been found at a number of other Inca sites. Apparently important leaders used it for public events of a political, administrative, or ceremonial nature. The large amount of pottery found in clearing the area around the *Ushnu* will not be considered here because of the high probability that it was brought to this location by the Spaniards rather than deposited here by the Inca in the course of some pre-Columbian activity.

In addition to the *Ushnu,* there are a number of multiple room structures in the plaza. Their seemingly irregular arrangement and the fact that they seem to our eyes to clutter the otherwise open plaza have led several people to attribute them to the brief Spanish occupation of the site from 1539-42, rather than to the Inca. So far, however, there is no archaeological evidence for assigning these structures to the Spanish tenants, and it would seem presumptuous to assume that our views on the utilization of open spaces were necessarily shared by the Inca.

The Residential Districts

The north and south *barrios* or quarters of Huánuco Viejo seem to have functioned largely as residential districts. Some sections are very formally arranged, for example the so-called *cuartel* in the northern *barrio,* which seems to resemble an army barracks to the European eye. Found in both sections are the typical Inca rectangular houses with trapezoidally-shaped niches in the interior walls. All such houses are built of *pirka* masonry, usually bifacial walls with rubble and mud fill. Niches and doors vary somewhat in size and shape, as do the houses themselves.

The houses are usually found arranged around a central courtyard. In some instances the pattern is quite regular; in others, quite haphazard. In either case, however, these buildings and their arrangement are Inca inspired; there is no resemblance to the domestic architecture of any of the local ethnic groups surveyed. Local Chupachu architecture, for example, consists of square rooms of slab masonry with rounded interior corners and steeply gabled roofs; Yacha architecture, of irregular multi-roomed structures with flat stone roofs, also of slab; and Wamali architecture, of large circular houses and tall towers (Thompson 1967, 1968a, 1968b, 1968c). Thus, although local people presumably provided the labor for construction, they worked under Inca supervision.

The only possible exception to the remarks made above comes from a number of circular structures found near the periphery of the site. Some of these appear to have served as houses, and circular houses, as previously noted, are known among some of the local groups in the area. Since these are few in number and tend to be on the outskirts of the site, we interpret them at the moment as being peripheral to the main plan of the site, perhaps inhabited by squatters or the like. In some cases they may even be postconquest in date.

The ceramics collected from the surface and excavated from pits in the residential zones were Inca inspired. Indeed, of the tens of thousands of sherds found at Huánuco Viejo, fewer than 5 sherds could be attributed to local peasant traditions. This is not to say that the pottery was made at Huánuco Viejo or that it was brought from Cuzco. Quite to the contrary, all evidence, documentary as well as archaeological, indicates that local potters in the villages made vessels to rather precise Inca specifications for tribute purposes, and this pottery is what makes up the bulk of the collections from Imperial Inca sites in this area. Thus, although many of the inhabitants of Huánuco Viejo might be villagers serving their labor service, they lived in Inca inspired houses and used Inca style pottery in their kitchens.

The Storage Area

The Spanish chroniclers have noted the presence of massive storage facilities at provincial centers like Huánuco Viejo. The city of Vilcas Waman, which probably was not greatly different from Huánuco Viejo in its nature and functions, is said to have had over 700 storehouses (Cieza de Léon 1959:127). The storage zone at Huánuco Viejo overlooks the site from a hill to the south, and contains 497 storehouses and a series of 30 non-storage buildings apparently connected with storage processing and administration.

A thorough study was made of the surface architecture in the zone; all structures were measured and a typology was developed. Two of the storehouses, selected on the basis of preservation, were first excavated to give preliminary indications of problems likely to be encountered, techniques required, and the kinds of data which could be obtained. A random sample of 50 storehouses was then selected for excavation. This sample was eventually expanded to 94, but only the original 50 were randomly selected, the remainder being chosen in terms of providing some specific information rather than enlarging a general sample representative of the zone as a whole. In particular, an attempt was made to determine if boundaries between different building types represented a difference in contents; therefore, as many storehouses as possible at these boundaries were excavated. Also most of the excavations beyond the original sample were in structures of architectural types which frequently yielded pottery, rather than in those where pottery was established to be absent early in the excavation. While this resulted in more botanical data from some types than others, it substantially increased the quantity of storage pottery recovered. Twenty of the 30 non-storage buildings were excavated in whole or in part. While eight of these were initially selected randomly, the larger number were selected on the basis of specific questions and field considerations.

Excavation first involved removing parts of the *pirka* walls which had fallen into the structures; this level was sterile in almost all cases. Below the wall debris, a culture bearing matrix of 8 to 20 cm. extended down to the floor. This matrix was excavated in 10-cm. levels where it was sufficiently thick. When charred, plant remains were well preserved and easily recovered, and the quantities recovered were increased by flotation of the matrix in which they occurred. Matrix samples of five liters were taken from the last 10 cm. above the floor of each storehouse excavated. The flotation of portions of several of these proved unproductive except in samples from storehouses where carbonized material had been noted in the field.

A study of functional variability within the storage zone was based on both the architectural data and the material recovered in excavation. The aim was to isolate functionally specific areas and to associate these with the storage of certain commodities and with differences in the uses for which the goods were intended.

The data were collected in connection with a broader study of Inca storage (Morris 1967) and specifically to test alternative hypotheses regarding the function of storage at Huánuco Viejo, and in major Inca provincial centers in general. One of these hypotheses derives from the work of Polanyi (1957), and more directly from the ethnohistorical work of John V. Murra on the Inca economy (Murra 1956, 1962b). It suggests that the expansion of a redistributive economy leads to a large and complex system of storage, and in terms of it one of the most important functions of Huánuco Viejo would have been that of a redistributive center supplying the provincial villages of the area it administered with the products of other regions. In a physical sense the storage zone would have been the equivalent of a large market place, which the city almost certainly lacked.

The storehouses, or *qollqa*, are constructed in a series of 11 rows, some of which are quite irregular due to the contour of the hill. All of the storage buildings were made of *pirka* masonry, essentially identical to that employed in the site's domestic architecture. Storehouses are easily distinguished from other structures by their small windows (or doors) with thresholds well above the surface of the ground. There are two main types of storehouses, rectangular and circular. But these may be further subdivided on the basis of floor characteristics, and the rectangular *qollqa* were constructed in both single room and multiple room varieties. The non-storage area adjoining the storehouses included three relatively large *kallanka,* a group of "houses," and a number of small buildings of types not identified in other parts of the site.

The 497 storehouses provided a total of 12,680 square meters of floor space and a maximum volume capacity of over 37,900 cubic meters. The drawing of fine distinctions and accurate boundaries between functionally specific groups of storehouses was difficult because of the rarity of preserved botanical specimens and the effects on artifact distribution of the lotting and disorganization following the Spanish Conquest. But on the basis of the patterning of the various types of storage architecture and ceramics we were able to tentatively isolate several groups and, in cases where botanical materials were preserved, to determine what goods had been stored in them. The groups of structures included: (1) a small zone of storehouses which may have held the stores, of the Sun, the state religion; (2) minor groups or single storehouses apparently devoted to special shrines or ceremonial activities; (3) an ill-defined section of buildings which may have held a wide variety of goods in temporary storage for more immediate uses; and (4), by far the largest group, which was committed to the long-term storage of various food stuffs and other goods in technologically specialized facilities. Differences in the storage methods for various products appear in all of these divisions or groups. The best documented of these differences is indicated by the associations of root crops and maize. Root crops were placed between layers of straw, bound into bales with rope, and placed in rectangular structures. Maize was usually stored shelled, in large jars placed in circular storehouses with stone floors.

It is estimated that between 50 and 80% of the total space was given to the storage of highland root crops (potatoes, sweet potatoes, oka, and mashwa have been identified) and between 5 and 7% was probably devoted to maize. The products stored in the remainder of the facility cannot be suggested except for an isolated occurrence of what may have been charcoal. The small zone which perhaps stored the goods of the Sun constituted a storage area of 270 square meters with a volume of about 825 cubic meters. This, obviously, is only a fraction of what appears to have been allotted for state or secular use. The smaller zone, however, closely mirrored the larger one in its internal architectural differentiation, in the proportions of space it provided in the different building types, and in the patterns of association between architecture and ceramics.

The non-storage structures contiguous with the storehouses were almost certainly related to storage administration, but the interpretation of their specific functions is difficult. On the basis of the architectural forms and the ceramics associated with them we can suggest that the group included small sentry posts, large buildings housing checking and processing operations, a large building where the specialized storage pottery was kept, and residences of storage administrators.

The heavy emphasis on highland root crops seems to indicate that storage at Huánuco Viejo mainly involved the products of the surrounding region. Had it been primarily related to redistributional activities we would have expected evidence of a greater abundance of non-local products. And specifically we would have expected more space to have been devoted to maize, which was both more storeable and more highly prized in the Andean scale of values (Murra 1960:398). Furthermore, we would expect a center of redistributive storage to have a relatively rapid turnover of goods. The evidence of Huánuco Viejo, on the other hand, suggests a major concern with fairly long term storage. Only a small zone at the edge of the storage area near the city proper showed suggestions of a rapid turnover of goods. This zone contained both rectangular and circular storehouses, and yielded botanical evidence of both maize and root crops. The best evidence that these structures may have witnessed a more frequent change of their contents than the remainder of the storehouses was the presence of noticeably eroded sherds from a much greater number of jars than would have been in use at a single time. This zone accounted for only about 15% of the total storage space.

A further test of the contribution of Huánuco Viejo to the local village economies, based on the presence in the villages of the Cuzco style pottery associated with Huánuco Viejo, failed to produce positive results. Significant quantities of that type of ceramics were found only in the village which was the seat of the most important local leader of the period. While it could not be expected that movements of some kinds of goods would be reflected in distribution of ceramics, it would seem that a quantitatively important dependence on state storage by the villages would be evidenced either in the archaeological materials or in the relatively detailed Ortiz *visita*.

These findings suggest that an explanation of the massive storage facilities at Huánuco Viejo lies primarily in something other than the stocking of large quantities of goods for redistribution to the villages. And of the alternative explanations, the most plausible seems to be that the bulk of the storage was used in support of the city itself. This is in harmony with our general interpretation of a rather marginal center almost totally dependent on outside sources of both provisions and population. It is probable that Cieza's (1959:109) figure of over 30,000 people who "served" Huánuco Viejo does not refer to the city's population at any given time. But the extent of the site suggests that as many as four to six thousand could have been in service there at the same time, and temporary stationing of troops might occasionally have brought the figure even higher.

Air photographs suggest there may have been a small area of fields adjacent to the city on its north and west sides. It is difficult to locate these on the ground, and we are uncertain of their nature or their date. But the area they cover is only about one-fourth the size of the area covered by architectural ruins, and it does not seem likely that this zone of possible fields was a major force in the sustenance of the center. There is, though, sufficient positive evidence in the *visita* of Iñigo Ortiz (1967) to document the major source of food on which Huánuco Viejo lived. The detailed village surveys list repeatedly the carrying of goods, predominantly comestibles, to the city. Supplies such as these were produced for the state as an aspect of the *mita* labor tax (Rowe 1946:265-268; Murra 1958).

We can assume that the influx of supplies was uneven. Normal seasonal variations were at times further complicated by famine or by breakdown in the socio-political mechanisms that assured delivery. The demand for goods also undoubtedly fluctuated. While some of the city's activities were performed on a year-round basis, others like military operations varied, resulting in alterations in both personnel and material needs. Large scale storage seems an obvious solution to these disjunctions between supply and demand. It was probably essential for maintaining a rather marginal city like Huánuco Viejo under conditions where both the technology of transportation and the organization of the economy were still primitive. This does not mean that storage was not involved in redistribution, but that, quantitatively, storage at Huánuco Viejo was concerned with products from its own hinterland, for its own consumption. Unfortunately we recovered no traces of cloth and other luxury goods known to have been of special redistributive importance (Murra 1962b). It is impossible to say whether post-conquest looting, poor preservation and our smaller than desirable sample prevented identification of these goods, or whether a highly centralized circuit of redistribution concentrated their storage in Cuzco. We feel relatively certain, however, that if they were kept in the main storage complex at Huánuco Viejo, their quantities were small in comparison with the foodstuffs.

Summary and Conclusions

It is clear from what has been said above that many of the specific functions of Huánuco Viejo and the details of life there remain hypotheses to be tested by further work. But our work has contributed to an emerging picture of some of the major activities carried out at the site, and of the center's role in the Inca scheme of provincial governance. We would like to stress two primary conclusions. First, Huánuco Viejo was a center created by the Inca rulers to serve a whole series of functions vital to the expansion and perpetuation of the state. Second, unlike some of the coastal cities occupied in Inca times (Menzel 1959; Thompson 1969:73) it was a highly artifical city, both in terms of the semi-transient population which largely inhabited it and its relationship with the supporting hinterlands.

Ceramics furnish the most striking archaeological evidence that Huánuco Viejo was a state creation, rigidly distinct from the villages of the ethnic groups which peopled the surrounding region. The pottery of Huánuco Viejo consists of local imitations of the ceramics of Cuzco. And in the almost 100,000 sherds examined from all sections of the site less than five were of types identified with the local traditions. Furthermore, the Cuzco style pottery of Huánuco Viejo was rarely found in the villages, as was mentioned above, although there were occasional incorporations of some of its features in local wares. This distribution suggests something approaching a "state pottery," produced by or for the state and used in official functions to the exclusion of wares indigenous to the region. The nearly exclusive occurrence of this "Inca" pottery at Huánuco Viejo seems to indicate a predominant concern with state activities and the lack of any substantial "casual" flow of people back and forth between the city and the surrounding region.

Architecture also emphasizes the vivid demarcation between the city and the villages. The architecture of Huánuco Viejo is basically an imitation of that of Cuzco; with the possible exception of circular houses, local house forms and masonry techniques are almost entirely absent. Even the choice of a site for the city ran counter to local tradition. Our survey showed that the high, grassy, relatively flat *pampa* on which Huánuco Viejo and other Inca centers in the area were located, was a type of locality foreign to the settlement patterns of the inhabitants of the region at the time the Inca arrived.

These rather firm archaeological indications that Huánuco Viejo was primarily an artificial center serving the state is further bolstered by the fact of its rapid depopulation after the upper levels of Inca organization were destroyed by the Spanish. After a short and abortive attempt to establish a Spanish settlement at the city, it was abandoned by Spanish and Andeans alike. The Spanish founded the modern city of Huánuco in the Huallaga Valley, and what remained of the original inhabitants presumably returned to their villages (Cieza 1959:108-9; Varallanos 1959:125-42).

From the activities we believe to have been carried out in the site's major zones, we can suggest some of the services it provided for the Inca. The eastern section with its monumental architecture and its great variety of building types and spatial arrangements, was a zone devoted largely to administrative and ceremonial activities and to elite residence. Further archaeological work is necessary before specific activities can be related to particular structures and compounds, but comparisons of the architecture with descriptions of Cuzco and other Inca cities give at least an impression of what the area's prime activities were. Its heart is formed by the complex of buildings and open plazas linked by large gateways, called the *Casa del Inca* by Harth-Terré (1964) and described above. With its focal point in the *kancha* enclosed buildings we have mapped, this large architectural unit seems to have incorporated royal lodgings into the setting for a much broader framework of activities, many of them of a ceremonial nature. The gateways provide an additional link between this entire *Casa del Inca* section and the Central Plaza with its *Ushnu*. Together these furnished both buildings and open spaces in many different sizes. While we will probably never be able to determine the exact uses served by such elaborate planning, the architectural comparisons with Cuzco are sufficient to suggest that many of the features of the capital had been replicated in Huánuco Viejo. This in part served the function of creating appropriate surroundings for travelers and residents, many of whom had come from Cuzco. But beyond that it must have been a showcase of Inca splendor for the benefit and edification of the peoples indigenous to the region.

The central ceremonial complex, the *Casa del Inca,* occupies less than half of the total area of Huánuco Viejo's eastern section. The remainder of the section is devoted to buildings in a variety of sizes, grouped around plazas which are small in comparison to those in the *Casa del Inca.* There is little comparative data to aid in interpreting these building groups, and in the absence of extensive work, conclusions about them are hazardous. Harth-Terré (1964:11-12) feels on the basis of his study of the architecture that the area just south of the *Casa del Inca* constituted a large *aqllawasi,* dwelling place of the *aqllakuna* the women selected for service to the Inca and the temples. We can probably assume that Huánuco Viejo had an *aqllawasi,* but the identification of it on the present evidence is difficult. Some of the eastern section gives the impression of being composed of house groups similar to, but significantly larger than, those in the main domestic zones of the city. It seems likely that much of the administrative personnel resided in this part of the city contiguous to its main ceremonial and administrative complex.

The major domestic areas to the north, south, and west of the Central Plaza were not explored sufficiently to allow us to uncover very much of the variation within and between them. There is throughout the pervasive absence of indications of the varying ethnic identities of the inhabitants. Even the crudest houses tested by excavation contained only the local Cuzco style pottery found throughout the city. Even if members of the various ethnic groups serving the city resided in segregated zones, those zones can probably never be defined archaeologically.

The most obvious distinction in domestic architecture is between the house groups in walled compounds in the major zones surrounding the plaza and the small circular structures clinging to the edges of the ruin not unlike the unplanned squatter settlements of some modern cities. Whether these differences denote distinctions in status, in the composition of the domestic unit, or in the kind of relationship the residents had with the state, can only be determined through additional work. It is tempting to see the crude circular buildings as the houses of people who were not fully incorporated into the planned regime of the city—people whose presence was not required by the *mita,* somehow taking personal advantage of the city's presence. This, however, is not indicated by the exclusively Inca style domestic pottery found in the three of these houses which were excavated.

The zone north of the plaza differs from those to the south and west in that it was not so predominated by domestic house compounds. For example there are 43 structures, larger than the typical "house," arranged along narrow streets near the Central Plaza. Harth-Terré's (1964:13) interpretation of these as barracks seems a reasonable one, and we might postulate that those structures, as well as some of the *kallanka* surrounding the Central Plaza, provided housing for the army or other persons whose residence was temporary and did not involve family units.

We did not make an accurate house count in the domestic zones, but there were at least 500 domestic structures. When these are combined with the numerous larger buildings perhaps used for transient residence and the small circular houses at the periphery of the site, the city could easily have housed more than 5,000 persons. The point which should be emphasized however, is that since most of the inhabitants were only part time residents serving their *mita,* the population probably fluctuated somewhat in relation to the agricultural cycle and other features of the state's organization and activities. The nature and extent of these fluctuations, as well as more reliable population figures, must await further research.

The artificial character of the center which we have emphasized created special problems of economic support for this relatively large population. From our understanding of the working of the Inca economy, there is little doubt that the state shouldered most of the responsibility for the sustenance of those laboring for it (Murra 1958:32). If our conclusion that Huánuco Viejo was largely inhabited by people engaged in one form or another of state service is correct, then the state was obliged to provide for them with the products of its fields. The city was thus sustained through the overall system of reciprocity between state and village, mediated through an elaborate storage system.

Since there is no evidence in either documents or the archaeological data to suggest that there was an important marketplace at Huánuco Viejo, the zone where storage was located must have been the focal point of the city's economic activity. The rather thorough investigation of that zone combined with data from the villages has not given us as full and reliable an understanding as we would like of the importance of Huánuco Viejo as a center for regional and inter-regional redistributive exchange. However, the positive evidence for such an economic role is meager, and it does not seem that we should list this as one of the city's major functions at this time.

The image of an artificial, essentially imposed, population center supported through a system of exchange based on reciprocity and redistribution contrasts markedly with some of our notions of "urban" and "city." Huánuco Viejo did not rise because of an important concentration of natural resources or because of a propitious position as a center of inter-regional exchange. It appears rather to have been a link in an elaborate network of communication, transportation, and administration which was established to bind together the state's authority structure centered in Cuzco and the numerous ethnic groups it sought to control in the provinces. It supported military and political objectives and helped channel goods and services to the state. In fulfilling these functions, Huánuco Viejo, and the many other provincial administrative centers, were vital to the expansion and maintenance of the most extensive political unit of the pre-Columbian Americas.

Acknowledgments

The field and laboratory work on which this paper is based was carried out between 1964 and 1967 with the support of two grants from the National Science Foundation: GS 42 and GS 1136, and under the sponsorship of the Institute of Andean Research and the University of Wisconsin, respectively. Permission to undertake excavations in Peru was granted under Resoluciones Supremas Nos. 58 (10 de Febrero, 1964); 637 (13 de Mayo, 1965); 962 (13 de Julio, 1966). In addition, a semester of research leave was granted to Donald E. Thompson by the Ibero-American Studies Program of the University of Wisconsin from the Ford Latin American Training and Research Grant. For aid in the course of our research, we would like to thank especially John V. Murra, Peter Jenson, Luis Barreda Murillo, Daniel Shea, Robert Bird, John Cotter, and Delfin Zúñiga.

References

Cieza de Leon, Pedro. 1959. *The Incas of Pedro de Cieza de León*, translated by Harriet de Onis and edited by Victor W. von Hagen. University of Oklahoma Press.

Enock, Reginald. 1905. The ruins of Huánuco Viejo, or Old Huánuco, with notes on an expedition to the upper Marañon. *The Geographical Journal* 26:153-168.

———— 1907. *The Andes and the Amazon.* T. Fisher Unwin.

Harth-Terre, Emilio. 1964. El Pueblo de Huánuco-Viejo. *Arquitecto Peruano* 320/21:1-20.

Ishida, Yazawa, Sato, Kobori, Chavez, and Others. 1960. *Andes. Report of the University of Tokyo scientific expedition to the Andes in 1958.* Andean Institute. University of Tokyo.

Menzel, Dorothy. 1959. The Inca occupation of the south coast of Peru. *Southwestern Journal of Anthropology* 15:125-142.

Morris, Craig. 1966. El Tampu Real de Tunsucancha. *Cuadernos de Investigación*, No. 1,

Antropología, pp. 95-107. Universidad Nacional Hermilio Valdizán.

———— 1967. *Storage in Tawantisuyu.* Doctoral dissertation. Department of Anthropology, University of Chicago.

Murra, John V. 1956. *The economic organization of the Inca State.* Doctoral dissertation, Department of Anthropology, University of Chicago.

———— 1958. On Inca political structure. In *Systems of political control and bureaucracy in human societies,* edited by Vern F. Ray, pp. 30-41. University of Washington Press.

———— 1960. Rite and crop in the Inca state. In *Culture in history: essays in honor of Paul Radin,* edited by Stanley Diamond, pp. 393-407. Columbia University Press.

———— 1962a. An archaeological "restudy" of an Andean ethnohistorical account. *American Antiquity* 28:1-4.

———— 1962b. Cloth and its functions in the Inca State. *American Anthropologist* 64:710-728.

Murra, John V., and Gordon J. Hadden. 1966. Apéndice; informe presentado al Patronato Nacional de Arqueología sobre la labor de limpieza y consolidacíon de Huánuco Viejo. *Cuadernos de Investigación,* No. 1, Antropología, pp. 129-44. Universidad Nacional Hermilio Valdizán.

Ortiz de Zuñiga, Iñigo. 1920-25, 1955-61. Visita fecha por mandado de su magestad.. [1562]. *Revista del Archivo Nacional del Perú.*

———— 1967. Visita de la Provincia de León de Huánuco en 1562. *Documentos para la historia y etnologia de Huánuco y la Selva Central* 1. Universidad Nacional Hermilio Valdizán.

Polanyi, Karl, Conrad M. Arensberg, and Harry W. Pearson. 1957. *Trade and market in the early empires.* The Free Press.

Raimondi, Antonio. 1874. *El Perú.* Emprenta del Estado.

Rowe, John H. 1946. Inca culture at the time of the Spanish Conquest. In "Handbook of South American Indians," edited by J. H. Steward, Vol. 2, pp. 183-330. *Bureau of American Ethnology,* Bulletin 143.

Shea, Daniel, 1966. El conjunto arquitectónico central en la Plaza de Huánuco Viejo. *Cuadernos de Investigación,* No. 1 Antropología pp. 108-116. Universidad Nacional Hermilio Valdizán.

———— 1968. *The plaza complex of Huánuco Viejo.* Master of Science Thesis, Department of Anthropology, University of Wisconsin.

Sobreviela, Padre Manual, and Lorenzo de la Sierra. 1786. *Plan del Palacio destinado para Baño de los Yncas sito en el Partido de Huamalies, con nombre de Huánuco el Viejo.* Manuscript Collection, British Museum.

Squier, E. George. 1877. *Peru. Incidents of travel and exploration in the land of the Incas.* Macmillan and Co.

Thompson, Donald E. 1967. Investigaciones arqueológicas en las Aldeas Chupachu de Ichu y Auquimarca. In "Visita de la Provincia de León de Huánuco en 1562," pp. 357-362. *Documentos para la historia y etnología de Huánuco y la Selva Central* 1. Universidad Nacional Hermilio Valdizán.

———— 1968a. Huánuco, Peru: A survey of a province of the Inca Empire. *Archaeology* 21:174-181.

———— 1968b. An archaeological evaluation of ethnohistoric evidence on Inca culture. In *Anthropological Archaeology in the Americas,* edited by Betty J. Meggers, pp. 108-20. The Anthropological Society of Washington.

———— 1968c. Peasant Inca villages in the Huánuco region. Paper presented at the 38th International Congress of Americanists, Stuttgart. In Press.

————— 1969. Incaic installations of Huánuco and Pumpu. In *El Proceso de urbanización en America desde sus orígenes hasta neustros días* (Papers presented at a symposium at the 37th International Congress of Americanists, Mar del Plata), edited by Jorge Hardoy and Richard Schaedel, pp. 67-74.

Thompson, Donald E., and John V. Murra. 1966. The Inca bridges in the Huánuco region. *American Antiquity* 31:632-639.

Varallanos, Jose. 1959. *Historia de Huánuco*. Imprenta Lopez.

Vasquez de Espinosa, Antonio. 1942. Compendium and description of the West Indies [1629], translated by Charles Upson Clark. *Smithsonian Miscellaneous Collections* 102.

Melvin L. Fowler received his Ph.D. from the University of Chicago in
1959 and is now professor of anthropology at the University of Wisconsin,
Milwaukee. He has done fieldwork in both Middle and North America.
He is known particularly for his studies at Modoc Rock Shelter and
Cahokia in Illinois. In this interesting paper, he compares two Pre-
columbian towns in North America and Mexico in order to see if he
can discover cultural regularities in communities which appear to have
the typological criteria but which are situated in two very different
cultural and environmental settings.

The Temple Town Community:
Cahokia and Amulucan Compared

Melvin L. Fowler

Introduction

It is a common weakness among archaeologists to use the term village interchangeably with the term site, that is, locality where archaeological materials are found. This
usage overlooks the sociological implications terms such as village or town can have.
In this type of symposium the sociological implications of terminology are important
and need to be well developed.

For the concept of village I prefer a combination of two definitions extant in the
literature. Haury (1962:118) has said:

> I see [villages] . . . as distinct from the earlier long occupied camps . . .
> whether in caves or in the open, because of formalized architecture perhaps
> a closer clustering of houses, usually the presence of a larger apparently
> non-domestic structure, and a greater complexity of the material posses-
> sions . . . The house pits . . . reflect a solidity of construction and an
> investment of labor that would arise only from need for prolonged residence.

Haury has stressed the physical aspects such as clustering of houses, a specialized
structure, and the relative permanence of occupation. On the other hand, Mumford
(1961:18) adds a social dimension to the definition when he states:

> Everywhere, the village is a small cluster of families, from half a dozen to
> three score perhaps, each with its own hearth, its own household gods, its

Reprinted from *Actas y Memorias del XXXVII Congreso Internacional de Americanistas,* Vol. I (1968),
by permission of the publisher and author.

own shrine, its own burial plot within the house or in some common
burial ground.

. . . [Each family follows the same way of life and participates in the
same labors.

Mumford's stress is on the commonality of life in a village and the lack of specializations.

Other dimensions to the definition of village would depend upon the context in
which it is found. It is possible for villages of the type outlined above to be the peak of
socio-political organization and territorial dominance in an area, or, for such villages to
be satellites to larger more complex communities. In the latter context a village may be
a specialized craft center participating in the great tradition of the larger centers. In the
former context the village represents a point of social-political development made possible by agriculture or some other stable food supply.

An even more distressing misapplication of the term village is when it is applied to
large and complex archaeological sites. These are sites that show evidence of functionally
distinct precincts within their boundaries, of a large hinterland which they seem to
dominate and of related and smaller satellite communities. One of the details that puts
these large communities apart from their satellites is a central precinct set aside for
religious and political purposes and manifested in specialized architecture. Among other
characteristics there is probably craft specialization within the community so that segments of the population are participating in only part of the total life as compared to
the commonality Mumford stressed for the village. There may also be centers and
mechanisms for redistribution of goods and services both for the community itself and
for the hinterland. For these types of communities I prefer the term "town." Such
towns could have arisen as a manifestation of the growing need for social and political
control of increasing populations resulting from effective agriculture subsistence. Agriculture is not necessary for village life but it is a prerequisite for town life in its sociological implications.

In North America archaeological sites that can be classed as towns are found in
three different cultural settings. One is that they can be found as satellites to urban
centers. This will not be discussed in this paper.

Another context is that towns, especially in central Mexico, can be found preceding the period when urbanism appears as a facet of developing territorial control. In this
context are sites of the late Preclassic or Formative period (or proto-Classic in Michael
Coe's terms). Braidwood and Willey (1962: 350 ff) refer to these as "temple centers"
and a "kind of incipience to urbanization" which is present in the New World but which
is not clear from the archaeological record of the Old World. Willey (1960) in a different
article used the term Temple Town to refer to this type of development. I accept this
term and will use it henceforth in this paper attributing to it the characteristics I have
briefly outlined above.

The third context for such towns in North America is in areas peripheral to Nuclear
America where they appear as the pinnacle of social-political development. This
appears to be especially true of the Mississippi Valley and Southeastern areas of the
United States. In this area the chroniclers of the De Soto expeditions described many

such communities and their hinterlands. These men were conscious of moving from one political province to another and of going to each principal town. They met merchants who were traveling from community to community with goods to trade. They marveled at the towns with their walls and moats, dug to bring water from the river around the town. They saw the mounds upon which temples and houses of the notables were constructed. Archaeological research has confirmed much of what was reported by these men.

In a move to contribute to our understanding of urbanism and its development this paper is designed to examine two archaeological sites and compare them in terms of the concept of the Temple Town that has been outlined above. One of these communities will be the Cahokia site near east St. Louis, Illinois, that has long been known as the largest, and perhaps the earliest, of this type of site in Eastern North America. The other site is Amalucan near the city of Puebla in the central highlands of Mexico. This site is of the Middle to Late Preclassic period. More detailed descriptions of these sites will follow.

> The main purposes of this comparison can be stated as follows: Can superficially similar sites such as Amalucan in Mexico and Cahokia in Illinois be meaningfully compared? In what ways, if any, is it illuminating to consider these two communities to be "temple towns"? Does such a grouping elucidate the concept of "temple town," bound it, and specify more clearly the area of its possible usefulness?

> A subsidiary question is:

> What is the effect of cultural-historical (for example, marginality) and ecological (dry highland versus humid lowland) factors on the nature of communities which have been provisionally called "temple towns"?

The following comparison will not be able to answer these questions definitively since the kinds of data available are not yet sufficiently inclusive. The comparison will yield suggestions and a programatic definition of goals for developing research.

Cahokia

The first site to be considered in this comparison is the Cahokia site near East St. Louis, Illinois. The central feature of this locality is a large terraced mound covering 16 acres and rising to a height of over one hundred feet above the surrounding valley floor. Grouped around this large mound in a series of avenues and plazas were over eighty other mounds of varying sizes and shapes.

This group of mounds and related occupation covers an area of about 15 square kilometers (about 5 square miles). The total area thought to have been utilized aboriginally is bounded by two types of data. One is that there are outlying mounds that are suggestive of limits to the major site area. At least two of these mounds, Rattlesnake and Powell, were of essentially the same shape, a long rectangular mound with a ridge like top. There are no other mounds of this shape within the limits we have suggested. There are two mounds at the southernmost and westernmost areas included within the site limits. At roughly corresponding points on the north and east are other mounds.

Another factor suggesting limits to the site are certain lines which appear on old serial photographs suggestive of palisade and ditch lines surrounding the area. One of these lines has been tested and proven to be such a palisade. These lines converge at points on the main north-south axis of the site.

Within these limits are several areas of apparent functional difference. There is data now coming out of the ground to suggest that the main mound and the mounds immediately around it were walled off from other parts of the town thus setting them apart. This is doubly interesting, if further excavation confirms this, since the big mound is the only mound with four terraces and it is thus possible that it represents a structure of special importance not only for the town itself but for the surrounding areas. At one time there was a conical eminence on the third terrace of this mound. This is suggestive in light of the data we have on the Natchez that the Sun or major leader of a Natchez territory would ascend an eminence near his house every morning to greet the sun at sunrise. Perhaps the big mound and its enclosed compound represents the residence and precinct of the chief political leader of the area.

Other functional areas are suggested by the different shapes of mounds that are within the site area. There is only one other multiple stage or terraced mound and that is just west of the big mound, outside of the proposed enclosed compound. Besides these, there are several rectangular and square flat-topped mounds that are obviously platforms. Another form of mound is a conical and round topped type. There is some suggestion that these may be burial mounds although this possibility has not been thoroughly investigated. A study is currently underway classifying the types of mounds at the Cahokia site in order to determine the distribution of the types and the possible functional significance of the differing types and their distributions.

Besides the mound types mentioned above, recent excavations have demonstrated that there are other functional areas within the site. Some of these excavations have shown the residential areas to be quite intense with rebuilding of houses on the same locality several different times. In some cases these houses are well aligned with each other and form sections with street like areas between the houses. Other areas have yielded data on what were probably plazas and ceremonial and communal structures. In some cases residential areas were built over what had earlier been public plazas.

Of particular interest is one area where a large circle of posts had been placed in the ground. This circle of evenly spaced posts had at its center another large post. Dr. Warren Wittry (1964) who excavated this structure has carried out studies indicating that this circle of posts, called wood henge by him, may well have been an observatory for noting both the rising and setting of the sun and moon to determine critical days for measuring the year. In line with this kind of data suggesting a concern for things astronomical is the fact that the site seems to be aligned on an axis about three degrees east of true north. The main axes of the site, the big mound and the other larger mounds seem to follow this alignment. Currently a precise map of the entire site is being made which will give us data enabling a more precise definition of this orientation.

The question of craft specialization within Cahokia has not been studied as yet. At the present time surface distribution studies of materials are being undertaken by investigators from two different institutions. Hopefully these studies will give us data on this and other problems. There is some suggestion of such specialized areas in the finding of artifacts called micro drills in a rather limited area of the site. Gregory Perino suggests that these might have been used to drill shells in the process of bead manufacture. The implication would be that this then was a craft specialized area.

Petrographic thin section studies of ceramics from the Cahokia site and surrounding area have been carried out in the past several years. Suggestions from these studies are that there were several local areas of pottery manufacture using clays locally available. Perhaps more detailed studies of this type will make it possible to trace an interchange of such local ceramic wares.

That Cahokia participated in a larger interchange of goods with not only the surrounding area but with other regions as well is an accepted but poorly documented hypothesis. There are certain exotic materials such as galena and conch shells which suggest this. That trade routes were established and goods interchanged in the southeast United States as early as three thousand B.C. has recently been demonstrated.

How the goods were distributed within Cahokia is another unanswered question. A structure very suggestive of a market area was excavated about 250 meters west of the big mound. This apparently was a large square enclosure of upright log construction. Spaced at regular intervals along the walls of this enclosure were circular rooms opening in toward the center of the area. Only the size and shape of this suggest a market as no other data exists to confirm this idea. Another such enclosure is indicated on the early serial photographs of the site about 500 meters to the east of the big mound.

Several other sites exist in the area surrounding Cahokia suggesting a series of smaller towns, villages, and farm steads related to the larger center. Among these are Pulcher about ten miles to the south and Mitchell about 7 miles to the north. Although these sites are rather large in themselves none are as large and complex as Cahokia and none have terraced mounds. It is my hypothesis that these are satellite communities dominated by the larger town. It may well be that there was a well defined political territory which was immediately controlled by Cahokia.

In this territory there were probably two distinct ethnic groups as is suggested by ceramic and other data. These ethnic groups lived at the same time within the confines of Cahokia and in separated communities outside as well.

Cahokia exerted an influence over a much larger area, in fact most of the Mississippi Valley, but this is a problem beyond that which we have chosen to discuss.

As a final note on this discussion of Cahokia some mention should be made of the time of its occupation. Radiocarbon dates suggest that human habitation of the site area began as early as 800 AD and continued until at least 1500 AD. However, it is my opinion that it reached its peak and functioned as a temple town between 900 and 1200 A.D. After that time it was a different type of community and had a qualitatively different relationship to the surrounding area.

Amalucan

The description of the Amalucan site will be much shorter since much less archaeological research has been conducted at that site. Some investigations were carried out by Linne (1942) and Noguera (1940) as well as Krieger and Sanders (1951).

Amalucan is the name of a large hacienda located just to the east of the City of Puebla and south of the volcanic peak of Malinche. Most of the archaeological site is now in the *ejido* lands of the village of Chachapa. The natural features dominating the landscape in this immediate area are two conical hills arising abruptly from the valley floor. The largest of these, Cerro Amalucan, has a large mound group and plaza area on its peak and the slopes of the hill were terraced. The smaller hill, Amaluquillo, apparently was not utilized.

The main cultural feature of the site is a large mound group to the east of Cerro Amalucan. This group is made up of one large multiple stage mound, a long rectangular platform mound, and some smaller mounds forming a plaza area. Besides this main group there are several smaller groups of mounds.

Since the whole valley floor seems to have been occupied in Preclassic times it is difficult to delimit the site. Using data such as continuity of surface distribution and natural features such as barrancas I estimate that the site covers an area of 10 square kilometers (3 square miles). The surface material scattered over this area is uniformly middle to late Preclassic.

Similar Late Preclassic sites literally surround Amalucan. To the east is a site at Chachapa. To the north is a site of similar nature and mound types near Parecio. To the south is the site of Totimehuacan recently excavated by Dr. Bodo Spranz of the Freibourg Ethnographic Museum. In terms of site distribution and density one might say that one of the major features of the distribution of archaeological sites in the Puebla valley is that some 90% of them are Preclassic. The settlement pattern of that period seems to have been of a series of towns and their supporting lands almost cheek by jowl with each other. This pattern of settlement seems to have changed in Classic times with the domination of Cholula over this entire area.

Returning to the site of Amalucan itself there seems to have been functionally distinct areas within the site. The major precinct seems to have been that of the main mound group and plaza. Only one mound at the sites multiple stage suggesting some special function for it. This mound is nearly identical in shape to mound 1 of Totimehuacan (Spranz, 1966). This includes a similar depression on one side of the upper terrace which Spranz found at Totimehuacan to be a room that had been filled in.

Excavations in three different areas of the site have suggested other specialized areas. One of these excavations was carried out in the wall of a barranca to the south of the main pyramid group. Refuse pits and possibly house floors were noted in this barranca. Excavation demonstrated that there had been a series of refuse pits here and that there were several levels of occupation. Nearby were large flat-bottomed pits suggesting houses. Since these types of features were not found in other sections of the site that were excavated it is suggested that this was an area of habitation throughout the history of the site.

Another specialized area was discovered through the study of aerial photographs. On the photos a straight dark line was noted extending in a northeasterly direction from near the central part of the large mound of the major group to an old stream channel. Further study of the photo indicated that there were similar lines nearly perpendicular to the first at regularly spaced intervals. A trench was put across the main line of this series. The excavations demonstrated that these lines were the remains of an ancient series of canals. These canals were utilized over a long period and as they silted in were re-excavated to clear the channel. This happened at least five different times. Finally it appears that the canals were filled in and the ground leveled, probably in preparation for the building of the big pyramid. Indications are that these lines continue under the main pyramid. Thus there is evidence not only of a water distribution system but of a changed function for this section of Amalucan through time.

There is no evidence as yet to suggest the actual use to which the canals were put other than the distribution of water. One good possibility of course is irrigation. Another possibility is that they were used to distribute water to the residents of the town.

In the northwest portion of the site, at the foot of Cerro Amalucan are other markings on the aerial photos of the same dark discoloration of the soil. These have not yet been investigated by excavation but undoubtedly represent a major aboriginal feature of the site.

The time when Amalucan was occupied can be defined by three lines of evidence. One is that the bulk of material found on the surface and in the excavations to date is Preclassic. The one exception to this is the southeast portion of the site where some Classic material has been found. By far the most common form of figurine found to date is one similar to Vaillant's type E-2. This suggests a Zacatenco-Ticoman affiliation for the site.

In the stratigraphy of the site there is a dark black zone found in all excavations which caps all other strata below. This was found over the canal area as well as over the area of refuse pits. It appears that this is an old humus line and apparently represents a time when the site was abandoned. The material below this line is all Preclassic. This suggests that before Classic times the site was completely abandoned and not utilized intensively again until colonial times.

The third line of evidence is a radiocarbon date from Totimehuacan Mound 2 (Spranz personal communication). While appraisal of this date must await Dr. Spranz's detailed analysis it suggests an age of ca. 100-300 B.C. for some of the activity at that group.

Comments

Superficially both Amalucan and Cahokia seem to have been the same *type* of community. Both contained a central precinct which probably represents a center of social, religious and political control. Both had other public works of community importance. There is some evidence of craft specialization at Cahokia but this type of data has not yet been collected at Amalucan. Both seem to be involved in a relationship with their own hinterlands and with a broader network. In this aspect there appear to be differences in their individual relationships with the total settlement pattern. Amalucan seems to have participated in a more densely settled area with other similar communities close at hand. Cahokia was a larger community but with a much less densely settled hinterland and with more space between communities. These conclusions are speculative since very little study or thought has been given to this type of problem. In neither of the communities are we able to make estimates of population since sufficient control over occupation unit data has not been achieved. In both cases however we would surmise that population was in the order of thousands rather than hundreds.

Further studies need to be made in order to truly define temple town communities and to adequately compare or contrast these two. These types of studies need to take lines suggested by Schaedel, Mann and Longacre in the first session of this symposium. Particularly important to arriving at the kinds of data needed for such studies and conclusions is an application of the methods outlined in Crawford's *Archaeology in the Field*. Attention in this type of approach should be given to delineation of site area, collecting distributional data from the surface, defining specific factures on the basis of serial photos, distribution data and excavation, and a reconstruction of the history of the site area. From this should develop a description of the community through time with special emphasis on functional divisions within the community and population growth. Developed along with this would be a concern for understanding the setting, both cultural and ecological, in which the community is found. Interpretation of the above types of data will be of necessity based upon ethnographic data on communities of types comparable to that thought to be represented by the archaeological sites being investigated.

When these studies are carried out we will be able to go somewhat beyond the hypothesis and descriptions presented above.

References

Braidwood, R. J., and G. R. Willey. 1962. *Courses Toward Urban Life*. Aldine.

Haury, E. W. 1962. "The Greater American Southwest," in Braidwood and Willey.

Linne, S. 1942. *Mexican Highland Cultures*. Statens Ethnografeska Museum 7.

Mumford, L. 1961. *The City in History*. Harcourt, Brace.

Noguera, E. 1940. "Excavations at Tehuacan," in *The Maya and Their Neighbors*. Appleton-Century.

Spranz, B. 1967. "Descubrimiento en Totimehuacan," *Instituto Nacional de Antropologia e Historia, Boletin* 28: 19-22.

Willey, G. R. 1960. "New World Prehistory," *Science* 131: 73-86.

Wittry, W. 1964. "The American Woodhenge," *Cranbrook Institute of Science, Newsletter* 33: 1

Philip Phillips (Ph.D., Harvard University, 1940) is Honorary Curator of
Southeastern Archaeology at the Peabody Museum, Harvard University.
He is coauthor of the pathbreaking *Archaeological Survey in the Lower
Mississippi Alluvial Valley, 1940-1947* (1951) and the author of the recent-
ly published *Archaeological Survey in the Lower Yazoo Basin, Mississippi, 1949-1955* (1970). The question of independent invention versus
spread by diffusion is one found in many anthropological contexts when
parallel developments occur among different peoples. In this paper,
Phillips discusses the evidence for contact between the Old and New
Worlds, seeking to determine whether the older civilizations of the
Eastern Hemisphere influenced the development of New World civilizations. For an excellent up-to-date, book length summary of current
evidence and views, the reader is referred to *Man Across the Sea* (1971),
edited by C. L. Riley et al. While this topic used to be one of the most
hotly debated subjects in New World archaeology, the new attention
on systemic models has tended to shift the emphasis from where new
cultural items came from to why and how they were integrated into
the recipient system, no matter what their original provenience.

The Role of Transpacific Contacts
in the Development of New World
Pre-Columbian Civilizations

Philip Phillips

With a few notable exceptions writings on the subject of pre-Columbian contacts
across the Pacific take the form of comparisons of specific elements shared by Asiatic
and American cultures without reference to geographical, chronological, or cultural contexts. The rationale is that if parallels are sufficiently close, the only possible explanation
is transmission across the Pacific by means that do not require to be specified. The writers
are generally referred to as "diffusionists," a not altogether appropriate designation. All
anthropologists are diffusionists whether they believe in transpacific contacts or not.
The usage goes back to a time when Americanists were divided by a controversy over
the roles of diffusion and invention in the building of cultures. Diffusion as now understood covers the transmission of cultural ideas by any sort of means; but anthropologists
increasingly tend to think of it in terms of small-scale interaction requiring nothing more

Reprinted from *Handbook of Middle American Indians*, edited by R. Wauchope, Vol. 4, pp. 296-315,
University of Texas Press, 1966, by permission of the publisher and author.

than short-range movements of individuals or small groups of people. In this sense the proponents of transpacific contact are not really diffusionists at all. They have been obliged by various considerations (that we cannot go into here) to abandon the idea of island-to-island diffusion across the Pacific in favor of direct sea voyages over vast distances. This has forced them back into the kind of thinking that explained everything by migrations. Voyages are not migrations, to be sure, but from the point of view of anthropological theory they are the same kind of phenomena. They are events, not processes. As such they give us the right to demand not only evidence that they occurred but where, when, and how.

If the proofs of transpacific diffusion have fallen short, the implications drawn from them have been of a most far-reaching nature. It has occurred to me that a useful approach to this complicated subject might be to consider first the implications and then to proceed to an examination of the evidence that would be required to support them. As a point of departure I take a recent paper by Wilhelm Koppers (1957) on the concept of an universal world history.[1] This all-important project, he holds, is impossible of fulfillment without demonstration of the worldwide unity of culture—this being the special task of cultural anthropologists and prehistorians. Professor Koppers states that on the levels of high culture this task has already been achieved by Heine-Geldern and others, the crux of the demonstration being the proof of the unity of the civilizations of the Americas with those of the Far East, and ultimately of course the Middle East, the cradle of all civilization. He refers to this "breakthrough" as though there could be no two opinions about it. All that remains is to demonstrate a similar unity at lower levels of cultural development.

Not many American archaeologists will accept this claim, but with the proposition that the problem must be dealt within a deeper context of development there can be no disagreement. Gordon Ekholm, one of the few American scholars who has not ignored the transpacific question, has expressed a similar view (1953, p. 72). In slightly different terms, the question is not whether there have been contacts across the Pacific but whether such contacts could have been determinant at critical moments in the development of American culture. For example, it signifies little in terms of development that a lotus design of presumed Asiatic origin appears in certain Maya centers in the 8th century A.D. long after Maya civilization achieved its classic expression. It is necessary to reject the assumption that inheres in both isolationist and diffusionist positions, to wit, that acknowledgment of the transpacific provenience of one, several, or even many, particular elements settles the question *against* the integrity of American civilizations once and for all. The isolationist appears to believe that if he lets anything in, the trickle will irresistibly become a flood. The diffusionist cannot be blamed for exploiting this convenient situation; all he has to do is prove the existence of a trickle. In my opinion this is the most he can so far claim to have done. Before any assertions can be made about the unity of New and Old World civilizations, it will be necessary not only to produce evidence of historical contacts, with some degree of precision as to time, place, and means of transport, but also to show that the role of such contacts was decisive in the development of Nuclear American civilizations *in their formative stages,* that without such contacts the level of civilization would not have been attained.

The views expressed here involve two familiar assumptions about the nature of culture change. The first is that it does not proceed at a constant unvarying rate, but rather by a succession of sharp advances separated by intervals of less rapid change, stagnation, or even recession. The causes of such advances may be manifold, not to say mysterious, but always to be reckoned with is the possibility of new ideas from an external source. The second assumption is that the appearance of new features tends to coincide with other changes not necessarily related in a direct and ascertainable way. The culture seems to move forward on a broad front. In a recent seminar on culture contact situations this kind of diffusion was somewhat ponderously described as "trait unit intrusion, type B4: fusion with emergence of new traits which have no obvious antecedents in the trait units or the receiving culture" (Willey *et al.,* 1956, pp. 22-23). It was the view of the conferees that this is the usual way one civilization influences another.

With these assumptions in mind it would seem reasonable to approach the problem of transpacific diffusion by locating the important breaks in the development of Nuclear American civilizations and then to scan the western horizon for signs of contact at these times and places. By focusing on the archaeological features that mark the breaks, they may be thought of as "events" and thereby rendered intelligible in a culture-historical context. The events that appear to have specific significance in this context are: (1) the domestication of plants; (2) the introduction (or invention) of pottery; (3) the establishment of the village farming socio-economic pattern; (4) the addition of minor ceremonial centers to the village pattern; (5) the emergence of major ceremonial ("great temple") centers. In this article we shall attempt to see to what extent these events can be related to the kind of events envisioned by the diffusionists, i.e. contacts of culture-bringing voyagers from Asia. The main emphasis will be on Middle America, but none of these developments can be dealt with adequately without reference to North and South American data.

Beginnings of Plant Domestication

If we seem to be starting the argument about transpacific diffusion at a stage well along in the development of New World culture, it is not because nothing of consequence to that development happened before, but because there is no serious argument about what did happen. It is almost universally held by isolationists and diffusionists alike that the original seepage of peoples into the New World was by way of Bering Strait, and that by a time conveniently estimated at 10,000 B.C. both continents were fully albeit sparsely occupied. As to what sort of cultural impedimenta the earlier migrants brought with them, there is less agreement. A commonly accepted theory is that the Arctic environment was an effective screen against all traits not compatible with a hunting-fishing-collecting mode of life. The isolationist could grant the Asiatic origin of all the technologies of the pre-agricultural levels in the New World without seriously affecting his position. This, however, would be giving away too much. We know that a considerable amount of indigenous development did in fact take place on these levels.[2]

The first real brush between isolationist and diffusionist comes with the stage that is marked by the beginnings of plant domestication. It is now believed that the "agricultural revolution" in the Near East was preceded by a long period of incipient cultivation, in which the chief reliance continued to be on hunting and collecting but experiments leading to the cultivation of cereals were taking place (Braidwood, 1958, 1960). The creation of an agricultural system is certainly one of the greatest achievements in human history, and Neolithic culture (in the sense of village agricultural subsistence) was made possible by its spread from the Near Eastern hearth to most parts of the Old World where cultivation of cereals was possible.[3] Finds of domesticated plant remains in early New World contexts now afford the view of a similar period of incipient farming, not as early in its inception, but lasting as long if not longer. This is not the growth pattern one would expect if the knowledge of plant domestication came to the New World fully developed.

Botanical arguments for transpacific diffusion are usually in the form of evidence that specific plants were known on both sides of the Pacific in pre-Columbian times, the assumption being that the transfer must have been by the agency of man. A further implication not always expressed is that the entire development of American agriculture originated in such a transaction. Such views were considerably shaken by the early dating of domesticated plant remains in the Huaca Prieta midden on the north coast of Peru (Bird, 1951) and will be even more so by recent developments in the archaeology of Tamaulipas, Mexico (MacNeish, 1958; Mangelsdorf and Reeves, 1959). Without insisting on the somewhat doubtful evidence of domesticated plant remains in the Infiernillo phase (7000–5000 B.C.) in Tamaulipas, it appears that by the Ocampo phase (5000–3000 B.C.) cultivation of gourds, squash, peppers, and beans is fairly certain. No one has produced acceptable evidence, or even an hypothesis, of sea-borne contacts across the Pacific at this remote period.

Leaving aside the question of domestication in general to focus on the plant that furnished the economic basis for Nuclear American civilization, we find the temporal context is only slightly later. The most primitive maize so far discovered is from Bat Cave, New Mexico, with a series of radiocarbon dates on associated charcoal running back to about 4000 B.C. (Libby, 1951; Dick, 1952). Precise data on the association of the corn and charcoal have not been published, so this early date may be justly regarded with suspicion. A safer date perhaps for the considerably less primitive maize of the La Perra phase in Tamaulipas is 2500 B.C. (Libby, 1952). These finds of early maize have taken much of the steam from the hotly debated question of Asiatic origin of maize (Stonor and Anderson, 1949; Carter, 1950; Mangelsdorf and Oliver, 1951; Ho, 1955).[4] The emphasis now has shifted to the possibility of pre-Columbian diffusion of maize from America to Asia.

Less important from our standpoint is the argument about the grain amaranths, anciently cultivated in the New World and also known from certain regions of southern and central Asia. So far as I am aware it has not been stated with confidence that the amaranths were cultivated in Asia before they were in America, so the outcome of this particular question has little bearing on the origins of American agriculture.

Ever since the pioneer papers of Hutchinson and Stephens (Hutchinson, Silow, and Stephens, 1947; Stephens, 1947) suggesting relationships of Old and New World cottons, the interested layman has watched from the sidelines a botanical dispute of terrifying complexity. Discovery of cotton and cotton cloth in the pre-maize levels of Huaca Prieta added some nonbotanical complications. Hutchinson's theory requires the crossing of an American wild cotton with a cultivated Asiatic cotton, the latter having been carried across the Pacific by man, and the Huaca Prieta dates require that this event be pushed back to some time before 2500 B.C. According to Heine-Geldern's findings, cotton was introduced into southeast Asia from India some time after the beginning of the Christian Era and reached China even later. It was cultivated at Mohenjo Daro in the Indus Valley as early as the latter half of the third millennium B.C., perhaps earlier still in the Near East, but even to Heine-Geldern the notion of a direct transfer by sea from India or Arabia to South America as early as 2500 B.C. "sounds fantastic" (1952, p. 347). The only comfort he can find is in the possibility that Huaca Prieta cotton was not like other American cottons, that the crossing hypothesized by Hutchinson and his colleagues actually took place at a later date, but in a more recent paper (1958, p. 397, note 101) he points out that this solution involves some difficult botanical problems. His final conclusion, that we must await for more evidence from the botanists, is one with which no one can fail to agree.

My impression is that the same conclusion can be extended to all botanical aspects of the transpacific question, but I cannot refrain from commenting further on the paper just cited because it exhibits a remarkable shift of strategy. Heine-Geldern is now pre-pared to accept, even to welcome, the American origins of corn and the grain amaranths. Their introduction into Asia, he contends, was by the return voyages of his south Chinese and Dongson adventurers of the first millennium B.C. Thus in the special case adverse findings are turned to positive account. But the general implication seems to be that it is a matter of slight concern whether the original impulse to cultivation in America came from within or without,[5] a position not heretofore taken by proponents of transpacific diffusion. This goes far beyond the question of the independence of American agriculture. If the first and most decisive step toward civilization was taken without stimulus from cultures further along that road, it becomes more difficult to reject the possibility of other steps of similar independent nature. In a more specific sense, if the characteristics of Nuclear American maize economy—and I think Heine-Geldern would agree that associated religious and social features would have to be included—were already set before the first transpacific influences could have been brought to bear, it raises a serious ques-tion as to how decisive such influences (if proved) could have been at any subsequent stage of development.

First Appearance of Pottery

It cannot be said that the earliest pottery in Nuclear America marks a turning point save in the sense that from here on the archaeologist is provided with an analytical tool dear to his heart. Nevertheless, pottery is relevant to the present inquiry as one element that we have some hope of tracing to its ultimate source, or sources, and this might tell us something about diffusion in general.

In Nuclear America it had been customary to equate the earliest pottery with the beginnings of the village farming pattern in an "Archaic" "Formative" or "Preclassic" period, but more recently archaeologists have been finding pottery in coastal shell middens under conditions similar to those of North America, where the equation of pottery with agriculture has long since broken down. However, the temporal frontiers of agriculture have been pushed back also. The general concensus is that the first ap-pearance of pottery was long after the beginnings of plant domestication but before the consolidation of the village farming pattern (Willey, 1960). The threshold of pottery has been pushed back, but this has not brought the problem of origins any nearer solution. The most influential theory at the moment is that Nuclear American pottery is the result of a fusion of two separate developments: the Woodland tradition of North America, with its ultimate origins in Asia; and an indigenous Nuclear American tradition the dispersal center of which has not yet been located. Another theory would derive all Nuclear American pottery from the Woodland tradition. Thus both explanations involve the possibility of ultimate Asiatic origin in whole or in part.

At present (1961) certain data must be accommodated in any hypothesis of origin: (1) The earliest dated potteries in South America and lower Central America are in the third millennium B.C.: Puerto Hormiga, Columbia, ca. 2900-2500 B.C. (Reichel-Dolmatoff, 1961); Valdivia, Ecuador, with three dates on shell ranging from ca. 2500-2100 B.C. (Evans, Meggers, and Estrada, 1959); Rancho Peludo, Venezuela, ca. 2500 B.C. (Cruxent and Rouse, 1958-59); Monagrillo, Panama, ca. 2100 B.C. (Willey, 1958, 1960). Of these potteries Monagrillo is perhaps the most primitive, but none are what might be expected of the initial stage of pottery technology. (2) The earliest pottery in Middle America, from Tehuacan, Puebla, ca. 2300-1300 B.C., has not yet been described. It is sufficiently crude to have prompted a hypothesis of local origin from stone proto-types of the underlying preceramic stage (MacNeish, 1961). The earliest pottery in the Valley of Mexico, Early Zacatenco, is considerably later (ca. 1360 B.C.) and more advanced technologically (Vaillant, 1930; Johnson, 1951). (3) The oldest pottery in North America is the plain fiber-tempered phase on the Georgia coast with five dates ranging from about 3500 to 1000 B.C. The earliest and latest of these dates appear to be out of line; the three in between are in the order of 2100 to 1700 B.C.[6] This fiber-tempered pottery does look technologically primitive. Specialists have suggested that it may have been a local development sparked by stimulus diffusion from the Woodland tradition of the Great Lakes region to the north (Sears and Griffin, 1950), but the dating now available runs counter to such an explanation. (4) The earliest Woodland pottery, Vinette I, dates from about 1000 B.C.[7] Many of the characteristic features of Woodland pottery are believed to have diffused from Asia via Bering Strait (Tolstoy, 1953, 1958b), but the specific type Vinette I has no close counterpart in Asia or the North American Arctic (Griffin, 1960a, p. 811). Oddly enough, the most striking Eurasian parallels to later Woodland pottery (of the Point Peninsula type) seem to be as far away as possible from Bering Strait, in north Russia and Scandinavia (Ridley, 1960), a circumstance that no one has yet been able to explain.

Juxtaposition of these findings is not favorable to the theory of Woodland origin of Nuclear American pottery in any specific sense. To leave aside for the moment the fiber-tempered ware, which seems to be a problem all to itself, the chronological data do not support diffusion in a north-south direction. Even as between Middle and South America, the temporal gradient seems to slope the other way. Individual features considered as Woodland, particularly rocker-stamping and zoned rocker-stamping, have been reported from many early phases including Valdivia, but the features in question are not among the earliest or the most fundamental features of Woodland pottery in the home area. So the dating actually favors the theory that these features came into Woodland from the south, as some North American archaeologists have maintained (Griffin, 1952b, p. 126). One pottery that has a slightly more authentic Woodland cast is the recently discovered Ocos phase of the Guatemala coast (M. D. Coe, 1960b, 1961). This has several of the more fundamental Woodland elements, such as cord- and fabric-marking, but also many other features that have close counterparts in Ecuador, and these have no relationship whatever to Woodland. The phase has not been dated, but on the basis of cross-ties M. D. Coe has given it an estimated time span of 1500–800 B.C. The youngest of these dates is not inconsistent with a North American Woodland connection but, as Coe himself has pointed out, the most specific Woodland traits in Ocos, i.e. those that might be considered as reliable time-markers, such as zoned shell edge and dentate rocker-stamping, are Middle Woodland or "Hopewellian" features. The earliest (Illinois) phase of Hopewellian is abundantly peppered with radiocarbon dates falling within the period from 500 B.C. to A.D. 1. It seems that even Coe's terminal estimate is too early for the theory of Woodland derivation.

It might be observed, however, that more thoughtful comparisons are required before any of these Nuclear American features can be called Woodland or Asiatic. As Paul Tolstoy pointed out some time ago (1953, p. 36), before the possibility of Woodland influences in Nuclear America became an issue, progressive attenuation of Asiatic features with increase of distance from their source is to be expected. Perhaps the emphasis on specifically Woodland connections in Nuclear America has been misplaced. Woodland is after all a refocalization of Asiatic traits that came into eastern North America not as a complex but separately and at different times. Some of them, particularly the earlier arrivals, might be unrecognizable as Asiatic today. Fiber-tempering may be a case in point. It has been reported from both Asia and Alaska (Chard, 1958a). Does this not suggest a similar origin for other ceramic features that are not specifically Woodland?

Whatever the ultimate origins, it is becoming clear that the earliest diffusion of pottery in North America was in a nonagricultural context, and this may have been true for Nuclear America as well. At some as yet unspecified point in time it was incorporated into an incipient farming culture and there began the well-known American agriculture-pottery association that has been the subject of so much generalization in the past. If this is the correct view, the effect of an admission of remote Asiatic origin of pottery on the integrity of Nuclear American civilizations would be just about nil.

Establishment of Village Farming

Tangible evidence for the transition from incipient cultivation to village agriculture is available in only two regions in Nuclear America, Tamaulipas and the north coast of Peru.[8]

In his long stratigraphic sequence in the Sierra de Tamaulipas, MacNeish (1958) has been able to show a steady increase in percentages of domesticated plant remains (in terms of volume of all food remains) from about 5 per cent in the upper deposits of the Nogales phase (ca. 3000 B.C.) to 40 per cent in the Laguna phase (ca. 500 B.C.). This figure of 40 per cent apparently represents agricultural stability in this rugged but not forbidding environment, where game and wild plant foods must always have been plentiful. There was a gap, however, in the sequence preceding the Laguna phase, and MacNeish thinks it likely that agricultural stability was reached here before 500 B.C. In other not yet fully reported excavations in the Sierra Madre of southwestern Tamaulipas this gap appears to have been filled. Here, as we have seen, the shift to cultivation may have begun as early as the Infiernillo phase (ca. 700-5000 B.C.). The 40 per cent stability figure was reached in the Mesa de Guaje phase equated with the pre-Laguna gap mentioned above (ca. 1500–500 B.C.). Food plants in this phase included a number of varieties of beans, warty squash, pumpkin, sunflower, cotton, and bottle gourds. Pottery and cotton cloth appeared for the first time in the sequence. There is little information on settlements, but what there is suggests small villages of scattered houses without specialized ceremonial or religious structures (MacNeish, 1958, pp. 168–69).

The chief interest of this peripheral evidence to the present inquiry lies in the extent to which it may be assumed to reflect what happened in the more central parts of Mesoamerica, where the earliest agricultural phases so far known are already firmly established on a village farming level. Before we consider these, it will be well to glance briefly at the situation in Peru.

Almost all the relevant Peruvian information is from the north coast where, at the mouths of the many rivers coming down from the Andes, small areas of water-holding soil made some cultivation possible. Combination of this and the more dependable resources from the sea was sufficient to permit the growth of fairly large and stable villages. In terms of our nomenclature, under these rather special conditions, village settlement patterns developed on an incipient agricultural base. About 1400 B.C. (the date is not securely fixed) maize was incorporated into this economy, and shortly thereafter, pottery. Soon there began a shift of population up into the valleys away from the sea, where more land was available for cultivation. It is an arid country, even in the valleys. Whether this shift could have taken place without the aid of irrigation is a point that has not been settled. In any case, this is the threshold of village farming that we are seeking. The earliest chronological datum for this new economic pattern is the Cupisnique phase in the Chicama Valley, with a radiocarbon date of ca. 700 B.C. But Cupisnique is a coastal phase of the Chavin culture of the highlands, the type site of which Chavin de Huantar is a cult center in no uncertain terms. It is now believed that other elaborate centers farther down the coast, such as Las Aldas, may date from a still earlier pre-maize period (Engel, 1957b). Thus the courses of development in Peru and Mesoamerica are clearly not the same. By the time the threshold of village farming as herein defined (on the basis of Mesoamerican data) has been reached in Peru, there are already indications that some cultures at least have passed beyond it. The explanation of this apparent anomaly may lie in the fact that the first appearance of maize in Peru cannot be dated earlier than about 1400 B.C. (Collier, 1959). The corresponding date in Middle America (backed up by the United States Southwest) is more than a thousand years earlier. Technical analyses of early Peruvian maize have not been published, but it has recently been suggested by the most qualified experts that its great diversity resulted from the hybridization of Peruvian and Mexican popcorns (Mangelsdorf and Reeves, 1959, p. 422). If our assumption is correct that it was maize that made possible the shift to a village farming economy in Mesoamerica, it might be argued that a similar shift in Peru had to wait for the Mexican component of the hybridization postulated by Mangelsdorf and Reeves, and by the time this happened advances toward more complex social and religious organization had already taken place. We do not have to assume that these other developments also diffused from Mesoamerica, although it is a possibility. This of course is a flagrant oversimplification, taking no account of the Peruvian highlands, where data on early agricultural developments are not yet available.

In any case on present evidence it is clear that priority, so far as this particular turning point is concerned, rests with Mesoamerica. This is the ground on which the case for transpacific diffusion, if there is a case, must be argued.

The earliest dated occurrence of the village farming pattern in Mesoamerica is Vaillant's Early Zacatenco phase in the Valley of Mexico (Vaillant, 1930) with a radio-carbon date of 1360 B.C. ± 250 (Johnson, 1951).[9] The earliest phase of the closely related El Arbolillo site (Vaillant, 1935) is thought to be slightly older. This is of no great importance here except as a further indication that a date of 1360 B.C. for the beginning of the village farming era is probably on the conservative side. What is important is that these cultures show no signs of fumbling beginnings or sudden development under the stimulus of new ideas. One has a strong impression that this is not the threshold of village farming but merely its first appearance in the archaeology of a particular region. It is in fact held that the emergence of fully settled village farming took place somewhere in the southern part of Mesoamerica. The reason for this supposition is that the earliest known Preclassic cultures of the highlands and Pacific coast of Guatemala, though not as yet securely dated, seem to have been further along in social and economic development as evidenced by the presence of fairly large temple mounds.

At the present time, however, the El Arbolillo I-Early Zacatenco culture seems to be as close as we can come to the threshold of village farming in Nuclear America while still remaining on firm ground so far as documentation and chronology are concerned. It remains now to see what are the salient features of this culture and what the chances are that any of them can be attributed to influence from across the Pacific. For this purpose the barest outline will suffice.

Settlements were small lakeside villages, that can certainly be characterized as "permanent," to judge from the depths of the refuse. Total area of the Zacatenco site was about 3.5 acres, that of El Arbolillo somewhat larger. Vaillant gave no population estimates. A more recent authority suggests 200 inhabitants as a probable village limit (Piña Chan, 1955, p. 25). Houses were small, rectangular, constructed on a framework of poles with walls of wattlework daubed with mud and roofs of thatch, a type of dwelling that remained in vogue throughout all the periods of Middle American prehistory and is still in use today. There is no evidence of any other kind of structures, religious or secular, no defensive works, and no special repository for the dead, who were simply placed in shallow graves scooped into the soft and pungent refuse that accumulated around the dwellings. Burials were not oriented consistently and no rigid canons with respect to position of the body were in evidence, though tight flexure was the most common form. Some burials were covered with red ochre, a custom that may have a remote Asiatic origin. Its early occurrence in North America, however, is not favorable to a transpacific route. Grave offerings were not lavish; at Zacatenco they were very often lacking altogether.

Technological aspects of El Arbolillo I-Early Zacatenco culture were equally un-distinguished. It was plainly an era of household arts, with few signs of specialized crafts-manship. Implements of ground or chipped stone, the latter mainly of obsidian, conform to patterns that are practically universal in New World cultures at a comparable level of development. Nevertheless, the presence of a few simple but well-finished ornaments of jade and small flat bits of turquoise reveal the beginnings of crafts that are to show charac-teristic development in succeeding periods. Pottery, to quote Vaillant, shows a "smug competence uninspired by artistic yearnings." Ninety per cent was a purely utilitarian "bay ware," but there were also more specialized black, white, and painted wares. Shapes were simple bowls and jars with rounded bottoms, but a few vessels had small tripod supports, a feature of interest in the present inquiry. Decoration was by means of incision, sometimes paint-filled, and white-on-red painting. Designs of simple linear motifs showed little if any symbolic content.

Pottery was the preferred material for many small objects—rattles, whistles, bells, spindle whorls—but the outstanding products from any point of view were the figurines. These fresh and lively little objects of problematical function display something more than the "smug competence" of the pottery, although they were to receive even more intense expression in subsequent periods.

Of religious and social aspects of the culture not much can be inferred. A great deal of nonsense has been written about figurines as expressions of an "earth mother" or "fertility" cult. True enough, in El Arbolillo I-Early Zacatenco times they were exclusively female, but it is noteworthy that the interest is centered on the heads, with an endless and charming variety of hair style and headdress, rather than on those portions of the female anatomy devoted to procreation. A sounder inference can be based on the lack of symbolism—this applies to pottery decoration as well—as compared with later figurines (e.g. Tlatilco) which, in addition to being often male, appear as magicians or priests with masks or god-animal attributes, or as ball-players with helmet, pads, and other ritual paraphernalia. The contrast suggests that there was a lack of complex religious organization in the earlier period.

Now what can the transpacific diffusionist make of this? If I am correct in supposing that it is important for him to be able to show that this village farming point was not independently "turned," what specific features of this culture can he point to as trace elements of Asiatic intervention? The basic technologies—agriculture, stone and bone, pottery, weaving—were already present in the incipient farming era. The only features that might be considered as new that have figured in transpacific writings are jade carving, turquoise mosaics, tripod vessel supports, and figurines.

Jade and Turquoise

Now that sources of jadeite have been located in the Guatemala highlands (Foshag and Leslie, 1955), there is no further basis for the supposition that the raw material as well as the techniques of jadeworking came from Asia. Nevertheless jade does continue to figure in the transpacific question in a slightly different way. According to Heine-Geldern (1954), his Chinese voyagers of the 8th century B.C. were in search of gold, which was found in Peru but not in Middle America. For their interest in the latter area other lures must be assumed. "Where," asks Krickeberg (1956, p. 567), "did the Olmecs get their advanced techniques of working jade?" The simple little El Arbolillo jades are not to be overlooked in this question. I would merely point out that 1360 B.C. is a half-millennium too early for the Heine-Geldern hypothesis. The technique of inlaying turquoise has been treated in the same offhand fashion (Covarrubias, 1954, p. 54) as though its mere presence on both sides of the Pacific were sufficient evidence of contact.

Tripods

Vessel supports have an immensely long history in China and the New World, in the course of which all possible changes have been rung on this basically simple invention. It would be surprising if, out of countless variations on both sides of the Pacific, some remarkable parallels were not to be found. Covarrubias has done so (1954, fig. 25). His earliest Middle American example is from the Las Charcas phase at Kaminaljuyu. There is every reason to believe that Las Charcas is later than El Arbolillo I. Covarrubias would derive the Las Charcas tripod from China because he has been able to find an example from Kansu that it closely resembles. If tripods were already in existence in Middle America, I would think it more economical to derive the Las Charcas example from them, never mind how close the resemblance.

Figurines

I would be disinclined to mention figurines and "fertility cults," but the subject comes up in transpacific writings that are not to be ignored (e.g. Ekholm, 1955, p. 103). The unsuitability of El Arbolillo I-Early Zacatenco figurines as expressions of fertility has already been noted. The Valdivia figurines (Evans, Meggers, and Estrada, 1959), probably the oldest in the New World, are either unsexy females or androgynous. More significant perhaps is the possibility that Valdivia was not an agricultural phase. On the other hand, the evidence for figurines in known incipient agricultural phases is negative because these had no pottery. In short, the theory that figurines participated in the original spread of agricultural practices in the New World is entirely unsupported by the facts.

Perhaps in this sketch of what is currently believed to be the earliest village farming culture in Nuclear America there are other less trivial items of possible Asiatic origin that I have overlooked. But even if the case for such intrusions were clear and irrefutable, it would still remain to show that they could have been crucial in a developmental sense. This, so far as I know, has not even been attempted. We can say therefore with some degree of confidence that the course of development toward civilization in Nuclear America reached the stage of village farming at a time probably not later than 1360 B.C. without serious intervention from across the Pacific.

Village Ceremonial Center

At the present time it cannot be stated with certainty that village ceremonial centers marked by "temple" mounds of earth were not present in some places in Mesoamerica as early as the threshold of village farming. They are claimed to be associated with the earliest known Preclassic cultures in Guatemala: the Arevalo phase at Kaminaljuyu (Shook, 1951) and the Ocos phase on the coast (M.D. Coe, 1960b, 1961). Although these have not been dated earlier than El Arbolillo I-Early Zacatenco, it cannot be considered an impossibility. In my view there is no serious anomaly in the existence of platform mounds in simple village farming communities, but this does not accord with the view that such mounds imply the existence of societies more complexly organized than is consistent with the concept of simple village farming. If this is correct, the concept of a simple village farming era in Mesoamerica may be a fiction. I have already called attention to the difficulty of establishing such an era in Peru, so the whole proposition is in danger.

In my opinion the Guatemala evidence does not support this pregnant interpretation.[10] The expression "temple mound" has implications of complex religious institutions. Actually we know nothing about the kind of buildings supported by these primitive earthen platforms. The only inference backed by any concrete evidence is that they were funerary. If we were to call them "burial mounds," the implication of multi-village organization might disappear. There is no clear indication that the mounds in question exceed in size or numbers what might be expected in the public architecture of simple village communities. In the Ohio and Mississippi Valley we find earthen mounds of considerably larger dimensions associated with cultures that are perhaps not even "up to" the village farming level.

This is not a matter, however, that any one can afford to be dogmatic about. We certainly must reckon with the possibility that future research in southern Mesoamerica will reflect the existence of complex multivillage patterns at the very beginning of the Preclassic. If so, the diffusionist could with perfect reason seize on this as *the* turning point in the Middle American prehistory, a rags-to-riches leap from the stage of incipient cultivation to something approaching civilization—a change containing the seeds of all subsequent developments in Middle American culture. For such a forward bound what more natural than to look for an external stimulus? A diffusion hypothesis might go something like this: Experiments with plant domestication began very early in America but led to nothing until a more advanced people appeared, bringing the degree of social and religious organization necessary to establish, on the basis of the food crops made available by said previous experimentation, a stable farming economy. The visible symbol of this revolutionary change is the tomb or temple platform mound of earth. The round date of 1500–1000 B.C. would indicate China as the only possible source of the intrusion. This would be followed by the usual encomiums on Chinese seafaring at this remote period based on evidence of 2000 years later.

The arguments that could be deployed against this hypothesis are not despicable. (1) Early Preclassic art does not support a theory of complex religious development. This is not to say that religion played a secondary role at this time, but simply that it gives no indication of having reached the "cult" stage, reflected in archaeology by the dissemination over wide areas of art styles characterized by the dominance of symbolic over purely decorative and naturalistic forms. (2) There is no present evidence of platform mounds in China from which these early Middle American structures could have derived.[11] (3) It has not yet been demonstrated that platform mounds appeared in Middle America fully developed and with dramatic suddenness. A strong case could be made in favor of the proposition that they developed slowly from very small beginnings. In many parts of the world structures of whatever purpose—residential, public, or religious—have tended to be placed on foundation platforms. Given the ever-present tendency for height above ground to be an expression of prestige, such platforms are certain to grow by accretion. So long as their size and number in any one site does not exceed what could be estimated as the capacity for moving dirt and stone of a single village community, implications of further social and religious complexity are gratuitous. When that capacity is plainly exceeded, there are usually other accompanying features to show that more complex institutions have been achieved.

Early Temple Centers

Up to this point we have seen nothing but difficulties for the diffusionist. The agricultural beginnings lie in a period too remote for diffusion by any other than the forbidding Arctic route. Pottery may have come in by this route but its influence in a developmental sense is negligible. The union of agriculture and pottery and the formation of simple village settlements with or without small-scale ceremonial or funerary structures seem to have required no impulse from overseas. We conclude that village farming culture in the New World is neolithic only in a homotaxial sense.

When it comes to the point, or points, where civilization begins to rear itself upon this substructure, the question of diffusion becomes acute. The criteria of civilization have been listed elsewhere in this *Handbook,* with particular reference to the fully developed Classic civilizations of Middle America. The point of view of this article is necessarily not so limited. These critical elements did not appear all at once and in one place. If they had, there would be ample reason to suspect a massive cultural invasion from an external source. I do not think it necessary to spend any time proving that this is not what happened. Civilization is neither a tight association of cultural elements traveling about the world as a "complex" nor a haphazard aggregation of random achievements with no functional relationship between them. If a culture finds the way to one or several such achievements, through its own creativity or by diffusion, or both, others are pretty sure to follow. This permits us to focus on the first appearance of any of the critical elements of civilization instead of waiting for all of them. These first appearances are in the Middle Preclassic period of Mesoamerica and the Early Formative (Chavin horizon) of Peru, coincident with the emergence of "great temple centers," the last turning point I shall consider in this article.

It could be argued that the transition from village ceremonial centers to great temple centers is more a matter of growth than change, but this would be to ignore a number of elements, among them some of the criteria of civilization, that seem to have come into existence only with the rise of these great centers. These are: (1) monumental architecture, (2) planned assemblages, (3) sculpture, (4) metallurgy (Peru), (5) hieroglyphic writing (Mesoamerica), (6) great art styles. This is a strictly archaeological list. Reflected in these features are intangibles such as widespread religious movements, complex sociopolitical institutions, craft specialization, and trade. These figure only implicitly in the transpacific question.

It will be noted that nothing has been said on the demographic side. The evidence is murky, but so far nothing seems to indicate that the rise of early temple centers was attended by, or dependent on, any far-reaching changes in cultivation and settlement patterns. A new kind of relationship between villages and temple center is obvious, but as yet there are no signs that populations were being drawn to these centers. In short, I am taking the position, without attempting to prove it, that the early great temple centers afford a context for consideration of the beginnings of civilization, and the possibilities of Asiatic influences therein, without involvement in the complex issue of urbanism.

Uncertainties of dating make it impossible to focus the discussion on any single site. We cannot even confine it within one or the other of the two nuclear areas. A point that I should think worth making, if I were on the diffusionist side, is that great temple centers appear to have arisen in Mesoamerica and Peru about the same time. Most securely dated is La Venta in Tabasco, the outstanding site of the Olmec culture, with a series of radiocarbon dates ranging from about 800 to 400 B.C. (Drucker, Heizer, and Squier, 1959, pp. 264-67). Kaminaljuyu in Guatemala and Monte Alban in Oaxaca had almost certainly attained the scale of great temple centers before the end of this interval, perhaps also Uaxactun in the Chicanel phase. Chavin de Huantar in the north Peruvian highlands is cross-dated, through the related Cupisnique on the coast, at about 700 B.C. Thus 700 B.C. may be taken as a round date for the rise of great temple centers in Nuclear America. It could hardly have been much later, but might have been somewhat earlier. It is about this time, Heine-Geldern thinks, that the maritime kingdoms of South China developed the seafaring capability to cross the Pacific. The apparent synchroneity, however, cuts both ways. If these early temple centers developed in response to the same stimulus, one would expect to be impressed more by the similarities than by the differences between them. The most I can do here is to refer briefly to some of the differences under the headings suggested above.

There is an understandable reluctance to consider as "monumental" those structures that do not involve the use of brick or stone masonry. In the context of this discussion we certainly have to do so. The builders of the great center of Kaminaljuyu used nothing but packed earth, a form of construction so elemental that it is scarcely worthwhile to discuss its origins. At La Venta massive blocks of columnar basalt were used exactly as though they were logs of wood. The similarity to the way stone was handled in Polynesia (at a much later time) is striking. The theory of local development of the Polynesian structures seems eminently reasonable, and the arguments in its favor apply to La Venta with equal force (Emory, 1943). The contrast between these primitive techniques of construction and the beautiful ashlar masonry of Chavin de Huantar is only equaled by the difference in the structures themselves. One searches Mesoamerica in vain for anything remotely resembling the great Castillo of Chavin with its multistoried rooms and galleries. The relatively modest temple platform known simply as E-VII-sub at Uaxactun is constructed on another system entirely different from any of the foregoing (Ricketson and Ricketson, 1937), a plaster coating over a hearting of earth and rubble, foreshadowing the stone veneer construction of later periods.

It may be out of place but I cannot refrain from commenting on the parallel, seldom omitted in transpacific writings, between the Classic period Maya lowland temple-pyramid and similar structures in southeast Asia, especially Cambodia. For example, a specific comparison has been made between the stone-covered Temple II at Tikal and the brick funerary temple of Baksei-Chamkrong in Cambodia (Ekholm, 1950). The first dates from about the 5th century A.D. and the second from the 10th century A.D. It goes without saying that the builders of Tikal Temple II could not have been influenced by Baksei-Chamkrong. What is said, or inferred, is that both derive from some earlier Asiatic proto-type. The exact whereabouts and dates of such prototypes are not given. According to students of Cambodian architecture, Baksei-Chamkrong is in an early or transitional phase of classic Cambodian architecture, a period of rapid development and change (Briggs, 1951, p. 126). If there are prototypical structures, in Cambodia or elsewhere, dating say five centuries earlier, is there any likelihood that they would resemble Temple II at

Tikal as closely as does Baksei-Chamkrong? To ask the question is to answer it. The Tikal structure is also in an early classic stage. Behind it lie several centuries of development, going back perhaps to the lowly prototype, Str. E-VII-sub at Uaxactun; behind that, according to present dating estimates, the earth and adobe pyramids of the Arevalo and Las Charcas phases at Kaminaljuyu. To my way of thinking the real point brought out by this comparison is quite different from what was intended. It seems that two widely separated and noncontemporaneous architectural traditions have been able to produce, at given stages of their own internal development, buildings that are remarkably similar. If this proves anything, it is that convergence is a factor to be reckoned with in long-range cultural comparisons.

Planned Assemblages

The plans of the early temple centers under consideration vary as much if not more than the architecture. La Venta in Mesoamerica and Las Aldas in Peru have vaguely similar axial plans, but Chavin de Huantar bears no resemblance to either. We do not know much about the plan of Kaminaljuyu when it first became a temple center, but at its peak it consisted of a number of tightly integrated units, each consisting of several pyramidal structures grouped about a central court. This is the basic Mesoamerican plan.

Every list of Asiatic parallels finds room for pyramidal mounds, but no one so far as I know has considered them in terms of total assemblages and possible cosmological inferences. This might be a useful approach. If, for example, they were grounded in the same Asiatic tradition, it would be reasonable to expect in the planning of the Maya some reflection of the cosmic symbolism implicit in the planning say of the Khmer, i.e. the concept of a celestial mountain, center of the universe, consisting of a pyramid or quincunx of tower sanctuaries with surrounding wall, moats, gates, and avenues leading to the central feature (Coedès, 1947, 1948; Heine-Geldern, 1956a; M. D. Coe, 1957a). One sees no sign of this in the typical Maya plan. It might be argued that nothing is left but the pyramid itself, the sacred mountain.[12] But Maya pyramids are not usually centrally placed. If there is a central feature, it is the plaza with pyramids grouped tangentially around it. More often there is no consistent organization of plan that would invite speculation in terms of cosmology. Enclosing walls are rare and never placed in reference to a single mound; gates and avenues equally so.[13] These are profound differences, quite outranking any similarities that may be seen in the individual structures.

Is this a case of divergence from concepts of planning that were formerly similar? On the Asiatic side the central principle is fundamental, I believe, going back, it is said, to the ziggurat of Mesopotamia. On the American side the tangential principle seems also to be rooted in the past. The plans of La Venta and Chavin de Huantar differ markedly from the classic Maya assemblage but not in the direction of the centralized temple-mountain concept of Asia. In both cases the largest structure—pyramid at La Venta, castillo at Chavin—dominates the composition by size alone, not by a central position in relation to other structures of the assemblage.

Sculpture

The Olmec and Chavin cultures also appear to have priority in the production of monumental sculpture.[14] Again there is little similarity in the forms or the techniques of carving. Relationships of style present intriguing problems. Many Classic and Postclassic Maya forms have their prototypes in La Venta and other Olmec sites, including some that have figured in transpacific writings. For example, Ekholm compared atlantean figures from Chichen Itza and the great stupa of Sañci, India, admitting that the case was somewhat complicated by the existence of an Olmec example from San Lorenzo Tenochtitlan (1953, p. 81, fig. 16). What he failed to point out was the uncanny resemblance between the little potbellied old men of San Lorenzo and Sañci, a good deal closer than between the latter and those of Chichen. The west gate of Sañci, where the figures are located, is said to date from the early first century A.D. (Zimmer, 1955, pl. 20, caption), almost certainly too late to have inspired the San Lorenzo sculpture. The theoretical implications of this parallel are not insignificant. The Olmec culture is held by diffusionists to be the result of Chinese contacts in a period necessarily antedating Indian expansion into southeast Asia. The San Lorenzo-Sañci parallel must be fortuitous or it makes nonsense of this hypothesis.

Metallurgy

The exquisite gold ornaments in the Chavin style that have been found from time to time (Lathrop, 1941, 1951) have been overlooked in the transpacific controversy. The artistic quality and design of these possibly earliest examples of goldworking in the New World, do not seem to have been surpassed in any subsequent periods, and this is what one might expect if the techniques, if not the actual artisans, were Asiatic. The objects, however, do not specifically figure in Heine-Geldern's monograph (1954), from which I conclude that he was unable to find close Chinese parallels. A greater difficulty for the diffusionist position, it seems to me, is the complete lack of metals in the early temple centers to the north. With one or two trifling exceptions metallurgy comes into Mesoamerica about the end of the Classic period. For some regions lack of raw materials may have been a factor, but this is small comfort to the diffusionist who is trying to show that the impetus to civilization was in the form of direct and repeated contacts with metal-using cultures of the Far East. If, on the other hand, he is content to show that these contacts operated only indirectly on Mesoamerica via South America (a position that is beset by other difficulties that we cannot go into here), it is not less incredible that metallurgy, or at least objects of metal, were not relayed along with other elements of civilization of alleged Asiatic provenience.

Hieroglyphic Writing, Numeration, and the Calendar

One might expect that a decisive impact of one civilization on another would be most clearly revealed in the domain of intellectual culture. The outstanding archaeological expressions in this domain are, of course, the hieroglyphic inscriptions of Mesoamerica and what they reveal of an extraordinary preoccupation with the passage of time—a limited but highly characteristic body of mathematical and astronomical knowledge. The complete lack of a comparable development in Peru is one of the most striking differences between the two nuclear areas. If this body of knowledge derived from an Asiatic source it ought to be possible to prove it. Yet it seems that research in this field has been so far remarkably barren of results.

However, I must point out that the diffusionist looks at this question in an entirely different way. For him the possibility of anything so complex as a system of writing being invented more than once simply does not exist. For example, in a recent paper on the perennial question of the origin of the Easter Island script, Heine-Geldern asks (freely translated): "Can we admit for a moment that Mexican and Maya writing were invented in complete independence without any suggestion from the systems of writing in the Old World? . . . What proofs do we have of this?" (1956-57, p. 19). I ask, what sort of proofs does he demand? In a historical question how does one prove that something did not happen otherwise than by pointing to the lack of evidence that it did? It is not clear to me that Heine-Geldern accepts this burden of proof, but he does indicate what sort of evidence he would bring to bear. The earliest examples of hieroglyphic writing, he holds, are the gylphs associated with the danzantes of Monte Alban I. The style of these remarkable bas-reliefs, he promises to show in a forthcoming paper, is Asiatic. Their date, possibly as early as the 8th century B.C., indicates as source the maritime states of south China, whose archaeology is so little known that direct comparisons cannot be made. Since the Monte Alban script cannot have been indigenous, it is not necessary to show its derivation from any specific Chinese script, but merely to indicate by a general stylistic comparison where that source would have to lie. It seems to me that from the standpoint of method this leaves something to be desired. Even if the stylistic affinity of the danzantes was beyond question, it would not preclude the possibility that the glyphs had a totally different history. Consider for a moment that it is by no means certain that these are the earliest glyphs in Mesoamerica. Pedantic as it may appear, I submit that the way to prove the relationship of one script to another is to compare the scripts.

Great Art Styles

A considerable share of transpacific "evidence" rests on comparisons in the domain of style. Close stylistic parallels are triumphantly proclaimed by the diffusionists as clinchers and greeted by the isolationists in embarrassed silence. Few attempts are made to consider the theoretical implications involved in such comparisons.

It may make things clearer to begin with an extreme example, although it has nothing to do with early temple centers. Ekholm (1950) presents a very telling comparison between a Marajoara pot from the mouth of the Amazon dating about A.D. 1200-1500 (Meggers and Evans, 1957, fig. 149) and a bronze drum of the Shang period which must date some time before 1028 B.C. (Grousset, 1959, p. 315). Here we have two objects decorated in a remarkably similar way and separated by a prodigious gap of time and space and we are asked to believe that they "hint at a common artistic tradition." Ekholm does not furnish any theory to account for the supposed relationship. For this we may turn to others. Thus Covarrubias (1954, p. 32): "The time difference is really no obstacle to the soundness of the theory. On the one hand the true age of American civilization is still undetermined. On the other there is a great probability that the cultural waves that started from eastern Asia between 1200 and 200 B.C. spread gradually across the Pacific by successive infiltration of styles from one place to another from various sources and at various times, a process that must have taken very long. What traveled, consequently, was the styles acquired second-hand by different peoples, not the actual objects from Asia."

One of the way-stations Covarrubias had in mind was the Marquesas where, according to Heine-Geldern (1937), elements of the Shang style were preserved down to the 19th century.[15] But style is a complex phenomenon like culture itself. One style can be influenced by another with a result that is unlike either, but that a style can be taken over by an alien people without serious modification is a doubtful proposition. And that it can be preserved in essential purity for thousands of years is another. How, it may be asked, does a style diffuse? Through movement of objects or of people capable of making them, or of showing other people how to make them? Covarrubias does not favor the first alternative because objects of proven Asiatic provenience have not been found in pre-Columbian America,[16] but it is at least conceivable. If Shang bronzes found their way to and across South America to the mouth of the Amazon, they could have been imitated by Marajoara potters. Highly improbable but not impossible. But if they had to get the idea from people, who in turn got it from other people and so on for thousands of years, it is simply inconceivable that the end product would still be recognizable as Shang. Here is a problem that cannot be laid to rest by formulae such as "successive infiltration of styles" or "lost intermediaries."

Such is the theoretical background of a comparison more pertinent to the present discussion, one that invariably figures in diffusionist writings, i.e. the similarity of ornamentation in the Classic Veracruz or Tajin style to that of ritual bronzes of the late Chou period in China. The time gap (some 500-800 years)[17] is not so great as in the Shang-Marajoara parallel. In this case, however, the interest is not primarily in the time gap, but in the indications that the Tajin style is grounded in the Olmec style, which is approximately contemporaneous with Middle Chou. If there were contacts with China at this time, either direct or by way of South America, they should be reflected in the Olmec style, not in Classic or Postclassic outgrowths from it. This is a problem for the diffusionist. I do not say that no such reflection can be seen, only that so far all suggested parallels have related to the later post-Olmec styles. The point that interests me is this: if there was a connection between the art of Chou and Preclassic Olmec, why did the style get to look more Chou-like with the passage of time? "Convergence" is a forbidden word in diffusionist literature, but I cannot think of any other explanation.[18]

Chavin, Olmec, and the Hypothesis of Early Chinese Contacts

Most of the facets of the transpacific question commented on in this study, and others that might have been, are involved with the Chavin and Olmec cultures of the Early Formative or Middle Preclassic periods. These are proper testing grounds for theories of early Chinese contacts with America. In the most formidable monograph on the transpacific question yet to appear Heine-Geldern proposed an hypothesis of direct voyages to South America by merchant adventurers from the maritime kingdoms of southern China in the period from the end of the 8th century B.C. to some time in the 4th century B.C.

(Heine-Geldern, 1954, pp. 383-87). The object of the voyages was the search for gold, the result was the Chavin culture. Krickeberg, I believe, was the first to point out in print that this hypothesis could be extended to the Olmec culture (1956, p. 575). Chavin and Olmec occupy similar developmental niches in their respective areas. Connections between them have been postulated (Porter, 1953) but not thoroughly explored. Chronological relationships are not very firm, but offer no serious difficulty. If I understand it correctly, the priority of Chavin over Olmec would be assumed in the expanded hypothesis because of the importance of gold as motivation for the voyages and the knowledge of goldworking in Chavin as evidence that they occurred. Influences from Chavin would have been responsible for a second florescent culture in Mesoamerica, the Olmec. Subsequent development on the foundation provided by these two affiliated cultures would have been fostered by continued contacts from China, and later from Southeast Asia, resulting in the classic civilizations of Peru and Mesoamerica.

It is a grand hypothesis. Merely to state it gives one a vicarious thrill. But there are enormous difficulties, as I have attempted to show. Not the least is that Chavin and Olmec are not similar enough to have derived, one from the other, or both from the same Asiatic source.

Recapitulation

For purposes of summary the issues that have figured in the controversy over transpacific diffusion may be grouped into three categories: (1) Items having to do with the Preformative and Early Preclassic cultures of Nuclear America in the long period that saw the beginnings of agriculture and settled village life. In this category the evidence for direct Asiatic influence is practically nonexistent. Except for pottery, I have not considered possibilities of direct diffusion via Bering Strait and North America, which may have been not insignificant. (2) Items having to do with the emergence of civilization, which I have equated with the rise of great temple centers in the Peruvian Early Formative and Mesoamerican Middle Preclassic periods. Here is a formidable transpacific hypothesis based on stylistic comparisons and conjectures about Chinese seafaring capabilities in the first millennium B.C. Whether this is "evidence" is a matter of opinion. I have done my best to indicate that something more substantial is required. In any case the importance of this hypothesis is not to be minimized. If I were a diffusionist, this is where I would concentrate my efforts. (3) Items, by far the largest number, that have to do with the fully developed Classic period civilizations of South and Middle America or with their less advanced contemporaries in between. In this category are included most of the famous parallels of transpacific literature, from Tylor's patolli-pachesi (Tylor, 1879; Erasmus, 1950) down to the recently reported Ecuadorian finds (Estrada, 1960). These I have not considered at all. They are fascinating problems of culture history, but from the point of view of this article they are of minor interest. We could concede them all without affecting the integrity of Nuclear American civilization in a strictly developmental sense.

My final conclusion is that Professor Koppers, in the passage cited at the beginning of this article, has greatly overstated the position. The diffusionists have *not* proved the unity of Far Eastern and American civilizations, and as for the lower levels of cultural development, they have not even made a case.

Notes

[1]This paper makes clear in a most interesting fashion why continental European scholars have taken the lead in transpacific studies. Koppers holds that the concept of an universal world history, the product of 19th-century German historians, is the "main line" of historical research. Anglo-Americans, under the influence of empirical philosophy and evolutionary natural history, have been drawn off into sidetracks: materialism, determinism, parallelism, and evolutionism, conceded to be valuable in their own way but not contributing to the main task of history.

[2]If recent opinions of Americanists who also know something about Siberian archaeology are correct, the bifacial projectile point tradition which was the mainstay of the early American hunters has temporal priority as well as technical superiority over comparable Siberian developments (Tolstoy, 1958b; Chard, 1958b; Griffin, 1960a). This might be taken as an earnest of American inventiveness at later stages more important from the standpoint of civilization, but we need not insist on it here.

[3]This of course is not the whole story of agriculture in the Old World. In the area of southern and southeastern Asia an agriculture based on an entirely different assemblage of plants came into being (Sauer, 1952), and recently the possibility of a third center in Africa has been suggested (Anderson, 1960). The priority and relationships of these Old World centers of agricultural dispersal are subject to dispute, but some connection between them is probable. Here the diffusionist does not have to reckon with the possibility of wholly separate and independent "invention" of plant domestication. It is interesting but not germane to the present issue that in lowland South America there may have been a separate center of agricultural dispersal based on root crops, as in southeast Asia, and here also the relationship with the Nuclear American seed-plant center is in question (Sauer, 1952; Rouse, 1960b).

[4]The discovery of fossil maize pollen in drillcores from 200 feet below Mexico City (Barghoorn and others, 1954) appeared to settle any doubts about the American origin of maize; but possibility of misidentification of the pollen has recently been suggested (Kurtz, Tucker, and Liverman, 1960).

[5]"Beim gegenwartigen Stand der Forschung lässt sich die Frage nicht entscheiden. Gleichgültig aber, ob der Pflanzenbau in Amerika selbständig ist oder auf Angregungen zurückgeht, die aus der Alten Welt gekommen waren: Zur Zeit als die ersten starken Einflüsse asiatischer Hochkulturen sich gelten machten, wahrscheinlich im 8 Jahrhundert v. Chr., hatte er in Mexico, Zentralamerika und Peru beriets sein charakteristisches Gepräge mit dem Mais als Hauptfrucht angenommen" (1958, p. 382).

[6]Only one of these dates has been published (Crane, 1956). The others are Humble Oil Company dates (information by William G. Haag). I understand there are now additional unpublished dates from Florida in the same order of magnitude.

[7]Following Griffin (1958, p. 10) in rejection of the date of ca. 2500 B.C. for Vinette I pottery at the Red Lake site in New York State.

[8]MacNeish has also found evidence of this transition in caves in Puebla, central Mexico (personal communication, 1960).

[9]A slightly earlier date of 1456 B.C. $\pm$ 250 from the famous burial site of Tlatilco (Johnson, 1951) has not been confirmed by recent dates run on more carefully selected samples, but is perhaps not entirely worthless. According to M. N. Porter (1953), there were Zacatenco sherds scattered through the soil of the burial area and in bottle-shaped pits nearby, so it is altogether possible that this date relates to an Early Zacatenco component at the site.

[10]In neither case has the full evidence for dating the mounds been published. I understand that at Kaminaljuyu dating was by means of sherds on the surface and in the mound fill, at the site near Victoria from surface sherds alone. Both methods of dating are

subject to the same possibilities of error, i.e. sherds from an earlier occupation may be contained in soil used in building the mound, and these may subsequently be washed out by erosion and left on the surface.

11Ekholm (1955) says that "the early pyramid tombs of the Miraflores period in Highland Guatemala have an unusual resemblance to the Shang tombs of China," but gives no particular references. According to information from Kwang-chih Chang, only one small platform "altar" dating from the Shang period has been reported (but not yet published). The great tombs of Anyang (Chu'ü-hsun, 1959) are in deep pits with sloping sides and ramps, very like a Maya pyramid in intaglio. Heine-Geldern (1956b) offers as prototypes the "gigantic grave pyramids of Chinese rulers of the last half of the first millennium B.C." but these are not early enough.

12Krickeberg (1950) states with assurance that Maya pyramids symbolize the celestial mountain, but in the same paper he has already pointed out that symbols diffuse but their meanings change.

13The sacbés of Yucatan and their "gates" seem to have no relationship to any specific pyramidal structures.

14A statement made possible by the lack of chronological information about San Agustin and other sites with monumental sculpture in Colombia.

15Heine-Geldern has more recently argued that the Chinese contacts with South America were by way of the North Pacific, bypassing Polynesia, where there could have been no way-stations to speak of.

16There are numerous references to finds of Chinese objects in post-Columbian contexts, which shows that things do get transported once contacts have been established. See Meighan, 1950; Mason, 1951; Meighan and Heizer, 1952; Heizer, 1953; Camman, 1952; Borhegyi, 1955; Kamer, 1955; H. G. Smith, 1955.

17We may take as a means of estimating the time gap the two pairs of examples figured by Ekholm (1950). I have no information about the precise date of the Chou bronzes but assume that they were made before 221 B.C., the end of the period of the Warring States (Grousset, 1959, p. 315). The Tajin examples are Yoke 9 and Palma 11 in Proskouriakoff's numbering (1954, figs. 1, 6). Yoke 9 is classified in her Yoke Group A, which has features that she finds reminiscent of Olmec jades (p. 74). She also calls attention to similar treatment on a carved mirror-back found in an Esperanza phase tomb at Kaminaljuyu cross-dating with Teotihuacan III, Monte Alban III, and Late Tzakol, in other words the end of the Early Classic period about A.D. 350 or 600, depending on the correlation used. Palma II is in the Tajin style of Proskouriakoff, the treatment "particularly suggestive of an advanced date" (p. 82). The human sacrificial scene on the reverse, she says, is similar to that of the late ball-court sculpture at Tajin. Parenthetically, if Ekholm had illustrated both sides of this palma, the Chou resemblance would have been rather overshadowed by this gruesome presentation. Proskouriakoff says that so far there is no evidence that palmas were made before the Postclassic period. So the time gap between these objects and the Chou bronzes is 550 or 800 years, depending on the Maya-Christian calendrical correlation used.

18A suggestion that the Tajin style is a persistence of an earlier style which may have been confined to woodcarving has the inestimable advantage that it cannot be confirmed or denied.

References

Anderson, E. 1960. The evolution of domestication. In Tax, 1960, 2: 67-84.

Barghoorn, E. S., M. K. Wolfe, and K. H. Clisby. 1954. Fossil maize from the Valley of Mexico. Bot. Mus. Leafl., Harvard Univ., 16: 229-40.

Bird, J. B. 1951. South American radiocarbon dates. *In* F. Johnson, 1951, pp. 37-49.

Borhegyi, S. F. 1955. Chinese figurines in Mesoamerica. *Amer. Antiquity,* 20: 286-88.

Braidwood, R. J. 1958. Near Eastern prehistory. *Science,* 127: 1419-30.

———— 1960. The agricultural revolution. *Sci. Monthly,* 203: 131-48.

Briggs, L. P. 1951. The ancient Khmer empire. *Trans. Amer. Phil. Soc.,* vol. 41, pt. 1.

Camman, S. V. R. 1952. A chinese soapstone carving from Yucatan. *Amer. Antiquity,* 18: 68-69.

Carter, G. F. 1950. Plant evidence for early contacts with America. *SW. Jour. Anthr.,* 6: 161-82.

Chard, C. S. 1958a. Organic tempering in northeast Asia and Alaska. *Amer. Antiquity,* 24: 193-94.

———— 1958b. An outline of the prehistory of Siberia. Part 1: The premetal period. *SW. Jour. Anthr.,* 14: 1-33.

Chu'ü-hsun, Kao. 1959. The royal cemetery of the Yin dynasty at Anyang. *Nat. Taiwan Univ., Dept. Archaeol. and Anthr.,* Bull. 13, 14. Tapei.

Coe, M. D. 1957a. The Khmer settlement pattern: a possible analogy with that of the Maya. *Amer. Antiquity,* 22: 409-10.

———— 1960b. Archaeological linkages with North and South America at La Victoria, Guatemala. *Amer. Anthr.,* 62: 363-93.

———— 1961. La Victoria: an early site on the Pacific coast of Guatemala. *Papers Peabody Mus., Harvard Univ.,* Vol. 53.

Coedes, G. 1947. Pour mieux comprendre Angkor. Libraire d'Amerique et d'Orient. Paris.

———— 1948. Les états hindouisés d'Indochine et d'Indonésie. *In* Histoire du Monde, vol. 8, ed. by M. E. Cavaignac. Paris.

Collier, D. 1959. Agriculture and civilization on the coast of Peru. Paper presented to annual meeting, Amer. Anthr. Assoc., Mexico City. Mimeographed. Chicago.

Covarrubias, M. 1954. The eagle, the jaguar and the serpent: Indian art of the Americas, New York.

Crane, H. R. 1956. University of Michigan radiocarbon dates, I. *Science,* 124: 664-72.

Cruxent, J. M., and I. Rouse. 1958-59. An archeological chronology of Venezuela. 2 vols. *Pan Amer. Union, Social Sci. Monogr.,* no. 6.

Dick, H. W. 1952. Evidences of early man in Bat Cave and on the plains of San Augustin, New Mexico. *In* Tax, 1952, pp. 158-63.

Drucker, P., R. F. Heizer, and R. J. Squier. 1959. Excavations at La Venta, Tabasco, 1955. *Ibid.,* Bull. 170.

Ekholm, G. F. 1950. Is American Indian culture Asiatic? *Natural Hist.,* 59: 344-51, 382.

———— 1953. A possible focus of Asiatic influence in the late classic cultures of Mesoamerica. *Mem. Soc. Amer. Archaeol.,* 9: 72-89.

———— 1955. The new orientation toward problems of Asiatic-American relationships. *In* Meggers and Evans, 1955, pp. 95-109.

Emory, K. P. 1943. Polynesian stone remains. *In* Coon and Andrews, Studies in the anthropology of Oceania and Asia, pp. 9-21. *Papers Peabody Mus., Harvard Univ.,* vol. 20.

Engel, F. 1957b. Sites et établissements sans céramique de la côte Péruvienne. *Jour. Soc. Amer. Paris,* 46: 65-155.

Erasmus, C. J. 1950. Patolli, pachisi, and the limitation of possibilities. *SW. Jour. Anthr.,* 6: 369-87.

Estrada, E. 1960. Newspaper article. Guayaquil.

Evans, C., B. J. Meggers, and E. Estrada. 1959. Cultura Valdivia. *Mus. Victor Emilio Estrada*, Pub. 6.

Foshag, W. F., and R. Leslie. 1955. Jadeite from Manzanal, Guatemala. *Amer. Antiquity*, 21: 81-83.

Griffin, James B. 1952b. Some early and middle Woodland pottery types in Illinois. *In* Deuel, 1952, pp. 93-129.

———— 1958. The chronological position of the Hopewellian culture in the eastern United States. *Univ. Michigan, Mus. Anthr., Anthr. Papers*, no. 12

———— 1960a. Some prehistoric connections between Siberia and America. *Science*, 131: 801-12.

Grousset, R. 1959. Chinese art and culture. London.

Heine-Geldern, R. 1937. L'art prébouddique de la Chine et de l'Asie du Sud-Est et son influence en Océanic. *Rev. Arts Asiatiques*, 11: 177-206.

———— 1952. Some problems of migration in the Pacific. *In* Koppers, Heiné-Geldern, and Haekel, eds., Kultur und Sprache. *Wiener Beiträge zur Kulturgeschichte und Linguistik*, 9: 313—62.

———— 1954. Die asiatische Herkunft der südamerikanischen Metalltechnik. *Paideuma*, 5: 347-423.

———— 1956a. Conceptions of state and kingship in southeast Asia. *Southeast Asia Program, Dept. Far Eastern Studies, Cornell Univ.*, Data Paper 18.

———— 1956b. Herkunft und Ausbreitung der Hochkulturen. *Osterreichische Akad. Wissenschaften*, Almanach (1955), Jahrgang 105, pp. 252-67.

———— 1956-57. La escritura de la Isla de Pascua y sus relaciones con otras escrituras (observaciones al articulo del Dr. Thomas Barthel). *Runa*, 8: 5-27.

———— 1958. Kulturpflanzengeographie und das Problem vorkolumbischer Kulturbeziehungen zwischen Alter und Neuer Welt. *Anthropos*, 53: 361-402.

Heizer, R. F. 1953. Additional notes on Chinese soapstone carvings from Mesoamerica. *Ibid.*, 19:81.

Ho, Ping-Ti. 1955. The introduction of American food plants into China. *Amer. Anthr.*, 57: 191-201.

Hutchinson, J. B., R. A. Silow, and S. G. Stephens. 1947. The evolution of Gossypium and the differentiation of the cultivated cottons. London.

Johnson, F. 1940. The linguistic map of Mexico and Central America. *In* The Maya and their Neighbors, pp. 88-114.

———— 1951. [ed.] Radiocarbon dating. *Mem. Soc. Amer. Archaeol.*, no. 8.

Kamer, Aga-Oglu. 1955. Late Ming and early Ch'ing porcelain fragments from archaeological sites in Florida. *Florida Anthr.*, 8: 91-110.

Koppers, W. 1957. Das Problem der Universalgeschichte im Lichte von Ethnologie und Prähistorie. *Anthropos*, 52: 369-89.

Krickeberg, W. 1950. Ostasien-Amerika: Bemerkungen eines Amerikanisten zu zwei Büchern.

Kurtz, E. B., H. Tucker and J. L. Liverman. 1960. Reliability of identification of fossil pollen as corn. *Amer. Antiquity*, 25: 605-06.

Libby, W. F. 1951. Radiocarbon dates, II. *Science*, 114: 291-96.

———— 1952. Radiocarbon dates, III. *Ibid.*, 116: 673-81.

Lothrop, S. K. 1941. Gold ornaments of Chavin style from Chongoyape, Peru. *Amer. Antiquity*, 6: 250-62.

———— 1951. Gold artifacts of Chavin style. *Amer. Antiquity*, 16: 226-40.

MacNeish, R. S. 1958. Preliminary archaeological investigations in the Sierra de Tamaulipas, Mexico. *Ibid.*, 48: 1-209.

———— 1961. First annual report of the Tehuacan archaeological-botanical project.
Robert S. Peabody Found. Archaeol., Phillips Acad. Andover.

Mangelsdorf, P. C. and D. L. Oliver, 1951. Whence came maize to Asia? *Ibid.*, 14: 263-91.

———— and R. G. Reeves. 1959. The origin of corn. *Ibid.*, 18: 329

Mason, J. A. 1951. On two Chinese figurines found in Mesoamerica. *In* Homenaje Caso,
pp. 271-76.

Meggers, B. J. and C. Evans. 1955. [eds.] New interpretations of aboriginal American
culture history. *Anthr. Soc. Washington,* 75th anniv. vol.

———— 1957. Archeological investigations at the mouth of the Amazon. *Smithsonian.*

Meighan, C. W. 1950. Excavations in sixteenth century shell-mounds at Drake's Bay,
Marin County. *Univ. California Archaeol. Survey,* Rept. 9, pp. 27-32.

———— and R. F. Heizer. 1952. Archaeological exploration of sixteenth-century Indian
mounds at Drake's Bay. *California Hist. Soc. Quar.,* 31: 98-108.

Piña Chan, R. 1955. Las culturas preclásicas de la cuenca de Mexico. Fondo de Cultura
Económica. Mexico.

Porter, M. N. 1953. Tlatilco and the pre-classic cultures of the New World. *Viking Fund
Pub. Anthr.,* no. 19.

Proskouriakoff, T. 1954. Varieties of classic central Veracruz sculpture. *Ibid.,* Pub. 606,
Contrib. 58.

Reichel-Dolmatoff, G. 1961. Puerto Hormiga: un complejo prehistórico marginal de
Colombia. *Ibid.,* 10: 349-54.

Ricketson, O. G. and E. B. Ricketson. 1937. Uaxactun, Guatemala: Group E—1926-1931.
Carnegie Inst. Wash., Pub. 477.

Ridley, F. 1960. Transatlantic contacts of primitive man: eastern Canada and northwestern
Russia. *Pennsylvania Archaeol.,* 30: 46-57.

Rouse, I. 1960b. Recent developments in American archaeology. *In* Wallace, 1960, pp.
64-73.

Sauer, C. O. 1952. Agricultural origins and dispersals. Amer. Geog. Soc.

Sears, W. H. and J. B. Griffin. 1950. Fiber-tempered pottery of the southeast; fabric-
marked pottery in eastern United States. *In* J. B. Griffin, ed., Prehistoric pottery
of the eastern United States. Mus. Anthr., Univ. Michigan.

Shook, E. M. 1951. The present status of research on the pre-classic horizons in Guatemala. *In* Tax, 1951, pp. 93-100.

Smith, H. G. 1955. Archaeological significance of oriental porcelain in Florida sites.
Florida Anthr., 8: 111-16.

Stephens, S. G. 1947. Cytogenetics of Gossypium and the problem of the origin of New
World cottons. *In* Advances in genetics, 1: 431-42.

Stonor, C. R., and E. Anderson. 1949. Maize among the hill peoples of Assam. *Ann.
Missouri Bot. Garden,* 36: 355-404.

Tolstoy, P. 1953. Some Amerasian pottery traits in north Asian prehistory. *Amer.
Antiquity,* 19: 25-39.

———— 1958b. The archaeology of the Lena basin and its New World relationships.
Pt. 1. *Amer. Antiquity,* 23: 397-418; pt. 2: *Ibid.,* 24: 63-81.

Tylor, E. B. 1879. On the game of patolli in ancient Mexico, and its probable Asiatic
origin. *Jour. Anthr. Inst. Great Britain and Ireland,* 8: 116-29.

Vaillant, G. C. 1930. Excavations at Zacatenco. *Amer. Mus. Natural Hist., Anthr. Papers,* vol. 32, pt. 1.

———— 1935. Excavations at El Arbolillo. *Amer. Mus. Natural Hist., Anthr. Papers,* vol. 35, pt. 2.

Wauchope, R. 1956. [ed.] Seminars in archaeology: 1955. *Mem. Soc. Amer. Archaeol.,* no. 11.

Willey, G. R. 1958. Estimated correlations and dating of South and Central American culture sequences. *Amer. Antiquity,* 23: 353-78.

———— 1960. New World prehistory: the main outlines of the pre-Columbian past are only beginning to emerge. *Science,* 131: 73-86.

———— and others. 1956. An archaeological classification of culture contact situations. *In* Wauchope. 1956, pp. 5-30.

Zimmer, II. 1955. The art of Indian Asia. *Bollingen Ser.,* no. 39.

Part III

The Old World: Mesopotamia

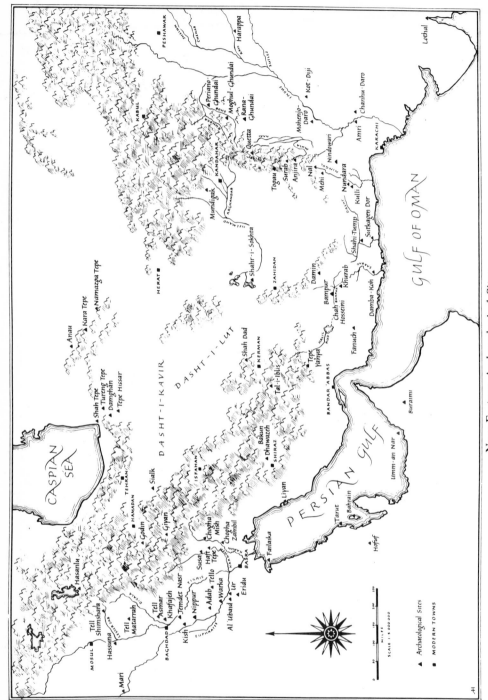

Near Eastern Archaeological Sites.

K. V. Flannery is one of the few archaeologists who has worked in both
the Old and New Worlds. His collaboration with Frank Hole in south-
western Iran provided the first fully eco-systemic approach in Near
Eastern archaeology. In this article he provides a masterful summary
on the origins and effects of domestication in the Near East.

Origins and Ecological Effects of
Early Domestication in
Iran and the Near East

Kent V. Flannery

Introduction

Late in the Pliocene period there began a series of movements of the earth's crust,
which caused the central plateau of Iran to be drawn closer to the stable massif of Arabia.
The land between, caught in the grip of these two far-heavier formations, was compressed
and folded into a series of parallel mountain ridges or anticlines. Gradually the centre of
this compressed zone collapsed and subsided, so that the parallel ridges, trending from
north-west to south-east, appear to rise out of it like the successive tiers of a grandstand,
eventually reaching the Arabian and Iranian plateaus to either side. The sunkland in
between, still settling and filling with the erosion products of the mountains, became
the rolling and irregular plain known as Mesopotamia; the parallel ridges to the east of it
are the Zagros Mountains.[1]

The result was an area in which altitudinal differences produce a great number of
contrasting environments in a relatively limited geographic area—a mosaic of valleys at
different elevations, with different rainfall, temperature, and vegetational patterns. Like
some of the other areas where early civilizations arose—Mesoamerica and the Central
Andes, for example—the Near East is a region of "vertical economy", where exchanges
of products between altitude zones are made feasible and desirable by the close juxtaposition of four main environmental types: high plateau (c. 5000 ft.), intermontane
valleys (1500-4000 ft.), piedmont-steppe (600-1000 ft.), and alluvial desert (100-500 ft.).
A similar pattern arose in the Levant, where the same later Pliocene tectonic movements
produced the great Jordan Rift Valley, flanked by the wooded Lebanon-Judean mountains and the arid Syrian Plateau. It was in this kind of setting that the first steps toward
plant and animal domestication were made.

Reprinted from *The Domestication and Exploitation of Plants and Animals,* ed. Ucko and Dimbleby,
by permission of the publishers Gerald Duckworth & Co. Ltd. ©1969 Peter J. Ucko and G. W. Dimbleby.

Stages in Near Eastern prehistory

In a recent article, Frank Hole and I have divided the prehistory of Western Iran into three main adaptive eras.[2] The first was a period of semi-nomadic hunting and gathering, which lasted until roughly 10,000-8000 B.C. The second era we have called the period of early dry-farming and Caprine domestication, and it seems to have involved predominantly emmer wheat *(Triticum dicoccum),* two-row hulled barley *(Hordeum distichum),* goats *(Capra hircus),* and sheep *(Ovis aries).* This period lasted until about 5500 B.C., and its hallmarks are already familiar to members of this symposium: permanent villages, early hornless sheep, goats with medially-flattened and/or helically-twisted horn cores, and cereal grain samples which show a mixture of wild (tough-glumed, brittle rachis) and domestic (brittle-glumed, tough-rachis) characteristics. The third adaptive era was one which involved the previously-mentioned cultivars plus bread wheat *(Triticum aestivum);* six-row barley which might be either hulled or naked *(Hordeum vulgare);* lentils; grass peas; linseed; domestic cattle *(Bos taurus);* pigs *(Sus scrofa);* and domestic dogs *(Canis familiaris),* and featured irrigation in those zones where its use was feasible without elaborate technology. This era culminated, in the lowlands at least, in the rise of walled towns, about 3000 B.C.[3]

There is no reason to believe that the entire Near East went through these eras synchronously; in addition, evidence suggests that each of the cultivars may have appeared earlier in some areas than in others. Nevertheless, with these caveats in mind, I find this framework useful enough so that I will follow it in this paper, and apologize in advance for viewing the rest of South-western Asia through Iranian eyes. The stages are, it should be emphasized, ones of farming adaptation: they imply nothing about level of social and political development. They allow, in other words, for the simultaneous existence of tiny four-acre villages in Kurdistan and immense, 32-acre sites like Catal Hüyük in Anatolia.

The basic argument of the paper is as follows. An important change in subsistence pattern, midway through the Upper Palaeolithic in the Near East, set the stage for domestication of plants. This shift, which represented a trend toward "broad spectrum" wild resource utilization, continued long after cultivation had begun. In this sense, our Western view of early cultivation as a drastic change or "improvement" in man's diet is erroneous, as is the frequently-cited notion that early agriculture gave man a "more stable" food supply. Given the erratic nature of rainfall in south-west Asia, the era of early dry-farming was still one of unpredictable surpluses and lean years, with considerable reliance on local wild products. I suggest that early caprine domestication, apart from its food aspects, represented a way of "banking" these unpredictable surpluses in live storage, analogous to the use of pigs by Melanesian peoples[4] or the exchange of imperishable, exotic raw materials which characterized early village farmers in Mesoamerica.[5] Early irrigation modified this pattern, and also aggravated environmental destruction to the point where the return to a wild resource economy would have been nearly impossible. It also set the stage for both dramatic population increases in the lowlands and "ranked" or stratified societies in which a hereditary elite controlled the small percentage of the landscape on which the bulk of the food was produced. A bit of indulgence on the reader's part will be required by the fact that in a paper of this length only the meagrest documentation can be offered for these points of view.

Prime movers and subsistence change

A basic problem in human ecology is why cultures change their modes of subsistence at all. This paper, while not relying on the facile explanation of prehistoric environmental change, is hardly destined to settle that problem. The fact, however, is that for much of South-west Asia we have no evidence to suggest that late Pleistocene or post-Pleistocene environmental changes forced any of the significant subsistence shifts seen in the archaeological record. I will therefore use, as one possible mechanism, a model of population pressure and disequilibrium relative to environmental carrying capacity, drawn from recent enthnographic data on hunting and gathering groups.

A growing body of data supports the conclusion, stated with increasing frequency in recent years, that starvation is not the principal factor regulating mammal populations.[6] Instead, evidence suggests that other mechanisms, including their own social behaviour, homeostatically maintain mammal populations at a level *below* the point at which they would begin to deplete their own food supply. The recent conference on "Man the Hunter", held at Chicago in 1966, made it clear that this is probably also true of human populations on the hunting-gathering level.[7] In addition, a number of current ethnographic studies indicate that, far from being on a starvation level, hunting-gathering groups may get all the calories they need without even working very hard.[8] Even the Bushmen of the relatively desolate Kalahari region, when subjected to an input-output analysis,[9] appeared to get 2100 calories a day with less than three days' worth of foraging per week. Presumably, hunter-gatherers in lusher environments in prehistoric times did even better. This is not to say that palaeolithic populations were not limited by their food supply; obviously, they were. But *in addition,* they engaged in behaviour patterns designed to maintain their density below the starvation level.

What, then, would persuade a hunter-gatherer to modify his subsistence pattern significantly—for example, to adopt agriculture? In the course of this paper I would like to apply the equilibrium model recently proposed by Binford[10] as a means of explaining post-Pleistocene changes in the archaeological record. This model will be used to offer tentative explanations for subsistence changes which took place in the Near East at the three critical points mentioned in the start of this paper: the Upper Palaeolithic, the beginning of domestication, and the beginnings of irrigation.

Binford, drawing on both Birdsell and Wynne-Edwards, postulates that prehistoric hunting populations, once reasonably well-adapted to a particular environment, tended to remain stable at a density below the point of resource exhaustion. He argues that their adaptation would change only in the face of some disturbance of the equilibrium between population and environment. Two kinds of disturbances might take place: either (1) a change in the physical environment which would bring about a reduction in the density of chosen plant and animal foods, or (2) a change in demography which would raise local human populations too close to the carrying capacity of the immediate area. The first kind of disturbance might be reflected in the palynological record; the second might be reflected in a shift in site density and settlement pattern in the archaeological record. Disturbances of both kinds occurred in the prehistoric Near East, but it is perhaps the second kind which is most useful theoretically, because it does not rely on the *deus ex machina* of climatic change, an event which does not seem to have taken place with sufficient frequency to explain all (or even most) prehistoric cultural changes.[11]

Binford points out that, even in the hunting-gathering era, certain areas supported higher populations than others because of their high level of edible resources. Butzer[12] makes the same point, singling out the "grassy, tropical deciduous woodlands and savannas; the mid-latitude grasslands; (and) the lower latitude Pleistocene tundras" as having the optimal carrying capacity for hunting-gathering populations. In the case of the Near East, for example, it would appear that the mixed oak woodland of the Levant Coast supported higher upper palaeolithic populations than some of the treeless inland steppe areas, at least where survey has been comparably extensive. One sees, therefore, a mosaic of "optimal" habitats, with a somewhat higher carrying capacity and population density, separated by "less favourable" habitats with a somewhat lower carrying capacity and population density. Binford argues that one source of stimulus for culture change is the cyclical demographic pressure exerted on these marginal habitats by their optimal neighbours. It is the optimal habitats which are regional growth centres; it is in them that populations rise, followed by buddings-off and emigrations of daughter groups before the carrying capacity has been strained.[13] They are the "donor systems"; the marginal habitats are the "recipient systems". And it is in the marginal habitats that the density equilibrium would most likely be periodically disturbed by immigrations of daughter groups, raising populations too near the limited carrying capacity. Thus Binford argues that pressures for the exploitation of new food sources would be felt most strongly *around the margins* of population growth centres, not in the centres themselves.

The "Broad Spectrum" Revolution

The first change I would like to deal with took place in the upper palaeolithic period, before 20,000 B.C., and amounted to a considerable broadening of the subsistence base to include progressively greater amounts of fish, crabs, water turtles, molluscs, land snails, partridges, migratory water fowl (and possibly wild cereal grains in some areas?).

The Upper Palaeolithic of the Near East has a number of chronological phases and regional variants, from the "Antelian" and "Kebaran" of the Mediterranean Coast[14] to the "Baradostian" and "Zarzian" of the Zagros Mountains.[15] Its environmental context in the coastal Levant may have been an open Mediterranean woodland not unlike today's,[16] while the Zagros Mountains seem at that time to have been treeless *Artemisia* steppe. [17] In both areas, hunting of hoofed mammals accounted for 90% of the archaeological animal bones, and when weights of meat represented are calculated, it appears that ungulates contributed 99%.[18] In the Zagros, archaeological settlement patterns suggest that the basic residential unit was a "base camp" composed of several families, which shifted seasonally; from this base, hunting parties made periodic forays to "transitory stations", vantage points from which they stalked and eventually killed game, which was then cut up into portable sections at temporary "butchering stations".[19] There are indications that a similar pattern may have characterized the Levant. On the basis of multivariant factor analysis of flint tools, Binford and Binford[20] have described the various living floors of Rockshelter I at Yabrud as brief "work camps" made at varying distances from a base camp, sometimes for hunting, sometimes for processing plant material. Near the Wadi Antelias, where Ksar Akil was presumably the "base camp", Ewing[21] describes "hunting sites on the surface higher up in the mountains", some of which may be analogous to the transitory stations or butchering stations of the southern Zagros.

Midway through the "Antelian" or "Baradostian" phases, one can see the afore-mentioned trend toward increasing use of small game, fish, turtles, seasonal water fowl, partridges, and invertebrates—the latter including terrestrial and marine snails, freshwater mussels, and river crabs. It would be oversimplified to view this as a "shift from large to small game", for even at late palaeolithic sites, ungulates contributed 90% of the meat supply. The trend is rather from exploiting a more "narrow spectrum" of environmental resources to a more "broad spectrum" of edible wild products. This "broad spectrum" collecting pattern characterized all subsequent cultures up to about 6000 B.C., and I would argue that it is only in such a context that the first domestication could take place. It is a pattern in which everything from land snails *(Helix* sp.) to very small crabs *(Potamon* sp.), and perhaps even cereal grasses, was viewed as potential food. It was also accompanied by a number of "pre-adaptations" for early cultivation.

One of these was the development of ground stone technology. At sites like Ksar Akil in Lebanon[22] and Yafteh Cave in Iran,[23] small coarse grinding stones occasionally appear; abraders are increasingly common in later Zarzian sites in the Zagros, where they come to include grooved rubbing stones.[24] Evidence suggests that these implements were at first used mainly (but not necessarily solely) for milling ochre. However, the ground stone technology was there, and when man eventually turned to the cereal grasses, he had only to adapt and expand a pre-existing technology in order to deal with grain processing.

Still another "pre-adaptation" for what was to follow can be detected in the later stages of the Palaeolithic in the Near East: the development of storage facilities, which are not at all well-represented in earlier phases. In the Zarzian level at Shanidar Cave, for example, "several pits . . . which may have been storage pits" are reported by Soleki.[25] These features increase with time; many sites of the period 9000-7000 B.C. are reported to have subterranean pits, e.g. Zawi Chemi Shanidar,[26] Karim Shahir,[27] and Mureybat.[28] Some were plastered, evidently for storage, e.g. at Aïn Mallaha,[29] while others may have been used for roasting grain over heated pebbles, e.g. at Mureybat.[30] In any event, these subterranean pits seem to be a feature of the broad-spectrum collecting era, and would presumably have been more effective for storing or processing invertebrate or vegetal foods (snails, acorns, pistachios, etc.) than for any activity connected with ungulate hunting.

It seems unlikely that the shift to a broad spectrum pattern was a direct result of environmental change. It is true that the earlier Pleistocene "big game" of the Near East—elephant, rhinoceros, hippopotamus, and so on—had vanished, but as pointed out by Howell,[31] these species disappeared midway in the Mousterian period, that is, many thousands of years before we can see any substantial increase in the use of fish, inverte-brates, and (possibly) vegetal foods. Moreover, use of these latter foods is more striking in some areas than others. For example, in the Levant area none of the Mount Carmel caves shows much in the way of invertebrate foods,[32] while "thousands" of *Helix* snails are reported from Ksar Akil in the Wadi Antelias.[33] In the Zagros, certain caves like Palegawra[34] have more abundant remains of snails, mussels, and crabs than do those in other areas; we recovered virtually no land snails from our Khorramabad Valley caves.[35]

Regional variations like those mentioned above suggest that Binford's model of disturbed density equilibrium may not be far wrong: pressure for the use of inverte-brates, fish, water fowl, and previously-ignored plant resources would have been felt most strongly in the more marginal areas which would have received overflow from the expanding populations of the prime hunting zones, raising their densities to the limit of the land's carrying capacity. At this point they would tend to turn, I suggest, not to small *mammals*— which do not appear to be a very secure resource anywhere in the Near East—but to those smaller resources which are readily and predictably available in some quantity at certain seasons of the year. These are water fowl, fish, mussels, snails, and plants. Many of these resources are storable, and though small, are not to be scoffed at. Land snails, for example, although less rich in protein than ungulate meat, are actually much richer in calcium,[36] especially in limestone mountain regions, since they use lime to synthesize their protective mucous.[37] Mussels supply vitamin A and acorns and pistachios are very high calorie foods, much more so than wild game.[38] Present data tentatively suggest that the "broad spectrum revolution" was real, that it was nutritionally sound, and that it originally constituted a move which counteracted disequilibria in population in the less favourable hunting areas of the Near East. Once established, however, it spread to and was eventually taken up even by the favourable areas. And one other aspect of it might be noted: the invertebrate (and vegetal?) foods involved are ones which could easily have been collected by women and children, while the men continued ungulate hunting. The broad spectrum collecting pattern may therefore have contributed to the development of division of labour in the late Pleistocene and early post-Pleistocene era.

Early Dry Farming

The environmental context of early domestication

The "broad spectrum" revolution set the cultural stage for domestication, and with the close of the Pleistocene the oak woodland belt expanded over the upland Near East, even into areas of the Zagros which had formerly been treeless steppe.[39] This "optimum" wild resource zone, which includes the densest stands of edible nuts, fruits, and wild cereal grasses had apparently been present in the Levant throughout the last glaciation,[40] but was now available over a much wider area.

A number of environmental characteristics of this zone today (which presumably have characterized it since the Pleistocene drew to a close) should be mentioned here, for they are variables which affected man's use of the region and set the environmental stage for domestication. Low average precipitation inhibits dense forest growth, but cool, moist air from the Mediterranean in winter results in enough rain (or snow) to guarantee some spring growth of edible grasses and legumes. Hot, dry air circulating out of Eurasia in the summer (plus even hotter local winds off Arabia) produces a prolonged rainless period which inhibits the growth of perennials; most of the vegetation thus consists of annuals which have a peak growing season in March or April, after which they must be harvested in a three-week period. This set the seasonal collecting pattern. Further, like most arid or semi-arid regions, the zone has a low vegetation diversity index,[41] which means that certain species (like wild cereal grasses) may form nearly pure stands. This is true of the fauna as well; while the number of mammalian species is low (relative to wetter areas), many of these are species which tend to form herds, e.g. sheep, goat, gazelle, and onager. Harlan and Zohary[42] have discussed the implications of the nearly-pure cereal stands, and Reed[43] has considered the pre-adaptive role of "herd behaviour" in the ungulates which were first domesticated.

The origins of cultivation

The beginning of cultivation is a second shift which may have taken place in the less favourable valleys and wadis around the periphery of the zone of maximum carrying capacity.

For many years it was assumed, quite logically, that domestication must have begun in the zone where the wild ancestors of the domesticates are most at home. Then, in an eye-opening paper, Harlan and Zohary[44] revealed that "over many thousands of hectares" within this zone "it would be possible to harvest wild wheat today from natural stands almost as dense as a cultivated wheat field". Harlan[45] then proceeded to do just that: armed with a flintbladed sickle, he harvested enough wild wheat in an hour to produce one kilo of clean grain—and the wild grain, after chemical analysis, proved to be almost twice as rich in protein as domestic wheat. Harlan and Zohary[46] therefore closed with a warning: "Domestication may not have taken place where the wild cereals were most abundant. Why should anyone cultivate a cereal where natural stands are as dense as a cultivated field? . . . farming itself may have originated in areas adjacent to, rather than in, the regions of greatest abundance of wild cereals."

Harlan's wild wheat harvest also suggested that a family of experienced plant-collectors, working over the three-week period when wild wheat comes ripe, "without even working very hard, could gather more grain than the family could possibly consume in a year."[47] Such a harvest would almost necessitate some degree of sedentism—after all, where could they go with an estimated metric ton of clean wheat?

This was, of course, what archaeologist Jean Perrot[48] had been saying for years about the Natufian culture in Palestine—that they had been semisedentary, based on intensive wild cereal collection. A further suggestion of this nature has since come from Tell Mureybat, a site on the terrace of the Euphrates River in inland Syria, dating to c. 8000 B.C. Preliminary analyses of carbonized barley and einkorn wheat from pre-pottery levels at the site—which have clay-walled houses, grinding stones, and roasting pits presumably used to render the cereal glumes brittle for threshing—suggest that the grain may be all wild.[49] Such data indicate that sedentary life based on wild cereal collecting and hunting may be possible, and that consequently pressures for domestication may not be as strong in the heart of the wild cereal habitat as elsewhere.

This impression is reinforced by the fact that some of our most ancient samples of morphologically domesticated grain (e.g. emmer wheat) come from "marginal" habitats well outside the present wild range of that plant; for example, in the Wadi Araba region[50] and the Khuzistan steppe,[51] in areas where dense stands could only be produced by deliberate cultivation. It is possible, therefore, that cultivation began as an attempt to produce artificially, around the *margins* of the "optimum" zone, stands of cereals as dense as those in the *heart* of the "optimum" zone. Binford had already suggested that this might have taken place in response to population pressure exerted on the marginal habitats by expansion of sedentary food-collectors from the heart of the wild cereal zone. It appears that efforts at early cultivation were probably soon reinforced by favourable mutations in the cereals themselves, such as toughening of the rachis, polyploidy, and loss of tough glumes.

The spread of the early dry-farming complex across the Near East is striking; where surveys are adequate, it appears that very few environmental zones were without farming communities at this time, although population densities were higher in some areas than others. In the Zagros Mountains, densities of sites are highest in intermontane plains with a high sub-surface water table and frequent marshy areas,[52] suggesting that a critical resource sought by early farmers were lands of high water-retention, where soil moisture helped the planted cereals to survive annual fluctuations in rainfall. At Ali Kosh on the lowland steppe of south-west Iran, early farmers planted their cereals so near swamp margins that seeds of club-rush *(Scirpus)* were mixed in with the carbonized grain samples.[53] This is analogous to the practices of early farmers in parts of arid highland Mesoamerica, who also utilized permanently-humid bottomlands and high-water table zones.[54] Such types of farming may also have facilitated the spread of agriculture out of the Near East and into Europe, which took place sometime during this time period.

More complicated techniques accompanied the extension of early dry-farming to its limits in very marginal habitats to the north-east (e.g. the Turkoman steppe), and the south-west (e.g. the Wadi Araba region). At Beidha, in the south Jordan desert, it is possible that farming sites were located in such a way as to take advantage of rainfall run-off concentrated by steep nearby cliffs.[55] On the Turkoman steppe, early cultivators used small "oasis" situations where streams from the Kopet Dagh formed humid deltas along the base of the mountain range.[56] In all such cases, where rainfall agriculture must have been pushed to its absolute limit, barley seems to have been the main crop;[57] otherwise, wheat was preferred.

A detailed look at the early dry-farming diet

In archaeology, one concrete example is often worth more than a whole chapter of generalization. At this point, I would therefore like to present in some detail our dietary data from the site of Ali Kosh, a small early dry-farming village on the Khuzistan steppe of south-western Iran.[58] Excavations at Ali Kosh produced *c.* 45,000 carbonized seeds, which on analysis by Helbaek (n.d.) could be grouped into 40-odd species of plants; it also produced more than 10,000 identifiable bones from approximately 35 species of animals. I have listed only the most common categories in Table I. In addition, I have estimated the pounds of usable meat represented by minimum individuals of each type of animal, using the system proposed by White[59] and adult weights taken from Walker[60] and my own field notes (Table 2). A further chart (Table 3) gives average representative nutritional values for some of the important plant and animal foods at the site, taken from Platt,[61] plus some estimates of the amount of each food source needed to make a kilogram.

Three periods of the early dry-farming era were represented at the site of Ali Kosh. These have been called the Bus Mordeh (7500-6750 B.C.), Ali Kosh (6750-6000 B.C.), and Mohammad Jaffar (6000-5600 B.C.) phases.[62] Counts of the animal bones and carbonized seeds by species will be given in the final reports on the site.[63] I can present here only an abbreviated summary of the results.

The subsistence pattern in the earliest, or Bus Mordeh phase, had five main aspects: (1) the cultivation of cereals, whose grains amounted to only about 3% of the carbonized seeds, but because of their greater size constituted perhaps a third of the

TEPE ALI KOSH (7500-5600 B.C.)

(a) Emmer wheat	Caper
(a) Two-row barley, hulled	Pistachio
(a) (Rare traces of other cultivars)	Gazelle
	Onager
(a) Goats	Pig
(a) Sheep	Aurochs

Small wild legumes *(Astragalus, Trigonella,*	Fox (and other small mammals)
Medicago)	Miscellaneous birds
Wild two-row barley	Ducks and geese
Goat-face grass *(Aegilops)*	
Ryegrass *(Lolium)*	Water turtles
Wild oat grass *(Avena)*	
Canary grass *(Phalaris)*	Fish (carp, catfish)
Vetchling *(Lathyrus)*	
Shauk *(Prosopis)*	Freshwater mussels

Table 1. Most common foods recovered in debris at Ali Kosh,
an early village in the plain of Deh Luran, south-western Iran. (b)

(a) Domesticated items.
(b) See Helbaek, H. (In press). Plant-collecting, dry-farming, and irrigation agriculture in prehistoric Deh Luran, in Hole, F., Flannery, K. V. and Neely, J. A. Prehistory and human ecology of the Deh Luran plain, *Memoirs,* Univ. of Michigan, Museum of Anthropology; see Hole, F. and Flannery, K. V. (1967). The prehistory of southwestern Iran: a preliminary report, *Proc. Prehist. Soc.,* 33 (9), pp. 147-206.

total weight of plant food; (2) collecting of small wild legume seeds of clover-alfalfa type, which constituted about 94% of the carbonized seeds, but amounted probably to no more than a third of the total weight of plant food; (3) collecting of the seeds of wild grasses, constituting only about 1% of the carbonized seeds and about 15% of the weight of plant food; (4) herding of domestic goats and sheep, whose bones constituted about 67% of the faunal material, but which contributed only about a third of the total weight of meat represented (see Table 2); (5) hunting of wild ungulates, which accounted for only 25% of the animal bones, but contributed more than 60% of the total weight of meat.

The remainder of the food supply was made up by elements such as nut meats, fruit, small mammals, fish, water fowl, and mussels, which although nutritionally important constituted a small percentage of the total weight of meat and plant food. Unfortunately, in the absence of coprolites, we have no way of calculating what percentage of the diet was made up by plant foods and what percentage was meat. It appears, however, that the Bus Mordeh villagers ate a good deal more meat than the average modern Iranian peasant; Watson[64] reports that animal bones are "rather rare" on village dump heaps today.

Nowadays, as May[65] points out, "most Iranian meals are of the one-pot type", with many ingredients thrown in, such as grain, lentils, meat, onions, etc. This may also have been true prehistorically—at least during the later part of the dry-farming era, when cooking pots are known. The early cereals (emmer wheat and two-row hulled barley) are largely unsuitable for breadmaking, and their grains seem to have been pounded up and eaten right along with fragments of the woody spikelet base.[66] A lack of scorched or carbonized bone suggests that most meat was cooked after it had been cut off the carcass,

Animal	Estimated adult weight (kg.)	Kg. of usable meat	TEPE ALI KOSH						TEPE-SABZ (all phases)	
			Bus Mordeh Phase		Ali Kosh Phase		Moh. Jaffar Phase			
			Minimum no. of individuals	Kg. of usable meat	Minimum no. of individuals	Kg. of usable meat	Minimum no. of individuals	Kg. of usable meat	Minimum no. of individuals	Kg. of usable meat
Sheep/Goat	50	25	(49)	1225	(102)	2550	(40)	1009	(44)	1100
Gazelle	50	25	(16)	400	(59)	1475	(18)	450	(18)	450
Onager	350	175	(3)	525	(12)	2100	(4)	700	(8)	1400
Aurochs	800	400	(3)	1200	(6)	2400	(2)	800	—	—
Domestic cattle	500	250	—	—	—	—	—	—	(9)	2250
Pig	100	70	(2)	140	(3)	210	(3)	210	(5)	350
Wolf (?)	26	13	—	—	(2)	26	(2)	26	—	—
Red fox	9	4·5	(2)	9	(3)	13·5	(7)	31·5	(6)	27
Hyaena	40	20	—	—	—	—	(1)	20	—	—
Wild cat	1	0·5	—	—	(2)	1	(2)	1	(1)	0·5
Marten	1	0·5	—	—	—	—	—	—	(1)	0·5
Weasel	0·2	0·1	—	—	—	—	(1)	0·1	—	—
Hedgehog	0·8	0·4	—	—	(2)	0·8	(1)	0·4	(1)	0·4
Duck-size birds	1·5	1	—	—	—	—	(2)	2	—	—
Goose-size birds	2	1·4	(2)	2·8	(2)	2·8	(1)	1·4	(1)	1·4
Partridge-size birds	0·2	0·14	(1)	0·14	(6)	0·84	(7)	0·98	(6)	0·84
Hawk-size birds	1	0·7	—	—	—	—	—	—	(2)	1·4
Turtle	0·5	0·25	(8)	2	(4)	1	(4)	1	(4)	1
Fish	0·5	0·25	(29)	7·25	(49)	12·25	(44)	11	(4)	1
Crab	0·01	0·005	—	—	(3)	0·015	(3)	0·015	—	—
Mussell	0·01	0·005	(123)	0·62	(166)	0·83	(111)	0·56	(8)	0·04

(a) For method of calculation, see White, T. (1953). A method of calculating the dietary percentage of various food animals utilized by aboriginal peoples, *American Antiquity*, 18 (4), pp. 396–8.

Table 2. Estimated kilograms of usable meat represented in middens at Ali Kosh and Tepe Sabz, in the plain of Deh Luran, Iran. Broken down by category of animal, and cultural phase (except in the case of Tepe Sabz).(a)

Estimated value per kilogram of edible portion

Food	Calories	Protein (gm.)	Fat (gm.)	Carbohydrate (gm.)	Calcium (mg.)	Iron (mg.)	Vitamin A (IU)	Vitamin C (mg.)	Approximate amount needed for 1 kilo
Wheat	3440	115	20	700	300	35	—	—	±33,000 grains
Barley	3390	120	20	680	350	40	—	—	±45,000 grains
Lentils	3390	240	10	590	700	70	1000	—	±25,000 lentils
Lathyrus	2930	250	10	460	1100	56	700	—	Tens of thousands
Small wild legumes	3350	290	52	500	1800	220	—	—	>1,000,000 seeds
Miscellaneous wild grasses	3880	120	75	680	600	50	—	—	>30,000 grains
Pistachio	6260	200	540	150	1400	140	1000	—	±2750 nuts
Almond	6570	200	590	120	1500	35	—	—	±1000 nuts
Goat	1450	160	90	—	110	25	—	—	1/25 of one animal
Sheep	1490	170	90	—	110	25	—	—	1/25 of one animal
Gazelle	1450	160	90	—	110	25	—	—	1/25 of one animal
Onager	2020	190	140	—	100	30	—	—	1/175 of one animal
Aurochs	2020	190	140	—	100	30	—	—	1/400 of one animal
Domestic cattle	2020	190	140	—	100	30	—	—	1/250 of one animal
Pig	3710	140	350	—	100	20	—	—	1/70 of one animal
Ducks/Geese	1390	190	70	—	150	15	—	—	1 bird (or less)
Turtle	790	160	10	20	1000	10	—	—	4 turtles
Fish	950	180	25	—	500	10	—	—	4 fish
Mussels	700	100	20	30	1500	100	200	—	200 mussels

(a) Based on tables given by Platt, B.S. (1962). Tables of representative values of foods commonly used in tropical countries, *Medical Research Council, Special Report Series*, 302, H.M.S.O.

Table 3.   Estimated values of some of the foods commonly eaten at Ali Kosh and Tepe Sabz, in the plain of Deh Luran, Iran. (a)

or else boiled; there is little evidence to indicate direct roasting of the meat while still on the bone. Thus, it is possible that a typical meal of the early dry-farming era consisted of a gruel of cereal grains, spikelet bases, wild legumes, and chunks of ungulate meat cooked up together.

During the three periods represented at Ali Kosh, the only significant change in meat resources seems to have been an increase of sheep relative to goats; hunting was just as important when the site was abandoned as when it was founded. On the other hand, the changes in plant species percentages through time are more striking. They reflect (1) increases in cultivated cereal grains, (2) decreases in the use of local wild legumes, (3) increases in crop weeds, and (4) increases in plants typical of fallowed agricultural land (see below). In Tables 2 and 3 I have added comparative data from a nearby site, Tepe Sabz, which was occupied during the later era of simple irrigation farming (5500-3700 B.C.).

In terms of total food supply, hunting and wild plant collecting were not "supplements" to the Bus Mordeh diet; they were major subsistence strategies. Most of the total weight of meat and plant foods of this period came from wild resources. These resources had been available throughout the preceding Upper Palaeolithic period, and some of them (e.g. aurochs meat, pistachios, small wild legumes) are intrinsically richer in calories, protein (or both) than most of the domestic foods eaten in the Bus Mordeh phase. In this sense, there is no reason to believe that the early "food-producers" were significantly better nourished than their "food-collecting" ancestors. Nor was their subsistence base necessarily more "reliable"; attempts at dry-farming in the Deh Luran plain today meet with failure two or three years out of every five.[67]

The one real advantage of cereal cultivation is that it increases carrying capacity of the land in terms of kilograms per hectare. Dry farming of wheat in northern Khuzistan, for example, yields an average of 410 kilos per hectare.[68] This is equal to the weight of usable meat from sixteen sheep, or the weight of more than 400 million small legume seeds. There is probably no other food in the Bus Mordeh phase debris which will produce as many kilos from so small an area as the cereals. Cultivation thus represented a decision to replace the native, high-protein wild legume ground cover with a lower-protein grass which would grow more densely and probably was less work to harvest, in spite of the risk of crop failure.

Nutritional aspects of early dry-farming in Iran

Still another fact which emerges from an examination of Tables 1-3 is that the early farmers of south-western Iran were still in the "broad spectrum" era: they made a living by *diversifying* their subsistence strategies, rather than concentrating on one food source. In fact, the synergistic effect of their various food combinations—ungulate meat, grasses, legumes, nut meats, mussels and so on—probably resulted in better nutrition than would specialization on a narrower range of products.

Highest on the list of calorie-producing foods used at Ali Kosh and Tepe Sabz were the almonds and pistachios, followed by cereal grasses and wild legumes. The wild legumes, judging by analyses of *Trigonella*,[69] seem to have been higher in protein than most other food sources. Most calories probably came from these plant foods, since none of the meat sources (with the possible exception of pig) has a very high caloric value.

Minerals like calcium came from a variety of foods: mussels, water turtles, fresh water crabs, almonds, and pistachios. The mussels, pistachios, and various of the wild legumes are also good vitamin A sources. (It is interesting to note, however, that all these calcium-vitamin A sources probably became insignificant once the milking of domestic animals was established—an event for which we still have no archaeological evidence.)

None of the foods listed in Table 3 is a decent vitamin C source; the fruit of the wild caper *(Capparis)* probably filled this role. Other sources existed in the environment, and probably were used, although it cannot be proved archaeologically. These include fresh ungulate liver, the fruit of the jujube tree *(Zizyphus),* and the growing shoots of *Medicago* and other wild legumes.[70] In short, combinations of the twenty or so major foods used by the early dry farmers probably left them far better nourished than today's Iranian villager.[71]

Cropping, herding and erratic rainfall in the dry-farming era

One aspect of dry-farming in western Iran—or elsewhere in the Near East, for that matter—is that its outcome is unpredictable. Our figure of 410 kilos per hectare for northern Khuzistan is an average; in a good year the yield might be 1000 kilos, in a bad year almost nothing.

We have already mentioned the hazards of dry-farming in the Deh Luran plain. Watson[72] gives roughly similar figures for Iranian Kurdistan, where annual rainfall is higher (but still erratic). There a farmer may plant 300 kilos of wheat, and if the rain comes on time and in sufficient amounts, he might even get a ten-fold yield (3000 kilos). On the other hand, Watson's informants lost their entire wheat crop in 1958, 1959, and 1960 because of insects. What early farmers needed, therefore, was a way of levelling out the years of unpredictable bumper crops.

Primitive peoples, in the prehistoric record and in the ethnographic present, seem to use three main methods for dealing with unpredictable surpluses. They can store them; they can convert them into craft items of imperishable, exotic raw materials, which can be used as media of exchange during lean years;[73] or they can convert them into live storage, i.e. domestic animals, which can be used either directly (as food) or for inter-group exchanges which set up reciprocal obligations and maximize sharing during lean years.[74] These second two alternatives amount to a kind of "banking" of surpluses.[75]

While early farmers in Mesoamerica relied fairly heavily on exchanges of exotic raw materials,[76] the early Near Eastern farmers seem to have used mainly storage and domestic animals. Sheep and goats, for example, may be purchased with agricultural surpluses in good years, then exchanged for grain in lean years. They may be allowed to graze on growing cereal grain fields in good years,[77] and at some time periods were fed stored or surplus barley.[78] Archaeological and ethnographic evidence suggests that plant cultivation and animal herding, far from being two separate subsistence activities, are interrelated in ways which help "bank" surpluses and even out the erratic fluctuations of the Near Eastern environment.

Effects of early cultivation on the wild plant cover

One effect of cultivation was an extensive alteration of the native plant cover of areas like the south-west Iranian steppe, which may actually have prevented a return to previous food-gathering patterns.

We have mentioned already the heavy dependence of Bus Mordeh phase farmers on local wild plants between 7500 and 6750 B.C. Nine-tenths of the seeds identified by Helbaek from these levels were from small annual legumes and wild grasses native to northern Khuzistan. Most abundant were the clover-like legumes *Medicago* (wild alfalfa), *Astragalus* (spiny milk vetch), and *Trigonella* (a small plant of the pea family, related to fenugreek); but they also collected oat grass *(Avena)*, Bermuda grass *(Cynodon)* and Canary grass *(Phalaris)*. However, these wild plants have the same general growing season as wheat and barley, which the Bus Mordeh people cultivated, and they also compete for the same alluvial soil with low salinity which the cereals require. As cultivation of wheat and barley increased, therefore, these wild legumes and grasses assumed the status of weeds, and were removed to make way for cultivated grains.

Their place did not remain unfilled for long, however—what happened was that new crop weeds from the mountains were introduced, probably in imperfectly cleaned batches of grain brought down to the steppe. These included various strains of *Aegilops* (goat-face grass), *Lolium* (ryegrass), and other grasses. Once established, the newcomers proved stubborn; Adams[79] reports that today ryegrass is one of the major crop weeds requiring eradication in the Mesopotamian lowlands.

One of the native plants which did not compete with the cereal crops was *Prosopis,* a woody perennial legume with an edible pod, related to the mesquite plant of the American West. Adams points out that *Prosopis* matures in a different season of the year from the cereals, and its deep root system survives even after ploughing. This woody wild legume may therefore even *increase* along with cultivation and fallow land, and Helbaek has in fact detected an increase in *Prosopis* seeds through time through three periods at Ali Kosh. Evidently the early cultivators responded in a reasonable way: as *Prosopis* increased, they ate more of it.

Fallowing practices also modified the landscape in other ways. Today in Khuzistan, three-fourths of all arable land is fallow during any given year. Helbaek's study of carbonized seeds from the Mohammad Jaffar Phase at Ali Kosh indicate that by *c.* 6000 B.C. such fallowing systems were already taking their toll of the previously dominant grasses and legumes, which were increasingly being replaced by pasture plants like mallow *(Malva),* plantain *(Plantago),* fumitory *(Fumaria)* and bedstraw *(Galium).*

The tiny annual legumes retreated to the margins of the cultivated land and the talus slope of the mountains. Their role as a major human food was played out by 6000 B.C. But they were not forgotten or ignored; they became food for sheep and goats. Today, from Iran west across the Near East, and even as far as the Tuareg Country of North Africa,[80] *Astragalus* and *Trigonella* have become two of the most common plants collected as fodder for domestic caprines. Man continues to derive energy from them, but through an animal converter.

Early Irrigation Farming

Origins of irrigation

Irrigation may be yet a third example of an innovation which took place in a less-favourable habitat adjacent to an area of population growth. Our earliest evidence for this new technology comes not from the well-watered uplands of Kurdistan and Luristan, where early dry-farming was so successful, but from the lowland steppe of Khuzistan, a treeless plain receiving only 300 mm. of annual rainfall.

There is some reason to believe that the Khuzistan steppe was, indeed, receiving overflow populations from the mountain woodland. One line of evidence is the afore-mentioned field weeds in early levels at Ali Kosh—including *Aegilops* and *Lolium,* which are more at home in the mountains than on the steppe. The implication is that the whole complex, both cereals and field weeds, came into the steppe from the uplands. Another line of evidence is the strong resemblance of steppe artifact assemblages to those in the mountains.[81]

Although survey has been far from exhaustive, what we know of the Zagros region at that time does suggest that population densities were higher in the large inter-montane valleys than on the steppe.[82] Under conditions of rainfall agriculture, the carrying capacity of the steppe is limited, soil salinity is an ever-present danger, and considerable fallowing is required. Parts of the steppe, however, had great potential for irrigation: areas like the upper Khuzistan plains, where "increased surface gradients and widespread underlying gravel deposits provide sufficient natural drainage . . . to minimize the problems of salinization and waterlogging that usually attend irrigation agriculture".[83] Once irrigation appeared, the steppe greatly increased in carrying capacity and became, in fact, the dominant growth centre of the Zagros region between 5500 and 4000 B.C. Yet, interestingly enough, this new mode of production did not spread rapidly out of south-west Asia as earlier systems of dry-farming had: it seems to have been a peculiarly Near Eastern development.

Early irrigation on the lowland steppe was accompanied by a shift in settlement pattern.[84] Instead of locating sites near the margins of swampy areas, where the high water table could be used to ameliorate fluctuations in rainfall, some villages now occurred in linear arrangements along fossil stream courses from which water could be drawn by small, shallow canals. Table 4 lists the major plant and animal food sources from Tepe Sabz, an early irrigation site in south-western Iran.

Archaeological evidence for early irrigation comes from a variety of approaches. It was Adams[85] who first pointed out that there were alignments of later prehistoric sites in Khuzistan (5500-3500 B.C.) which seemed to follow such water courses south into the zone where rainfall alone is inadequate for cultivation. Implications of the settlement pattern were that irrigation, consisting of the simple breaching of the natural levees of small streams flowing at the surface of the plain, enabled prehistoric farmers to partially counteract the erratic and frequently inadequate rainfall of the steppe. A similar survey by Wright,[86] recently undertaken in the vicinity of Ur, shows that Ubaid baked-clay sickles and sickle fragments found on the land surface tend to be restricted to a band five kilometres wide to either side of fossil stream channels, giving us an estimate of the area watered by the small canals serving the fields.

TEPE SABZ (5500-3700 B.C.)

(a) Emmer wheat   Shauk *(Prosopis)*
(a) Two-row barley, hulled   Caper
(a) Bread wheat   Pistachio
(a) Einkorn wheat   Almond
(a) Six-row barley, hulled
(a) Six-row barley, naked
(a) Linseed   Gazelle
(a) Lentils   Onager
(a) Grass peas   Pig

(a) Goats   Fox (and other small mammals)
(a) Sheep   Miscellaneous birds
(a) Cattle

    Goat-face grass *(Aegilops)*   Water turtles
    Ryegrass *(Lolium)*
    Vetchling *(Lathyrus)*   Fish

Table 4. Common foods recovered from Tepe Sabz,
in the plain of Deh Luran, south-west Iran.(b)

(a) Domesticated items.
(b) See Helbaek, H. (In press). Plant-collecting, dry-farming, and irrigation agriculture
in prehistoric Deh Luran, in Hole, F., Flannery, K. V. and Neely, J. A. Prehistory
and human ecology of the Deh Luran plain, *Memoirs* Univ. of Michigan, Museum
of Anthropology.

Ecological effects of irrigation

Irrigation in Khuzistan, according to Adams[87] tends to increase crop yields from
410 kilos per hectare to 615 kilos per hectare. In addition, the actual physical size of
the crop plants themselves seems to have been increased. For example, Helbaek's
studies suggest that seeds of flax or linseed *(Linum bienne)* grown by rainfall alone have
a maximum length range between 3·29-4·03 mm., while irrigated flax has a maximum
length range of 4·39-6·20 mm. Flax seeds of this large size do not appear in the Deh
Luran deposits until 5500-5000 B.C., after which they are present in large numbers.[88]
However, as many authors have already pointed out, irrigation if unaccompanied by
proper drainage may bring salt to the surface through capillary action in areas which
were not previously saline. Agriculture then necessitates a strategy in which the advantages of irrigation water are weighed against soil salinity. One strategy employed in the
lowlands of Iran and Mesopotamia was to concentrate on barley, which has a shorter
growing season and higher salt tolerance than wheat. It is no accident that barley and
sheep (see below), with their relatively greater ability to withstand the rigours of the hot,
dry, saline lowland steppe and alluvium, were among the most important food resources
of Elamite civilization.[89]

One by-product of irrigation was that the canal became a new semihumid niche on
which specialized plants could be grown, apart from those which the water was originally
intended to irrigate. It is known, for example, that onions and date palms were grown on

canal banks in early historic times in Mesopotamia.[90] Unfortunately, the canal vegetation is also served as a haven for crop pests such as the bandicoot-rat *(Nesokia indica)* which otherwise would have been less abundant in the region.

Sheep versus *Stipa:* a by-product of the origins of wool

An interesting chain of events followed the domestication of *Ovis orientalis,* an animal which still roams the foothills and intermontane plains of the Zagros and Taurus ranges in herds of up to fifteen individuals. These sheep have a coat which is reddish-buff above, white below, and is little different from that of a deer or gazelle. The coat is composed of hair from two kinds of follicles: "primaries", which produce the visible coat, and "secondaries", which produce the hidden, woolly underfur.[91]

In the wild, these sheep use a number of wild grasses as forage. One of the best of these is a plant known as *Stipa,* or "feathergrass", which grows over much of the area from the Khuzistan and Assyrian steppes to the high mountains of the Iran-Iraq border. Many species of *Stipa* are classed by Pabot[92] and others as among the better forage species in terms of nutrition. *Stipa* has a rather interesting seed implantation mechanism: the seed has a sharp callus, which easily penetrates the soil, and a number of short stiff hairs which oppose its withdrawal. The bent and twisted awn of the seed, which is hygroscopic, serves as a driving organ, twisting and untwisting with changes in humidity. Thus, over a period of alternating wet and dry days, the feathergrass seed literally "screws itself into the ground".

Now, to set the stage, let us domesticate *Ovis orientalis* in the Zagros area sometime between 9000 and 8000 B.C. It appears (at the present state of our knowledge) that the first genetic change following domestication was the loss of horns in some sheep, probably females. One hornless sheep specimen is known from the Bus Mordeh phase in the Deh Luran plain of Iran, dating to about 7500 B.C.,[93] and others are known from early villages near Kermanshah, Iran and in Anatolia.[94] A later change, and one still not radiocarbon dated,[95] was the appearance of wool in domestic sheep, which we know took place prior to 3000 B.C.[96] Ryder[97] has shown that this was brought about when the "secondary" follicles increased in number and changed their spacing, causing the "underfur" to become the principal component of the sheep's coat.

It has long been known that sheep survive high temperatures and desertic conditions better than most other domestic animals. Recent studies by Schmidt-Nielsen[98] and his associates suggest that this is due to a number of factors: a "panting" mechanism which "permits an efficient ventilation of the upper respiratory tract, where most of the evaporation takes place"[99] and also—believe it or not—their wool. Thermometers were used to measure the internal, skin-surface, and outer-wool temperatures of sheep exposed to extreme conditions of heat and sun. It was observed that while the wool temperature reached 87°C, skin temperature remained at 42°C; in other words, "4 cm. of wool sustained a gradient of 45°C between tip and skin".[100] It appears that while wool acts not only as a reflection to divert light and heat rays, but also as a layer of insulation which allows air circulation to cool the skin without exposing it to the sun. There may thus be some adaptive advantage for woolliness in domestic sheep maintained in captivity in hot climates, especially if they are deprived of a chance to spend the mid-day hours in the shade of a thicket, as they do in the wild. (Obviously, however, the *extreme* degree of woolliness in modern breeds is an artificial condition maintained by man, since feral sheep rapidly lose it.)

One of the side-effects of this process becomes apparent when woolly sheep are allowed to graze in meadows of *Stipa:* the feathergrass seed catches in the wool and often, through the same process of wetting and drying with which it plants itself, may burrow right into the animal's skin, causing considerable discomfort and even infection.[101] In some parts of Iran today, for example, shepherds even avoid taking their flocks into areas dominated by this plant,[102] which must have been one of the most useful foods of the hairy wild sheep. Such little ecological chains of events give us some idea of how complex the whole process of domestication must have been.

Effects of changing land-use on sociopolitical structure

An interesting relationship appears when one plots the increasing population of prehistoric Iran against today's figures for different kinds of land use. It would appear that while early dry-farming and irrigation were pushing population densities up at a rapid rate, the relative amount of land which could be considered "prime", or "highly productive" was decreasing with equal rapidity. Let me explain.

Hole and I[103] have already presented estimates of population densities for parts of south-western Iran during the prehistoric era. These estimates are based on numbers of sites recovered by our surveys and those of Adams,[104] using figures of approximately 100 persons per 1-hectare village site, and so on; it is presumed that whatever inaccuracies are present apply equally to all periods, so the general shape of the population growth curve should be reasonably reliable. Briefly, our estimates go from 0·1 persons per square kilometre in the late Palaeolithic, to 1-2 persons per square kilometre under conditions of early dry-farming, and up to 6 or more persons per square kilometre after irrigation appears in the archaeological record. In other words, population increased at least sixty-fold in the space of about six thousand years.

Now consider the figures given by May,[105] which are based on the 1956 Iranian Census, plus studies by FAO-WHO and the U.S. Foreign Agricultural Service. First of all, these studies indicate that a very large part of Iran—about 65%—is taken up by nearly uninhabitable deserts and lands of extremely marginal productivity. These may have been used by late Palaeolithic man, but surely it would have been the other 35% which provided him with the best hunting-gathering opportunities; included in the latter would be the intermontane plains of the limestone mountain area and the great winter grasslands of northern Khuzistan. These zones had the wild game, as well as the edible fruits, grasses, and legumes which supplied its sustenance and presumably also man's.

Begin dry-farming, however, and the picture changes; for only 10% of Iran's land surface is considered "arable".[106] This means that although population increased by twenty times, most of its food was now produced on one-tenth of the land surface. And with the start of irrigation the ratio changed drastically again; today, only 10% of the arable land in Iran, or 1% of the total land surface, is irrigated (and that includes large areas irrigated today by underground chain wells or *qanats,* for which we have no evidence in pre-history; the area over which stream or canal irrigation can be practised is even smaller). Add to this the fact that in any one year three out of every four hectares of arable land are fallow, and it appears that a very small area feeds many millions of people. In fact, the irrigated 1% of the country produces 30% of the yearly crop.[107]

Such an inverse ratio between population and "most productive" land characterized other areas where early civilizations arose—Mesoamerica, for example. As Palerm and Wolf[108] have suggested, early agriculture in Mexico and Guatemala probably depended on rainfall alone; but as time went by, increasingly more productive techniques arose, such as flood-water farming, canal irrigation, dams, and *chinampas* or "floating gardens". As these techniques appeared they were "applicable to an ever-decreasing number of areas".[109] The area over which the most productive techniques could be applied was miniscule relative to Mesoamerica as a whole—yet such areas fed millions of Indians.

Perhaps the most important consequence of the inverse ratio is that it set the stage for social stratification. As May[110] has pointed out, one of the salient characteristics of Near Eastern agriculture is what he politely calls "inequitable systems of land ownership and tenure". It is not just that 100% of the food is produced on 10% of the land; it is the fact that in some cases 1% of the population owns the 1% of the land which produces 30% of the food. This kind of differential access to strategic resources, including the means of production, is at the heart of "ranked" or "stratified" society. It is not a result of agricultural success, or "surplus", but a product of the widening gap between the size of the population and the size of the critical land surface on which it was most dependent. It is probably no accident that highly stratified societies followed this adaptive era in the alluvial lowlands of the Near East.

Conclusions

Like many semi-arid mountain regions, the Near East is a mosaic of woodland or parkland areas, relatively rich in wild products, surrounded by steppes or grasslands which are less rich in wild products. The changes leading to intensive food production are here viewed as a series of responses to disturbances of density equilibrium in human populations around the margins of the favoured areas, caused by the fact that those areas were the zones of population growth and emigration. Obviously, a definition of "favourable" depends on the technological level at the time: i.e. hunting, wild plant collecting, early dry-farming, or early irrigation.

Recent ethnographic studies do not indicate that hunters and gatherers are "starving", or that starvation is the major factor limiting their populations. Nor does the archaeological record in the Near East suggest that the average Neolithic farmer was any better nourished than the average Palaeolithic hunter. Moreover, over much of the Near East, farming does not necessarily constitute a "more stable" subsistence base or a "more reliable" food supply. The real consequence of domestication was to (1) change the means of production in society, (2) make possible divisions of labour not usually characteristic of hunter-gatherers, and (3) lay the foundations for social stratification by continually reducing the zone of "optimum" productivity while allowing the population to expand at a geometric rate. It also (4) increased man's potential for environmental destruction, so that eventually it would have been impossible for him to return to his former means of subsistence, had he wanted to.

In this respect, early Near Eastern agriculture represents yet another example of the "second cybernetics".[111] Starting with a relatively stable configuration of plant and animal species at 10,000 B.C., early cultivation took two genera of cereal grasses and two genera of small ungulates out of their habitat and artificially increased their numbers while they underwent a series of genetic changes, many of which were favourable from man's standpoint. These favourable changes made feasible a still greater investment of human labour in the cereals and caprines, and a greater artificial expansion of their range at the expense of other species. At this point, the ecosystem was no longer cybernating, or "stable"; all former rules which had kept species in check were off. What had been a minor deviation from equilibrium at 8000 B.C. had been amplified into a major subsystem at 5000 B.C., by which time irrigation had been employed to produce single-species stands of cereals where none had even existed in the wild. When equilibrium was momentarily reached again, perhaps around the time of the Sumerian state, a great many species—like the aurochs, the onager, and the red deer—had been driven completely on to marginal land. Today they are locally or universally extinct in the Near East. The new niches opened up by agriculture and irrigation were not for them, but for the crop pests and weeds which accompanied the cereals into foreign habitats and became, in some cases, part of the dominant biota. So great was the change in the Near East that today we see its original configuration only in the pollen record and the Palaeolithic bone debris.

Notes

[1]Lees, G. M. and Falcon, N. L. (1952). The geographical history of the Mesopotamian plains, *Geo. J.,* 118, pp. 24-39.

[2]Hole, F. and Flannery, K. V. (1967). The prehistory of south-western Iran: a preliminary report, *Proc. Prehist. Soc.,* 33 (9), pp. 147-206.

[3]Adams, R. M. (1962). Agriculture and urban life in early south-western Iran, *Science,* 136, p. 114.

[4]Lees, S. H. (1967). Regional integration of pig husbandry in the New Guinea highlands, *Paper presented at the Michigan Academy of Sciences, Annual Meeting 1967.*

[5]Flannery, K. V. (1968). The Olmec and the Valley of Oaxaca: a model for interregional interaction in Formative times, *Conference on the Olmec, Dumbarton Oaks,* Washington, D.C., 27th October 1967.

[6]Wynne-Edwards, C. V. (1962). *Animal Dispersion in relation to Social Behaviour.* Edinburgh.

[7]Birdsell, J. D.(1966). Some predictions for the Pleistocene based upon equilibrium systems among recent hunters, Statement for conference, *"Man the Hunter",* University of Chicago, 6-9th April 1966.

[8]McCarthy, F. D. (1957). Habitat, economy, and equipment of the Australian Aborigines, *Aus. J. of Sci.,* 19, pp. 88-97; Bose, S. (1964). Economy of the Onge of Little Andaman, *Man in India,* 44 (4), pp. 298-310, Calcutta; Lee, R. B. (1965). Subsistence ecology of !Kung Bushman, *Ph.D. Dissertation, University of California, Berkeley.*

[9]Lee, R. B. (In press). !Kung Bushmen subsistence: an input-output analysis. To appear in Vayda, A. P. (ed.) *Human Ecology: an anthropological reader,* American Museum of Natural History.

[10]Binford, L. R. (1968). Post-Pleistocene adaptations *in* Binford L. R. and Binford, S. R. (eds.) *New Perspectives in Archaeology,* Chicago.

11Binford, L. R. (1968). ibid.

12Butzer, K. W. (1964). *Environment and Archeology: an introduction to Pleistocene geography.* Chicago.

13Birdsell, J. B. (1957). Some population problems involving Pleistocene man, *Cold Spring Harbor Symposia on Quantitative Biology,* 22. The Biological Laboratory, Cold Spring Harbor, pp. 47-69.

14Howell, F. C. (1959). Upper Pleistocene stratigraphy and early man in the Levant, *Proc. of the American Phil. Soc.,* 103, (1), pp. 1-65.

15Solecki, R. S. (1964). Shanidar Cave, a late Pleistocene site in northern Iraq, *Rep. of the VIth Inter. Congress on the Quaternary,* 4, pp. 413-23.

16Rossignol. M. (1962). Analyse pollinique de sédiments marins Quaternaires en Israël, 11—Sédiments Pleistocènes, *Pollen et Spores,* 4 (1), pp. 121—48; Rossignol, M. (1963). Analyse pollinique de sédiments Quaternaires dans la plaine de Haifa, Israel, *Israel J. of Earth Sciences,* 12, pp. 207-14.

17van Zeist, W. and Wright, H. E., Jr. (1963). Preliminary pollen studies at Lake Zeribar, Zagros Mountains, south-western Iran, *Science,* 140, pp. 65—9; van Zeist, W. (1967). Late Quaternary vegetation history of western Iran, *Rev. of Palaeobot. and Palynol.,* 2, pp. 301—11.

18Flannery, K. V. (1965). The ecology of early food production in Mesopotamia, *Science,* 147, pp. 1247—56.

19Hole, F. and Flannery, K. V. (1967). ibid.

20Binford, L. R. and Binford, S. R. (1966). A preliminary analysis of functional variability in the Mousterian of Levallois facies, *Amer. Anthrop.,* 68 (2, part 2), pp. 238—95.

21Ewing, J. F. (1949). The treasures of Ksar 'Akil, *Thought,* 24, Fordham University, p. 276.

22Ewing, J. F. (1951). Comments on the report of Dr. H. E. Wright, Jr., on his study of Lebanese marine terraces, *J. of Near Eastern Studies,* 10, p. 120.

23Hole, F. and Flannery, K. V. (1967). ibid.

24Hole, F. and Flannery, K. V. (1967). ibid.; Garrod, D. A. E. (1930). The Palaeolithic of southern Kurdistan: excavations in the caves of Zarzi and Hazar Merd., *Bull. of the American School of Prehistoric Research,* 6, pp. 9—43.

25Solecki, R. S. (1964). op. cit. p. 417; Solecki, R. L. (1964). Zawi Chemi Shanidar, a post-Pleistocene village site in northern Iraq, *Rep. of the VIth Inter. Congress on the Quaternary,* 4, pp. 405—12.

26Solecki, R. S. (1964). ibid.; Solecki, R. L. (1964). ibid.

27Braidwood, R. J. and Howe, B. (1960). Prehistoric investigations in Iraqi Kurdistan, *Studies in Ancient Oriental Civilization,* Oriental Institute, Chicago, 31.

28van Loon, M. (1966). Mureybat: an early village in inland Syria, *Archaeology,* 19, pp. 215—16.

29Perrot, J. (1966). Le gisement Natufien de Mallaha (Eynan), Israël, *L'Anthropologie,* 70 (5—6), pp. 437—84.

30Braidwood, R. J. and Howe, B. (1960). ibid.

31Howell, F. C. (1959). op. cit. table 10.

32Garrod, D. A. E. and Bate, D. M. A. (1937). *The Stone Age of Mt. Carmel: excavations at the Wadi el-Mughara,* I. Oxford.

33Ewing, J. F. (1949). op. cit. p. 262.

34Reed, C. A. and Braidwood, R. J. (1960). Towards the reconstruction of the environmental sequence in north-eastern Iraq, *In* Braidwood, R. J. and Howe, B. op. cit. p. 169.

[35]Hole, F. and Flannery, K. V. (1967). ibid.

[36]Platt, B. S. (1962). Tables of representative values of foods commonly used in tropical countries, *Medical Research Council, Special Report Series*, 302, Her Majesty's Stationery Office.

[37]Hesse, R., Allee, W. C. and Schmidt, K. P. (1951). *Ecological Animal Geography*. New York.

[38]Platt, B. S. (1962). ibid.

[39]van Zeist, W. and Wright, H. E. (1963). ibid.

[40]Rossignol, M. (1962). ibid.; Rossignol, M. (1963). ibid.

[41]Odum, E. P. and Odum, H. T. (1959). *Fundamentals of Ecology*, 2nd ed. Philadelphia. p. 281.

[42]Harlan, J. R. and Zohary, D. (1966). Distribution of wild wheats and barley, *Science*, 153, pp. 1075–80.

[43]Reed, C. A. (1959). Animal domestication in the prehistoric Near East, *Science*, 130, pp. 1629–39; Reed, C. A. (1960). A review of the archaeological evidence on animal domestication in the prehistoric Near East, *in* Braidwood, R. J. and Howe, B. op. cit. pp. 119–46.

[44]Harlan, J. R. and Zohary, D. (1966). op. cit. p. 1078.

[45]Harlan, J. R. (1967). A wild wheat harvest in Turkey, *Archaeology*, 20 (3), pp. 197–201.

[46]Harlan, J. R. and Zohary, D. (1966). ibid.

[47]Harlan, J. R. (1967). op. cit. p. 198.

[48]Perrot, J. (1966). op. cit. pp. 480–3.

[49]van Loon, M. (1966). ibid.

[50]Kirkbride, D. (1966). Five seasons at the pre-pottery Neolithic village of Beidha in Jordan, *Palestine Exploration Quarterly*, 98 (1), pp. 8–72.

[51]Helbaek, H. (In press). Plant-collecting, dry-farming, and irrigation agriculture in prehistoric Deh Luran, *in* Hole, F., Flannery, K. V. and Neely, J. A. Prehistory and human ecology of the Deh Luran plain, *Memoirs,* Univ. of Michigan, Museum of Anthropology.

[52]Hole, F. and Flannery, K. V. (1967). ibid.

[53]Helbaek, H. (In press). ibid.

[54]Flannery, K. V., Kirkby, A. V., Kirkby, M. J. and Williams, A. W., Jr. (1967). Farming systems and political growth in ancient Oaxaca, *Science*, 158, pp. 445–54.

[55]Kirkbride, D. (1966). ibid.

[56]Masson, V. M. (1965). The Neolithic farmers of Central Asia, *Acts, VI Inter. Congress of Pre- and Proto-historic Sciences*, 2, pp. 205–15.

[57]Helbaek, H. (1966). Commentary on the phylogenesis of *Triticum* and *Hordeum*, *Econ. Bot.*, 20, pp. 350–60; Helbaek, H. (1966). Pre-pottery Neolithic farming at Beidha, in Kirkbride, D. Five seasons at the pre-pottery Neolithic village of Beidha in Jordan, *Palestine Exploration Quarterly*, 98 (1), pp. 61–6; Masson, V. M. (1965). ibid.

[58]Hole, F. and Flannery, K. V. (1967). ibid.

[59]White, T. (1953). A method of calculating the dietary percentage of various food animals utilised by aboriginal peoples, *American Antiquity*, 18 (4), pp. 396–8.

[60]Walker, E. P. (1964). *Mammals of the World*. Baltimore.

[61]Platt, B. S. (1962). ibid.; Obvious difficulties were encountered in finding values for some of the wild foods at Ali Kosh. For gazelle meat, I have used the values for lean goat meat; for onager, those for lean beef. Small legume values are those given for fenugreek *(Trigonella* sp.), etc.

62Hole, F. and Flannery, K. V. (1967). ibid.

63Halbaek, H. (In press). ibid.; Hole, F., Flannery, K. V. and Neely, J. A. (In press). ibid.

64Watson, P. J. (1966). Clues to Iranian prehistory in modern village life, *Expedition*, 8 (3), p. 13.

65May, J. M. (1961). *The Ecology of Malnutrition in the Far and Near East.* New York. p. 370.

66Helbaek, H. (In press). ibid.

67Hole, F. and Flannery, K. V. (1967). op. cit. footnote 6.

68Adams, R. M. (1962). op. cit. p. 110.

69Platt, B. S. (1962). ibid.

70Platt, B. S. (1962). ibid.

71May, J. M. (1961). op. cit. p. 373; the synergistic value of food combinations was brought home to me in 1963 while I worked closely in the field with my friend and colleague, Frank Hole, excavating the paleolithic caves of Iran's Khorramabad Valley. As we sat in our camp in the evening—partaking of barley in its most appealing form— we used to share a large paper sack of Kurdistan pistachios *(Pistacia atlantica)*. Wild products being what they are, the 1963 pistachio crop was riddled with small live caterpillars which had bored into the nuts and lay waiting for the unwary eater. I examined each pistachio carefully as I opened it, and as a consequence had to discard about half; but I noticed that Hole was able to eat 100% of the ones he selected, and I commented on his luck. To which he replied: "I'm just not looking." I later learned that a kilo of dried caterpillars may contain 3720 calories, 550 grams of protein, 2700 milligrams of calcium, and a generous supply of thiamine, riboflavin, and iron (see Platt, B. S. (1962). ibid.). In fact, the protein content is double that of the pistachios themselves, and a combination of the two foods probably has a synergistic effect exceeding the value of the nuts alone. Hole's wise decision to diversify his subsistence base brought him out of the field season a good thirty pounds heavier than me.

72Watson, P. J. (1966). ibid.

73Harding, T. G. (1967). *Voyagers of the Vitiaz Strait: a study of a New Guinea trade system.* Seattle; Flannery, K. V. (1967). ibid.

74Lees, G. M. (1967). ibid.; Rappaport, R. A. (1967). Ritual regulation of environmental relations among a New Guinea people, *Ethnology,* 6 (1), pp. 17–30.

75Lees, S. H. (1967). ibid.

76Flannery, K. V. (In press). ibid.

77Adams, R. M. (1965). *Land behind Baghdad: a history of settlement on the Diyala plains.* Chicago. p. 14.

78Adams, R. M. (1962). op. cit. p. 115.

79Adams, R. M. (1965). op. cit. p. 5.

80Nicolaisen, J. (1963). Ecology and culture of the pastoral Tuareg, *Nationalmuseets Skrifter,* 9, Copenhagen.

81Hole, F., Flannery, K. V. and Neely, J. A. (In press). ibid.

82Hole, F. and Flannery, K. V. (1967). ibid.

83Adams, R. M. (1962). op. cit. p. 110.

84Hole, F., Flannery, K. V. and Neely, J. A. (In press). ibid.

85Adams, R. M. (1962). op. cit.

86Wright, H. T. (1967). The administration of rural production in an early Mesopotamian town. *Ph.D. Dissertation. University of Chicago.* pp. 38–9.

[87]Adams, R. M. (1962). ibid.

[88]Helbaek, H. (1960). The paleoethnobotany of the Near East and Europe, *in* Braidwood, R. J. and Howe, B. (1960). op. cit. pp. 99-118; Helbaek, H. (1960). Ecological effects of irrigation in ancient Mesopotamia, *Iraq*, 22, pp. 186-96; Helbaek, H. (In press). ibid.

[89]Adams, R. M. (1962). ibid.; Hole, F. and Flannery, K. V. (1967). ibid.

[90]Adams, R. M. (1960). Early civilizations: subsistence and environment, *in* Kraeling, C. H. and Adams, R. M. (eds.) *City Invincible: a symposium on urbanization and cultural development in the ancient Near East.* Chicago. pp. 269-95.

[91]Ryder, M. L. (1958). Follicle arrangement in skin from wild sheep, primitive domestic sheep and in parchment, *Nature, Lond.* 182, pp. 781-3.

[92]Pabot, H. (1960). *The Native Vegetation and its Ecology in the Khuzistan River Basins.* Khuzistan Development Service, Ahwaz, Iran.

[93]Hole, F. and Flannery, K. V. (1967). op. cit. fig. 8.

[94]Personal communication from S. Bökönyi and D. Perkins, Jr.

[95]Textiles from Çatal Hüyük, once thought to be perhaps the earliest wool known, have been examined now by Ryder, M. L. (1965). Report of textiles from Çatal Hüyük, *Anatolian Studies*, 15, pp. 175-6, and it appears that they are mostly flax fibre.

[96]Hilzheimer, M. (1941). Animal remains from Tell Asmar, *Studies in Ancient Oriental Civilization*, 20, Univ. of Chicago, Oriental Institute.

[97]Ryder, M. L. (1958), ibid.

[98]Schmidt-Nielsen, K. (1964). *Desert Animals: physiological problems of heat and water.* Oxford.

[99]Schmidt-Nielsen, K. (1964). op. cit. p. 99.

[100]Schmidt-Nielsen, K. (1964). op. cit. p. 97.

[101]Reeder, J. R. (1967). Grasses, *Encyclopedia Britannica*, 1967 edition, 10, p. 700.

[102]Pabot, H. (1960). ibid.

[103]Hole, F. and Flannery, K. V. (1967). ibid.

[104]Adams, R. M. (1962). op. cit.

[105]May, J. M. (1961). op. cit.

[106]May, J. M. (1961). op. cit. p. 357; Cressey, G. B. (1960). *Crossroads: land and life in South-west Asia.* Chicago.

[107]May, J. M. (1961). ibid.

[108]Palerm, A. and Wolf, E. (1957). Ecological potential and cultural development in Mesoamerica, *in Studies in Human Ecology, Social Science Monographs,* 3, Pan American Union, Washington, D. C. pp. 1-37.

[109]Palerm, A. and Wolf, E. (1957). op. cit. p. 36.

[110]May, J. M. (1961). op. cit. p. 343.

[111]Maruyama, M. (1963). The second cybernetics: deviation-amplifying mutual causal processes, *American Scientist* 51 (2), pp. 164-79; Flannery, K. V. (1968). Archaeological systems theory and early Mesoamerica, *in Anthropological archaeology in the Americas,* Anthropological Society of Washington.

Frank Hole received his Ph.D. from the University of Chicago in 1961
and now is professor of anthropology at Rice University, Houston, Texas.
He is coauthor of the standard text: *An Introduction to Prehistoric
Archaeology* (3rd edition, 1973) and has recently become editor of the
major journal, *American Antiquity*. He has participated in archaeological
investigations at Oaxaca, Mexico and has, over the past several years, been
director of numerous expeditions to Iran. The results of his research in
Deh Luran, Iran, some of which are included in this article, have added
significantly to our understanding of man's earliest dependence on domesticated animals and plants.

Investigating the Origins of
Mesopotamian Civilization

Frank Hole

In southwest Asia, between 8000 and 3000 B.C., human society developed from self-
sufficient bands of nomadic hunters to economically and politically integrated city dwellers
who specialized in a variety of occupations. A central archeological problem is to try to
discover the factors that triggered these fundamental changes in man's way of life. For want
of evidence and for want of a satisfactory model of the conditions existing during the
period in question, searching for origins and attempting to discover the course of events
that led to civilization is difficult. Prehistorians deal with nameless cultures, trusting to
reconstructions from physical remains for their picture of life in ancient times. They must
work directly with geographic, technological, and demographic factors and only indirectly
infer ideologies and philosophical concepts. Archeologists are thus limited in what they
can hope to learn by the nature of their data and the tools they have for interpreting
them. Within these limits, however, it is possible to construct some plausible theories
about the origins of civilization and to test them through controlled programs of excavation and analysis. In this article I define the problem under consideration in ecological
terms, review the current evidence, and suggest topics for further study.

Mesopotamian (Sumerian) civilization began a few centuries before 3000 B.C. and
was characterized by temples, urban centers, writing, trade, militarism, craft specialization,
markets, and art. Inferred characteristics are a class-stratified society and well-defined
mechanisms for regulation of production and distribution of resources. To be sure,
Sumerian civilization must have had many other important but intangible characteristics,
but most of these cannot be inferred from archeological data.[1]

The early Mesopotamian civilizations were restricted to southern Mesopotamia, the alluvial plain that stretches south from Baghdad to the Persian Gulf. Remains of immediately antecedent cultures have been excavated in the same area, and still older cultures have been excavated in the surrounding Zagros mountain valleys of Iraq and Iran and on the steppes at the verge of plain and mountain in Khuzistan, southwest Iran.[2]

Intensive agriculture is a precondition for civilization. The Sumerian societies for which we have some historical records were sustained by cultivation of irrigated barley and wheat, supplemented by crops of dates, and the production of sheep, goats, cattle, pigs, and fish. In 8000 B.C. people were just beginning to plant cereals, raise animals, and live in permanent villages; their societies were small, self-sufficient, egalitarian groups with little differentiation of occupation or status. These people had fewer of the artifacts and qualities of civilization than the Sumerian city dwellers had 5000 years later. In this article I use 8000 B.C. as a convenient base line and attempt to assess some 5000 years of culture history (see Table 1).

Theories of Development

Recognizing the obvious changes in society that occurred during the 5000 years, archeologists and others have proposed causal factors such as characteristics of geography to account for them. The most detailed examination of the relationship between geographic features and social forms has been made by Huntington,[3] but other scholars working with data from Southwest Asia have had more influence on archeologists. For example, in attempting to explain the origins of agriculture, Childe proposed climatic change, specifically desiccation, as the initiating event and set off a chain of thought that is still favored by some authors.[4] Childe argued that "incipient desiccation . . . would provide a stimulus towards the adoption of a food-producing economy. . . ." Animals and men would gather in oases that were becoming isolated in the midst of deserts. Such circumstances might promote the sort of symbiosis between man and beast implied in the word *domestication.* Although Childe's theory is attractive, there is no conclusive evidence that the climate in Southwest Asia changed enough during the period in question to have affected the beginnings of agriculture and animal husbandry.[5]

It was once fashionable to think of culture as inevitably rising or progressing, and this trend was thought to be analogous to biological evolution. Except in a most general way, however, modern prehistorians do not think of universal stages of cultural development.[6] Rather than focusing on evolutionary stages, many scholars have examined the role of particular social and economic activities in triggering the emergence of complex forms of society. For instance, Marxists have explained the form of society (government, broadly speaking) on the basis of modes of production. Marxist evolutionists even today explain the development of social classes and political states in similar terms. They argue that, as people gained control over the production of food, the concept of private property crept in, and later the mass of people were exploited by the propertied few. "The creation of a state was necessary simply to prevent society from dissolving into anarchy due to the antagonisms that had arisen."[7] Information on the emergence of Sumerian civilization that might support this idea, however, is lacking.

Another attempt to correlate technological systems and social advances was made by Karl Wittfogel in *Oriental Despotism*. He contended that, where people had to depend on irrigation, they inevitably led themselves into an escalating dependence on an organizational hierarchy which coordinated and directed the irrigation activities. "The effective management of these works involves an organizational web which covers either the whole, or at least the dynamic core, of the country's population. In consequence, those who control this network are uniquely prepared to wield supreme political power."[8] Although Wittfogel's analysis seems valid in many instances, archeological investigation in both Mesopotamia and the Western Hemisphere leads to the conclusion that there was no large-scale irrigation at the time of the emergence of the first urban civilization.[9]

An Ecological Approach

Single factors such as technology are unquestionably important, but they can be understood only within the cultural, social, and geographic context. A more comprehensive view that takes into account the interrelation of many factors is called human ecology. In a consideration of cultural development, the relevant concept in human ecology is adaptation, hence the approach is to try to discover how particular factors influence the overall adaptation of a society. By means of the general approach, human ecology attempts to understand what happened in the histories of particular cultures. It does not address itself to making general statements about cultural progress or evolution.

In an ecological approach, a human society is treated as one element in a complex system of geography, climate, and living organisms peculiar to an area. To ensure survival, various aspects of a human society must be complementary and the society itself must be successfully integrated with the remainder of the cultural and physical ecosystem of which it is a part.[10] From the ecological view, such factors as technology, religion, or climate cannot be considered apart from the total system. Nevertheless, some parts of the system may be considered more fundamental in the sense that they strongly influence the form of the other parts.[11] Anthropologists, through their study of modern societies, and archeologists, through inference, find that such factors as geographical features, the distribution of natural resources, climate, the kinds of crops and animals raised, and the relations with neighboring peoples strongly influence the forms that a society may take. These factors comprise the major elements of the ecosystem, and societies must adapt themselves to them.

Archeological Evidence

For the period 8000 to 3000 B.C., archeological data are scattered and skimpy. This naturally limits the generality of any interpretations that can be made and restricts the degree to which we can test various theories. Ideally we would wish to work with hundreds of instances representing the range of environmental and cultural variation; instead, for the whole of Southwest Asia we can count fewer than 100 excavated and reported sites for the entire range of time with which we are dealing. Of course the number of unexcavated or unreported sites about which we know something is far greater, but we cannot but be aware of how little we know and how much there is to find out.

In all of Southwest Asia only about 15 villages that date to 8000 B.C. have been excavated, and only two of these, Zawi Chemi and the Bus Mordeh levels at Ali Kosh, give good evidence of the use of domesticated plants or animals.[12] In short, data for the time of our base line are woefully inadequate. We have much fuller information about the villages of 5000 B.C., but, unfortunately, for periods subsequent to 5000 B.C. the *kind* of data we have changes drastically. Thus, although there is historical continuity in the series of known sites, there is discontinuity in some of the data themselves because few archeologists have worked sites spanning the whole period from 8000 to 3000 B.C. Most of the sites dating to about 3000 B.C. were excavated by "historic" archeologists who struck levels that old only incidentally as they plumbed the depths of the cities they were digging. These scholars depended far less on artifacts than on history for their interpretations. The earliest sites were dug by prehistorians who based their inferences on results generated by an array of scientific experts. In order to understand the origins of civilizations, we thus need to bridge two quite different "archeological cultures." Archeologists and their various colleagues working in the early villages painstakingly teased out grains of charred seeds, measured metapodials and teeth of early races of sheep or cattle, and analyzed the chemical and mineral constituents of obsidian and copper; their counterparts working in the historic sites busied themselves with the floor plan of temples, the funerary pottery in the graves, the esthetics of an art style, and the translation of cuneiform impressions in clay.[13]

Bearing in mind the reservations I have already expressed, we can begin to try to pick a coherent path through 5000 years of history. In dealing with Mesopotamia, it is usual to regard the presence of towns, temples, and cities as indicative of civilization. If we do so, we can divide our history into two parts, beginning with small food-producing villages and following with more complex societies that include towns and cities. In the ensuing discussion I assess the available evidence and, for both forms of community, outline the characteristics and indicate how the community developed.

Food-Producing Villages

Small food-producing villages have had a long history, but here we are chiefly interested in those that existed between 8000 and 5000 B.C. None of these communities is known thoroughly, and the following descriptions are based on data from several excavated sites and from surface surveys. The fullest data come from the phases represented in Ali Kosh and Tepe Sabz, in southwest Iran, and from Jarmo, Sarab, and Guran in the Zagros mountains. Additional data derive from extensive surveys in Khuzistan and the valleys of the Zagros.[14, 15]

During this period villages are small and scattered, typically less than 1 hectare in size and housing perhaps 100 to 300 people. They are situated on the best agricultural land in regions where farming is possible without irrigation. From a handful of sites known to be about 10,000 years old, the number of settlements had increased by 5000 B.C., when many villages were within sight of one another and almost every village was within an easy day's walk of the next. There is no evidence of great migrations or any serious pressure of population during this time. By 4000 B.C. some villages occupy areas as large as 2 hectares.[14, 16]

The increase in population appears to have been a direct consequence of improved agricultural techniques. In 8000 B.C., only primitive, low-yield races of emmer wheat and two-row barley were grown; sheep and goats were both in the early stages of domestication. By 5000 B.C. a modern complex of hybrid cereals and domesticated sheep, goats, cattle, and pigs were being exploited, and irrigation was practiced in marginal agricultural areas such as Deh Luran.[17] The effects of developed agriculture are soon apparent, for, by 4000 B.C., settlement of new areas by prehistoric pioneers can be shown clearly in such places as the Diyala region to the east of Baghdad.[18, 19] The age of the earliest settlements in southern Meso-

Table 1. Generalized chart showing the chronology of phases and sites mentioned in the text (39).

Date (B.C.)	Settlement subsistence type	Cultural phase	Ethnic group
2500		Early Dynastic III	Sumerians
		Early Dynastic II	Sumerians
		Early Dynastic I	Sumerians
2900	Walled cities	Jamdet Nasr	Sumerians
3500	Cities	Uruk	?
4000	Towns	Ubaid	?
5300	Temples	Eridu	?
5500	Irrigation	Sabz	
5800		Mohammad Jaffar	
6500	Food production	Ali Kosh	
8000	Food production aid small, settled villages	Bus Mordeh	
Pre-8000	Nomadic hunters	Zarzian	

potamia proper is unknown, but it would be surprising if groups of hunters and fishers had not lived along the rivers or swamps prior to the introduction of agriculture. The oldest settlement, Eridu, has been dated to about 5300 B.C., but there are no contemporary sites. In fact, there are few villages known in southern Mesopotamia that antedate 4000 B.C.

Towns and Cities

The millennium between 4000 and 3000 B.C. saw the rapid growth of towns and cities. Villages were also abundant, but some evidence suggests that they were less numerous than in earlier periods. "In part at least, the newly emerging pattern must have consisted of the drawing together of the population into larger, more defensible political units."[14] The trends I describe here pertain almost exclusively to southern Mesopotamia; in the north and in the valleys of the Zagros, the pattern remained one of small villages and— emerging later than their counterparts in the south—townships.[20]

From southern Mesopotamia, archeological data for the period before 3000 B.C. are skimpy. Deep soundings at the bases of such sites as Eridu, Ur, Uqair, Tello, Uruk, and

Susa and test excavations at Ubaid, Ras al-Amiya, and Hajji Mohammad are about all we have.[2] Only at Ras al-Amiya is there direct evidence of agriculture, although at Eridu a layer of fish bones on the altar of temple VII suggests the importance of the sea and of fishing. Archeological evidence from several of the remaining sites consists either of temple architecture or pottery, the latter serving more to indicate the age of a site than the social or cultural patterns of its inhabitants. Some temple plans are known, but published data on domestic architecture are few, and the sizes of the communities can be inferred only roughly.

There are extensive enough excavations at sites like Urak, Khafajah, Kish, Ur, and Nippur to indicate the scale of urbanism and many of its more spectacular architectural and artistic features for the period after 3000 B.C. The largest Early Dynastic site was evidently Uruk, where 445 hectares are enclosed by the city wall; contemporary Khafajah and Ur comprise 40 and 60 hectares, respectively. By contrast, the Ubaid portion of Uqair had about 7 hectares.[2]

Historical Reconstructions

Pictographic writing began by about 3400 B.C., but it is difficult to interpret, and in any case early writing tells little about society; it is confined to bookkeeping.[21] Nevertheless, by depending on myths, epics, and tales written some 1000 years later, scholars have attempted historical reconstructions of the emerging urban societies.[22-24]

The oldest texts that characterize the Sumerian community are no earlier than 2500 B.C. and were written at a time when the "Temple-city" had already become the characteristic feature of the Mesopotamian landscape.[25] In the view of many authors,[26] the city was an estate belonging to gods of nature and maintained on their behalf by completely dependent and relatively impotent mortals. Controversy centers around the degree to which the temple controlled the economy. The extreme view is that it controlled everything while the more popular moderate view is that it controlled only part of the economy. In the Early Dynastic period, it seems clear, some, if not all, people were responsible to a temple which in turn directed most of the production and redistribution of goods and services. For practical purposes there was no distinction between the economic and the religious roles of the temples, but their administrators may not have had much political influence. Some temples listed large staffs of attendants, craftsmen, laborers, and food producers, but the precise relationship of these people to the temple is by no means clear. Moreover, such staffs would have been associated with the largest temples and not with the host of lesser temples and shrines that seem to have been present in the larger cities. Political control was vested variously in the *en* (lord), *lugal* (great man, or king), or *ensi* (governor-priest), depending on the historical period, the city referred to, and the translator of the text. In early times religious and secular titles seem not to have been held by the same person. Jacobsen describes, for pre-Early Dynastic times, a "primitive democracy" with the leader appointed by and responsible to an assembly of citizens.[27] The arguments about the nature of Sumerian cities are summarized by Gadd:[28] "The issues barely stated here have been discussed with much elaboration and ingenuity, but only a notable increase of contemporary evidence could raise the conclusions to a possibility of much affecting our conception of Sumerian government."

Environment and Subsistence

By combining the geographic, economic, and historical data, we can construct some plausible theories about the course of development and the situations that triggered it.[29] The remarkable thing, from an ecological view, is the change in relations between men and products, and then between men and their fellows during the 5000 years. If we return for a moment to the pre-agricultural ways of life, we find small bands of hunters exploiting the seasonally available resources of a large territory by wandering from one place to another. Each community was self-sufficient, and each man had approximately the same access to the resources as his fellows. The earliest villagers seem to have maintained this pattern, although, as agriculture and stock breeding became more developed and important economically, the villagers tended more and more to stay put. People settled down where they could raise large amounts of grain, store it for the future, and exchange it for products they did not produce. In return for dependability of food supply, people gave up some of their dietary variety and most of their mobility. From a pattern of exploiting a broad spectrum of the environment, there developed a pattern of exploiting a relatively narrow spectrum.[30]

As long as people stayed where they could find sufficiently varied resources through hunting and gathering, they could be self-sufficient. When people settled in villages away from the mountains, out of the zone of rainfall agriculture, they were no longer independent in the sense that they personally had access to the varied resources they desired or needed. Psychologically and sociologically this marked a turning point in man's relations with his environment and his fellows. Southern Mesopotamia is a land with few resources, yet in many ways this was an advantage for the development of society. In a land without timber, stone, or metals, trade was necessary, but the role of trade in the emergence of civilization should not be overemphasized. Date palms and bundles of reeds served adequately instead of timber for most construction, and baked clay tools took the place of their stone or metal counterparts in other areas. On the other hand, travel by boat is ancient, and extensive land and sea trade is attested in early documents. It was easy to move goods in Mesopotamia.[31]

In order to live as well as the farmers in Deh Luran did, the Sumerians had to cooperate through trade, barter, or other means with their fellow settlers. We should remember that the barren vista of modern Mesopotamia on a dusty day does not reveal the full range of geographic variation or agricultural potential of the area. Swamps and rivers provided fish and fowl and, together with canals, water for irrigation and navigation. With sufficient water, dates and other fruits and vegetables could be grown. The unequal distribution of subsistence resources encouraged the beginnings of occupational specialization among the various kinds of food producers, and this trend was further emphasized after craftsmen started to follow their trades on a full-time basis.[32]

Economics and Management

Because of the geographic distribution of resources and the sedentary and occupationally specialized population, a social organization that could control production and redistribution was needed. Clearly, any reconstruction of the mechanics of redistribution in emerging Mesopotamian civilization is subject to the severe limitations of the evidence. If we recognize this, however, we may then seek in contemporary societies analogs that may help us imagine appropriate redistributional structures. In modern economies, money markets act as the agency of redistribution, but in virtually all "primitive" societies where surpluses or tradeable goods are produced, a center of redistribution of another kind grows. The "center" can be a person (for example, the chief); an institution, like a temple and the religious context it symbolizes; or a place, like a city with some form of free markets.[33] Jacobsen suggests that in Sumeria temples served as warehouses, where food was stored until times of famine.

Sahlins's[34] studies in modern Polynesia are also relevant to this point. He found that there is a close relation between surplus production and the degree of social stratification in Polynesia—that in a redistributional economy, the greater the surplus is, the greater is the degree of stratification. Of course we can only speculate about Mesopotamia, but, granting this and following Sahlins's findings, we may say that the chief of the Mesopotamian town would have acted as the center of redistribution. In Mesopotamia, most of the surplus labor or food went directly or indirectly into building and maintaining temples. One would also have expected the chief to use a good bit of the surplus to support himself and his family, to pay the wages of craftsmen, and to buy the raw materials that were turned into artifacts, such as jewelry and clothing, that served to distinguish his rank. Others in the lord's biological or official family would also have profited from his control of the resources and ultimately have become recognized as a social class entitled to special prerogatives. This social stratification would have been associated with a similarly burgeoning system of occupational differentiation.

In an emerging system where both technology and governmental forms are relatively simple but susceptible of improvement, there is a maximum opportunity for feedback. That is, if a certain level of production will support a certain degree of social stratification, efficient management by the social elite may result in more productivity.[34] It is interesting to speculate on how much the construction of enormous irrigation systems during later Mesopotamian history may have depended on the rising aspirations of the ruling elite.

Although the need for management of production might in itself have been sufficient cause for a developing social stratification, other factors were probably contributory. Turning now to law and politics, I should point out that, with the establishment of irrigation and the concentration of population in urban centers, man's basic attitudes toward the land must have changed. The construction of irrigation systems, even if primitive, makes the land more valuable to the builders, and this, if it did nothing else, would lead to some notions of property rights and inheritance that had not been necessary when abundant land was available for the taking. An irrigation system also implies that some men may have more direct control over the supply of water than others. This could have led to an increase in the power of individuals who controlled the supply of water, and it certainly must have led to disputes over the allocation of water. It seems inevitable that a working system of adjudicating claims over land would then have been necessary, and the task may have fallen to the chiefs (lords).[35]

The presence of "neighbors" also has ecological implications; it is worth recalling that property invites thievery. Adams argues that the "growth of the Mesopotamian city was closely related to the rising tempo of warfare," and Service points out that the inte gration of societies under war leaders is common, and clearly an adaptation to social-environmental conditions. Several Early Dynastic II cities had defensive walls, attesting to conflict between cities and perhaps between settled farmers and nomadic herders, but the historical evidence for warfare begins only about 2500 B.C.[36]

If we consider both the agricultural system and the wealth, we see conditions that enhanced opportunities for leadership and, ultimately, for direction and control. With these situations, the emerging systems of rank and status are understandable without our resorting to notions of "genius,""challenge and response,"or immigration by more advanced peoples.

Religion

The role of religion in integrating emerging Mesopotamian society is frequently mentioned. By 3000 B.C. texts and temples themselves attest to the central place of religion in Sumerian life; theoretically, at least, cities were simply estates of the gods, worked on their behalf by mortals.[26] How closely theory corresponds to fact is a question that cannot be answered. Although we cannot date their beginnings precisely, we know that temple centers were well established by 5000 B.C., and that towns and temples frequently go together. Whether towns developed where people congregated because of religious activities or whether temples grew in the market centers where the people were cannot be decided without more data. Both interpretations may be correct. Historic evidence suggests that economic activities were controlled by the temples, but this evidence says nothing about the original relationships between the two. Furthermore, the interpretation of the historical documents is open to question. As Gadd[28] points out, the picture of Sumerian economy that the various authors use is based on the "detailed records of one temple (Lagash) over a rather short period."

In regard to this limited view of the role of religion, it is well to recall that major settlements had several temples. At Khafajah, for example, perhaps as early as 4000 B.C. there were three temples, and a fourth was added later. Our image of the Sumerian temple is nevertheless likely to be that of the large temple oval at Khafajah or Ubaid rather than that of the smaller temples that were contemporary and perhaps just as characteristic. The temple oval appears to have housed a society within a city, but many temples had no auxiliary buildings. More impressive even than the temple ovals were the great ziggurats erected on artificial mounds—at Uruk 13 meters high and visible for many kilometers. Again this was only one of several temples at the same site. In Ubaid, Eridu, and Uqair, for example, where temples were originally associated with residential settlements, the towns were later abandoned and only the temples with cemeteries were maintained.[37]

Summary

It seems unlikely that Mesopotamian society took a single path as it approached the rigidly organized, hierarchal civilization of Early Dynastic times. Rather, we imagine that there was considerable experimentation and variety in the organization of society as people adapted to their physical environment and to the presence of other expanding communities.

Some towns and cities probably arose as the demographic solution to the problem of procuring and distributing resources. It would have made sense to have central "clearing houses." Similarly, it would have made sense to have the craftsmen who turned the raw materials into finished products live close to their supply (probably the temple stores). Temple centers are natural focal points of settlements. Cities and towns, however, are not the only demographic solutions to the problem of farming and maintaining irrigation canals. Both of these tasks could have been carried out by people living in more dispersed settlements. City life in Mesopotamia probably also presented other benefits. For example, as warfare came to be a recurrent threat, the psychological and physical security of a city must have been a comfort for many. Finally, to judge from some historical evidence, Mesopotamian cities were places of diversity and opportunity, no doubt desiderata for many people as long as they could also gain a suitable livelihood.[38]

In considering the development of civilization, an ecological approach forces us to consider multiple factors. Seeking isolated causes among the many factors possibly involved ignores the central concept of adaptation, with its ramifications of interaction and feedback. Still, we are a long way from fully understanding the emergence of Mesopotamian civilization. In particular, we need a great deal more archeological data that relate to the 2000 years preceding 3000 B.C. in southern Mesopotamia. Specifically, there are three projects which ought to have high priority in the planning of future archeological work in this area. First, we need thorough surveys in order to determine the early history of settlement in Mesopotamia. By means of these surveys in and around the early cities, we would try to determine the duration of occupation, and the variety and location of additional sites. Second, we need extensive excavation of selected smaller sites and portions of larger ones in order to determine the characteristics of different settlements. We would like to know in what way the cities, towns, temple centers, and villages were integrated to form a socioeconomic network. A third question, which gets at the crux of the matter, is, What structural form did the emerging Sumerian society take? Answers to this question must depend in large part on the results of future surveys and excavations of the kind suggested above. Then, selective excavations focusing on successive periods should yield data on the relative roles of economic and religious activities and on social differentiation and stratification. These data, after they are eventually pieced together, will comprise the story of the emergence of the world's first civilization.

References and Notes

[1] Archeological criteria: V. G. Childe, *Town Planning Rev.* 21, 3 (1950). Sociocultural criteria: R. M. Adams, in *City Invincible*, C. H. Kraeling and R. M. Adams, Eds. (Univ. of Chicago Press, Chicago, 1960), pp. 30-31; E. R. Wolf, *Peasants* (Prentice-Hall, Englewood Cliffs, N. J., 1966) ["It is the crystallization of executive power which serves to distinguish the primitive from the civilized . . . when the cultivator becomes subject to the demands and sanctions of power-holders outside his social stratum" (p. 11)]. The "form" of civilization: H. Frankfort, *The Birth of Civilization in the Near East* (Doubleday, Garden City, N. Y., 1956), chap. 2.

[2] Relevant sites are Ubaid, Eridu, Ras al-Amiya, Ali Kosh, Guran, Sarab, and Jarmo. For a bibliography of publications on Mesopotamia and Iran, see articles by E. Porada and R. H. Dyson in *Chronologies in Old World Archaeology*, R. W. Erich, Ed.

(Univ. of Chicago Press, Chicago, 1965), pp. 133-200, 215-256.

[3]E. Huntington, *Mainsprings of Civilization* (Wiley, New York, 1945).

[4]V. G. Childe, *New Light on the Most Ancient East* (Praeger, New York, 1952), p. 25; J. Mellaart, *Earliest Civilizations of the Near East* (Thames and Hudson, London, 1965), pp. 19-20.

[5]Studies based on archeology, paleontology, geography, palynology, and geology fail to disclose post-Pleistocene climatic changes that would have been of major cultural significance. See R. J. Braidwood and C. A. Reed, *Cold Spring Harbor Symp. Quant. Biol.* 22, 19 (1957); K. W. Butzer, in *Cambridge Ancient History* (Cambridge Univ. Press, Cambridge, 1965), vol. 1, chap. 2; K. V. Flannery, *Science* 147, 1247 (1965); H. E. Wright, Jr., *Eiszeitalter Gegenwart* 12, 160 (1960); W. van Zeist and H. E. Wright, Jr., *Science* 140, 65 (1963). Moreover, as I discuss more fully later, the development of urban civilizations doubtless depended more on sociocultural factors such as trade, surplus production, and economic interdependence than on geography *per se* [see R. M. Adams, in *City Invincible*, C. H. Kraeling and R. M. Adams, Eds. (Univ. of Chicago Press, Chicago, 1960), p. 291].

[6]For a general discussion of these ideas, see R. J. Braidwood in *Evolution and Anthropology: a Centennial Appraisal* (Anthropological Society of Washington, Washington, D.C., 1959), pp. 76-89; S. Piggott, in *Evolution After Darwin,* S. Tax, Ed. (Univ. of Chicago Press, Chicago, 1960), vol. 2, pp. 85-97.

[7]M. W. Thompson, *Antiquity* 39, 108 (1965).

[8]K. A. Wittfogel, *Oriental Despotism* (Yale Univ. Press, New Haven, Conn., 1957), p. 27.

[9]R. M. Adams, in *City Invincible,* C. H. Kraeling and R. M. Adams, Eds. (Univ. of Chicago Press, Chicago, 1960).

[10]It is misleading to think that at any moment all parts of a system are necessarily functioning harmoniously, let alone perfectly. One finds situations that can only be understood as a result of historical accident. For example, immigrants may carry with them customs and practices that are inappropriate to new circumstances.

[11]For examples of the effect of environmental conditions on socio-political integration, see J. H. Steward, *Bull. Bur. Amer. Ethnol.* 120 (1938); M. D. Coe, *Comp. Studies Soc. Hist.* 4, 65 (1961).

[12]R. I., Solecki, *Intern. Congr. Quaternary, 6th* (1964), vol. 4, pp. 405-412; F. Hole, K. V. Flannery, J. A. Neely, *Current Anthropol.* 6, 105 (1965). Since this article is restricted to Mesopotamia, I have ignored such spectacular and large early sites as Çatal Hüyük in Anatolia and Jericho in Jordan. These developments were essentially independent of Mesopotamia and must be explained in their own contexts.

[13]Kramer expressed the view of·many Sumerologists when he spoke of "Mesopotamian archeology in all its aspects: architecture, art, history, religion, and epigraphy" [S. N. Kramer, *The Sumerians* (Univ. of Chicago Press, Chicago, 1964), p. 28]. Historical archeologists often base their interpretations of culture on less tangible factors than those discussed in this article—on catastrophe, invasion and destruction, migration, religious inspiration, inventive genius, moral decadence, and the like.

[14]R. M. Adams, *Science* 136, 109 (1962).

[15]R. J. Braidwood, *Illustrated London News* 237, 695 (1960); F. Hole, *Science* 137, 524 (1962).

[16]For an example of the spacing of settlements and their relation to subsistence patterns, see F. Barth, "The land use pattern of migratory tribes of South Persia," *Norsk Geograf. Tidsskr.* 17 (1959).

[17]K. V. Flannery, *Science* 147, 1247 (1965).

[18]R. M. Adams, *Land Behind Baghdad* (Univ. of Chicago Press, Chicago, 1965).

[19]As agricultural techniques improved and the social organization for exploiting them developed, the population increased and settlement expanded slowly into the less favorable areas, a process that continues even today with the introduction of moldboard plows, tractors, and motor-driven water pumps.

[20]A. J. Jawad, *The Advent of the Era of Townships in Northern Mesopotamia* (Brill, Leiden, 1965).

[21]A. Falkenstein, *Archaische Texte aus Uruk* (Harrassowitz, Berlin, 1936).

[22]A. Deimel, *Sumerische Tempelwirtschaft zur Zeit Urukaginas und seiner Vorgänger* (Päpstlisches Bibelinstitut, Rome, 1931).

[23]A. Falkenstein, *Cahiers Hist. Mondiale* 1, 784 (1954).

[24]H. Frankfort, *The Birth of Civilization in the Near East* (Doubleday, Garden City, N. Y., 1956), chap. 3; S. N. Kramer, *The Sumerians* (Univ. of Chicago Press, Chicago, 1964); T. Jacobsen, *Z. Assyriol.* 52, 91 (1957). For a criticism of the Templewirtschaft, see N. M. Diakonoff, *Sumer: Society and State in Ancient Mesopotamia* (Academy of Sciences, Moscow, 1959) (in Russian, with English summary). A summary of the views of Russian scholars is given in F. I. Andersen, *Abr-Nahrain* 1, 56 (1959-60).

[25]For a general review of Sumerian history, see C. J. Gadd, in *Cambridge Ancient History* (Cambridge Univ. Press, Cambridge, 1962), vol. 1, chap. 13. General accounts of Sumerian life are given in S. N. Kramer, *The Sumerians* (Univ. of Chicago Press, Chicago, 1964) and ——, *History Begins in Sumer* (Thames and Hudson, London, rev. ed., 1961). The cuneiform texts take Sumerian history back to the ruler Mesilim, about 2500 B.C. A summary of the kind of texts available is given in T. Jacobsen, *Z. Assyriol.* 52, 91 (1957).

[26]See especially A. Deimel (22) and A. Falkenstein (23).

[27]T. Jacobsen, *J. Near Eastern Studies* 2, 159 (1943); *Z. Assyriol.* 52, 91 (1957).

[28]C. J. Gadd, in *Cambridge Ancient History* (Cambridge Univ. Press, Cambridge, 1962).

[29]Many of the ideas in this section are derived from the work of R. M. Adams; see 9, 14, 18.

[30]For an analogous situation, see M. D. Coe and K. V. Flannery, *Science* 143, 650 (1964).

[31]The desirability of trade is an effective stimulus to demographic consolidation and political integration; see M. D. Coe, *Comp. Studies Soc. Hist.* 4, 65 (1961). A clay model at Eridu gives the earliest evidence for boats; see S. Lloyd, *Illustrated London News* 213, 303 (1948). For a summary of early trade, see C. J. Gadd (28, p. 41).

[32]R. M. Adams (9, p. 276) discusses the Sumerian subsistence base. Sumerian texts make poignant reference to famine and the insecurity of life in Mesopotamia [see T. Jacobsen, *Proc. Amer. Phil. Soc.* 107, 476 (1963)].

[33]K. Polanyi, in *Trade and Market in the Early Empires*, K. Polanyi, C. M. Arensberg, H. W. Pearson, Eds, (Free Press, Glencoe, Ill., 1957), pp. 250-256; for a discussion of chiefdoms, see E. R. Service, *Primitive Social Organization* (Random House, New York, 1962), pp. 144-152. The practical consequence of redistribution in the Mesopotamian case was the development of a tributary peasant society as a distinct social stratum [see E. R. Wolf, *Peasants* (Prentice-Hall, Englewood Cliffs, N.J., 1966), pp. 10-11; T. Jacobsen, *Proc. Amer. Phil. Soc.* 107, 476 (1963)].

[34]M. D. Sahlins, *Social Stratification in Polynesia* (Univ. of Washington Press, Seattle, 1958).

[35]On the role of lords, see C. J. Gadd (28, p. 13); T. Jacobsen, *Z. Assyriol.* 52, 91 (1957). On the development of political authority, see R. M. Adams (9, p. 278); K. A. Wittfogel (8); M. Fried, in *Culture in History*, S. Diamond, Ed. (Columbia Univ. Press, New York, 1960), pp. 713-731.

[36]Part of Jacobsen's reconstruction of kingship emerging from a base of primitive

democracy is based on the need for a rapidly mobilized defense and the holding of power by war leaders; see T. Jacobsen, *Z. Assyriol.* 52, 91 (1957); R. M. Adams, *Sci. Amer.* 203, 153 (1960); E. R. Service, *Primitive Social Organization* (Random House, New York, 1962), p. 114.

[37]Abandonment of any city with irrigated fields would be unlikely unless the water failed or the fields became too salty for use. Both of these circumstances have been important in Mesopotamia since settlement began, and we may not be able to infer much about the role of religion in society from the lack of settlements around temples that were probably maintained for a time out of a sense of tradition by people living elsewhere.

[38]S. N. Kramer, *The Sumerians* (Univ. of Chicago Press, Chicago, 1964), p. 89.

[39]Table 1 is based in part on E. Porada, in *Chronologies in Old World Archaeology,* R. W. Erich, Ed. (Univ. of Chicago Press, Chicago, 1965). Since there is archaeological continuity from Eridu times into the Sumerian period, there is probably biological continuity in the population, too. Strictly speaking, however, *Sumerian* is a term that refers to the language and not to the people.

[40]The research in Iran was supported by NSF grants GS-67 and 724 and by the University of Chicago and Rice University. The Archaeological Service, Musee Bastan, Tehran, granted permission to excavate and provided assistance in the field. I thank Edward Norbeck and Barbara Stark for advice in preparing the manuscript and Steve Wood for the drawings.

T. Jacobsen, one of the most distinguished students of ancient
Mesopotamian civilization, has made extensive and fundamental
contributions to the study of Sumerian and Akkadian languages
and archaeology. He has participated in numerous archaeological
surveys and excavations as past Director of the Oriental Institute
at the University of Chicago. Presently, he is professor of
Assyriology at Harvard University.

Robert McC. Adams (Ph.D., University of Chicago, 1956), past
director of the Oriental Institute, University of Chicago, is professor
of anthropology and Dean of the Social Sciences at the University
of Chicago. He has conducted extensive field work in both the
Near East and Mexico, and has published numerous books and
articles including *The Evolution of Urban Society* (1966) and
The Uruk Countryside (with H. J. Nissen, 1972). In this important
paper the authors suggest that an increasing salinization greatly
affected agricultural production and settlement patterns in lower
Mesopotamia. A final analysis of the surveys upon which this
article was based appears in Adam's *Land Behind Baghdad* (1965).

Salt and Silt in Ancient Mesopotamian Agriculture

Thorkild Jacobsen
Robert M. Adams

*Progressive changes in soil salinity and sedimentation contributed to the breakup
of past civilizations.*

Under the terms of a farsighted statute, 70 percent of the oil revenues of the Iraq
Government are set aside for a program of capital investment which is transforming many
aspects of the country's predominantly agricultural economy. As compared with the
subsistence agriculture which largely has characterized Iraq's rural scene in the past, new
irrigation projects in formerly uninhabited deserts are pioneering a rapid increase in land
and labor productivity through crop rotation, summer cultivation in addition to the
traditional winter-grown cereals, and emphasis on cash crops and livestock.

But these and similar innovations often have disconcerting effects in a semiarid,

Reprinted from *Science*, Vol. 128, pp. 1251-1258, by permission of the publisher and authors. Copyright 1958 by the American Association for the Advancement of Science.

subtropical zone—effects which cannot be calculated directly from the results of experiment in Europe and America. At the same time, old canal banks and thickly scattered ruins of former settlements testify to former periods of successful cultivation in most of the desert areas now being reopened. The cultural pre-eminence of the alluvial plains of central and southern Iraq through much of their recorded history provides still further evidence of the effectiveness of the traditional agricultural regime in spite of its prevailing reliance on a simple system of fallow in alternate years. Accordingly, the entire 6000-year record of irrigation agriculture in the Tigris-Euphrates flood plain furnishes an indispensable background for formulating plans for future development.

At least the beginnings of a comprehensive assessment of ancient agriculture recently were undertaken on behalf of the Government of Iraq Development Board. In addition to utilizing ancient textual sources from many parts of Iraq which today are widely scattered in the world's libraries and museums, this undertaking included a program of archeological field work designed to elucidate the history of irrigation and settlement of a portion of the flood plain that is watered by a Tigris tributary, the Diyala River.[1] Here we cannot report all the diverse findings of the project and its many specialists, but instead will outline some aspects of the general ecological situation encountered by agriculturalists in the Mesopotamian alluvium which seem to have shaped the development of irrigation farming. And, conversely, we hope to show that various features of the natural environment in turn were decisively modified by the long-run effects of human agencies.

Historical Role of Soil Salinization

A problem which recently has come to loom large in Iraqi reclamation planning is the problem of salinity. The semiarid climate and generally low permeability of the soils of central and southern Iraq expose the soils to dangerous accumulations of salt and exchangeable sodium, which are harmful to crops and soil texture and which can eventually force the farmer off his land.

For the most part, the salts in the alluvial soils are presumed to have been carried in by river and irrigation water from the sedimentary rocks of the northern mountains. In addition, smaller quantities may have been left by ancient marine transgressions or borne in by winds from the Persian Gulf. Beside the dominant calcium and magnesium cations, the irrigation water also contains some sodium. As the water evaporates and transpires it is assumed that the calcium and magnesium tend to precipitate as carbonates, leaving the sodium ions dominant in the soil solution. Unless they are washed down into the water table, the sodium ions tend to be adsorbed by colloidal clay particles, deflocculating them and leaving the resultant structureless soil almost impermeable to water. In general, high salt concentrations obstruct germination and impede the absorption of water and nutrients by plants.

Salts accumulate steadily in the water table, which has only very limited lateral movement to carry them away. Hence the ground water everywhere has become extremely saline, and this probably constitutes the immediate source of the salts in Iraq's saline soils. New waters added as excessive irrigation, rains, or floods can raise the level of the water table very considerably under the prevailing conditions of inadequate drainage. With a further capillary rise when the soil is wet, the dissolved salts and exchangeable sodium are brought into the root zone or even to the surface.

While this problem has received scientific study in Iraq only in very recent years, investigation by the Diyala Basin Archeological Project of a considerable number and variety of ancient textual sources has shown that the process of salinization has a long history. Only the modern means to combat it are new: deep drainage to lower and hold down the water table, and utilization of chemical amendments to restore soil texture. In spite of the almost proverbial fertility of Mesopotamia in antiquity, ancient control of the water table was based only on avoidance of overirrigation and on the practice of weed-fallow in alternate years. As was first pointed out by J. C. Russel, the later technique allows the deep-rooted *shoq (Proserpina stephanis)* and *agul (Alhagi maurorum)* to create a deep-lying dry zone against the rise of salts through capillary action. In extreme cases, longer periods of abandonment must have been a necessary, if involuntary, feature of the agricultural cycle. Through evapotranspiration and some slow draining they could eventually reduce an artificially raised water table to safe levels.

As to salinity itself, three major occurrences have been established from ancient records. The earliest of these, and the most serious one, affected southern Iraq from 2400 B.C. until at least 1700 B.C. A milder phase is attested in documents from central Iraq written between 1300 and 900 B.C. Lastly, there is archeological evidence that the Nahrwan area east of Baghdad became salty only after A.D. 1200.

The earliest of these occurrences particularly merits description, since it sheds light on the northward movement of the major centers of political power from southern into central Iraq during the early second millennium B.C. It seems to have had its roots in one of the perennial disputes between the small, independent principalities which were the principal social units of the mid-third millennium B.C. Girsu and Umma, neighboring cities along a watercourse stemming from the Euphrates, had fought for generations over a fertile border district. Under the ruler Entemenak, Girsu temporarily gained the ascendancy, but was unable to prevent Umma, situated higher up the watercourse, from breaching and obstructing the branch canals that served the border fields. After repeated, unsuccessful protests, Entemenak eventually undertook to supply water to the area by means of a canal from the Tigris; access to that river, flowing to the east of Girsu, could be assured without further campaigning against Umma to the northwest. By 1700 B.C. this canal had become large and important enough to be called simply "the Tigris," and it was supplying a large region west of Girsu that formerly had been watered only by the Euphrates. As a result, the limited irrigation supplies that could be drawn from the latter river were supplemented with copious Tigris water. A corresponding increase undoubtedly occurred in seepage, flooding, and overirrigation, creating all the conditions for a decisive rise in groundwater level.

Several parallel lines of evidence allow the ensuing salinization to be followed quantitatively:

(1) Beginning shortly after the reign of Entemenak, the presence of patches of saline ground is directly attested in records of ancient temple surveyors. In a few cases, individual fields which at that time were recorded as salt-free can be shown in an archive from 2100 B.C. to have developed conditions of sporadic salinity during the 300 intervening years of cultivation.

(2) Crop choice can be influenced by many factors, but the onset of salinization

strongly favors the adoption of crops which are more salt-tolerant. Counts of grain impressions in excavated pottery from sites in southern Iraq of about 3500 B.C., made by H. Helbaek, suggest that at that time the proportions of wheat and barley were nearly equal. A little more than 1000 years later, in the time of Entemenak at Girsu, the less salt-tolerant wheat accounted for only one-sixth of the crop. By about 2100 B.C. wheat had slipped still further, and it accounted for less than 2 percent of the crop in the Girsu area. By 1700 B.C., the cultivation of wheat had been abandoned completely in the southern part of the alluvium.

(3) Concurrent with the shift to barley cultivation was a serious decline in fertility which for the most part can be attributed to salinization. At about 2400 B.C. in Girsu a number of field records give an average yield of 2537 liters per hectare—highly respectable even by modern United States and Canadian standards. This figure had declined to 1460 liters per hectare by 2100 B.C., and by about 1700 B.C. the recorded yield at nearby Larsa had shrunk to an average of only 897 liters per hectare. The effects of this slow but cumulatively large decline must have been particularly devastating in the cities, where the needs of a considerable superstructure of priests, administrators, merchants, soldiers, and craftsmen had to be met with surpluses from primary agricultural production.

The southern part of the alluvial plain appears never to have recovered fully from the disastrous general decline which accompanied the salinization process. While never completely abandoned afterwards, cultural and political leadership passed permanently out of the region with the rise of Babylon in the 18th century B.C., and many of the great Sumerian cities dwindled to villages or were left in ruins. Probably there is no historical event of this magnitude for which a single explanation is adequate, but that growing soil salinity played an important part in the breakup of Sumerian civilization seems beyond question.

Silt and the Ancient Landscape

Like salt, the sources of the silt of which the alluvium is composed are to be found in the upper reaches of the major rivers and their tributaries. Superficially, the flatness of the alluvial terrain may seem to suggest a relatively old and static formation, one to which significant increments of silt are added only as a result of particularly severe floods. But in fact, sedimentation is a massive, continuing process. Silt deposited in canal beds must be removed in periodic cleanings to adjoining spoil banks, from which it is carried by rain and wind erosion to surrounding fields. Another increment of sediment accompanies the irrigation water into the fields themselves, adding directly to the land surface. In these ways, the available evidence from archeological soundings indicates that an average of perhaps ten meters of silt has been laid down at least near the northern end of the alluvium during the last 5000 years.

Of course, the rate of deposition is not uniform. It is most rapid along the major rivers and canals, and their broad levees slope away to interior drainage basins where accumulated runoff and difficult drainage have led to seriously leached soils and seasonal swamps. However, only the very largest of the present depressions seem to have existed as permanent barriers (while fluctuating in size) to cultivation and settlement for the six

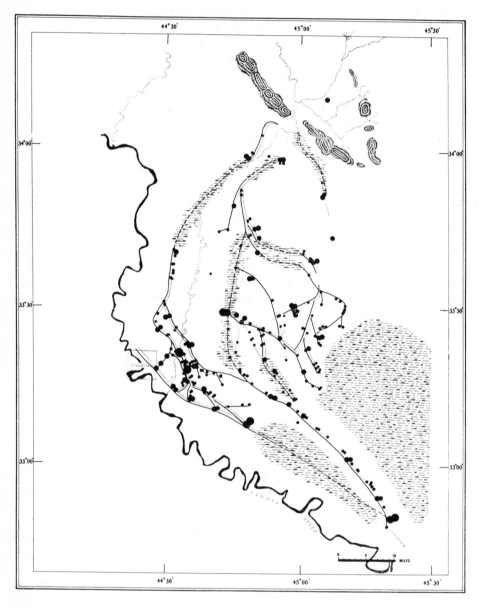

Fig. 1. Early watercourses and settlements in the Diyala region. The system shown in grey was in use during the Early Dynastic period, about 3000-2400 B.C. Sites and watercourses shown in black, slightly displaced so that the earlier pattern will remain visible, were occupied during the Old Babylonian period, about 1800-1700 B.C. In this and subsequent figures, size of circle marking an ancient settlement is roughly proportional to the area of its ruins. Modern river courses are shown in grey.

millennia since agriculture began in the northern part of the alluvium. More commonly, areas of swamp shifted from time to time. As some were gradually brought under cultivation, others formed behind newly created canal or river levees which interrupted the earlier avenues of drainage.

As the rate of sedimentation is affected by the extent of irrigation, so also were the processes of sedimentation—and their importance as an agricultural problem—closely related to the prevailing patterns of settlement, land-use, and even sociopolitical control. The character of this ecological interaction can be shown most clearly at present from archeological surveys in the lower Diyala basin, although other recent reconnaissance indicates that the same relationships were fairly uniform throughout the northern, or Akkadian, part of the Mesopotamian plain.[2] To what degree the same patterns occurred in the initially more urbanized (and subsequently more saline) Sumerian region further south, however, cannot yet be demonstrated.

The methods of survey employed here consisted of locating ancient occupational sites with the aid of large-scale maps and aerial photographs, visiting most or all of them—in this case, more than 900 in a 9000-square-kilometer area—systematically in order to make surface collections of selected "type fossils" of broken pottery, and subsequently determining the span of occupation at each settlement with the aid of such historical and archeological crossties as may be found to supplement the individual sherd collections.[3] It then can be observed that the settlements of a particular period always describe networks of lines which must represent approximately the contemporary watercourses that were necessary for settled agricultural life. For more recent periods, the watercourses serving the settlements often still can be traced in detail as raised levees, spoil banks, or patterns of vegetation disturbance, but, owing in part to the rising level of the plain, all of the older watercourses so far have been located only inferentially.

A number of important and cumulative, but previously little-known, developments emerge from the surveys. By comparing the over-all pattern of settlement of both the early third and early second millennium B.C. (Fig. 1) with the prevailing pattern of about A.D. 500 (Fig. 2) these developments can be seen in sharply contrasting form. They may be summarized conveniently by distinguishing two successive phases of settlement and irrigation, each operating in a different ecological background and each facing problems of sedimentation of a different character and magnitude.

The earlier phase persisted longest. Characterized by a linear pattern of settlements largely confined to the banks of major watercourses, it began with the onset of agricultural life in the Ubaid period (about 4000 B.C.) and was replaced only during the final centuries of the pre-Christian era. In all essentials the same network of watercourses was in use throughout this long time-span, and the absence of settlement along periodically shifting side branches seems to imply an irrigation regime in which the water was not drawn great distances inland from the main watercourses. Under these circumstances, silt accumulation would not have been the serious problem to the agriculturalist that it later became. The short branch canals upon which irrigation depended could have been cleaned easily or even replaced without the necessary intervention of a powerful, centralized authority. Quite possibly most irrigation during this phase depended simply on uncontrolled flooding through breaches cut in the levees of watercourses (like the lower Mississippi River) flowing well above plain level.

It is apparent from the map in Fig. 1 that large parts of the area were unoccupied by settled cultivators even during the periods of maximum population and prosperity that have been selected for illustration therein. An extended, historical study of soil profiles would be necessary to provide explanations for these uninhabited zones, but it is not unreasonable to suppose that some were seasonal swamps and depressions of the kind described above, while others were given over to desert because they were slightly elevated and hence not subject to easy flooding and irrigation. Still others probably were permanent swamps, since it is difficult to account in any other way for the discontinuities in settlement that appear along long stretches of some watercourses. One indication of the ecological shift which took place in succeeding millennia is that permanent swamps today have virtually disappeared from the entire northern half of the alluvium.

Considering the proportion of occupied to unoccupied area, the total population of the Diyala basin apparently was never very large during this long initial phase. Instead, a moderately dense population was confined to small regional enclaves or narrow, isolated strips along the major watercourses; for the rest of the area there can have been only very small numbers of herdsmen, hunters, fishermen, and marginal catch-crop cultivators. It is significant that most of the individual settlements were small villages, and that even the dominant political centers in the area are more aptly described as towns rather than cities.[4]

An essential feature of the earlier pattern of occupation, although not shown in a summary map like Fig. 1, is its fluctuating character. There is good historical evidence that devastating cycles of abandonment affected the whole alluvium. The wide and simultaneous onset of these cycles soon after relatively peaceful and prosperous times suggests that they proceeded from sociopolitical, rather than natural, causes, but at any rate their effects can be seen clearly in the Diyala region. For example, the numerous Old Babylonian settlements shown in Fig. 1 had been reduced in number by more than 80 per cent within 500 years following, leaving only small outposts scattered at wide intervals along watercourses which previously had been thickly settled. An earlier abandonment, not long after the Early Dynastic period that is shown in gray in Fig. 1, was shorter-lived and possibly affected the main towns more than the outlying small villages. Village life in general, it may be observed, remains pretty much of an enigma in the ancient Orient for all "historical" periods.

Under both ancient and modern Mesopotamian conditions, a clear distinction between "canals" and "rivers" is frequently meaningless or impossible. If the former are large and are allowed to run without control they can develop a "natural" regime in spite of their artificial origin. Some river courses, on the other hand, can be maintained only by straightening, desilting, and other artificial measures. Nevertheless, it needs to be stressed that the reconstructed watercourses shown in Fig. 2 followed essentially natural regimes and that at least their origins had little or nothing to do with human intervention. They were, in the first place, already present during the initial occupation of the area by prehistoric village agriculturalists who lacked the numbers and organization to dig them artificially. Secondly, the same watercourses persisted for more than three millennia with little change, even through periods of abandonment when they could not have received the maintenance which canals presuppose. Finally, the whole network of these early rivers describes a "braided stream" pattern which contrasts sharply with the brachiating canal systems of all later times, which are demonstrably artificial.

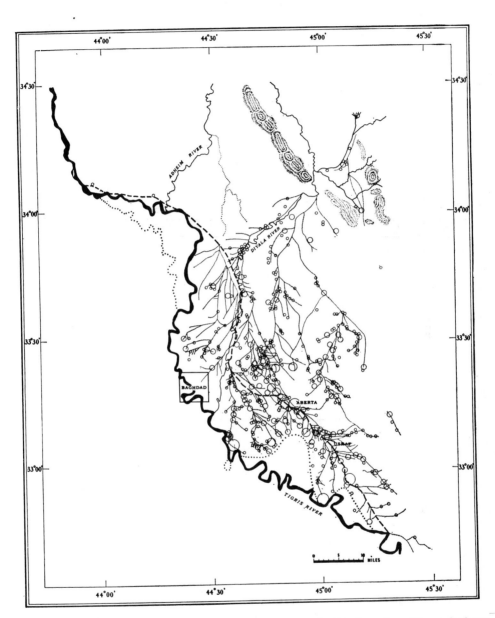

Fig. 2. Maximum extent of settlement and irrigation in the Diyala region. All canals shown by lines with minute serrations were in use during the Sassanian period, A.D. 226-637. However, expansion to the full limits came only with construction of the Nahrwan Canal shown as a dashed black line) late in the period. Settlements shown as black circles are also of Sassanian date. The different course probably followed in places by the Tigris River during the Sassanian period is suggested by black dotted lines.

Specific features of the historic geography of the area are not within the compass of this article, but it should be noted that the ancient topography differed substantially from the modern. Particularly interesting is the former course of the Diyala River, flowing west of its present position and joining the Tigris River (apparently also not in its modern course) through a delta-like series of mouths. A branch that bifurcated from the former Diyala above its "delta" and flowed off for a long distance to the southeast before joining the Tigris has been identified tentatively as the previously unlocated "River Dabban" that is referred to in ancient cuneiform sources.

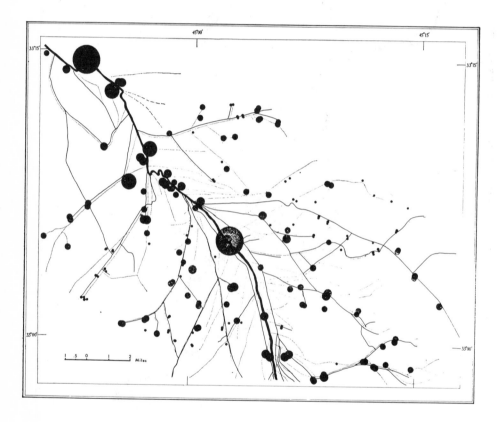

Fig. 3. Branch canal sequence along the Nahrwan. Branches shown as dashed grey lines date to the later Sassanian period (about A.D. 500-637). Settlements shown as grey circles and branch canals shown as continuous grey lines belong to the Early Islamic and Samarran periods, prior to about A.D. 900. Settlements and branch canals shown in black are those in use during the final phase of irrigation in the lower Nahrwan district, about A.D. 1100. The weir excavated by the project was located at the junction of numerous branch canals northwest of the city of Uskaf.

The pattern of occupation illustrated in Fig. 2 began to merge in Achaemenian times (539-331 B.C.), after nearly 1000 years of stagnation and abandonment. Perhaps the pace of reoccupation quickened with the conquest of Mesopotamia by Alexander, but the density of population reached during much older periods was attained again, and then surpassed, only in the subsequent Parthian period (about 150 B.C.-A.D. 226). New settlements large enough to be described as true cities, on the other hand, were introduced to the area for the first time by Alexander's Macedonian followers—demonstrating, if doubt could otherwise exist, that the onset of urbanization depends more on historical and cultural factors than on a simple increase in population density.

A central feature of this second phase of settlement is the far more complete exploitation of available land and water resources for agriculture. There is some evidence that the irrigation capacity of the Diyala River was being utilized fully even before the end of the Parthian period, and yet both the proportion of land that was cultivated and the total population rose substantially further, reaching their maxima in this area, for any period, under the Sassanian dynasty (A.D. 226-637) that followed. A rough estimate of the total agricultural production in the area first becomes possible with records of tax collections under the early Abbasids, perhaps 300 years after the maximum limits of expansion shown in Fig. 2 had been reached. From a further calculation of the potentially cultivable land it can then be shown that (with alternate years in fallow and assuming average yields) virtually the entire cultivable area must have been cropped regularly under both the Sassanians and early Abbasids.

Increased population, the growth of urban centers, and expansion in the area of cultivation to its natural limits were linked in turn to an enlargement of the irrigation system on an unprecedented scale. It was necessary, in the first place, to crisscross former-ly unused desert and depression areas with a complex—and entirely artificial—brachiating system of branch canals, which is outlined in Fig. 2. Expansion depended also on the con-struction of a large, supplementary feeder canal from the Tigris which, with technical proficiency that still excites admiration, and without apparent regard for cost, brought the indispensable, additional water through a hard, conglomerate headland, across two rivers, and thence down the wide levee left by the Dabban River of antiquity. Enough survives of the Nahrwan Canal, as the lower part of this gigantic system was called, even to play a key part in modern irrigation planning. Excavations carried out by the Diyala Basin Archeological Project at one of several known weirs along the 300-kilometer course of this canal provided a forceful illustration not only of the scale of the system but also of the attention lavished on such ancillary works as thousands of brick sluice gates along its branches. In short, we are dealing here with a whole new conception of irrigation which undertook boldly to reshape the physical environment at a cost which could be met only with the full resources of a powerful and highly centralized state.[5]

In spite of its unrivaled engineering competence, there were a number of undesirable consequences of the new irrigation regime. For example, to a far greater degree than had been true earlier, it utilized long branch canals which tended to fill rapidly with silt because of their small-to-moderate slope and cross-sectional area. Only the Nahrwan Canal itself—and that only during the first two centuries or so of its existence—seems to have maintained its bed without frequent and costly cleaning. Silt banks left from Parthian, Sassanian, and Islamic canal cleaning are today a major topographic feature not only in the Diyala region but all over the northern part of the Mesopotamian alluvium; frequently they run for great distances and tower over all but the highest mounds built up by ancient towns and cities. Or again, while massive control installations were essential if such a complex and interdependent system was to operate effectively, they needed periodic reconstruction at great cost (six major phases at the weir excavated by the Diyala Project) and practically continuous maintenance. Moreover, the provision of control works of all sizes acted together with the spreading networks of canal branches and subbranches to reduce or eliminate flood surges which otherwise might have contributed to the desilting process.

None of these consequences, to be sure, vitiated the advantages to be obtained with the new type of irrigation *so long as there remained a strong central authority committed to its maintenance.* But with conditions of social unrest and a preoccupation on the part of the political authorities with military adventures and intrigues, the maintenance of the system could only fall back on local communities ill equipped to handle it. These circumstances prevailed fairly briefly in late Sassanian times, leading to a widespread but temporary abandonment of the area. After an Islamic revival, they occurred again in the 11th and 12th centuries A.D., accompanied by such storm signals of political decay as the calculated breaching of the Nahrwan during a military campaign. On this occasion there was no quick recovery; it still remains for the modern Iraqis to re-establish the prosperity for which the region once was noted.

A closer look at the role of sedimentation along the Nahrwan during the years of political crisis under the later Abbasids is given in Fig. 3. In the first illustrated phase, in late Sassanian times, irrigation water was drawn from the Nahrwan at fairly uniform intervals and applied almost directly to fields adjoining its course. During a second phase, roughly coinciding with the rise of the Abbasid caliphate, irrigation water tended to be drawn off further upstream from the field for which it was destined. This is best exemplified by the increasing importance of the weir as a source for branch canals serving a considerable area. For some distance below the weir the level of the Nahrwan apparently no longer was sufficient to furnish irrigation water above the level of the fields.

By the time of the final phase, soon after A.D. 1100, practically all irrigation in the very large region below the weir had come to depend on branch canals issuing from above it; it is worth noting that two of the largest and most important of these branches simply paralleled the Nahrwan along each bank for more than 20 kilometers. The same unsuccessful struggle to maintain irrigation control is shown by the shrinkage or disappearance of town and city life along the main canal and the depopulation of the initial 5 to 10 kilometers along each major branch issuing from it, while lower-lying communities at the distal ends of the branches continued to flourish.

This cumulative change in the character of the system probably was a consequence of both natural and social factors. On the one hand, silt deposition had raised the level of the fields by almost 1 meter over a 500-year period. Since the natural mechanisms for maintaining equilibrium between the bed of a watercourse and its alluvial levee were largely inoperative in such a complex and carefully controlled system, this rise in land surface may have reduced considerably the level of water available for irrigation purposes. At the same time, inadequate maintenance and subsequent siltation of the Nahrwan's own bed in time sharply reduced its flow and surely also reduced the head of water it could provide to its branches. But whatever the responsible factors were, the result was an especially disastrous one. At a time when the responsibility of the central government for irrigation was eroding away and when population had been reduced substantially by warfare and by prolonged disruption of the water supply, the heavy burden of desilting branch canals remained constant or even increased for the local agriculturalist. If the accumulation of silt was no more than a minor problem at the beginning of irrigation in the Diyala basin 5000 years earlier, by the late Abbasid period it had become perhaps the greatest single obstacle that a quite different irrigation regime had to deal with.

With the converging effects of mounting maintenance requirements on the one hand, and declining capacity for more than rudimentary maintenance tasks on the other, the virtual desertion of the lower Diyala area that followed assumes in retrospect a kind of historical inevitability. By the middle of the 12th century most of the Nahrwan region already was abandoned. Only a trickle of water passed down the upper section of the main canal to supply a few dying towns in the now hostile desert. Invading Mongol horsemen under Hulagu Khan, who first must have surveyed this devastated scene a century later, have been unjustly blamed for causing it ever since.

References and Notes

[1] The Diyala Basin Archeological Project was conducted jointly by the Oriental Institute of the University of Chicago and the Iraq Directorate General of Antiquities, on a grant from the First Technical Section of the Development Board. It was directed by one of us (T. J.), with the other (R. M. A.) and Sayyid Fuad Safar, of the Directorate General of Antiquities, as associate directors. Excavations were under the supervision of Sayyid Mohammed Ali Mustafa, also of the Directorate General of Antiquities. Field studies of paleobotanical remains were undertaken in association with the project by Dr. Hans Helbaek, of the National Museum, Copenhagen, Denmark. Intensive study of the cuneiform and Arabic textual sources on agriculture was made possible through the collaboration of scholars of many countries. Especial thanks for assistance to the field program in Iraq, and for advice in the interpretation of its results, are due to Mr. K. F. Vernon, H. E. Dr. Naji al-Asil, Dr. J. C. Russel, and Sayyid Adnan Hardan.

[2] R. M. Adams, *Sumer,* in press.

[3] A preliminary application of this approximate methodology to conditions prevailing in Iraq was introduced by one of us (T. J.) in the Diyala basin in 1936-37, and the results of that earlier survey have been incorporated in the present study. Fortunately for the archeologist, there is sufficient disturbance from routine community activities (for example, foundation, well, and grave digging, and mud-brick manufacture, and so forth) for some traces of even the earliest of a long sequence of occupational periods to be detected on a mound's surface.

[4] Partial town plans for the political capital of the region at Tel Asmar (ancient Eshnunna) and for the two other slightly smaller centers are available from extensive Oriental Institute excavations carried out in the Diyala region between 1930 and 1937. See P. Delougaz, *The Temple Oval at Khafajah* [Oriental Inst. Publ. 53 (Univ. of Chicago Press, Chicago, 1940)]; P. Delougaz and S. Lloyd, *Pre-Sargonid Temples in the Diyala Region* [Oriental Inst. Publ. 58 (Univ. of Chicago Press, Chicago, 1942)]; and H. Frankfort, *Stratified Cylinder Seals from the Diyala Region* [Oriental Inst. Publ. 72 (Univ. of Chicago Press, Chicago, 1955)], plates 93-96. For recent general overviews of the history and culture of the earlier periods, see A. Falkenstein "La cité-temple Sumérienne" [*Cahiers d'Histoire Mondiale* 1 (1954)] and T. Jacobsen, "Early political developments in Mesopotamia" [*Z. für Assyriologie* (N.F.) 18 (1957)].

[5]General accounts of political, social, and cultural conditions in Mesopotamia during the Persian dynasties and under the Caliphate are to be found in R. Ghirshman, *Iran* (Pelican, Harmondsworth, Middlesex, England, 1954) and P. K. Hitti, *History of the Arabs* (Macmillan, London, ed. 6, 1956).

A. L. Oppenheim, professor of Assyriology at the University of Chicago
and past president of the American Oriental Society, has studied Mesopotamian
tablets for over 35 years. He is the author of numerous articles, monographs, and books, all of which have added new dimensions to our understanding of Mesopotamian society and political and economic structures.
His book *Ancient Mesopotamia* (1964) provides one of the most lucid
syntheses of this civilization. In the selected letters below, written 4000 years ago,
the citizens of Sumer, Akkad, and Babylon record the trials and tribulations of
their own 'rise and fall.'

Letters from Mesopotamia

A. L. Oppenheim

Old Akkadian Letters

A Solemn Warning

> This is from Iškun-Dagan to Puzur-Ištar:
> You are bound herewith by the oath I swear by the gods Inanna and Aba, and the
> gods Ašširgi and Ninhursag, and the oath by the life of the king and the life of the queen,
> that not until you (come here and) have seen me face to face must you touch either
> bread or beer, and that not until you have arrived here must you even sit down on a chair.

Before the Invasion of the Guti

> This is from Iškun-Dagan to Lugalra:
> Cultivate the field and watch over the cattle! And, above all, do not tell me:
> "The Guti are around, I could not cultivate the field." Man outposts at one-mile intervals
> and you yourself go on and cultivate the field! The men will go about their business(?).
> If the Guti attempt an attack against you, then bring all the cattle into town. Formerly(?)
> when the Guti men drove away the cattle I have never said a word; I have always given
> you silver (for the damages). But now(?) I swear by the life of King Šar-kali-šarrī that
> should the Guti men have driven away the cattle, and you cannot pay out of your own
> pocket, I shall give you no silver when I come to town. Now, won't you keep watch over
> the cattle!
> I have already claimed from you the regular delivery of barley in piles.
> This is a warning(?)—take cognizance of it.

Trade

Tell Ea-ñasir: Nanni sends the following message:

When you came, you said to me as follows: "I will give Gimil-Sin (when he comes) fine quality copper ingots." You left then but you did not do what you promised me. You put ingots which were not good before my messenger (Sīt-Sin) and said: "If you want to take them, take them; if you do not want to take them, go away!"

What do you take me for, that you treat somebody like me with such contempt? I have sent as messengers gentlemen like ourselves to collect the bag with my money (deposited with you) but you have treated me with contempt by sending them back to me empty-handed several times, and that through enemy territory. Is there anyone among the merchants who trade with Telmun who has treated me in this way? You alone treat my messenger with contempt! On account of that one (trifling) mina of silver which I owe(?) you, you feel free to speak in such a way, while I have given to the palace on your behalf 1,080 pounds of copper, and Šumi-abum has likewise given 1,080 pounds of copper, apart from what we both have had written on a sealed tablet to be kept in the temple of Šamaš.

How have you treated me for that copper? You have withheld my money bag from me in enemy territory; it is now up to you to restore (my money) to me in full.

Take cognizance that (from now on) I will not accept here any copper from you that is not of fine quality. I shall (from now on) select and take the ingots individually in my own yard, and I shall exercise against you my right of rejection because you have treated me with contempt.

Tell Ahuni: Bēlānum sends the following message:
May the god Šamaš keep you in good health.

Make ready for me the myrtle and the sweet-smelling reeds of which I spoke to you, as well as a boat for (transporting) wine to the city of Sippar. Buy and bring along with you ten silver shekels' worth of wine and join me here in Babylon sometime tomorrow.

Tell Sin-iddinam: Sillī- [. . .] sends the following message:

I have written you repeatedly to bring here the criminal and all the robbers, but you have not brought them here nor have you even sent me word. And so fires started by the robbers are (still) raging and ravaging the countryside. Since you have not brought the robbers to me although I have sent you word repeatedly, I am holding you responsible for the crimes which are committed in [the country].

Tomorrow, I shall dispatch this sealed letter of mine; inform me [break]

Tell the Lady Alītum: Aplum sends the following message:
May the god Šamaš keep you in good health.

The ladies Lamassûm and Nīš-īnišu came to me in tears, their heads bowed. They said: "You want to abandon us by going to Babylon without leaving us food for a single day!" When you receive my letter [send them thirty] kor-[measures of barley] in addition to the provisions which I have promised you for the girl.

They shed tears and urged me, saying: "Help me, this year I am on the brink of starvation." They (text: she) have made me give my consent concerning the payment of thirty *kor*-measures of barley besides the provisions for the girl. So do have thirty *kor*-measures of barley loaded on a boat for your sisters; otherwise, they will not quit complaining to us during the entire year.

Tell Uzalum: Your son Adad-abum sends the following message:
May the gods Šamaš and Wēr keep you forever in good health. I have never before written to you for something precious I wanted. But if you want to be like a father to me, get me a fine string full of beads, to be worn around the head. Seal it with your seal and give it to the carrier of this tablet so that he can bring it to me. If you have none at hand, dig it out of the ground wherever (such objects) are (found) and send it to me. I want it very much; do not withold it from me. In this I will see whether you love me as a real father does. Of course, establish its price for me, write it down, and send me the tablet. The young man who is coming to you must not see the string of beads. Seal it (in a package) and give it to him. He must not see the string, the one to be worn around the head, which you are sending. It should be full (of beads) and should be beautiful. If I see it and dislike(?) it, I shall send it back!
Also send the cloak, of which I spoke to you.

Tell my little Gimillum, whom my lord (the god Šamaš) keeps in good health: the *nadītu*-woman Awat-Aja sends the following message:
May my Lord and my Lady (the goddess Aja) keep you for my sake in good health forever.
When I saw you recently, I was just as glad to see you as I was when (long ago) I entered the *gagûm*-close and saw (for the first time) the face of my Lady (the goddess Aja). And you too, my brother, were as glad to see me as I to see you. You said: "I am going to stay for ten days." I was so pleased about it that I did not then report to you on my situation; I did not want to tell you here personally what I used to write to you about, before, from a distance. But you left suddenly and I was almost insane for three days. I did not touch food or even water.
You well know the amount of barley which I received before, and which you yourself had sent me. (If we continue) in this manner we will not wrong each other and I will not die of hunger with my household. Just send me the amount of barley which it was customary to send so that I can keep my household provided with food, that cold and hunger should not plague me (during the coming cold season).
PS: Have a heart, my dear Gimillum, let me not die of hunger. I was more pleased with you than I was ever with anybody else.

Tell Bēlšunu: Qurduša sends the following message:
May the god Šamaš keep you in good health.
As you have certainly heard, the open country is in confusion and the enemy is prowling around in it. I have dispatched letters to Ibni-Marduk, to Warad- . . ., and to yourself. Take a lamb from the flock for the diviner and obtain a divination concerning the cattle and the flocks, whether they should move into my neighborhood; if there

will be no attack of the enemy and no attack by robbers the cattle should come to where
I am—or else bring them into the town of Kish so that the enemy cannot touch them.
Furthermore, bring whatever barley is available into Kish and write me a full report.

Tell Sinnī: Your sister Akatija sends the following message:
   May' the gods Enlil, Ninlil, and Ninšubur keep you for my sake in good health forever.
   For the god who would make me see your face again, (I would gladly provide)
incense with lavish hands.
   For three years the field has not been thirsting for water, and I myself have been
in good health, and the field is now full of barley.
   You are the sun, let me warm myself in your rays; you are the cedar, in your shade
let me not be burnt. Why (should I worry)? Where there is a field belonging to my father,
there is sustenance for me!
   Now, I have (acquired and) am raising a boy, telling myself: Let him grow up, so
that there will be somebody to bury me. But the merchant confronts me now with the
demand: Hand over to me the "pestle" (to indicate that the boy legally belongs to the
merchant)!

Tell the boss: Sin-nādin-aḫḫī sends the following message:
   May the gods Šamaš and Marduk keep you in good health forever. Stay well, stay
healthy! May your protective god allow only good things to happen to you. I am writing
to you to learn about your well-being; may your well-being be lasting, before the gods
Šamaš, Marduk, and our lord, King Ammiṣaduqa.
   In regard to the lawsuit between Sin-rīmenni and his brother Ibni-Adad which I
have investigated in Sippar-Jaḫrurum, and concerning which I have handed down to
them a sealed tablet containing an agreement (which) you have sealed with the seal of
the high priest of Šamaš and the high priest of Aja, and your own seals, (I know that)
the sealed tablet with this agreement was in the possession of Sin-rīmenni. When this
Sin-rīmenni went to his fate, his brother Ibni-Adad made claims against the estate of
Sinrīmenni. Now, if the seal of the high priest of Šamaš and of the high priest of Aja
and also your own seals are contested, whose seal can be accepted (as incontestable)?
They should bring that Ibni-Adad before you; challenge him, he should be made to
make a statement under oath so that he will no longer make any claim against the estate
of his brother Sin-rīmenni.

Agricultural Management

Tell the boss: Šunuma-ilū sends the following message:
   May the gods Šamaš and Marduk keep you in good health forever. Stay well, stay
healthy! May your protective god allow only good things to happen to you. I am writing
to you to learn about your well-being; may your well-being be lasting before the gods
Šamaš and Marduk.
   I have written you previously asking you to deliver to me ten *kor*-measures of barley for seed, and ten *kor*-measures of dry bran as feed for the plow bulls; why have
you delivered only five *kor*-measures of barley and five *kor* measures of dry bran so

that for lack of seeds my plow bulls were idle for two days? From here the distance to the field is so great that I was unable to send dry bran there. Is it because I am not able to pay (now) that you have done this to me?

I am sending herewith this request of mine. Give another five *kor*-measures of barley and the (missing) five *kor*-measures of dry bran to my man Sin-bēl-dumqi so that he should not be fined. Write me whether I should return the barley in kind or do whatever else you will ask me to do up to the counter value of the barley.

Tell Lugā: Sin-putram sends the following message:
May the gods Enlil and Ninurta keep you in good health.
Lugatum moved his bulls to the fortified area in order to plant sesame, and (my man) Ubar-Lulu was going along with them as ox driver. One of the bulls in his care died, so they came to me with this dispute; I questioned the ox drivers who accompanied Ubar-Lulu, and they declared as follows: "The bull strayed away (from the herd) to eat grass; he fell down and died." I said: "Go to Nippur, to the city where there are judges; let them decide your case!" The judges in Nippur gave them their decision and handed Ubar-Lulu over to the Garden Gate in order to take the oath there. Lugatum, however, is not accepting this decision. Please take good care of Ubar-Lulu so that he does not suffer a loss.

Tell Nūr-Šamaš, Awēl-Adad, Sin-pilah, Sillī-Adad, and the overseer of the ten-man team: Šamaš-nāsir (the governor of Larsa) sends the following message:
This is really a fine way of behaving! The orchardists keep breaking into the date storehouse and taking dates, and you yourselves cover it up time and again and do not report it to me.
I am sending you herewith this letter of mine; bring these men to me—after they have paid for the dates. And also the men from the town Bad-Tibira [*end broken*]

Tell my lord: your servants Enlil-bāni, Sin-abī, and Sin-kāšid send the following message:
As to what our lord has written to us concerning the releasing of irrigation water, (we report that) the water has not yet reached us. Our ditches are cleaned out. Should Utu.si.sa withold water from us when the water comes, we shall report to our lord.

Letters from Mari

The Administration of the Realm

Tell Yasmaḫ-Addu: Your father, Šamšī-Addu, sends the following message:
I have listened to the messages you have sent me. You have asked me about the waiving of all administrative and legal claims incumbent on the northern tribes. (I answer:) It is not appropriate to waive these claims. Should you waive the claims against them, their relatives, the Rabbaya tribes, who are (now) staying on the other side of the river Euphrates in the country of Yamḫad, will hear (about this preferential treatment) and be so angry with them that they will not come back here to their home grounds. Therefore do not waive the claims against the northern tribes under any

circumstances. (On the contrary), reprimand them severely in the following terms:
"If the king goes on an expedition, everybody down to the youngsters should immediately assemble. Any sheikh whose men are not all assembled commits a sacrilege against the
king even if he leaves only one man behind!" Reprimand them in exactly this way. Under
no circumstances should you cancel the claims against them.

Now to another matter: When I sent you orders concerning the allotting of the
fields along the Euphrates as well as the taking over of these fields by the soldiers, you
asked me the following: "Should the auxiliaries from Hana who live in the open country
take over fields from among those (who live) along the Euphrates, or not? " This is what
you wrote me. I have asked Išar-Lim and other experts for advice, and it is not advisable
to reallot the fields along the Euphrates, or even to check on (the rights of the present
holders). Should you allot anew and check (on these fields) there will be too much complaining. Under no circumstances should you reallot the fields which are along the
Euphrates. Every man should keep his holding exactly as in the past. The fields must
not become mixed up. Check only on the fields of those who died or ran away, and
give them to those who have no fields at all.

At the waiving of claims itself, be most rigorous and have the soldiers ready.
The waiving you perform should be well checked.

Also, the Hana auxiliaries who live in the open country should keep the fields
which are along the bank of the Euphrates just as they did before.

Furthermore, as to what you have written me about having many large boats
built together with the small ones, one should construct (only) large boats [whose cap] acity
is ten or thirty for(?) the (very) large ones. Moreoever, wherever these boats go, they
will always be available to you to carry your own barley.

Tell my lord: your servant Bahdi-Lim sends the following message:
I have been waiting now for five days for the Hana auxiliaries at the place agreed
upon, but the soldiers are not assembling around me. The Hana authorities did come out
of the open country but they are now staying in their own encampments. I sent messages
into these encampments once or twice to call them up, but they did not assemble; in fact,
it is three days now and they still are not assembling.

Now then, if this meets with the approval of my lord, one should execute some
criminal kept in the prison, cut off his head, and carry it around outside the encampments
as far away as Hutnim and Appān, so the soldiers will become afraid and will assemble
here quickly.

As to the urgent message which my lord has dispatched to me, I will quickly send on
a contingent of troops.

Tell my lord: Your servant Yasim-Sumū sends the following message:
With respect to the barley boats which are to collect (barley) in the city of Emar
(I report that) they could not collect it at a better moment than right now. The harvest
time is here but they (the boats from Mari) are not arriving to load the barley for the
palace. And for the next five months boats will not be able to collect barley (here).

Now either they (the boats from Mari) will have arrived here after (the barley) is
collected, then one could fill up only 2 boats with barley so that not (all) should have

to return (to Mari) empty—or, if my lord finds this proposal more acceptable, he should send me 5 minas of silver; then I myself and the merchants (of Mari) living in Emar will hire 10 boats of 300 *kor* capacity (each) [co]lle[ct barley] and dispatch thus 3,000 *kor* of barley to Mari. Then one should give either to Idinyatum or to another official 600 *kor* of barley for the 5 minas of silver at a rate of 2½ *kor*-measures per shekel so that the 5 minas of silver return to the palace. The wages for the 60 *talilu*-men of the crew (needed) are 2½ shekels per man, hence 2½ minas of silver which amounts to 300 *kor* of barley. And the balance of 2,100 *kor* barley should go into the palace.

If that silver is to come here, two expert scribes and ten trustworthy persons should come with it.

May my lord send me an answer to my letter.

Tell my lord: Your servant Kibri-Dagan (the governor of Terqa) sends the following message:

The gods Dagan and Ikrub-El are fine; the city of Terqa and the districts are fine.

Now to the matter at hand: the very day I sent this tablet to my lord I have an extispicy made concerning the harvesting of the barley in the lowlands around Terqa, and the extispicy was propitious for up to three days. So I quickly assembled the entire city down to the youngsters and sent them out to harvest the barley in the lowlands. Moreover, I provided well-to-do citizens of Terqa with food, and placed them in the police outposts, giving them strict orders (to be on guard against brigands).

Now, as my lord has already forewarned me, the soldiers from the country Yamhad who are stationed in the town Šalabbatim appeared here, and I had an extispicy made (on that occasion); the prognosis was propitious. So I reprimanded them in the following terms: "You have to stay in the town Mulhê until the barley of the lowlands has been gathered in!" This is what I said to them, but they did not obey me; isn't it said(?) [. . .] no soldiers are to enter the town of Terqa? Yet they do not obey and are staying at the edge of the town. Now, my lord should send an unequivocal order to the general of these soldiers so that the soldiers will remain in the town of Mulhê.

The role of trade and the extent of cultural relations between the
contemporary Mesopotamian and Indus civilizations has been a favorite
subject of much debate. In this article the author reviews the evidence,
presents a new model, and provides new substantive evidence from his
own excavations at Tepe Yahya which bear on the role of trade and
the rise of civilizations.

Trade Mechanisms in
Indus-Mesopotamian Interrelations

C. C. Lamberg-Karlovsky

Trade may be understood in its widest sense as the reciprocal traffic of materials or
goods directed by human agency from one place and/or individual to another. Polyani
(1957:159) divides the mechanics of trade into four major constituents which provide a
suitable framework within which to examine trade: two-sidedness, goods, personnel and
carrying. Our emphasis will be upon the first three. Our information on the last for the
time period involved, save for the presence of sea-faring, is virtually *nil.* Additionally at
least three different processes in long distance trade can be profitably distinguished.

1. *Direct Contact Trade:* face to face contact is established between two different
places for the purposes of trade. Goods are traded between places A and B without
direct assistance by or relations with intermediary sites. This may include the actual
presence of trading colonies established by peoples of place A at site B for the trade of
specific materials of standardized value. This type of trade is usually centrally organized
and administered by one of the principals involved.

2. *Exchange:* this form in the dissemination of goods differs from the above by
lacking a definite organization or standardized value of specific materials. Goods are
passed from place to place without specific design or purpose. Thus materials from
site A and their arrival at site B represent an arbitrary exchange of merchandise from site
to site. It is often difficult to isolate whether an object was brought into a site through
exchange or independently produced through stimulus diffusion of a style or functional
tool type.

3. *Central Place Trade:* is evident when goods are either produced, or resources
present, at a few necessarily central points. Thus site C may be located beyond the spheres
of influence of sites A and B and control the means of production and/or resources which
are desired by sites A and B. Site C, acting as a Central Place, may then either transship
materials produced in other centers or export its own materials or resources. Alternatively,
the resources and/or transshipment of goods may be under the control and direction of
peoples from either site A or B residing among the foreigners of site C. In this respect
there is Direct Contact Trade between the Central Place (site C) and either A and/or B.
The important factor is that the Central Place (C) is of a different culture than either

Reprinted from *Journal of the American Oriental Society,* Vol. 92, No. 2, pp. 222-230 (1972) by
permission of the publisher and author.

A or B. It becomes immediately apparent that the archaeologist must attempt to distinguish whether peoples from sites A or B are physically present, i.e., in the form of a trading colony at the Central Place or whether material remains of A or B are present at C as a result of trade.

Insufficient emphasis has been placed on the economic development of trade in what may have been independent systems or mechanisms. Three such systems are described above and diagrammed in Chart I. They appear most profitable as isolated mechanisms in discussing Indus-Mesopotamian relations. It must be recognized, however, that these are not mutually exclusive systems—all three types may be coexistent. The task of the archaeologist is to distinguish which process is involved in any trade mechanism at a given point in time. Because of the high.cost of transportation, long distance trade is mainly restricted to materials and goods which are of great value or produced and/or available in limited areas. The role that trade may have had in generative processes leading *toward* urbanization is unknown. It is unreasonable to dismiss long distance trace on *a priori* grounds as derivative from the growth of urban civilization rather than having perhaps helped bring the latter into existence.

Until recently archaeologists have argued for the predominance of *Direct Contact Trade* between the Indus and Mesopotamia, either by sea (Oppenheim 1954) or by land (Mallowan 1965).

Direct Contact Trade

Direct contact between traders or colonies within the Indus and Mesopotamia cannot be supported or negated by the archaeological evidence. Clearly a handful of seals (Gadd 1932; Wheeler 1968), etched carnelian beads (Wheeler 1968; Dikshit 1949), terracotta statues and dice (Dales 1968) in Mesopotamia cannot be used as concrete evidence to support the presence of Indus traders in Mesopotamia. Conversely, the presence of perforated, knobbed and 'reserve slip' ware (Delougaz 1952), spiral and animal headed pins (Piggott 1948) or segmented beads (Wheeler 1968) cannot support the evidence of Mesopotamia in the Indus.

Direct Contact Trade through the presence of Assyrian trading colonies at the Anatolian sites of Hattush (Bittel 1970) and Kultepe (Ozguc 1962) have been concrete examples derived from excavations of this type of trade. At both sites the excavators argued for distinctive activity areas inhabited by foreign trading colonists, set apart from the living quarters of the indigenous inhabitants. It is instructive to see the evidence which suggested this situation to the excavators. The intrusive nature of the colonists was not obtained by identifying the distinctive nature of their architecture or ceramics, which were similar to those of the indigenous inhabitants. At both the karum of Kultepe and Hattush the presence of the colonies were indicated by the presence of cylinder seal impressions and textual data. Thus at Kultepe the excavator admits,"If the tablets and their sealed envelopes had not been found, in fact, we might never have suspected the existence of a merchant colony." (Ozguc 1962). At Hattush of sixty-three Old Assyrian documents, sixty were found in the residential quarters of the colony and "These documents contain only Assyrian names no native ones. The impression of cylinder seals on the envelopes show, without exception Mesopotamian non-Anatolian motifs."

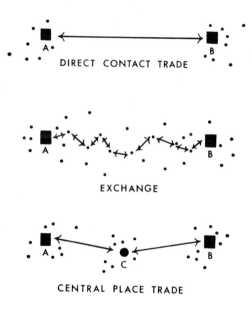

On analogy, the principle evidence for Direct Contact Trade between Mesopotamia and the Indus should be seen in the seals, sealing impressions and textual data of one culture found in another. No surprise, for, if Indus traders were in Mesopotamia, or the reverse one would expect them to seal goods shipped back by their own seals. Three points become immediately evident:

1. No Mesopotamian seals, sealings or texts have ever been found in Harappan context.

2. Only one Indus type seal impression with ten Indus signs has been found in Mesopotamia (at Umma, Scheil 1925).

3. No distinctive architectural complex of Mesopotamian characteristics has ever been excavated in the Indus. The reverse being also true.

4. On no Mesopotamian site is there a clustering of Indus objects in association with architecture, save for Tell Asmar (see below). We are left only to consider the scattered Indus-type seals in Mesopotamia—by itself weak evidence to suggest Direct Contact Trade.

Indus seals have supported the main evidence for Direct Contact Trade between the Indus and Mesopotamia, as well as for establishing contemporaneity of both civilizations during pre and post Sargonid times. It is unfortunate that the chronology is rendered doubtful by either unstratified or uncertain context of the majority of the seals.

A re-assessment of the context of the Indus seals in Mesopotamia in no way supports their association within a trading colony context. For the most part the seals are single finds without clusterings of additional Indus type materials in association and, we might add, in an almost universally bad context.

The list below does not include the Persian Gulf types included by Gadd (1932).

Indus Type Seals

Ur:

  1. Unstratified (Woolley 1928:26, Pl. XI, Fig. 2; Gadd 1932, No. 1).

  2. From Bur-Sins Tomb or mixed in later filling (Woolley 1932:362-64, Pl. LXII, No. 2; Gadd 1932, No. 16).

  3. From a vaulted tomb of Larsa Period (Gadd 1932, No. 6; Legrain 1951:632).

  The remainder of the Ur seals published by Gadd (1932) have been seen as Persian Gulf variants (Wheeler 1968).

Tell Asmar:

  1. From an Akkadian house, a cylinder seal (only six cylinder seals have been found in Harappan context) depicting elephant, rhinoceros, crocodile (Frankfort 1923:51; 1938:305).

  2. Akkadian context but without further association (Frankfort 1923:52).

Kish:

  1. Square steatite seal with "unicorn" and the Indus signs. Found "nine meters below the surface" (Langdon 1931:593-96).

  2. Square Indus seal with unicorn and Indus inscription, "below the pavement of Samsuiluna, son of Hammurabi (Langdon 1931:593).

Umma (Tell Jokha)

  1. An impressed square clay sealing with at least ten Indus signs (Scheil 1925).

  The seals thus present not only doubtful chronological markers but minimal support for the presence of Indus trade in Mesopotamia. Only the Umma sealing indicates a receipt of goods received from the Indus. It is indicative, however, that such evidence as does exist, supports the presence of Indus traders in Mesopotamia rather than the reverse. Thus, if there were Direct Contact Trade it would seem to be Indus traders in Mesopotamia.

  A review of the contextual association of unmistakeably Indus seals in Mesopotamia does not support the clustering of such material on any given site, nor more particularly, without a specific activity or habitation area. A single exception could be Tell Asmar where the seals are reinforced by ceramics; knobbed ware, etched beads and kidney shaped inlay of bone, all of Harappan types and found in Akkadian houses at Tell Asmar. If anywhere in Mesopotamia we have evidence for Indus Direct Contact Trade it would be best supported at Tell Asmar.

  Furthermore, when the material evidence for Direct Contact Trade between the Indus and Mesopotamia is compared quantitatively against the Direct Contact Trade as it existed at the Assyrian karum of Hattush and Kultepe, Egyptian-Minoan or Egyptian-Syro-Palestinian (i.e., Byblos) it becomes evident that neither a single Mesopotamian nor Indus site indicates a comparable clustering of materials in association to suggest Direct Contact Trade between these two areas.

  One cannot, however, deny the existence of materials other than Indus seals in Mesopotamia which suggest some form of relations. These objects, few in number and varied in type cannot be argued as standardized or valued trade objects (see below). Such objects may be taken as either possessions of Indus traders in Mesopotamia or having arrived through an indirect contact trade, i.e., Exchange. These materials: terracotta statues, dice, etched carnelian beads, stone vessels (see below) are not found on any single Mesopotamian site in sufficient numbers and in clustering association to support the presence of trade in these items or the presence of an Indus colony. Again, we note that incontestable Mesopotamian products simply have not been found in the Indus (see below).

The presence of single objects of Indus derivation found on Mesopotamian sites may well have been brought to Mesopotamia by hand-to-hand (site-to-site) exchange. It is unfortunate that few sites of Eastern Iran and Baluchistan between the Indus and Mesopotamia have been excavated, and those that have clearly support their role in *Central Place Trade* (see below) controlling either the given resources of an area or the transshipment of goods from the East to the West, or the reverse.

Exchange (Indirect Contact Trade)

The evidence for Exchange, an informal non-centrally administered stimulus diffusion of materials, can be supported in the distribution of materials appearing as rare occurrences both in the Indus, Mesopotamia and on sites between both areas. They are not objects or materials upon which a reciprocal trade would be structured, i.e., necessary resources or desirable luxury goods. They are single and varied objects, as animal headed pins, beads, etc. not classes of distinctive functional materials as seals. Such an Exchange, unlike Direct Contact Trade, would not be under administrative control, but the varied materials in passing from hand-to-hand (site-to-site) would appear randomly on sites between the Indus and Mesopotamia as well as on Mesopotamian and Indus sites.

One of the best explications of an exchange system in antiquity is contained in Herodotus *(The Histories;* Book IV, Chap. 33);

> But the persons who have the most to say on this subject are the Delians. They declare that certain offerings, packed in wheaten straw, were brought from the country of the Hyperboreans into Scythia, and that the Scythians received them and passed them on to their neighbors upon the West, who continued to pass them on, until at last they reached the Adriatic. From hence they were sent southward and when they came to Greece, were received first of all by the Dodoiceans. Thence they descended to the Maliac Gulf, from which they were carried across into Euboea, where the people handed them on from city to city, till they came at length to Carystus .... Such according to their own account was the road by which the offerings reached the Delians .... Afterwards the Hyperboreans when they found their messengers did not return, thinking it would be a grievous thing always to be liable to lose the envoys they should send, adopted the following plan: They wrapped their offerings in the wheaten straw and bearing them to their borders, charged their neighbors to send them forward from one nation to another, which was done accordingly, and in this way the offerings reached Delos.

Objects often believed to be of Western Asian and/or Indus origin found outside either area and in the past used as evidence for Exchange include:

1. *Metal Types.* From the depth of 18.4 feet at Mohenjo-daro in DK area (MacKay 1938:539, Vol. II, Pl. C, No. 4) and from Chanhu-daro (MacKay 1943:195, Pl. LXVIII, 9) belonging to the last phase of occupation were found two spiral headed pins, while two animal headed pins from Area J, Trench III at Harappa (Vats 1940:390, Pl. CXXV, 34, 36) and one from DK area of Mohnejodaro (MacKay 1938: Vol. II, Pl. C, 3) were recovered. Piggott (1948:26-40) has argued that these pins were imported into the Indus Valley. The presence of this generalized type at Troy II, Alaca Huyuk (Grave L), Naram Sin's palace at Brak, a mid-second millennium tomb of Mari, Hissar II, IIIc, *et al* indicated to Piggott the eastward migration of this type. Their presence in the Koban and Korca in 13th-9th century context make them at best a questionable chronological marker. Piggott's examples from Iran alone range from 4th to 2nd millennium date. We reject the evidence of spiral and animal headed pins as evidence for trade between East and West. Doubtful it is that they were even representative of an Exchange. We believe them best explained as the transmission of a generalized pin type. Among the many examples cited by Piggott no two examples are really alike. The pins from Alaca, the Caucasus, Mainland Greece, Luristan, Khurab, Kish, etc. are all similar in that animals form their head—the animals differ however as do their individual styles. We dismiss them as evidence of trade, but see in their popularity throughout late 3rd millennium Western Asia an indication of a common tradition in the manufacture of pins.

An unpublished bronze or copper knife of distinctly Harappan type was found in Hissar IIIB (Wheeler 1947:80), while a copper axe-adze is noted from Mohenjo-daro (6 feet below the surface) and said to be paralleled at Hissar III. It has been argued that Indus metallurgy owes a great deal to that of Iran—but not, we believe, through trade in objects, but through stimulus diffusion in the development of a metallurgical technology and the production of similar functional tool types (Lamberg-Karlovsky 1967:145-62).

2. *Ceramics.* Ceramics are poor indicators for documenting the existence of trade relations but have been used to suggest cultural contacts between the Indus and Meso-potamia.

A few types of pottery have been thought to indicate contact between the Indus and Mesopotamia. The evidence is at best shaky—the selected attributes indicating typological similarities are too generalized, namely (a) perforated, (b) knobbed and (c) 'reserved slip' ware. Perforated wares appear on several Mesopotamian sites and in Iran at Hissar, Tureng Tepe, Shah Tepe, Yahya, Bampur and Shahr-i-Sokhta. Of different shapes and date this ware in no way can be marshalled to support the existence of Mesopotamian-Indus contact or relations.

Knobbed ware is rare in Mesopotamia, Iran and the Indus. Several sherds with knobs on the external surface at Tell Asmar and Khafajeh are dated to Jemdet Nasr and Early Dynastic III and have been paralleled to the knobbed ware in the Indus (Delougaz 1952:188). The carefully made knobbed vases of Mohenjo-daro contrast with the roughly made knobs on those of the Diyala. The general resemblance of the plastic decoration is far too vague to establish contacts between the two areas. Rare examples of knobbed ware in Iran: Shah Tepe (Arne 1945: Fig. 167, 168, Pl. XXVII, 6); Sialk

(Ghirshman 1938: Vol. I, Pl. XXVIII, 6) and Yahya (Lamberg-Karlovsky 1970, Fig. 29, 0), differ in shapes as much as those from the Indus and Mesopotamia. This type of ware cannot be used to strengthen any argument for Indus-Mesopotamian relations. Two sherds of 'reserve slip' ware were found at 31.8 feet below datum at Mohenjo-daro. MacKay (1938:184) compared these to a common 'reserve slip' pottery from Kish and Ur. The evidence of two sherds indicating similar surface treatment simply cannot be used as evidence for any type of relationship or chronological contemporaneity.

Several unique objects have been used to indicate an interrelationship between the Indus and Mesopotamia. Again, they are principally Indus objects found in Mesopotamian context and would not seem to be objects of commercial value for trade. These are figurines, dice and beads.

3. *Figurines.* Three figurines found in Mesopotamia are said to compare stylistically with ones from the Indus (Dales 1968). All three figurines come from Nippur, two were found in the 'Scribal Quarter' and one from the floor of a contemporary house (TBVZ). Although one cannot deny the stylistic affinity of these figurines with those known from Harappan context (Dales: *op cit*) the evidence from Nippur and the Indus cities does not show an intrusive character of these figurines, thus, despite few similarities in the style of representation, they could more readily be quite independent creations.

4. *Dice.* Dales (1968) has presented convincing evidence that one of the Indus die types (1/2, 3/6, 4/5) was actually exported or duplicated in Mesopotamia. In Mesopotamia, where dice are less common than in the Indus, the above type die has been found in the Royal Cemetery, Pit X at UR (Woolley 1955:44, 79, Fig. 7a, b), Nippur in Akkadian context (McCown 1960, Pl. 153, 11), at Tell Asmar beneath an Akkadian floor, incompletely described, and perhaps not of Indus type (Frankfort 1933:48). One cannot be certain that the die were actually imported to Mesopotamia from the Indus: stimulus diffusion of a game-type followed by independent development of die seems as likely, and is supported by the unique die type of Gawra IV (2/3, 4/5, 6/1) (Speiser 1935:82, Pl. XXXVII) which may have been copied from a southern Mesopotamian counterpart with the retention of 4 opposite 5 (the single consistent opposition on all Mesopotamian die), but varying other oppositions.

5. *Beads.* Distinctive shapes and decorative designs of several bead types have been regarded as further evidence of connections between the Indus Valley and Mesopotamia. Beads from Chanhu-daro with single, double or triple circular designs as well as ones with a figure of 8, afford close resemblances to those from Kish (compare MacKay 1943 Pl. LXXIX, Nos. 1-3, 8, 11, 15 with MacKay 1925 (29) Pl. X, 2, 3, p. 698). Similarly the rare segmented beads in the Indus (Wheeler 1968) have been compared to those more widely distributed in Mesopotamia between 3100 B.C.-1800 B.C. (Mallowan 1947: 254, Pl. LXXXIV, 2; MacKay 1925: Pl. 60, 39, 40). The evidence of segmented beads tends to distort rather than clarify Indus-Mesopotamian interrelations. It seems unsafe to rely on a widely scattered bead type in both space and time for documenting Mesopotamian-Indus contacts.

These frustrating bits of information, despite large scale excavations in the Indus and Mesopotamia, do not provide evidence for a co-ordinated effort toward mutual contacts and/or trade. Objects such as pins, dice, statuary, etched carnelian beads, stamp and cylinder seals are not an impressive list of exchanged or traded articles. Certainly it does not seem that a single class of objects were in preferential demand in either area which resulted in objects for standardized trade. We cannot turn to a single site where there is a clustering of Indus objects in Mesopotamia, or the reverse. More often than not we have seen only one to three objects of allegedly Indus derivation in Mesopotamia, and their context does not suggest a clustering in a specific area of the excavation. Perhaps, significantly, we have noted that Indus objects are found in Mesopotamia— never the reverse. The Harappan contacts with Mesopotamia, as evidenced by the scattered evidence, suggest a casual and indirect exchange. It has been argued that the Kulli people seem not to have been the exclusive middle men, i.e., merchant-venturers (Lamberg-Karlovsky 1971). Trade between the Indus and Mesopotamia is best seen through our model in Central Place Trade—evidenced at Bahrein and Tepe Yahya.

Central Place Trade

Locational analysis, more specifically, Central Place Theory offers a conceptual and theoretical framework relevant to a discussion of Indus-Mesopotamian relations. Fundamental to Central Place Theory is the assumption that goods and services are produced and offered at a few necessarily central points in order to be consumed at many scattered points. These central points are Central Places, their role the dissemination of goods (transshipment), or the production of goods from a given resource which they control. We have already indicated that trade, rather than a result of urbanization may have been one of the major establishing factors in the rise of urban centers. We turn to two Central Places, both important to Mesopotamian-Indus interrelationships. One, Tepe Yahya, has an early village occupation (ca. 4500 B.C.) with direct cultural continuity toward a later fluorescence (contemporary) with Mesopotamian Late Uruk sites, ca. 3300 B.C.). The fluorescence at Yahya can be attributed to its role in East-West trade and its control of a natural resource—steatite, which was exported to the West (see below). At Bahrein a contemporary fluorescence appears to have been brought about by its role in the transshipment of goods rather than control of resources.

At Tepe Yahya in Period VA (ca. 3200-3400 B.C.) we have recovered Nal pottery, a ware long known to pre-date the Harappan Civilization. Period VA indicates a prosperous rural community which already makes use of local and imported resources: steatite, carnelian, turquoise, obsidian, alabaster, Persian Gulf shells, *et al.* In the immediately later Period IV C we have an increase in the architectural complexity and material wealth of the site—we believe brought about by its increasing trade relations with both East and West. In IV C we have recovered from what would appear to be an administrative building (previous architecture would appear to be entirely domestic in function) Proto-Elamite tablets, Susa C cylinder sealings, distinctive cylinder seals of a type indigenous to Yahya and Uruk bevelled rim bowls. Carved steatite bowls identical in shape and motif to those found in Mesopotamia (Kish, Tell Asmar, Mari, Khafajeh, Ur, Ubaid, etc.) and at Mohenjo-daro have been recovered. At Yahya, over 1500 steatite pieces represent both finished and incompletely manufactured objects—this together with the discovery of a steatite mine some 25 km. away strongly support the manufacture and export of steatite from Yahya. We might add that the pottery represents largely an indigenous type strongly paralleled at Bampur (de Cardi 1970), Shahr-i-Sohkta (Tosi 1970) and Iblis (Caldwell 1967) but only vaguely paralleling the painted Baluchistan pottery (Lamberg-Karlovsky 1970, 1971, 1972, for discussion).

The work and recovery of the Late 4th millennium Proto-Elamite settlement at Tepe Yahya has obvious and important implications for our understanding of the chronological and cultural reconstructions throughout this large area of Baluchistan, the Persian Gulf and Mesopotamia (Lamberg-Karlovsky 1971). Firstly, on chronology: we will be able through a series of radiocarbon dates to establish fixed dates to the Late Uruk, Proto-Elamite configuration in this area; Susa C, and indirectly for the Early Dynastic steatite parallels in Mesopotamia. Our dating will also establish the first understanding of the period of export of steatite from Yahya and Southeastern Iran to the West. The carved steatite bowl fragments in House V, Room 53 in DK area and House III, Room No. 76 at Mohenjo-daro can be precisely paralleled at Yahya (MacKay 1938, Pl. CXCII; Marshall 1931; Pl. CXXXI; Lamberg-Karlovsky 1970, Fig. 21: B, D, E, F and Pl. 23, A, F). It would appear that these pieces can now be dated to the first quarter of the 3rd millennium. This together with the presence of Nal sherds in our Period V suggests that the pre-Harappan painted pottery (Nal) dates to as early as the end of the 4th millennium while the Early Harappan surely starts earlier than the reasonably supposed 2500 B.C. Certainly we cannot accept the lowering and restricting of Harappan chronology to 2300-1700 B.C. (Agrawal 1966). We would prefer to see sites as Kulli, Rana Ghundai, Mundigak, Amri, Kot Diji and the even earlier Shahr-i-Sokhta, Yahya, *et al* of the late 4th and early 3rd millennium as directly related in a causative manner to the later consolidation of the mature Harappan. The above sites being in fact where the sociopolitical processes were established and later adopted in the consolidation of the Harappan Civilization.

The presence of a "Persian Gulf" type seal in Yahya IV B supports a beginning 3rd millennium date for the beginning of the Bahrein sequence, already indicated by the presence of Jamdet Nasr sherds in the Barbar Temple (Mortensen 1970). The evidence for Bahrein as a Central Place engaged in the transshipment of goods between the Indus and Mesopotamia is evidenced from both textual and recent archaeological materials, i.e., Indus weights in the "customs house" at Bahrein, a Persian Gulf seal at Lothal (see Bibby 1969). Our strong parallels to Bampur I-IV in Period IV C indicate an end 4th millennium date for the beginning of the important Bampur sequence and a mid 3rd millennium date for its end (based on IV B parallels with the end of the Bampur sequence). Thus substantially revising the proposed chronological framework for this site (de Cardi 1970; Lamberg-Karlovsky 1970, 1971, 1972).

Secondly, we would like to point out that our site has no evidence for the presence of the Kulli Culture. Much has been made of and suggested for the Kulli "Merchant venturers" of the 3rd millennium (Dales 1965:268-74; 1969:15ff). We find it indicative that at Tepe Yahya with obvious evidence for long range exchange patterns there is a lack of an identifiable Kulli element. Until we hear from the important work of Professor J.-M. Casal at the Kulli site of Nindowari it is best to call a moratorium on ascribing to Kulli the responsibility for "international trade"—a conception without evident support.

Thirdly, it becomes evident that with the distribution of Tepe Yahya, Bampur, Shahr-i-Sokhta, Tal-i-Iblis and Shahdad we have an expansive distribution of contemporary and ceramically related sites. We suggest that there is here a shared cultural "ecumene" identifiable as Proto-Elamite. Clearly, the nature of the settlement pattern, the degree of uniformity between the sites, their socio-political and economic configurations (Yahya's export of steatite, Shahr-i-Sokhta's export of lapis lazuli and alabaster, etc.) need individual attention before the above hypothesis becomes wholly acceptable (Lamberg-Karlovsky 1971). It appears likely that a trade mechanism was established which in recognizing the value of local resources brought the Iranian highlands into a supply-demand relationship with resource-poor Mesopotamia. Mesopotamian demand for lapis, steatite and mineral ores would have provided in part the economic base for the urban development of Shahr-i-Sokhta, Yahya and Iblis. This relationship as in a feedback mechanism would have in turn aided in bringing about the developing complexity of socio-political and economic structure of the Late Uruk Mesopotamian city-state.

Fourthly, the presence of a late 4th and early 3rd millennium proto-literate settlement in distant Southeastern Iran, evidencing an indigenous and centralized socio-political structure, some 300-400 years prior to the 'Early Harappan' suggests that the area of Southeastern Iran and Baluchistan may have played an important role in generating the processes which resulted in the later Harappan Civilization. Thus, we believe that at Yahya during Late Uruk and Jemdet Nasr times the natural resources which it possessed and traded both East and West contributed to its urban and concomitant socio-political development, while as in a systems feedback, a similar development took place in the resource-poor demand center of Mesopotamia. Through a similar systems mechanism we see the early development of the Harappan Culture, beginning as early as 3000 B.C. Under the stimulus of desired resources and reciprocal trade throughout Baluchistan we can see an increasing nucleation of sites (Kulli, Amri, Kot Diji, Mundigak, Shah-i-Tump, etc.) which find a culmination in the mature Harappan Civilization.

Fifthly, the role of Elam and the Elamites in Indus-Mesopotamian relations has been too long overlooked. In the 3rd millennium, situated between the Indus and Mesopotamia, was the poorly known but important Elamite Civilization. Clearly, any overland routes would have had to pass through their territory, which we now know extended eastward at least to Tepe Yahya. The relations of Elam and Mesopotamia have been well summarized by Hinz (1963):

> ... the historian can recognize the leitmotiv of relations between Elam and Mesopotamia, one of hereditary enmity, mitigated at the same time by equally persistent economic and cultural exchanges, for Mesopotamia needed the products of the Elamite highlands, timber, metallic ore (lead, copper, tin and silver), stone (alabaster, diorite, and obsidian), semiprecious stones and also horses. The countless campaigns of the Sumerians and Akkadians against Elam were due to the need to control these important materials. At the same time they followed the political aim of warding off and keeping in check the Elamites, who were always ready to plunder the lowlands.

It is entirely possible that Direct Contact Trade between the Indus and Mesopotamia was prevented by the Elamites. It is equally possible that the development of sea trade was brought about in Mesopotamia through a necessity to bypass overland routes through hostile Elamite territory. Thus, the absence of port sites of 3rd millennium date along the Iranian shores of the Persian Gulf may have also been dictated by Elamite hostility toward their establishment.

Lastly, the presence of a proto-literate site at Tepe Yahya, some 600-800 miles from the Indus Valley and 200-400 years prior to the formation of the Harappan Culture has clear implications in generating the processes which led toward not only the development of later Indus-Elamite-Mesopotamian relations, but for the very formation of the Harappan Civilization! Thus the explosive evolution traditionally argued for the Harappan Culture (Wheeler 1968) can be seen as misleading. At such sites as Yahya, Shahr-i-Sokhta, Mundigak, Amri, *et al* one can see the embryonic urban forms of social organization from which the later Harappan Culture was to evolve. Wheeler (1968) has pointed out that the "idea of civilization" crossed from West (Mesopotamia) to East (the Indus). One might well ask why civilization did not occur between. We believe this is a false question; for it is evident today from such a wide distribution of proto-urban sites in eastern Iran and Baluchistan, of the late 4th and early 3rd millennium, that there was an established dialectic between these resource rich areas with resource-poor Mesopotamia on the one hand and the Indus on the other which brought about a mutually dependent parallel and contemporary process toward urbanization. The absence of a political/cultural consolidation in the area of the eastern Iranian highlands and Baluchistan may be due to the absence of a unified environment, as the essentially similar riverine environments which saw the consolidation of Mesopotamian and Indus Civilizations.

In conclusion we note that the same causal factors that create a civilization often serve to identify it. Anthropologists have used the word "intensify" to signify the heightening of cultural activity which produces this complexity (Fairservis 1960:14). We have argued here that one of the important "intensifiers" motivating the parallel but essentially distinctive rise toward urban complexes in Mesopotamia and the Iranian highlands, and the later Harappan Culture was trade. As a working hypothesis it has gathered considerable support with the new excavations undertaken in Southeastern Iran, Sistan, Baluchistan and Turkmenia.

References

Arne, T. J. 1945. *Excavations at Shah Tepe, Iran,* Stockholm.

Bibby, G. 1969. *Looking for Dilmun,* A. Knopf, New York.

Bittel, K. 1970. *Hattusha, The Capital of the Hittites,* Oxford Univ. Press.

Caldwell, J. 1967. *Investigations at Tal-i-Iblis,* Springfield, Illinois.

Dales, G. 1965. "A Suggested Chronology for Afghanistan and the Indus Valley", in Ehrich, R. *Chronologies in Old World Archaeology,* Univ. of Chicago Press.

————— 1968. "Of Dice and Men", *Journal of the American Oriental Society,* Vol. 88, No. 1, pp. 14-22.

de Cardi, B. 1970. *Excavations at Bampur, A Third Millennium Settlement in Persian Baluchistan, 1966.* American Museum of Natural History, Vol. 51, Pt. 3.

Delougaz, P. 1952. *Pottery from the Diyala Region,* Univ. of Chicago Oriental Instit. Publication, Vol. LXIII, Chicago.

Dikshit, M. G. 1949. *Etched Beads in India,* Univ. of Poona, India.

Frankfort, H. 1923. "Tell Asmar, Khafaje, Khorsabad Seals", Oriental Instit. Communications No. 16, Chicago.

————— 1939. *Cylinder Seals,* Macmillan, London.

Gadd, C. J. 1932. "Seals of Ancient Indian Style Found at Ur", *Proceedings of the British Academy,* Vol. XVIII, London.

Ghirshman, R. 1938. *Fouilles de Tepe Sialk,* Paul Geuthner, Paris.

Lamberg-Karkovsky, C. C. 1967. "Archaeology and Metallurgical Technology in Prehistoric Afghanistan, India and Pakistan", *American Anthropologist,* Vol. 69, No. 2 pp. 145-162.

———— 1970. *Excavations at Tepe Yahya 1967-1969,* American School of Prehistoric Research Bulletin 27, Peabody Museum, Harvard Univ.

———— 1971. "The Proto-Elamite Settlement at Tepe Yahya", *IRAN,* Vol. IX, pp. 87-96.

———— 1972. "Tepe Yahya 1971. Mesopotamia and the Indo-Iranian borderlands," *IRAN,* Vol. X.

Langdon, S. 1931. "A New Factor in the Problem of Sumerian Origins", *Journal of the Royal Asiatic Society,* pp. 593-596.

LeGrain, L. 1951. *Ur Excavations,* Vol. X, Seal Cylinders, British Museum.

MacKay, E. 1925. *Report on the Excavations of the "A" Cemetery at Kish Mesopotamia,* Parts I, II, Field Museum, Chicago.

———— 1938. *Further Excavations at Mohenjo-daro,* Vol. I, II, Gov't. of New Delhi Press.

———— 1943. *Chanhu-daro Excavations,* American Oriental Society, New Haven.

Mallowan, M. 1947. "Excavations at Brak and Chagar Bazar", *IRAQ,* Vol. IX.

———— 1965. "The Mechanics of Ancient Trade in Western Asia", *IRAN,* Vol. III, pp. 1-9.

McCown, D. E., Haines, R. C. Hansen, D. P. 1960. *Nippur I. Temple of Enlil, Scribal Quarter and Soundings,* Oriental Instit. Publications, Chicago.

Oppenheim, A. L. 1954. "The Seafaring Merchants of Ur", *Journal of American Oriental Society,* Vol. 74, pp. 6-17.

Ozguc, T. 1962. "An Assyrian Trading Outpost", *Scientific American,* pp. 97ff.

Piggott, S. 1948. "Notes on Certain Metal Pins and a Macehead in the Harappan Culture", *Ancient India,* Vol. I, pp. 26-40.

Polyani, K. 1957. "The Economy as Instituted Process", *Primitive, Archaic and Modern Economics,* Ed. George Dalton, Anchor Books.

Scheil, V. E. 1925. "Un Nouveau Scean Hindon Pseudo-Sumerian", *Revue d'Assyriologie et d'Archeologie Orientale,* Vol. XXII, pp. 55-56.

Speiser, E. A. 1935. *Excavations at Tepe Gawra,* Vol. I, Univ. of Penn.

Tosi, M. 1970. "Excavations at Shahr-i-Sokhta, Preliminary Report on the Second Campaign September December 1968", *East and West,* Vol. 19, Nos. 3-4, pp. 283-386.

Vats, M. S. 1940. *Excavations at Harappa,* New Delhi, 2 Vols.

Wheeler, M. 1948. "Harappa the Defenses and Cemetery R37", *Ancient India,* No. 3, pp. 58-130.

———— 1968. *The Indus Civilization,* Cambridge Univ. Press, 3rd ed.

Woolley, L. 1928. "Excavations at Ur 1926-27", Part II, *The Antiquaries Journal,* Vol. VIII, No. 1, pp. 1-29.

———— 1932. "Excavations at Ur 1931-32", *The Antiquaries Journal,* Vol. XII, No. 4, pp. 355-392.

———— 1955. *Ur Excavations: The Early Periods,* Vol. IV, British Museum and Univ. of Penn.

Part IV

The Old World: Indus

Bridget and Raymond Allchin are, respectively, Fellow of University College
and Lecturer at Churchill College, Cambridge University, and both
received their doctorates from Cambridge. The former's principal
research has been on the Stone Age of India and Pakistan, while the
latter has excavated a number of Neolithic sites in India. The following
article is taken from their book *The Birth of Indian Civilization* (1968)
and presents the traditional theory for the collapse of the Indus
civilization.

The Indus Civilization
and the Aryan Invasions

Bridget and Raymond Allchin

It has been remarked that books on the prehistory of India and Pakistan are often
Indus valley centered. If this be true, it is understandable, for until recently the Indus
civilization occupied the centre of our knowledge. The past two decades have changed
this, and we venture—at the risk of erring in the other direction—to try to put the civilization in a better perspective. Its importance is however still unique, both because it
represents a great and astonishing cultural achievement and because it may be seen as
the formative mould for many aspects of classical and even modern Indian civilization.
In this chapter we shall direct our discussion mainly to questions of sequence, and of
the extent of the civilization, and in later chapters we shall touch upon various salient
features. The preceding pages have shown how the stage is set in the Indus valley and
Punjab and how there is a direct cultural continuity between the pre-Harappan and the
Harappan periods. It is in the light of this that we may now proceed.

The present evidence, either of archaeological sequence or of absolute dating, does
not permit any certain conclusion of the rate at which the Harappan culture expanded
nor of where the new culture traits first evolved, apart from the pre-Harappan cultures
of the Indus valley. There is some evidence both at Mohenjo-daro and Harappa of a
general cultural evolution, but the earlier excavations of Marshall and Vats are not helpful
on this point. We feel that the expansion was something of an 'explosion' and that it
represented among other things an outcome of the successful control of the tremendous
agriculturally productive potentialities of the Indus plains. The refinement of the
archaeological evidence concerning the development of the civilization and of its
regional variants, and the consequent possibilities of discovering the first centres of the
culture and of tracing its diffusion, are thus desiderata of the research programme of
the coming decades.

We have already mentioned the environment of the Indus valley and the opportunities it offered once the annual inundation had been understood. There is no good evidence of any drastic change in climate during the past four or five millennia in this region. Thus while it is reasonable to expect a slightly higher rainfall throughout the area before the natural vegetation cover was reduced by man's steady intensification of agriculture and grazing, no major shift in climate need be postulated. A vital necessity of settlement on the Indus plain itself would have been flood defence, and here it seems that burnt-brick must have played an important role. For in those areas where stone was not readily available (and this includes the majority of Harappan sites) mud-brick would have been rapidly destroyed by rain or flood water. Thus the discovery and utilization of burnt-brick was one factor. It has sometimes been suggested that the Indus valley could not have produced sufficient timber for this operation, unless the climate were damper than today. But Lambrick, writing with many years of administrative experience of the Sind, has shown that timber growing along the riverine tracts today is sufficient for all the burnt-bricks made in the province, and anciently cannot have been less abundant.

The area enclosed by a line joining the outermost sites at which the material culture of this civilization has been discovered is little less than half a million square miles, considerably larger than modern West Pakistan. Within this area over seventy sites are known, of which the great majority lie on the plains of the Indus and its tributaries, or on the now dry course of the Hakra or Ghaggar river which once flowed to the south of the Sutlej and then southwards to the east of the Indus, with the Sind desert on its left bank. Outside the Indus system to the west a few sites occur on the Makran coast, the farthest being Sutkagen Dor near the modern frontier of Pakistan and Iran; these were probably ports or trading posts in a separate culture region. The uplands of Baluchistan appear to have been outside the Harappan zone. To the east of the Indus further sites occur on or near the coast beyond the marshes of Cutch (Kacch), the most impressive being the trading post at Lothal, on the gulf of Cambay; while at the mouth of the Narbada river the small settlement at Bhagatrav marks the southernmost extent of the culture so far recognized. One other significant extension is beyond the Indus system towards the north-east, where the site of Alamgirpur lies beyond Delhi, between the Ganges and Jamuna rivers.

Of all the Harappan sites two stand out, both on account of their size and of the diversity of the finds excavations have revealed. These have generally been hailed as cities, the twin capitals of this extensive state.[1] The southern is Mohenjodaro on the right bank of the Indus. Here the Indian Archaeological Survey under Sir John Marshall, and later Mackay, excavated between 1922 and 1931; after the partition of India and Pakistan in 1947 further work was done by Sir Mortimer Wheeler, and more recently by Dr. George Dales of Pennsylvania University. In all these excavations the bottom of the Harappan occupation has never been reached, let alone the level of the first settlement, because, as we have already seen, the alluvial deposition of the centuries has raised the level of the plain by more than thirty feet, and the water table has risen correspondingly, so that reaching the lower levels presents special difficulties. The second and northern city is Harappa on the left bank of the now dry course of the Ravi in the Punjab. The vast mounds at Harappa were first reported by Charles Masson in 1826, and visited by General Cunningham in 1853 and 1873. Their rediscovery some sixty years later led to the

Archaeological Survey's excavations between 1920 and 1934, directed by Pandit M. S. Vats. A short but important further excavation was made in 1946 by Sir Mortimer Wheeler: the natural soil was reached and evidence of a pre-Harappan culture phase revealed. In the earlier excavations of both these sites a mass of information was obtained relating to their planning and architecture, and much material relating to arts and crafts and to the way of life of the people was recovered. However, the excavations prior to 1947 did not achieve a satisfactory picture of the development of the cities, and in the absence of radiocarbon dating no absolute chronology was obtained.

A second series of sites have in some cases features which recall the basic layout of the cities, and although smaller, they may reasonably be regarded as provincial centres of government. Among them several have been excavated. Most recent in point of time is Kalibangan, where extensive excavations of the Harappan township are still in progress. From the viewpoint of technical excellence this work is among the finest so far done in the subcontinent and does credit to the Indian Archaeological Survey. Kalibangan shares with Harappa and Mohenjo-daro the layout of citadel and lower town, and it has produced a series of radiocarbon datings. At Kot Diji the excavators also treat the site as comprising a citadel and outer town of Harappan style. It was excavated in 1958, but the publication is somewhat unsatisfactory. Other large sites which may also be included in this category are Sandhanawala in Bahawalpur and Judeirjo-daro in Sind north of Jacobabad, but these have not as yet been excavated, nor has the great mound at Dabar Kot in the Loralai valley of north Baluchistan, apart from trial trenches made by Sir Aurel Stein. Farther south in Sind are Amri and Chanhu-daro, the former on the right and the latter on the left plains of the Indus. The French excavations have revealed much interesting information at Amri and have shown not only the pre-Harappan development, but also three distinct phases of Harappan occupation, as well as an immediately post-Harappan period. Chanhu-daro was excavated in 1935-6 by Mackay and produced a great deal of interesting material relating to the two latter periods.

Among other excavated sites we may mention Sutkagen Dor on the Makran coast where Sir Aurel Stein dug some trial trenches. More recently Dales has shown the existence of a great fortification around the Harappan outpost there. Perhaps the most important excavation of the post-war period has been that at Lothal. Here the Indian Archaeological Survey's team, under the direction of S. R. Rao revealed a great artificial platform with streets and houses of regular plan, and a series of building phases which have been dated by a number of C14 samples. Beside the township was discovered a remarkable brick dockyard connected by a channel to the gulf of Cambay. Two other smaller sites excavated in recent years are Rojdi in Saurashtra, and Desalpar in Cutch (Kacch) district. Both provide evidence of an initial occupation in the Harappan period, and of continuing occupation during post-Harappan times. Finally mention may be made of two outlying sites at Rupar in the Punjab and at Alamgirpur in Uttar Pradesh, at both of which recent excavations have established the presence of Harappan or late-Harappan settlements. The extension of the civilization eastwards towards the Ganges-Jamuna Doab raises various interesting possibilities which must await the research of coming years.

As a result of more than thirty years of excavations at these sites, there is a great body of evidence relating to the life of the civilization which produced them. Much of the detailed description will be given in later chapters, but here we shall summarize the main outlines which present themselves to the observer. Our overwhelming impression is of cultural uniformity, both throughout the several centuries during which the Harappan civilization flourished, and over the vast area it occupied. This uniformity is nowhere clearer than in the town-planning. The basic layout of the larger settlements, whether cities or towns, shows a regular orientation, with a high citadel on the west dominating the lower town. Probably the latter was originally more or less square. Equally careful was the oriented grid of streets which intersected the blocks of dwellings. The widths of the streets seem to have been determined by a modulus. The imposition of this new layout on the older pre-Harappan settlement at Kalibangan, with its haphazard disposition, dramatically emphasizes the suddenness and completeness of the change. A similar uniformity is found throughout the Harappan structures. There is a remarkable standardization of brick sizes, both of burnt- and mud-bricks, and this too is in basic contrast to that of the pre-Harappan period. The skill of the bricklayers is particularly clear in the great public buildings of the citadel complexes, for example in the great bath at Mohenjo-daro, and in the granaries at both cities. On the other hand one cannot but be struck by the monotonous regularity of the plain undecorated brickwork of the acres of uniform houses of the lower town at Mohenjo-daro. Another feature of the towns that calls for attention is the care expended on domestic bathrooms and latrines, and on the chutes which linked them to brick drains running down the streets. At intervals the drains were connected with soakage pits or sumps, and their maintenance implies some sort of highly effective municipal authority.

The mainstays of life must have been extraordinarily like those of recent centuries in the Indus valley. Wheat and barley were the main crops; leguminous plants, field peas and dates were other items of diet. Sessamum and mustard were used, presumably for oil. We shall have more to say regarding the system of agriculture in a later chapter. Among domestic animals were sheep, goats and cattle, and the domestic fowl was also kept. It is not clear whether bones of pig and buffalo indicate the presence of domesticated stock, or only that these animals were hunted for food. Several varieties of deer were certainly hunted. The discovery of fragments of woven cotton is of great interest, attesting the antiquity of an industry for which in later times India has been particularly famous.

A similar uniformity of culture can be observed in the technology of the Harappans: indeed it is as strong as in the town-planning, and so marked that it is possible to typify each craft with a single set of examples drawn from one site alone. It is not yet established whether this uniformity was achieved by the centralization of production, linked with efficiency of distribution, or whether by other factors, but in either case it calls for special study. A standard range of tools of copper and bronze is recorded at site after site. Many among them set the pattern for later Indian types for centuries to come. The majority exhibit what Piggott called 'competent dullness', a simplicity of design and manufacture linked with adequate, but not great functional efficiency. The range of bronze and copper vessels is technically more worthy of remark. There is little doubt that such special objects as the cast bronze figures of people or animals, or the little model carts (of which nearly identical examples come from sites as far apart as Harappa and Chanhu-daro) were the products of specialists' workshops in one or other of the cities. In spite of the commonness of metals, stone was not abandoned, and chert blades were prepared from cores which in turn had probably been exported from such great factories as that at Sukkur (Sakhar).

This craft, which demands comparison with the stone-blade industry of the Neolithic-
Chalcolithic cultures of peninsular India, shows a sort of effortless competence, without
apparently any desire to produce novel or special results. On the other hand the products
of the potters must have been mainly local, and the uniformity of forms and painted
decorations which they display cannot be accounted for by trade. How it was achieved
is not easy to determine; mere uniformity of wheels or equipment cannot alone supply
the answer, even though it must have played a substantial role. The ubiquitous terracotta
figurines of people and animals, both male and female, deserve no special mention. They
may have been toys, or in some cases cult figures of mother goddesses.

There were numerous highly developed arts and crafts. Among them that of seal-cut-
ting calls for comment. The seals were sawn from blocks of steatite and cut as intaglios,
then toasted in a small furnace to harden and glaze the surface. Their importance was
doubtless linked in some way with their role in trading activities, but for the modern
observer of even greater interest are the short inscriptions in the unknown Harappan
script and the subjects of the intaglio, many representing scenes of a cultural or religious
character. The bead-maker's craft was also remarkable, and the long barrel beads of
carnelian rank among the technical achievements of the Harappans. So too must have
done the art of shell inlay, unfortunately known only from fragments of shell; and the
manufacture of objects of faience. Of stone and metal sculpture very few examples are
known, but these range in quality between excellence and comparative crudity. Summing
up we may say that technical uniformity over so great an area is probably unique in the
ancient world and that Harappan technology deserves Childe's acclaim as 'technically
the peer of the rest' (that is, of Egypt and Babylonia). But its limitations should not be
overlooked. The majority of the products are unimaginative and unadventurous, in
some ways reminiscent of the products of the Roman provinces, but also suggesting
that the people of Harappa had their eyes on things not of this world. There are signs of
an innate conservatism, which in many respects demands comparison with Indian conservatism of later times.

Other categories of information are less easily obtained by excavation, but include
aspects of life and culture which are essential if a full and balanced picture is to be obtained:
thus from variations of house sizes, and from localization of groups of 'barracks', some
scholars have inferred class differences even amounting to slavery. The same evidence has
been used to suggest the presence of a 'caste' structure like that of later times. Again the
presence of great granaries on the citadel mounds and of the 'citadels' themselves, have
suggested, partly by analogy with Middle Eastern cities, the presence of priest-kings or
at least of a priestly oligarchy who controlled the economy, civil government and religious
life of the state. The intellectual mechanism of this government and the striking degree
of control implicit in it are also very worthy subjects of research.

The language of the Harappans is at present still unknown, and must remain so
until the Harappan script is read. Broadly there would appear to be two main contestants:
that it belonged—however improbably—to the Indo-European or even Indo-Iranian family;
or that it belonged to the Dravidian family. In spite of the careful analysis of the corpus
of Harappan inscriptions—now in the region of 2,500—by Hunter, Langdon and others,
the task of decipherment remains problematic. Numerous attempts have been—and are
still being—made, but none so far can inspire much confidence. In recent years the most

significant advance has been the certain proof, offered by B. B. Lal, that the script was written from right to left. The shortness of the inscriptions, nearly all on seals or amulet tablets, further renders decipherment difficult. The uniformity of weights and measures is another indication of the efficiency of state control throughout a large area.

There are many traits which appear to anticipate features of the religion of Vedic times or later Hinduism. We shall notice below the probable existence of temples and stone cult icons in the cities. The seals have been generally agreed to contain a body of information on religious beliefs. It is evident that such motifs as the *pipal* leaf, or the *svastika,* were already of religious significance for the Harappans. There is a suggestion of a religion dominated by one great God, who convincingly shares many of the traits of the later Śiva, being a *Yogi,* a Lord of Beasts, whose cult was associated with fertility and the *lingam,* and who in later times had the epithet *Mahādeva* (great God), and by a great Mother who equally shares traits of Parvati, the spouse of Śiva known also as Mother, and Devi, the Goddess. There is an indication of the cult of trees or tree-spirits, and of the special significance of various animals. Taking all in all, we are left with a very clear sense at least of elements of the Harappan religion, and we cannot fail to see in them much that continues in subsequent Hinduism.

The information that has been gathered on such topics as the economy, social system, government or religion, was largely the product of chance finds in the earlier excavations. It is to be hoped that as archaeological research in India and Pakistan advances further excavations may be conducted with the aim of answering specific questions and elucidating specific problems.

The earlier excavations at Mohenjo-daro and Harappa revealed surprisingly little clear evidence of the Harappan burial customs. However, in the final seasons at the latter site Vats discovered the post-Harappan Cemetery H (to be discussed below), and between 1937 and 1941 a second, Harappan burial ground known as Cemetery R 37. Both these were further investigated by Wheeler in 1946. Since 1940 three other Harappan cemeteries are reported, although none is yet published; at Derawar in Bahawalpur, discovered by Stein, at Lothal, and at Kalibangan. The two latter have been excavated. It appears that the predominant burial rite was extended inhumation, the body lying on its back with the head generally to the north. Quantities of pottery were placed in the graves, and in some cases the skeleton was buried with ornaments. A number of graves took the form of brick chambers or cists, one at Kalibangan being of unusual size (4 x 2 metres), and from Harappa is reported a coffin burial with traces of a reed shroud. At Kalibangan two other types of burial were encountered: smaller circular pits containing large urns, accompanied by other pottery, but, perplexingly, no skeletal remains, at any rate in the examples so far excavated; and more orthodox burial pits with what are evidently collected bones. From the Lothal cemetery comes evidence of another burial type with several examples of pairs of skeletons, one male and one female in each case, interred in a single grave. It has been suggested that these may indicate a practice akin to *sati.* Until more is published, or further research is done, it does not seem possible to add to Marshall's speculations regarding the burials inside Mohenjo-daro itself, but it is evident from all these other finds that the regular cemeteries wherever they have been discovered were disposed around the perimeter of the settlement.

We shall now turn to a more detailed discussion of Harappan chronology and internal development, and the circumstances of the downfall of the civilization. The first estimate of the duration of the occupation at Mohenjo-daro was made by Sir John Marshall in 1931. His estimate, based upon general concordances with Mesopotamia, was from 3250 to 2750 B.C. In the following year C. J. Gadd published a paper listing a number of Indus, or Indus-like, seals discovered in Mesopotamian sites, particularly Ur, and discussing their ages. Here, apart from two examples which were listed as pre-Sargonid, the majority of finds of seals belonged to the Sargonid and Isin-Larsa periods, and might therefore be expected to indicate active trade contacts between 2350 and 1770 B.C. A few seals were also found in Kassite contexts indicating a yet later date. Since then Piggott (1950) and Wheeler (1946, 1960, etc.) have reviewed the evidence, including cross-dates to the as yet imprecisely dated sites of Iran (Hissar, Giyan, etc.), and other categories of objects apparently imported into Mesopotamia, etched carnelian beads, stone house-urns, etc. There has been general agreement upon an overall span of 2500-1500 B.C. with principal trade contacts with Mesopotamia between 2300 and 2000 B.C. In the past twenty years little additional evidence has come to light to change this view, so far as archaeological crossdatings are concerned. However, in 1955 Albright concluded that the end of the civilization must have been around 1750 B.C. in order to coincide with Mesopotamian evidence. The advent of radiocarbon has provided a welcome new source of information on what must otherwise have remained a very vague position, and may well necessitate a revision of the earlier views. Already by 1956 Fairservis had seen in the radiocarbon dates of his excavations in the Quetta valley a need to bring down the dating of the Harappan culture to between 2000 and 1500 B.C. In 1964 Shri D. P. Agrawal, of the flourishing radiocarbon laboratory attached to the Tata Institute of Fundamental Research in Bombay, was able to plot some two dozen dates, including those from Kot Diji, Kalibangan and Lothal, and to draw the conclusion that the total time span of the culture should be between 2300 and 1750 B.C. This evidence appears to us to be on the whole most plausible.

In view of the proximity of Kot Diji to Mohenjo-daro, it seems improbable that any great time lag would be experienced in the culture sequence of the two. Thus the radiocarbon dates relating to the general destruction by fire which heralds the intermediate period following the end of the pre-Harappan at Kot Diji, and any dates relating to the subsequent developments, would be of tremendous interest. Unfortunately the published report on Kot Diji leaves some vital gaps. The detailed description of the layer numbers of two of the four samples is not clearly stated, but we gather that only one date, 2090 + 140 B.C., relates to the final destruction at the end of the Kot Dijian occupation. With this we may compare the series from Kalibangan, where a cluster of dates between 2100 and 2070 B.C. indicates the beginning of the Harappan period, and two dates around 1770-1670 B.C. indicate its conclusion. At Lothal another series gives dates between 2080 and 1800 B.C. (± 115 and 140 years respectively), and a single date from a late level at Mohenjo-daro gives 1760 ± 115 years.[2] There is a surprising conformity in these dates. They suggest a period of not more than four centuries for the Harappan civilization, between 2150 and 1750 B.C. We are inclined to accept them with the proviso that unknown variables may be found which demand some general modification. Yet even allowing a margin of 100 years, an initial date of 2250 B.C. would seem acceptable and in no way goes against the admittedly imprecise evidence afforded by the Mesopotamian finds. Acceptance of this chronology carries with it the implication that trade contacts with the Middle East prior to 2150 B.C. would have been with the towns of the pre-Harappan Amrian culture in the lower Indus.

There is another category of dating evidence which may be invoked, in the textual references from Mesopotamia to objects imported from Meluhha (probably the Indus Valley or Western India), or the entrepots of Tilmun (probably in the Persian Gulf, perhaps Bahrain) and Magan (perhaps in Southern Arabia or on the Makran coast). There is good reason to suppose that many of these objects originated in India, and therefore the dates of this literature are likely to be significant, at least of the period of maximum trade activity on the part of the Harappans, if not of the duration of the civilization. The first reference is in the time of Sargon of Agade (c. 2300 B.C.), but the volume of literature only grows during the third dynasty of Ur (2130-2030 B.C.) and the subsequent Larsa dynasty (2030-1770 B.C.). Thereafter they markedly decline. They therefore suggest that the maximum trade contacts coincide almost exactly with the duration of the civilization indicated by the radiocarbon samples. It seems likely that a critical reassessment of dates ascribed to seals and other Indus objects from Mesopotamia would also tend to confirm these results. The discovery of a 'Persian Gulf' seal at Lothal highlights the interest attached to finds at Failaka, Bahrain and other sites on the southern shores of the Persian Gulf. In recent years the Danish expedition working in this area has discovered a large number of these distinctive seals, some almost identical to imported specimens found at Ur and other sites in Mesopotamia. Most recently Buchanan has reported the impression of one such seal on a dated cuneiform tablet of the tenth year of king Gungunum of Larsa, that is about 1923 B.C. according to the middle chronology. Thus almost for the first time, a find from a Harappan site, although unhappily not from a well-stratified context, can be crossdated to the historical chronology of Iraq; and is not found to conflict with the radiocarbon chronology we are following. Of all the findspots of these seals and of objects supposedly imported into Mesopotamia from the Indus region, Frankfort's excavations at Tell Asmar in the Diyala valley supply perhaps the most convincing evidence of the age. But there seems even so to be some latitude in the interpretation of the evidence. According to Buchanan the earliest seals and imports are not earlier than the late Agade period, and he concludes that 'the Mesopotamian evidence therefore does not require a date for the mature Indus civilization much, if at all, before the twenty-third century B.C.' If this conclusion is correct, it means that there is no substantial conflict between the Indian and Mesopotamian evidence.

At almost every site of the Harappan period there is at least some evidence of internal development. Unfortunately much of the earlier work at Mohenjo-daro and Harappa was of such a kind that its analysis is now scarcely possible, while the more recent work at Kalibangan or Lothal is still incompletely published. It is thus not easy to make a close comparison of the development at each site, although one is led to feel that parallels might be found, if only more evidence were available. At those sites where excavation has revealed a pre-Harappan phase below the Harappan (Amri, Kot Diji, Kalibangan) there is in each case an indication of cultural continuity. Even when at Kot Diji a massive burnt layer intervenes, the evolution of decorative motifs on pottery continues. At the same three sites there is further a transitional level in which both styles of pottery are found together. Of this level there is no evidence at Chanhu-daro or Mohenjo-daro, as the height of the subsoil water prevented excavation below a certain point, but at Mohenjo-daro Mackay's deep digging in Block 7 of the DK area revealed an early period, related by him to the 'Early' eighth stratum of Marshall on the Citadel mound, which produced some pottery of non-Harappan type, for example some incised comb decoration, recalling the pre-Harappan Fabric D at Kalibangan. This may indicate that the early period reached in the excavation at Mohenjo-daro goes back to the transitional phase of the other sites.

At Harappa, Mohenjo-daro and Chanhu-daro the early period ends with the massive brick platforms of the citadel areas, and above are found the remains of the high period of the civilization. At Mohenjo-daro this included three principal structural levels of Marshall's intermediate period and was succeeded by a great and disastrous flood, and by three levels of the late period; at Harappa there were six structural levels of which the uppermost produced some pottery of Cemetery H type. At Kot Diji there are also apparently six or seven building phases within the Harappan period, while at Kalibangan nine are reported. At almost every site there succeeds a 'late' period during which planning and construction decline, brickbats from former houses are reused, new motifs appear on pottery, etc. This is generally seen as a decline, though whether associated with natural calamities or with political factors is still far from clear.

Around 1750 B.C. the uniform culture of this great area broke up: apparently with different results in Sind and the south, and in the Punjab and the north. What was the cause of this breakdown? Several causes have been suggested. Lambrick has recently proposed that calamitous alterations of the course of the Indus above Mohenjo-daro may either have driven population from desiccated areas to Mohenjo-daro, or have caused the desiccation of the lands around the city, and thereby weakened it, making it an easy prey to barbarians from the west. Marshall and Mackay stressed the repeated flooding of the city, and saw too in the vagaries of the Indus a possible cause of decay. This view has recently been modified by Raikes who, as a result of his study of the exposed flood-deposits and borings made at Mohenjo-daro, and of related observations elsewhere, has invoked tectonic movements downstream as responsible for mighty lake formation and silting. All three of these theories need not entirely exclude one another. But Raikes's theory raises serious difficulties which require elucidation before we are ready to accept it. Marshall, who dated the civilization almost a thousand years earlier than we have done, saw no connexion between its downfall and the Aryans. But Childe (1934) and Wheeler (1946) have shown that with revised chronology there is every possibility of invoking Aryan, if not Rigvedic Aryan, agency for the destruction. The unburied skeletons lying in the streets of Mohenjo-daro are very suggestive. We may now, from the position suggested by radiocarbon dates, envisage yet another possibility—even if a remote one. If, as we have seen, the Harappan civilization with its remarkable cultural unity, came into existence only around 2150 B.C., it is necessary to admit that not only the end of the cities, but even their initial impetus may have been due to Indo-European speaking peoples. It is interesting to notice that recent work in Greece and Asia Minor suggests that the earliest movements traceable to Indo-European peoples there—those associated with the Minyan ware—may also be assigned to a nearly similar date.

The Aryan Invasions

As we have already seen, not only are languages of the Indo-European family the most widely spoken in modern India and Pakistan, but also the Rigveda is revered as the fountainhead from which all later Indian religion and philosophy developed. It is therefore of great interest to know when the Indo-European speakers entered the subcontinent and whence they came; and we now propose to consider briefly the archaeological evidence relating to their arrival. It is generally agreed that the expansion of the Indo-European languages in some way coincided with the domestication of the horse and its subsequent use with light war chariots. The wild species of horse appears in late Pleistocene times on the south Russian and Ukrainian steppes, and thence eastwards towards Kazakhstan and Central Asia. It is therefore to be expected that domestication would have taken place somewhere in this region. According to Zeuner the evidence formerly adduced from such sites as Anau and Sialk for a date in the fifth or fourth millennia B.C. relates to bones of half-asses (hemiones) and not to true horses. At present all that can be said is that domestication probably took place some time before 2000 B.C. and that the adoption of the war chariot dates from the opening of the second millennium. One of the earliest references to this spread is in the Chagar Bazar tablets of Samsi-Adad (c. 1800 B.C.), in the Khabur of north Syria. There is also inscriptional evidence about that time for Indo-European languages spreading into the Iranian region. The Kassite rulers of Babylon at the opening of the sixteenth century bore Indo-European names, as did the Mitannian rulers of the succeeding centuries. A treaty of the Hittite King Subiluliuma and the Mitannian Mattiwaza of c. 1380 mentions the names of Mitra, Varuna and Indra, gods of the Rigvedic Aryans themselves, and among the Boghaz Keui tablets is a treatise on horse-training by Kikkuli of Mitanni using chariot-racing terms in virtually pure Sanskrit.

The archaeological evidence relating to all these movements, both in Iran and in India and Pakistan, is much less precise, and indeed it almost always lacks any clear hallmarks to establish its originators as Indo-Europeans. In north Baluchistan, Piggott has drawn attention to the thick layers of burning which indicate violent destruction of whole settlements at about this time at Rana Ghundai, Dabar Kot, etc. In South Baluchistan the cemetery at Shahi-tump, dug into an abandoned Kulli settlement, shows copper stamp seals, a copper shaft-hole axe and footed and legged bowls. The seals may be compared with Iranian examples from Anau III and Hissar III; the shaft-hole axes, unknown until this time in the Indian subcontinent, are of west Asiatic type and compare with those from Maikop and Tsarskaya in south Russia. A date of c. 1800 B.C. is quite acceptable. At Mundigak in period V the picture is rather different. On the main mound a considerable reconstruction of a massive brick structure is found over the ruins of the palace of period IV. The massive structure is perhaps in some way connected with the brick granaries of the Harappans and may well indicate a need for fortified storage of grain. Copper stampseals, of patterns sometimes reminiscent of those of Shahi-tump, make their first appearance during period IV, and continue into V. Copper pins with spiral loops, also reminiscent of Shahi-tump and Chanhudaro, appear in IV (although related types are reported already in II, while shaft-hole axes and adzes are already present in III.6). None of these finds however is datable in itself.

Evidence of a rather different kind is available in Sind, where at Amri, Chanhu-daro, Jhukar, Lohumjo-daro and other sites, the occupation continues, apparently without a major break, with a distinct culture named after the type-site of Jhukar. The most extensive evidence of invasions was discovered at Chanhu-daro. Here a shaft-hole axe and copper pins with looped or decorated heads recall Shahi-tump and more significantly Hissar III*b*. Circular, or occasionally square, stamp-seals of stone or faience again recall Hittite parallels from Asia Minor, and also Shahi-tump. Another foreign trait is a small cast bronze cosmetic jar (or mace head) comparable to examples from Luristan and Hissar III. In contrast to such objects the distinctive Jhukar pottery, a buff ware with red or cream slip often in bands, and bold painting in black, suggests a real degree of continuity with local Harappan and even west Indian traditions, and leads us to infer that a substantial element of the population survived the invasion. The picture in this way is generally comparable to that of Saurashtra although the two regions show important differences. By contrast with the Harappan pottery, a fair proportion of the Jhukar ware gives evidence that it was finished by beating, after removal from the wheel. This later becomes a typical Indian potting technique.

At Mohenjo-daro direct evidence of a Jhukar occupation is wanting, perhaps because of natural causes, but on the other hand the numerous groups of hastily buried or unburied corpses left in the streets of its final occupation, and the buried boards of jewellery and copper objects seem testimony enough to the proximity of foreign barbarians. More precise evidence of their presence at Mohenjo-daro in the upper levels is found in the copper shaft-hole axe-adze, whose Iranian parallels date from *c.* 1800 to 1600 B.C. while two dirks and two daggers with thickened mid-rib and rivet holes, are also of this time. We shall see below that thickened mid ribs of bronze and copper appear to have spread into the peninsula of India between 1500 and 1300 B.C. The bronze pin with spiral loop, found by Mackay at a depth of 18·4 feet in the DK area, must indicate an earlier importation, and so too may the animal-headed pin discovered in the same part of the site. Their Iranian or Caucasian origin nevertheless seems established.

At Chanhu-daro and at the mound of Jhangar on the other side of the Indus, the Jhukar phase is succeeded by one producing a poor grey-black burnished pottery with incised decoration. This ware is quite different from the earlier painted traditions, and no other evidence of the material culture of its makers is known. An inferior painted ware is also found. Some of the Jhangar forms, and more particularly the incised patterns, are reminiscent of those occurring in paint in Saurashtra at Rangpur and Somnath, during our phase 4 and may thus be expected to date to *c.* 1000 B.C. In Saurashtra too, incised grey ware, often of crude make and of related forms is found. The most distinctive 'Jhangar' form from Chanhudaro was a triple jar whose analogues are at Shahi-tump and Sialk, Necropolis B, thus reinforcing our view of the date.

The period coinciding with the end of the Harappan civilization in the north of the region, in the Punjab, is of a rather different character from that of the Sind, and may well prove of fundamental importance to our understanding of later Indian civilization. A bronze animal-headed pin found at Harappa near the surface in area J suggests connexions with western Iran and the Caucasus between 1500 and 2000 B.C. All over the citadel mound at Harappa, and in the topmost stratum of the area F immediately to the north, Vats discovered a decadent period of structures of reused brick, and pottery including a significant quantity similar to that discovered in Cemetery H. Even in the second stratum of the citadel mound instances of pottery of this sort were noted. As this pottery is clearly identified only in the cemetery, we propose to refer to the culture to which it belongs as the Cemetery H culture. Wheeler showed conclusively by his excavation in 1946 that the cemetery bore a stratigraphic relationship to the cemetery (R37) of the Harappan period. Between the two there intervened a great mass of debris, mainly Harappan pottery, including some late-Harappan forms such as footed goblets. Above and into this debris burials of Cemetery H were dug at two levels. In the lower (stratum II) were extended inhumations accompanied by quantities of pottery, while in the upper (stratum I) were fractional burials in large urns, without accompanying grave goods. It has not so far been definitely established whether these two are contemporary, or whether the lower is earlier, as Vats believed. The latter would clearly represent an important change in burial customs during the period.

We are given almost no information by the excavators about the other aspects of the related material culture: thus at present all we have to go by is the pottery. Our view is that the differences between it and the earlier Harappan pottery have been overemphasized, while the many technical similarities and even the forms have not been given sufficient attention. A substantial range of forms—the urns themselves, the carinated vessels, the graceful footed vases—are no doubt foreign to the Harappans; the painted decoration with its distinctive stars and ring-and-dot patterns, is also foreign. On the other hand the whole feeling of the pottery, with its monotonous red slip and black painting, suggests a continuity of potting tradition, and must indicate an integration of existing potter communities with the newcomers, whoever they were. This conclusion was reached by Vats, who supported it by a careful consideration of relative stratigraphy. He stated that the Cemetery H culture was the final stage of the Harappan, and continuous with it; but that it must indicate the presence of foreign conquerors or immigrants. In our view this is a fact of great interest, suggesting the sort of cultural fusion which may be represented by the Cemetery H culture itself. The date of this event is not easy to estimate with precison. It may be expected to open at about the time when the Harappan period ends (i.e. c. 1750 B.C.). The pottery shows affinities with wares from far to the west in Iran, near the borders of Mesopotamia, particularly Tepe Giyan (Strata II-III), and Djamshidi II, dated between 1400 and 1550 B.C. or somewhat earlier, and with Susa D. At these sites stars and birds occur in registers in a manner strikingly recalling those of Cemetery H. This unfortunately does not help us to a very precise date. Certain of the evolved Harappan forms, particularly the offering stands, may be compared with those from Rangpur IIB and C. Altogether, we feel that this period may extend over some two centuries or more in the Punjab, probably between 1750 and c. 1400 B.C. Its geographical extent is suggested by sites reported in Bahawalpur, and by pottery from Rupar and Bara to the north-east. The pottery from the latter site shows some resemblances of painted decoration to that of Giyan IV. It is also probable that among the sites with Harappan or late-Harappan affinities recently reported from Saharanpur district to the east, some may belong to this phase.

From the Punjab we turn to the north-west to consider the growing body of evidence of folk movements into this area during the second millennium. From Fort Munro in the foothills west of Dera Ghazi Khan comes a beautiful bronze dirk with a fan-shaped decoration on the pommel of its hilt. This piece is very close to dirks from Luristan and Sialk VI and should date to c.1150 B.C. At Moghul Ghundai, in the Zhob Valley, Sir Aurel Stein excavated cairn graves which Piggott assigns to the period of Cemetery B at Sialk (c. 1000-800 B.C.). These graves produced an array of bronze objects typical of the latter site, including a tripod jar, horse bells and a bangle. In some of the graves iron arrow-heads were found, but these are in no way out of keeping with the probable date. At Shalozan, high up in the Kurram valley, a characteristic trunnion axe of copper was discovered, belonging to type III of Maxwell-Hyslop's classification, and comparing with examples from Hasanlu and other Iranian sites, where they belong to the second millennium and indicate contacts between Anatolian and Iranian smiths. A somewhat perplexing surface find is a golden stag from the Hazara district of the Punjab, now in Peshawar museum. This piece has a distinctly Caucasian appearance and may be compared with many examples of various metals from the south-west Caspian at such sites as Talyche, Samthavro and Lenkoran, where they date from c. 1450 to 1200 B.C.[3]

In 1958 Professor Jettmar photographed the residue of a large hoard of bronze objects discovered shortly before at a spot far up the Indus valley, high in the Gilgit Karakoram. This included several good specimens of trunnion axes of a similar type, along with shaft-hole axes with narrow necks. This hoard also suggests Iranian contacts during the second half of the millennium. It may be argued—however improbably—that the stray items of copper and bronze found in these western border regions indicate trade contacts rather than movements of peoples. This can scarcely be said of the grave sites with their thoroughly Iranian equipment. Taking the two categories of evidence together, the outline is beginning to emerge of a series of waves of immigration from the direction of Iran during the second half of the millennium, some penetrating deep into the valleys of the northern mountains. The graves of a group of people who may be taken as the descendants of one such wave of Indo-Iranian-speaking immigrants have recently been discovered in considerable numbers by the Italian expedition working at such sites as Butkara and Barama in Swat, and by Professor Dani and his associates of Peshawar University at Thana in Swat and at Timurgara in Bajaur. The graves are usually drystone cists built on the lower slopes of the valleys. The grave goods include plain grey and red pottery with pedestal goblets, flasks and bowls whose nearest parallels are in Giyan I and in the two Necropoles at Sialk. Partly burnt bones are deposited in some of the urns, while other graves have complete skeletons. Iron is a rare occurrence. This may be taken to indicate new waves of Indo-European speaking peoples entering the Indian subcontinent towards the end of the second millennium. Radiocarbon dates from Butkara and Barama range between 713 and 440 B.C.

We shall be returning to the archaeological evidence for Aryan movements east of the Indus later, but a few more stray metal finds may be mentioned here. A copper hoard from Khurdi in the Nagaur district of Rajputana included a fine bowl with long protruding channel spout, of a form with numerous analogues in both pottery and metal at Giyan I, Sialk (Necropolis B), etc.; another simple bowl of copper reminiscent of examples from Sialk, and a flat double axe of copper. From copper hoards at Fatehgarh and Bithur in Uttar Pradesh, and from a site in the neighbourhood of Kallur in Raichur district, well to the south in the peninsula, have come swords or dirks of copper or bronze with midribs and 'antennae' hilts, compared by von Heine-Geldern to examples from the Koban culture of the Caucasus and there datable to *c.* 1200-1000 B.C. A copper spearhead with somewhat similar hilt from Chandoli in Maharashtra comes from strata dated by radiocarbon to *c.* 1330 B.C., and a fragment of a similar piece comes from Navdatoli. Identical spearheads were found in a grave at Gezer in Palestine, datable to the close of the XVIII Egyptian dynasty, and therefore contemporary with the Chandoli piece. All of these stray finds may do no more than indicate indirect contact, but they appear to be consistent with the movement of peoples from Iran and perhaps even from the Caucasus region into India.

It is in the light of this archaeological evidence that the Rigveda must be read. It has hitherto been tantalizingly difficult to point to any archaeological culture which may be that of the Vedic Aryan tribes; but now at last there appears to be a probability that the two categories of evidence may shortly be superimposed upon each other. It is believed that the Veda—on account of its great sanctity—was not reduced to writing until the time of Sayana (in the fourteenth century A.D.), and thus that it was passed down in oral traditions for about thirty centuries. None the less, from the time when its hymns were collected and arranged, probably before 1000 B.C. they have been preserved syllable by syllable with incredible accuracy, and while the language changed with time so that their original meaning became more and more obscure, the hymns were passed down immutably from Brahman teacher to pupil. The picture the hymns present is of barbarian tribes, glorying in their swift horses and light chariots, with sheep, goats and cattle, cultivating at first barley and wheat and later rice. They made tools and weapons of *ayas,* a metal which, being occasionally described as red in colour, must have been either copper or bronze. Iron (at first known as black metal to distinguish it) is not mentioned in the Rigveda, but in later Vedic literature, from the time of the Atharvaveda and the *Samhitas* of the Yajurveda, it becomes increasingly common.

The Vedic hymns are addressed to Indo-European gods such as Indra, the warrior charioteer whose thunderbolt destroyed their enemies and who brags of his inebriation on the sacred *soma* drink; Agni, the fire god, who also shares something of this warlike character as the consumer of the enemy, as well as being the intermediary between gods and men; Varuna, the Asura or righteous king; Mitra, with solar characteristics, and so on. Their cult revolved around the fire sacrifice. The Aryan funeral rites are of interest: cremation and burial were evidently both in vogue.

The geographical horizons of the Rigveda are relevant to our inquiry. On the west they are bounded by the western tributaries of the Indus, the Gomatī (modern Gomal), the Krumu (modern Kurram) and the Kubhā (modern Kabul) rivers. Other rivers are mentioned even to the north of the Kabul, notably Suvāstu, the modern Swat. This latter signifies 'fair dwellings' and may therefore indicate Aryan settlements in this beautiful valley. The centre of Rigvedic geography is the Punjab. The rivers most often referred to are the Indus itself, the Sarasvatī and the Drishadvatī and the five streams which collectively gave their name to the Punjāb (five waters), the Śutudrī (Sutlej), Vipās (Beas), Parushnī (Ravi), Asiknī (Chenab), and Vitastā (Jhelum). The eastern horizons are the Jamunā river and at the end of the period the Ganges.

From the Veda it is evident that the Aryans were not the only inhabitants of the region, for which they themselves used the name *Sapta-Sindhava* or land of seven Indus rivers, and that their original stay was not entirely peaceful. We learn of a people called *Dāsas* or *Dasyu* (the word later means 'slave') who were dark-complexioned, snub-nosed, worshippers of the phallus *(śiśna deva)*, etc. They were rich in cattle and lived in fortified strongholds, *pura*. We learn of another people, the *Panis*, who were also wealthy in cattle and treasures. Although many of the hymns refer to battles between one Aryan tribe and another there is an underlying sense of solidarity in the fight against the Dāsas, and Indra is named *Purandara*, the 'breaker of cities'. Already in the Veda the first encounters of Indra (the Aryan people personified) and the fortified settlements of the Dāsas were being forgotten and the Dāsas rulers were regarded as demons. We hear of a city named Nārminī destroyed by fire, and of a battle on the banks of the Ravi at a place named Hariyūpiyā (which Indologists are ever more confidently identifying with Harappa). Professor Burrow has recently shown the unambiguous character of such references as, 'Through fear of thee the dark-coloured inhabitants fled, not waiting for battle, abandoning their possessions, when, O Agni [fire], burning brightly for Puru [an Aryan tribe], and destroying the cities, thou didst shine' (VII.5·3). He has further recognized the importance in both the Rigveda and later Vedic texts of the word *arma, armaka,* meaning ruin. For instance, in the Rigveda we read, 'Strike down, O Maghavan [Indra], the host of sorceresses in the ruined city of Vaila-sthānaka, in the ruined city of Mahāvailastha [Great Vailastha]' (I. 133·3). There were then, in the time of the Rigveda, great ruin-mounds which the Aryans associated with the earlier inhabitants of the area. The same idea recurs in a later Vedic text, the *Taittirīya Brāhmana* (II. 4, 6, 8), in the statement that, 'The people to whom these ruined sites belonged, lacking posts, these many settlements, widely distributed, they, O Agni, having been expelled by thee, have migrated to another land.' Also in one of the later Vedic texts we read, 'On the Sarasvatī there are ruined sites called Naitandhava; Vyarna is one of these'; and, for the archaeologist perhaps even more suggestively, 'He should proceed along the right bank of the Drishadvatī, having reached the ruined site near its source he should proceed towards the right,' etc.

Such, briefly, is the picture presented by the Rigveda. It provides us with a geographical provenance and with two fairly sure termini, the overthrow of the Harappan cities, in *c.* 1750 B.C., and the introduction of iron around 1050 B.C. Against this evidence we must consider that of archaeology, both the earlier and less positive part discussed in this chapter and the later part discussed in the following chapter. Archaeology is as yet only on the threshold of revealing the information which will be needed to pin down the authors of the Rigveda, but we feel fairly confident that the researches of the last decade or so have made a large contribution towards this end.

Notes

[1] It is perhaps hardly necessary to mention that this glib sentence conceals the cold archaeological truth, that up to today there is no positive evidence that the cities were capitals, either of separate states or of a unified 'empire'. For any society lacking written records, or whose script is still undeciphered, evidence of such matters as political conditions is clearly hard to come by, and is at best inferential. Generations of archaeologists have felt that some such interpretation better fits the Harappan evidence than any other, but necessarily it remains hypothetical. The reader must therefore draw his own conclusions from the available data: the apparent uniformity of weights and measures, the common script, the uniformity—almost common currency—of the seals, the evidence of extensive trade in almost every class of commodity throughout the whole Harappan

culture zone, the common elements in architecture and town-planning, the common elements of art and religion. Even if the political and economic unity is admitted, there remain the profound and tantalizing problems of how it came about and how it was maintained. These have yet to be tackled satisfactorily.

2A recently published series of dates from Mohenjo-daro, obtained by G. F. Dales, gives the Mature Harappan a span of 2154-1864 B.C.

3The age of this piece is open to debate. M. Bussagli has assigned it to the Animal style of the Scytho-Sarmatian period, and dates it accordingly to the last centuries B.C. (La Civilta dell'Oriente,4, pp. 137-8, and Pl. 191). We can only comment that it is far removed from other Indian objects which exhibit the influence of the Animal style at that period (for example, some of the pierced ring-stones of Mauryan date), and appears to us to be considerably earlier. It is difficult to believe that at so late a date it would exhibit no trace whatsoever of contemporary Indian influence.

H. T. Lambrick is the author of *Sind: a general introduction* (Vol. I, 1964).
He worked in the Indian civil service from 1927 to 1947 at which time he
was appointed Spalding Senior Research Fellow at Oriel College, Oxford,
where he continues to teach historical geography. The present article
represents a geographer's response to an archaeologist's explanation
for the demise of the Indus civilization. Several archaeologists suggested
the demise of Mohenjo-daro, and thus the Indus civilization, resulted
from a cataclysmic flood. The reader will note this differs considerably
from the explanation of the fall of the Indus civilization provided by
the Allchins. Mr. Lambrick addresses his article to the geological and
geographical improbability of such flooding. The argument remains
unresolved.

The Indus Flood-Plain
and the 'Indus' Civilization

H. T. Lambrick

    In the past few years increasing attention has been attracted to the problem: what
caused the apparently sudden decline and extinction of the prehistoric Harappa or 'Indus'
civilization in its southern sphere, viz., the province of Sind?
    One theory ascribes the ruin of Mohenjo-daro to drastic geomorphological occur-
rences in the Lower Indus plain. The evidence hitherto adduced in support of the
alleged occurrence of these particular physical changes seems to me utterly inadequate.
Moreover, had such changes taken place as and when suggested, there would inevitably
have been consequences other than, or additional to, those assumed by the protagonists
and supporters of this theory. The absence of traces left by these *other* consequential
processes must cast doubt on the occurrence of those events thought to be reflected in
the phenomena actually noticed. The whole conception clearly requires to be reviewed
in the light of the ascertained behaviour of the river Indus, and of the physical nature
of the Lower Indus plain; and this paper represents an attempt to apply those tests, and
to show that other serious objections deserve to be taken into account.
    The theory briefly (and, I trust, fairly) stated is as follows: at some period when
the Indus civilization was well established and Mohenjo-daro a large and populous city,
a violent tectonic disturbance took place in the country many miles down stream. This
resulted in a great uplift of the plain, along an axis roughly at right angles to that of the
river Indus. It took the form of a swell of ground, many miles broad across its base on

Reprinted from *Geographical Journal*, Vol. 1, Part 4, pp. 483-495 (1967), by permission of the Royal
Geographical Society and author.

the level of the flood-plain, with a height along its crest of more than 100 feet above that of the plain. This swell or bank is assumed to have extended over thirty miles from the rocky rising ground on the western or right-hand limit of the flood-plain to the sand-covered rising ground on its eastern or left-hand limit. The effect of this barrier was to arrest the normal progress of the river Indus to the sea. The flow, held up against it, gradually 'ponded' backward up the 'valley', forming a very large lake. In due course the rising water level in this lake surrounded, penetrated, and finally submerged the city of Mohenjo-daro. After a period, the length of which may have been of the order of a century, the waters of the lake succeeded in overtopping or breaching the barrier, the river again flowed into the Arabian Sea, and a period of rejuvenation began, at the end of which the Lower Indus flood-plain had (as I understand the argument) resumed its former configuration.

According to one version of the theory, this process of tectonic uplift, arrest of the Indus, creation of the great lake, and submergence of Mohenjo-daro, must have occurred two or three times, at intervals of perhaps as many centuries. In another version, barriers of this nature, productive of like effects, are thought to have been thrown up across the Indus plain at points much nearer the sea than the position of that assumed to have caused the ruining of Mohenjo-daro.

The fundamental idea—of tectonic uplift in the Lower Indus plain causing, or contributing to cause, the destruction of Mohenjo-daro by complete submersion—seems to have been first suggested by the palaeontologist Dr. M. R. Sahni in 1952 (Sahni, 1952, p. 153). He developed his views in an article published in 1956 (Sahni, 1956). The data on which his theory was based had been observed by him in 1940-41: namely, a thick mass of alluvium containing shells of freshwater snails, lying on Budh-jo-Takar, a flat-topped rocky hill about 24 miles south of Hyderabad, Sind, at a level at least sixty feet above the bed of the Indus flowing near by. Attributing this alluvium to prolonged flooding above this height, Dr. Sahni made mention also, as relevant to his theory of down-stream uplift, of the fact that the great earthquake of 1819 had thrown up a swell of ground many miles in length, though of no great height, across the plain elsewhere in Lower Sind—the Allahbund.

In 1960 other investigators observing geomorphological effects in the neighbouring territory of Makran began to consider the possibility of similar natural changes in Sind having had an influence in the ruining of Mohenjo-daro. Dr. G. F. Dales, an archaeologist, reported signs that the coast of Baluchistan had been 'gradually rising for thousands of years at least', and Mr. R. L. Raikes, a hydrologist, sketched out a provisional theory, ascribing the end of Mohenjo-daro and other settlements of the Indus civilization in that quarter to the effect of such earth movements. For discussion of the theory reference will be made chiefly to a subsequent article, 'The Mohenjo-daro floods', in which Mr. Raikes expounds the theory in greater detail after investigation on the spot (Dales, 1962; Raikes, 1964; 1965).

He would tentatively locate the zone of uplift in the plain opposite Sehwan—north of Amri and Chanhudaro'. He describes in some detail the form and composition of his barrier; the influence of percolation and evaporation in delaying for perhaps a hundred years the attainment of a level in the resulting lake that eventually submerged or silted up Mohenjo-daro; and his conception of the manner in which the *status quo* would have been restored. Then 'the previously buried parts of the city re-emerged, enabling the inhabitants to build on the slopes as well as on the tops of the older mounds'. He adds,

'The possibility must be considered of more than one uplift episode separated by a period or periods of tectonic repose' (Raikes, 1965, p. 201). Dr. Dales, whose views in general coincide with those of Mr. Raikes, has also this to say: 'Both the multiple layers of silt at Mohenjo-daro and the evidence of multi-level construction suggest that the city was flooded in this prolonged and damaging fashion no less than five times and perhaps more' (Dales, 1966, p. 98).

If this remarkable sequence of events is to be taken as more than imaginative speculation, we obviously require good evidence that Mohenjo-daro was submerged under water or overwhelmed by mud; and that uplift did occur, producing a barrier of the requisite dimensions, in the vicinity of Sehwan. Before proceeding to examine the data presented as evidence, attention is invited to the accompanying map based on surveys some fifty years old.

This configuration of the Lower Indus flood-plain[1] reflects the characteristic behaviour of a great alluvial river in natural conditions. The Indus has always built up its bed and run along broad 'ridges' of its own creation, till it slips off to one or other side and starts the process anew. The modern contours afford clear evidence of the different courses taken by it over a period of several thousand years. The axial gradient of the plain as a whole is almost constant from above Sukkur to the delta. In the few places where the slope corresponding with the existing axis of the river shows a steeper than average fall for a few miles, the change may be attributed to a particularly abrupt avulsion in the distant past from a previous course of very long standing, e.g., a break-out to the right hand from a W to E reach, and consequent adoption of a N to S direction from that point.

Mr. Raikes in his article 'The Mohenjo-daro floods' gives an account of the data—numerous occurrences of 'silty clay' in the ruins of the city at various heights up to twenty-nine feet above the existing flood-plain—which he holds to indicate stillwater flooding up to and above that level. While distinguishing 'silty clay' from 'clayey silt' he does not define these or other terms he uses—'sterile material', 'silty sand', etc. One cannot but feel chary of admitting as evidence of lacustrine deposition observations described in such vague language. I can best explain myself by outlining the physical composition of such materials as I understand it.

The entire alluvial plain of Sind, from its surface down to any stipulated depth, may be regarded as a virtually infinite number of 'skins' of Indus silt, each overlying its predecessor. Each such skin represents the deposit of one year's inundation, possibly with some admixture of similar wind-borne material, and may differ in composition from its predecessor. Nor need this predecessor be deposit from the immediately preceding year's inundation, but may date from many years previously. Thus 'non-conformity' may exist in a given depth of Sind alluvium just as among composite beds of rock. Variety in composition of Indus silt will accord with the relative speed of movement of the particular flood which deposited it. Thus the coarsest and most angular particles will be shed by the water and will form on the ground over which it flows while that flow is relatively fast. As the speed decreases, lighter particles will be shed, forming a layer of finer texture; and when the water reaches the limit of its flow and becomes stationary, the very lightest grains which have been borne along in suspension while the water was in motion will at last drop. These are so minute that they coagulate readily into an argillaceous substance. 'Nonconformity' in alluvium is liable to be found a feature in bore-holes sunk anywhere in the Indus plain, due to the fact that deposition by overspill was not constant in every area, but would vary from year to year according to differences in the inundation discharge, and also in the theatre of overspill, which from the characteristic behaviour of the river was liable to change from year to year. It is also worth remembering that a large proportion of the silt carried by the Indus water in the inundation is eroded from its own banks (which at the cold-weather level stand up like ten- or twelve-foot cliffs on that side to which the main current was setting in the previous flood season) and thus consist of the composite deposits of perhaps several centuries together. Such silt is liable to be a mixture of large, medium and minute particles. If the large predominate to a considerable depth, the inference would be that the material (representing 'early' deposition) was built up close to a reach of the river in which it has maintained a virtually unchanged course over a long period.

Reverting to the occurrence of silt high up among the ruins of Mohenjo-daro, one must of course agree with Mr. Raikes that this can hardly have been deposited by direct river flood. Again, one recognizes the definite evidence at Mohenjo-daro of periodical rebuilding over former building levels, and may agree that it is reasonable to infer that there were intervals of time in which the city was deserted and to some extent deteriorated. Mr. Raikes and Dr. Dales assume that these intervals were of the order of a century in length and that during them the city was almost entirely submerged, the strata of natural deposits in the ruins representing siltation by Indus water after it had come to a virtual standstill in their postulated lake. But is it necessary to deduce, from the available data, lacustrine deposition, with all the remarkable implications of that hypothesis?

It is necessary to quote Mr. Raikes's ideas on these processes. He says, 'When siltation was nearly completed there would have been an enormous terrace area extending upstream from the uplift zone'; and again, 'Mohenjo-daro and inevitably all other sites in the same general area of the Indus flood-plain were gradually engulfed by mud' (Raikes, 1965, pp. 200, 202). If by this he means that the silted bottom of his lake would have been raised practically parallel with, and eventually not far below, the surface of the water, it must be pointed out that the main theatre of siltation would be over that area in which the inflow of silt-bearing Indus water was slowed up by the resistance of the water already impounded in the lake. The zone of considerable deposit would thus move progressively backward up the 'valley' *pari passu* with the extension thither of the surface of the lake. Therefore the natural progress of sedimentation within the lake would seem to be, not parallel with the rising surface of its water, but more or less even along its bottom, and thickest along the submerged former course of the river.

How, then, could the siltation of the uplift-dam have reached as high a level as Mr. Raikes requires? Why should the rising water bring any silt to seal the upper part of the dam? It would already have shed its burden many miles up stream. If this reasoning is correct, and the dam remained (to quote Mr. Raikes) 'presenting to such water as was stored above the deposited sediments a very easy percolation passage', the Indus would surely have cut through it long before the surface of the impounded water had risen high enough to submerge Mohenjo-daro. At the outset this obstacle was, *ex hypothesi,* of readily permeable substance; it would in consequence have been unlikely to withstand in the first few years the enormous impact on a relatively narrow front of water arriving at the rate of five hundred thousand cubic feet per second in the flood season. The Allahbund—the swell of ground raised by the earthquake of 1819—was breached by a mere flood of spill water coming down the Nara in 1826; perhaps the first such flood to arrive since the 'bund' was raised. Next year Alexander Burnes describes it, 'composed of soft clay and covered all over with shells, and has quite the appearance of having been broken through by some torrent' (Burnes, 1827, 1834).

If the argument is valid, that the face of Mr. Raikes's dam could not have been sealed up to the required hundred-foot level (and more) by lacustrine sedimentation, it follows that the silt observed high up in Mohenjo-daro could not have been deposited by such a process. If, however, the argument be deemed erroneous, and the proposition of a dam sealed by siltation up to the requisite height is acceptable, we are faced by another problem. The greater the degree of impermeability postulated (and it would have to be impermeable over the whole face of the dam—thirty miles at least, and perhaps very much more) the less likely that all traces of this barrier would have disappeared. The conception of multiple cutting down, etc., is unrealistic. We know only too well by practical experience[2] that, though a "bund" may be overtopped or breached in several places by an abnormal food, the main exit soon locates itself in one of these, resulting in very deep scour through a single breach. And by experience also we know that the substance which would presumably have been the sealing agent for the face of the hypothetical dam, namely the finest colloidal clay such as was at one time deposited by the Indus in an area of slack water in the original canal approach-channel at Sukkur, is particularly resistant to erosion or scouring.[3] At least the butt-ends of such a dam, resting against e.g. the northern end of the Lakhi range and the edge of the Registan beyond Kot Lalu, ought to be visible. What is there at all remarkable at these places? The great fracture in the Lakhi range near Bhagotoro is held to have been caused by the earthquake of 1819 (Blanford, 1880). The other local faulting has the same north-south strike as all faulting in the Sind Kohistan. There is the mass of calcareous tufa deposited by the Lakhi sulphur spring, and some isolated sand-hills on the plain towards Kot Lalu. None of these, surely, can be accepted as evidence of existence of the great dam. The geological processes which have affected Makran and Las Bela are irrelevant to the Lower Indus plain; better guidance might be provided by the effects of the Bihar earthquake of 1934 in the Lower Ganges plain (*Rec. geol. Surv. India,* 1934). But we require *local* data.

Take next the period or periods of rejuvenation of the flood-plain by the Indus after overcoming the barrier. Mr. Raikes says, "This, starting with a system of dendritic gullies, would have reached *fairly quickly* [my italics: H.T.L.] the present regime along the main stem of the system'. This conception seems to be far too facile. Moreover it is not a question only of what went on along 'the main stem of the system'. What was the effect on the flood-plain far away on either side, above the position of the barrier? How was Mr. Raikes's enormous terrace area' removed? If the silt deposits at Mohenjo-daro 29 feet above the existing plain are the vestiges of its flat surface, his terrace must subsequently have been cut right down to the previous bottom of his lake; for the existing flood-plain, to a depth of over twenty feet, has been built up by ordinary alluvial aggradation since the epoch of Mohenjo-daro. Surely other portions of such a terrace ought to be visible, especially along its western side—if it ever existed.

As to the actual profile of the whole flood-plain of Sind, as recently ascertained, it is difficult to see how this could have been produced except by several thousand years' unimpeded alluvial action of the Indus in natural conditions, i.e., with its characteristic changes of course. The mean axial slope of this plain from Sukkur to sea level is roughly 1 in 8200. The bed gradient of the river is flatter, about 1 in 10500, or six inches' fall per mile. The configuration of the contours indicates that this regime is of very long standing. According to Mr. Raikes's diagram included in his article (Raikes, 1965, p. 198), the slope of the existing flood-plain is 1 in 7000. On what basis is this calculated? As to the slope he deduces and extrapolates for the 'pre-Harappan flood-plain'—1 in 3500— it is extremely difficult to imagine the Indus accommodating itself to such a relatively steep slope. If the composition of the alluvium was similar to that of today, the river's oscillations in the effort to maintain the regime-slope of 1 in 10,500 would have been catastrophic.

The reasons why Mr. Raikes suggests such a slope are evident from his diagram. First, he believes the pre-Harappan mouth of the Indus to have been at or not far below Amri; and secondly, he assumes the river to have flowed in Harappan times, as now, through the 'gorge' at Sukkur ('bed-rock control'). Taking up the latter point first— what grounds are there for such an assumption?

The general configuration of the contours considered in relation to the marked kink in the axis of the river at this point suggests that the event reflected by that kink—the capture of the Indus by the Sukkur gorge—was of relatively recent occurrence. This conclusion is reinforced by the clear indications a few miles north-west and south-west of Sukkur of a former bed crossed by the present one. Apart from this, not one of the geographies, chronicles or histories dealing with the country makes mention of this passage of the Indus through a rocky gorge earlier than the thirteenth century A.D.

As to the idea of the sea extending nearly up to Amri shortly before Harappan times: the plain opposite this place is now about ninety feet above sea level. If we allow seven inches per century as the average rate of aggradation of the Indus flood-plain and delta (Inglis, 1949, p. 172), and refrain from mixing in such a conjectural factor as some difference between the levels of the sea in Harappan and modern times, we should expect the Harappan coastline of c. 3000 B.C. to approximate to the modern 30-foot contour. That contour lies on the average about sixty miles inland from the sea (corresponding with the river's regime slope of six inches per mile), and not far short of one hundred miles below Amri, measured axially along the plain. But if we postulate a considerably higher sea level in Harappan times so as to extend up to Amri, how are we to explain the presence of the pre-Harappan 'Amri' people on the site of Tharro Gujo? The plain adjoining this place is about twenty feet above the existing sea level, and the rocky 'inhabited' area only some twenty-five or thirty feet higher—roughly the same elevation as the prehistoric site of Garho Bhiro near Nohto, over one hundred miles to the eastward. The plain opposite Amri stands now at double the height of these places (Cousens, p. 46; Majumdar, pp. 20-21; *J. Sind hist. Soc.* 8 (1946) 60 for Nohto).

I have entered into these peripheral matters because they provide additional tests of the validity of the main theory. Mr. Raikes claims that it is 'a geologically plausible and hydrologically acceptable interpretation of the flood evidence . . . that fits the known archaeological facts'. This begs the question whether the observed data really amount to 'flood evidence'. But if they are susceptible of a different interpretation it may appear that there is no evidence of flooding beyond that which can be interpreted as the effects of ordinary river-flood; in which case the whole theory must be rejected.

It is incumbent on the critic who views the matter in this light to propound his own interpretation of the data. Accepting that natural Indus silt of some kind is present in the ruins of Mohenjo-daro at various heights up to twenty-nine feet above the existing flood-plain, how did it get there?

The site of Mohenjo-daro, before any excavation had been undertaken, consisted of several large mounds of grey-white earth, with a pinkish tinge from the burnt brick-bats scattered over them or protruding from the surface, among occasional bushes and shrubs (Marshall, pl. 3, opp. p. 10). In other words, it looked just like dozens of other old sites in Sind though on a larger scale than most of them. How were these masses of grey-white earth piled up over ruins of man's habitation and handiwork in the plains of Sind—prehistoric like Chanhudaro; Buddhist like Kahujo-daro near Mirpur Khas; medieval like Tharri Mohbat? (Majumdar, 1934, pl. IVb, opp. p. 26; Cousens, 1929, pl. XXII, Fig. 1; *J. Sind hist. Soc.*, 8 (1946) p. 62). After allowing a proportion to be the debris of disintegrated mud walls, etc., a vast quantity from some other source must have contributed to produce the characteristic configuration of these mounds. If we ascribe it to lacustrine flood-sedimentation, we have to postulate individual uplift mechanisms at work virtually everywhere in Sind; and are next obliged to ask ourselves, were the similar mounds over ruined habitation sites in Bahawalput and the south-west Punjab the result of yet other lakes, and further spheres of tectonic uplift? And we must not forget that Dr. Sahni requires uplift of this kind down stream from Budh-jo-Takar, to produce the phenomena at that place.

Clearly, some other influence must have been at work; and the obvious one is the wind, periodically whipping sand, silt and dust off the surface of the grey-white alluvial plain, and depositing it in every hollow or interstice among the ruins. Over the centuries rainfall, with further disintegration of the mud buildings, consolidates the mound into the form which is such a familiar feature in the Indus plain. The important fact must be borne in mind that wind-borne silt naturally tends to be composed of the lighter grains; and when these are consolidated by rain, the texture of the resulting 'silty clay' (or ? 'clayey silt') is liable to resemble very closely the substance resulting from deposition in a lake or by a very slow-moving river flood.

Or take the detached sand-hills standing on the flood-plain of the Indus; those, for instance, about the latitude of the hypothetical barrier. These surely are accumulations of wind-borne silt from the banks and islands of the river exposed at its cold-weather level. Many a village in Sind has been obliterated, in modern times, by air-borne river silt.[4]

In the light of such general observations and of the data which Messrs. Raikes and Dales give us in regard to the silty deposits high up in the ruins of Mohenjo-daro, it is suggested that these may be due to:

(1) Disintegration of sun-dried brick-work, solid mud plinths, etc., which we know existed among the burnt brick buildings. A certain amount of subsidence of structures of all kinds around the outskirts of the city is likely to have occurred in seasons when a particularly copious inundation temporarily insulated the city; and such movements, with seepage, would tend to affect the stability of buildings further inward.

(2) Consolidation under rain, and pressure by subsequent buildings, of windborne silt which, if the climate of Sind in the days of Mohenjo-daro was anything like that of

which we had (unpleasant) experience,[5] would have been blown all over the city periodically. Let it be remembered that the burnt bricks, the sun-dried bricks, the man-made consolidated mud fillings, the clay, the 'natural' silt whether river-borne, lacustrine or air-borne, the sand-hills—all this material in the plains of Sind was *originally* water-borne, the offspring of the Indus, deposited somewhere. When the mud bricks were disintegrated and the wind-borne silt consolidated, by what criteria could they be distinguished with certainty?

It may fairly be asked, why then did the Mohenjo-daro people allow their city to be cluttered up with wind-blown silt? And what induced them to undertake all this periodical rebuilding, so that the place was raised higher and higher, the top-most structures eventually reaching a level sixty or seventy feet above the then existing flood-plain? It is thought that the city existed, from the first Harappan settlement till its abandonment, for less rather than more than 1000 years. The aggradation seems out of all proportion, even allowing for the recurring subsidence of peripheral buildings whenever the city was insulated by heavy seasonal overspill. Moreover, in view of the drainage system, and ancillary municipal scavenging, the general rise cannot have been due, as at Ur, primarily to constant raising of the street levels. Nor can the mere passage of this span of time account for deterioration of the buildings on successive levels at intervals which, when fitted into the total period, must seem short in comparison with the lasting quality of the burnt-brick masonry. Mr. Raikes and Dr. Dales ascribe the deterioration to long, and it seems recurring, periods of total immersion. This explanation seems untenable on other grounds. Is there an alternative?

The concept of Mohenjo-daro flourishing continuously for nearly a thousand years constitutes an exception to what we know to have occurred in every other old town on the Sind flood-plain. Clearly the site must originally have had great natural advantages; the Indus running on an apparently stable course within easy reach, and in the annual inundation fertilizing the adjoining plains with copious overspill, but not tormenting them or invading the city with deep, swift and destructive floods. The wonder would be if such conditions remained constant. It is safe to assume that they did not so remain; that the Indus, though not changing course violently during this long period, did occasionally deny to the vicinity of the city the overspill on which its agriculture mainly depended. We know by experience (in pre-Barrage days) what problems a short-fall in the *abkalani*[6] used to cause, locally if not generally. There are virtually certain to have been many lean years among those thousand. It was for such years that the great granary was provided; but how were the people to obtain subsistence if there were several successive absences of serviceable inundation locally—perhaps for a whole decade? The Indus in natural conditions usually provided overspill *somewhere* along its lower course, and on such occasions the recourse of these thousands of citizens would have been to evacuate Mohenjo-daro temporarily and set up camps in the nearest quarter where favourable conditions for cultivation still obtained. But understanding, as they may be presumed to have understood, the idiosyncrasies of their river, they would be slow to give up hope of a recurrence of favourable conditions near the city. Unless there had been a major change of course, the prospect remained that the Indus would once more show itself benign; and when this occurred they would return to recolonize the city. What, then, were they likely to find? That in their absence silt and sand had blown all over Mohenjo-daro, and was now piled up in houses and streets; that there had been looting and damage done in the deserted city by the subject races of the Indus Empire.[7] Roofs and doors had been carried off, drains had become choked, and rain-water had seeped in where it should not, shrubs seeded from the jungle tracts had begun to grow up in odd corners; hyenas and other animals had been digging and rooting and fouling the place. It was in a sorry state. A large measure of rebuilding would be necessary; so labour is conscripted on a grand scale; masses of mud and mud-brick infilling are introduced and the banked up accumulations of silt smoothed down, to provide a new level. New houses rise on the stubs of former walls, additional courses of brick-work bring the half-buried well-heads up to the new height required, and soon the city's life is back in its old routine. Interruptions of this kind, shorter or longer in duration, may have occurred many times during the span of Mohenjo-daro's existence. So long as the Indus maintained its stable course a few miles away, the original advantageous conditions of the site could be expected to be reproduced, and to last much longer than the interruptions.

Compare with this picture that implicit in the theory of Mr. Raikes and Dr. Dales. Mohenjo-daro has been surrounded by a vast lake, submerged, and finally engulfed in mud—a process lasting at least a century. At an early (?) stage the inhabitants evacuate the city, and live for several generations elsewhere. Eventually Mr. Raikes's 'enormous terrace area . . . marshy during the annual flood' is somehow transformed back to the ante-diluvian conditions; and the descendants of the flood-refugees return and reoccupy the mud-sodden site. Why? Attracted by what advantages as a place of residence? What could possibly have induced them to act so on a *single* occasion, let alone several times— five according to Dr. Dales! (Dales, 1966, p. 98). Such a concept implies that the people of Mohenjo-daro, pioneers of civilization, were totally lacking in commonsense.

At this point I may outline my own theory of the cause of the *final* ruin and extinction of Mohenjo-daro.[8] I conceive that an avulsion and major change of course by the Indus took place considerably up-stream of the city. The new bed being (*ex hypothesi*) lower than the old one and, say, thirty miles away to the eastward, close to the western flank of the Khairpur hills, inundation spill thereafter did not approach within twenty miles of Mohenjo-daro, and the surrounding country, starved of water, immediately began to deteriorate. This theory is not susceptible of proof. But there is strong circumstantial evidence in its favour:—

(1) A drastic change of course had become *prima facie* probable from the very fact of the Indus maintaining the same general course past Mohenjo-daro for 900 years or so, with the consequent build-up of its bed.[9]

(2) There is a historical instance, recorded by the geographer Strabo, of this actually occurring in part of the plain dependent on the Indus. That acute observer, Aristobulus, came in 326 B.C. upon a tract which had recently been reduced to ruin in this manner. He explains exactly what the Indus did and what the results were. (see Strabo, XV, i, 19).

It has already been mentioned that the general theory under examination was first adumbrated by Dr. M. R. Sahni. The data from which he deduced a flood of 'unprecedented magnitude' occurred in a four-foot thickness of 'bedded . . . though more or less unconsolidated' alluvium resting on the surface of the rocky hillock of Budh-jo-Takar in Lower Sind, many feet above the bed of the Indus which runs nearby. This alluvium contained the shells of freshwater mollusca. Its thickness suggested to Dr. Sahni that the flooding by which it had been deposited must have been prolonged, and this in turn led him to suppose that such conditions could only have been produced by uplift down stream, due to earth movements.

By a curious chance I happened to examine the hillocks of Budh-jo-Takar in December 1941, a few months after Dr. Sahni's visit, of which I was unaware. My object was archaeological.[10]

There are two distinct hills at this place. On the conical one nearest to the Indus no ancient man-made objects were observed. The other hill is oblong in shape with a flat top, and on the summit, at the end furthest from the river, a patch of earth occurs, where I noticed a number of chert flakes and some painted pottery. Close by there is a regular mound of earth, like a tumulus, with what is evidently a Muslim grave on top. Immediately below, but not apparently an integral part of the tomb, several courses of burnt brickwork like a quadrate plinth were traced; the bricks thin but measuring at least a foot square superficially. Adjoining the mound on the west was a large excavation revealing a depth of earth at this point, on the surface of the hill, of about four feet, and exposing a certain amount of pottery.[11]

One of the photographs I took at the time of my visit is here reproduced, with its original caption. The view of the earth-face looks as if it was taken from the right of, and nearly at right-angles to, the view appearing as Fig. A. in the plate accompanying Dr. Sahni's article (Sahni, 1956, pl. 14, opp. p. 106). If this 'excavation' was identical with the four-foot depth of earth examined by Dr. Sahni (1956), I have to confess that I did not notice the snail shells he reports. But what I saw suggested to me that here, both in the tumulus and in the thick mass of 'excavated' earth below it, was the debris of man-made mud-brick buildings, very probably Buddhist, perhaps a *stupa,* the disintegration of which over twelve or more centuries might have been assisted by the iconoclastic zeal of Muslims, one of whom had elected, as in instances elsewhere in Sind, to be buried on top of the ruins of this 'infidel' structure.[12]

As for the presence of snail shells: shells of small mollusca are to be seen resting upon or embedded in Indus alluvium all over the Sind flood-plain; indeed their occurrence is so commonplace that one hardly notices them. Since river snails exist in the Indus, some are bound to be deposited on the plain by its overspill. And if present in the natural alluvium they are liable to be dug up with it, especially by the Odhs wielding their large *khodars* to hack out building material for mud walls and sun-dried bricks. Snail shells are often to be seen embedded in walls made of these materials.

Thus there are strong grounds for doubting whether the earth on this particular hill represents a natural deposit of alluvium; and before we can accept that explanation of its presence, we should wish to have supporting evidence of similar strata of silt at corresponding levels on other hills in the neighbourhood. It would be strange if the postulated exceptionally high flood left such traces in only one place.[13] Similarly the absence of reports of deposits of 'silty clay' in other places within the perimeter of Mr. Raikes's lake, at levels corresponding with the 29-foot mark at Mohenjo-daro, must be deemed significant.

The great tectonic uplift-lake-submergence theory of the causes of Mohenjo-daro's decline and fall, thus subjected to critical examination, would appear to rest on entirely inadequate evidence. Meanwhile its promoters and supporters claim, not only that it is 'both hydrologically and archaeologically acceptable' but, in so many words, that further researches should be based on it. It is to be hoped that the opposing views, and the grounds on which they are held, presented here *faute de mieux* by a non-scientist, may demonstrate the need for greater objectivity in the search for data and for fresh thinking on what is admittedly a complex and obscure subject.

Notes

[1] It is convenient to speak of the 'valley of the Indus', but one should bear in mind that in Sind this 'valley', viewed transversely, is convex instead of concave, so that longitudinally the lowest lines run along the extremities of the flood-plain on either hand, not down its middle.

[2] The writer was actively engaged in measures to avert as far as feasible damage in Upper Sind by the great Indus floods of 1929 and 1930 (before the Sukkur Barrage was in operation), and also witnessed the devastation caused by that of 1942.

[3] Information from Mr. S. B. Hickin, Executive Engineer, Barrage Division, 1937-1943.

[4] There is an example near Sheikh Bhirkio, about twenty miles south east of Hyderabad. This is close to the well-marked former bed of the Indus—'Phitto'— that runs from a little north of Matiari past Nasarpur and Khesano. Great masses of river silt are piled to a considerable height along this bed as the effect of the strong seasonal wind.

[5] The reference is to the *chaliho,* the forty trying days in May-June; and again to the shorter but very violent dust storms which often usher in a little rainfall later in the hot weather.

[6] The 183-day period which includes the main annual inundation.

[7] I conceive these people—semi-nomadic herdsmen, fishermen and fowlers—to have formed the bulk of the population of the plain, living in brushwood huts or *pish*-mat shelters.

[8] It was developed in more detail in my *Sind: a general introduction* (Lambrick, 1964), see pp. 81, 84-5, 104.

[9] For this characteristic of alluvial rivers, and particularly the Indus, see Sir Claude Inglis 1949, part I, p. 204).

[10] Viz., to resolve the contradiction between the reports of Mr. G. E. L. Carter and Mr. N. G. Majumdar on this place; the former having mentioned finding flints 'upon two tumuli of brick debris which look like the remains of Buddhist buildings, possibly stupas', while Majumdar declared that nothing of the kind had come to his notice on a visit some years later. In explanation of Majumdar's negative report: his published account mentions his difficulty in crossing the river to Budh-jo-Takar with the evening drawing on. He must have given up his inspection before reaching the eastern end of the summit of the further hill.

[11] My account of this examination of Budh-jo-Takar was included in a paper read to the Sind Historical Society on 27 Aug. 1942, which was published in the Society's *Journal* in Oct. of that year. J. Sind hist. Soc. 6 (1942) 110-112.

[12] The concluding paragraph of my article reads, 'Mr. Manoo Gidwani, in the last number of this Journal, mentions the legendary association of Budh-jo-Takar with Sultan Bul Bul. May we assume that the tomb on the mound, which is of heroic dimensions, is the Sultan's last resting place?''

[13] Dr. Sahni alludes to Jhirrak in his account, but no specific data appear to have been noticed there. Indeed it is far from clear which data were observed by him and which by Mr. Nagappa, or what was the exact location of any of them.

References

Blanford, W. T. 1800. The geology of western Sind. *Mem. geol. Surv. India* 17: 126, note 1.

Burnes, A. 1827. 'Memoir of a map of the eastern branch of the Indus', para. 17 (Bombay Government File 763 of 1828) Cf. *Travels into Bokhara, etc.* (1834) John Murray. Vol. 2, pp. 315-6.

Cousens, H. 1929. *Antiquities of Sind.* Archaeological Survey of India, Vol. 46.

Dales, G. F. 1962. Harappan outposts on the Makran coast. *Antiquity* 36:86 *et seq.*

———— 1966. The decline of the Harappans. *Sci. Amer.* 214, 5:93-100.

Inglis, Sir Claude 1949. *The behaviour and control of rivers and canals.* Government of India Research Publication no. 13, Poona.

J. Sind hist. Soc., 6 (1942) 104-112; 8 (1946) 60 (for Nohto).

Lambrick, H. T. 1964. *Sind: a general introduction.* Vol. I of the History of Sind series, published by the Sindi Adabi Board (distributed in U.K. by Oxford University Press).

Majumdar, N. G. 1934. *Explorations in Sind.* Memoirs of the Archaeological Survey of India, no. 48.

Marshall, Sir John 1931. *Mohenjo-daro and the Indus civilization.* Vol. 1.

Raikes, R. L. 1964. The end of the ancient cities of the Indus. *Amer. Anthropol.* 66: 284-9.

———— 1965. The Mohenjo-daro floods. *Antiquity* 39:196-203.

Rec. geol. Surv. India 68:2 (1934) 177-239.

Sahni, M. R. 1952. *Man in Evolution.* Orient Longmans.

———— 1956. In *J. palaeontol. Soc. India* 1, 1: 101 *et seq.*

Strabo, *Geographia,* XV, 1, 19.

Gurdip Singh is at the Australian National University in the Research
School of Pacific Studies, department of biogeography and geomorphology.
This important paper, based on his original research in Rajasthan, India,
presents the first evidence suggesting environmental changes coincident
with the rise and fall of the Indus civilization—thus providing a wholly
new perspective from that of the Allchins and Lambrick.

The Indus Valley Culture

Gurdip Singh

The Indus Valley culture, or the Harappa culture as it is called from the name of the
village occupying the site of its northern capital, on the river Ravi in West Pakistan, is
known to the world as the largest of its three most ancient civilizations (Wheeler, 1953).
The known remains of this culture, with all its ramifications, occupy a broad triangular
area in north-west India and West Pakistan, extending from the foot of the Himalayas to
the Makran Coast, Gujarat, Bahawalpur and north-western Rajasthan, measuring nearly
1,000 miles from Sutkāgen Dor near the coast 300 miles west of Karachi to Rupar at the
foot of Siwaliks in the extreme north-east. Further explorations have now pushed the
limits of this culture from Cambay in the south to the Jumna Basin, about 30 miles
north of Delhi. The Harappa culture is essentially a riverine culture as the remains of
its towns and villages, with rare exceptions, occupy the banks of the present river
systems or former ones now occurring as dry river beds. The culture was initially considered to have extended over much of the third millennium B.C. up to the mid-second
millennium B.C., but in recent years it has been assigned a much more limited time
range, 2300-1750 B.C. (Agrawal et al., 1964), by means of close radiocarbon datings
from Kot Diji, Kalibangan and Lothal. The civilization itself is shown to have been based
on a secure foundation of an agricultural-cum-urban economy (cultivating wheat, barley,
cotton, field-peas, melon, sesame and dates), but the conditions leading to the immediate
development of such an advanced economy have tended to remain obscure. It has often
been assumed that a civilization such as that of the Indus cannot be visualized as a slow
and patient growth (Wheeler, 1966, p. 61), an assumption which has been accepted
generally in view of the sudden appearance of the culture in an accomplished form all
over north-west India.

It is known for certain that the practice of cereal farming was in force in the "fertile
crescent" in the Near East several millennia before the advent of the Indus culture, and
that two great riverine civilizations had started ahead of it in Mesopotamia and in Egypt.

Reprinted from *Archaeology and Physical Anthroplogy in Oceania,* Vol. VI, No. 2 pp. 177-188 (1971),
by permission of Professor A. P. Elkin, editor, and of the author.

But, strangely enough, there is no physical evidence to base any direct derivation of the Harappan culture from either of these civilizations. The arts, crafts and the characteristic Harappan technology, manifested in the most highly individualized form of script, stand out clearly from any other known culture, either preceding or following this period. While the origin of the Indus culture is still shrouded in mystery, the mode and the prime causes leading to its sudden decline are still less understood.

One of the most debated of the issues concerning the Indus people in recent years has been regarding the postulated occurrence of higher rainfall conditions during the period they are known to have flourished in north-west India. Ever since Stein (1931), on the basis of the occurrence of "gabar bands" (dam-like structures constructed artificially by prehistoric man), suggested the possibility of a significant decline in rainfall of Baluchistan since prehistoric times resulting from climatic change, other authors have produced additional evidence, in one form or another, to support the hypothesis (Marshall, 1931; Vats, 1940; Wheeler, 1953, 1966, 1968; Chowdhury and Ghosh, 1951). Deductions on the nature of climate during Harappan times have so far, however, rested on indirect evidence provided by human artifacts, such as sculptures, drawings and engravings of animals and plants on potsherds and steatite seals, burnt bricks, animal bones, wood and charcoal remains, flooding horizons and the occurrence of "gabar bands". In recent years, the testimony to higher rainfall argued for each of these lines of evidence has been questioned by some authors (Raikes, 1964, 1965a, 1965b; Raikes and Dyson, 1961; Dales, 1966).Without going into details either for or against the issue at this stage, it may suffice to say that sufficient weight had been attached to the counter-arguments for Dales (1966, p. 131) to say: "Convincing evidence, collected from both archaeological and natural science investigations, refutes the popular theories of appreciable climatic change in the South Asian area during the past four to five thousand years (Raikes, 1965a; Raikes and Dyson, 1961). Climate has thus been practically eliminated as a major factor in the environmental fortunes of the Harappan civilization."

The interests of the present author, who is primarily a plant palaeoecologist, do not rest directly in the line of archaeology. Recently, however, a series of new evidences has emerged from pollen-analytical studies of salt-lake deposits carried out by the author in an area centring on the Rajasthan desert in north-west India, which reflects closely on the nature of climate of the period of the Indus Valley culture and has largely prompted the present contribution (Singh, 1970).Besides the post-glacial climatic sequence, the studies have also brought out evidence suggesting the possibility of early primitive agriculture in north-west India, antedating the Harappan culture by about five thousand years.

The present contribution is an attempt to open the question of the nature of climate governing the Indus culture once again and to consider the rise and fall of this culture in a palaeoecological context, with special reference to the possibility of a gradual evolution of the art of agriculture in north-west India since early post-glacial times.

The Area Investigated

The area covered by the present investigations is broadly comprised of the State of Rajasthan (20° 3′ N.–30° 12′ N. latitudes and 69° 30′ E.–78° 17′ E. longitudes), and some bordering areas in the adjoining States of the Punjab, Haryana and western Uttar

Pradesh, in north-west India. The investigations comprising studies on the late-Quaternary
history were confined to the Rajasthan territory, whereas the work on surface samples
for determining basic criteria for the interpretation of pollen diagrams was extended to
the other provinces.

(1) Physiography

The territory is broadly subdivided into two geographical units by the Aravalli Range,
which runs in a north-east—south-west direction. The eastern half, which constitutes the
northern part of the Central Highlands, is endowed with comparatively higher rainfall, and
its south-eastern parts conform very closely to the pattern of tropical humidity found
in central India. The western half, also called the Western Sandy Plains (Misra, 1967), on
the other hand, is a part of the Great Indian Desert, most of the western part of which
is now in Pakistan. The part included in the State of Rajasthan is mostly an arid, sterile
and sandy desert in the west which grades into a semi-arid steppe in the neighbourhood of
the Aravalli Range. The only river of any consequence in this region is the Luni, which rises
in the hills near Ajmer and flows west by south-west into the Rann of Kutch. The Ghaggar
(Saraswati of Vedic times) once flowed through the northern part of Rajasthan and is said
to have joined the river Indus, but now it is dry except during the rainy season, when its
water loses itself in sand a mile or two west of the town of Sadulgarh.

(2) Climate

The area is characterized by a progressive fall in the mean annual rainfall towards its
core, centring on the Thar desert, with less than 10 cm. average annual rainfall. One
witnesses the occurrence of more or less eccentrically placed zones of increasing rainfall
round the central core which, proceeding outwards, are here described as Arid (10-25 cm.
average annual rainfall), Semi-Arid (25-50 cm.), Semi-Humid (50-60 cm.) and Humid
(60-100 cm.). The climate of north-west India as a whole is divisible into four seasons:
winter (cool and dry), spring or pre-monsoon (hot and dry), summer or monsoon (hot and
wet) and autumn or post-monsoon (warm and dry). Geographically, the area is situated in
the normal latitudes of sub-tropical anticyclones in winter and the deserts associated with
them. In general terms, the aridity in the core area may be ascribed to the rather sharp
north-westward boundary to the moist current of the monsoon, as the area lies a little
too far west of the main monsoonal upper air flow to receive such monsoonal rainfall,
save in exceptional years. The air circulation in winter is marked by subsiding, low-level
anticyclonic flow (Raman and Dixit, 1964; Frost and Stephanson, 1964). On the far
north-west, however, the winds are of continental origin and come from the north-west.
The winter rainfall resulting from western disturbances is mainly confined to the area
north and north-west of Delhi and tends to decrease progressively towards the Thar
desert. The Aravalli Range acts as a great divide between the western and eastern climatic
provinces of north-west India. The province to the west of the Aravallis is characterized
by extremes of temperature, severe drought, high velocity winds and low relative humidity.
The region east and south of the Aravallis shows considerable variation in the amount of
rainfall and temperature distribution even though, as a whole, the area is denoted by
strong periodical rains and more or less uniform temperatures.

(3) Vegetation

It is beyond the scope of this paper to give a detailed background of the vegetation of the area but it is necessary to point out some of the critical aspects of the distribution of plant life which have allowed the use of the past distribution of certain individualized plant species as climatic indicators for the present investigations.

As is true of most other natural phenomena, the vegetation of the area is greatly influenced by the placement of the Aravalli Range, which divides the plant life into two unequal parts: a smaller one (generally mesophytic) east of the Aravallis, and the larger (mostly xerophytic) to their west (King, 1879). The vegetation of the dividing range itself can be considered to resemble much more the eastern than the western tract. In general terms, three distinct elements can be distinguished: a Western (Perso-Arabian) west of the Aravallis, an Eastern (Indo-Malayan) east of them, and a more general element (including Indian species also) in the Aravallis themselves (Biswas and Rao, 1953). The line dividing the two major phytogeographical units, the Perso-Arabian and the Indo-Malayan, passes along the Aravalli Range from the gulf of Cambay in the south-west to Delhi in the north-east (Drude, 1890). In addition to the placement of the mountain barrier, this line is also determined approximately by the 50 cm. isohyet line within the State of Rajasthan. In view of the critical nature of the above boundary, any recognizable shift observed in the past vegetation, *vis-a-vis* the two floras, becomes diagnostic of a change of climate in the distant past. The selection of the sites investigated is clearly motivated by the above considerations.

(4) Sites Examined

Pollen-analytical studies were carried out on three salt lakes in western Rajasthan, at Sambhar, Didwana and Lunkaransar, and one freshwater lake in eastern Rajasthan, at Pushkar in the Aravallis. Both the lakes at Sambhar (27° N. 75° E.) and Didwana (27° 20′ N. 74° 35′ E.) lie in the Semi-Arid belt (25-30 cm. average annual rainfall), while the lakes at Lunkaransar (28° 30′ N. 73° 45′ E.) and Pushkar (26° 29′ N. 74° 33′ E.) are respectively in the Arid (less than 25 cm. rainfall) and the Semi-Humid (50-60 cm. rainfall) belts. Of the four lake-site investigations the evidence from Pushkar, which refers mainly to the post-Harappan period, is not considered in the present paper. Soil samples from pre-Harappan levels at Kalibangan, the only Indus Valley site excavated in Rajasthan, were examined for pollen-analysis. A brief summary of the palaeoecological results from one of the salt lakes, namely Sambhar, has already been published (Singh, 1967).

Stratigraphical, Palaeoecological, and Cultural Considerations

The known time range of the Indus culture, which is about five hundred years, is only a small fraction of the Holocene period. While it would be quite futile to dwell in detail on the findings pertaining to the entire post-glacial period, it is necessary to have a long-range perspective of the climatic sequence for a consideration of the development of the late-Holocene cultures, including the Harappan culture, in their natural settings. It is therefore proposed to present an outline of post-glacial environmental history preceding the Indus Valley culture, together with some of the basic evidence, and to discuss the same in the light of the known cultural history.

The environmental sequence which is built up here from the vegetational history deduced from pollen analysis has been grouped into six phases, of which all but phase I belong to the Holocene period. Phase I, which is primarily inferred from the general stratigraphy of the salt-lake basins, is pre-Holocene. Phases III, IV and VI are further subdivided into subphases IIIa, IIIb, IVa, IVb, IVc, VIa and VIb, following the zonation of the pollen diagrams. The pollen record comes wholly from the Holocene, as fossil pollen is not preserved in the pre-Holocene sandy material. The post-glacial pollen sequences from the sites investigated are divisible into five zones termed A, B, C, D and E, of which zones B, C and E are subdivided into subzones B_1, B_2, C_1, C_2, C_3, E_1 and E_2. The original pollen diagrams, together with their detailed descriptions, will be published elsewhere. In the present discussion only phases I, II, III and a part of phase IV, which are relevant to the Indus Valley culture, are considered.

Phase I: Before 8000 B.C.

The evidence for phase I comes mainly from the stratigraphy of the salt-lake basins. The earliest lake sediments, which date from early Holocene times at all the sites, are underlain by a thick bed of loosely packed, wind-borne sand. In each case the sand bed is seen to extend horizontally to meet the sand dunes (which are now stabilized) encircling the individual salt-lake basins. This suggests that the basins were probably formed during pre-Holocene times by the damming of ancient valleys by wind-borne sand, at a time when the sand dunes were still active. While the beginning of this phase of severe, pre-Holocene aridity is uncertain, there is evidence that the phase ended with an increase in rainfall at about the beginning of the Holocene period. This is shown by two radiocarbon assays obtained separately from Sambhar (9250 ± 130 B.P., TF-887) and Lunkaransar (9260 ± 115 B.P., WIS-405), from levels about 30-40 cm. above the sand/clay boundaries at the two sites. From these results a date for the infilling of the lake basins can be extrapolated of around 10,000 B.P.

There is practically nothing known of the human cultures occupying north-west India during this phase. At present there appears to be a somewhat abrupt break between the largely Upper Pleistocene Middle Stone Age cultures and the exclusively post-glacial microlithic Late Stone Age cultures in north-west India. This is quite unlike the situation prevailing in southern India, where the change from Middle to Late Stone Age, that is to say from the flake to the microlithic tradition, appears to have been a process of continuous development rather than of sudden change (Allchin and Allchin, 1968, p. 78). Whether the hiatus between the Middle Stone Age and the Late Stone Age cultures in north-west India was in some manner influenced by the severe aridity prevailing during pre-Holocene times is not certain. From the present evidence it would, however, appear that the central core of north-west India was affected by severe aridity and that the territory would have been unsuitable for habitation for a long time during at least the later part of the last glacial.

Phase II: Pollen zone A: c. 8000 B.C.–c. 7500 B.C.

This phase starts with the first sedimentation of freshwater lacustrine deposits in the lake basins, a development that appears to have occurred at about the beginning of the Holocene period around 10,000 B.P. The lake sediments consist of laminated clays and contain a fair amount of fossil pollen at all the sites, thus allowing the reconstruction of the vegetational history of the post-glacial period.

The vegetation as deduced from the pollen record in phase II, represented by pollen zone A, is comprised of high values for sedges and grasses and low values for halophytes denoted by Chenopodiaceae/Amaranthaceae. *Artemisia,* which now grows abundantly under a higher rainfall régime (above 50 cm. average annual rainfall) mostly in the Himalayan foothill plains and which is at present rarely seen in the Rajasthan desert, appears to have flourished in large numbers during this phase in both the contemporary Arid and the Semi-Arid belts. Mesophytic plants such as *Mimosa rubicaulis* and *Oldenlandia,* which now grow mostly east of the Aravalli Range and upcountry in Punjab and Haryana, are indicated as having occupied the Semi-Arid belt in western Rajasthan. There is little desert vegetation represented in the Semi-Arid belt in this phase: small quantities of *Ephedra* pollen, which is notorious for being wind-transported over long distances (Maher, 1964), is, however, seen regularly; a few grains of *Maytenus,* a desert plant species, make their appearance in the later part of the sequence in this phase. As there is no further inter-calation of sand layers in the lake sediments, it is suggested that the sand dunes had started to stabilize. That the rainfall was considerably more than that of the present day, with freshwater conditions prevailing in the lake basins, is apparently testified by the presence, in both the Arid and the Semi-Arid belts, of *Typha angustata,* a freshwater aquatic species no longer seen in the Rajasthan desert beyond the 50 cm. isohyetal line. The present evidence would thus indicate that there was an excess of at least 25 cm. (10 in.) of precipitation over the present in the Arid belt in phase II.

Phase II corresponds in time to the pre-Boreal period in Europe, when temperatures are known to have started rising throughout the world, including north-west India, following the final recession of the last glacial (von Post, 1946; Godwin, 1956; Iversen, 1954; Singh, 1963). In the Rajasthan desert, as is seen above, the climatic change is suggested to have taken the form of an increase in rainfall.

The state of human cultures occupying the Rajasthan desert during this phase is largely a matter of conjecture, as work on Late Stone Age microlithic cultures in India is still in its infancy. Nevertheless, the climatic conditions of the Rajasthan area, as inferred above, appear to have been favourable enough to support freshwater bodies and perennial river courses, which in turn can be expected to have supported animal and human populations.

Phase III: Pollen zone B: c. 7500 B.C.–c. 3000 B.C.

The initial rise in precipitation in phase II appears to have given way to a slight lowering of rainfall around 7500 B.C., which was, however, not severe enough substantial-ly to alter the overall ecological patterns already established during the earlier phase. While the sedges decline, the halophytic vegetation, represented by Chenopodiaceae/Amaranthaceae, starts a gradual rise. Desert shrubs, such as *Maytenus* and *Capparis,* begin to occur more regularly in the Semi-Arid belt. The freshwater aquatic vegetation, consisting of *Typha angustata, T. latifolia* and *Potamogeton,* was apparently not affected, suggesting the continuation of freshwater environments in the lake basins. Mesophytic plant species, *Artemisia, Oldenlandia* and *Mimosa rubicaulis,* are also suggested to have continued flourishing in the Semi-Arid belt, and all except *Mimosa rubicaulis* occurred, to a lesser degree, in the Arid belt.

Phase III, which is represented by pollen zone B and ranges between *c.* 7500 B.C. and *c.* 3000 B.C., can be broadly equated chronologically with the combined Boreal and Atlantic periods of Europe (Godwin, 1960). Its lower limit is determined by two radiocarbon analyses mentioned earlier from Sambhar (9250 ± 130 B.P., TF-887) and Lunkaransar (9260 ± 115 B.P., WIS-405), dating the boundary between pollen zones A and B to about 7500 B.C. at both sites.

Early Agriculture. The late Stone Age microlithic culture (or cultures) which preceded the Neolithic-Chalcolithic cultures in north-west India and is most likely to have been dominant in the Rajasthan area, unfortunately remains undated for most of the part. At a few places where the remains of this culture have been found in stratigraphical context, it tends to overlap the known Neolithic-Chalcolithic cultures in its upper levels, whereas its early history remains almost unfathomed. The earliest radiocarbon dated horizons go back to approximately 5500 B.C., in the rock shelters excavated at Adamgarh hill in the Narbada valley (Allchin and Allchin, 1968). These sites, together with another microlithic site at Langhnaj, in Gujarat, show evidence of contemporaneity for a considerable period with Neolithic or later settlements in adjacent regions (Allchin and Allchin, *loc. cit.*). Speaking of Langhnaj, Joshi (1963, p. 3) remarks that "on the basis of this site, it may be said that this phase is characterized by communities which have a mixed economy and might be practising some sort of primitive agriculture along with hunting and fishing, domestication of animals to some extent, burying their dead and having a slightly more settled pattern of life than the wandering folks".

In the salt-lake profiles from western Rajasthan one witnesses an extraordinary rise in carbonized vegetable remains (mostly wood fragments) in the sediments at about the beginning of phase III (pollen zone B) at all the sites. The phenomenon cannot be explained in terms of natural causes as the enhanced rate of the occurrence is maintained in layer after layer of the lake sediment, starting with phase III. It can be strongly argued that the increase in the burnt remains resulted from the introduction of the practice of scrub burning at the hands of early man, for this alone can explain the synchronous rise in their occurrence in the lake profiles of sites separated by hundreds of kilometres. It is seen that the practice of scrub burning as attested by the above evidence remained at a high level in phases III and IV (pollen zones B and C) and then dwindled away in phases V and VI (pollen zones D and E). It is of considerable interest to note that Cerealia-type pollen (grass pollen more than 40μ; size range $40\text{-}50\mu$) also starts occurring in the lake sediments early in phase III (pollen zone B) and continues to appear intermittently throughout phases III and IV at all the sites in close harmony with the enhanced occurrence of carbonized remains. The evidence of scrub burning, together with the first occurrence of Cerealia-type pollen in the lake profiles, is dated at 9260 ± 115 B.P. (WIS-405) at Lunkaransar in the extreme west and 8300 ± 135 B.P. (TF-738) at Sambhar in the extreme east. The close correlation between the occurrence of Cerealia-type pollen on one hand and the evidence of scrub burning on the other raises the obvious question as to whether some sort of primitive cereal agriculture was introduced into the area as far back as 7500 B.C.

Before proceeding any further one may, however, ask whether the Cerealia-type of pollen seen in the salt-lake profiles from Rajasthan does in fact represent cereal pollen. In this regard studies of present-day pollen spectra from 114 samples coming from 64 different sites spread all over north-west India have demonstrated that cereal pollen, mainly because of its large size, is not carried a great distance from its mother source, so that the pollen type is not seen in areas which are free of cereal cultivation. Some wild grasses can indeed be expected to contribute large-sized pollen similar to the Cerealia-type, but the introduction of such wild grasses through purely natural means over an axis of 200 kilometres (separating Lunkaransar from Sambhar) during the same time interval at the beginning of phase III and in conjunction with the first introduction of scrub burning in the territory, seems rather far-fetched. On the other hand, it would appear from the evidence that man had already started interfering with the natural vegetation in western Rajasthan at the beginning of phase III and it is not unreasonable to believe, therefore, that the burning of scrub was probably involved in the practice of some form of primitive cereal agriculture, the like of which was still prevalent with several tribal communities until quite recently in Rajasthan. It goes without saying, however, that the present evidence suggesting an exceptionally early start for cereal agriculture in north-west India needs to be supported with material evidence from excavations at the numerous microlithic settlements found scattered all over the Rajasthan desert, and outside.

Phase IV: Pollen zone C: c. 3000 B.C.–c. 1000 B.C.

At the beginning of this phase, about 3000 B.C., the climate seems to have taken a sudden change to wetter conditions. The period of maximum wetness, however, appears to have lasted only up to about 1800 B.C. Thereafter, the climate shows a small-scale oscillation to drier conditions between c. 1800 B.C. and c. 1500 B.C., followed by a slight reversal to a relatively weak wetter interval, lasting up to about 1000 B.C. This period of change is considered as phase IV, which is subdivided into subphases IVa, IVb, and IVc, denoting the above threefold oscillation of climate during the mid-post-glacial. Of the three subphases, only subphases IVa and IVb are relevant to the present discussion.

(i) Subphase IVa: Pollen subzone C_1: c. 3000 B.C.–c. 1800 B.C. The beginning of subphase IVa, which is marked by the boundary between pollen zones B and C, is dated around 3000 B.C. from two radiocarbon analyses, 5060 ± 70 (WIS-387) and 5420 ± 70 (WIS-386), from above and below the zonal boundary respectively at Lunkaransar. At Sambhar the date for the same boundary is extrapolated to 3000 B.C. from two radio-carbon determinations, 4665 ± 115 and 4510 ± 110 (TF-739 and TF-883), from about the middle of subphase IVa (subzone C_1).

Palaeoecologically, the subphase starts with a sudden rise in the frequencies of sedges and those of three and shrub vegetation. The latter rise for the first time in the post-glacial sequence, at all the sites. The trees and shrubs mainly consist of *Syzigium cuminii, Mimosa rubicaulis, Acacia* sp., *Prosopis cineraria, Capparis* sp. and *Tamarix* sp. in the Semi-Arid belt, and of *Calligonum polygonoides, Zizyphus* sp., *Prosopis cineraria, Maytenus* sp. and *Syzigium cuminii* in the Arid belt. The sedges reach their maximum frequencies of more than 500% of all other land-plant pollen in the Semi-Arid belt and are almost as prominently represented in the Arid belt. The present evidence would indicate that *Syzigium cuminii*, a mesophytic tree now growing naturally in India in areas having in excess of 85 cm. (35 in.) average annual rainfall (Troup, 1921), enjoyed a luxuriant growth in the Semi-Arid belt and that it even penetrated the western extreme of Rajasthan, as far as Lunkaransar in the Arid belt. Similarly, *Mimosa rubicaulis,* a mesophytic shrub mentioned earlier in phases II and III, rises to its highest frequencies in the Semi-Arid belt in subphase IVa. *Typha angustata* continues to grow in both the Arid and the Semi-Arid belts as before. The above palaeoecological picture of subphase IVa goes to suggest that relative precipitation over the Rajasthan desert had risen considerably and that the annual average rainfall may have been in excess by at least 50 cm. (20 in.) of the present-day rainfall in the Arid belt. In the light of all this evidence the doubts expressed earlier with respect to a relatively higher rainfall in north-west India during Harappan times (Raikes, 1964, 1965*a*, 1965*b*; Raikes and Dyson, 1961; Dales, 1966) can perhaps now be set aside.

Pollen of Cerealia type, of the same size range as seen in the earlier phase, continues to be met with at all the sites in subphase IVa, without any recognizable hiatus. At the same time evidence for scrub burning in the form of carbonized remains also continues into this subphase.

(ii) Expansion of Neolithic-Chalcolithic Cultures. It is of profound interest to note that subphase IVa, in terms of chronology, sees the rise of the pre-Harappan and, later on, of the Harappan culture throughout north-west India. It is generally agreed that in the plains of Sind, the Punjab and northern Rajasthan, around the end of the fourth or the beginning of the third millennium B.C., the major expansion of the Neolithic-Chalcolithic way of life took place (Allchin and Allchin, 1968, p. 112). The earliest radiocarbon evidence so far available is the date of pre-Harappan settlement at Kot Diji, placed at 2605 $\pm$ 145 B.C. The testimony of Cerealia-type pollen for the existence of cereal agriculture in the latter half of subphase IVa cannot be doubted as the Harappan people are definitely known to have practised cereal cultivation. The question is, however, relevant when the pollen is encountered in earlier horizons.

Here it may be of interest to point out that Cerealia-type pollen of the same size range is encountered in good numbers (58% of total land-plant pollen) in the pre-Harappan levels of the Indus Valley site at Kalibangan, excavated by the Archaeological Survey of India. This, together with the unbroken record of Cerealia-type pollen in the pollen profiles and the evidence of forest burning from three different sites, would lead one to believe that the practice of cereal cultivation perhaps does not start with the Indus Valley culture after all but that the practice had existed in the region for a long time, indeed, as has been suggested, from the beginning of phase III. It can in fact be argued that the significant increase in rainfall at the beginning of the third millennium B.C., attested by the palaeoecological evidence, played an important part in the sudden expansion of the Neolithic-Chalcolithic cultures in north-west India, ultimately leading to the prosperity of the Indus culture.

(iii) Subphase IVb: Pollen subzone C_2: *c.* 1800 B.C.–*c.* 1500 B.C. The end of subphase IVa and the beginning of subphase IVb can be dated around 1800 B.C. by extrapolation from two radiocarbon determinations mentioned earlier (TF-739 and TF-883), from subphase IVa at Sambhar. For subphase IVb the palaeoecological evidence points to a short dry period. The sedges undergo a sudden decline. All the mesophytic plant species found in subphase IVa, such as *Syzigium cuminii, Mimosa rubicaulis* and the freshwater aquatic species, disappear for good from the pollen sequence. At Lunkaransar, in the Arid belt, the horizontal stratification of laminated clays breaks down and pollen is no longer preserved in the sediment, both factors indicating that the lake had started drying out.

In the Semi-Arid belt, with the disappearance of freshwater aquatic vegetation, it would appear that the lakes had started turning saline. Indeed there is some rise in the frequencies of halophytic plant species at Sambhar. All this goes to indicate that a dry period of some intensity had set in about 1800 B.C. It is a rare coincidence that the Harappan culture is known to have started declining around 1750 B.C. (Agrawal *et al.,* 1964). The archaeological evidence has been interpreted to suggest that the Harappan culture met with a sudden end. The same evidence, however, also indicates that a general decline had already set in much before the final blow (Wheeler, 1966, p. 75; 1968, p. 127), which some believe to have been struck by the Aryan invaders (Wheeler, *loc. cit.*; Allchin and Allchin, 1968, pp. 144-156). The present evidence would suggest that the onset of aridity in the region around 1800 B.C. probably resulted in the weakening of the Harappan culture in the arid and semi-arid parts of north-west India but that the peripheral areas of the culture, such as in Gujarat and the Himalayan foothills, were not affected to the same degree. The extinction of the Indus culture may have thus been initiated through gradual decline as a result of climatic change, but the process may yet have been completed by successive invasions from the north-west by the Aryans.

References

Agrawal, D. P., Kusumgar, S., and Sarna, R. P. 1964. "Radiocarbon Dates of Archaeological Samples", *Current Science,* Vol. 33 (9), p. 266.

Allchin, B., and Allchin, R. 1968. *The Birth of Indian Civilization,* Harmondsworth, Middlesex: Pelican Books.

Biswas, K., and Rao, S. 1953. "Rajputana Desert Vegetation", *Proceedings National Institute of Sciences, India,* Vol. 19 (3), pp. 411-421.

Chowdhury, K. A., and Ghosh, S. S. 1951. "Plant Remains from Harappa", *Ancient India,* Vol. 7, pp. 3-19.

Dales, G. F. 1966. "Recent Trends in the Pre- and Proto-historic Archaeology in South India", *Proceedings of the American Philosophical Society,* Vol. 110 (2), pp. 13-139.

Drude, O. 1890. *Handbuch der Pflanzengeographie,* Stuttgart.

Frost, R., and Stephanson, P. M. 1964. "Main Streamlines from Standard Pressure Levels Over the Indian Ocean and Adjacent Land Areas", *Proceedings WMO-IUGG Symposium on Tropical Meteorology, Rotorua, New Zealand,* November, 1963. Ed. J. W. Hutchings, Wellington: New Zealand Meteorological Service, pp. 96-97.

Godwin, H. 1956. *The History of the British Flora,* Cambridge University Press.

Godwin, H. 1960. "Radiocarbon Dating and Quaternary History in Britain", The Croonian Lecture. *Proceedings of the Royal Society,* B, Vol. 153, pp. 287-320.

Iversen, J. 1954. "The Late-glacial Flora of Denmark and Its Relation to Climate and Soil", *Danmarks Geologiske Undersøgelse,* II, Raekke, Vol. 80, pp. 87-119.

Joshi, J. P. 1963. *Comparative Stratigraphy of the Protohistoric Cultures of the Indo-Pakistan Subcontinent,* Lucknow: Ethnographic and Folk-Culture Society, U.P.

King, G. 1879. "The Sketch of the Flora of Rajputana", *Indian Forester,* Vol. 72, pp. 213-225.

Maher, L. J. 1964. "Ephedra Pollen in the Sediments of the Great Lakes Region", *Ecology,* Vol. 45 (2), pp. 391-395.

Marshall, Sir John 1931. *Mohenjo-daro and the Indus Civilization,* London: A. Probsthain.

Misra, V. C. 1967. *Geography of Rajasthan,* New Delhi, India: National Book Trust.

Post, L. von 1946. "The Prospect of Pollen Analysis in the Study of the Earth's Climatic History", *New Phytologist,* Vol. 45, pp. 193-217.

Raikes, R. L. 1964. "The End of the Ancient Cities of the Indus", *American Anthropologist,* Vol. 66 (2), pp. 284-299.

Raikes, R. L. 1965*a*. "Tne Ancient Gabar-bands of Baluchistan", *East and West,* Vol. 15 (1-2), pp. 3-12.

Raikes, R. L. 1965*b*. "The Mohenjo-daro Floods", *Antiquity,* Vol. 39, pp. 155, 196-203.

Raikes, R. L., and Dyson, R. H. 1961. "The Prehistoric Climate of Baluchistan and the Indus Valley", *American Anthropologist,* Vol. 63 (2), pp. 265-281.

Raman, C. R. V., and Dixit, C. M. 1964. "Analysis of Mean Resultant Monthly Winds for Standard Pressure Levels over the Indian Ocean Adjoining Continental Areas", *Proceedings WMO-IUGG Symposium on Tropical Meteorology, Rotorua, New Zealand,* November, 1963. Ed. J. W. Hutchings, Wellington, New Zealand, Meteorological Service, pp. 107-118.

Singh, G. 1963. "A Preliminary Survey of the Post-glacial Vegetational History of the Kashmir Valley", *The Palaeobotanist,* Vol. 12 (1), pp. 73-108.

Singh, G. 1967. "A Palynological Approach Towards the Resolution of Some Important Desert Problems in Rejasthan", *Indian Geohydrology,* Vol. 3(1), pp. 111-128.

Singh, G. 1970. "History of Post-glacial Vegetation and Climate of the Rajasthan Desert", unpublished Report, submitted to the University of Wisconsin, Madison, U.S.A.

Stein, Sir Aurel 1931. "An Archaeological Tour in Gedrosia", *Memoirs of the Archaeological Survey of India,* Vol. 43.

Troup, R. S. 1921. *The Silviculture of Indian Trees,* Oxford.

Vats, M. S. 1940. *Excavations at Harappa,* Delhi: Manager of Publications.

Wheeler, Sir Mortimer 1953. *The Cambridge History of India. The Indus Civilization.* Cambridge University Press.

Wheeler, Sir Mortimer 1966. *Civilization of the Indus Valley and Beyond,* London: Thames and Hudson.

Wheeler, Sir Mortimer 1968. *The Cambridge History of India: The Indus Civilization,* 3rd Ed., Cambridge University Press.

Part V

The Old World:
Egypt and Africa

Barbara Bell (Ph.D., Radcliffe College) is Scientific Assistant to the Director
of the Harvard College Observatory and is the author of numerous works
in the field of astronomy. Her contribution underscores the debt
archaeology owes to scholars in other disciplines. Dr. Bell contends that
the decline of Egyptian civilization coincides with, and is caused by,
climatic change. This article is the first of a long range research program
on the role of climatic factors in the rise and fall of Near Eastern civilizations undertaken by the author.

The Dark Ages in Ancient History

Barbara Bell

Introduction[1]

In the history of the ancient Near East two striking Dark Ages have occurred. They
occurred more or less simultaneously (within the limits of current dating accuracy) over
a wide area extending at least from Greece to Mesopotamia and Elam, from Anatolia to
Egypt, and probably beyond. In Egypt, where the chronology is best established, the first
Dark Age began around 2200 B.C., when at the end of Dynasty VI Egypt, until then a
very stable society, with seeming suddenness fell into anarchy. About the same time the
Akkadian Empire disintegrated. Byblos and a number of other sites in Syria and Palestine
were destroyed by fire and some were abandoned for a time. Troy II, the wealthy citadel
of Schliemann's gold treasure, was destroyed by fire and rebuilt on only a very shabby
scale. Lerna and other prosperous Argolid centers were burned and their destruction was
followed by greatly lessened prosperity. In western and southern Anatolia "the end
of the E.B. [Early Bronze] 2 period is marked . . . by a catastrophe of such magnitude
as to remain unparalleled until the very end of the Bronze Age" (Mellaart, 1962); widespread destruction is followed by a general decline in material culture and a decrease by
about 75 percent in the number of known settlements. We may probably include also
the decline of the Indus Valley civilization. The radiocarbon dates of Phase F (mature
Harappan) lie between 2100 and 1900 B.C. (Dales 1965; half-life 5730), with an average
of 1975 B.C. from 12 measurements. But when these dates are corrected for the systematic
error in C-14 dates of this period, as determined by Suess (1967) and by Ralph and
Michael (1969), the dates fall between about 2500 and 2250 B.C.

The second Dark Age began around 1200 B.C. It was marked by the disappearance
of the Hittite Empire of Anatolia and the collapse of the Mycenaean civilization of Greece.

Reprinted from *American Journal of Archaeology,* Vol. 75, No. 1, pp. 1-26 (1971), by permission of
the publisher and author.

About the same time, or a little later, Egypt went into a prolonged decline, while Babylonia and Assyria were also weak for most of the 1100's and 1000's.

When we turn to the revised *Cambridge Ancient History (CAH)* or other modern studies for explanation, we find numerous references to evidence of destruction by fire. The destruction is often attributed to invasions by barbarians about whom little is known, however, and for whose activities the archaeological evidence is often meager or nonexistent. Moreover Adams (1968) has pointed out that the interpretation of seemingly violent destruction and discontinuous layering in a habitation site is more complex and ambiguous than previously recognized, and cannot be considered clear evidence of either intermittent occupation or enemy attack. He thus urges more caution in inferring invasions when there is no clear positive evidence for the presence of invaders. But even where it is clear that barbarian invasions did occur, we are left with the question of whether they are a sufficient cause or explanation for the destruction of a number of apparently powerful and prosperous states, and why so many different barbarian tribes were stirred to attack centers of civilization about the same time. Any one or two of the above disasters, standing alone, might be sufficiently explained by political factors. But the concentration in time of so many disasters and the universal absence of prosperity throughout the area strongly suggest a common underlying cause.

Of "historical truth," Frankfort (1951) wrote that a concept whereby "many seemingly unrelated facts are seen to acquire meaning and coherence is likely to represent a historical reality." It is the thesis of this study that the two Dark Ages, and the numerous disasters in the periods c. 2200-2000 and c. 1200-900 B.C., can be given coherence and can all be explained at once by a single primary cause. The cause I postulate as "historical reality" is drought—widespread, severe, and prolonged—lasting for several decades and occurring more or less simultaneously over the entire eastern Mediterranean and adjacent lands. This is not to deny the significance of contemporary political and social factors; it is, however, to assert that a climatic-economic deterioration of sufficient magnitude can set in motion forces beyond the strength of any society to withstand.

Such an hypothesis has indeed already been advanced by Rhys Carpenter (1966) for the Second Dark Age, c. 1200-900 B.C.; his argument is based primarily on study of the decline of Mycenaean Greece and the Hittite Empire. And in a subsequent paper I plan to discuss this period with primary reference to Egypt.

The present paper will examine the evidence for the hypothesis that the First Dark Age of Egypt, the so-called First Intermediate Period, was brought on by a similar prolonged and intense drought. Later papers will examine the evidence from other lands, but there are several advantages in beginning with Egypt:

First, Egypt was in ancient times a relatively isolated civilization, generally unified and free of civil war and, because of its formidable and well-defined natural frontiers, of foreign invasions. Thus we have here the best chance of tracing the interaction of man and his natural environment, and making plausible inferences from the level of economic prosperity about fluctuations in the resources provided by the natural environment.

Second, the chronology of Egypt, in the historical period from c. 3100 B.C. onward, is known with greater precision than that of any other ancient land. Thus whatever climatic fluctuations we deduce from Egyptian history will be relatively well dated. Moreover we can test them by looking for contemporaneous patterns, that is for fluctuations in the direction of greater aridity or of greater moisture, in other lands; and if similar sequences can be found, there is a possibility of improving the chronology of other lands.

Third, Egypt was a literate society, so that we may hope to find texts bearing on the conditions of the times, and it is in fact the discussion of such texts which forms the main section of this paper. Mesopotamia also offers the advantage of literacy, but its chronology is less certain; more importantly, the picture there is obscured by frequent warfare between the cities, the lack of natural frontiers, recurrent invasions on a large scale, and a greater complexity in climatic factors. In Egypt we have to do essentially with the volume of the Nile, and particularly of its annual flood; that is, we have a single climatic factor to consider, rather than the combination of river-floods and rainfall characteristic of Mesopotamia.

It may appear a bizarre hypothesis, even to those sympathetic to the concept of climate fluctuations as a factor in history, to link drought in the lands of the eastern Mediterranean, which derive their moisture mainly from winter rainfall, with Egypt which depends for its water on the Nile River—that is on the rainfall over central Africa (White Nile) and on the summer monsoon rains over the East African highlands (Blue Nile). Nevertheless there is a growing body of evidence that such a correlation does at times occur, and indeed that it has occurred over the past century. Studies by Kraus (1954; 1955a, b; 1956) and by Butzer (1961) indicate that the average rainfall was less in many regions in the first four decades of this century than in the late decades of the nineteenth century. This decline occurred over a wide area of the Near East and North Africa, including both the northern and southern fringes of the Sahara, northwest India (Jaipur) and Pakistan (Quetta), and the drainage basin of the Nile. The decrease in average rainfall occurred also in a number of other lands far beyond our present interest, such as parts of Australia (Kraus 1954) and the Dust Bowl of the United States (Butzer 1961). The change over from the moister to the drier climate regime occurred quite abruptly in many places between 1893 and 1908, with the exact date depending upon the region concerned. For the Nile, the annual average volume of water passing Aswan was about 25 percent less for the years 1899-1957 than for the years 1871-1898, with a clear and abrupt shift to the drier regime in 1899 (see Kraus 1956). "Without the tempering effect of dams and barrages, agriculture in the Nile Valley would have suffered badly" (Butzer 1961:50); and as a consequence of the widespread decline in rainfall, "Droughts of economic importance plagued the Levantine area in the 1920s and the entire Near East in the 1930s. Lake Aksehir in Central Anatolia dried out entirely in 1933. Similar conditions can be noted for the peripheries of the Sahara." And similarly in the Red Sea Hills of eastern Egypt, "vegetation was . . . more common prior to the desiccation that has taken place during the present century" (Trigger 1965:11).

This evidence from the past century makes it more plausible that most of the Near East and the Nile catchment basin were afflicted more or less simultaneously by some decades of severe drought at certain times in the past.

It is the prime thesis of my investigation, indeed, that a widespread drought, considerably more severe than the present one, occurred at intervals in the past and that it was precisely these droughts which precipitated the Dark Ages of Ancient History. Even a moderate drought can bring famine to the marginally productive lands on the edges of the deserts and can thereby motivate tribal migrations and invasions of the better-watered river valleys, a phenomenon discussed by numerous scholars (e.g. Brooks 1949). But a severe drought, such as postulated in this paper, and by Carpenter (1966), will bring crop failures and famine and varying degrees of civil disorder even to the richer lands. If sufficiently severe, a drought may not only incite invasions from marginal lands but may weaken the power of the major states to resist invasion, and in some cases may even plunge them into a Dark Age without any serious foreign threat. In the case of Egypt the evidence which we shall consider presently favors the latter condition.

The first of the postulated Great Droughts in the Ancient Near East occurred from about 2200 to 2000 B.C. More precisely, as we shall see from a detailed consideration of the historical evidence, it occurred in two parts, at least in Egypt—and almost certainly in Iraq—the first around 2180 to 2150, and the second for a few years around 2000 B.C. In Egypt the crisis was not a failure of local rainfall, which was already at a very low level, but a severe failure of the annual floods of the Nile. It is as if Nature set two great exclamation points to emphasize the end of the Neolithic Wet Phase (NWP); or, to reverse Eliot, the NWP ended not with a whimper but with a bang.

Prehistoric Climate

A brief review of the earlier climate fluctuations may be useful before we take up the Dark Age itself, to put our central event in its paleoclimatic setting. It is now a fact beyond dispute that climate has been subject to change since the earliest times known to geologists. Because geology is a relatively young science, however, this fact has been recognized for only about a century; and at first only the larger fluctuations, the extremes of Ice Age and Interglacial, were recognized. But soon geologists found evidence that ice sheets, both in their expansion and their recession, were subject to interruption—that is, neither advances nor recessions proceeded smoothly and linearly, but each was from time to time interrupted by a reversal of the primary trend, a reversal lasting some hundreds to thousands of years. The Pleistocene Ice Age, now thought to cover some two to three million years, has been studied extensively in northern and central Europe and in North America, and much attention in Europe particularly has been given to the larger fluctuations that accompanied the retreat of the latest (Würm) ice sheet. We obtain an impression of damped oscillations, of gradually diminishing amplitude and duration, over the past ten to fifteen thousand years.

Although many details and dates remain to be fixed, it has been established beyond any reasonable doubt that significant fluctuations in climate have occurred in post-glacial times in northern and central Europe (see Brooks 1949, for a convenient[2] semi-popular summary; for more recent, and more technical, reviews, see Starkel 1966 and Frenzel 1966). It is, to me at least, *a priori* incredible that the climate should not also have fluctuated over all other areas of the earth. This, of course, is not to claim that there is anything *a priori* obvious about the direction and amplitude, or even the timing, of such fluctuations, which cannot be inferred by analogy, but must be determined from paleo-ecological, geological, and archaeological evidence.

The Mediterranean Basin, the Near East, and northern and central Africa, which are the regions of concern to us here, have received much less attention from natural scientists, primarily, it would seem, because the evidence is more subtle and difficult to detect. A number of isolated studies of particular areas were made, but only within the past decade have the relatively meager available facts been synthesized into a coherent picture for the area as a whole. This synthesis was made by Karl W. Butzer (1958, etc.), on whose work most of the following summary of climate variation is based. One of Butzer's most important and interesting contributions is his clarification of the relation in time between the larger subtropical and European climate changes.

For some time it has been recognized that central Africa and the margins of the deserts had a number of pluvial periods, but the relation in time of these tropical and subtropical wet periods to the northern ice sheets was much disputed. The probably most popular view held the two to be contemporaneous, and considered that the increased wetness in lower latitudes, particularly in Africa, was a simple and direct consequence of mid-latitude storm tracks being deflected southward by the presence of the ice sheets. Thus the maximum subtropical wetness would coincide with the maximal extent of the ice sheets. And indeed a number of scholars, beginning with Childe (1929:42, 46) and Toynbee (1934:304f), have linked the development of the great river-valley civilizations to the challenge of a gradually increasing desiccation following upon the recession of the ice sheets.

However this view is no longer tenable. After the work of Büdel and of Schaefer, it now appears that only the expansion phase had heavy rainfall, while the full and late glacial phases were relatively dry in middle-latitude Eurasia. Recent work also indicates that the last major pluvial in Africa is to be dated to the early Würm period, and that this was a period of advance and growth for the central-east African mountain glaciers (Butzer 1963), although the most recent work (Butzer and Hansen 1968) indicates that the actual situation has many complexities. And finally, Butzer (1963) found that the period of glacial advance was the pluvial period in the Mediterranean Basin as well, whereas the terminal phases of the Pleistocene were quite dry. Thus he concluded (ibid. p. 212) that "subtropical pluvials cannot be genetically interpreted as secondary effects of the presence of continental ice sheets in higher latitudes . . . [but] . . . must be attributed to a primary change of the general circulation, presumably in immediate association with glacial advance in higher latitudes."

Contrary to the views of Childe (1929), Toynbee (1934), and most subsequent scholars who have mentioned prehistoric climate, including Carpenter (1966)—but excluding Hayes (1964), Trigger (1965), and the revised CAH (Butzer 1965)—the lands of the Near East and northern Africa were already as dry or drier 15,000 years ago than they are today. Recent evidence from Lake Zeribar in Iran, from the lowlands of Macedonia, and from the mountains of northwestern Greece, indicates that much of this region was then apparently a treeless landscape, perhaps resembling the semi-arid steppe of modern Anatolia (Wright 1968).

Since that time numerous fluctuations have occurred between relatively wetter and drier conditions, on a time scale of hundreds to thousands of years. In amplitude, and hence in terms of geological effects, these fluctuations are small and difficult to detect in the arid and semi-arid lands of interest to us here. However fluctuations that are too small to leave geological evidence can still be large enough to produce highly significant ecological effects, which may be reflected in archaeological evidence.

Early in his studies Butzer (1958) noted a curious parallelism between moisture trends in Europe and in the Near East. Every fluctuation to greater or lesser precipitation, the duration of which is measured in millennia, has been more or less parallel in Europe and in lower latitudes. In addition to the parallelism between Europe and the Near East, Butzer (1961) emphasizes that the major paleoclimatic shifts north and south of the Sahara have been, insofar as evidence is available, synchronous and not alternative. That is, the evidence (see also Kraus 1955a:202-204) supports an expanding and contracting Sahara Desert. Thus the ultimate meteorological explanation, Butzer points out, must be sought in terms of a mechanism that will enlarge or shrink the extension of the dry trade-wind circulation zone, which is responsible for the subtropical deserts, in both latitudinal directions at once.

The existence of a Neolithic Wet Phase, and a preceding very dry period, has been suspected in Egypt for several decades by various scholars, including Caton-Thompson and Gardner, Huzayyin, and Murray (1951), but in the absence of any systematic study of the overall evidence, there was little agreement on the duration, extent, and character of the NWP (Butzer 1958). It is outside the scope of the present study to review in any detail the evidence for the NWP in the Near East (see Butzer 1958; 1959b, c; 1965), a period which corresponds approximately to the relatively warm and wet Climatic Optimum or Atlantic Period (see Brooks 1949; Starkel 1966) in northern Europe. For northern Africa much of the evidence is archaeological, such as neolithic artifacts found in desert areas where man cannot now live, rock drawings of animal species that require at least a savanna type of vegetation, and fossil roots and tree stumps in wadi bottoms and the low desert where no trees grow today.

Decline of the Neolithic Wet Phase

"Overall, the Nubian and Egyptian evidence indicates a complex moist interval beginning before c. 7000 B.C., interrupted by some drier spells and terminating in stages between 2900 and 2350 B.C." (Butzer 1966:75). These stages have been documented (Butzer 1959c) by indirect archaeological evidence, including a study of the relative frequencies of various species of animals appearing in rock drawings, tomb and temple wall reliefs, and other art forms. At this time in northern Europe we have a transition to the Sub-Boreal period, which "may be characterized as warm but rather dry, with considerable variations in humidity . . . ." The study of lake levels gives evidence for "the occurrence of great oscillations in precipitation," as does also the periodic desiccation of peat bogs (Starkel 1966:27).

An interesting point for the present study is the extent to which the time-synchronism of wet and dry periods holds, or held in earlier times, over shorter time periods—periods of decades to centuries. The data on these smaller fluctuations are obscure and will remain so at least until the systematic errors (Suess 1967; Ralph and Michael 1969) have been fully determined and corrected for, or other more accurate methods of dating can be developed. We should nonetheless regard it as encouraging if a severe dry spell were found to occur in Europe in the same century as that for which we are postulating one in the Near East. Such may well be the case, for Brooks (1949:296f) cites evidence, from lake levels and peat bogs, for unusually dry conditions in central Europe around 2300-2000 and 1200-1000 B.C., although modern pollen studies (Frenzel 1966) cast doubt upon this picture. However this may eventually be resolved, conditions in Europe have no *necessary* bearing on the validity of our conclusions about conditions in Egypt.

Butzer considers that the NWP rains over Egypt had pretty well declined to their modern low level by the beginning of Dynasty VI, c. 2350 B.C. This conclusion is based in part on a change at this time in the character of hunting and desert scenes depicted on tomb and temple reliefs, a change both in the game hunted and in the background landscape. There appears also to have been a general exodus from the Libyan Desert in Dynasty VI times, evidenced by the cessation of rock paintings and the abandonment of Neolithic sites, together with the appearance, according to O. H. Myers, of Tehenu Libyans in the Nile Valley (Butzer 1958).

The specter of famine first clearly appears towards the end of Dynasty V, when a well-known relief from the causeway of the Pyramid of Unis depicts a group of severely emaciated people, evidently dying of hunger (Drioton 1942; Smith 1965:pl. 48B). Unfortunately no inscriptions have survived to reveal the circumstances of this scene, and nothing is known of either the nationality of the starving people or the cause of their plight—whether a failure of the Nile floods (an unlikely event for the King to wish to commemorate) or the ending of the NWP rains, which drove starving desert-dwellers to seek refuge in the Nile Valley.

It is not unlikely that the decline of the Early Bronze 2 culture in Greece and in Anatolia set in with the ending of the NWP, particularly in regions where many settlements were permanently abandoned, as in western and southern Anatolia (Mellaart 1962). To support more than speculation, of course, much additional study is needed. We may note, however, that four pieces of charcoal from the House of Tiles at Lerna (late EH II) give an average radiocarbon date of 2126 B.C. (from Weinberg 1965; half-life 5730); but this becomes c. 2500 B.C. when corrected for systematic error (see Suess 1967; and Ralph and Michael 1969). Also possibly relevant is the evidence (Wright 1968) for a reduction in percentage of pine pollen around Pylos shortly after 2000 B.C., and evidence for a reduction in the beech-fir forest of northwestern Turkey, dated to around 2000 B.C., changes which might "reflect either a change to a drier climate or deforestation." The dates here are a little late, but they are also quite uncertain (Wright, personal communication), so that the changes could well reflect the ending of the NWP.

But in Egypt the Old Kingdom civilization continued, under Dynasty VI, to flourish for some 150 years after the ending of the NWP. Most Egyptologists agree that the Pyramid complex of King Neferkare Pepi II, the last major monument of the Old Kingdom, exhibits the same high quality of craftsmanship as its predecessors and gives no hint of the Dark Age soon to engulf all aspects of Egyptian civilization. Moreover it appears that the climate of northeastern Africa remained severely arid, probably averaging slightly less rainfall than today, for at least some fifteen centuries, during which time Egypt had two periods of high civilization and three ages of decline.

This serves only to emphasize once again the well-known dependence of Egypt upon the Nile. Without a failure of the floods, it seems unlikely that the ending of the NWP would have caused Egypt more than some inconvenience and local disturbances, when desert nomads of necessity sought to settle in the Valley. Inscriptions indicate that many of them did settle in the Valley, finding employment with the army as mercenaries (Breasted 1906:311; Borchardt 1905), increasing the population and adding to the potential for trouble in any famine that might occur.

The Nile

A few words on the annual Nile floods may be useful here. Because rainfall over all but the northern Delta has long been rare and irregular, Egyptian farmers have depended for at least some 5000 years upon the annual flood of the Nile River to water their fields and prepare the soil for cultivation. The amount of any particular inundation—at least before the building of the modern system of dams and barrages—determined whether that year would bring plenty of famine or something intermediate. These annual floods are the direct consequence of the summer monsoon rainfall over the catchment basin of the Blue Nile and the Atbara in the highlands of Ethiopia. The maximum level of the flood waters in Egypt thus provides a measure of the amount of this rainfall.

According to Hayes (1964), in Middle Egypt the average difference between high and low water is 22' (6.7 m), with a yearly variation that depends on the volume of the equatorial rains; 4-5' (1.2-1.5 m.) below average is a "bad Nile" and in antiquity a succession of these usually resulted in crop failures and famine, while a flood of 30' (9 m.) or more would cause widespread destruction.

Deposits south of Wadi Halfa suggest that flood levels in early predynastic times were about 10 m. higher than today, that they declined in an oscillatory way to about 5 m. above today in early dynastic times, and to the present level by the time of the New Kingdom (Trigger 1965:31). It is hoped that the present study, in this and subsequent papers (now including Bell 1970), will provide additional details on the flood levels in historical times.

Fluctuations in climate during the past 4000 years have generally been either too small in amplitude or too short in duration to leave behind much geological evidence, as Butzer (1958, 1961) points out, so that it becomes increasingly necessary to resort to archaeological and literary sources, as we shall do in the main section of this paper. But on the fringelands of deserts the drifting of sand is a particularly sensitive indicator of changes in aridity and in aeolian activity. In Middle Egypt, Butzer (1959a, c) found evidence that a chain of dunes from the western desert invaded the valley and covered the alluvium with several meters of sand over a stretch about 175 km. in length and 0.5 to 3.5 km. in width. These fossil dunes are now covered by a few meters of mud, deposited mainly between about 500 B.C. and A.D. 300. The dune invasion was facilitated by weaker Nile floods and consequent shrinkage of the floodplain, as well as by increased aeolian activity and by an eastward retreat of the Bahr Yusef, a secondary branch of the Nile in Middle Egypt which drains into the Fayum lake. The dunes cannot be dated precisely, but a number of passages in the literary evidence to be examined presently, indicate that they were actively invading during the First Intermediate Period. A knowledge of their existence clarifies the meaning of a number of otherwise rather enigmatic passages.

Although the adequacy of the Nile flood is the main determinant of Egypt's prosperity, there are also phrases in the ancient texts, as we shall see, which seem to indicate that the low-water level was at times abnormally low, which in turn implies a deficiency of rainfall over sources of the White Nile in east-central Africa. This is not unlikely, for Brooks (1949) points out that in the records of the Nile floods available from A.D. 641 to 1800 there is a fair correlation between low-water level and flood height, although the low-water levels show the more violent fluctuations. Brooks' conclusion derives from his analysis of the tables of low- and high-water levels published by Toussoun (1925). Toussoun's volume also contains a chronological list of quotations on the level of the Nile and related events, compiled from Arab authors. Several times in years of abnormally low floods there is mention also of a remarkably low level of the "old waters" or pre-flood Nile. And conversely there is a tendency for the old waters to be high before a very large flood. More important, one obtains from these quotations also an impression that the total volume of flood water fluctuates more than the height of the flood. One frequently reads that the flood attained a normal height, then declined at once and there was famine, or at least scarcity, in Egypt.

The First Dark Age in Egypt

It is now widely believed (Hayes 1961, 1962b; Wilson 1956; Gardiner 1961) that the real Dark Age lasted only some 20-25 years, from the end of Dynasty VI to the start of Dynasty IX, or from about 2180 to 2160. Although the details remain obscure and the primary cause open to dispute, some aspects of the trouble which occurred at the end of Dynasty VI seem clear: texts from the period indicate that hardly any form of civil disorder was absent, ranging from strife between districts, to looting and killing by infiltrating Asiatics in the Delta, to individual crime run riot, to revolution and social anarchy. Reference to famine occurs in several texts. This fact has of course been noted by a number of Egyptologists, including those cited immediately above, and the texts themselves have been intensively studied by Vandier (1936). But none of these scholars gives to famine the importance which I hope to show it deserves as an explanation of the collapse of the Old Kingdom. Butzer (1959c:68; 1965) points out that a number of these documents refer to "famine resulting from low Niles rather than from human negligence," but analysis of the historical implications lay outside the scope of his investigation.

Although the real Dark Age was short, it had a severely traumatic effect on the psyche of the Egyptian educated classes; it produced a radical change in values and outlook that can only reflect severe shock and disillusionment. In the words of W. S. Smith (1965:87), "The earlier complacent sense of stability had been rudely shaken, and Egypt never regained that simple confidence in an enduring continuity." The collapse of the Old Kingdom was reflected in a new pessimistic literature "foreign to the spirit and thought of earlier times" (Smith 1962:55). This pessimistic literature, Černý (1952:79) emphasizes, "was not the result of philosophical meditation but a reflection of historical events . . . and is in direct contradiction to the habitual optimistic attitude of the Egyptians to life."

In the absence of unambiguous evidence, various nonclimatic causes have been suggested for this time of trouble; none of them however seem sufficient to explain the magnitude of the effect.

The evidence for famine in ancient Egypt, given by written texts, has been studied by Vandier (1936), who points out that such evidence is scarce because the Egyptians had not the habit of recording their misfortunes for posterity. The principal data for his study are the autobiographical inscriptions of nomarchs (rulers of nomes or districts) who, their personal vanity having overcome national pride, boasted of having fed their towns and districts during the years of famine. Vandier found very few documents on famine during the Old Kingdom, and he attributed this to the strength of the central government—which made it relatively easy to store up large surpluses in years of good Niles and dispense them in years of poor Niles. I do not question the essential soundness of this point, but would add two qualifications. First, in these earlier times the provincial officials were neither as independent in the content of their inscriptions nor as firmly attached to a particular district. And second, as we have seen above, the Neolithic Wet Phase was ending gradually during the time of Dynasties V and VI. Thus while famine probably did threaten from time to time in the earlier years, the danger was unlikely to have been as prolonged or severe, and was less likely to have exhausted the stores of surplus grain.

Vandier lays great stress on the correlation between weakening of the authority of the central government and the disastrous consequences of insufficient floods. His study shows clearly that such a correlation exists. The problem then is to distinguish the symptoms of the disease from its cause. Because of the meager evidence from these troubled times, the question cannot be answered with absolute certainty, but I hope to show that a more consistent picture of "historical truth" results from the hypothesis that prolonged insufficiency of the floods destroyed a somewhat weakened central government than vice versa. The claim can indeed be made that there is no other adequate explanation for the complete and seemingly sudden disintegration of both the government and Egyptian society that occurred at the end of the reign of Pepi II of Dynasty VI, about 2180 B.C. In considering the ancient texts, I follow the viewpoint of Gardiner (JEA 1:36) that one should avoid undue skepticism about ancient documents, and should rather "use their statements, in the absence of conflicting testimony, as the best available evidence with regard to the periods of history to which they relate."

Texts relating to the first great famine, c. 2180-2130 B.C.

Turning now to the written evidence itself, we may first consider Ankhtifi, who is known from the inscriptions in his tomb at Mo'alla, some 20 miles south of Luxor. This tomb has been thoroughly studied by Vandier (1950) who is the source for the quotations[3] which follow. Ankhtifi's claim to his position is obscure—whether he held it by birth or simply by his effective leadership in troubled times—but he was nomarch of Hierakonpolis and of Edfu, two of the southernmost nomes of Upper Egypt. It is generally agreed that he lived early in the First Intermediate Period (First Dark Age), before Inyotef I of Thebes unified the South and proclaimed himself King of Upper Egypt about 2134 B.C. Inyotef would surely not have tolerated a hostile prince so near at hand, and Ankhtifi's inscriptions describe a war he initiated against the Theban nome, although the outcome is obscure. Beckerath (1962, JNES 21:140) points out that Ankhtifi must have lived at the virtual start of the first Intermediate Period, because his inscriptions give evidence that when he was young Abydos was still the residence of an "Overseer of Upper Egypt" who was recognized by the nomarchs. Toward the end of Dynasty VIII that office had lost all importance. Thus we may consider that Ankhtifi's inscriptions provide a picture—probably the best available— of conditions in the darkest part of the Dark Age.

Most significant for our purpose is his vivid description of the famine that afflicted

Upper Egypt: . . . *I fed/kept alive Hefat (Mo'alla), Hormer, and (?) . . . at a time when the sky was (in) clouds/storm (igp) (was a tumult?) and the land was in the wind* (probably the clouds of a memorably severe season or seasons of dust storms), *(and when everyone was dying) of hunger (ḥḳr*, the common word for hunger) *on this sandbank of Hell (tzw of Apophis*, a place in the underworld where the dragon-serpent, Apophis, nightly threatened to devour the sun god, Re).

As supporting evidence for the dust-storm interpretation,we note Butzer's (1959b: 66) finding that at Hierakonpolis, nearby, a predynastic cemetery was denuded by wind action, which removed up to 2 m. of fairly resistant silt and exposed the burials, probably some time after the end of Dynasty VI. At Abydos, some 100 km. to the north, the "funerary palace" of Queen Merneith of Dynasty I suffered such intense denudation (and perhaps also deliberate destruction) that its walls were reduced to only a few courses of bricks, partly buried beneath a layer of sand by the time of Dynasty XII, when a few small mastabas were constructed over the ruins (B. J. Kemp 1966, JEA 52).

Vandier considers the above-quoted sentence of Ankhtifi's to be a particularly inspired masterpiece of erudition, made up essentially of phrases from the Pyramid Texts, aptly selected to describe the current local troubles. The reference to the *tzw of Apophis* is useful in helping to give us a clearer idea of a key word, *tzw,*[4] which occurs in several of the famine texts of this period and merits some discussion. The word *tzw* is generally translated *sandbanks* by Egyptologists. For the famine texts, Vandier (1936:75) considers two hypotheses: either the *tzw* are the sandbanks of the Nile that men cultivate at low waters and that are submerged through most of the inundation; or they are the higher lands on each bank of the Nile susceptible to being flooded for some weeks at the time of the inundation. If the flood is weak, the *tzw* in the first hypothesis (lower sandbanks) do not remain long covered by water, and in the second (upper sandbanks) they are not covered at all. Although preferring the "upper" hypothesis, Vandier translates *tzw* as *year(s) of low Nile,* and thus of famine by metonymy. However, the texts in which *tzw* appears seem to describe quite dire conditions of famine, so that I find the first of Vandier's hypotheses, the lower sandbanks, the one more probably correct. Also for this reason, I do not accept Vandier's suggestion that *tzw* was already at this time a stale over-used image meaning simply famine from whatever cause, but consider it highly probable that *tzw* was an image meaning *poor Nile* by metonymy, and famine by consequence.

Moreover it is not clear, either from the examples we shall encounter below or from those cited by Vandier without a context of famine, that the *tzw* have to do with any sort of cultivated land. They may be simply sandbars in the river, which are exposed in the season of low water, and remain exposed, more or less, according to the degree of deficiency in the flood. This interpretation would still leave *tzw* as an appropriate figure of speech to mean famine due to insufficient flood, but not for famine from other causes. This view is supported also by the phrase from the Book of the Dead from whose prototype Vandier (1950) believes that Ankhtifi's scribe derived the terms of the tomb inscription: *O master of the stormclouds (igp) . . . O thou who sailest the bark (of Re) by this sandbar (tzw) of Apophis . . .* Thus the appearance of *tzw* in a context of famine may, and indeed should be taken as evidence of a very low flood, quite sufficient in itself to cause severe famine without any political complications.

Returning now to the inscription of Ankhtifi, we find a very severe famine indeed:
. . . *All of Upper Egypt was dying of hunger (ḥḳr), to such a degree that everyone had
come to eating his children, but I managed that no one died of hunger in this nome.
I made a loan of grain to Upper Egypt. . . . I kept alive the house of Elephantine during
these years, after the towns of Hefat and Hormer had been satisifed.. . . The entire
country had become like a starved (?) grasshopper, with people going to the north and
to the south (in search of grain), but I never permitted it to happen that anyone had to
embark from this to another nome . . . .*
          Vandier (1936:8) points out that this is one of only two known references to
cannibalism in Ancient Egypt, an act of desperation that also occurred during famines
in mediaeval Arab Egypt (see Toussoun 1925:458-474, for details). Vandier, and Gardiner
too (1961:111), are inclined to doubt that we should take this part literally, in spite of
the numerous other contemporary references to a lack of grain. I suggest that while the
"everyone" is surely an exaggeration, instances of cannibalism did occur, else why should
it even occur to Ankhtifi's scribe to record such an atrocity? The rarity of the practice,
and the probability that it occurred at all, only serve to make more vivid the desperation
of the people in these years of low Niles *(tzw)*.
          It is noteworthy that virtually none of the famine inscriptions from the Dark Age
mention the name of any king, a drastic change from the style of Old Kingdom inscriptions.
Ankhtifi, indeed, does make passing mention of a king in the isolated inscription: *Horus
brings/brought (or, May Horus bring) a (good) inundation for his son Ka-nefer-Re.* The
identity of this king (Nefer-ka-Re?) is quite uncertain and useless for dating the tomb more
precisely. But I suggest that Ankhtifi probably had no faith in any king for whom Horus
sent no good inundation; but when a good flood did finally come he may have thought
it prudent preparation for the afterlife to offer a phrase of recognition. Or, if we translate
the verb in the past tense, the king could be Neferkare Pepi II of Dynasty VI, who ruled
in Ankhtifi's youth, before the bad times, and the phrase intended as a criticism of present
kings. Or it may be simply a magic wish.
          For vividness of phrasing and interest in natural conditions (sandstorms), no one
equals the author of the tomb inscriptions of Ankhtifi. Another famine text, however,
that Vandier (1950) considers to be contemporary with it or only slightly later is the
stele of Iti (Cairo 20.001) of Gebelein: . . . *I made Gebelein live during the years of
misery (ḳsnt), at a time when 400 men found themselves in . . (?) . . I gave wheat from
Upper Egypt to Iuni and to Hefat* (Ankhtifi's town) *after Gebelein had been sustained;
at a time when Thebes descended and ascended the stream to search for grain . . . I never
let men of Gebelein go up and down the stream to another nome to look for grain . . .*
(Vandier 1936).
          Also probably from this period is the stele of Merer (Černý 1961) in the Cracow
Museum and of unknown provenance. Merer calls himself . . . *overseer of the slaughterers
of the House of Khuu* (probably nomarchs of Edfu, according to Fischer 1962, *Kush*
10:333) and recounts how he took care of his family during the famine, and offered for
thirteen rulers: . . . *I was a pure one to slaughter and to offer in two temples on behalf of
the ruler; I offered for thirteen rulers . . . I acquired (property) . . . I fed my brothers and
sisters, I buried him who was dead and fed him who was alive wherever I alighted in this
famine (on this sandbar, tzw) which occurred. I shut off all their fields and their mounds*

*in town and in the country, I did not allow their water to inundate for someone else . . .
I caused Upper Egyptian barley to be given to the town and I transported for it a great
number of times. . . .* Here we have one of the clearer linkings of *tzw,* a shortage of
irrigation water, and famine.

The stelae of Iti and of Merer contain clues that may explain much of the fighting
which occurred early in this Dark Age, in the references to Thebes searching upstream
and downstream for grain, and to Merer's efforts to increase his family's supply of the
meager floods at the expense of others. Raids on the granaries of neighboring districts
probably occurred, as well as violent disputes over water rights.

Another interesting text comes from Middle Egypt, where the nomarch of Assiut,
Khety, refers to building new irrigation works and to providing for his people in a time
of famine *(tzw)* in his tomb inscriptions. His date has not been fixed with certainty, but
he evidently grew up at the royal court in a time of relative calm, if we may judge from
the inscription stating that he learned swimming with the royal children. There is no mention of war with Thebes, and Breasted (1906: 405) accordingly suggests that he lived
before the nomarch Tefibi and the latter's son Khety, each of whom mention war with
the south in which they played an active role on behalf of the Herakleopolitan king of
Lower Egypt. Vandier (1936) and Hayes (1961) also agree in placing this Khety before
Tefibi. Thus we may tentatively consider that he grew up in the late years of Pepi II,
spent his adult life in the Dark Age, and was able to maintain a degree of order in his
nome and preserve his people from the worst suffering of the famine. The relevant
passages, as kindly translated for me by N. B. Millet, read:

. . . I made a monument (probably, a canal) *in -- a substitute for the river, of
10 cubits; I excavated for it upon the ploughlands; I provided a gate . . . in brick . . . in
one (act of) building, without dispossessing anyone of any house/property. . . .*

*I nourished my town, I acted as (my own) accountant in regard to food (?) and
as giver of water in the middle of the day, in order to be very wary of ? ? ? . . in the
island(?) I made a dam for this town, when Upper Egypt was a desert(?), when no water
could be seen. I closed my (?) frontiers . . .(to outsiders) . . . I made (agricultural) highlands out of swamp and caused the inundation to flood over old ruined sites. I made
ploughlands out of --? -- all people who were in thirst drank. . . . I was rich in grain
when the land was as a sandbank (tzw), and nourished my town by measuring grain . . . .*

We have in this inscription two of the clearer references to a low Nile: *. . . when
no water could be seen . . .* suggesting that the White Nile too was very low at times;
and *. . . when the land was as a sandbank (tzw) . . .* which suggests that Khety was a
contemporary of those others above who lived in the time of the *tzw.* Khety's dam was
most probably a barrier on the alluvial flats designed to retain on his fields as much
water as possible in the event of a too-brief flood, a not uncommon cause of scarcity
or semi-famine in the Islamic era (see Toussoun 1925:455ff; and above, under Ankhtifi).

The word *tzw* appears in four additional texts collected by Vandier (1936), three
of which are graffiti from Hat-Nub, a quarry in the Hare Nome in Middle Egypt. (The
fourth is Turin 1310, discussed in the following section.) Graffito 20, from the 6th year
of the nomarch Neheri, reads in its relevant part: *(I was a man) who . . . kept alive
(nourished) his town during the years of low Niles (tzw), who supplied it when there
was nothing, who gave aid to it without making any distinction between the great and the*

small . . . Graffiti 23 and 24, by two different sons of Neheri, and within a year or two of 20 in date, state in almost identical words: *. . . I nourished my town, so that it was supplied wholly during the low Niles (tzw) of the country, when there was nothing . . .*

References to warfare form another major topic of these same graffiti from Hat-Nub. Egyptologists have not agreed on the identity of the primary combatants nor on the dates of Neheri and his sons, for one depends upon the other. Faulkner (1944) gives reasons to interpret the war as a rebellion by Neheri and his sons against an early Herakleopolitan King (of Dynasty IX?), that is, before c. 2133 when the nomarch of Thebes established an independent kingdom in Upper Egypt. Hayes (1961), however, believes that the texts refer to a battle in the final war by which, c. 2050, the Theban King Nebhepetre Mentu-hotep brought about the forcible reunification of Upper and Lower Egypt and established the Middle Kingdom. If we accept the interpretation of Faulkner, we have all known *tzw*-famines together within a period of 50 years or less, between c. 2180 and c. 2130. The interpretation of Hayes (1961) would give us a second, presumably brief, *tzw*-famine around 2050. While this is not impossible, it is not substantiated by any other evidence. Moreover, the word *tzw* has not been found in famine texts (Vandier 1936:158) outside the First Intermediate Period. The appearance of the word in these Hat-Nub graffiti thus lends support to the early dating and to Faulkner's interpretation of the warfare as a revolt by Neheri against the king. It is natural then to wonder if the revolt may not have been motivated, at least in part, by Neheri's unwillingness to pay taxes, that is, to send any of his nome's scarce grain to the capital.

A tantalizing reference to another sort of violence appears in the tomb stele of Nefer-Yu, from Dendera, probably early in the Dark Age (Hayes 1953:139), who calls himself *Chancellor of the King of Lower Egypt*, in this period often a purely honorary title. Nefer-yu recounts, in addition to his acts of conventional charity, that he aided his superiors during the troubled times. Unfortunately the translation of the critical line, and thus the exact nature of the trouble, are not agreed upon. As translated by Hayes (1953), Nefer-yu claims: *. . . I gave bread to the hungry (ḥḳr) and clothes to the naked . . . I succored the great ones until the year when slaughter was ended. I wrought mightily with my oxlike arm in order to be established.. . . .* But according to Fischer (1968:207): *. . . I nourished the great in the year of famine. I wrought greatly with my arm that I might endure with my children . . .*

However, the slaughter referred to in Hayes' translation is depicted in several verses (e.g.: *Nay but the children of princes, men dash them against walls.. . . The highborn are full of lamentations, and the poor are full of joy. Every town saith: "Let us drive out the powerful from our midst.. . . ."*) in the lament of Ipuwer, more commonly known as the Admonitions of an Egyptian Sage. Since both the beginning and the ending of the manuscript are lost, the circumstances evoking the poet's lament are unknown. Although van Seter (1964, JEA 50) presents arguments for assigning the work to the Second Intermediate Period, most Egyptologists consider it more probably belongs to the First. The most compelling argument is given by Erman (1927), who points out that the work is undoubtedly older than the "Instruction of Amenemhet," since the latter quotes a passage, interpolated in corrupt form where it makes no sense, from the "Admonitions" where, on external grounds, the passage certainly belongs.

Gardiner, Posener, Hayes, and others consider that Ipuwer was most probably an eye witness of the anarchy he laments—civil strife and social revolution (of a people made desperate by famine), lawlessness of every sort, including tomb robbery, and infiltration of the Delta by Asiatics. To the modern Western mind, the text gives an impression of disorganization as great as that existing in Egypt itself at the time. It illustrates what W. S. Smith (1962:61), in speaking of the Pyramid Texts, called the Egyptian "tendency to assemble an accumulated mass of material without synthesis. Contradictions are not resolved but presented side by side." The Lament of Ipuwer contains a number of such contradictions; one of the more glaring appears when we read in one verse that everyone is starving, and in another that he who formerly had nothing now has many good things.

I quote below at some length from this important account probably by an eye-witness. I have aimed to include every verse that seems to pertain to natural, as opposed to purely social, conditions, but have included a few of the latter also to give a more representative impression. The translation is taken primarily from Faulkner (1964, 1965), with some phrases and notes from Erman (1927) and Wilson (1955).[5] Explanatory notes in parentheses are identified by the initial of the translator (F, E, and W); in the absence of any initial, the comments are my own.

But first, to stimulate imaginations that have never witnessed severe famine, we requote from Carpenter (1966:69) part of a description of an actual famine that occurred not so long ago in northeast Brazil: "In 1953, following three preceding years of unremitting drought, the people of the burnt-out countryside descended en masse, armed with every available weapon, to sack and pillage the settlements where any food had been stored. Always . . . there comes a time, a homicidal moment, when the famished cannot longer endure the sight of the well-nourished. Kinsman and friend alike must succumb to their desperation."

We turn now to Ipuwer and his lament over the state of Egypt in this Dark Age: . . . *The inhabitants of the Delta carry shields . . . the tribes of the desert have become Egyptians everywhere. . . . Indeed, the plunderer is everywhere and the servant takes what he finds. . . .*

Indeed, the Nile overflows, yet none plough for it. Everyone says: "We do not know what will happen throughout the land." (E: No one has enough confidence in these times of uncertainty to till the fields.) Perhaps this was the year that Ankhtifi took over Edfu, and found certain areas flooded due to the incompetence of his predecessor. Even in a period of prolonged drought a more or less adequate flood will surely occur from time to time, as an occasional deficient flood will occur in a period of generally liberal ones. A general comment by Frankfort (1951:105) may be illuminating here: "Agriculturalists are inevitably the prey of occasional calamities because they are dependent on weather and water. But if disasters follow one another frequently without relief . . . there is no inducement for the peasant to continue his labours at all."

Indeed, women are barren and none conceive.[6] *Khnum fashions (men) no more because of the condition of the land . . . hearts are violent, plague is throughout the land, blood is everywhere . . . many dead are buried in the river; the stream is a sepulchre and the place of embalmment has become a stream* (E: the corpses are too numerous to be buried; they are thrown into the water like dead cattle) *. . . Squalor is throughout the land, and there is no one whose clothes are white in these times. . . .*

Indeed, the land turns round as does a potter's wheel. The robber possesses riches. . . .

(Considering the second sentence, the first would seem to refer to the social order; but I wonder whether it might not refer also to the land itself, keeping in mind Ankhtifi's sandstorms, and Butzer's invading dunes, and possible shiftings in the course of the Nile.)

Indeed, the river is blood, yet men drink of it. Men shrink from human beings and thirst after water ... (Perhaps, the river is full of corpses, but men are so desperate for water that they drink anyway).

Indeed, the ship of (the Southerners) has broken up; towns are destroyed and Upper Egypt has become an empty/dry waste ... ("dying of hunger on the sandbanks of Apophis"; Butzer [1959b] himself suggests this passage may refer to invading sand dunes).

Why really, crocodiles (sink) down because of what they have carried off, for men go to them of their own accord (W: suicide in the river). *It is the destruction of the land.... Men are few. He that lays his brother in the ground is everywhere* (E: gravediggers are everywhere).

Indeed, the desert is throughout the land, the nomes are laid waste (probably another reference to the invading dunes, although previously [E,W] interpreted as "desert dwellers"). *Barbarians from outside have come to Egypt, there are really no Egyptians anywhere .... Good things are throughout the land, yet house-wives say: "Oh that we had something to eat!"*

None sail north to Byblos today (due no doubt largely to the chaotic conditions in Egypt; however Byblos itself was destroyed by fire about this time [Wilson 1956:100; R. de Vaux 1966, *CAH* fasc. 46]).

Nay, but the entire Delta marshland is no (longer) hidden. The confidence (trusted defense?) *of the Northland is now a trodden road* (E: the natural protection of the Delta afforded by its swamps is no longer of avail). *The inaccessible place ... belongs now as much to them that knew it not, as to them that knew it, and strangers are versed in the crafts of the Delta.* (Probably, because of low waters, including the White or non-flood Nile, strangers can get about easily in the Delta which is no longer protected by being islands and marshlands; cf. Neferty, Texts from c. 2002 ... below, *The river of Egypt is empty, men cross over the water on foot.)*

... *"Cakes are lacking for most children; there is no food.... What is the taste of it like today?" Indeed, magnates are hungry and perishing ... cattle moan because of the state of the land ... the children of princes are dashed against walls, and the children of prayer are laid out on the high ground* (E: want drives people to expose them). (More likely, many young children, who are always particularly susceptible to famine, are dying and people cannot afford proper burials for them.)

Indeed, the ways are watched; men sit in the bushes until the benighted traveller comes in order to plunder his burden.... He is belabored with blows of a stick and murdered.... Indeed, that has perished which yesterday was seen ... commoners coming and going in dissolution (F: at the point of death).

Nay, but men feed on herbs and drink water; neither fruit nor herbage can be found any longer for the birds and ... (?) ... is taken away from the mouth of the swine, without it being said (as aforetime): "This is better for thee than for me," for men are so hungry. (E: men are now themselves eating that which they used to feed to the poultry and the pigs.)

Indeed, everywhere barley has perished and men are stripped of clothes, spice, and oil; everyone says: "There is none." The storehouse is empty and its keeper lies stretched on the ground (dead) . . . *The writings of the scribes of the cadaster (?) are destroyed, and the grain of Egypt is common property* (F: looted). (The granaries have been attacked and looted by the starving people.)

Behold, things have been done which have not happened for a long time: the king has been deposed by the rabble. . . . He who was buried as a falcon (is devoid?) of biers, and what the pyramid concealed has become empty (F: the living king is deposed and the dead one is disinterred). (The ingenuity expended by the kings of Dynasty XII to build robber-proof burial chambers lends further support to the idea that the royal tombs of the Old Kingdom were vandalized during this Dark Age [Edwards 1961]) . . . .*The land has been deprived of the kingship by a few lawless men . . . .The residence is afraid because of want, and (men go about?) unopposed to stir up strife . . . .The possessor of wealth now spends the night thirsty . . . he who had no shade is now the possessor of shade, while the erstwhile possessors of shade are now in the full blast (?) of the storm . . . .The statues are burnt and their tombs destroyed* (a further reference to vandalism in the cemeteries).

. . . *Authority, Knowledge, and Truth are with you* (the King), *yet confusion is what you set throughout the land, also the noise of tumult . . . You have acted so as to bring those things to pass. . . . You have told lies* (E: *lies are told thee), and the land is brushwood* (E: kaka, elsewhere a plant that easily catches fire). (Thus the vegetation is so dry it easily catches fire.) *All these years are strife, and a man is murdered on his house-top even though he was vigilant in his gate-house . . . .*The King is here blamed for the condition of the country, presumably before he was deposed, but in such general terms that his sins of omission or commission remain altogether obscure. However, see below, Discussion.

. . . *The troops whom we marshalled for ourselves have turned into foreigners and have taken to ravaging.* (The native recruits, or the mercenaries [Decline of the Neolithic Wet Phase, above] are quite out of control.) . . . *What has come to pass through it is informing the Asiatics of the state of the land* (that they can invade it with impunity). (This suggests that the collapse or revolt of the Egyptian army preceded any invasion or infiltration by Asiatics that added to the woes of the Egyptians.)

The basic cause of all the troubles lamented by Ipuwer is singularly obscure if we consider this text alone. There are several references to famine, to the land becoming as desert, and one to plague, but we look in vain for a direct lament about the level of the floods or even a reference to *tzw*. In the light of other inscriptions, indeed, we wonder if the Egyptians had some religious taboo, or at least a superstitious disinclination, about speaking critically of the Nile. Or one might agree with Vandier (1936) that civil disorder was the primary cause of the famine, but then one is left with no adequate explanation for the civil disorder. Ipuwer's reproaches to the King are in the most general terms; he gives no clue to the grievances which may have transformed the normally peaceful and docile Egyptian peasants into a violently rebellious rabble. Nor does he reproach any nomarch in particular (or nomarchs in general) with carrying on civil war, for destroying the state with his selfish ambitions. The traditionally unwarlike, unmilitary character of the Egyptian peasant (Kees 1961:141) provides an additional plausibility-argument that famine was originally the cause of civil disorder rather than the result of it, although then civil disorder may well have delayed recovery from the famine. Spontaneous combustion into civil war of such extreme destructiveness as must be assumed if we are to account for so major a famine, seems to me decidedly un-Egyptian, and not to be accepted without more clear and compelling evidence. On the other hand, some of the other texts, especially those designating famine as the time of the *tzw,* seem to indicate clearly a link between very low floods (*tzw*) and severe famine.

Although I have emphasized the word *tzw* because of its clear implication of "low Nile" and its appearance in texts describing the most severe conditions of famine, *tzw* is not the only word that has been interpreted to mean famine in ancient Egypt. Vandier (1936:59-93) identifies and discusses a number of other words, some of which are even more indirect. One of the more interesting (kindly called to my attention by Dr. Millet) which is found in famine contexts of this period is *snb-ib,* literally *the heart is healthy.* The use of this euphemism or "antiphrase" translated by Vandier (1936:90) as *years of courage*–and which could well be imagined, although we have no evidence, as a condensed reference to some currently popular phrase such as "The heart is healthy, though the body is weak"–may be taken as further evidence of the reluctance of the ancient Egyptians to speak plainly of a failure of the Nile floods.

It is noteworthy that not only do our texts fail to speak directly of the Nile, but also they never indicate that any deity is in any way concerned with the disaster. In Egyptian disaster-literature, the gods are neither held responsible for the disaster nor prayed to for relief. Their absence may easily pass unnoticed by the modern western mind. Yet it is quite otherwise in Mesopotamian disaster-literature, where the disaster may be explicitly described as an affliction sent by a god, particularly by the chief god, Enlil– for no evident reason as in the Lament over the Destruction of Ur, or to reduce the human population which had become so numerous and noisy that they interfered with the sleep of the gods as in Atrahasis (*ANET*, pp. 455-463 and 104, respectively).

There are a few additional texts which may throw an indirect light on the condition of the Nile and on related social conditions. One of these is a Hymn to the Nile (Wilson 1955:372) which was originally composed, most probably, in the Middle Kingdom. Although not strictly an historical document, it is worth quoting for an impression of the conditions which the Egyptians, not long after the Dark Age, associated with a low Nile:

   . . . *If he is sluggish, the nostrils are stopped up* (because it is so dry and dusty?), *and everybody is poor. If there be (thus) a cutting down in the food-offerings of the gods, then a million men perish among mortals, covetousness is practiced, the entire land is in a fury, and great and small are on the execution-block . . . . (But) when he rises, then the land is in jubilation . . . .*

   . . . *If thou are (too) heavy (to rise), the people are few, and one begs for the water of the year. (Then) the rich man looks like him who is worried, and every man is seen (to be) carrying his weapons. There is no companion backing up a companion. There are no garments for clothing; there are no ornaments for the children of nobles . . . .He* (the Nile) *who establishes truth in the heart of men, for it is said: "Deceit comes after poverty"* (W: poverty from a low Nile brings lawlessness) . . . .

Some of the consequences of a low Nile cited here seem reminiscent of Ipuwer's laments and quite excessive for one year under a strong government, and it is natural to infer that the Hymn reflects memories of the many years of very low Niles of the First Intermediate Period.

Texts from the years c. 2150-2000 B.C.

By 2130 or a little earlier there were signs of improvement in natural conditions and in political stability. In the north, Dynasty X came to power, with a King Neferkare and his two strong and long-lived successors, Wahkare Khety and Merikare ruling from Herakleopolis over Lower Egypt. In the south, the nomarch of Thebes, Inyotef, established a rival dynasty (XI), declaring himself King of Upper Egypt, c. 2133, as the Horus Sehertowy; he was followed by Inyotef II, Horus Wahankh, who reigned for some 50 years (c. 2117-2069), and by Inyotef III, Horus Nakhtnebtepnefer for 8 years (c. 2068-2061) according to the chronology of Hayes (1961).

Although political stability had clearly improved, Vandier (1936:12) points out nine funerary stelae which he dates to the period of the Inyotef (Antef) kings and which contain an assertion that the owner saved his district or town by distribution of grain in a time of famine (most commonly, *burdensome years, or years of misery, ksnt*). Hayes (1961) also discusses a number of these Upper Egyptian stelae.

The word *tzw* appears in only one (Turin 1310) of these inscriptions, in an enigmatic passage which reads (Vandier 1936): *He* (the king?) *repelled (?) the years of famine (tzw) from the land. He,* Vandier suggests, is most probably the founder of the dynasty, Inyotef I. In the light of my general thesis, this may be interpreted to mean that the years of very low Niles *(tzw)* and of severe famines came to an end under his rule, as it is reasonable to believe on other grounds, and King Inyotef, as a true Horus King, is claiming credit for the improvement (see Discussion, below).

This group of inscriptions seem to describe conditions less severe than the time of the *tzw,* and apparently we should imagine that climate conditions improved in a fluctuating manner, with years of good inundation becoming more frequent and deficient years less frequent and less severely deficient. For completeness I include the most relevant passages, translated from Vandier (1936), although because of uncertainties in dating they contribute no great amount of additional information. The first seven (following Vandier's numbering) come from the time of Inyotef I, or slightly earlier, that is, to the later years of the first great drought.

(1) Stele of Djari, of Qurneh: . . . *I was a great provider for their houses, in the year of famine (rnpt snb-ib), I gave to those whom I did not know as well as to those whom I did know. . . .*

(2) The stele of Iti of Gebelein, already quoted above, is considered by Hayes to be somewhat later than the inscriptions of Ankhtifi, but not necessarily as late as Inyotef I.

(3) Stele of Heka-ib (BM 1671), also of Gebelein, and according to Vandier (1936, 1950), contemporary with Iti: . . . *I have provided this entire town with Upper Egyptian grain for several years, without counting (?) . . . . I gave oil to Hierakonpolis after my town had been provided for . . . .*

(4) Stele of Djehouti of Qurneh: . . . *I supplied the temple of Amun during the years of misery (ksnt). . . .*

(5) Turin 1310: *He* (the king?) *repelled the years of low Niles (tzw) from the land.*

(6) Stele of Antefoker (BM 1628): . . . *I possessed barley and wheat; I gave barley and wheat to the hungry, and I supported everyone in my vicinity during the famine (ḥkrw), acting in such a way that no one died. . . .*

(7) Stele of Senni (Cairo 20500): . . . *I measured out life-giving grain of Upper Egypt for this entire town in the palace of the count . . . during the miserable years of famine (ksnt nt snb-ib).*

The last two of the nine stelae are several decades later; one of them is clearly dated by the name of King Inyotef III. This one (8), the stele of Ideni of Abydos (Cairo 20502), reads in part: . . . *I was a man who gathered his energy in the day of misery (hrw n ksnt) . . . a man of whom the Horus Nakhtnebtepnefer, King of Upper and Lower Egypt, son of Re, Inyotef (III), living forever, (said?) on the subject of the plan to keep alive (nourish) this town: "He has done all that I ordered throughout the entire country."*

And finally (9) the stele of . . (?) . . . (Cairo 20503): . . . *I kept alive (nourished) my town, in the year of misery (ksnt), so that my name would be good. . . .*

These two stelae indicate a year of scarcity, although not necessarily of severe famine, during the rein of Inyotef III.

Turning now to Lower Egypt, we find that this period remains a Dark Age in terms of available information, in spite of the improvement in political stability. But around 2080 the father of King Merikare, probably Wahkare Khety, is able to say in his Instructions to his son (Wilson 1955): . . . *There is no enemy within the compass of thy frontier. . . . I pacified the entire west, as far as the coast of the sea. . . . But the east is rich in bowmen . . . turned about are the islands in the midst* (later, under Dynasties XVIII-XX, this would mean the islands of the Aegean but whether the phrase had this meaning already c. 2100 is uncertain) . . . . *Lo, the wretched Asiatic . . . he has been fighting since the time of Horus, he does not conquer nor yet can he be conquered. He does not announce a day in fighting, like a thief. . . . I made the Northland smite them, I captured their inhabitants, and I took their cattle, to the disgust of the Asiatics against Egypt. Do not trouble thyself about him: he is only an Asiatic. . . . He may rob a single person, but he does not lead against a town of many citizens. . . .* Somewhat puzzling is his description of the land of the Asiatics as both *afflicted with water, difficult from many trees,* unless "water" here means "rain," which the Egyptians may have considered an inferior and unreliable source of water.

Merikare is advised to deal firmly with agitators: *A talker is an exciter of a city . . .,* and traitors, to liquidate them before they can stir up trouble (Wilson 1955; Erman 1927); to be skillful in speech; and to rule benevolently and justly, . . . *but keep thine eyes open, one that is trusting will become one that is afflicted. . . .*

More directly relevant to our main theme: *Thou sufferest not from the Nile, that it cometh not, and thou hast the products* (taxes) *of the Delta . . .* (Erman 1927). This I take as evidence that some of his predecessors, within vivid memory, had suffered from the Nile, that its flood had failed to come.

Another interesting verse seems to refer to the large number of young people among the population: *Behold thy commonalty is full of those newly grown up, of such as are 20 years old. The young generation is happy in following its heart. . . . Increase the younger generation of thy followers, that it may be provided with property, endowed with fields and rewarded with cattle . . .* (Erman 1927). While the meaning of this passage is uncertain, it suggests to me that there has been no serious famine for at least twenty years, and that since the end of the famine there has been a great increase in the population.

We should not expect, however, that a return to normal floods would be followed promptly by a full political and cultural revival and the building of fine large monuments. Both the king and his subjects would be too busy reorganizing the kingdom, and repairing and restoring the irrigation system of canals and dikes. Even if the king desired to build a large monument, after a severe and prolonged famine the population would be so much reduced that he would be prevented by a shortage of skilled labor. As for reunification of the Two Lands, of Upper and Lower Egypt, this would have to await the appearance on the throne of a local king who possessed the necessary dynamic qualities.

Merikare was further advised to deal tactfully with the South and not to provoke it. Apparently he disregarded this advice, went to war and recovered the nome of Abydos, with substantial help from another Khety of Assiut. His triumph was shortlived, however, for by 2040 his kingdom had been overthrown, and Upper and Lower Egypt forcibly reunited by King Nebhepetre Mentuhotep of Thebes, who is traditionally regarded as the founder of the Middle Kingdom.

The floods were evidently adequate, or better, during the 50-year reign (2060-2010) of King Mentuhotep II. The large and original funerary monument built by this king at Deir el Bahri near Thebes gives evidence of a high level of prosperity. And Vandier (1936) finds only one possible reference to famine, in the stele of a certain Mentuhotep, son of Hepi: *When a little inundation (ḥcpy) happened, in the year 25* (probably of Mentuhotep II, although Griffith favors Senwosret I of Dynasty XII, and Goedicke [JEA 1962] favors Inyotef II), *I did not allow my nome to suffer hunger; I gave it wheat and barley and I did not allow a famine to occur in it before the years of big inundations returned.* Whatever its date, this does not suggest anything as serious as those we have considered above, but only a poor year in the midst of a series of good floods. It is also more forthright in speaking openly of a *little inundation.*

Texts from the years c. 2002-c. 1950 B.C.

With the death of King Seankhkare Mentuhotep III about 1998, Dynasty XI came to an end in a second period of disorder, brought on, I suggest, by another period of low Niles, drought and sandstorms, a second "exclamation point" emphasizing the end of the Neolithic Wet Phase. It is generally considered that the twelve-year reign of Mentuhotep III was peaceful and prosperous, but there is one document that, in retrospect, may be considered an omen of trouble to come. This is a letter written to his family by a certain Hekanakht when he was on a business journey during a famine caused by a low Nile. This document, recently translated by James (1962) and by Baer (1963), states that . . . *the whole land is perished, but you have not been hungry. . . . When I came hither southwards I fixed your rations properly. (Now) is the inundation very high? Now our food is fixed for us in proportion to the inundation. So be patient, all of you who are listed here. . . . I have managed to keep you alive until today. . . . Take heed lest you be angry . . . everything is mine. It must be said, "Being half alive is better than dying altogether."Now one should say hunger only is regard to real hunger. They have begun to eat people here. . . .*

This last, Vandier (1936) and others consider to be an exaggeration intended to impress those to whom Hekanakht is writing; in absence of other evidence for very bad times, and considering the general tone of Hekanakht's letters, I must agree. But I would also suggest that the statement derives from a memory of the earlier time of more terrible famine, when Ankhtifi speaks of cannibalism.

These terrible times were soon to come again, although more briefly. Following the death of Mentuhotep III come five to seven years of darkness, about which very little is known. A King Nebtowyre Mentuhotep IV apparently occupied the throne for at least two years of this period, but he is known only from the inscriptions in Wadi Hammamat by his Vizier Amenemhet, and seems subsequently not to have been considered a legitimate ruler. Following Seankhkare, the Turin Papyrus mentions seven kingless years. During the period a fresh outbreak of raids by the Libyans of the western desert and by the Asiatics from the northeast apparently occurred.

The primary document on the confused and obscure period between the end of Dynasty XI and the start of Dynasty XII is the so-called Prophecy of Neferty, composed during the reign of Amenemhet I. In the words of Posener (CAH fasc. 29, p. 8) this document "combines in one sinister picture these recent memories with older memories of the depredations of the Asiatics during the First Intermediate Period." And not only of the Asiatics, but also of the chaotic social and natural conditions in both periods, for Neferty has a good deal to say about the natural conditions of the land, and gives a rather clearer picture than did Ipuwer. The quotes are mainly from Erman (1927), with occasional phrases from Wilson (1955). The invading sand dunes should be kept in mind while reading the words of Neferty.

. . . *That which was made is as if it were never made, and Re must begin to found anew* (E: begin creation over again). *The whole land has perished, there is none left, not the black of the nail survives of what should be there* (W: Not so much of the Black Land of Egypt survives as might be under a fingernail). Probably it was buried under blowing sand and invading dunes.

This land is ruined; no one concerns himself about it any more, no one speaks, and no eye weeps (E: That is no longer worthwhile). . . . *The sun is veiled and will not shine that men may see. None can live when the storm veils it* (the sun), *all men are dulled (?) through want of it.* (E: By this obscuring of the sun, of which he also speaks below, not a single eclipse is intended, but dust- and sand-storms, suiting, as they do, the following descriptions of the drought.) (Cf. also the dust storms of Ankhtifi, above.)

The river of Egypt is empty, men cross over the water on foot. (This implies a failure of the White Nile, thus of the rains over east-central Africa.)[7] *Men search for water upon which the ships may sail; its road is become a bank, and the bank is become water.* Probably this refers to shiftings in the location of the river bed, accompanying the erratic and abnormal fluctuations in the volume of water, and the drifting sands; it is well established (Butzer 1959a, 1960) that shiftings did occur from time to time.

The south wind drives away the north wind (E: which brings coolness and humidity), *and the sky has still only the one wind* (meaning, the north wind failed to come at its normal season?). *The birds no longer hatch their eggs in the swamps of the Delta, but the bird hath made her a nest nigh unto men* (E: The birds migrate from the dried-up swamps to inhabited regions, where water still exists). . . .

Foes are in the East, Asiatics are come down into Egypt. . . . *By night one will suddenly be fallen upon (?).* . . .

. . . *This land is taken away and added to* (W: *is brought-and-taken*) (by the varying course of the river and the drifting dunes?), *and no one knows what the issue will be. . . .*

. . . Men take up weapons of war, the land lives in confusion (E: In the prevailing distress all live on robbery). *. . . They beg for bread with blood. Men laugh with a laughter of disease . . . and one slayeth another. . . . Men take the goods of a man of high estate from him and give them to one from without. . . . The possessor is in deprivation and him from without is contented.*

. . . The land is diminished and its governors are many. The field is bare, and its taxes are great; little is the grain and great the grain measure (of taxes), *and it is measured to overflowing.*

The sun separates himself from men (E: by sandstorms); *he arises when it is the hour. No one knows when it is midday, for his shadow cannot be distinguished* (E: on the sundial). *. . . . He is in the sky like the moon, and yet he does not deviate from his accustomed time. . . .*

But finally, *a king shall come from the south, called Ameni,* and he put the country to rights again, particularly by driving out the Asiatics, and building the "Wall of the Prince" to keep them out. Fortunately, Nature cooperated and the Nile floods returned more or less to normal, and King Amenemhet I was able to launch his country into one of the most glorious periods of its long history, known as the Middle Kingdom.

Since virtually nothing is known of this brief Dark Age at the end of Dynasty XI, we may speculate briefly in the light of the climatological hypothesis. It is generally agreed that the future King Amenemhet I was the same man as the Vizier Amenemhet who led an expedition to the Wadi Hammamat in year two of King Mentuhotep IV. Hayes (1961) has noted that the tone of the inscriptions of Amenemhet suggest a loyal servant of his king, not a man plotting imminent revolt. I suggest that Amenemhet may have been driven to reconsider whether this Mentuhotep was in truth a proper and legitimate king, approved by the gods, when the floods failed so severely. Or perhaps Mentuhotep himself developed such doubts of his own legitimacy that he abdicated or died (see Discussion, below), since his claim to the throne is anyway obscure.

Further support to the idea of a serious failure of the Nile preceding the reign of Amenemhet I is provided by the quotation from his Instructions to his son: *. . . I was the one who made barley, the beloved of the grain-god. The Nile honored me on every broad expanse* (the inundations were good). *No one hungered in my years; no one thirsted therein. . . . Everything which I had commanded was in the proper place* (Wilson 1955).

Regarding the relations between the king and the feudal nomarchs in the early years of Amenemhet I, Hayes (1961:35) states that the new king saw to it that "the boundaries of the nomes were rigorously established and regulations were enacted covering each district's share in the supply of Nile water available for purposes of irrigation" (see also Gardiner 1961:128; and Breasted 1906:628). This again suggests not only that water was not abundant at the very start of his reign, but also that much of the fighting in the times of great trouble may have been over access to the severely limited water supply. We have already seen that Merer shut off certain fields and did not allow his family's water to irrigate for someone else, and that Khety of Assiut built new irrigation works the better to utilize the meager water available. And we may speculate whether Ankhtifi's ability to supply other towns in the time of worst famine, in spite of living in a relatively poor part of the country, may have been related not only to the organizing efficiency and resourcefulness of which he boasts, but to the fact that his nomes had first access to the water. In normal times of course this would not matter, but if the river fell so low that one could walk across it, there could be some advantage in first access.

In this context we may note two items from the "Protestations of Guiltlessness" (Wilson 1955:34) by the soul appearing before a posthumous court: A31: *I have not held up the water in its season* (W: denied the inundation waters to others); and A32: *I have not built a dam against running water.* No doubt there were many who did, including Merer, and Khety of Assiut, as noted above.

With the reign of Amenemhet I, we come to the end of the First Dark Age in Egypt— an age bracketed by two particularly troubled and dark intervals, each associated with a severe drought, about 2180 to 2130, and 2000 to 1990 B.C. Dynasty XII, c. 1991-1786 B.C. was a period of strong government, cultural advance and general prosperity. There was no significant revival of the rains over the desert (Butzer 1958), no return of the Neolithic Wet Phase, but the inundations were evidently adequate. I shall discuss else-where what can be known of their levels. Vandier (1936) was able to find only one text referring to famine in these years, an inscription in the tomb of Ameny, Nomarch of Beni Hasan, during the reign of Senwosret I. The Nomarch Ameny states (Breasted 1906: 523): . . . *When years of famine came, I plowed all the fields of the Oryx Nome, as far as its southern and northern boundaries, preserving its people alive, and furnishing its food so that there was none hungry therein. . . . Then came great Niles, producers of grain and of all things, (but) I did not collect the arrears of the field* (taxes). . . . This inscription no doubt gives a picture of the normal situation in years of low Nile, which must have occurred from time to time throughout Egyptian history, though rarely with such severity as in the Dark Ages at the end of Dynasty VI and between Dynasties XI and XII. Vandier notes that Griffith considers that the inscription of Mentuhotep, son of Hepi, refers to the same famine as Ameny's inscription.

Discussion

Most Egyptologists who attempt to explain the collapse of the Old Kingdom stress the declining power and wealth of the king and the growing power and independence of the provincial nobility. Evidence of this trend through Dynasty VI is too plentiful to be questioned and need be mentioned here only briefly: from as early as the end of Dynasty IV, the royal pyramids decrease in size while the mastabas of the great nobles grow in size and splendor; in Dynasty VI many a noble abandoned the earlier custom of a tomb near the royal pyramid in favor of a tomb in his own province; governorships became hereditary, with "only a perfunctory nod in the direction of Memphis" (Hayes 1953). This much is beyond dispute. What is questionable is whether such a trend is sufficient explanation for a disaster of the magnitude that overwhelmed Egypt at the end of Dynasty VI.

I have suggested rather than dire famine, due to prolonged (on the historic, though very brief on the geologic, time scale) failure of the rains over the central and eastern African sources of the Nile—a sort of "exclamation point" emphasizing the ending of the Neolithic Wet Phase—was the crisis that shattered a weakened central government utterly unable to cope with the problem, and decimated the Egyptian people. We have considered a number of ancient texts that support this point of view, and the meaning of which becomes clearer when read in this light. Moreover, the literature "voicing the bewilderment and despair with which Egyptians faced the overturn of their once stable world" (Wilson 1956) is more readily understood if we conceive of a cause that they were essentially helpless to remedy.

Let us explore some further political aspects of this hypothesis. Of the time of Dynasty VI, the decades before the disaster, Hayes (1953:131) writes: ". . . One cannot help but feel that it was only through personal loyalty that the great rulers of Upper Egypt [served] the crown. Once the king, incapable of controlling his provincial governors by force, found himself unable to win their loyalty through favors and wisely chosen concessions, the whole fabric of the pharaonic government fell to pieces."

We consider this situation against the background of the Egyptian concept of Kingship, particularly as described by Frankfort, Wilson and Aldred. In the words of Frankfort (1951:120): "The Egyptian system . . . [in which] . . . a god had consented to guide the nation . . . gave a sense of security which the Asiatic contemporaries of the ancient Egyptians totally lacked . . . a pledge that the forces of nature would be well disposed and bring prosperity and peace." "That Pharaoh was of divine essence, a god incarnate" is fundamental to the Egyptian concept of Kingship, "and this view can be traced back as far as texts and symbols take us" (Frankfort 1948:5); the attitude can be seen most readily in art—in war scenes, hunting scenes, and scenes involving the other gods—from the time of Narmer.

Introducing a text from Dynasty XII, Wilson (1955:431) writes: "The king of Egypt ruled the land as a god, as the Son of Re, or as the Horus, or as the incorporation of the deities of Upper and Lower Egypt. He was also a synthesis of other gods who represented forces of proper rule, a blend of force and intelligence, of terror and nurture, or of sustenance and punishment. . . . Some of the divine elements which went into the composition of a pharaoh" are set forth in a poem of instruction addressed to his children by Sehetepibre, Chief Treasurer under King Ni-maat-Re Amenemhet III: *Worship King Ni-maat-Re, living forever, within your bodies, and associate with his majesty in your hearts. He is Perception* (W: cognitive intelligence, an attribute of good rule), *which is in the hearts, and his eyes search out everybody. He is Re, by whose beams one sees. He illumines the Two Lands more than the sun. He makes the Two Lands more verdant than does a high Nile. For he has filled the Two Lands with strength and life. . . . He giveth vital force to them that serve him . . .* (Wilson 1955; Erman 1927).

Under Dynasty XVIII this attitude was expressed in an inscription in the tomb of Rekhmire, vizier under King Thutmose III (Frankfort 1948:47): *What is the King of Upper and Lower Egypt? He is a god by whose dealings one lives, the father and the mother of all men, alone by himself, without an equal.* Moreover the King's power and his concern for his realm do not cease with his death, for we read in another inscription (Frankfort 1948:195): *Thutmose III is in heaven like the moon. The Nile is at his service. He opens its cave to give life to Egypt.*

Aldred (1963, 1965) particularly stresses the relation between king and Nile, and writes that the Egyptian concept of the god-king derived from the "prehistoric rain-maker who kept his tribe, their crops, and beasts in good health by exercising a magic control over the weather ... [who was] ... transformed into the Pharaoh, able to sustain the entire nation by having command over the Nile flood. . . . The Kingship and the Nile are intimately associated. . . . The earliest kings were associated with the control of the flood waters . . ." (Aldred 1963:157). "The never-failing inundations of the river were more predictable in their occurrences, though not in their volume, and therefore more amenable to control than the weather" (Aldred 1965:50). Indeed, the climatic conditions of Egypt were almost uniquely suited to inspire the confidence of the people in any divine power claimed by their kings, far more so than in western Asia; and the predictability of the Nile probably played no insignificant role in the successful development of the dogma of divine kingship.

In the earliest Pyramid Texts, inscribed on the walls of the tomb chamber of the Pyramid of Unis, the king is poetically identified with the Nile flood (Černý 1952:85): *It is Unis who inundates the land and who has come forth from the lake, it is Unis who plucks the papyrus plant.* Pyr. 388; and in Pyr. 507-8: *Unis came today from the fullness of the flood, he is Subek, with a green feather, watchful face and uplifted fore-part of the body. . . . He came to his pools which are on the shore inundated by the Great Fullness, to the place of satisfaction, with green fields (the place) which is in the realm of light.* Pyr. 509 (transl. N. B. Millet) continues: *Unis causes the plants to become green on the two banks of the realm of light.* Černý points out that in later Pyramid Texts the god Osiris is connected with the flooding of the Nile on several occasions, and from the Middle Kingdom onward is often referred to as the god of floods and vegetation. Since the earliest texts, those of King Unis, refer thus to the king and not to Osiris, Černý suggests that Osiris received his flood-vegetation attributes from his identification with the dead king.

King Amenemhet I of Dynasty XII includes the occurrence of good floods among the reasons why he deserves the loyalty and gratitude of all his subjects: *. . . I was the one who made barley, the beloved of the grain-god. The Nile honored me on every broad expanse. No one hungered in my years, no one thirsted therein. . . . Everything which I had commanded was in the proper place* (Wilson 1955:419). Frankfort (1948:57) emphasizes that the king here asserts that he "partakes of the essence of these natural phenomena. . . . The king 'produced barley,' not merely in an indirect way, for instance by caring for the farmers or furthering agriculture, but through his own actions—by maintaining Maat, the right order which allowed nature to function unimpaired for the benefit of man. Hence the Nile rose effectively at the inundation so that the arable land reached its maximum extent and the people prospered."

Frankfort instructively compares this Dynasty XII text with a song written for the accession of King Merneptah of Dynasty XIX, more than 700 years later, as translated by Erman: *Rejoice, thou entire land, the goodly time has come. A lord is appointed in all countries . . . great of kingship like Horus . . . Merneptah. . . . Truth has repressed falsehood* (W: The Egyptian concept of *ma'at* "truth, order, right" was of the essential order of the universe, given by the gods at the beginning and maintained and reconfirmed by the god-king). *The sinners are fallen on their faces. . . . The water standeth and faileth not, the Nile carrieth a high flood. The days are long, the nights have hours, the months come aright* (W: Order is found also in the regularity of times and seasons, restored by the new king). *The gods are content and happy of heart, and life is spent in laughter and wonder.*

Frankfort (1948:58) points out that "The comparison of the two texts enhances their significance. The song might be thought to contain merely the hyperboles of a festive mood, were it not that they recur in the grim context of Amenemhet's teaching. There the beneficial influence of the king is stressed only to bring out his utter loneliness, for notwithstanding it he was betrayed. And yet, though the two texts differ in both mood and age, we find them describing regal power with the same attributes, as strong a proof as we are likely to find that the Egyptians really believed these attributes to pertain to their king. This power, then, includes the remarkable capacity to dominate and further natural processes, especially the inundation of the Nile on which the prosperity of Egypt depends. Because the king, who has established Maat, who has defeated falsehood, comes to the throne, there are abundant inundations; and the seasons—that is, the months and days and nights—follow each other in orderly procession. So the song. But the teaching of Amenemhet says practically the same thing; none was hungry, for the king made the corn grow; and the Nile, in obedience, rose to all accessible places so that they could be tilled. Even as late an author as Ammianus Marcellinus knew that the Egyptians ascribed plenty or famine to the quality of their king— not, in a modern sense, to his quality as an administrator, but to his effectiveness as an organ of integration, partaking of the divine and of the human and intrusted with making the mutual dependence of the two a source of 'laughter and wonder.'"

The concept of the king's influence over nature also appears behind the words of flattery addressed by Sinuhe to King Senwosret I: *Whether I am in the Residence or in this place, it is ever thou that obscurest this horizon, and the sun ariseth at thy pleasure; the water in the river is drunk when thou willest, and the air in heaven is breathed when thou biddest* (Erman 1927:25). Probably this is merely an Egyptian way of saying "I recognize and accept you as the legitimate god-king of Egypt, as the true Horus."

Let us now link together the factors described in the preceding pages of this section: the great nobles of Upper Egypt waxing in independent power and bound to the throne by increasingly fragile ties; the fundamental link between the divinity of the king and his control over the floods; and to this combination add the prolonged and severe failure of the floods, to the extent that people throughout Egypt were dying of starvation—the *tzw*-famines of several ancient texts. Imagine an average king on the throne, a man with no outstanding qualities of leadership but adequate to normal conditions. With these ingredients, I suggest, we have a quite sufficient and entirely plausible explanation for the troubles that afflicted Egypt in its First Intermediate Period, or First Dark Age. The central government, unable to deal effectively with so severe a famine and drought, and undermined at its ideological core by the very existence of this revolt by nature, simply collapsed. The local nobility became as free in spirit as in fact to cope locally with the famine to whatever extent their various individual abilities permitted, and also free to ignore the supposed king in their tomb inscriptions, a practice general in this period and utterly contrary to earlier usage.

There remains one major characteristic of Egyptian Dark Ages in need of explanation, the short reigns and the very large number of kings to be fitted into relatively few years. Here I shall venture a step beyond what seems to me the realm of sound probability, into the realm of speculation, to propose a hypothesis that I believe makes sense of these numerous short reigns, in the context of a Dark Age caused primarily by deficient Nile floods in a land ruled by god-kings.

When we consult the revised *CAH* (Smith 1962; Hayes 1961, 1962) we find at least 31 Kings, and possibly as many as 40, in the interval from the death of Pepi II to the end of Dynasty IX, a period now believed to cover no more than about 60 years, c. 2190 to c. 2130; and this disregards the description by Manetho of Dynasty VII as composed of 70 Kings who reigned for 70 days. From the death of Pepi II to the end of Dynasty VIII, c. 2160, we have at least 18 Kings in some 30 years. Dynasty VI itself ended with several ephemeral reigns following that of Pepi II; the Turin Papyrus appears originally to have listed eight Kings (Gardiner 1961) but the names of only three have survived, and only these three are included in the total of 18. For Dynasty IX, c. 2160-2130, the Turin Papyrus indicates thirteen Kings. With Dynasty X conditions finally became more stable, with five Kings in some 90 years.

In addition to the evidence from the various King Lists, it is of interest to recall the statement of Merer that he *offered for thirteen rulers (ḥk3w),* in a single adult lifetime, during which *tzw*-famines occurred. Unfortunately the word *ḥk3w* does not enable us to distinguish between kings and nomarchs, nor is it certain that thirteen living rulers are meant (N. B. Millet, private communication); Černý (1961) interprets it, with some unease, as thirteen living nomarchs. But thirteen living kings seems the most plausible interpretation within the historical context.

Almost nothing is known of the genealogy of the Kings of the First Dark Age. The popularity of the praenomen "Neferkare" in Dynasty VII-VIII, and to a lesser extent in Dynasty IX, is often taken as evidence that the Kings of Dynasties VII-IX regarded themselves as legitimate successors of Neferkare Pepi II (Hayes 1961). Since Pepi II had four known Queens, and an unknown number of sons, daughters and grandchildren, and moreover is believed to have lived to be 100, it is quite likely that he outlived most of his children, and it is easy to imagine that the order of the succession became uncertain and controversial at or shortly after his death, or at the end of Dynasty VI. Then Manetho's tradition of 70 Kings who ruled for 70 days might be imagined as a council of royal princes, descendants of Neferkare Pepi II, ruling collectively while they tried to resolve the question of which of them should become king.

The next Dynasty, be it properly called VII or VIII, evidently began with a King Neferkare "the Younger," a son or grandson of Pepi II by Ankhesen-Pepi, the Queen of his late years; Neferkare the Younger was credited by the Turin Papyrus (Hayes 1953) with a reign of just over four years, leaving only fourteen years for his fourteen successors of Dynasty VII-VIII. It is clear that there can be no question of a succession of generations among these Kings, and it has been suggested (Millet, 1968 lecture) that for some reason in this period the succession passed from brother to brother. While resulting in shorter reigns, even this hardly seems adequate to account for fourteen Kings in fourteen years, nor even some 31+ Kings in no more than 60 years. (A similar difficulty occurs also in the Second Intermediate Period with Dynasty XIII, and in the early part of the Dark Age around 1200 B.C.)

The need to explain these very numerous short reigns invites a radical hypothesis, which however fits well into our general picture of the situation. In brief, I suggest that the reigns of many of the kings in these periods were terminated rather promptly by death, either by suicide or by secret murder, when their performance of all the correct rites failed to produce any significant alleviation of the drought.

Although there is no evidence from ancient Egypt, there is evidence from recent times in various regions of Africa about what happens to a rainmaker king in a time of unusual drought. From C. G. Seligman's *Egypt and Negro Africa, a Study in Divine Kingship,* p. 38, Frankfort (1948:34) quotes that the African "king of Juken is . . . able to control the rain and winds. A succession of droughts or bad harvests is ascribed to his negligence or to the waning of his strength, and he is accordingly secretly strangled." And there are other tribes, "like the Shilluk [who] will destroy their king when he threatens to become an imperfect link between man and the gods. . . . It has repeatedly been maintained that the Egyptians, too, killed their king and for the same reason; but of this there is no proof at all. The Egyptians, however, did regard their king in the same manner—a bond between nature and man" (Frankfort 1948:47).

Childe (1953) points out that the Pharaoh is a type of divine king, described by Frazer, who "holds his sovereignty by virtue of his magic power," and as its price must submit to ritual death before his body, and hence his magic power, grows feeble with age. In Egypt he was ritually revitalized by the sed-festival from the time of Menes onward. Egyptologists agree that the Egyptians did not as a regular practice kill their king, and that ritual revitalization played at least some role in the sed-festival. In spite of the magic-symbolic renewal of the king's power by the sed-festival, however, Aldred (1963:157) considers it significant that . . . "the tradition that the king should die for his people persisted in folk-lore and in the more primitive spells of *The Pyramid Texts;* and there are anthropologists who believe that the ceremonial killing of the Pharaoh was sometimes revived in moments of crisis."

If ever there was a crisis calling for such extreme measures, the First Dark Age, the period of the *tzw*-famines, was surely such a time. Frankfort (1948) emphasizes that there is no proof that any such thing ever occurred in Egypt. But then, there is little proof for anything—except famine, civil disorder, and too many kings—from the Dark Ages. Moreover, in addition to influencing the powers of Nature, "the king was the personification of ma'at, a word which we translate as 'rightness' or 'truth' or 'justice,' but which also seems to have the meaning of 'the natural cosmic order.' The forces of evil could upset ma'at until restoration had been effected by some appropriate act—a magic rite, or the advent of a new king" (Aldred 1963:161). A prolonged and severe failure of adequate floods, the *tzw*-famines, must have represented to the ancient Egyptians a uniquely profound upset of the natural cosmic order which might well seem to demand a drastic remedy, and might well lead them to try one new king after another, as each conspicuously failed to restore *ma'at*—particularly if the drought should occur at a time when there was an unusual degree of uncertainty about the identity of the prince chosen for the next incarnation of Horus.

We noted above that Ipuwer seems to blame the king for the sorry state of the land, but completely fails to specify what the king was doing wrong. In the light of the above discussion it appears probable that Ipuwer actually had no specific idea what the king was doing wrong. But since maintaining *ma'at*, by some supernatural power, was the primary duty of the king, the occurrence of disorder, or famine, and of failure of the floods, would mean that the god-king had somehow failed in his prime duty.

Without any particular reference to the Dark Ages, Anthes (1959, *JNES* 18:180) considers that "the Pyramid Texts indicate conclusively that there existed a supreme court of sorts who nominated the king. It is hard to imagine that their activity would have been restricted to the mere acclamation of the new king." I am not able to offer an opinion on the validity of this concept. But if it has any validity, we may imagine the indecision and confusion in this council as year after year the floods failed to rise above famine levels—particularly if there was no one prince who by the usual standards had a claim much superior to those of his rivals. Such a condition could easily occur after so long a reign as that of Pepi II, with at least four queens. One can imagine the council approving one prince after another, as to each Horus brought no good inundation, in an increasingly frantic effort to discover the true Son of Horus, and persuading or coercing each prince in turn to kill himself after he had performed the proper rites and received no recognition from the god. Now and then there would be a year or two or three of hope, with at least meagerly adequate flooding, and then again failure. In all probability the prince himself would lose confidence in his right to be king, and only the most irreligious, or cowardly, would resist the pressure to kill himself.

If this picture corresponds in any way to reality—and the reality of the hypothetical council is not essential to the correspondence—we should surmise that the same situation recurred at the end of Dynasty XI, with the seven-year darkness that followed the death of Seankhkare Mentuhotep III. Hayes (1953:167) mentions three names in addition to Nebtowyre Mentuhotep IV who may have reigned briefly in this interval. The practice in Dynasty XII, whereby each king appointed his chosen heir co-regent in his lifetime, may have been motivated in part by a desire to reduce the influence of the council in the naming of a new king. The power of the council would wax and wane, inversely with the prosperity and stability of the country.

A problem meriting fuller discussion than would be appropriate here is the possible influence of climatic crises on the evolution of religious concepts in Egypt. There can be little doubt that the climate of Egypt, with the normally dependable regularity in the seasonal flooding of the Nile, provided conditions uniquely suitable for the development of the concept of divine kingship. The predictability of natural conditions would readily inspire the people to believe any claims to magic powers and divinity that a king might make.

Furthermore, there can be little doubt that the concern expressed by local nomarchs for the material wellbeing of their subjects in the First Intermediate Period, and the later Middle Kingdom idea of the King as a good shepherd watching over his flock, developed naturally out of the crisis of famine that impoverished and killed the industrious as well as the lazy and shiftless, so that poverty could not be blamed on a deficiency of character.

It is tempting also to link the great increase in the popularity of Osiris, "a divinity who had himself suffered death and resurrection in the process of transfiguration" (Lloyd 1961:118) during the first Dark Age to the nature of the crisis through which the Egyptians themselves were passing. This god, "as one of the forces of nature, personified the growth of plants through the stimulus of the lifegiving water of the Nile" (Smith 1962), both of which were in critically short supply. Smith further notes that Osirian beliefs began to appear in private tombs about the middle of Dynasty V, while Gardiner (1961) points out that the Pyramid Texts of Dynasty VI emphasize Osiris, in contrast to the Vth

Dynasty emphasis on Re. And the Nile floods, first poetically identified with King Unis, came in Dynasty VI to be often identified with Osiris (Černý 1952). This change coincides with Butzer's dating for the end of the Neolithic Wet Phase.

Another god whose popularity, or in this case unpopularity, may have been influenced by the end of the NWP is Seth. Wainwright (1963, *JEA* 49) states that Seth is to be considered as originally a storm god, and of great antiquity (Nagada I), and thus to have originated well within the NWP, as "a god of the blessed yet dangerous storm." As the rains became rare, his rites became only a nuisance, and he eventually slipped from his high estate and became the personification of evil. With the decline of the NWP, everything from the desert became sinister to the Egyptian peasant. "Out of the south-western desert come sandstorms and bad weather, sent by Seth, Lord of the Libyan Desert. . . . The hot south and west winds in summer bring 'the pestilence of the year' which kills people" (Kees 1961:37).

And finally we may note a legend according to which "Sekhmet, the lioness god-dess dwelling in the desert near Memphis, by order of Re, once destroyed nearly all the first race of men when they were beginning to make settlements, until the god saved the remainder by a stratagem" (Kees 1961:37). It may well be that this legend reflects a dim and distant memory of an earlier fluctuation to aridity, or drought, within the NWP.

We conclude with a brief return to the broader picture of the First Dark Age of Ancient History outlined in the Introduction. We have considered in some detail a num-ber of texts from the First Intermediate Period which clearly establish that Egypt was afflicted by severe famine, and that this famine was caused primarily by failure of the Nile floods rather than by human negligence. Most of these texts, and particularly those relating to the severest drought *(tzw-*famines), can be dated within a period of no more than 50 years, c. 2180 to c. 2130 B.C. A second drought, less prolonged, and perhaps less severe, occurred between 2002 and 1991 B.C.

If the more general thesis of a *widespread* drought, as set forth in the Introduction, is correct, it would be the first of these great droughts which brought an end to EB2 civilization throughout the eastern Mediterranean Basin. It would be the first drought also which in Mesopotamia contributed to the destruction of the Akkadian Empire, and the second drought which contributed to the downfall of the Third Dynasty of Ur. I plan to investigate the evidence from Mesopotamia in detail in a later paper. The conclusions reached in the present paper should, however, be judged primarily on the internal Egyptian evidence. They do not depend in any necessary way on the correctness of the hypothesis of a widespread drought.

Notes

[1] I wish to take this opportunity to thank Dr. Nicholas B. Millet (Harvard University) for his interest, encouragement, and numerous helpful discussions throughout the course of this study; his critical reading of the semi-final draft and advice on the various trans-lations was an aid of particular value because I do not myself have a reading knowledge of ancient Egyptian. The various theories set forth herein are, however, solely my responsibility.

I wish to thank also Professors Sterling Dow (Harvard University), Karl W. Butzer (University of Chicago), and Rhys Carpenter, each of whom kindly read the semi-final draft and made suggestions and comments which enabled me to improve the manuscript.

The chronology followed in this paper is that of the revised *Cambridge Ancient History*, particularly Smith (1962) and Hayes (1961). References (with a few exceptions in the text) will be found at the end of the paper, alphabetically by author, and by date.

[2]But unfortunately in some respects obsolete.

[3]All quotations attributed to Vandier are my translations from his French.

[4]The correct printing of this term, I understand, is *tzw* with the t underlined. The line under the t, however, would have to be set by hand and because the word occurs so frequently it proved impractical to include the hand-set underline.

[5]My choice of which translation to use for each line was determined by my general concept of environmental conditions, a concept which is supported by the less ambiguous texts that we have already discussed.

[6]"In times of famine . . . the birth rate is greatly reduced, largely, it seems, because of the actual physiological effect of food shortage in its various aspects . . .," India *Famine Inquiry Commission, Final Report* (Delhi 1945) 86.

[7]In the modern fluctuation to greater aridity that set in around 1900, the flow diminished from both the Blue and the White Nile; see H. H. Lamb, *GeogrJ* 132 (1966) 188.

References

Adams, William Y. 1968. Invasion, diffusion, evolution?, *Antiquity* 42:194-215.

Aldred, Cyril. 1963. *The Egyptians,* Praeger, New York.

———— 1965. *Egypt to the End of the Old Kingdom,* McGraw-Hill, New York.

Baer, Klaus, 1963. An Eleventh Dynasty Farmer's Letters, *JAOS* 83:1-19.

Bell, Barbara. 1970. The oldest records of the Nile floods, *GeogrJ* (in press).

Breasted, James Henry. 1906. *Ancient Records of Egypt,* vol. I, University of Chicago Press.

Brooks, C. E. P. 1949. *Climate through the Ages,* McGraw-Hill, New York.

Borchardt, Ludwig. 1905. Ein Königserlass aus Dahschur, *ZAeS* 42:I-II.

Butzer, Karl W. 1958. *Quaternary Stratigraphy and Climate in the Near East,* Bonner Geogr. Abh., Heft 24, Bonn.

———— 1959a. Some recent geological deposits of the Egyptian Nile valley, *GeogrJ* 125:75-79.

———— 1959b. Environment and human ecology in Egypt during predynastic and early dynastic times, *BullSocGeogr.d'Egypte* 32:43-87 (a condensed English transl. of 1959c, q.v. for documentation).

———— 1959c. Die Naturlandschaft Ägyptens während der Vorgeschichte und der Dynastischen Zeit, *AbhAkWissLit* (Mainz) *Math.-naturw.Kl.* No. 1, 80 pp., Wiesbaden.

———— 1960. Archeology and geology in ancient Egypt, *Science* 132:1617-24.

———— 1961. Climate change in arid regions since the Pliocene, pp. 31-56 in *A History of Land Use in Arid Regions,* ed. L. D. Stamp, UNESCO Arid Zone Research XVII.

———— 1963. Changes of climate during the late geological record; and The last "pluvial" phase of the Eurafrican sub-tropics, pp. 203-206, and 211-218 in *Changes of Climate,* Proc. Rome Symposium, UNESCO Arid Zone Research XX.

———— 1965. Physical conditions in Eastern Europe, Western Asia, and Egypt, *CAH* I, ch. 2 (fasc. 33).

———— 1966. Climate changes in the arid zones of Africa, pp. 72-83 in *World Climate from 8000 to 0 B.C.,* Symposium Proc., Roy. Meteorol. Soc., London.

Butzer, Karl W., and Carl L. Hansen. 1968. *Desert and River in Nubia,* University of Wisconsin Press, Madison.

Carpenter, Rhys. 1966. *Discontinuity in Greek Civilization,* Cambridge University Press.

Černý, Jaroslav. 1952. *Ancient Egyptian Religion,* Hutchinson, London.

———— 1961. The Stele of Merer in Cracow, *JEA* 47:5.

Childe, V. Gordon. 1929. *The Most Ancient East,* London.

————,1953. *New Light on the Most Ancient East,* Praeger, New York.

Dales, George F. 1965. A suggested chronology for Afghanistan, Baluchistan, and the Indus Valley, pp. 257-284 in *Chronologies in Old World Archaeology,* ed. R. W. Ehrich, University of Chicago Press.

Drioton, Etienne. 1942. Une représentation de la famine sur un basrelief égyptien, *BIE* 25:45-53.

Erman, Adolf. 1927. *The Ancient Egyptians:* a sourcebook of their writings, Harper Torchbooks, transl. from German by A. M. Blackman.

Faulkner, R. O. 1944. The rebellion in the Hare Nome, *JEA* 30:61-63.

———— 1964. Notes on "The Admonitions of an Egyptian Sage," *JEA* 50:24-36.

———— 1965. The Admonitions of an Egyptian Sage, *JEA* 51:53ff.

Fischer, Henry G. 1968. *Dendera in the third Millennium B.C.,* New York.

Frankfort, Henri. 1948. *Kingship and the Gods,* University of Chicago Press.

———— 1951. *The Birth of Civilization in the Near East,* Bloomington.

Frenzel, B. 1966. Climate change in the Atlantic/sub-Boreal transition on the Northern Hemisphere, pp. 99-123 in *World Climate from 8000 to 0 B.C.,* Symposium Proc., Roy. Meteorol. Soc., London.

Gardiner, Sir Alan. 1961. *Egypt of the Pharaohs,*Clarendon Press, Oxford.

Hayes, William C. 1953. *The Scepter of Egypt,* vol. I, Harper, New York.

———— 1961. The Middle Kingdom of Egypt. *CAH* I, ch. 20 (fasc. 3).

———— 1962. Chronology: Egypt; Western Asia; Aegean Bronze Age, *CAH* I, ch. 6 (fasc. 4).

———— 1964. *Most Ancient Egypt,* University of Chicago Press.

James, T. G. H. 1962. *The Hekanakhte Papers and other early Middle Kingdom Documents,* New York.

Kees, Hermann, 1961. *Ancient Egypt,* University of Chicago Press.

Kraus, E. B. 1954. Secular changes in the rainfall regime of SE Australia, *QuartJ. Roy. Meteorol. Soc.* 80:591-601.

———— 1955a. Secular changes of tropical rainfall regimes,*ibid.* 81:198-210.

———— 1955b. Secular changes of east-coast rainfall regimes, *ibid.* 430-439.

———— 1956. Graphs of cumulative residuals, *ibid.* 82:96-98.

Lloyd, Seton. 1961. *The Art of the Ancient Near East,* Praeger, New York.

Mellaart, James. 1962. Anatolia, C. 4000-2300 B.C., *CAH* I, ch. 18 (fasc. 8).

Murray, G. W. 1951. The Egyptian climate: an historical outline,*GeogrJ* 117:424-434.

Ralph, Elizabeth K. and Henry N. Michael. 1969. University of Pennsylvania radiocarbon dates XII, *Radiocarbon* 11:469-81.

Smith, William Stevenson, 1962. The Old Kingdom in Egypt, *CAH* I, ch. 14 (fasc. 5).

———— 1965. *The Art and Architecture of Ancient Egypt,* Penguin Books, Baltimore.

Starkel, L. 1966. Post-glacial climate and the moulding of European relief, pp. 15-33 in *World Climate from 8000 to 0 B.C.,* Symposium Proc., Roy. Meteorol. Soc., London.

Suess, Hans E. 1967. Zur Chronologie des alten Ägypten, *ZfPhysik* 202:1-7.

Toussoun, Prince Omar. 1925. *Memoire sur l'Histoire du Nil,* Cairo.

Toynbee, Arnold J. 1935. *A Study of History,* vol. I, Oxford University Press.

Trigger, Bruce. 1965. *History and Settlement in Lower Nubia,* Yale Univ. Publ. in Anthropology, No. 69.

Vandier, Jacques. 1936. *La famine dans l'Egypte Ancienne,* Cairo.

———— 1950. *Mo'alla,* Cairo.

Weinberg, Saul S. 1965. The Relative Chronology of the Aegean in the Stone and Early Bronze Ages, pp. 285-320 in *Chronologies in Old World Archaeology,* ed. R. W. Ehrich, University of Chicago Press.

Wilson, John A. 1955. translations from *Ancient Near Eastern Texts (ANET),* ed. J. B. Pritchard, Princeton University Press.

———— 1956. *The Culture of Ancient Egypt,* University of Chicago Press.

Wright, H. E., Jr. 1968. Climate change in Mycenaean Greece, *Antiquity* 42:123-127.

Kurt Mendelssohn, F.R.S., is Reader in Physics at Oxford University and
a Fellow of Wolfson College. He has been a visiting professor in the
United States, Japan, Ghana, and India. Among the many honors in
his distinguished career are the Hughes Medal of the Royal Society
and the Simon Memorial Prize of the Institute of Physics and Physical
Sciences. His research interests lie in the fields of cryogenics (he is
the editor of *Cryogenics*), medical physics, and Egyptology. The
author of numerous books and articles in the physical sciences, his
wide ranging interests are underscored in this unique interpretation
for the rise of Egyptian civilization.

A Scientist Looks at the Pyramids

Kurt Mendelssohn

The pyramids of Egypt are immensely large, immensely ancient, and, by general
consensus, immensely useless. The very dawn of human history and civilization is marked
by a set of monuments so gigantic that nothing even faintly approaching their grandeur
has ever been attempted again in our cultural orbit. Silent and mysterious, the pyramids
have kept their secret for the better part of five thousand years. The mystery surrounding
them mainly concerns the purpose for which they were built. It has been suggested that
they were observatories, or grain stores, or refuges from the Flood, or depositories of
Divine revelations expressed in geometrical terms.

Archaeological evidence, however, leaves no doubt that the pyramids served as
funerary monuments for the early pharaohs. Since the only undisturbed sarcophagus, in
an unfinished pyramid, was found empty and since all the other tomb chambers had
been robbed in antiquity, we cannot be certain that the kings of Egypt were actually
buried in them. Possibly the pyramids were only cenotaphs but, even so, their connection
with funerary rites and sacrifices is attested by contemporary literary evidence. On the
basis of this inescapable conclusion the matter has been turned over to the professional
Egyptologists whose aim it is to show why an early civilization should have mobilized all
its resources and directed its entire labor force at nothing better than a royal tomb.

It is the object of this article to suggest that this generally accepted conclusion may
result from faulty logic. While it is readily admitted that the pyramids served as royal
mausoleums, it is not necessarily true that this was the only purpose for their construction.
In fact it may not even have been the principal purpose.

Reprinted from *American Scientist,* Vol. 59, pp. 210-220 (1971) by permission of the publisher and
author.

However, before discussing the problem of why the pyramids were built, something has to be said about the state of Egyptian civilization at that time. Also, a short account of the pyramids themselves has to be given in order to provide the factual basis for our considerations.

The Old Kingdom

Several centuries before the first pyramid was built, the scattered settlements along the Nile Valley seem to have coalesced into two groups: Upper Egypt, situated south of present-day Cairo, and Lower Egypt, comprising the tribes of the delta. Possibly an invading "dynastic race" was responsible for this process, but very little is known about it. Eventually, by conquest and marriage, the two kingdoms were gradually united over a period to which archaeologists allot three or four hundred years, covering the first two dynasties of pharaohs in Egyptian history. The tombs of some of these early pharaohs, which have been excavated by Flinders Petrie and W. B. Emery, are shallow underground chambers, surmounted by fairly low oblong and rectangular structures. These resemble in shape the low bench in front of the local farmers' houses, called a mastaba, and this term has been adopted by the Egyptologists.

The building material of the mastabas was mud brick and, in order to lend stability to the outside walls, they were made to slope inward at an angle of about $72°$, which simply means a tangent of 3. As we shall see, this slope of 3 in 1 was adopted by the pyramid builders for all their buttress walls. Toward the end of the first two dynasties limestone, sometimes well cut and polished, begins to appear as building material for selected features of the tomb. However, there was no gradual increase in size or magnificence leading up to pyramid building. Emery in his description of the fairly modest and badly planned tomb of the last pharaoh of the Second Dynasty remarks on the curious fact that the huge Step Pyramid at Saqqara was built only a few years later.

On the other hand, there is no evidence whatever of any technological breakthrough in the methods of quarrying or cutting stone which might account for the onset of pyramid building. All the tools and techniques used by the pyramid builders were in existence well before their time. In fact, the nature of the work involved underwent no change at this time, but the extent of it was subject to a sudden escalation of fantastic proportions.

It appears that the reign of Zoser, the first king of the Third Dynasty with whose name the Step Pyramid is associated, was marked by far-reaching political and social changes. He evidently was the son of an Upper Egyptian king and Princess Nemathap of Lower Egypt, and there are many indications that this marriage finally sealed the unification of the two kingdoms. It is important and significant that it was not the pharaoh who was credited by the Egyptian historians with building the Step Pyramid but his vizier, Imhotep. To Imhotep is ascribed not only the design of the first stone buildings but also the first teaching of astronomy, magic (science?), and medicine. Egyptian tradition deified him as the supreme sage of all times, and the Greeks equated his worship with that of Asklepios, their god of healing. Imhotep is unique in Egyptian history as being a much venerated personality who was not a king.

The place chosen by Imhotep for Zoser's mausoleum was the desert plateau on the west bank of the Nile above Memphis, the capital of the united Egypt, just south of present-day Cairo. This is the famous Step Pyramid of Saqqara, which to this day dominates the western skyline of the valley. In spite of being about five thousand years old, the building is in a remarkably good state, and only the edge of the lowest step and the smooth casing stones have disappeared. The Step Pyramid gives the impression that six stone mastabas, of diminishing size, have been piled on top of each other, but this is architecturally misleading. Instead, the construction is that of a tower whose masonry is held in place by outer buttress walls of diminishing height. The inclination of the buttresses follows the standard pattern of a 3 in 1 elevation, as used on the earlier mastabas.

The next pyramid was built at Meidum, about 35 miles south of Saqqara, also at the edge of the western desert. This pyramid, which is the only one of the seven great pyramids that is heavily ruined, will become the most important one for our considerations. It was originally planned as a step pyramid, on an even grander scale than Zoser's, but then the plan was changed and the step pyramid was covered with a smooth mantle which transformed the edifice into a true pyramid. The angle of elevation of the sides is $\sim$52°, and this results in a shape for which the ratio of circumference to height is 2π. This large-scale exercise in squaring the circle may have been chosen for aesthetic reasons or, more probably, it may have had magical significance.

It is obvious that the change from the Meidum step structure to the true pyramid took place very late in its construction, when the step pyramid was essentially finished. This is evident from the towerlike structure we see today, in which some of the underlying steps are exposed. These steps had already been given their outer casing, and this casing had even received its final polish when the outer mantle was added. Of the outer mantle only the lowest part, covering the two bottom steps, now remains intact.

The third and fourth pyramids are at Dashur, just a few miles south of Saqqara. Number three was planned on a still grander scale than its predecessors. It appears to have been designed from the beginning as a true pyramid of 52° elevation. However, when it had reached a third of its intended height the angle of elevation was lowered to 43½°, which incidentally, makes the ratio 3π. Its curiously stunted shape has earned it the name of Bent Pyramid. Whether this and the other great pyramids also were constructed on top of an underlying buttressed step structure is impossible to say without dismantling substantial parts of them. A certain amount of evidence for the continued use of this basic architectural pattern is provided by the smaller and later pyramids of the Sixth Dynasty, which in their ruined state expose a clearly visible step structure.

Egyptologists have suggested that the change of elevation in the Bent Pyramid was due to the premature death of the Pharaoh and the need to finish the building in a hurry. This explanation is not very convincing, and again it is a point to which we will return later. The use of a slide rule shows that the amount of masonry saved in this manner is less than 10 percent of the total. Moreover, the next pyramid to be built was designed from the very beginning with the lower elevation angle of 43½°. This fourth pyramid, also at Dashur, is the first one preserved in its true pyramid shape. Unlike its predecessor it has been completely stripped of its white limestone casing and has become known as the Red Pyramid. There is, as we shall see, good reason why the three pyramids following that of Zoser are not associated with the name of a pharaoh.

It is different with the remaining three great pyramids, all at Giza, which are known as that of Khufu (Cheops), Khafra (Chephren), and Menkaure (Mykerinos). The first two of these, numbers five and six in our series, are the well-known colossal edifices over-looking Cairo. They each cover roughly the same area as the Red Pyramid but are much more impressive because they revert to the elevation angle of ~52°. The third pyramid in the Giza group is, by comparison, a runt, with only a tenth of the cubic content of its predecessor. The pyramid age had come to an end, having lasted for a little more than a century. Pyramids were still being erected for about a thousand years, but they rapidly became smaller and shoddier, and it is quite clear that with the third Giza pyramid the zest had gone out of pyramid building forever.

From the Meidum Pyramid onward, these structures were all aligned remarkably accurately in the cardinal directions, and they all have entrance passages pointing toward the celestial pole. The arrangement of these internal passages is an absorbing subject but is beyond the scope of this article. Here it must suffice to say that they lead to comparative-ly small "burial" chambers and that their cross-section is only about one meter square, too low to walk through and just about large enough to admit a dead body.

Disaster at Meidum

It should not be thought that I went to Egypt with the intention of finding out why the pyramids were built. On the contrary, as will be presently explained, the final conclusions were drawn quite unexpectedly and much later in a sequence of steps, largely based on the photographic material I had gathered. On my first trip I visited all the usual Egyptian tourist sites, including most of the pyramids. I then became intrigued by the magnitude of technological organization that had been mastered at this early phase in human civilization, and on my second visit I was kindly granted facilities by the Egyptian Antiquities Service for a closer scrutiny and an inspection of the interiors not open to the public.

My first aim was to see the Meidum Pyramid, which is beyond the standard tourist itinerary and is rarely visited. Even in its heavily ruined state it is a most impressive structure: the remaining central core of the step pyramid still rises to a height of over 40 meters. In fact, the disappearance of the outer mantle and some of the lower buttress walls enhances its height, having left a tower with an elevation of 3 in 1. Bands of smooth and rough surface show, as Borchardt has pointed out, that the step pyramid below the mantle was built in at least two stages, each of which had dressed external walls when the next enlargement was decided upon. Egyptologists ascribe the ruined state of the monu-ment to quarrying by later generations, and Flinders Petrie, who made the first survey, mentions that he saw fellahin carting away stones on donkeys.

This again is a problem for the slide rule. The immense bulk of the pyramids will allow severe inroads by quarrymen without showing much effect on the shape of the structure. Most of Cairo's great mosques and essentially the whole city wall were built with casing stones from the Giza pyramids without any noticeable effect on their size. In fact, while Napoleon's companions were climbing these pyramids, he calculated that the stone used in them would suffice to build a wall ten feet high and one foot thick around the whole of France. Keeping this in mind, even whole donkey caravans cannot provide an explanation for the reduced shape of the Medium Pyramid. Moreover, this pyramid is the only one which never had a large town in its neighborhood where the pillaged stones could have been used.

However, there is no need to search for the stolen masonry since it is still there, surrounding the pyramid in huge mounds of rubble. In fact, a very rough estimate suggests that not much of the original bulk is missing. Equally, it is hardly likely that anyone will have expended immense labor in reducing the pyramid to ruins for no useful purpose. Leaving out willful destruction, we must conclude that the collapse of the Meidum Pyramid was the result of a disaster.

Once this view is accepted, we find ample reason to support it. The prototype at Saqqara had shown that a step pyramid is stable and, indeed, the polished buttress walls at Meidum indicate that two successive phases of a step pyramid at that location, too, had been finished successfully. The disaster evidently occurred when the building was given a novel, and as yet untried, shape by adding the mantle in order to transform it into a true pyramid. Fortunately the existing remains of the pyramid and three successive surveys, by Petrie, Borchardt, and Rowe, permit an excellent reconstruction of this third building phase. After the outer step pyramid was completed, stones were laid onto the steps in order to smooth the shape of the building. At this stage the resulting structure was probably still fairly stable since the weight of these packing blocks was supported by the buttress walls of the steps. However, then further stones were laid on, beyond the edge of the buttress wall and forming an outer mantle. This addition was evidently required in order to achieve the desired elevation of $52°$. At the height of the, at present exposed, second step, the thickness of this outer mantle was about 7 meters and it was completely unsupported by buttress walls. It is most likely that the failure occurred when, during the third building phase, the weight of this unsupported layer was gradually increased.

The average pressure at the base of a large pyramid is, at the center, of the order of 50 kg cm^{-2}, with the thrust acting vertically downward. This is high but not destructive for limestone and cannot cause failure if the load is evenly distributed. However, whereas the blocks forming the buttress walls and the outer casing were well squared, this is not true for the bulk of the pyramid masonry. Thus for blocks which, owing to surface irregularities, touch in only a few places, pressure at the joins might rise to 1,000 kg cm^{-2} or higher, and this is enough to cause limestone to crumble. In fact, there is evidence from inside the passages that some of the pyramids slightly "settled" while building was in progress. This mild bedding down of the masonry would not have catastrophic consequences in an otherwise sound structure, but things were different at Meidum, where the pyramid had two serious architectural weaknesses: the unsupported outer mantle and the smoothed internal surfaces of the buttress walls. These provided no frictional adhesion for the surrounding masonry and thus became dangerous slip planes.

At whichever of these weak features the original fault on loading developed, the resultant motion of huge masses of stone is likely to have triggered off catastrophic changes at the other as well. The ruin, in any case, shows clearly that an appreciable fraction of the whole pyramid masonry slipped off along the polished inner walls. Moreover, the disaster appears to have occurred with considerable rapidity since the wide extent of the rubble heap testifies to the fact that the slipping mass must have acquired appreciable kinetic energy.

Structural failure in a pyramid will lead to phenomena that are quite different from the collapse of a conventional building. The kinetic energy liberated in the motion of this enormous mass will alter the shape of the individual building blocks in such a way as to encourage further movement, and the whole body of the structure begins to behave like a fluid rather than a solid. In fact, the edifice will undergo changes that are quite similar to plastic flow. Whereas before the catastrophe the thrust was essentially downward, severe structural failure must result in lateral forces that tend to flatten out the affected portions of the edifice. As a result the material will behave very much like a slipping mine tip, a type of disaster which is only too well known.

That pyramids are prone to plastic flow is shown by at least two examples. A later and rather poorly built pyramid, that of Pepi II at Saqqara, had been provided with a strong girdle of limestone completely surrounding its base. Archaeological evidence leaves no doubt that this girdle was added at a late stage in the building operations. It evidently was built as a containing buttress because the pyramid showed a tendency to spread outward under its own weight. The other instance occurred fairly recently when excavators removed the stone covering from some sections of the largest Mexican pyramid. The core of the structure, built of adobe brick, began to exhibit plastic flow after heavy rain, and emergency action had to be taken.

Once it is realized that the ruined state of the Meidum Pyramid was not caused by later pillaging but was the result of failure during construction, additional evidence for it can easily be found. The memorial stelae in the mortuary temple attached to the base of the pyramid have remained uninscribed. In addition, the large slabs of limestone forming the corbeled roof of the tomb chamber, although fitted perfectly together, were never dressed. That smooth polishing of internal surfaces was not only possible but customary at that time is shown by the perfect finish of the burial chamber of an adjacent and contemporary mastaba. This all goes to show that the Meidum Pyramid was abandoned before completion.

However, the strongest and most interesting evidence for the disaster comes from Dashur. We have seen that the explanation for the curious shape of the next pyramid, the "bent" one, is quite unconvincing. The true reason now becomes apparent through the failure at Meidum. When it occurred, the builders at Dashur immediately took action in order to avoid a similar catastrophe. They reduced the angle of elevation to a less perilous value, making sure that lateral thrust was not likely to develop. In this way, and although they spoiled the appearance of the structure, they were able to complete their task safely. Again playing safe, they built the Red Pyramid from the beginning at the same lower angle that had proved reliable for the upper part of the Bent Pyramid.

Further proof for this sequence of events is to be found in the peculiar manner of laying the casing stones in the Bent Pyramid. In fact, this peculiarity has puzzled the Egyptologists so much that, for a time, they dated the Bent Pyramid before that of Meidum until other evidence led them to the correct order. At Meidum, as in the Step Pyramid at Saqqara, the blocks forming the buttress walls are laid perpendicular to the face of the wall; that means the courses slope backward into the pyramid at an angle of about 1 in 3. In fact, it is this camber which, by the inward thrust of the masonry, lends added strength against collapse. When at Meidum the outer step pyramid was completed, the tops of the steps were made level, and later, on transformation into the true pyramid, the packing blocks were laid onto them in horizontal courses. Moreover, this horizontal packing was continued in the outer, unsupported mantle, making it easier for failure to occur by the complete absence of inward thrust.

The shape of the Bent Pyramid shows that, when the building plan was altered, the core of the structure must have been completed up to one-third of the intended height and could not be changed. When the Meidum Pyramid collapsed, every possible means had to be employed to save the Dashur edifice from a similar fate. One of these was the lowering of the angle of elevation at the upper levels. The other was to lay the packing and casing stones with an inward camber, similar to that of the buttress walls, thereby providing added inward thrust. Understandably, the Egyptologists who surveyed the pyramid regarded this arrangement of the outer courses as an early method reminiscent of Zoser's first step pyramid. No casing blocks have survived at the Red Pyramid, but the packing stones were laid horizontally. This evidently was considered quite safe in view of the lower angle of elevation.

Having successfully played safe with the lower elevation at the two Dashur pyramids, the Egyptian architects appear to have left confident that they could again attempt structures embodying the desirable ratio of 2π. The last three great pyramids, all at Giza, were built at an elevation of $52°$ and have not only been constructed without disaster but also have stood the test of time successfully. We cannot, of course, know whether novel methods were employed in designing the core, but the external features of the Great Pyramid show clearly what means were adopted to ensure safety. First of all, very much larger packing blocks, of about one meter cube, were used. Secondly, these blocks were very well squared, and these two features counteract the development of plastic flow. Finally, additional inward thrust was provided not by letting the masonry courses slope backward but by making them slightly concave toward the top of the pyramid. This was achieved by grading the size of the blocks in the lower courses so that the edges are somewhat raised with respect of the center of the faces. This last precaution, incidentally, was evidently considered unnecessary after completion of the building since it was not repeated in the two remaining pyramids.

The object of pyramid building

So far our considerations have revealed a large-scale technological failure in the second pyramid the Egyptian architects built and the precautions they took in order to avoid another catastrophe. However, the sequence of events we have traced leads to further conclusions which go far beyond the problems of pyramid design.

Most important of all, the Bent Pyramid had already reached a third of its intended height when its predecessor at Meidum collapsed in the final building stage. This shows that, contrary to accepted ideas, the pyramids were not built consecutively but their building periods overlapped very substantially. Therefore the concept that a pharaoh, after coming to the throne, built his pyramid in which he was eventually buried and then the next king repeated this process has become untenable. Indeed, as we shall see presently, this sequence of events in any case turns out to be technologically impossible.

The erection of a pyramid required a very large labor force, probably an appreciable fraction of the whole male population. No contemporary records have been found, and our only information comes from Herodotus, who visited the pyramids two thousand years later. The priests told him that 100,000 men were employed for twenty years in erecting the Great Pyramid, and Flinders Petrie, when making his famous survey at Giza, considered this estimate reasonable. Herodotus mentions shifts of three months' duration but, unfortunately, the relevant passage is ambiguous. It is now generally assumed that these were three months in each year, coinciding with the annual inundation of the Nile, when agricultural work was at a standstill. For these three months, at least, a large part of the whole Egyptian population was employed by the state and became completely dependent on it for their maintenance.

Before considering this last question further, let us turn to the variation of the size of this labor force during the construction of a single pyramid. The work consists in quarrying the stone, shaping the blocks, transporting them to the building site, raising them up, and laying them into place. Most of this is unskilled or semiskilled work, requiring no special craftsmanship. A much smaller number of highly skilled masons, for cutting and dressing the casing blocks, was probably permanently employed. Petrie excavated workmen's dwellings at Giza suitable for housing four to five thousand of these artisans. Again this appeared to him a reasonable number for the work required. In our considerations we will disregard these relatively few skilled men and deal only with the huge seasonal labor force.

In order to finish the immense structure of a pyramid within a reasonable time, the maximum available labor force would be brought to bear on the task. However, throughout construction this would not necessarily be equal to the maximum employable force. The layers near the base require the largest number of blocks to be quarried and transported. As blocks forming these layers can be placed with comparative ease and from all sides, the maximum available labor force would be fully employed for the first few years. Then, as the pyramid is growing, conditions begin to change. Fewer blocks per layer are required, but now access is becoming progressively restricted and slow. This feature is quite independent of the particular system of ramps that was actually used, about which we know little. Accordingly, the employable labor force begins to drop after the first few years of pyramid construction from its constant level, finally tapering off gradually; after the edifice is eventually completed, the labor force would become inactive until, in the following reign, the pattern must be repeated. Then again the maximum number of men is required for several years.

Whatever the state of the Egyptian economy was at the turn of the Third to the Fourth Dynasty, it could never have stood the strain of this employment pattern; neither could any other economy since. As pyramid building started, a profound change had to take place in the living conditions of the population, affecting more and more people as the work proceeded. They and their families became completely dependent on the central administration which employed and fed them. At the same time the administration must have made annual levies to obtain the grain needed to supply their workers. These deliveries too had to increase steadily, until in the end an entirely new system of supply and distribution was established. This system, operating for a period of years, would have made a complete break with the previous isolated village economy, ushering in a basically different phase in the life of the whole country. It is quite inconceivable that after twenty years or so, when the pyramid had been completed, the Egyptian economy should have reverted to the old pattern. The change that had been brought about by pyramid construction was far too radical to permit this. The only possibility was to embark on the next pyramid at the time when the labor force on the preceding one was tapering off. Pyramid building became an economic necessity whether or not there was a pharaoh ready to be buried.

The astonishing conclusion that pyramid building was an activity in its own right removes one difficulty which has baffled the Egyptologists for a long time. There are more pyramids than pharaohs. The reason why the Meidum Pyramid, the Bent Pyramid, and the Red Pyramid are known under these names rather than names of pharaohs is that they all have been tentatively ascribed to Seneferu, the last pharaoh of the Third Dynasty. Unconvincing efforts have been made to invoke obscure names from Manetho's list of kings, referring to quite short reigns in order to solve this problem. With the realization that it was not the pharaoh but the pyramid that led the pace of construction, this problem has disappeared. From the evidence presented earlier in this article we know that the pharaoh, possibly Seneferu, when finishing the pyramid at Meidum, had already built the major part of the next pyramid at Dashur.

When I say that pyramid building had become an economic necessity, I am not suggesting that the Egyptians were caught up in a vortex of architectural activity from which they did not know how to escape. On the contrary, it seems that they had embarked consciously on the construction of these enormous monuments in order to achieve a highly organized political and economic structure of their society. In fact, they invented the state, a form of centralized and efficient organization which up to then was unknown to the human race.

Until then Egypt had consisted of separate tribal units, each with its local god, which were loosely connected by the gradual imposition of a unifying Horus cult. The parents of this falcon god, Osiris and Isis, gave emphasis to the importance of the continuance of life after death, leading to elaborate tombs and funeral rites. The potentialities of this form of religiopolitical federation had probably been exhausted in the course of the first two dynasties. With firm unification at the time of Zoser, the stage had been set for the next phase in the development of society. In this new stage, which we call the state, centralization of power and administration became the key object. It was achieved by the ingenious device of creating a large communal task, engulfing eventually a large fraction of the population: pyramid building.

That the pyramid was chosen is not surprising. Heaping up an impressive man-made mountain is the simplest and most basic great communal task that can be imagined. All that is required for its achievement is a worthwhile reason. The existing Osiris cult easily lent itself to an interpretation in which the ascent of the dead pharaoh to the sun was of paramount importance for the afterlife of every member of the community. The pyramid, as is known from contemporary inscriptions, was the means of achieving this ascent.

It would not be very rational to assume that Imhotep, with almost fiendish ingenuity, had worked out this master plan for the creation of the state and then set out on the design of the Step Pyramid of Saqqara. In fact, we know that this was not the case. The original funeral monument that he built for Zoser was a traditional type of mastaba on the west bank of the Nile above Memphis. Its only difference from earlier structures of this type was its greater size and its entirely stone construction. After its completion, this mastaba was twice successively enlarged. It was possibly at this stage that the organization of labor marshalled for this big tomb began to suggest a new economic pattern with desirable political consequences. Again the exploitation of this new scheme was gradual, taking place in two consecutive stages. The first was the erection, on top of the existing mastaba, of a pyramid composed of four steps. It seems that the provision of labor for this great enterprise, far from exhausting the working capacity of the community, was proving very practicable and perhaps economically beneficial. This is shown by the fact that Imhotep was encouraged to enlarge the building still further, increasing its cubic content three times and reaching an even greater height by constructing the final pyramid of six steps.

Details of the subsequent development cannot be discussed in the space of this article but it seems clear that, after two—probably never completed—step pyramids, Seneferu embarked on the true pyramid age with the continual employment of a huge labor force. It seems that now the organization of the centralized state through the drafting of ever-increasing numbers of workers was consciously exploited. It is significant that the main emphasis was shifted toward numbers and away from skills. The elaborate surrounding walls and subsidiary buildings of the earlier step pyramids were dispensed with and the bulk of the pyramids themselves was continually increased.

Five enormous pyramids were built in less than a century, and then, with the Menkaure Pyramid, this fantastic activity tapered off within a comparatively short time. Pyramid building has achieved its object; the organization of the state had been created. From now on the labor force, accustomed to centralized organization and well disciplined, could be turned to other, economically more rewarding activities within the new state. As for the pharaohs, they still got their pyramids but they now had to ascend to the sun on mud bricks, thinly covered with a limestone casing. Neither did control of expenditure for their monuments allow them to ascend very high.

Space does not permit more than passing remarks on two other problems of the pyramid age: the shape of the monuments and the question of forced labor. That the monument of the communal task had to be a mountain, as steep and as high as circumstances permit, goes without saying. The structure was a mountain and not a building, as is attested by the great difficulties the Egyptians encountered in providing even a little space inside it. A mountain is something one can ascend, and a passage in the pyramid texts suggests ascent to heaven by a staircase, which may be the meaning of the step pyramid. The true pyramid may suggest ascent along the sun's rays.

Connected with this interpretation was evidently a change in the religious position of the pharaoh, ushered in under Seneferu by the priests of Heliopolis. A conical stone was the emblem of the sun god, and this cult change, exemplified by the alteration of the Meidum Pyramid, may be associated with a closer link of the pharaoh with the god he was supposed to accompany on his daily journey across the sky. This would mean enhanced importance for the whole community of the pharaoh's person and of the part he had to play after death for the wellbeing of all, in this and the next life. The building of this cult symbol on a stupendous scale must have appeared to the Egyptians as an essential and worthwhile task.

This leads straight to the question of despotic "slavery," to which the pyramid builders are supposed to have reduced their people. Even a serious Egyptologist like Borchardt will interrupt a scholarly dissertation on building ramps to conjure up the spectacle of exhausted slaves toiling under the whips of overseers. In our age of automatic weapons we are accustomed to large numbers of people being terrorized by a small well armed group. No such disparity existed between worker and overseer five thousand years ago, and in order to enforce unwilling labor, a very sizable army would have had to be employed to control a hundred thousand workers and their disgruntled relatives scattered over the country. Moreover, the workers would have had to be rounded up each year anew, and this subjugation had to last for a century.

This is not very probable, and the alternative, that the work was undertaken willingly, sounds a good deal more likely. When enquiring about the labor force used for large projects in present-day China, I learned that a sufficient number of volunteers is always available. The pay is good, there is a sporting rivalry between work gangs, and when the workers return, they are the heroes of their village, telling evening after evening "how we built the dam" stories. Inscriptions on the pyramid blocks give the name of working groups such as Vigorous Gang and Enduring Gang. Moreover, the cooperative effort of villagers, brought together from a great number of different tribal communities, some with traditional enmity, must have played an important part in the creation of a centralized state.

Altogether our analysis suggests that, far from being a period of abject slavery and exhaustion, the pyramid age represented a new form of communal living by common work for the benefit of all. One even may have doubts whether it was spiritual benefit only. Such information as has come down to us indicates that at the time when the pyramids were erected, Egypt's prosperity increased rapidly. Seneferu is credited with building the first sea-going ships that traded along the Syrian coast, and he and his successors established for the first time a hold over territories beyond the Nile Valley, in the Sinai peninsula.

The Mexican pyramids

There exists another set of large pyramids in the world, at Teotihuacan and Cholula in Mexico. It has often been maintained that a connection must exist between the two sets of striking monuments in Egypt and Central America. This I am inclined to believe, but not in the way it is usually suggested. Even if, though that seems unlikely, the Egyptians had navigated papyrus boats across the Atlantic, they would hardly have induced the Mexicans to engage in an activity they themselves had given up two thousand years earlier.

Carbon dating and similar methods show that the great Mesoamerican pyramids were built just before the beginning of the Christian era. There is even greater paucity of information about this period than about the Egyptian pyramid age since no script had been developed. Neither is there any reference in Mexican tradition to the people who built the pyramids. They were overgrown and in ruins when more than a millennium later the Aztecs entered the Valley of Mexico. They thought that the double line of mounds at Teotihuacan, hiding ruined pyramids, were tombs and called it the Avenue of the Dead. They also named the two large pyramids that of the sun and of the moon, but none of these descriptions have any link with the true significance of the monuments, about which we know, as yet, practically nothing.

The Aztecs displaced the civilization of the warlike Toltecs, whose capital was probably at Tula, and it may have been the Toltecs who earlier conquered the people whom we now call Teotihuacanos. What their real name was is unknown and the archaeological research into their civilization is still in its infancy. However, it is worthy of note that in Mexico, as in Egypt, legend ascribes the building of the large pyramids to the inspiration of an outstanding sage who further taught them many of their arts and crafts. He later was deified under the symbol of the plumed serpent, Quetzalcoatl, and Cortez benefited by a tradition that this god would return to Mexico from the east.

Pyramids were still being built when the Spaniards conquered Mexico, but the true Central American pyramid age had come to an end 1,500 years earlier. Again, as in Egypt, the colossal pyramids mark the beginning rather than the height of Amerindian civilization. Their precursors were some fairly modest circular mounds, such as that at Cuicuilco just outside Mexico City. Cuicuilco can be roughly dated because it was partly covered by a flow of lava from the volcano Xitle, which erupted some 2,000 years ago. Pottery found there classes Cuicuilco into Mexico's late Archaic period, characterized by agricultural village communities, each with its own tradition, as is shown by the different styles of the little female idols found in abundance. The mound at Cuicuilco marks the onset of cult ritual, serving a large number of villages. From the little we know, it can be concluded that life in the Valley of Mexico at about 300 B.C. was not unlike that in Egypt under the first two dynasties.

Then, quite suddenly as in Egypt, we find a number of gigantic pyramids, the largest of which, at Cholula, exceeds in cubic content that of Khufu at Giza. The angle of elevation is lower than in Egypt, because in Mexico the building material was mud brick which was stabilized and protected against heavy rains by a thick mortar made from pounded volcanic stone. Embedded in the mud brick are numerous small idols, which show that the large Mexican pyramids followed immediately upon the mound at Cuicuilco and that the culture was identical with that of the villagers who built the mound. Thus, we have no reason to ascribe the pyramids to the initiative of some conquering race, and we must assume that village settlement in the Valley of Mexico had reached a stage at which it had become ripe for urbanization and centralization of power. Just as the people of the Nile had invented the institution of the state 3,000 years earlier in the Old World, the Teotihuacanos performed the same task in the Western Hemisphere. They, too, achieved the necessary organization of the villagers by creating a labor force for a striking communal task, and again the most obvious undertaking, the building of an artificial mountain, was chosen.

In Egypt the avowed reason for constructing pyramids was to provide the pharaoh with a funerary monument, but the Teotihuacan pyramids were not primarily burial mounds. A number of tunnels have been bored through these mud bricks and earth structures and these have not as yet revealed the existence of a tomb although there are indications that one may exist in the Pyramid of the Sun. The main object of the Amerindian pyramid was to provide a stage for a ritual, usually a human sacrifice, to be watched by a large number of people. The top of the pyramid was always flat, carrying a temple and an altar, an arrangement which already exists on the mound at Cuicuilco and was continued until the Spanish conquest.

It is interesting to note that in Mexico, just as in Egypt, the period of building very large pyramids not only occurs at the onset of urbanization but that it also lasted for a relatively short time. Like the burial of pharaohs, human sacrifice, required to keep the sun alive by feeding it with blood, remained a social activity of essential importance to the population throughout the Amerindian civilization. Pyramids carrying altars continued to be built, but it was no longer necessary to concentrate large labor forces as a means to create the state. As soon as the basic pattern of the state had been developed, the Mexican pyramids were built no larger than necessary to provide a good view of the spectacle for a large crowd.

Instead, architectural features other than size, and sometimes not compatible with it, were given greater importance. With the continual increase in the number of sacrifices in Toltec and particularly in Aztec times, rapid disposal of the victims became necessary. Their corpses were rolled down the pyramid steps, to be received by their captors or buyers for cannibalism, and this purpose was best served by relatively small but rather steep structures. Thus, while retaining their ritual function, the later edifices could be erected by a modest labor force. As in Egypt, no large pyramids were attempted after the early Mexican pyramid age, although in both cases the community became larger and more prosperous, and the technological means were more advanced.

In this article I have purposely left the sequence of conclusions in the order in which they occurred to me. This is to show that I did not approach the subject with any preconceived idea; it developed on the basis of what I consider to be compelling logic. Faced with the same basic material, the scientist and technologist draws different conclusions from the archaeologist simply because he is looking for different things. In doing so, he may occasionally arrive at results that are at variance with the archaeologist's ideas merely because in these particular instances the problems are essentially technological ones.

Naturally, I have discussed some of these ideas with my Egyptologist friends, particularly with Professor Emery of University College, London, the successor of Flinders Petrie, and with Dr. Edwards of the British Museum, whose famous book *The Pyramids of Egypt* is the standard work on this subject. I am much indebted to their helpful advice and I am encouraged by the fact that they have raised no objections to my suggestion of a disaster at Meidum and the subsequent events. Whether Old Kingdom experts in general will accept my thesis that the pyramids were more important than the pharaohs whose names they immortalize remains to be seen.

It might be possible to atone for this heresy by drawing the archaeologists' attention to a small section of Seneferu's world which lies entombed under the rubble at the foot of the Meidum Pyramid. The physicist's analysis of the spread of the debris suggests that the catastrophe was too rapid for people to save themselves in time, and they most probably are still there, after almost 5,000 years, waiting for the excavator's bulldozer.

David O'Connor is associate curator of the Egyptian Section, University Museum, and assistant professor in the Oriental Studies Department of the University of Pennsylvania. He holds a diploma in Egyptology from University College, London, and a Ph.D. from Cambridge University (1969). Over the past decade he has spent considerable time on excavations and survey in Egypt and the Northern Sudan. He is Co-Director of the Pennsylvania-Yale Expedition to Egypt and currently directing excavations at Luxor, Southern Egypt.

Ancient Egypt and Black Africa— Early Contacts

David O'Connor

In 1955 a west African scholar, Marcel Diop, argued vehemently that professional Egyptologists had been concealing a startling fact for over half a century; Diop claimed that the ancient Egyptians were Negroes and their characteristic civilization was a Negro achievement. It is in fact a not uncommon belief that Egypt was part of Black Africa, but as far as physical appearance goes this is not true. Thousands of sculpted and painted representations from Egypt and hundreds of well preserved bodies from its cemeteries show that the typical physical type was neither Negroid nor Negro. The second part of Diop's thesis however was that Egyptian civilization had been spread throughout Africa by emigrants from Egypt and presented in dramatic form a genuine and fascinating historical problem. Geographically ancient Egypt was an African country and her civilization was part of a mosaic of African cultures distributed over the face of that vast continent. Was there any serious contact between ancient Egypt and Black Africa, that is the Negroid and Negro peoples of western and central Africa; and, if there was, how important was the flow of influences in either direction?

This is not just an academic question, for many Africans and Afro-Americans, intensely interested in the history of early African cultures, often feel that the creativity of these cultures has been unfairly minimized by European scholarship. This is not true of prehistorians and historians of Africa today; the old habit of attributing any unusually sophisticated idea or technique appearing amongst Black Africans to the influence or the presence of a racially "superior" Hamite or other non-Negro has rightly been abandoned. However, as the achievements of Black Africa are recognized and increasingly better documented, and the distinctive characters of its many cultures emerge, the role of Egyptian influence becomes even more problematical. Are there any significant similarities between Egyptian and ancient African cultures; if so, how much are they due to a general "African" nature, and how much to cultural interaction?

Reprinted from *Expedition*, Vol. 14, No. 1, pp. 2-10 (1971) by permission of the publisher and author. Copyright 1971 The University Museum, University of Pennsylvania.

Egyptian civilization was in fact peculiarly resistant to outside influence, but many ancient people, including Africans, borrowed from it. This was not however indiscriminate borrowing from an overwhelmingly superior culture and was varied in its effects. The Greeks, for example, were impressed by Egypt; their statuary and architecture were at first strongly influenced by Egypt and, according to the Greeks themselves, some of their leading philosophers and scientists went to Egypt to study its ancient knowledge as well as the new learning established after 320 B.C. in the Hellenistic city of Alexandria. Yet developed Greek art and thought cannot be mistaken for Egyptian. Similarly, amongst ancient Black Africans there must have been varied reactions to Egyptian contact, affected both by the cultural strength of each African group and by the role in which the Egyptians appeared. Egyptians in Africa were sometimes traders and employers, sometimes conquerors and colonists, sometimes defeated enemies.

Physical hindrances to contact must also have affected the potential spread of Egyptian influence. It is generally agreed that in late prehistoric times, between 5000 and 3000 B.C., the chances for contact between the Egyptian Nile valley, the Sahara and Africa south of the Sahara and along the upper reaches of the Nile, were better than in later periods. The Sahara at this time had a moister climate and supported a comparatively large and mobile population, which included Negroid and Negro physical types, as did the communities living near modern Khartoum. Certainly, domesticated animals appear to have spread during this period from Egypt (which had derived them from the Near East) throughout North Africa, deep into the Sahara and as far south as Khartoum; agriculture was established in Egypt at the same time but spread more slowly. However, there was no comparable spread of Egyptian cultural influence. The many communities along the Egyptian Nile had no political or religious cohesiveness, and the common material culture and neolithic economy that they shared was not very different in its nature from that of contemporary African cultures. The typical pottery and artifacts of prehistoric Egypt are not found outside of the Nile valley or south of the Second Cataract, and only along the upper Nile is some influence perceptible.

Between the Second Cataract and Khartoum at this time a typical product of the indigenous population, called the "Khartoum Neolithic" people, was pottery with impressed designs, a tradition inherited from their hunting and gathering predecessors. By contrast, the wares of contemporary Egypt were sometimes painted but rarely incised, while the commonest fabric was plain red polished, often with an added black top. This decorative idea was copied on a small scale in the Khartoum Neolithic and eventually became an important feature of later pottery styles in Lower and Upper Nubia. Otherwise, borrowing was restricted to a simple tool, the "gouge" found in fact throughout the Sahara as well as along the Nile.

The civilization of historical Egypt developed so rapidly in the first centuries of the third millennium B.C. that some have suggested that the creative inspiration came from the already developed cultures of Mesopotamia. Literacy, centralized political control, an elaborate religious system, a metal (copper, later bronze) technology and a developed style in art and monumental architecture were firmly established in Egypt by 2700 B.C. However, it was just at this time that contact with other parts of Africa became more difficult. The Sahara was arid by 2500 B.C. and while its retreating population introduced agriculture and domesticated animals into western and central Africa, the desert routes to Egypt became more difficult to traverse. Even the chief remaining corridor for human movement, the Nile valley, was to a large extent blocked in the south by a vast swamp, the Sudd.

Some scholars therefore doubt that there could have been any significant contact between Egypt and most of Black Africa after 3000 B.C. They suggest that apparent similarities such as the appearance of centralized political structures and divine kingship, which appear in some Black African groups in the first and second millennia A.D., are general and coincidental. Other historians believe such similarities are ultimately derived from ancient Egypt, probably via the "Egyptianized" kingdom of Meroe in the Sudan (591 B.C.-A.D. 320), and are perhaps linked to the diffusion of iron technology from the same source. Recently however the appearance of iron-working in western Africa has been dated to about 500 B.C., and is unlikely to have come from Meroe where iron was still rare at the same date. It can no longer be automatically assumed that the iron-working which appears in central Africa in the early first millennium A.D. was derived from Meroe, since an alternative source is now known to have existed.

The controversy will be resolved only by extensive archaeological exploration, which so far has taken place only in the extreme north of the principal contact area, the modern Republic of the Sudan. Lower Nubia, the area between the First and Second Cataracts (now shared between Egypt and the Sudan), has been thoroughly explored; since 1900 it has served as an ever-growing reservoir to the Aswan Dam, a fact which has stimulated periodic bursts of salvage archaeology, culminating in an extraordinary international effort in 1961-1964. Upper Nubia, the valley between the Second and Fourth Cataracts, has been less well explored; recent surveys have reached as far as the Third Cataract and a handful of early historical sites are Napatan (706-591 B.C.), Meroitic or later. Archaeological coverage is not yet full enough to trace the possible diffusion of Egyptian influence beyond the Sudan in these or earlier times.

However, the accumulation of data over the last sixty years and its continuous reinterpretation have enabled us to study the earliest effects of ancient Egypt on its nearest southern neighbors, who included considerable numbers of Negroid and Negro peoples, and to guess what the effect may have been on more remote Black Africans. For nearly 1500 years (3000-1570 B.C.) the indigenous cultures of Lower Nubia were markedly different from those of historical Egypt, and in Upper Nubia the distinctions carried on into the Meroitic period. The differences are most easily to be seen in the pottery, in which the varied and inventive traditions of the ancient Sudan contrast strikingly with the unimaginative wares of historical Egypt, but are to be found also in most other aspects of material culture, in language, and surely, in social and political organizations and in religious beliefs. These latter aspects are poorly documented, since the Sudan did not become literate in its own language until ca. 180 B.C. and even now the earliest script, Meroitic, remains untranslatable.

Lower Nubia was unlikely to support a highly developed culture. It has access to some important resources (copper, gold and some valued types of stone) but only a small amount of cultivable land, and throughout history it has acted as a buffer zone between Egypt and the inhabitants of Upper Nubia. Nevertheless, the indigenous population of this region (which, certainly by 2200 B.C., consisted of a mixture of brown and black-skinned peoples, according to Egyptian depictions) was remarkably resistant to Egyptian cultural influence in spite of close and sometimes oppressive contact with the Egyptians. Already by *ca.* 3050 B.C. Egyptian expeditions had reached the Second Cataract while the people of the contemporary Nubian culture, labeled A-group by archaeologists, buried with their dead foods and liquids in imported Egyptian pots and Egyptian-made copper implements. These were obtained as a result of A-group control over the trade in luxury items, such as ebony and ivory, from further south. The material culture of the Nubians however remained basically non-Egyptian right up to the point (*ca.* 2600 B.C.) when they were decimated, enslaved and expelled by Egyptian troops intent on securing full control of the trade routes and natural resources of the area.

From *ca.* 2590 to 2420 B.C. the Egyptians controlled Lower Nubia from a few weakly defended settlements between the First and Second Cataracts, but these were eventually abandoned partly because of political instability in Egypt itself and partly because of an incursion of African people into Lower Nubia. These people, who may well have been related to the A-group, are called C-group by the archaeologists and came possibly from the now rapidly drying deserts to the east and west; during their period of occupation, part of, and finally all Lower Nubia came to be called Wawat. Organized under chieftains, the C-group were war-like enough to be hired as mercenaries by the Egyptians and they also hindered Egyptian trading expeditions, which until *ca.* 2185 B.C. were still reaching Upper Nubia. Eventually the C-group secured complete control of this trade and as a result, early C-group graves often contain Egyptian artifacts representing both booty and payment.

By *ca.* 1930 B.C. the Egyptians had reasserted their control over Lower Nubia, and consolidated it with a series of great forts eventually reaching to the southern end of the Second Cataract. These forts, with massive walls thirty to forty feet high, are eloquent testimony to the military threat offered by the C-group and the other African peoples in the general area. During the period of domination the C-group continued to live in flimsily built settlements, to bury their dead in substantial and un-Egyptian tombs with circular stone superstructures and to produce a variety of distinctive artifacts showing no Egyptian influence. When Egypt once again underwent an internal decline, the Egyptians did not abandon the forts but the C-group clearly regained some economic and political independence. Late C-group graves are often rich and include a number of especially large examples which probably belong to chieftains; some Egyptian influence may have affected burial customs, but as a whole the native culture of Wawat maintained its individuality.

At this point there was a dramatic incursion from Upper Nubia. Upper Nubia, with considerable amounts of cultivable land, was capable of supporting a larger and more complexly organized population than Lower Nubia. Already in the mid third millennium B.C. an important chieftainship, called Yam, existed in the area; it was visited by Egyptian traders and it provided them with armed escorts who protected the traders from the interference of the C-group people of Lower Nubia. After the Egyptian re-occupation of Lower Nubia however, the relationship became more complex; Upper Nubia, now called Kush, was regarded as a military threat and the great forts were meant in part to prevent Kushite attacks. The Egyptians fought several campaigns south of the Second Cataract and a contemporary inscription, while contemptuous of the Kushites, reveals by its very vehemence a fear and respect for Kushite fighting ability. In a recent translation by Gardiner, the text reads, in part:

When one rages against him [the Nubian] he shows his back; when one retreats he starts to rage. They are not people worthy of respect; they are cowards, craven-hearted.
But the Nubians were formidable enough for the royal author of the inscription to envisage that his troops might fail to resist them:

... he who shall destroy [the frontier] and fail to fight for it, he is not my son and was not born to me.

Despite the sporadic hostilities, trade continued to flow between Kush and Egypt, although the entry of Kushites into Lower Nubia was carefully regulated. Finally, in *ca.* 1650 B.C., the Kushites took the opportunity offered by declining Egyptian power, invaded Lower Nubia and occupied the Egyptian forts. Kushite political organization had reached the point where a single king, called by the Egyptians the "ruler of Kush," controlled not only Lower Nubia but probably Upper Nubia, the Kushite home-land, as well. Egypt by now was divided between an Asiatic dynasty in the north and an Egyptian dynasty in the south, and the Kushite and Asiatic rulers entered into an alliance against the Egyptian king. In a unique contemporary inscription, the Egyptians revealed the political reality of the situation by referring to the Kushite ruler as an equal of the Asiatic and Egyptian kings, in marked contrast to the Egyptian custom of referring to all foreign rulers as inherently inferior to the pharaoh.

Unfortunately, we cannot yet trace through archaeology the development of this important Kushite state, but in 1912-1914 a partially excavated cemetery at Kerma revealed what are almost certainly the royal burials of the "rulers of Kush" of the period *ca.* 1670-1570 B.C. and some of their predecessors. The latter probably did not exercise as much power, since the Kushites we know were originally divided into a number of tribes and the consolidation of control must have been gradual. The latest royal burials are extraordinary structures. The king was placed, with rich funerary equipment, in a central chamber or pit, and at the same time large numbers of women, presumably from his family, were sacrificed and buried in a nearby corridor or chamber. Over the burial complex was heaped a vast earth mound, sometimes held together by a mud-brick framework and a brick paving over the surface; a large stone cone was sometimes placed at the top.

These Kushite rulers no doubt maintained control over Upper and Lower Nubia through their exalted positions within the community, with however the support of warrior retainers, whose burials are found in and around the royal tumuli. Typically a warrior's funeral equipment includes a formidable metal dagger and he is usually accompanied by two or three sacrificed women. There are also indications that the Kushites had a fleet of boats, which would have secured them control over the river, the chief means of communication; boats are depicted in some buildings at Kerma and, earlier, the Egyptians had regulations against Kushite vessels entering Lower Nubia.

Kushite culture was in essentials non-Egyptian. The Kushites were dark-skinned people with their own language or languages, and their burial structures and customs were, for the most part, unparalleled in contemporary Egypt. The great mass of the artifacts from Kerma are of Kushite manufacture; they include excellent pottery, mainly a very fine red polished black-topped ware in beaker and bowl forms, leather garments, and mica and ivory inlays in animal or geometric form. Nevertheless, the long period of contact inevitably resulted in some cultural interaction with Egypt, the evidence for which needs to be carefully considered.

Hundreds of objects, mostly fragmentary but certainly of Egyptian origin, were found at Kerma, consisting of statues and statuettes of Egyptian kings and officials, faience and stone vessels, metal and wood objects, jewelry, and pottery. This led the excavator, Reisner, to believe that an Egyptian garrison and manufacturing center had dominated the Kushites, but it is now clear that some of these objects were plunder from Lower Nubia and the rest were secured through trade. The Kushites evidently were impressed by some aspects of Egyptian civilization; they collected Egyptian artifacts, refurbished some of the Egyptian temples in Lower Nubia and engaged the services of Egyptian scribes and craftsmen, some of whom must have been at Kerma. However, the technical knowledge of these Egyptians was applied to giving material form to Kushite conceptions and one may suspect that any intellectual influence from Egypt was similarly transformed. Thus the knowledge of building in mud-brick may have been derived from Egypt, but three massive brick structures found at Kerma are not of traditional Egyptian design. Their enormous walls take up between 80% and 90% of each structure and were meant to support an extensive second story, none of which survived. The ground floor rooms are quite small. One of these buildings, near the river, was perhaps the residence of the Kushite king; the two others, in the cemetery, were chapels and contained wall paintings in Egyptian style but of quite un-Egyptian content. Rows of painted hippopotami, giraffes and ships indicate a close connection with indigenous beliefs and experience.

In and around the denuded Kushite town at Kerma there was evidence for considerable industrial activity, including the making of pottery, faience and copper or bronze objects. The Kushites were skilled potters, but the faience-workers and metallurgists were probably Egyptian; their products however reflected Kushite culture. Faience (a powdered stone composition covered with a glassy glaze) occurs frequently but an un-Egyptian glazing of stone objects is also not uncommon, and some of the material produced, such as lions in blue faience or blue-glazed stone, are of Egyptian form but are not paralleled easily in Egypt itself. The famous Kerma daggers are based on an Egyptian prototype fitted however with a peculiarly Kushite pommel of ivory and tortoise shell, and there are occasional metal copies of typical Kushite pottery shapes.

The subsequent history of Kushite culture is not yet known. Between 1570 and 1500 B.C. the resurgent Egyptians rapidly re-occupied Lower Nubia and campaigned into Kushite territory until a new Egyptian frontier was established at Napata. For the next 400 years Wawat (Lower Nubia) and Kush were colonial possessions, governed by an Egyptian bureaucracy and sending an annual tribute, primarily of gold, to Egypt. The Nubians of Wawat now became Egyptianized and their chieftains, absorbed into the administrative system, are found depicted and buried in completely Egyptian style. In the larger and more diverse province of Kush the interaction was undoubtedly more complex, but unfortunately only Egyptian centers have so far been excavated. Resistance to Egyptian control is indicated by serious revolts throughout Dynasty XVIII (1570-1320 B.C.) and may have persisted into later periods. On the other hand, large numbers of Kushites were absorbed into the Egyptian army and some probably gained high rank in the provincial administration. The last effective viceroy of Kush, for example, was called Penehasi, "the Nubian" and although this name was also given to Egyptians he may well have been a Sudanese. In any case, Penehasi remained in Kush, presumably as its independent ruler, when the Egyptians abandoned the province in *ca.* 1085 B.C.

There is no textual or archaeological evidence on the transition to the later and better known Napatan and Meroitic periods. It is surely significant however that the earliest Napatan royal burials were of an earth-mound type, reminiscent of the Kushite customs at Kerma, and that Egyptian influence did not become strong until the Napatans conquered and, for a brief period (751-656 B.C.), ruled Egypt. Thereafter it is true that certain Egyptian cultural forms in art and religion become evident, but the many differences in detail and emphasis, and the eventually exclusive use of the native Meroitic language and script emphasize once again the individuality of these early Sudanese civilizations.

Turning briefly to the question of African influence on Egypt, it is sometimes said that ancient Egyptian institutions and social structure were, in a general way, "African." This however, implies a uniformity of thought and experience throughout the continent which in fact is unlikely to have existed. More specifically, Egypt seems to have been little affected by African or other foreign cultural influences. Their trading and military expeditions certainly must have enabled the Egyptians to learn much about their southern neighbors, but only one or two Nubian gods were absorbed, as minor deities, into the Egyptian pantheon while a few Nubian words appear in the Egyptian language. From early historical times it is true that a steady though proportionately small stream of Nubians entered Egypt as slaves or mercenaries; however, even when immigrants settled down as a community they rapidly absorbed Egyptian culture and within a few generations are virtually indistinguishable from Egyptians in the textual and archaeological record. There is evidence that in the New Kingdom especially individual Nubians were appointed to important posts at the royal court in Egypt and, in view of the fact that the pharaohs maintained harems which included Nubian women, it is not unlikely that a few of the Egyptian kings may have been at least partly Nubian. Nevertheless, no resulting cultural influence can be detected arising from this form of contact. The significant Black African influence on Egypt was indirect. The mineral and other natural resources of the northern Sudan attracted the Egyptians into the area where they encountered numerous and sometimes well organized and formidable human groups; contact stimulated a variety of commercial, diplomatic and military reactions which meant that the southern lands played a role in Egyptian foreign policy approaching in importance that of western Asia.

The cultural interraction between Egypt and her nearest Black African neighbors was then a complex matter from very early times; Egyptian influence was sometimes resisted and, if absorbed, underwent a transformation in the process. If it did penetrate into Africa beyond the Nile the transformation was probably even more radical and the resistance of the indigenous cultures to it even stronger.

Part VI

The Old World: The Aegean

Richard Wyatt Hutchinson was born in 1894 and educated at St. John's
College, Cambridge, where in 1952 he was appointed lecturer in
Classical Archaeology. He directed and took part in a great number
of major excavations, not only on Crete, but in Poland, Macedonia,
and the Near East. The selection included here appears as Chapter 11
of his book: *Prehistoric Crete* (1962).

The Decadence of Minoan Crete:
The Mycenaean Empire

Richard Wyatt Hutchinson

Minoan power terminated in a sudden and widespread but rather mysterious disaster.
At Knosos Evans found abundant evidences of the destruction of the Palace of Minos by
fire, and of its systematic looting, but very few human bones. If its inhabitants were not
carried off wholesale into captivity, they must have had time to escape. Moreover the
Minoan culture did not vanish overnight like the Minoan empire. After an interval
refugees of the same race and religion apparently, and indeed with the same culture but
on a much lower standard, began to squat and even build shrines in the ruins of the
palaces and villas of the princes and nobles. It is possible that the upper classes were
nearly wiped out by the great disaster, but it is clear that a large number of the common
people must have survived.

A lucky chance enabled Evans to date this disaster with considerable accuracy.
Painted pottery of the type found in the reoccupation period at Knosos was found
in Egypt in the city of Akhetaten at Tell-el-Amarna founded by the heretic Pharaoh
Akh-en-aten and abandoned after his death. Such pottery must therefore be dated between 1375 and 1350 B.C., and even though we now know that this pottery is a Mycenaean
not Late Minoan fabric, this does not affect the chronology, since the same Mycenaean
pottery is found at Knosos in strata immediately on top of the debris from the great fire.

But what was the cause of this catastrophe, which was not confined to Knosos but
seems to have been experienced all over the island? The same destruction (followed,
accompanied, or preceded by looting) seems to have affected Phaistos and Hagia Triada
in the Mesara, Tylisos, Amnisos, Nirou Khani, Mallia, Pseira, Gournia, and Mochlos in
the north, and in the east, though perhaps to a lesser degree, Palaikastro and Zakros.

What was the cause of so widespread a disaster? Was it caused by foreign invasion,
by internal revolutions, or by natural causes such as earthquakes and floods (which

curiously often cause fires as well)? It is clear that Mycenae benefited by the collapse of Crete, but this does not prove that the mainland Greeks were the primary cause of it.

Sir Arthur Evans, after considering the possibility that the great Cretan catastrophe at the end of the Late Minoan II period might have been caused by an invasion from the mainland, had rejected this idea in favour of the theory that the disaster was due to a terrible earthquake or series of quakes, and to the floods and fires that so often follow in their train. The most celebrated flood legend in Greece, that of the Thessalian Deucalion (not to be confused with the Cretan hero of that name), was traditionally supposed to have taken place about 1330 B.C. There were flood stories also on some other islands, such as Rhodes and Samothrace. If we could follow the suggestion made by Frost, and supported by Marinatos and Seltman, that Plato's story of Atlantis, that civilized island overwhelmed by a marine flood, was a garbled account of the destruction of Minoan Crete preserved in Egyptian records, then indeed we might have a folk memory of the catastrophe of 1400 B.C., but this interpretation at present lacks confirmatory evidence.[1]

Marinatos has supported the theory of the destruction of the Minoan empire by natural causes, but in a new form. He would associate the abandonment of Amnisos, and of other sites on or near the north coast of Crete after the Late Minoan I period, with the great eruption that blew up a large part of the Cycladic island of Thera and submerged a large area, leaving three islands, Thera, Therasia, and Aspronisi, as the only portions of what had been known as *Kalliste,* the 'fairest' of the Cycladic Isles. A large part of the present Thera is now buried in volcanic ash and pumice to a depth of thirty metres, and one of the strangest sights I have ever seen is the fields of flourishing vines and tomato plants growing out of lumps of pumice stone with apparently no other soil to support them.

Theophanes, the Byzantine historian, in describing the much smaller eruption on the same island in A.D. 726, tells how the pumice reached the shores of Asia Minor and Macedonia, and to this day it is easy to pick up small lumps of pumice anywhere along the north coast of Crete.

Marinatos, arguing from the size of the prehistoric crater (eight-three square kilometres in extent and six hundred metres deep), maintains that the great eruption which he assigns to about 1500 B.C. must have exceeded that of Krakatoa in A.D. 1883, and must therefore have been accompanied by an even greater series of tidal waves and earthquakes affecting all the neighbouring islands, including Crete. I should prefer to have dated this eruption of Thera about 1400 B.C. (though there may of course have been two serious outbreaks of the volcano) since the absence of Late Minoan II pottery except at Knosos can now be explained on other grounds. Otherwise I favour the theory of Marinatos, who points out that the Krakatoa eruption, with its much smaller crater of only 22·8 kilometres, caused tidal waves twenty-seven metres high, devastated the coasts of Java and Sumatra, and was responsible for the loss of 36,000 lives. Now Thera is only one hundred kilometres north of Crete, but at one point the sea reaches a depth of over 1800 metres, so that the tidal waves of the Cycladic earthquake should have been considerably higher and more frequent than those of Krakatoa.

A Cycladic settlement on Thera, with pottery imitating Late Minoan I types, was overwhelmed and buried in the debris from this earthquake, and it is not unnatural to suppose that the island and coastal settlements on the north of Crete, such as the harbour town of Knosos, Amnisos, Nirou Khani, Mallia, and Gournia were destroyed at the same time or shortly afterwards by the tidal waves and earthquakes.

Marinatos had supposed that Knosos had escaped serious destruction by reason of its greater height and distance from the sea, but I think the palace may have been destroyed by earthquake and fire at that time, even though it may have escaped the tidal waves.

The absence of the Late Minoan II culture (1450-1400 B.C.) from sites other than Knosos, except for an occasional import, can now be better explained by the presence of an Achaean dynasty at Knosos, rather than by assuming that Knosos persisted later than the other Cretan cities. The late Sir William Ridgeway always maintained stoutly that the Minos of the legend of Theseus and the Minotaur must have been an Achaean king, and his theory, till recently rather unpopular, has now been magnificently vindicated by Ventris's reading of the Linear Script B tablets as documents in 'Achaean' Greek, using the term Achaean not in the limited sense in which it was applied in classical times but in the wider sense in which it is used by Homer in the *Iliad*.

Among other causes which may have contributed to the abandonment of Cretan sites was the failure of Minos's naval expedition to Sicily. This story was already known to Herodotus, probably from his Samian sources, who would be familiar with the west Cretan version of the legend as told in Kydonia. Kleidemos again knew of it in the fourth century, but his attempt to conflate it with the tradition that Daedalus was born in Athens makes his story unconvincing.[2] Diodorus Siculus, who completed his history in the reign of Augustus, gives a coherent and reasonable account, which would appear to be derived partly from fifth-century sources like Herodotus, partly from Cretan historians of the Hellenistic period, and partly from the folklore of his native island of Sicily. How strong those Sicilian traditions were in the second decade of the fifth century B.C. is proved by the action of Theron, the tyrant of Akragas, who discovered what he claimed to be the bones of Minos, and sent them back to Crete to be reburied there. Herodotus, in the seventh book of his history, gives an account of this western expedition of Minos in pursuit of his runaway engineer, Daedalus, but does not mention the name of the Sicilian king, Kokalos. Herodotus, presumably drawing on his Samian-Cretan sources, gives some interesting details, such as the five years' unsuccessful seige of the city of Kamikos by the Cretans after the death of Minos, and the very interesting local detail that all the peoples of Crete had taken part in this expedition except the citizens of Polichne and Praisos. The most interesting item provided by Diodorus, obviously derived from the Sicilian legends, is his description of Minos's burial place as 'a tomb of two storeys, in the part which was underground they placed the bones, and in that which lay open to gaze they made a shrine of Aphrodite', a description which reminded Evans of the form of the Temple Tomb at Knosos, a royal tomb that the classical Cretans never saw, since it was buried for some three thousand years. The resemblance between the tomb and Diodorus's description may be a coincidence, but it is easier to explain it by supposing there had been a genuine tradition of such a tomb underlying the Sicilian folklore.

The fire that destroyed Minoan halls would have had less effect if the central pillars had not been of wood, and this accounts for the good preservation of most of the pillar crypts with central piers of ashlar stonework. The account of Samson's destruction of the Philistine palace at Gaza becomes less fantastic and more credible if we imagine him as pulling together two central Mycenaean wooden columns probably affected by dry rot.[3]

Ruined adobe houses tend to retain their walls. The material—clay—unlike stones, is not worth the trouble of carting away to be used elsewhere for other constructions. If the inhabitant of a destroyed adobe house should return and desire to build another on the same spot he simply levels the walls and builds his new house at a slightly higher level. This is the explanation why mounds consisting of the accumulation of prehistoric villages of mudbrick houses are so much higher as a rule than sites of the classical and historic periods, where building materials were re-used and the levels of the new buildings did not differ much from that of their predecessors. I think, therefore, that the great disaster approximately dated 1400 B.C. may probably have been due to natural causes, such as earthquakes followed by fires and in the coastal cities tidal waves, without excluding the possibility that it may have been aggravated by human actions, such as raids and revolutions following the collapse of the Sicilian expedition. In the nineteenth century A.D., when Ireland was struggling for Home Rule, it used to be stated that 'England's misfortune was Ireland's opportunity,' and we may perhaps claim that in the fifteenth and fourteenth centuries B.C. Knosos's misfortune was Mycenae's opportunity.

During the fourteenth century B.C. Achaean settlers seem to have colonized most of the more fertile parts of the island, and enslaved many of the native population. The more virile elements of the native Cretans fled to the hills and founded new villages, such as Axos in the Mylopotamos district, Prinias on the watershed between the northern plains and the Mesara, Karphi in Lasithi, and Vrokastro and Effendi Kavousi in the Merabello district.

Effects on Minoan Trade

Even in the sixteenth century, trade with the western Mediterranean seems to have been in Mycenaean rather than in Cretan hands, while in the fifteenth century Mycenae managed also to capture most of the trade with Egypt, Cyprus, and the Levant in general.

In Crete, however, the Minoan culture persisted in a weakened and decadent form. There are few imports of Egyptian alabaster vases, little jewellery or engraved gems in comparison with the previous period, and no painted frescoes, with the one curious and abnormal exception, the painted sarcophagus of Hagia Triada. Fresco painters and all the best gem cutters seem to have emigrated to the mainland, where there were richer patrons and a better market for their work. The pottery immediately succeeding the catastrophe in Crete, which in Furumark's classification is Late Minoan III A 2, I would term simply Late Minoan III A, preferring to regard the shortlived style which he terms Late Minoan III A I as simply the last pottery of the Late Minoan II B period. This is merely a matter of convenience, so that we may keep Evans's correlation of the great disaster with the end of the second Late Minoan period. The contemporary Late Helladic III A I style of the mainland is a well-balanced if rather dull style, with ornaments, derived mainly from the Late Helladic I repertoire, usually confined to the shoulder and with only horizontal girding bands decorating the belly and foot of the vase.

Revival of Minoan Shrines

Of the larger settlements in the lowlands perhaps the only examples we can quote as surviving without great change through the fourteenth century are Palaikastro and Zakros in the far east. There was more continuity, however, in the religious than in the civic life of the Minoan towns, and shrines of the reoccupation period can be quoted from most of the great Minoan centres. At Knosos two small rooms in the south-east part of the ruined Palace of Minos were reconstructed and converted into a shrine of the Household Goddess, dubbed by Evans the Shrine of the Double Axes. Here were preserved all the essential features of a Minoan shrine, but in the cheapest form. We gain the impression on the whole that the reoccupation of the lowlands of Crete by Minoan refugees was rather a gradual process, and that the first movement came from the priests. The worship at the old shrines revived before the civil life did, but by the thirteenth century B.C. civil life was also beginning to recover. At Mallia the structure that the French excavators cautiously describe as 'the diagonal building' should also, I think, be regarded as a shrine of the reoccupation period, though no sacred utensils or vases from it seem to have survived. These small shrines recall the simplest form of the 'megaron house' and look forward to the simplest form of the classical temples, the so-called *templum in antis,* which is simply a long narrow room entered through a porch with two columns between the *antae,* or side-posts, though the Late Minoan examples usually have either only one column or else none at all between the *antae.* But if the architectural form of these shrines has been affected by northern models, the ledge at the back and the figurines and other furniture, when preserved, remain solidly Minoan, to remind us that the deity and the ritual are Cretan.

The furniture of these Late Minoan III shrines is a travesty of those that had existed in the Minoan palaces. The figurines of the goddesses are of pottery, or occasionally of bronze, but not of ivory or faience, though small faience beads of ladies or goddesses in flounced skirts are found. There are few stone vases, except at Palaikastro, which seems to have escaped the worst of the disaster; pedestal lamps in stone still occur there, but the pedestals are shorter than formerly and have a moulded band half-way up. Steatite bowls of the 'bird's nest' and 'blossom' type still continue at Palaikastro, but many, perhaps most, of these may probably have been family heirlooms made in Middle Minoan times and still in use. Occasionally stone vases are found on other sites also.

In general the Eteo-Cretan country east of Seteia seems to have escaped from the worst effects of the floods, and earthquakes, and so to have been better able to hold out against Achaean colonists. Thus Zakros has one of the best-constructed and most comfortable houses of the period.

Pottery of the Reoccupation Period

The Late Minoan III A pottery of this reoccupation period starts with stirrup jars, deep bowls, cups, jugs, and *larnakes* adorned with degenerate versions of Late Minoan II 'Palace Style' motifs, and combines them in a loose, rather tasteless fashion developing into a 'close style' in which the main object of the painter seems to be a *horror vacui,* a terror of leaving any part of the vase undecorated, in great contrast to the rather industrialized, but very competent, decoration of the contemporary Late Helladic III A vases introduced by the Achaean colonists, who usually confined their main ornaments to the neck and shoulder, and only painted well-spaced girding bands on the body and foot of the vase.

Mainland influences are discernible, however, also in the Late Minoan III pottery, especially in the increasing popularity of certain shapes such as the squat alabastron, the 'pilgrim bottle', the *kylix* (a champagne cup), and the small pear-shaped amphora with three handles, all forms occurring in Crete at an earlier date, but hitherto much more popular on the mainland.

During this period we may observe the gradual adoption of the Minoan-Mycenaean style based on the Late Minoan II of Knosos by other Cretan areas which had been wont to use and manufacture pottery of Late Minoan I A and Late Minoan I B types during the second half of the fifteenth century. Furumark has discerned two main groups in this Late Minoan III A pottery, one basing its decoration on the old 'free-field unity' system native to Minoan Crete, and the other on the banded-zone system introduced by the Achaean immigrants. At first the whole vase was covered by horizontal zones of ornament with no special regard to the tectonic divisions of the vase, but this was soon replaced by a more balanced system whereby the main decoration was confined to the broadest part of the vase, where the handles and spouts were placed. Later still this tectonic arrangement was further emphasized by subdivisions into vertical panels, or by breaking up the intervals between the handles and spouts into triangular quadrants. The vertical panel division is particularly characteristic of many of the larger vases of the Late Minoan III A style. Western Crete, where the Minoan population, though well distributed, had always been relatively sparse, naturally succumbed more easily to the Achaean infiltration. The first extensive Mycenaean settlement in the west of which we have archaeological evidence would appear to be that at Atsipadhais, where the tombs are filled with Late Helladic III A and B pottery and contain a number of Mycenaean 'dollies', the little clay figurines so typical of Late Helladic III B sites on the mainland and easily distinguishable from Cretan figurines.

Another cemetery of chamber tombs in the west, outside Khania, contained both Late Minoan III A and Late Helladic III A vases, and the same mixture occurred in the Zapher Papoura cemetery excavated by Evans near Knosos. Typical Late Minoan III A pottery was also found in chamber tombs at Kalyvia in the Mesara, in *larnax* burials at Gournia, Hierapetra, Seteia and other sites in eastern Crete, and in the 'Bathroom' in block C at Palaikastro.

The Late Minoan III A *kylices* differ from their mainland contemporaries in having hollow pedestals.[4] The 'Vapheio cup' has died out and been replaced by 'tea-cups' and by small cups with straight sides and a handle perched on the flaring rim. Bridge-spouted saucers with a handle at one side, or opposite the spout, or without any handle at all, are quite common.

The circular *pyxis* reappears as a Cretan vase-shape, and for the first time we encounter domed covers for lamps as in Rhodes.

In the luxury arts of the Late Minoan III A period it is often hard to distinguish between Minoan and Mycenaean work, but the best patrons were the Achaean princes and the best Cretan workman had probably emigrated to the mainland. Frescoes appear on various sites on the mainland, but no frescoes have survived in Crete except the unique and very interesting painting adorning a sarcophagus in a Late Minoan III chamber tomb at Hagia Triada. No other sarcophagus is decorated in this fashion, but we are entering on a period when pottery ones with designs painted on the clay were to become normal, and Nilsson has suggested that this was the grave of a Mycenaean chief and that the local Minoan painter employed to decorate the sarcophagus had used the technique and the motifs which he would have employed to decorate a Minoan shrine.

A few engraved gems have been found associated with Late Minoan III A pottery (for example Tomb 99 at Zapher Papoura), but most seals assigned to this period are dated purely on grounds of style. They include some haematite cylinder seals with a mixture of Minoan and oriental subjects, reflecting influences from Syria or Cyprus. A tomb at Aptsa, dated 1400-1350, contained a prism seal that looks about 500 years older than the objects associated with it.[5]

The Late Minoan III B style of pottery[6] (1300-1200 B.C.) is rather more uniform than its predecessor. The absorption by the Achaean power of those areas of Crete where the Late Minoan I style had reigned resulted in the development of a pottery style in which were mingled late Mycenaean elements along with motifs derived from the older traditions of the Late Minoan I A and Late Minoan I B styles and others derived from the Knosian Palace Style of the Late Minoan II period. The general effect is rather dull, and neither the ornaments nor the paint are the equal of the contemporary Mycenaean pottery imported from the Peloponnese.

Gems

Gem engraving still continued, as is illustrated by the remains from the lapidary's workshop at Knosos. The shapes are normally lentoid, the material steatite, and the designs include not only such old favourites as the cow suckling its calf and the lion springing on a bull, but also representations of dogs attacking goats, sheep, or oxen. A seal from Arkhanes illustrates the motif of a well-known Mycenae dagger, namely the hunting cat attacking wild duck.

A certain amount of jewellery also occurs in Late Minoan III B chambers. Thus Tomb 7 at Zapher Papoura had a gold-plated bronze ring with the design of a sphinx, and a necklace of beads with the double argonaut design, which appears also on beads from a tomb near Phaistos. Further jewellery was found in Tombs 66 and 99 at Zapher Papoura, in Tombs 3 and 6 at Isopata, and in the Mavrospilaion cemetery.

The Middle-East Style

By 1200 B.C., or perhaps a little earlier, we are conscious of a new form of pottery decoration, a last dying flicker of the old Minoan spirit, in what Pendlebury terms the 'Middle-East Style'. It certainly was absent from western Crete, which seems to have been almost completely Hellenized and where the best pottery is all Mycenaean, but the new style was current in central Crete, both at Knosos and in the Mesara, and was exported in some quantities to Rhodes, while isolated examples have been found at

Kalymnos, in Attica, Asini, and Delphi and even as far west as Scoglio del Tonno near Taranto.[7]

Not many vases of this style from Crete have been published, and the examples from Karphi were often so affected by weathering that it was impossible to illustrate their designs, but the published examples from Crete include a small stirrup jar from the Royal Tomb at Isopata, a tankard from the Psychro Cave,[8] and some sherds from Hagia Triada.[9]

The characteristics of this style as defined by Pendlebury are 'the use of thick solid elements in the decoration usually fringed and combined with a forest of fine lines and closely hatched subordinate figures. The octopus motive is a favourite one and though clearly distinguishable it has become divorced from all reality and is treated as a pure pattern.' The most imposing vases adorned in this style are some large stirrup jars from Rhodes, and it is of course quite possible that these were local Rhodian imitations. The Cretan origin of the style, however, may be inferred from the fact that vases in this style from other districts are always stirrup jars, and only in Crete do we find different shapes, such as deep bowls and bridge-spouted tankards, in this same style. Elsewhere, both in the west and in the east, we find simply a gradual decay of the Late Minoan III and Late Helladic III styles.

A Syro-Phoenician Cult in Crete

The trade routes with Egypt and the East, however, were still open, and the Achaean merchants were quite ready to exploit them.

To the Late Minoan III period in general belongs a series of metal statuettes representing the Syrian god Reshef, usually in bronze but occasionally in some other material such as silver. They have been found in various parts of the Levant and must have been made, neither in Crete nor in the Peloponnese, but in some Phoenician or Syrian factory.

Recently an example of such a bronze figure with round shield and sickle-bladed sword, of the type which the Egyptians called a *khepesh* (and which some archaeologists wrongly dub a *harpe*) was found by the French excavators at Delos. H. G. de Santerre and J. Tréheux, in publishing this figurine, give a list of similar statuettes, which they do not claim to be complete, but which seems much fuller than any other.

This list of de Santerre and Tréheux emphasizes the overwhelming evidence in favour of a Phoenician or south Syrian factory for these works, but they were popular imports into Greece and Crete in the Late Minoan III period, as may be seen by the following supplement to this list of thirty-eight figurines:

39, 40	bronze statuettes in Athens from Mycenae and Tiryns
41	figurine from Sybrita, Crete, in the Ashmolean Museum, Oxford
42	silver figurine in the Ashmolean from Nezero in Thessaly
43	bronze figurine from Thermon
44	bronze figurine found at Schernen in east Prussia
45, 46	two statuettes found at Olympia
47, 48	four geometric statuettes from Delphi
49	the 'Karapanos' statuette from Dodona

His title in the Karatepe inscription, 'Reshef of the Birds', suggests a comparison with the Minoan 'Master of the Animals' and with figures such as the gold figurine from 'the Aegina treasure'.

This deity was the young 'Baal' of Phoenicia and could be hailed as Teshub, Hadad, Mot, or Seth according to the nationality of his worshippers. It is possible of course that the Mycenaeans and the Cretans of Late Minoan times may have equated him with Apollo, or the Minoan 'Master of the Animals'.

The Folk-Migrations of the Twelfth Century B.C.

The twilight of the Minoan and Mycenaean cultures is illuminated by some references to the peoples of the Aegean in the contemporary records of the Hittites and the Egyptians. In the third year of the reign of Mursil, Great King of the Hatti (about 1331 B.C.), the official records refer to a country called Ahhiyawa, associated with the name of a city called Millawanda. Many scholars believe that the country in question was an Achaean state, either in the Peloponnese or in one of the Aegean islands such as Cyprus, and that Millawanda was Miletus, which claimed to be a colony of Milatos in Crete. Some years later, perhaps still in the reign of Mursil II or perhaps in that of his successor Muwatallis (1306-1282 B.C.), often referred to as Mutallu, a letter was written by the Great King of Hatti concerning Tawagalawas, son of Antarawas, a vassal of the King of Ahhiyawa, based on Millawanda. This letter has received rather more publicity than it deserved because the Swiss scholar Forrer identified these princes with Eteokles, son of Andreus, legendary kings of Orchomenos. Most scholars, however, now reject both this identification and also Forrer's attempt to identify a certain Attarissyas, King of Ahhiyawa and a contemporary of the Hittite king Tudhalias IV (1250-1220 B.C.), with Atreus, the father of Agamemnon. The dates fit, but neither the form of the words nor the places associated with these names seem suitable. G. L. Huxley compared Attarissyas to Teiresias, and Sayce even preferred to identify Attarissyas with Perseus. Tudhalias may be the same name as the Greek Tantalus, but it does not follow that we can identify the father of Pelops with any particular Tudhalias, or Achilles's opponent Telephus with any particular Hittite prince named Telepinush.

The one inference that we can draw from these Hittite records with some degree of probability is the existence, somewhere in the Levant, of an important Achaean power during the thirteenth century B.C., and this is confirmed by the archaeological evidence. How many such states there were is more debatable, but that of Mycenae was certainly the most important, and those of Pylos, Orchomenos, and Thebes also of considerable standing.

The Hittite empire collapsed about 1190 B.C. and we therefore hear no more about Achaeans in the records from Boghaz Koi. Here, however, the Egyptian records help us with some references to the extraordinary ferment that was brewing in the international affairs of the Near East at this time, a ferment that began with the destruction of Hatti and the racial movement of the Phrygians from Macedonia into Asia Minor, and culminated in the attacks of the sea raids and the land raids on Egypt. Priam's campaign against the Amazons on the Sangarius River and Agamemnon's capture of Troy are all part of the same story, but so many pieces of the jig-saw puzzle

are missing that we cannot form a coherent picture of the whole. The first invasion of
the northerners broke against the shores of Egypt even before the collapse of Hatti when,
in 1221 B.C., the Egyptian Pharaoh had to repel a Libyan fleet that attacked the Delta
supported by a motley group of allies whose names suggested that they came from Asia
Minor. The only national contingent we can identify with absolute certainty is that of
the Lycians, though the Tursha are perhaps to be identified with the Tyrsenoi, the
Asiatic nation which colonized Etruria.[10] The Shakalsha have been identified with the
people of Sagalassos and the Shardana with Sardians or Sardinians. In favour of the last-
named identification is the fact that the Shardana wore helmets with two horns and
carried very long swords and small round shields like the figures found in the Nuraghe
cemeteries of Sardinia (though the Nuraghic culture is not supposed to begin before
1000 B.C.) Some of the Shardana, whoever they were, remained in Egypt and were
incorporated as mercenaries in the Egyptian army.[11] Some of the raiders used cut-and-
thrust swords with narrow tang of a type that became popular in Europe.[12]

The most interesting to us, however, of the Libyan allies are the Akwasha, who
are identified by most historians with the Achaeans and the people of Ahhiyawa in the
earlier Hittite records. The very same year (1221) Meneptah had had to contend with
revolts in Palestine in the cities of Gaza and Askalon, later celebrated as strongholds
of the Philistines. Indeed the Philistines may have already been infiltrating into this
coastland since, under the name Pulasati, they appear as one nation among the motley
horde of northerners that overran Syria and Palestine and attacked Egypt from the north-
east in 1190 B.C.[13] Of the previous raiders from the west only the Shakalsha appear
again, and the Akwasha are not mentioned. Of the new names the identifications for
Thekel and Weshesh are very uncertain, but fresh evidence has appeared in support of
the theory that the people termed Denyen in the Egyptian records were those that
Homer calls Danaoi, a term he used as a rather loose equivalent of Achaeans. The recent
decipherment of a Phoenician text at Karatepe in Cilicia suggests that these Denyen
were the inhabitants of the plain of Adana, a district which still recalls their name and
which was traditionally colonized by Mopsos of Argos, shortly after the fall of Troy.[14]
The same people also appear as Danuna in the Assyrian records. The curious stories of
Danaus and his brother Aegyptus, to which we owe the Greek and modern European
names for Egypt (which its inhabitants have always termed Musri), must go back to
the traditions of the land raid of the northern peoples on Egypt. The old Bronze Age
powers of the Aegean had disappeared or were in a state of collapse. Hatti, Knosos,
Troy, and even Mycenae became heaps of ruins, but the successors of these powers had
lived long enough in contact with the Bronze Age civilization of these cities to have
absorbed much of their culture, and the new states that emerged from the ruins, Phrygia,
the late Hittite states such as Carchemish, and the small city states that arose in Greece,
though simpler than their predecessors, preserved much of their cultural heritage.

Wace and Albright, for different reasons, would date the transition from the Sub-
Mycenaean to the Protogeometric Period not later than 1000 B.C. Desborough's 970 B.C.
depended on the date formerly assigned to stratum IV at Tall Abu Hawam in Palestine,
now dated fifty years earlier by Van Beek (see Wace and Albright in *The Aegean and the
Near East,* edited by S. Weinberg, pp. 134 and 163 respectively). The period between the
Dorian invasion and Homer remains very obscure. Whatever we may think of the validity

of Ventris's system, there seems little doubt that Greek was spoken in Crete in 1500 B.C. and that the percentage of Greek speakers rapidly increased. Why then was the native script abandoned, and was there a period of complete illiteracy at the end of the Bronze Age before the introduction of the Phoenician alphabet which, with the addition of a few letters, was to become the official Greek alphabet and the ancestor of all the modern alphabets of Europe? The date and the method of this transmission is still a matter of dispute, but a recent survey of the evidence by Margot Falkine has suggested a date between 900 and 863 for the transmission, which she thinks may have come via Rhodes.[15] Signorina Guarducci, however, has suggested that Crete may rather have been the medium. By 750 B.C. the modified Phoenician script was in use in Athens, Thebes, Corinth, Thera, and Melos as well as Crete and Rhodes.

It would appear that the *Iliad* and the *Odyssey* must have been composed during the eighth century. 'Homer, then,' says Sir Maurice Bowra, 'stands at a point where an ancient poetical tradition has just been touched by the new art of writing and to this we may owe some of his subtlety and aptness. But it is to the purely oral art behind this that we must turn when we wish to examine his relation with the past.'[16] This statement needs to be qualified. The art of writing was not 'new' in the eighth century B.C., but, even if it had not died out, it seems that the number of writers must have diminished and that oral transmission played an important role in epic poetry.

'Heroic poetry', Finley remarks, 'is always oral poetry; it is composed orally, often by bards who are illiterate, and it is recited in a chant to a listening audience. Formally it is at once distinguishable by the constant repetition of phrases, lines, and whole groups of lines.'

The procedure of the composition of an epic lay by an illiterate poet who dictates it to a literate scribe is illustrated by the Cretan poem *The Song of Daskaloyannis,* composed in A.D. 1796 by an illiterate cheesemaker and taken down in writing by a literate shepherd.[17]

Notes

[1]K. T. Frost, 'The Critics and Minoan Crete', *Journal of Hellenic Studies,* 1939, p. 189; S. Marinatos, 'Perí toú thrýlou tis Atlantidos', *Kretika Chronika,* 1950, p. 195; C. Seltman, 'Life in Ancient Crete', *History Today,* 1952, p. 332.

[2]For the confusion between a legendary artist named Daedalus of Bronze Age date and the alleged founder of the Dedalic School of sculpture see p. 340; and for Samians in Crete see p. 350 of *Prehistoric Crete.*

[3]Professor Mallowan, however, points out that the Mesopotamian records reveal many evidences of such destruction; probably palaces and temples were easier to fire than cottages, because there would be more timber and more air space.

[4]Two-handled goblets with characteristic decoration and fabric are found in Late Helladic II deposits on the mainland and occasionally at Knosos, but not elsewhere in Crete.

[5]S. Xanthoudides, 'Ek Kretes', *Ephemeris Archaiologiki,* 1904, p. 1 and Fig. 4.

[6]Furumark calls this Late Minoan III B I and his Late Minoan III B 2 corresponds to my Late Minoan III C.

[7]W. Taylour, *Mycenaean Pottery in Italy,* 1958, pp. 108, 131 considers most of these to be Rhodian, as some may well be, but not, I think, all of them.

[8]D. G. Hogarth, 'The Dictaean Cave', *Annual of the British School at Athens,* 1900, p. 103.

[9]M. Borda, *Arte Creteo-Miceneo del Museo Pigorini di Roma,* 1946, Plates XXXVII, XXXVIII.

[10]But when and how many? For the theory that the Etruscan nation grew up in Italy, see M. Pallottino, *The Etruscans* (Penguin Books, 1955), Chapter 2.

[11]See also R. Dussaud, *La Lydie et ses voisins,* 1930, p. 37.

[12]C. F. A. Schaeffer, 'A Bronze Sword from Ugarit', *Antiquity,* 1955, p. 226.

[13]For J. L. Myres's suggestion that Pulusati = Pelasgians, see *Who Were The Greeks?,* 1930, p. 143.

[14]R. D. Barnett, J. Leveen, and C. Moss, 'A Phoenician Inscription from Eastern Cilicia', *Iraq,* 1948, p. 56; see also G. L. Huxley, 'Mycenaean Decline and the Homeric Catalogue of Ships', *University of London Bulletin,* 1956, p. 19.

[15]M. Falkine, *Frühgeschichte und Sprachwissenschaft,* 1948.

[16]*Homer and his Forerunners,* 1955, p. 14.

[17]See V. Laourdas, *Tó Tragoudhi toú Dhaskaloyánni,* I , 991-8.

M. I. Finley (Ph.D., Columbia University) is Reader in Ancient Social and
Economic History at the University of Cambridge, England, and Fellow
of Jesus College. He is the author of a number of influential books,
including *The Ancient Greeks: An Introduction to Their Life and Thought*
(1963) and *Early Greece; The Bronze and Archaic Ages.* The reading published
here appears as Chapter 7 in the latter book.

The Dark Age

M. I. Finley

Unless life itself is destroyed in a region, there must always be continuity of some
kind. In that sense, Greek history was a continuation of its Bronze Age prehistory. To make
too much of that truism, however, is to put the stress in the wrong place and to overlook
how fundamentally new the new society was to become. The Greeks of historical times
had no tradition of a break and therefore no concept of a different civilization in the
millennium before their own, although they did know in a vague and inaccurate way
that other languages had once been spoken in Greece and the islands. Their 'heroic age',
familiar to them from the Homeric poems and from much legendary material (such
as the Oedipus story), was merely an early stage in Greek history. That is why Theseus
could be credited with destroying the minotaur and with unifying Attica, both legendary
actions, but one more appropriate to the Bronze Age, the other to the very different
world of the Dark Age. Modern archaeology has discovered a prehistoric world never
dreamed of by the Greeks of the historical era.

Archaeology brings to the forefront breakdown and decline about 1200 B.C.,
followed by poverty and a low quality of artistry and technology. What it reveals much less
clearly, and in certain critical respects not at all, is that the centuries after 1200 point
ahead, not only materially with the emergence of iron as the new and most advanced
metal, but also socially, politically and culturally. The future of the Greeks lay not in
palace-centred, bureaucratic states but in the new kind of society which was forged out
of the impoverished communities that survived the great catastrophe. We cannot follow
that process of growth in its formative stages, except in scattered hints strewn in the
archaeological record and in later traditions, and we are not helped by the fact that in
the contemporary written documents from Syria, Mesopotamia and Egypt there is no
reference whatever to the Greeks. In the sense, therefore, that *we* grope in the dark,
and in that sense only, is it legitimate to employ the convention of calling the long period
in Greek history from 1200 to 800 'a dark age'. And like the other 'ages' we are con-

---

Reprinted from *Early Greece: The Bronze and Archaic Ages,* Chap. 7, pp. 71-90 by permission of
W. W. Norton & Co., Inc., and the author. Copyright © 1970 by M. I. Finley.

cerned with, subdivisions must be noted, one about 1050, a second in the course of the ninth century.

The confused archaeological record in Cyprus, already described, shows that the generations immediately after 1200 saw more than one movement of people, whether as a further influx from the north, or as internal transfers within the Aegean area itself, or both. The break-up of the Mycenaean states, the Hittite Empire and the small North Syrian states created a power vacuum, which made movement relatively easy, especially into depopulated districts. One new arrival of particular importance for Greek history was that of the Dorians in the Peloponnese and Crete. There are no archaeological identifying marks of Dorians, which is not surprising, since different dialects are sometimes spoken by groups who otherwise share the material culture that archaeologists discover. However, Doric is the one classical Greek dialect that requires us to assume an actual migration into Greece: some of the peculiar word-formations and phonetics cannot be explained, on strictly linguistic grounds, as an evolution from the Greek of the Mycenaean period. Presumably it was a dialect which emerged separately in the more isolated northwestern region of the Greek peninsula, outside the Mycenaean sphere, before it was brought into southern Greece and Crete. The eleventh century is as good a guess as any for the date of that movement. Elsewhere in the then Greek-speaking world, the catastrophe of 1200 did not introduce any new linguistic factor, but the process of local differentiation that followed had its effects, which we can see in the end-product, the historical Greek dialect pattern.

Regional variations also make it difficult to present the archaeological picture of the Dark Age succinctly. True, a uniform dullness sets in everywhere (apart from an occasional find which is strikingly exceptional). Pictorial representation of human and animal figures is abandoned; there is no grandeur of scale, and hardly any building in stone at all; nor is there delicacy in the small objects, as gems are no longer manufactured. Luxury articles, all non-essential imports, virtually disappear: the absence of amber has already been noted, and the rare gold ornament indicates no more than a tomb robbery or a chance discovery of a Mycenaean hoard. Scarcely anything in the remains has religious associations we can grasp, apart, of course, from the fact itself that the dead were buried with a few objects of utility. There is little enough which reflects war or the warrior. For a century or a century and a half, everything still tends to look like 'debased' Mycenaean work. The pottery in particular maintains a continuity of style and technique, though Mycenaean III C and then 'sub-Mycenaean' ware had not only changed sufficiently to be differentiated from III B products, but also varied from place to place.

It is in the course of the eleventh century that genuine innovations first loom large in the archaeological record. There is 'protogeometric' pottery most easily recognizable from the compass-drawn circles and half-circles painted with a multiple brush. Experts see it as a 'descendant' from the Mycenaean, but the style is different enough to warrant a new classification (unlike 'sub-Mycenaean'). New tools, weapons and small objects (such as long metal dress-pins in place of buttons, indicating a change in both men's and women's clothing) are increasingly made of iron instead of bronze. In the critical class of cutting tools and weapons the shift is fairly abrupt and complete, as the following simple table of finds from mainland Greece (excluding Macedonia) for the period 1050–900 shows:[1]

	Bronze	*Iron*
Swords	1	20+
Spearheads	8	30+
Daggers	2	8
Knives	0	15+
Axe-heads	0	4

There are, in most areas, changes not only in the grave structure but also in burial practices. Notable is the replacement of inhumation by cremation, completed in Athens, where the evidence is extensive and continuous, by about 1050.[2] All these changes were foreshadowed earlier in one way or another, and it would be wrong to suggest that about 1050 there was a sudden and uniform transformation throughout the Aegean world. Nevertheless, when the different kinds of evidence are taken together, a significant change becomes apparent at that point of time.[3]

Then, by the end of the same century, still another new feature emerges, the significance of which is far more obvious, namely the establishment by migrants from the Greek peninsula of small communities along the coast of Asia Minor and on the offshore islands. Eventually the whole western edge of Asia Minor became Greek, and the Aegean was converted for the first time into a Greek waterway, so to speak. The eastern settlements were grouped by dialect in three bands from north to south, Aeolic, Ionic and Doric, in that order. But that required some three hundred years of complicated history which is largely lost to us—years of quarrelling and fighting with each other, and of ambiguous relations with the older inhabitants. We may suspect that few women were among the migrants, at least in the earlier days. In Miletus, writes Herodotus (I 146), the noblest of the colonists from Athens brought no women, 'but took Carian women, whose kinsmen they murdered. Because of the killing, the women laid down a law for themselves, which they swore an oath to observe and which they passed on to their daughters, never to dine with their husbands or to address them by name.' Just how Herodotus came to this story or what he was trying to explain is unclear, but in his own day intermarriage with Carians was a common practice in his native Halicarnassus. And we know (as Herodotus did not), thanks to recent and still preliminary archaeological investigation, that there were many separate migrations in small groups; that these were new settlements and not continuations or reinforcements of old Bronze Age or Mycenaean communities in Asia Minor (even where there was a return to previously occupied places, as at Miletus or Rhodes), that the first wave left Greece soon after the development of protogeometric pottery. Indeed, it is the discovery of quantities of protogeometric sherds in half a dozen or so sites which has enabled archaeologists to date the movements and to link some of the eastern sites with specific regions in Greece.[4] Aeolic and Ionic settlements were the earliest, the Doric somewhat later (not before 900, perhaps).

Exactly why any particular group chose to cross the Aegean *when* it did is anyone's guess, but there is no need to guess why they went where they did. The Asia Minor coast is a series of promontories with natural defences, backed by fertile river-valleys and plains, and in the eleventh, tenth and ninth centuries there were no strong powers or even large populations to block new settlers from establishing themselves. One site—Old Smyrna, so called to differentiate it from the later city of Smyrna, modern Izmir, nearby—provides a picture of what these early communities looked like: small, mean, cramped and huddled behind their fortified city-wall. At the end of the Dark Age, when, presumably, it had grown substantially from its earliest size, Old Smyrna counted no more than 500 small houses inside and outside the walls, representing a population of perhaps 2000.

This was also a 'dark age' as far as most of the native populations of western Asia Minor are concerned, and there is little on which to base a firm opinion about the relations between them and the Greek newcomers. It has been suggested that the Greeks were able to subjugate the people in their immediate neighbourhood and employ them as a dependent labour-force. This is a plausible guess—certainly Greek migrants did just that in historical times in Asia Minor, on the shores of the Black Sea, and in the west—but no more than that. We cannot even put names to the natives. The mysterious Carians were presumably there, though perhaps not yet the Lydians. Only the Phrygians have now come to light and they were in this early period too remote to be called neighbours. They came into Asia Minor across the Dardanelles at a time that was probably close to that of the earliest Greek migrations, but they were concentrated further inland. By the eighth century B.C., their greatest centre, Gordion, more than 200 miles from the Aegean coast, was large, rich and powerful, with a culture, partly inherited from the Hittites, technologically and materially more advanced than that of the Greeks. For the latter, Phrygia was the king-dom of Midas, whose touch turned everything to gold. Gordion was destroyed early in the seventh century by the Cimmerians sweeping in from the Russian steppes beyond the Caucasus, and that was the end of the Phrygian golden age. When we hear of Phrygians in classical Greek texts, it is as a major source of slaves for the Greeks, employed, for example, in the Athenian silver mines.

From the eighth century at the latest, Phrygian imports and Phyrgian artistic influences are visible not only in Greek Asia Minor but also in Greece proper, and there were close relations with the civilizations further east. The archaeologists have discovered what appear to be traces of the Hittite 'royal road' across Anatolia, which the Phrygians then maintained. That, however, was not the main route of eastern influence to the Greek world of the Dark Age, but the sea route from Syria, with Cyprus as a major intermediary. Contact between Greece and the Near East was never completely broken; it could not have been, if for no other reason than the imperative Greek need to import metal—copper, tin, and then, increasingly, iron—which at that time came largely, if not wholly, from the east.

Although Cyprus had been devastated by the 'Sea Peoples', copper mining almost certainly never stopped, and by the eleventh century the island was also important for its iron metallurgy, the influences of which are visible on the Greek mainland in weaponry. Significantly, the main Cypriot centres were henceforth to grow on the eastern and south-eastern coasts, closest to Syria. Enkomi was replaced by nearby Salamis, perhaps originally a Greek foundation of about 1100, and in the tenth century the Phoenicians made Citium their centre there. In the centuries to come, every Near Eastern empire conquered Cyprus in turn—first the Assyrians, then the Egyptians, and finally the Persians—though they could not always retain control. The result was a hybrid civilization which it is difficult to classify. Although Greek was the language of the majority of the population, an unidentified pre-Greek tongue remained in existence as well as Phoenician (the earliest Cypriot document in that language, a curse tablet, is dated to about 900). The art became more Levantine than Greek, as exemplified by the newly discovered 'royal tombs' of

Salamis of the eighth and seventh centuries.⁵ By then kingship had disappeared in the
Greek world, but it survived in Cyprus as long as the island retained any semblance of
autonomy.

It was presumably the close eastern connexion (and perhaps control) which enabled
Cyprus to outstrip the Anatolian Greeks during the Dark Age. The discovery in excavations
shortly before the last war of an ancient port at Al Mina, in the Orontes River delta in
northern Syria (actually within the borders of Turkey today), brought to light one of the
important link-posts on the Asiatic mainland. Cypriot and local pottery at Al Mina go
back to the ninth century, and possibly earlier. By about 800, Greek pottery appears and
then it becomes increasingly abundant, continuing after the Assyrian conquest of the
area in the late eighth century. The source of the earliest Greek ware was not in Asia
Minor but in Euboea and the Cyclades, later in Corinth and elsewhere. None of the evidence
indicates what was traded in return, but there can be little doubt that metal was, as usual,
a main Greek concern. The presence of so much Greek pottery suggests direct Greek
participation—though it should be stressed that this was only a trading-post, not a
permanent settlement of migrants as in Asia Minor—but it is not without relevance to
recall that in the Homeric poems overseas trade was virtually a monopoly of 'Phoenicians',
and that to Homer, as to Herodotus in the fifth century, 'Phoenicia' meant everything
from the Cilician-Syrian border to Egypt.

No writing has been found at Al Mina and therefore its ancient name is unknown.
It is just possible that it was the site of Posideion, according to Herodotus (III 91) the
city which in his day was the northern boundary of one of the Persian provinces or
satrapies. All that he could tell us about the past of Posideion was that it had been
founded by one of the legendary Greek heroes, Amphilochus. And, in general, when
the eastern Greeks finally came to write their history, which was not before the fifth
century B.C., the earliest period was represented by little more than foundation stories
built around individuals, and stories of isolated incidents, usually conflicts. They could
offer no narrative going back beyond the sixth century, and they had no interest in a
sustained account of social or institutional history. The picture they have left us is a
schematic, sentimental reading back into the past of the values and claims of a later age,
a 'mythical charter' for the present. Herodotus himself was uneasy. When he suggested
(III 122) that Polycrates of Samos was the first Greek to seek a maritime empire, he
explained that he was 'leaving aside Minos' and others like him, that Polycrates was
the first 'in what is called the time of men'. We should phrase it as the first in historical,
as distinct from mytheical, times.

Our only check, archaeology, cannot cope with stories about individual founders
or specific incidents. However, archaeology has exposed as false a fundamental element
in the traditions about the early Ionian colonization, imagined to have been a single
action, organized by and starting out from Athens, where many refugees from the
Dorians had congregated, including men from Pylos under King Neleus. That Athens
had a role in some of the Ionian settlements is certain, but little else stands up.
The Greek antiquarians who put the story into writing more than 500 years afterwards
had no notion of the great breakdown of about 1200 B.C., no idea of a Bronze Age,
and therefore no sense of the very considerable time-span of the Dark Age. They did
not, and could not, know that there had been a gap of perhaps 150 years between the

destruction of Pylos (which was not the work of the Dorians) and the earliest movements across the Aegean, far too long for a crowd of Pylian refugees to wait in Athens, an inherently improbable situation anyway. And the single colonizing expedition is pure fiction, whereas the paramount role of Athens in the development and diffusion of protogeometric pottery, which is fact, was completely forgotten (and it is doubtful that the later Greeks would even have recognized this pottery as their own).

It is fruitless to pursue in detail the later Greek traditions about the Dark Age in Asia Minor. Nor is the possibility substantially greater for Greece proper, where the traditions down to 800 or 750 B.C. are of the same kind and quality. We must turn instead to our earliest written documentation, the Homeric *Iliad* and *Odyssey,* two epic poems, some 16,000 and 12,000 lines in length, respectively. What are we to make of them as sources of historical information? There is perhaps no question about the early Greeks which provokes greater controversy and less agreement, and here it is not possible to do more than state the position adopted in this book.

The two poems were composed in Ionia, the *Iliad* perhaps in the middle of the eighth century, the *Odyssey* a bit later, by two different poets working in the same tradition. They were the culmination of a long experience in oral poetry, practised by professional bards who travelled widely in the Greek world. In the course of generations they knit together many incidents and local traditions, built round several main heroic themes, and they employed a highly stylized and formalized, artificial poetic language, in dialect basically Ionic but including Aeolic and other elements. No doubt there were bards in the Mycenaean world, too, but the tradition behind the Homeric poems was essentially a Dark Age one (and its existence provides an important corrective to judging the period solely from its *material* impoverishment). It was a tradition that deliberately looked back to a *lost* heroic age, and there are aspects of their own world which the poets successfully excluded. There is in the *Iliad* and *Odyssey* a considerable, though by no means perfect, knowledge of where the greatest Mycenaean centres had been located; there is not a hint that Asia Minor was now rather thickly settled by Greeks; there are no Dorians; there are indeed no distinctions, whether in dialect or in institutions, within the Greek world, other than differences in power. And there are the great palaces of the heroes, filled with 'treasure' *(keimelion).* When Agamemnon was finally persuaded to appease the wrath of Achilles, his offer included (besides seven cities and a daughter to wife with a great dowry) racehorses, captive women, 'seven tripods that have never been on the fire and ten talents of gold and twenty glittering cauldrons' and a shipload of bronze and gold from the anticipated Trojan spoils *(Iliad* IX, 121-56). The Dark Age possessed no treasure like that. Then, even the warriors were allowed only one sword or one lance-head after death, not both together; as time went on, indeed, arms of any kind became increasingly rare in the graves.

Thus far, one might imagine that the bards had transmitted, from generation to generation down to the eighth century, a recognizable picture of the late Mycenaean world. However, on closer analysis it turns out that their palaces are in structure and details not Mycenaean palaces (or any other known ones), that their understanding of the use of chariots in warfare has become uncertain, that the social system of the poems differs qualitatively from that of the Linear B tablets (and in particular from the palace economy recorded in the tablets), that the very terminology of administration and social structure has been radically altered. Even their 'realistic' accounts of treasure betray at least one remarkable anachronism. The dowries, racehorses and captive women of Agamemnon's offer of amends are timeless, or at least undatable, but not so the bronze 'tripods' and 'glittering cauldrons'. Although such objects existed in the Mycenaean world, they were rarities, whereas in the Dark Age they became notable treasures, above all to be dedicated to the gods, especially towards the end of the period, when the *Iliad* and *Odyssey* were composed. A few complete specimens and many fragments have been found in Olympia and Delphi, a smaller number in Delos, Crete and Ithaca, isolated examples elsewhere.

There is also significant change in religious practices. The Mycenaean world buried its dead; the Homeric poems cremated them, without exception. Again a difference within the Dark Age itself must be noted. By about 1050 cremation of adults had become universal in most of the Greek world (with the curious exception of the Argolid), but 200 or 250 years later, inhumation returned to the mainland while cremation continued in Crete, the Cyclades, Rhodes and Ionia. The *Iliad* and *Odyssey* remain firmly anchored in the earlier Dark Age on this point, although the paraphernalia and rites of mourning can be illustrated from later Dark Age graves and from scenes on 'geometric' pottery after about 800. That was the period when human and animal figures returned to Greek art for the first time since the Mycenaean age, a revival which did not go so far as an early return to portrayal of the divine. There were no epiphanies, no ritual dances, no initiation scenes; there are very few figures, either in sculpture or in the decorations on pottery, that one can imagine as gods even on a broad interpretation. This rarity in the plastic arts of the anthropomorphic spirit that dominates the Homeric poems is surprising (especially in contrast to the innumerable idealized Zeuses, Apollos and Aphrodites of later Greek art).

In sum, the Homeric poems retain a certain measure of Mycenaean 'things'—places, arms and weapons, chariots—but little of Mycenaean institutions or culture. The break had been too sharp. As the pre-1200 civilization receded into the past, the bards could not avoid 'modernizing' the behaviour and the social background of their heroes. All in all, there is an inner coherence in the way social institutions emerge from a study of the *Iliad* and *Odyssey,* despite the anachronisms at either end of the time-scale. That picture, it is suggested, is in general one of the Dark Age, and on the whole of the earlier half of that age, painted as a poet does and not a historian or chronicler, not precise or always accurate, surely exaggerated in scale, but not therefore a purely imaginary one.

The world of Agamemnon and Achilles and Odysseus was one of petty kings and nobles, who possessed the best land and considerable flocks, and lived a seignorial existence, in which raids and local wars were frequent. The noble household *(oikos)* was the centre of activity and power. How much power depended on wealth, personal prowess, connexions by marriage and alliance, and retainers. There is no role assigned to tribes or other large kinship groups. In the twenty years Odysseus was away from Ithaca, the nobles behaved scandalously towards his family and his possessions; yet his son Telemachus had no body of kinsmen to whom to turn for help, nor was the community fully integrated, properly organized and equipped to impose sanctions. Telemachus' claims as Odysseus' heir were acknowledged in principle, but he lacked the power to enforce them. The assassination of Agamemnon by his wife Clytaemnestra and her paramour Aegisthus placed an

obligation of vengeance on his son Orestes, but otherwise life in Mycenae went on unchanged, except that Aegisthus ruled in Agamemnon's place. The king with power was
judge, lawgiver and commander, and there were accepted ceremonies, rituals, conventions
and a code of honour by which nobles lived, including table fellowship, gift-exchange,
sacrifice to the gods and appropriate burial rites. But there was no bureaucratic apparatus,
no formalized legal system or constitutional machinery. The power equilibrium was
delicately balanced; tension between king and nobles was chronic, struggles for power
frequent.

Telemachus, it is true, summoned a meeting of the assembly in Ithaca to hear
his complaint against the noble 'suitors'. The assembly listened to both sides and
took no action, which is what the assembly always did in the two poems. In general, the
silence of the people is the most challenging difficulty presented to the historian by
the poems. They are there all the time, even in the battles, but as a vague mass whose
exact status is unclear. Some, chiefly captive women, are called slaves, but they do not
appear to be worse off than the others. A few specialists—seers, bards, metalworkers, wood-
workers, physicians—have a higher status. There is seafaring and a vital concern for trade,
more exactly for the import of copper, iron, gold and silver, fine cloths and other
luxuries. Even chieftains are permitted to go on expeditions for such purposes, but
generally trade and merchandising seem to be the business of foreigners, chiefly Phoenicians.
To be called a merchant was a grave insult to Odysseus; men of his class exchanged goods
ceremonially or they took it by plunder. In part, all this vagueness about the ordinary
people can be attributed to the poets' deliberate concentration on the heroic deeds of
heroes. But perhaps it is also to be explained by the absence, in reality, of the sharp status
categories of later societies, in particular of neat categories of 'freedom' and 'bondage'.
The fundamental class-line between noble and non-noble is clear enough. Above and
below that line the distinctions appear blurred, and perhaps they really were.

It would be idle to pretend that this provides the basis for a *history* of the Dark Age.
All that can be suggested is that, following the elimination of the rulers of the Mycenaean
world and with them of the whole power structure they headed, society had to reorganize
itself with new arrangements and new values appropriate to the new material and social
situation, in which migrants were presumably one factor to be reckoned with. If, as is
probable but not provable, the destruction of the Mycenaean world also involved
internal social upheavals, that would also have influenced the shape of the new arrangements. What happened in the centuries immediately following could not have been the
same everywhere, despite the Homeric image of uniformity. In Asia Minor from the
beginning (as in all subsequent Greek migrations to new areas), the settlements were
small territorial units around an urban core. Judging from the archaeology, similar units
existed from the beginning of the Dark Age on the Greek mainland and in some Aegean
islands as well. The poets assume them to be the rule, but still in their day and for several
centuries to come, whole areas of Greece—Thessaly and Aetolia, for example—in fact
lacked urban centres and were loosely organized agrarian and pastoral societies. What was
apparently uniform, however, was the class structure suggested by the poems, with an
aristocratic upper class and a king or chieftain who was a bit more than 'first among
equals'. How much more (or less) was a personal matter in each case, and, as we know from
other indications, by the time the *Iliad* and *Odyssey* were composed the 'equals' had

dispensed with the king almost everywhere and replaced monarchy by aristocracy. In some shadowy way, the common people also had an existence as a corporate body (whomever 'the people', the *demos,* may have included), but not as a political force in any constitutional sense.

Curiously, although the poets were conscious of a common bond uniting all the Greeks, a bond of language, religion and way of life (but not, either then or later, of a political bond or of a reluctance to war with each other), neither the *Iliad* nor the *Odyssey* refers to them by the name which has been theirs from at least the eighth century to our own day. They are Hellenes and their world is Hellas; 'their world', not in antiquity 'their country', because they were never politically united and therefore Hellas was an abstraction much like Christendom in the Middle Ages or Islam today. In the Homeric poems the Greeks have three different names, Achaeans, Argives and Danaans, the first two of which lived on as the names of specific localities in Greece while the third disappeared from use. It is virtually certain, however, that Hellas and Hellene were already current in the eighth century, and probably also the genealogies which were inevitably invented to explain the historical divisions according to dialect, 'race' or political organization: Hellen, son of Deucalion, had three sons named Dorus, Xuthus and Aeolus, and so on. In the eighth century, too, embryonic pan-Hellenic institutions were already in existence, notably certain oracles and the Olympic Games.

The eighth century, finally, saw the return of writing to the Greeks, in the form of the alphabet borrowed with modification from the Phoenicians. This fact the Greek tradition had right (though they had no idea of the date). We are in the position to pin the source down to the North Semitic script, and specifically the cursive writing used in business activity rather than the monumental characters of, for example, Byblos. Al Mina may have been the point of contact and diffusion, though that is only a guess, and the first borrowers were perhaps people from Euboea, Crete and Rhodes, more or less independently of each other, from whom the art then spread, by a complicated network of routes, to all the Greek communities. Neither the immediate reasons why the alphabet was acquired when it was (probably before 750) nor why it spread so rapidly are well understood. A long time was to go by before the Greeks made serious use of this new skill for chronicles or for religious texts, two of the chief uses of writing in the ancient Near East. Originally the Greeks seem to have concentrated on poetry and on what may be called labelling and mnemonic purposes, that is, inscribing names on pottery, gravestones and the like, on the one hand, and easing the burden of memory, on the other hand, by writing down lists that merited public notice and remembrance, such as Olympic victors.

The Homeric poems, in sum, looked back to the Dark Age and even a bit beyond, but they were composed at the beginning of a new era. By convention the next period (800-500 B.C. in round numbers) is known as 'archaic', a word taken from the history of art, and more narrowly of sculpture (as is the term 'classical' for the succeeding age). It is with Archaic Greece that the rest of this book will be concerned.

Notes

[1] From A. M. Snodgrass, 'Barbarian Europe and Early Iron Age Greece, *Proceedings of the Prehistoric Society, 31* (1965), pp. 229-240, at p. 231.

[2] Infants and very young children continued to be interred regularly, and not cremated.

[3] It is important to note that these dates are all archaeological, as explained in Chapter 1.Protogeometric pottery is pivotal in establishing the chronology.

[4] The unexpected recent discovery (see *Illustrated London News* for 6 April, 1968) of Mycenaean III C, sub-Mycenaean and protogeometric sherds in Sardis, the eventual inland capital of Lydia, raises new questions. There may be a link with the refugee movement of about 1200, as in Cyprus and Tarsus, followed by trading connexions, rather than another case of an actual Greek migration of the kind we are considering.

[5] *Illustrated London News* for 18 November, 2 and 16 December, 1967.

Part VII

The Old World: China

Kwang-chih Chang received his Ph.D. from Harvard University in 1960 and
currently is professor of anthropology and curator at the Peabody Museum
of Natural History at Yale University. He is the author and editor of a
number of important works including *Rethinking Archaeology* (1967) and
Settlement Archaeology (1968). He has undertaken numerous archaeological expeditions to Taiwan and is the author of the widely acclaimed *The
Archaeology of Ancient China* (1968) in which this reading appears as
Chapter 6. Several of the references in the original text have been deleted.

The Emergence of
Civilization in North China

Kwang-chih Chang

Despite the quality and complexity that distinguish the ancient civilizations from
their more barbarous antecedents, these early civilizations continue to be the object of
archaeological research, since they are known to us primarily through their material
remains: ruins, implements, utensils, and the visual arts. Nevertheless, with the emergence
of the Shang in North China, Chinese archaeology advances into a new phase, for in some important aspects the archaeology of the ancient civilizations differs significantly from that of
their Palaeolithic and Neolithic predecessors. Civilizations are the outcome of major qualitative
developments of culture, as were the other major qualitative transformations before them (e.g.
the first use of tools and the invention of agriculture), but in this evolution which produced
civilizations, social, political, and economic organizations played especially significant roles.
In grasping the essence of ancient civilizations, therefore, the archaeologist must give special
emphasis and attention to the articulation of his data as well as to the empirical aspects of the
data themselves. Moreover, in most civilizations the first written records emerged. As
Christopher Hawkes has pointed out, when texts become available, the scholar must be
responsible to them as well as to the archaeological data.

The Shang, the builders of the first verifiable civilization in China, were also the
first literate people of Asia east of the Urals. In the royal court of the Shang there were
archivists and scribes who recorded important events of the state. With brush and ink,
they transcribed characters onto slips of bamboo or wood, and bound them together
into book form (the so-called *ts'e*). We know of these books, however, only through
reference to them in other contexts, for they have not yet been found. Aside from
occasional inscriptions on pottery and other artifacts, the known written records of the

Shang that have been preserved intact to this day are primarily of two kinds: records of divination incised on the shoulderblades of animals (mainly oxen) and on turtleshells, the two principal media of divination, and signs of possession and offering cast on bronze vessels. The former are known as the *chia ku wen* (turtleshell and bone scripts), and the latter are known as *chin wen* (bronze scripts). The study of each kind of script is a highly specialized field of learning.[1]

The written records of the Chou, successors to the Shang at the center of the political stage of ancient China, are scarcely more abundant at the beginning. The custom of bone and turtleshell divination—scapulimancy and plastromancy—was continued by the Chou with much less interest; the practice of inscribing bones and turtleshells was in general discontinued and thus the *chia ku* scripts were no longer a source of textual information for the Chou. On the other hand, the bronze scripts of the Chou have longer texts than the Shang bronzes, often recording the political and ritual contexts in which the vessels were made and offered. The *chin wen,* therefore, became a major source of the Chou textual information. In addition, there have been rare discoveries of inscribed silk and bamboo and jade tablets, but the texts are in most cases short and the information they contain inconsequential.

Although archaeologically found Chou texts are scarce, literacy expanded to the local states during the second half of Chou history—the Eastern Chou period—and many more books, archives, and other written materials came into being throughout China. Many of these survived the Chou and were transcribed onto the newly invented paper during the Han Dynasty. Known as the pre-Ch'in texts, these became a part of the traditional literary heritage of China that was handed down through the subsequent two millennia of her historical period. Including such important volumes as the annals of the various states (e.g. *Ch'un Ch'iu* and *Chu Shu Chi Nien*), the *Book of History (Shu Ching)* and the *Book of Odes (Shih Ching),* the pre-Ch'in texts were the principal source from which Ssu-ma Ch'ien compiled his *Shih Chi,* the first comprehensive and objective history of China, in the beginning of the first century B.C. As sources of information, however, these pre-Ch'in texts are full of problems. Because of the Ch'in upheaval, few of these documents survived into the Han Dynasty intact; most had to be restored by Han scholars, many of whom had their own axes to grind and points to make and have been known to speak their own minds through their ancients. Each book must therefore be authenticated, section by section or even sentence by sentence, in order to be used as a piece of pre-Ch'in textual material. Moreover, few of these texts are accurately dated, and, owing to the scale of cultural change during the periods they represent, the date must be carefully estimated, often on very circumstantial evidence.

Thus, the study of ancient China can be divided into a prehistoric and a historic segment. For the study of prehistory, scholars must rely exclusively on archaeology, but the historical archaeologist has the advantage of the textual information that was available for both the Shang and Chou periods. Since the textual information pertains primarily to political and ritual aspects of the Shang-Chou cultures, aspects that are important concerns of civilizational studies, it is apparent that research into Shang and Chou culture and society cannot be a purely archaeological task.

It does not, however, necessarily follow that in the study of Shang and Chou China the archaeologist cannot play an independent part. All three main sources of textual information pertaining to the Shang and Chou are highly specialized fields of learning, each containing countless unsolved problems, many of which are perhaps unsolvable. To undertake research in depth in one of these fields one must become a chiakuologist, a chinwenologist, or a pre-Ch'in text specialist. Among the scholars of the last group there are even those who devote their lives to the study of single books. The archaeologist cannot be expected to become master of all these specialized fields, nor should he wait until all the textual information becomes known and all its problems solved before he undertakes his own study. On the other hand, many archaeological problems of ancient China are not only independent of textual study but are capable of contributing solutions to textual problems. The study of Shang and Chou China, therefore, calls for active and close collaboration between the archaeologist and the historian. Each must be aware of the other's results and conclusions and undertake his own research with them in mind, but he cannot be expected to be minutely responsible for the other's data and issues. In dealing with Shang and Chou China in this volume, I adhere strictly to my role as an archaeologist. Textual information and historical conclusions will be used only when and if they contribute to a better archaeological understanding.

A related issue in this connection is the matter of pre-Shang history. There may be two meanings to the phrase. The first refers to written records dated to an earlier period than the Shang. Since such records do not exist at present, and the problem is purely hypothetical, it requires no further discussion. The second meaning refers to the personages and events, recorded in Shang and Chou texts, that were regarded by the Shang and Chou themselves as having existed or taken place before their era.

Such data, collectively referable as the myths and legends of the Shang and Chou, are part of the material for the study of the Shang and Chou themselves, highly useful for an understanding of their views of cosmology and history. Undoubtedly they also included oral traditions that had been handed down from remote antiquity to the Shang-Chou period and are thus truly reflective of pre-Shang events and conditions. Two such events, the rise of the Huang Ti era and the whole history of the Hsia Dynasty, are illustrative.

The exact nature of Huang Ti, the celebrated Yellow Emperor, and the history of his career, are subjects of numerous studies. His supposed accession took place in 2697 B.C. He was the greatest of the cultural heroes of ancient China, and to him are credited the invention of all the essential elements of the civilization. He was also the greatest war hero of the Flower People, from whom all subsequent dynasties claimed descent. These stories are perhaps more important symbolically than historically: Huang Ti was more a symbol of an era than an actual ancestor.

> During the Age of Shen Nung, men cultivated food and women wove clothing. People were governed without a criminal law and prestige was built without the use of force. After Shen Nung, however, the strong began to rule over the weak and the many over the few. Therefore, Huang Ti administered internally with penalties and externally with armed forces [Chapter "Hua-ts'e," in *Shang Chün Shu*].

Thus is described a major transition of Chinese society from self-contained peaceful villages to warlike states with centralized government. Shen Nung ushered in an era with farming villages, but Huang Ti was responsible for the rise of cities and the state. These tales anticipated the modern archaeologists in giving due recognition to the Neolithic and the urban revolutions as epoch-markers of ancient history. How the ancient Chinese arrived at these notions is unimportant. It is significant that portions of the pre-Shang history in Shang-Chou texts contain grains of historical judgment that would have met the approval of a Gordon Childe.

The records concerning the Hsia Dynasty are of more than symbolic importance. A royal genealogy of the Hsia is known fragmentarily from pre-Ch'in texts and in organized form in *Shih Chi*. Tales about particular kings, events during the reigns of several, and the detailed process in which the Shang overthrew the Hsia are recorded in Ssu-ma Ch'ien's *Shih Chi*, whose credibility in recording some true history of the Three Dynasties is amply demonstrated by the reliability of its Shang and Chou portions. Was there a Hsia Dynasty as well? If so, what was its archaeological equivalent? Several points regarding these problems are self-evident.

In the first place, the archaeological sequence in the northern Honan area is reasonably complete in showing that the Shang civilization in that region was derived from the Lung-shan culture, and that there was no major break in the sequence. Unless this is a strictly local phenomenon (which is not at all impossible, since for other areas the record for this stage is incomplete), it is likely that the legendary history from Huang Ti through the Hsia Dynasty is included in the time span of the Lung-shan. Second, the Lung-shan stage of Chinese Neolithic cannot be considered to have achieved the kind of civilization that has been attributed to Huang Ti through Hsia. This need not, however, worry us particularly, for a strong political organization certainly appeared during the Lung-shan stage, probably along with some other items of civilization such as incipient metallurgy, intensified industrial specialization, and intensified status differentiation. On the other hand, we do not have to believe that the Huang Ti-Hsia interval had achieved a full-fledged civilization, as recorded in the traditional history, for this part of the tradition must have been tempered considerably in accordance with the historical perspectives of these early times. It is possible, therefore, that the Hsia Dynasty was one of the local cultural groups immediately preceding the Shang Dynasty. Finally, this identification may never be certain unless some archaeological finds belonging to the late Lung-shan stage are proved by written records to have been left during the Hsia Dynasty. Since we are still uncertain about the early history of Chinese writing, it is impossible to say now whether this is a likely prospect.

In any event, both archaeological and legendary Chinese prehistory preceded the Shang Dynasty. Earlier chapters have described the former, which ends where the Shang and Chou began. In other words, from two opposite directions Chinese prehistory and history meet at the beginning of the Shang civilization. The legendary prehistory is certainly contained in the archaeological prehistory, and may enrich and amplify it. A proper study of it, however, must be left to other volumes.[2]

Major Sites of the Shang

At a number of archaeological sites in North China it has been shown that lying above—and temporally subsequent to—strata of the Neolithic Lung-shan culture are remains of a much more advanced civilization that can be identified with the historical Shang civilization. In describing the Shang archaeology we must, at the outset, make a very careful distinction among the following terms. *Shang period* refers to a block of time, approximately from 1850 through 1100 B.C. In ascribing a site to the Shang period we simply date it to that block of time; the site itself may be at the dead center of the Shang civilization, or it may be a barbarous village contemporaneous with but independent of the Shang civilization. By *Shang Dynasty* one refers to a political entity and to the political epoch in Chinese ancient history when, after about 1750 B.C., the Shang royal house ruled the land. A site does not *date* from the Shang Dynasty, but it may have *belonged to* it; that is, it may have been a part of the Shang political sphere during that dynasty's reign. The totality of the Shang culture and society—including its material culture, social and political institutions, and its ideology in organic articulation—constitutes the *Shang civilization*. The archaeological localities where the Shang civilization is significantly manifested are *Shang sites*. Elements of the Shang civilization that are found archaeologically are the *Shang-type remains*. The discovery of Shang remains at a site does not necessarily make it a Shang site; these could have been trade objects in an alien community. It does not ensure that the site belonged to the Shang period; it could have been continuously in use after the twelfth century B.C. These distinctions are necessary at the outset in order to delimit the temporal and spatial expanse of the Shang civilization for my purpose. Shang remains have been found in most of China, but they should not be taken to mean that the Shang culture was similarly distributed. The Shang sites that form the nexus of the Shang civilization in its totality or essence, are much more limited. The center of the Shang is apparently in the northern part of Honan and its immediate surroundings. The best-known archaeological sites are in the following regions.

I. Yen-shih

The first "king" who founded the Shang Dynasty is known as T'ang or Ta Yi. T'ang overthrew the Hsia Dynasty and made Po the capital of his new state in 1766 B.C. The location of Po is uncertain; according to some scholars it is identified with places in easternmost Honan and adjacent northern Anhwei, but according to others it was near the modern city of Yen-shih in northwestern Honan. Shang sites were not found in the Yen-shih area until 1958, but in the last few years new data have accumulated in this region to indicate the existence here of a Shang settlement of major proportions at an early stage within the Shang period.

Yen-shih and the neighboring Lo-yang are the two major cities in the Loyang basin of western Honan, surrounded on all sides by low mountain ranges and drained by the rivers Yi and Lo, tributaries of the Huangho to the north. In the area of Yen-shih fourteen archaeological localities are known that date from the Shang period, but only at the sites of Erh-li-t'ou, Kao-yai, and Hui-tsui are brief descriptions of the excavated material available. The site of Kao-yai is of special significance in revealing a Neolithic stratigraphy of Yangshao-Lungshanoid—Lungshan sequence that suggests a continuous cultural development paralleling the sequence brought to light earlier at the Wang-wan site in neighboring Lo-yang. From the Shang stratum at Kao-yai a bronze knife was discovered.

At the Erh-li-t'ou site a developmental sequence continues from Kao-yai and suggests that out of the Honan Lung-shan culture grew an early phase of the Shang culture that can be referred to as the Erh-li-t'ou phase, which was apparently ancestral to the later

Shang phases known at Cheng-chou and An-yang. More than 8,000 square meters of the site were excavated between 1960 and 1964, with impressive results leading to the speculation that perhaps the T'ang capital of Po has been uncovered here.

At the center of the site a blunt T-shaped house floor, about 100 meters long and wide, of *hang-t'u* structure, was located. Along the sides on the floor are largely postholes containing stone postbases. Walls of wattle-and-daub were constructed on foundations of rock-filled ditches. About 50 meters south of the large floor—called a palatial foundation by the investigators—are three clusters of smaller house floors. Eleven houses have been excavated, rectangular in ground plan (one over 9 m long E—W), with stamped earth floors and stone post bases. At various parts of the site are 3 pottery kilns, 2 water wells, 48 human burials, and over 260 storage pits. Nineteen of the burials have recognizable grave pits and grave goods, and the bodies in them are all stretched, lying supine or on one side. The grave goods included various kinds of pottery (drinking vessels, cooking wares, containers, and serving vessels and dishes), a bronze bell, and turquoise, jade, and shell ornaments. The burials without grave goods are mostly found in habitation layers and storage pits, and are in various postures such as squatting, flexed, or stretched. Some were apparently victims of some sort, with hands tied and perhaps buried alive; some had heads or parts of the limbs missing. These burials indicate most vividly a stratified society in which members of a lower class were sometimes victims, perhaps of religious ceremonies.

Large numbers of pottery vessels at the site distinguish the Erh-li-t'ou phase as stylistically intermediate between the Honan Lung-shan culture and the later Shang phases. The paste of the pottery varies from very fine to very coarse and ranges in color from white and light yellow to red, gray, and black. Parts of the same vessel were often made in different ways: handmade, modeled, coiled, and wheel-made. Decorations were mostly impressed with cord, basket, and check designs, and appliqued and incised patterns are also found. Among the incised patterns are stylized animals such as dragons, serpents, fishes, and *t'ao-t'ieh*. In shape the vessels include pots, basins, and various kinds of ring-footed forms and tripods *(ting, li, chia, chüeh, ho, kui,* etc.) On the interior of the rims of some *tsun* vessels are incised signs of various shapes that may have been some kind of script. Of special significance is the appearance of specialized wine-serving vessels *(chüeh, chia, ku, ho, kui,* etc.), mostly found in graves with furnishings, indicating a leisurely social class.

Among the implements found at Erh-li-t'ou are hoes, sickle knives, and flat spades of stone, shell, and bone; arrowheads and spearheads of stone, bone, shell, and bronze; bone harpoons; fishhooks of bone and bronze; and clay sinkers and spindle whorls. Shoulderblades of oxen and sheep with burned marks are found, but no elaborate preparation or inscriptions are in evidence. There are also various art objects and ornaments of clay, stone, jade, turquoise, bronze, and shell. It is significant that bronze artifacts are few and simple (knives, awls, fishhooks, and a bell), but fragments of clay crucibles, bronze slugs, and clay molds indicate a bronze foundry at this site. Many bone fragments and half-finished bone artifacts tell of a developed bone industry.

Stratigraphic evidence at the site and at other sites with remains of the Erh-li-t'ou phase shows that this was earlier than the Erh-li-kang phase (to be described below); in fact, it is the earliest verifiable phase of a full-fledged Shang civilization with bronze metallurgy (of a possibly more primitive state), advanced forms of symbols on pottery, a Shang art, large *hang-t'u* structures, a highly stratified burial pattern, and specialized handicrafts. In pottery, the impressed decorations and such forms of *ku, chia, tou,* and deep pots suggest very close relationship with and probably direct descent from the Honan Lung-shan culture of the area. The importance of the Yen-shih sites cannot be exaggerated.

Remains of the Erh-li-t'ou phase have been located at the Tung-kan-kou site in neighboring Lo-yang. The distribution of similar remains elsewhere will be described below.

2. Cheng-chou

Discovered in 1950, the Shang remains in the vicinity of Cheng-chou, northern Honan, are still being excavated and studied. Enough has been discovered, however, for An Chin-huai to conclude that the "Shang Dynasty remains, except for those found in scattered spots in the western suburbs of Cheng-chou, are mostly concentrated within the ancient city site of Cheng-chou and its vicinity. Shang settlements spread continuously in an area of about forty square kilometers east from Feng-huang-t'ai west to Hsi-ch'eng-chuang, and south from Erh-li-kang to the north of Tzu-ching-shan." Before the Shang, the area of Cheng-chou was occupied by both Yang-shao and Lung-shan farmers, whose remains have been unearthed at Lin-shan-chai, Niu-chai, Ko-ta-wang, and other sites. Immediately subsequent to, and apparently evolving out of, the Honan Lung-shan culture were strata of the earlier stages of the Shang. The Shang history of settlements seems to be divisible, according to available evidence, into five stratigraphic phases, as shown in Table 1.

TABLE 1

Shang Culture Phases at Cheng-chou, Honan

Jen-min Park Phase	Jen-min Park III
	Ko-ta-wang III
Upper Erh-li-kang Phase	Erh-li-kang II
	Jen-min Park II
	Pai-chia-chuang II
	Nan-kuan-wai III
	Tung-chai III
Lower Erh-li-kang Phase	Erh-li-kang I
	Jen-min Park I
	Pai-chia-chuang I
	Nan-kuan-wai II
	Tung-chai II
	Ko-ta-wang II
Lo-ta-miao Phase	Lo-ta-miao
	Nan-kuan-wai I
	Tung-chai I
	Ko-ta-wang I
Shang-chieh Phase	Shang-chieh

The Shang-chieh phase, thus far represented only by the site at Shang-chieh in the westernmost portions of Cheng-chou, is on the very borderline between the Honan Lung-shan culture and the Shang. At the site several floors were found, all but one rectangular in shape. Over thirty storage pits, most with oval-shaped openings, were excavated. Among the artifacts, the polished stone spades and multiperforated knives particularly recall Lung-shan forms. In ceramics, jugs, *tou* fruit stands, bowls, basin, *li* tripods, and wide-mouthed jars are characteristic Shang items, but the flat-bottomed jugs with a high body resemble Lung-shan forms. No metal objects have been unearthed here. Ox and pig bones were found which had been utilized for oracle purposes, but evidence of preparation before heat application is lacking. Five human burials were located. Two of them have clearly outlined rectangular grave pits; one has a "waist-pit" in which are bony remains of animals, and the other has two pieces of cowrie-shaped bone objects. The other three burials were found in habitation layers, and their unpatterned postures suggest that the bodies were thrown into amorphous pits without ceremony.

Four sites so far can be grouped into the second, or Lo-ta-miao, phase. All seem to have been residential villages, but pottery kilns were also uncovered at Ko-ta-wang. Stratigraphy shows conclusively that this phase was chronologically situated between the Lung-shan and the Lower Erh-li-kang phase, although the relative dating between the Lo-ta-miao and the Shang-chieh phases is still typologically based. Metal objects are lacking in the cultural remains of this phase. In the cultural inventory, typical Shang traits increased, but there were still many Lung-shan features such as the great number of shell artifacts, bone hairpins with awl-shaped heads, pocket-shaped storage pits (which had become rare, however), and the generally unprepared oracle bones. Some diagnostic ceramic features are the round-bottomed and cord-marked jugs with high and nearly vertical bodies, vessels with large mouth openings, small basins and jars, and jugs with checker impressions. This stage is again known only imperfectly, but there is no question of its existence.

Cheng-chou of the Lower Erh-li-kang phase seems to have stepped suddenly into increased activity and expanded the size of its settlement. Sites of this phase contain dwelling houses, burials, workshops, and a city wall. It has been suggested that during this stage dwelling quarters and burials of the aristocrats were inside the city wall, and that the city itself was the center of living and administration, but that the commoners' residences, cemetery, craft shops, and farming fields were outside the wall. According to literary records, the ancient Shang kings changed their capital sites several times before finally settling at Yin, the site of the present city of An-yang. One of these earlier capitals, four capitals before An-yang, is said to have been the city of Ao or Hsiao, probably in the vicinity of the present town of Ying-tse, about 15 kilometers northwest of Cheng-chou. Intensive investigations were undertaken during the 1950s in the neighborhood of Ying-tse, but they failed to turn up any Shang Dynasty remains. In Cheng-chou, however, a full-fledged city site has been located, dating to the Lower Erh-li-kang phase, which, as will be shown, is considerably earlier than the dynastic phase of An-yang stratigraphy. Some scholars have suggested, therefore, that Cheng-chou may have been the site of the ancient capital of Ao.

The Shang city wall was roughly rectangular in shape, with a total perimeter of 7,195 meters and an enclosed area of 3.2 square kilometers. The maximum height of the surviving wall is 9.1 m, and the maximum width at the base is 36 m. The wall was built in successive compressed layers, each of which has an average thickness of 8 to 10 cm. On the surface of each layer are clear depressions made by the pestles used for compressing, and the soil making up the wall is hard and compact. The inner structure shows that it was built at two different periods, both within the time of the Shang, possibly corresponding to the Lower and the Upper Erh-li-kang phases. The wall was apparently used and mended during subsequent historic periods, but a new wall was built during the Han Dynasty around a smaller enclosure. The Shang wall shows without doubt that the city of Cheng-chou during the Shang Dynasty was of considerable importance and was constructed only with major effort. An Chin-huai estimates the original wall to have been 10 m in average height, with an average width of 20 m, which, multiplied by the total length of 7,195, required 1,439,000 m³ of compressed soil or (by a ratio of 1:2) 2,878,000 m³ of loose soil. Experiments carried out by archaeologists show that an average worker produces per hour 0.03 m³ of earth by means of a bronze pick or 0.02 m³ by means of a stone hoe. An concludes that to build the whole city wall of Cheng-chou, including earth-digging, transporting, and compressing, required no less than 18 years, with 10,000 workers working 330 days a year. This impressive figure, even though roughly calculated, indicates that Cheng-chou of the Shang Dynasty was no ordinary town.

The enclosure apparently marks the center of the administration and ceremony. Since it overlaps the present city site of Cheng-chou and has therefore been only spottily excavated, the layout of this site is not completely understood. But enough has been found to provide some ground for speculation. A large house floor has been identified at the northwestern corner of the city site, with a compressed, burned-hard, lime-plastered floor, with post holes 14 to 35 cm deep, 19 to 34 cm across. Such large buildings have not been found outside the city area. North of this building was found a platform of compressed earth, with an incomplete length of 25.5 m east to west, and an incomplete width of 8.8 m north to south. This reminds us of the earth altar at the center of Hsiao-t'un in the An-yang area. From a test trench in the northern part of the enclosure, south of the Tzu-ching-shan Hill, archaeologists found (in addition to potsherds) bone artifacts, stone implements, and scores of jade hairpins of excellent workmanship. Only two or three hairpins of this kind have ever been found in the vast area outside the enclosure.

Outside the city enclosure there were many residential sites and handicraft workshops, which can be attributed chronologically to the Lower and Upper Erh-li-kang stages. Two bronze foundry sites have been found thus far; one, north of Tzu-ching-shan Hill, is approximately 100 m north of the city wall, and the other about 500 m south of the wall at the point of the present South Gate (Nan-kuan). The workshop to the south covers an area of 1,050 square meters and has yielded crucibles of pottery, clay molds for both vessels and weapons, bronzes, debris of melted ocher, charcoal, and other stone and pottery remains. They are assigned to the Lower Erh-li-kang phase. The bronze foundry remains to the north are significantly connected with one of our stamped-earth house foundations: on the floor of the house is a layer of fine-grained and hardened light green earth containing copper, on which are some dozen conical depressions, each containing a layer of melted copper; outside the house is another area of verdigris 0.1 to 0.15 m thick; a heap of clay molds and relics of crucibles was placed beside a door connecting two rooms inside the house; a big lump of copper ocher was found 10 m west of the house.

This site belonged to the Upper Erh-li-kang phase. The last find is especially interesting, indicating that the bronzesmiths of the Shang Dynasty lived in stamped-earth houses and thus seem to have enjoyed a higher privilege than the common folk, who had to be satisfied with semi-subterranean houses.

Approximately 50 m north of the Tzu-ching-shan bronze foundry was a bone workshop. It is a good-sized pit, possibly of the Lower Erh-li-kang phase, containing over a thousand pieces of sawed and polished finished bone artifacts (arrowheads and hairpins), half-finished bone pieces, bone fragments used as raw materials, rejected pieces of bone, and eleven grinding stones. The bones are from human beings (about 50 per cent), cattle, deer, and pigs.

A pottery kiln site of the Erh-li-kang phases has been located on the west side of the Ming-kung Road, about 1200 meters west of the Shang city wall. In an area of 1,250 square meters, archaeologists have located fourteen kilns, near which are storage pits containing unfired and misfired pottery, pottery-making paddles and anvils, and stamps. Among the kilns are stamped-earth house foundations, which may have been the houses of the potters. Since all the pottery found at this site is of fine clay texture, there were presumably other kiln quarters for the manufacture of sand-tempered culinary wares, hard pottery, glazed pottery, and/or white pottery.

At Erh-li-kang, many large, coarse-textured pottery jars were found, on the inner surface of which is a layer of white substance which may indicate that they were containers for a kind of alcoholic beverage. The possibility that this was a wine-making industrial quarter has been suggested.

Besides those listed above, a large quantity of other kinds of remains has been unearthed both inside and outside the city enclosure. House foundations have been located at Pai-chia-chuang. Scattered water ditches have been found at Erh-li-kang, Pai-chia-chuang, Nan-kuan-wai, and the region on the west side of the Ming-kung-lu.

These ditches average 1.5 to 2.5 m in width and 1.5 m in depth. Those near Pai-chia-chuang have rows of small round depressions along both sides of the bottom. More than two hundred storage pits have been located throughout the area. Besides cultural debris and occasional pig and human skeletons, some of the pits contain large numbers of dog or cattle burials and apparently had some ceremonial significance. Burials have been located at Erh-li-kang, Tzu-ching-shan, Pai-chia-chuang, and Jen-min Park, and are particularly numerous at the last two sites. Some of the burials at Pai-chia-chuang (Upper Erh-li-kang phase) are described as large graves, with grave furnishings and (in two cases) human sacrifices; the others are small graves, which are numerous at the sites above named, and contain little or no grave furnishing.

These remains indicate that during the Erh-li-kang phases the city at Cheng-chou was a major political and ceremonial center. The population was apparently very large, in view of the extent of cultural distribution, the nature of settlement, and the depth of deposits (1 m average, with a maximum depth of 3 m). The artifacts found here include not only stone, bone, shell, and bronze implements and vessels, as well as pottery, but also bronze ceremonial vessels, glazed pottery, hard pottery, white pottery, jade and ivory artifacts, and three pieces of inscribed oracle bone. The dating of the inscribed bones is uncertain, but it has been suggested that they were intrusive from late strata and do not antedate the An-yang sequence of oracle records. The city enclosure was apparently occupied by a ruling aristocracy, while the craftsmen and farmers inhabited mainly the suburbs surrounding the city site. It is indeed highly probable that the traditional Shang capital of Ao was located here.

The Shang city life apparently continued into the final, Jen-min Park phase of the Cheng-chou sequence, for large graves of this phase have been located in the park, a short distance west of the Shang city wall. Aside from the findings here, however, Jen-min Park phase remains have thus far been found only in the upper stratum of the Ko-ta-wang site and in Ming-kung-lu. Whether this results from incomplete exploration of the area or indicates diminishing activities during this final phase of the Shang Dynasty, when the political center of the aristocracy had shifted away from the city of Ao, is a problem awaiting solution.

Some characteristic features of the Lower and Upper Erh-li-kang and the Jen-min Park phases are listed in Table 2.

3. An-yang

From King T'ang to King Ti Hsin, seven Shang capitals were recorded in the literature—Po, Hsiao (Ao), Hsiang, Keng (Hsing), P'i, Yen, and Yin. The locations of the first six, although generally assumed to be in northern Honan and its immediate neighborhood, are uncertain; the possibility that Po has been uncovered near Yenshih and that the Shang settlements near Cheng-chou are the remains of Ao has been discussed above. There is no question that the ruins of the last Shang capital, seat of power for twelve kings from P'an Keng to Ti Hsin for some 273 years until the fall of the dynasty, are situated on both banks of the Huan River northwest of the modern city of An-yang, northern Honan. They have been known to historians for ages past, and were referred to as Yin Hsü, the Ruins of Yin, by Ssu-ma Ch'ien in his *Shih Chi* (Hsiang Yü Biography). But it was not until 1899 when the remains of inscribed oracle bones were known to have been found in this area that the Ruins of Yin were brought to the attention of scholars. From 1928 to 1937, fifteen seasons of scientific excavation were undertaken in this region by the National Research Institute of History and Philology. After 1950, small-scale but intensive diggings have taken place continuously. Shang remains are now known in the An-yang region from no fewer than seventeen sites, covering an area of approximately 24 square kilometers.

The importance of the An-yang excavations in the history of archaeology in China cannot be exaggerated. The scale of the work, time, money, and manpower devoted to the excavations, and the scientific precision of the digging, are still unsurpassed in China. And it was the An-yang excavation, that settled, once and for all, the controversial problem of the existence of this dynasty, previously accredited only by legends. It was also the first site given a date in the earliest segment of Chinese written history, and thus ties written history to the prehistoric Neolithic cultures. However, work was interrupted by the Sino-Japanese War, leaving many sites in the An-yang group only partially excavated, and results have yet to be completely published. The center of Shang studies has tended to shift from An-yang to Cheng-chou, where a longer sequence has been uncovered and a series of preliminary and final reports has been made available. An-yang's fundamental importance, however, can never be doubted. Among other things, the oracle bone inscriptions from this area furnish much indispensable information concerning Shang culture and society that other Shang sites may never be able to match.

TABLE 2

Characteristic Features of Erh-li-kang and Jen-min Park Phases of the
Shang Culture at Cheng-chou

Lower Erh-li-kang Phase: The pottery has relatively thin walls, fine tempering materials,
fine cord marks, and is generally well made; the characteristic ceramic forms are *li* tripods
with elongated bodies, rounded rims curving outward and downward, high feet with long
conical ends; *hsien* tripods with fine tempering materials and breast-shaped feet; *chia*
tripods with out-turned rims; *kuan* jugs with fine cord marks and thin bodies; *tsun* jars
with squat bodies and short collars; *ting* tripods with basin- or bowl-like bodies; *tou*
fruit stands with shallow dishlike bodies. Oracle bones are similar to the Lo-ta-miao forms,
and bone hairpins are of the conical-head type.

Upper Erh-li-kang Phase: Pottery of this phase is similar to the previous phase, but the
tempering materials are generally coarser, the bodies thicker, and the cord marks made
of thicker strands. Many of the Lower Erh-li-kang ceramic forms continued into this
phase, but some of the forms that were initiated during the previous phase now became
prevalent, such as the *li* tripods with angular and up-turned rims, *hsien* tripods with
coarser cord marks and conical feet, *chia* tripods with in-turned rims, *ting* tripods imitating bronze forms, *tou* with bottoms considerably higher than indicated by the external
contours (false-bodied *tou*), and *tsun* jars with elongated bodies and long collars. Oracle
bones and bone hairpins are similar to the previous phase.

Jen-min Park Phase: The ceramic style has changed markedly, and the pottery is largely
of coarse tempering material, thick bodies, large-stranded cord marks, and crude workmanship. Few Erh-li-kang phase forms remain, while squat and short-footed *li* tripods, *tou* with
low pedestals, *p'o*, *yü*, and *yu* vessels appeared. There also appeared bone hairpins with
carved heads. Most of the oracle bones are turtleshells, and the preparation was elaborate.
The large graves containing human victims and rich furnishings which appeared in the
Upper Erh-li-kang phase continued here.

Similar to the settlement pattern of the Shang sites at Cheng-chou, the Shang sites
of the An-yang region were apparently articulated into a complex network of specialized
parts.

The Yin palaces south of Huanho (near the modern village of Hsiao-t'un)
constituted the center of the Yin Hsü, surrounded on all sides by habitation
clusters, workshops, and tombs. North of the Huanho, with Wu-kuan-ts'un
and the area north of Houchia-chuang [Hsi-pei-kang] as a center, there was
the area of the royal cemetery, burials of noblemen, and many thousand
sacrificial burials, an area also encircled by Yin settlements and burials.
Conditions of cultural deposits indicate that the neighborhood of Hsiao-t'un
was the region of the greatest abundance, and on its outskirts were settlements of varying sizes. Remains at these settlements do not occur in a
continuous area, but the distribution of the settlements was fairly dense.
Distances between settlements became greater as groups moved away from

the center. Palaces and the royal cemetery were apparently under the direct control of the ruling class, and the settlements surrounding Hsiao-t'un were probably habitations of [noblemen and the common people]. The latter classes were buried near where they lived, resulting in the intermixture of living and burial remains, although it is possible that [the noblemen] had their own cemeteries also. In the neighborhoods of the settlements were many workshops. For instance, large bronze foundry sites have been found at Miao-p'u-pei-ti and Hsiao-min-t'un, and bone workshops were identified at Pei-hsin-chuang and Ta-ssu-k'ung-ts'un. Even in the area of the palaces, many clay molds and bone materials were found. These may suggest that handicrafts were carried out under the direct control of the [upper classes,] and workshops often occurred in living areas but did not necessarily concentrate in their own quarters.

All this goes to show that the entire An-yang group formed a tightly organized unit, and the presence of the Royal House in this group is symbolized by the administrative and ceremonial center near Hsiao-t'un and the "royal cemetery" at Hsi-pei-kang.

The excavated part of the site at Hsiao-t'un is divided into three sections, A, B, and C. Section A, the northernmost, consists of fifteen parallel rectangular houses built on stamped-earth foundations. Section B, in the middle, includes twenty-one large houses, rectangular or square, built on stamped-earth foundations, and accompanied by a number of burials. These houses are arranged in three rows on a north-south axis, the central row consisting of three large houses and five gates. Section A and Section B are separated by a square stamped-earth foundation (of pure loess), which is thought to be a ceremonial altar. Section C, at the southwestern corner of the site, consists of seventeen stamped-earth foundations, arranged according to a preconceived plan and again accompanied by burials. Under the foundations in Section B is a complicated system of underground water ditches. The entire area of the Hsiao-t'un settlement includes about 10,000 square meters. According to the interpretation of Shih Chang-ju, Section A was probably the dwelling area of the settlement, Section B the royal temples, and Section C a ceremonial quarter. It is noteworthy, however, that these three sections seem to have been constructed during different time intervals, in the order A, B, and C. In view of the large scale of the construction, the elaborate planning of the houses, the extensive sacrifice of humans in the construction of the temples and the ceremonial altar, the innumerable inscribed oracle bones found at the site, and the mode of construction in stamped earth in contrast to the ordinary semi-subterranean dwellings, it appears reasonable to assume that this settlement was the center of the Royal House of the Yin Dynasty. These palaces and temples, as Tung Tso-pin describes them,

were all above-ground houses with stamped-earth foundations and stone pillar supporters. Although they were constructed of wattle-and-daub, these structures looked glorious and solemn enough. Near these foundations are often semi-subterranean pit houses, about 4 meters in diameter and the same in depth. These were presumably the service area of the Royal House subordinates. Inside the pit houses are round or rectangular bins, several meters deep and possibly places of storage.

These service areas included bronze foundries, stone and bone workshops, and pottery kilns. But some of these pit houses must also have served as domiciles. It is apparent that this Hsiao-t'un site served the same function as the city enclosure of Cheng-chou, but remains of a city wall have not been found. Nevertheless, it must be remembered that the Hsiao-t'un site was not completely excavated and that the excavators presumably did not look specifically for a city wall. Since the city walls appeared at Cheng-chou before the Hsiao-t'un phase, and continued into later historical periods, I would not be surprised if more intensive future investigations find that this site also had a walled enclosure.

Hsi-pei-kang, near Hou-chia-chuang, and the contiguous Wukuan-ts'un area, is best known for its burial complex that included 11 large graves (the royal cemetery) and 1,222 small graves, although dwellings and workshops have also been found here. The eleven large tombs are grouped into a western cluster of seven and an eastern cluster of four, happily coinciding in number with the eleven kings from P'an Keng to Ti Yi who ruled from An-yang. (The last king at An-yang, Ti Hsin, was supposedly burned to death when the capital fell to the Chou invaders.) Although it cannot yet be fully established that these were the kings' graves, we know that they were constructed on a large scale, with elaborate ceremonial procedures, and their furnishings represent the highest achievements of Shang technology and art. According to the estimates of Li Chi, the earth-digging alone required at least seven thousand working days for each of the large graves of Hsi-pei-kang. All the graves are square or oblong, oriented north-south, with long ramps on two (north and south) or four sides. The best known of the tombs, No. 1001, is shaped like a cross in ground plan and forms a pit about 10 m deep, with slightly sloping walls. The mouth of the pit is 19 m long north to south, and 14 m wide. A ramp leads from the ground to the bottom of the grave pit on each of the four sides; the southern ramp, the longest, measures about 30 m. Within the pit a wooden chamber was built; the chief coffin of the tomb was probably placed in the center. Many sacrificial burials occurred in various spots within the pit, but were concentrated within the chamber itself and in the southern ramp. Some of the sacrifices were provided with coffins and small grave pits, but most were without either coffin or pit, and many were separate burials of heads and trunks. The tomb was abundantly furnished with stone, jade, shell, bone, antler, tooth, bronze, and pottery artifacts, including many that are the best examples of Shang art. Li Chi has listed the following as the most significant contributions of the Hsi-pei-kang excavations to Shang archaeology: (1) importance of pisé construction in Shang architecture; (2) Shang burial institutions and the organization of manpower as indicated by the construction of single tombs; (3) the reality and magnitude of sacrificial burials; (4) the high level of achievement of the Shang material culture and the extent of leisure of the ruling class; (5) the discovery of stone sculptures and the sophistication of the decorative art; and (6) the representative products of bronze industry. To these we must add a point of chronological significance. If these eleven tombs were those of the kings and if these tombs can be chronologically seriated among themselves and together with Hsiao-t'un's habitation remains, then there is a complete sequence of artifacts and arts available at An-yang that covers the entire range of 273 years when An-yang was the royal capital. Therefore, the Hsi-pei-kang tombs represent a solid chronological segment of the Shang civilization and their sequence provides a basis for the study of cultural change within the segment.

Furthermore, if the Hsi-pei-kang tombs began with P'an Keng, then at the site of Hsiao-t'un the habitation floors and storage pits that are considered on typological grounds to be earlier than HPKM 1001 must belong to an earlier period than P'an Keng, the so-called Pre-Dynastic Period of Hsiao-t'un. In other words, in An-yang there is the segment of 273 years that can be referred to as the Yin or Hsi-pei-kang phase with which Hsiao-t'un II was contemporaneous. Hsiao-t'un I, therefore, must predate the Yin phase. The details of these Hsiao-t'un phases cannot be known until all the excavated materials become available. But excavations at other sites in the An-yang area are revealing. At Ta-ssu-k'ung-ts'un, remains of habitation floors and burials were found, and four stages of occupation were distinguished. A piece of oracle bone dated to King Wu Ting's reign or thereabouts was discovered from the earliest stratum, suggesting that the entire Ta-ssu-k'ung-ts'un sequence can be placed within the Hsi-pei-kang phase. At Mei-yüan-chuang, two cultural strata were recognized, the upper layer similar to the Hsiao-t'un phases but the lower layer similar to Cheng-chou's Lower Erh-li-kang. Thus, at An-yang the following stratigraphical sequence has been suggested: Mei-yüan-chuang I, the earliest: Hsiao-t'un I, possibly of the same phase or slightly later; and Hsi-pei-kang, contemporary with Hsiao-t'un II and Ta-ssu-k'ung-ts'un I–IV, a phase that should be susceptible to finer subdivisions.

Little is known concerning Shang sites in An-yang other than the above. Information is available at the sites of Hou-chia-chuang-nanti, Hou-kang, Hsüeh-chia-chuang, and Kao-lou-chuang. Remains of living floors, burials of varying scales and degrees of richness, bronze, pottery, and bone workshops, and storage pits have been reported from these sites, suggestive of the nature of the settlements in the An-yang group other than Hsiao-t'un and Hsi-pei-kang. All these sites are dated within the Hsi-pei-kang range.

The Yin settlement at An-yang may be summarized as follows: prior to the time of P'an Keng (1384 B.C., according to T. P. Tung's chronology), who made An-yang his capital, the Shang had already occupied the An-yang area. At any rate, at Hsiao-t'un, Hsüeh-chia-chuang as well as Mei-yüan-chuang remains were found that are similar to the Erh-li-kang phases of Cheng-chou. These are mostly of a domiciliary nature, but a bronze industry had already been established here. Whether the other settlements had been occupied cannot be established at present because of the lack of stratigraphic evidence. From the time of P'an Keng (so says the traditional history, which is supported by oracle bone records), the An-yang area was the capital of the Royal House of the Shang Dynasty. Most of the settlements of the An-yang group were probably occupied by the people of Yin and by nobility connected with the Royal House. Royal palaces and ceremonial centers were constructed at Hsiao-t'un and Hou-chia-chuang-nan-ti, and the cemeteries of the royal family were constructed at Hsi-pei-kang (and Wu-kuan-ts'un) and Hou-kang. The individual settlements were probably more or less self-sufficient in terms of basic subsistence and handicrafts, but as far as the control of the economy, political administration, and religious and ceremonial affairs is concerned, the entire An-yang settlement group appears to have formed a single unit.

4. Hsing-t'ai

Since 1954, Shang sites have been found widely in the neighborhood of Hsing-t'ai, in southern Hopei, directly north of An-yang. Neither literary tradition nor archaeological evidence itself gives this group of Shang sites a royal capital status, but this site is all the more important in the picture it gives of Shang civilization outside of the settlement groups which were politically prominent. Archaeological work in this area is still going on, and only preliminary reports have been published on the excavated sites. Some socioeconomic characteristics of these sites, however, are of immediate interest.

Over ten Shang sites have thus far been located in the regions north and west of the Hsing-t'ai city, in an area approximately 10 kilometers north to south and 7 kilometers east to west. The cultural deposits at some of the sites attain a maximum depth of 3 meters, testifying to the permanent nature of the settlement and the considerable duration of its inhabitation. Three cultural phases have been distinguished for the Yin-kuo-ts'un site, which correlate with other stratified sites in this region as follows:

Upper Yin-kuo-ts'un phase: Upper Ts'ao-yen-chuang. Upper Nan-ta-kuo-ts'un
Middle Yin-kuo-ts'un phase: Lower Ts'ao-yen-chuang, Lower Nan-ta-kuo-ts'un
Lower Yin-kuo-ts'un phase

Cultural remains from these Shang phases of Hsing-t'ai include many of the diagnostic Shang traits such as oracle bones, bone hairpins, and some characteristic pottery forms and decorative motifs. Pottery kilns were found at some of the sites, but a bone workshop was discovered at only one settlement, indicating that these settlements were tied together in terms of handicraft specialization, as was the case with An-yang and Cheng-chou. *Hang-t'u* house structures, inscriptions, and bronze foundries have not been unearthed, however. Stone was the raw material for all the implements, though bronze arrowheads, awls, adzes, and ornaments appear occasionally in the remains. Further investigations in the Hsing-t'ai area will undoubtedly throw much more light upon this settlement group, but the available data suggest that here in Hsing-t'ai the Shang people had an urban network similar to those at An-yang and Cheng-chou, even though there may not have been an outstanding aristocratic complex.

5. Other Shang Sites

Other sites of the Shang period providing sufficient information to warrant their classification as Shang civilizations include Ch'i-lip'u in Shan Hsien, Lu-ssu in Mien-ch'ih, Chien-hsi in Meng Hsien, a series of sites in the neighborhood of Lo-yang, Lu-wang-fen in Hsin-hsiang, several sites in Hui Hsien, Ch'ao-ko in T'ang-yin, Shih-li-p'u in Nan-yang, and Fu-kou in Yen-ling, all in Honan Province; Chu-chia-ch'iao in P'ing-yin, and Ta-hsin-chuang in Chi-nan, Shantung Province; and Chien-kou-ts'un in Han-tan, Pei-chai-ts'un in Ling-shou, and Feng-chia-an in Ch'ü-yang, Hopei Province. The sites in Lo-yang and Hui Hsien approach Cheng-chou and An-yang in extent, yielding bronze foundries and large graves with human victims. Bronze foundries have also been found in Nan-yang. The other sites, however, are like the Hsing-t'ai group, yielding networks that were probably economic, yet lacking a clearly defined aristocratic complex. A typological classification of the Shang sites as they are known at present also has a geographical significance: Shang sites with aristocratic complexes are confined to northern Honan, extending as far west as Lo-yang; those showing a similar urbanized structure but without a concentrated aristocratic complex extend to western Honan as far as Shan Hsien, southern Hopei as far as Ch'ü-yang, and Shantung as far as Chi-nan. Shang remains are also found outside this circle, notably in non-civilizational or non-Shang contexts. These facts are indispensable in delineating the cultural and social boundaries of the Shang civilization.

Chronology of the Shang Civilization and the Problem of its Origins

Shang history according to written records can be subdivided into four segments: legendary ancestors, from Ti K'u to Wang Hai; early ancestors, from Shang Chia to Shih Kui, the first six ancestors in the ritual genealogy recorded in the oracle scripts; the dynastic period from T'ang to Yang Chia, when the Shang were rulers of China but before they moved to An-yang; and the dynastic period from P'an Keng to Ti Hsin, when An-yang was the royal capital. Three dates are therefore of crucial significance in the chronology of the Shang: the accession of T'ang, the removal of the Shang capital to An-yang under P'an Keng, and the fall of the Shang dynasty under Ti Hsin. Exact dates for these events are still being debated among historians, but no conclusions have been reached. However, in this volume I shall adopt some round figures: 1750 for T'ang's accession, 1400 for P'an Keng's move to An-yang, and 1100 for the fall of the Shang Dynasty. For our purposes here, where broad chronological segments are adequate for studies of trends of cultural development and of cultural relationships, it is not necessary to take sides in this technical debate.

Before the Shang sites at Cheng-chou were excavated, the An-yang culture was the sole representative of the Shang civilization, and our understanding of it was accordingly restricted and conditioned. Since those excavations, however, the Cheng-chou sequence, by virture of its long and seemingly complete stratigraphy, has been used by archaeologists as the yardstick by which other Shang sites are measured. Tsou Heng, for instance, has classified the cultural remains at Hsiao-t'un of the An-yang group into three stages: pre-Hang-t'u, Hang-t'u, and post-Hang-t'u. The Hang-t'u phase of Anyang, according to Tsou, can be synchronized with the Jen-min Park phase of Cheng-chou, whereas the pre-Hang-t'u was earlier than the Jen-min Park phase but later than the Upper Erh-li-kang phase, and the post-Hang-t'u phase later than the Jen-min Park phase of Cheng-chou. The earliest phase at Hsing-t'ai, according to T'ang Yün-ming, was probably earlier than the Erh-li-kang phases, but the later phases correspond to them. For other sites, the terms Erh-li-kang and Hsiao-t'un are used freely for similar chronological and classificatory purposes. Carrying this scheme to the extreme, Cheng Te-k'un boldly attempts to synchronize all of the Shang sites, which he divides into five groups: Proto Shang, Early Shang, Middle Shang, Late Shang, and Post Shang.

It is true that cultural remains similar to this or that phase of the Cheng-chou sequence are found elsewhere, and this may have chronological significance. Until a number of sites other than Cheng-chou and An-yang are excavated intensively, however, it would be impossible for us to claim that the fivefold subdivision of the Shang sequence at Cheng-chou, as it is known at a certain period in the history of Shang archaeology, is universally valid. The Shang-chieh phase of Cheng-chou, for instance, may possibly be earlier than the Proto Shang phase of Cheng Te-k'un. What, then, should it be called? Cheng's Middle Shang includes both Upper Erh-li-kang of Cheng-chou and Hsiao-t'un I of An-yang, the two phases that are regarded by Tsou Heng as being chronologically successive rather than concurrent. Cheng's grouping them together apparently employs one set of criteria, then, whereas Tsou's setting them apart must use another. In the future, when a number of long sequences will presumably be determined for Shang sites that are not yet extensively excavated, the Cheng-chou sequence may not continue to be serviceable as the basic yardstick. Before we have knowledge of other sequences, any synchronization of all the Shang sites in North China according to the Cheng-chou sequence would seem to be dubious at best. For the time being, I believe that we are better off to confine discussion of the chronological development of the Shang culture to the few sites whose stratigraphy is reasonably well established.

The archaeological remains uncovered at the various Shang sites described above were plainly left during a long period that can be subdivided into a number of segments or phases according to the change of artifacts and styles. Stratigraphic evidence at Yen-shih, Cheng-chou, and An-yang, the three most important Shang sites both in the amount and quality of remains and in terms of the chronological information they provide, appears to warrant the tentative and broad correlation of the various phases indicated in Table 3. In other words, speaking of the total area of distribution of Shang sites in North China, three phases of Shang civilization are definitely indicated: *Erh-li-t'ou,* earliest; *Erh-li-kang;* and *Yin,* the phase of Yin Hsü occupation by the Royal House. Further subdivisions can certainly be made. For instance, several components occurred at the site of Erh-li-t'ou, at least Shang-chieh and Lo-ta-miao phases can be distinguished in Cheng-chou before Erh-li-kang, and the Yin phase contained at least the four minor subphases at Ta-ssu-k'ung-ts'un. These problems, however, require further study on the basis of additional information that is not yet adequate. For the time being, we can only speak of the following broad stages of the development of the Shang civilization.

The Erh-li-t'ou Phase

Up to 1965, Shang sites classified with the Erh-li-t'ou and the Shang-chieh and Lo-ta-miao phases had been known in Shan, Loning, Yi-yang, Lo-yang, Sung, Yi-ch'uan, Yen-shih, Teng-feng, Lin-ju, Kung, and Cheng-chou, all in northwestern Honan south of the Yellow River in an area drained by the Huangho and its tributaries Yi and Lo and the neighboring River Ju, an upper tributary of the Huaiho. *Shi Chi* states that the removal of P'an Keng to An-yang involved the crossing of the Yellow River, and it is likely that prior to P'an Keng all Shang capitals were south of the river, although historians are by no means agreed on this point. If T'ang indeed rose at the present site of Erh-li-t'ou, it appears probable that this earliest Shang phase represents the period immediately before and after the founding of the dynasty, a possibility that suggests a tentative date of 1850-1650 B.C. for the Erh-li-t'ou phase of the Shang civilization.

The important characteristics of the Erh-li-t'ou phase are: large *hang-t'u* floors of palatial buildings: division of human burials into those with grave pits and grave goods and those without them, some of the latter seeming to be sacrificial victims; the manufacture of bronze implements (knife, awl, fishhook, and bell); the incision of complex symbols on pottery; divination by the shoulderblades of oxen and sheep; the occurrence in graves of pottery wine utensils; the large number of stone, bone, and shell hoes, spades, and sickles; remains of domestic pigs, oxen, sheep, and horses; and bone shops, and bronze foundries. Characteristic also is a distinctive group of pottery vessels and decorative patterns that were absent in either the Lung-shan culture before or the Erh-li-kang phase

TABLE 3

Tentative Correlation of Shang Culture Phases at Major Sites

PHASES	YEN-SHIH LO-YANG	CHENG-CHOU	AN-YANG
ca. 1100 YIN	LATE SHANG SITES	JEN-MIN PARK	HSI-PEI-KANG HSIAO-T'UN II
——ca. 1400——	LO-YANG	UPPER ERH-LI-KANG	HSIAO-T'UN I
ERH-LI-KANG	ERH-LI-KANG PHASE LO-YANG	LOWER ERH-LI-KANG	MEI-YÜAN-CHUANG I
—— ca. 1650——	TUNG-KAN-KOU	LO-TA-MIAO	
ERH-LI-T'OU			
ca. 1850	ERH-LI-T'OU	SHANG-CHIEH	

after it (shallow dishes with three legs; flat-bottomed basins: characteristic types of *ting,
tou, ho, kui, ku, chüeh,chiao;* "filters"; steamers; deep pots with vertical walls: *ting* with
single handles; square *ting* with four legs; *chia* with handles; large check marks; a variety of impressed designs; developed appliqued designs; dotted patterns on the vessel interiors). The
forms and modes of some pottery vessels (especially those of wine vessels such as the lids
and handles of *ho*) give the impression that metal types were being imitated—the occurrence of bronze vessels in this phase cannot be ruled out. All these features point to a
highly stratified, complex society and a culture with advanced agriculture and handicrafts,
perhaps some rudimentary form of writing, and definitely a bronze industry at perhaps
a lower level of achievement than that of the An-yang bronzes.

Available data of the Erh-li-t'ou phase reveal a state of cultural development
intermediate between the Honan Lung-shan culture and the more advanced Shang
civilization of later phases that certainly has great bearing on the problem of origin and
process of growth of the Shang culture.

The Erh-li-t'ou type of culture apparently grew out of the foundation of the
Honan Lung-shan culture, having absorbed elements of the Shantung
Lung-shan culture. Some pottery types of this phase were common in both
the Honan and the Shantung Lung-shan cultures, such as the flat-bottomed
basins and the *kui* tripods. Some types find antecedents in the Shantung Lung-
shan culture, such as the shallow dishes with three legs and the *kui* tripods.
Other types and decorations grew out of Honan Lung-shan proto-forms, such
as the "filter," *ku*, deep pots with vertical walls, *wung, tou, chia,* and basket,
check, and cord marks.

The problem of Shang origins in the light of recent work at the Erh-li-t'ou phase sites is discussed below.

The Erh-li-kang Phase

By the time of the Erh-li-kang phase, Shang sites had already attained their maximal distribution, north as well as south of the Yellow River. If we use the Lower Erh-li-kang phase of Cheng-chou as the type site of this Shang phase and use the beginning of the capital status of An-yang to mark its upper end, then the Erh-li-kang phase of the Shang civilization can be placed between 1650 and 1400 B.C. If the site at Cheng-chou was indeed the capital city of Ao, the supposed date that Ao was made a capital (1557 B.C.) falls within this time span.

Aside from new types and modes of pottery there is little in the Erh-li-kang phase that is significantly different from the previous one. *Hang-t'u* constructions and bronze foundries existed, the latter producing primarily small and simple implements and ornaments but occasionally some ceremonial vessels. No writing has been found, and divination was carried out by means of shoulderblades of oxen and sheep. The pattern of settlement clearly indicates an urban network decisively different from the Neolithic village pattern. Since the Erh-li-t'ou phase is not well known it is difficult to assess how much progress it had achieved, but there is no question that it was still at a more primitive level, compared with the Yin phase, as far as cultural complexity and artistic achievement are concerned.

The Yin Phase

This is the phase represented by the Hsi-pei-kang royal tombs, dated to the period of 1400 to 1100 B.C. The center of the state had shifted to north of the Yellow River and there was a notable decline of cultural intensity at Cheng-chou, but the distribution of remains of this phase appears to be the same as in the previous phase, that is, in the northern half of Honan and adjacent regions in Honan, Hopei, and Shantung. This is the phase of the oracle scripts, divination by turtleshells, advanced bronze metallurgy, and artistic climax.

Before 1950, when the first pre-Yin sites were found in Cheng-chou, the fabulous spectacle of the Shang site at An-yang had no apparent antecedents in China, and the "origin" of the civilization—with its bronzes, stone sculptures, horse chariots, pisé houses, human sacrifices, and writing—was a major enigma in the ancient history of China. As Max Loehr pointed out, "An-yang represents, according to our present knowledge, the oldest Chinese metal age site, taking us back to ca. 1300 B.C. It displays no signs of a primitive stage of metal working but utter refinement. Primitive stages have, in fact, nowhere been discovered in China up to the present moment. Metallurgy seems to have been brought to China from outside." The same held true for other elements of Shang civilization than metallurgy: writing, chariot warfare, bronze types, and so forth. Many scholars, principally because they thought that civilization came to China suddenly and without previous foundation, argued that it came as a result of diffusion from the Near East, where civilization emerged some fifteen hundred years before it came to China. Now, during the last seventeen years, with the revelation of the Erh-li-kang phase and remains even earlier than Erh-li-kang, it appears that the foundation and the primitive stages of Shang civilization elements have been discovered. These have led Cheng Te-k'un to state: "the origin of some of the outstanding elements of the late Shang culture may now be told"; that, "after the recent extensive excavations . . . the problem of the origin of the Shang bronze industry may now be considered solved"; and that "Chinese historic culture of the Shang type stemmed directly from the Grey Pottery Culture."

The "origin" of a civilization or, for that matter, of any of its elements, is a complex and difficult problem that must be tackled with care in regard to data and to concepts. At what point in an archaeological sequence of artifacts can we consider, let us say, that the origin of bronze metallurgy in China has been established? Is it necessary to have available a sequence of bronze foundry sites and a sequence of bronze artifacts ranging from the most primitive and simple to the most advanced and elaborate before one can make such a claim? With writing, the horse chariot, and so on, the same question should be asked. If there is no complete sequence from the primitive to the advanced, does it then follow that this element came from without? And, finally, when and if the origins of a number of such important cultural elements have been "solved," has this also solved the problem of the origin of the civilization? Civilizations are articulations of cultural elements, each of which occupies a place in the whole but all of which do not occupy positions of equal importance—they are not summations of cultural elements. Knowing the origin of some elements of a civilization is not knowing the origin of the civilization and, conversely, we may know how a civilization began to emerge and form without knowing the history of all of its component elements.

Descriptions of the Lung-shan stage of the Chinese Neolithic have shown that the Shang civilization did not evolve out of a vacuum. As I have pointed out, a number of Lung-shan elements foreshadowed the birth of civilization in the Huangho Valley: (1) the permanent settlement and the large area of the farming villages, and the advancement of agriculture; (2) the specialization of industries which had been considerably developed, as shown by the appearance of wheel-made pottery in some of the areas; (3) the village fortifications indicating the need for defense, and hence the frequency of warfare between settlements; (4) the oracle bone, the prone burial, and the concentration of jade objects in certain places within the village, which may imply an intensification of the differentiation of individual status; (5) the regional variation of styles and the possible importance of the residential group at the community-aggregate level which foreshadowed, if it did not indicate, the formation of urban networks and the beginning of regional states, one of which eventually succeeded in expansion and conquest, and was known as the Shang.

The Shang civilization was indeed a new phenomenon in the Huangho Valley, an outcome of a quantum change, which put a full stop to the Neolithic way of life in the area of Shang distribution, and in doing so prefaced a new book which is entitled Chinese history instead of prehistory. But the main stream of this new civilization was evidently handed on from the previous Neolithic substratum. There were, in the Shang culture, new elements and new systems of organization for new and old elements of culture, but this does not necessarily mean that the Shang civilization was not a native growth. Table 4 shows, in a preliminary fashion, the Neolithic heritage of the Shang Bronze Age culture and its innovations. From this enumeration it becomes apparent that the "suddenness" of the emergence of the Shang civilization has been unduly exaggerated by past scholarly writing. In fact, few Shang ecosocial and stylistic elements

TABLE 4

North China Neolithic-Bronze Age Continuities and Discontinuities

Continuities	*Discontinuities*
Formation of village-aggregate	Mature urbanism and related institutions
Raid and warfare	(esp. formation of settlement groups)
Industrial specialization	Class differentiation
Differentiation of status, and prone burials	New government and economic patterns
Elaborate ceremonial complex (more lineage-ancestral than community-agricultural)	(conquest, tribute, redistribution, etc.)
	Wider trade, currency
Cultivation of millet, rice, kaoliang, wheat, hemp	New war patterns (capture of slaves and use of chariots)
Domestication of dog, pig, cattle, sheep, horse, chicken	Chamber burials and human sacrifices
	Domestication of water buffalo
Stamped-earth structures	Highly developed bronze metallurgy
Semi-subterranean houses and lime-plastered floors.	Writing
	Advanced stone carvings
Scapulimancy	New pottery forms
Some pottery forms (esp. ritual forms with ring feet and lids)	
Some decorative motifs	
Some stone implements and weapons (esp. semilunar knife, sickle, arrowhead, adz, ax, hoe, spade, perforated ax, halberd)	
Shell and bone craft	
Cord-marked pottery tradition	
Silk	
Jade complex	

did not have a Neolithic basis. Thus, one thing can be considered settled—that the Chinese civilization, on the whole, was built upon the Chinese Neolithic foundation. With this basic question out of the way, three problems still confront us: (1) the origins of the cultural elements that appeared during the Shang period for the first time, and the extent to which these new elements can be considered responsible for the appearance of the civilization; (2) the new structure and configuration of the Shang civilization which distinguish it from the Neolithic, continuities in cultural elements notwithstanding; and (3) the regional phase of the Lung-shan culture that is directly ancestral to the Shang. The second problem will be discussed at length in subsequent sections of this chapter. Evidence pertaining to the first and the third problems is still meager, but the following remarks may be of some help.

Most of the new features that appeared during the Shang and serve to mark it off from the Neolithic are largely developmental and functional in nature. Urbanism, class distinctions, political systems, and the like are poor indications of historical relationships; the use of currency, patterns of warfare, and many ceremonial practices can probably be said to be concomitant with particular functional contexts. Only bronze metallurgy, the use of writing, and the horse chariot are, therefore, of possible historical significance. Unfortunately, the history of these elements and their occurrence in China have yet to be studied. Horse bones have been found from some of the Lungshanoid sites. It is widely accepted that during the Shang, horses were used only for drawing chariots, and were neither ridden nor used for food. There is no reason to suppose that horses during the Lung-shan stage, if domesticated, were employed for purposes other than warfare. Since the riding of horses during the Lung-shan is highly unlikely, we might even be tempted to conclude that the horse chariot appeared during that period, but the evidence for this conclusion is dangerously thin. In the first place, horse bones have been found only rarely at Lung-shan sites, and the zoological characteristics of those that have been found remain to be specified. Second, chariot warfare does not seem to fit the Lung-shan context satisfactorily. Third, remains of chariots have never been found at Lung-shan sites. A great number of excavations and comparative studies of horse and chariot remains in China and in Mesopotamia must be made before we can be certain about the origin of the horse chariot in the Shang Dynasty.

The history of writing in China is another unknown factor. Palaeographers are agreed that a stage of writing existed in China before An-yang became the capital. The scripts during this pre-Anyang stage were supposedly more representational and elaborate than the An-yang oracle bone inscriptions which were highly simplified and conventionalized. Such archaic characters have been found on An-yang bronzes and oracle bones, along with the simplified and conventionalized form, probably for artistic and ceremonial use. Archaeologically, however, except for the complex symbols on pottery at both Yen-shih and Cheng-chou, this archaic writing has not been found in a stratigraphic context demonstrably earlier than the An-yang period.

The history of bronze metallurgy in China is now better known than previously, although it is not yet a solved problem. Based on recent findings, the following points can be made. An-yang does not represent the oldest Chinese metal age site; the existence of bronze metallurgy during the Shang before the period of An-yang has been established. Even the possibility that metallurgy began to appear in North China toward the end of the Lung-shan stage of the Neolithic cannot be ruled out. At Yen-shih and Cheng-chou, where bronze artifacts have been unearthed from a pre-Anyang stratigraphic context, bronzes are few and less refined than those at An-yang, although metallurgical details are not yet available. It is possible that this marks one of the "primitive stages" that Loehr said was lacking. An intensive investigation into the metallurgical techniques of the Chinese Bronze Age has convinced Noel Barnard that bronze foundry in China, showing little similarity to Western bronze metallurgy, was invented independently *in situ.* Deposits of copper and tin ores, according to the studies of Amano Motonosuke and Shih Chang-ju, are abundant in North China, and were easily accessible from northern Honan. This indicates that, given appropriate necessity and stimulus, the opportunity for independent metallurgical invention was available to the first Chinese bronze workers.

It is generally agreed that the Shang craftsmen used bronze as a new medium for working the traditional artifactual forms; in other words, the Shang bronzes manifested the traditional forms and functions by means of a new kind of raw material and technology. Considering all these points, we can say that much new light has been thrown upon the problem of the origin of bronze metallurgy in China, which renders likely the independent invention of this new technology in China. Much more information, to be sure, is required to transform this possibility into certainty, but the trend of available data is clear, and we are more sure of the various areas in which intelligent questions can be asked.

Furthermore, some new light has also been thrown upon the problem pertaining to the transition from the Lung-shan to the Shang. That the Lung-shan culture was the forerunner of the Shang civilization is certain, but we have yet to pin down the exact region where this transition took place, and—still more difficult—to determine exactly how it took place. The fact that, in the area of Yen-shih and Lo-yang of western Honan, stratified sequences of Honan Lung-shan culture and the Erh-li-t'ou phase of the Shang civilization have indicated a continuous development of culture, is certainly suggestive. One would be tempted to proclaim this area—the Yi and Lo River valleys—the cradle of the Shang civilization if it were not for the very inadequate amount of data available for the Erh-li-t'ou phase.

To conclude, one may find it possible to say that the foundation of the Shang civilization is the Honan Lung-shan culture; that the three phases of Shang civilization provide a preliminary sequence of its gradual development; that the transformation in question is primarily and essentially a societal growth and that its manifestations were rooted in the cultural history of the Yellow River basin itself; that the history of development of many of the Shang's essential elements are now clearly demonstrated by archaeological data in North China, but others remain unknown; that some important elements of the Shang civilization that had a role in stimulating its growth were possibly derivative; and, finally, that the actual process of growth of the civilization *in toto* and of its various constituent elements remains a topic for further research, for which future discoveries of Erh-li-t'ou sites will be essential.

Content and Style of the Shang Civilization

The earliest strata of the Shang civilization known at present in the form of the Erh-li-t'ou phase of western Honan are not adequately known, but it is already clear that by this time (ca. 1850 B.C.) the Neolithic economy had begun to give way to the formation of settlement groups as self-contained units. Bronze metallurgy was already well started, and at some sites one sees the beginning of a highly intensified and sophisticated aristocratic complex. This stage serves well as a transitional phase between the Neolithic and the climactic Shang civilization.

By the time the city wall was constructed at Cheng-chou, perhaps around 1650 B.C., there can no longer be any doubt that Chinese urbanization was mature and that a Shang style of Chinese art and culture is manifest in the archaeological record. Because the term "urbanization" is somewhat arbitrarily defined in the archaeological literature, we must carefully characterize the nature of city life of the Shang Dynasty in North China.

The foremost feature of the Shang sites is that individual villages were organized into inter-village networks in economy, administration, and religion. Each group depended upon others for specialized services, and offered services in return. There was a political and ceremonial center (a walled enclosure in the case of Cheng-chou), where the royal family and the nobles resided. It apparently served as the nucleus of the group and, when the capital of the dynasty was located there, as the center of political and economic control of the whole kingdom. Surrounding and centripetal to this nucleus were industrial quarters with high degrees of specialization, and farming villages. Goods apparently circulated among the various villages, with the administrative center serving also as the center for redistribution. The population of the entire settlement group was considerable, as indicated by the spatial dimensions and by the quantity and complexity of the cultural remains, and the social stratification and industrial specialization of the populace were highly intensified. We find in Shang China no physical counterparts to such large population and architectural configurations as Ur of Mesopotamia, Mohenjo-Daro on the Indus, and Teotihuacan of Mexico, yet the Shang capital sites performed all the essential functions of a city, indicating a definite break from the Neolithic community pattern. This basic Shang city pattern continued on into later historic periods. During the Eastern Chou period the capital sites grew into large commercial and political urban centers, as will be described in the next chapter.

Purely from an archaeological perspective, the populace of a Shang city seems to have been divided into three major groups: the aristocracy, the craftsmen, and the farmers.

The aristocracy

Archaeological excavations, oracle bone inscriptions, and historic records have jointly established the fact that the Shang capitals at Cheng-chou and An-yang were seats of a powerful centralized government in control of a number of settlement groups scattered over a part of North China. At one or a few of the sites within the same settlement group, an aristocratic complex of artifacts and architecture can easily be recognized. In architecture, this includes ceremonial altars, rectangular house structures with stamped earth floors, stone pillar foundations, and in some cases, stone sculptures used as pillar bases. Such sites have a complex system of graves, including tombs of gigantic dimensions and sophisticated structure, evidence of human sacrifice and accompanying burials of animal victims and horse chariots. This aristocratic complex is often associated with a sophisticated ritual complex, manifested by human sacrifice, animal sacrifice, scapulimancy, and ceremonial vessels of pottery (e.g. white pottery) and bronze. Horse and chariot fittings and other apparatus for ritual use help to mark the distinction of status, along with such artifacts as prepared and inscribed oracle bones, white, hard, glazed pottery, elaborately carved bone hairpins, jade weapons, and bronze ceremonial and household utensils. Groups of bronze and pottery vessels for use in wine drinking and serving occurred in the Shang burials for the first time. Remains of cowrie shells, probably used as media for exchange, may also be significant. Writing is apparently associated with the aristocracy, as are highly developed decorative arts like the *t'ao-t'ieh* style, mosaic designs, and stone and bone sculptures and engravings. Discovery of such artifacts points to a strongly consolidated aristocracy that was definitely absent prior to the Shang.

From the oracle inscriptions and the historic records, a little is known about the Royal House, the rule of succession to the throne, and the political relationships among the various settlement groups. Mythological sources relate that the Royal House of the Shang Dynasty was a grand lineage by the name of Tzu, attributed to a divine birth in Ssu-ma Ch'ien's *Shih Chi,* volume 3:

> The mother of Ch'i, founder of the Yin Dynasty, was called Chien Ti, a
> daughter of the tribe Yu Jung and second consort of Emperor K'u.
> Basking with two companions, Chien Ti saw an egg fall from a black
> bird [swallow or phoenix] and swallowed it. She then became pregnant
> and gave birth to Ch'i.

The grand lineage occupied a central position in the state's political, economic, and ceremonial structures, which were expressed and maintained with elaborate and solemn ancestor worship rites. There is little question about the relationship between the ancestor worship rites performed by and for the grand lineages and the origin myths of the descent of these lineages. According to the ancestor cult calendar worked out from the oracle inscriptions, Li Hsüeh-ch'in has been able to generalize that among thirty-five kings of the Shang Dynasty, whose rules of succession are relatively clear, the throne was assumed by sons for eighteen generations, and for seven generations (ten kings) it was taken over by brothers.

The settlement groups that were not under the direct rule of the monarch were administered by lords appointed by the central government. The lords were relatives of the monarch (sometimes junior sons), high officials who made great contributions to the cause of the Royal House, and the *de facto* rulers of regions that paid tribute to the central government but were out of the reach of the royal forces, and whose administrative status had to be recognized.

The central government and the local governments thus formed a tightly organized hierarchy, with the king at the top, assisted by officials of a royal court and priests who practiced scapulimancy, among other duties. Communications between the various settlement groups and the central administration were possible with the aid of a highly developed system of writing and a standardized currency. Raids and warfare between states were frequent, as judged by the war records in the inscriptions, the abundant remains of weapons, the sacrificial use of what were apparently war captives, and the chariots. The centralized power of government is most clearly indicated by the control of manpower. In addition, public works began to appear to a significant extent. The *hang-t'u* structures at Hsiao-t'un and Cheng-chou, such as the walled enclosure and the temples and altars, were probably built by large groups of people, organized and directed by administrative agencies. The construction of the large royal tombs at Hsi-pei-kang, An-yang, is of particular interest in this connection.

The social institutions that governed the aristocracy and its auxiliary groups, as indicated by the archaeological evidence and the oracle bone inscriptions, were as follows: Marriage in the royal family was as a rule monogamous. The families of the Royal House, the nobility, and some of the craftsmen were of the extended family type, probably patrilineal. Beyond the family, unilinear lineages may have been prevalent among the nobility and some of the craftsmen; these were possibly segmentary lineages based on patrilineality and primogeniture (see below). The lineage system may have been related to a part of the class structure. The kinship terminology of the royal family was possibly of the generation type.

The organization of the royal family is relatively clear. According to the Yin calendar of rituals, as recorded in the oracle bone inscriptions, each king had one particular spouse.

> *P'i* (grandmothers and female ancestors) was partnered to *tsu* (grandfathers and male ancestors), *mu* (mothers) partnered to *fu* (fathers), and *fu* (daughters-in-law) partnered to *tzu* (sons). Each man usually had only one official spouse. Among all the fathers, one, and one only, had an especially supreme status, and his spouse also had supreme status. The family descent and the calendar of rituals were both based on patrilineality.

The families of the nobility seem to be of the extended type. Their domiciliary house can be represented by the foundation A4 at Hsiao-t'un, which is 28.4 meters long and 8 meters wide, and is divided into two large halls and eleven small rooms, all connected by doors.

There is little question that lineages existed during the Yin Dynasty. But what kind of lineage organization it was is a baffling matter. It is clear that in Yin times the principle of primogeniture played an important role, and that the order of seniority of birth was duly symbolized in the order of rituals and the classification of temples and altars into grand and lesser lines. It is therefore possible that the so-called *tsung-fa* system of kinship, well known to be characteristic of the Chou Dynasty, had already started in the Yin stage, and that the Yin lineages were somewhat like the ramage system characterized by Raymond Firth and Marshall Sahlins, or the stratified lineage named by Morton Fried. This system is characterized above all by the close correlation of political status with kinship descent; i.e. an individual's rank within the clan is determined by his consanguineal proximity to the alleged main line of descent.

The highly organized ceremonial patterns of the Yin Dynasty essentially carried on the Neolithic heritage, as indicated by an institutionalized ancestor worship, the practice of scapulimancy, and the elaboration of ceremonial objects, especially vessels. But by Yin times, the ceremonial structure of society had been very much intensified and was unmistakably tied up with the aristocracy. Priests, whose main duty was probably to divine and foretell events, served the royal court; the elaborate and sophisticated ceremonial bronze vessels were apparently used for rituals performed for the Royal House according to an annual calendar, mainly rituals of ancestor worship; the ceremonial center of the An-yang settlement group was spatially identified with the administrative center (Hsiao-t'un); and large-scale human and animal sacrifice was offered for the royal family.

In this manner the ceremonial structure was possibly correlated with the kinship structure on the one hand and with the economic system on the other. Ancestral worship was stressed and the calendar of ancestral worship rituals was carefully scheduled, reminding of and reinforcing the rules of primogeniture, the supremacy of the grand lineages, and the ramification of the lesser lineages, which became more and more degraded with each succeeding generation. The king, at the top of the hierarchal clan, was the supreme ruler of the kingdom and of the clan and also the focus of attention for all rituals. The relationship among the various settlement groups of the Yin Kingdom was thus not only economically based (concentration and redistribution) but also accounted for in terms of kinship, and sanctioned and reinforced by rituals.

The craftsmen

At the Shang cities, craftsmen were physically identified with both farmers and the aristocracy, since the industrial quarters were distributed among the farming villages in the suburbs as well as near the palatial nuclei. Our knowledge about these men is rather limited, but we know that industry was a minutely specialized affair, that each settlement group had a number of industrial centers at the service of the aristocracy to provide for the whole settlement, that the craftsmen probably enjoyed a higher status than the farmers by virtue of their special skill and knowledge, and that various handicrafts may have been tied to kin groups. It is mentioned in the "Chronicle of the Fourth Year of Ting Kung" (of Lu State in the Spring-Atumn Period) in *Tso Chuan* that "after Wu Wang [of the Chou] conquered the Shang, Ch'eng Wang established the regime and selected men of wisdom and virtue and made them feudal lords to protect the Royal Chou." To each of the lords Ch'eng Wang is said to have given a number of *tsu* (= minimal lineage), and the names of the *tsu* mentioned here included words for a drinking utensil, pottery, flag, and pots and pans. This passage shows that during the Shang Dynasty, handicraft was possibly a kin group affair. Some of the lineages specialized in particular branches of handicrafts, either as a supplement to agriculture or full time. The Cheng-chou potters, as mentioned above, seem to have devoted full time to a special kind of pottery, whereas other kinds of ceramics probably were the business of other groups. The skills and special technical knowledge were probably passed down within the kin groups and, because of this, the members of the group may have enjoyed certain privileges that the farmers did not have. At Cheng-chou the bronzesmiths and potters lived in above-ground stamped-earth houses which were usually associated with the nobility. The bronzesmiths' dwellings found in the region north of Tzu-ching-shan in Cheng-chou consist of four houses:

> Each house is partitioned by a wall into two rooms. The two rooms are connected by a door. The two rooms may both have had a door to communicate with the outside, or only one of them may have had. Each room has an earth platform by the door, and a fireplace.

Furthermore, these four houses are arranged according to a definite plan, and each is separated from the next by a distance 10 or 11 meters. These facts may indicate that the bronzesmiths' families were of the extended type, and that their households belonged to the same patrilineage, a conclusion in complete agreement with the historic records concerning the lineage-occupation linkage.

Ground houses have also been uncovered at An-yang in association with the bronze technology. In 1959 and 1960 at the site of Miao-p'u-pei-ti, southeast of Hsiao-t'un, a number of ground-house floors were located, many of which were associated with clay molds. A large floor (more than 8 m long and 4 m wide), partitioned into two rooms, was built on a layer of *hang-t'u*, and the walls were also constructed by the *hang-t'u* technique. Posts were based on rocks here in the same manner as in the Hsiao-t'un palaces and temples. In the house, near the entrance, is a gourd-shaped pit, probably a hearth. Surrounding the floor were found many piece molds of clay and fragments of crucibles, indicating a close connection with bronze work.

From the large number of piece molds as well as the remains of clay models, crucible fragments, and the bronze artifacts themselves, the techniques of bronze-making are well understood. Flat bronze implements such as knives and *ko* halberds were probably manufactured with the aid of a single mold or a two-piece mold into which molten copper and tin were poured. Hollow implements of plain form, such as axes, were also relatively simply made, with an outer mold and an inner core. The complicated vessels, especially large ones and those with cast decorative designs (a square *ting* from An-yang is 137 cm high, 110 cm long, 77 cm wide, and 700 kg in weight), involved a more complex process.

> A bronze casting is simply a replica in bronze of a model created in another medium. In the Western tradition this model has typically been made of wax on a clay core, then sheathed in a solid clay outer mold, melted out and replaced with molten bronze [the so-called lost-wax method]. In ancient China, on the contrary, it appears that the model was made of *clay* (and perhaps of other infusible materials such as wood) around a clay core and that the outer mold was not solid and continuous but segmented. This seg- mentation (making the outer mold a "piece mold") was necessitated by the fact that the baked clay model, unlike its wax counterpart, could not be melted out but had to be removed bodily. Thus when the mold segments have received the imprint of the model they are detached from it, the model is broken or scraped away from the core, and the mold segments are reassembled around the core ready to receive the molten bronze in the now hollow interstice between the two.

This multiple piece-mold process of the Shang is what has convinced Noel Barnard that bronze metallurgy independently emerged in China, but Wilma Fairbank goes so far as to see it as a far more complex application of the rudimentary bronze metallurgical principles for processing ores and alloying, heating, and pouring the metal—which may or may not have been diffused into China from the West—made possible by the superior ceramic craftsmanship of the Chinese.

Perhaps the high social status apparently enjoyed by the bronzesmiths resulted from the association of bronze artifacts with the upper class. During the Yin phase of the Shang civilization at least, the bronze artifacts were made for the most part for exclusive pur- poses like ceremonies, warfare, and hunting. On the other hand, practically all the tools and implements for such basic subsistence purposes as agriculture and domestic utility continued to be made of wood, stone, clay, or bone. In all likelihood the industrial specialization at this time was tightly correlated with status differentiation.

Archaeologically substantiated handicrafts (whose "workshops" have been dis- covered) include manufacture of bronzes, pottery, and stone and bone artifacts, and possibly wine-making. Other professions that can be inferred from archaeological remains or have been mentioned in the oracle bone inscriptions include carpentry, sculpture, earth construction, masonry, manufacture of drinking utensils, chariots, and weapons, tailoring, fabric-making, and flag-making. Their extent of specialization seems to vary, and they had clienteles of differing social status.

The farmers

The Shang subsistence was based on agriculture and supplemented by hunting and fishing. Remains of crops of the Shang period have been found at Cheng-chou, An-yang, and Hsing-t'ai, but have not been specified. From the oracle bone inscriptions it can be determined that millet (probably both *Setaria* and *Panicum*), rice, and wheat were planted. Little is known about the cultivation techniques except that stone hoes, spades, and sickles were used, as well as a kind of large wooden digging stick which may have been pushed by men or pulled by cattle and dogs, and was possibly a prototype of the plow. Two crops of millet and rice were harvested each year, and irrigation was probably employed, although the connection of the water ditches discovered at An-yang and Cheng-chou with irrigation has not been satisfactorily demonstrated. Those at Hsiao-t'un, at least, are not likely to have been connected with irrigation. Fertilizers may have been used, but this again is by no means certain. An elaborate agricultural calendar was developed. Other archaeological finds connected with farming include pestles and mortars. Among the cultivated materials for fabrics were hemp and silk. In the domestication of animals the Shang carried on the Neolithic heritage (pigs, dogs, cattle, sheep, horses, and chickens), with some additions (water buffalo) and modifications (as the use of dogs, cattle, and sheep for sacrifice and horses for chariot warfare).

Fishing is indicated by fishbones, fishhooks, and the scripts for fishnets and fish-hooks. Hunting is indicated by the large quantity of wild animal bone remains (tiger, leopard, bear, rhinoceros, deer, water deer, hare, etc.), by the remains of stone and bronze arrowheads, by the hunting records in the oracle bone inscriptions, and by the animal designs in the decorative art. However, the part played in the basic subsistence by hunting may not have been very significant. According to Li Chi, the "game huntings mentioned in the ancient inscriptions were evidently pursued for pleasure and excitement rather than for economic necessity . . . Such pursuits were the monopolies of a privileged class."

There is no question that agriculture was the basis of Shang subsistence, or that the techniques were highly developed and the yield considerable. In the suburbs of Cheng-chou and An-yang, the many residential hamlets were presumably occupied by farmers who tilled the fields in the neighborhood. One controversial point among Shang specialists is whether the direct participants in agricultural production were free farmers or slaves. It is known that live slaves suffering from malnutrition, possibly war captives, were sacrificed in the construction of palaces, temples, and royal tombs, were buried dead or alive with the royal body in the royal tomb, and that their bones were used for the manufacture of artifacts. But whether slaves were the sole laborers in the farming fields is not known. Amano suggests that during the Yin Dynasty there were two kinds of fields: the royal field, cultivated by slaves under centralized management, and the clan fields cultivated by the lower classes of clan members. This theory may have some truth in it, but no thorough general conclusion is yet in sight.

Created and sustained by people of all these categories, in concert if not in harmony, the Shang civilization by the Yin period at the latest achieved both distinction and great-ness, placing it among the civilized giants of the ancient world. It can best be recognized through its art and religion—those complexes of culture through which the Shang ex-pressed their minds about the world around them and indicated to us how the various aspects of their lives could be articulated.

For much of the Shang religion and ritual we must resort to the information that only written records provide, but archaeology is rich in religious symbols and ritual art.

Shang domiciles, palaces, temples, and tombs alike were invariably square or oblong, governed in orientation by the four cardinal directions and dominated in design by a persistent attempt at symmetry. The ancestral temples in Section B at Hsiao-t'un were constructed in two north-south rows facing each other east and west, with an earthen altar at the northern end to provide focus; the Hsi-pei-kang royal tombs, neatly square and angular themselves, formed an eastern and a western half. In the decorative art of the bronzes "there is never any asymmetry," and in inscribing the plastral shells of turtles after a divination the messages were repeated on the left and the right sides. As shown in the *chia ku* scripts, the world is square, and each of the four directions probably had its own symbolic color and certainly its own deity with its own name; winds blown from the four directions were the deities' agents, and countries beyond the kingdom were grouped into four directional classes.

Above the four directional deities—and also deities of sun, moon, earth, mountains, clouds, rivers, and other natural beings—was a Shang Ti, Supreme God on High, who presided over a court consisting usually of five ministers. He was all-powerful, controlling human affairs large and small, but he was never directly sacrificed to or specifically located. With all deities and, especially with Shang Ti, ancestors of the royal lineages were in constant and easy communication, and plastromancy and scapulimancy were the means by which living man achieved communication with the ancestors in the other world. Probably carrying on an ancient shamanistic tradition, the Shang had access to the other world through animal agents. In death, the nobleman's living possessions were buried with him in his chamber of eternal rest; in life, he burned animal bones to reach the ears of his ancestors and performed ancestral worship rites, using utensils covered with animal images.

Shang art, in other media as well as in bronze, was "an art that exclusively worked with animal motifs." Images and forms of animals—serpent, dragon, phoenix, owl, falcon, tiger, sheep, oxen, buffalo, cicada, elephant, rhinoceros, among others—and their bodily parts, in realistic or stylistic motifs, permeated Shang ritual art on bronze vessels, stone sculptures, bone, jade, and ivory carvings, white pottery, plastic clay, and wood carvings with stone and bone inlays. Human images constituted another significant category of artistic work. The interrelationship of animal and human images in Shang art is an interesting topic whose significance, however, will not become explicit until after we have observed, in the next chapter, how it changed during the subsequent Chou period.

Bernard Karlgren has isolated a number of bronze decorative motifs and analyzed the distribution patterns of these motifs in the total decor of complete vessels of Shang types. Finding that some motifs tend to be associated with one another but to be excluded from other motifs, Karlgren has constructed two contrasting styles that he calls A and B, each consisting of a number of motifs. Both A and B styles were components of the same Shang art, for "the intimate connection between all the classes of both styles is emphasized by a series of 'neutral' elements which constitute constantly recurring paraphernalia of the bronze decor and which appear in various classes of both A style and B style vessels." But Karlgren also believes that they were perhaps chronologically distinct (A being earlier than B in the beginning) or that they were perhaps the art styles of two contending social groups of the ruling class, each claiming a style exclusive to its own families of artisans. An analysis of the bronze motifs of vessel assemblages discovered in

Shang graves has convinced me that the A and B styles were indeed not only favored by different artisans in making the bronze vessels but were also favored by different social groups who selected these ceremonial paraphernalia for burial with their dead members, because all bronze vessels found in each grave tend to exhibit either A or B style preferences.

These studies may have revealed a significant key to the meaning of a number of apparently interrelated phenomena of Shang art, archaeology, and history. The late Tung Tso-pin was the first scholar to discover the significant internal criteria that enabled the oracle texts, fragmentary and disjoint, to be placed in a chronological sequence within the 273 years of their history at An-yang and, in so doing, was the first to bring into focus the cyclical changes of the Shang institutions—ritual calendar for one, and court etiquette for another—which he characterized as two contending traditions. I have come to notice the cyclical pattern of distribution of the temple designations of the Shang kings and their spouses in their genealogical sequence, and from this I have worked out a dualistic scheme of royal succession whereby two parallel but different groups within the Royal House alternated in ascent to the throne. This would provide a basis not only for an interpretation of the A and B styles of Shang bronzes and the two institutional traditions in the *chia ku* scripts but also explain why Hsiao-t'un had two parallel rows of temples and Hsi-pei-kang had two clusters of royal tombs. The genealogical duality of the Shang kings would dictate a division of the eleven Shang kings at An-yang (again excluding the last king, who presumably was not buried in the same manner as his eleven predecessors) into a left (eastern) cluster of four and a right (western) cluster of seven, which is exactly what we find at Hsi-pei-kang. Many of these dualistic phenomena are identical with the essential features of the so-called *chao mu* institution of the Chou, a point worthy of attention in discussing the Shang—Chou cultural identity in the next chapter.

Notes

1For a comprehensive and authoritative survey of the pre-Ch'in literature see Ch'ien Tsun-hsün, *Written on Bamboo and Silk,* Univ. Chicago Press, 1962. See also Hsün Cho-yün, *Ancient China in Transition,* Stanford Univ. Press, 1965, pp. 183-92.

2For mythology in ancient China, see Marcel Granet, *Danses et légendes de la Chine ancienne,* Paris, Felix Alcan, 1926; Henri Maspero, *Jour. Asiatique, 204* (1924), 1-100; Bernhard Karlgren, *BMFEA, 18* (1946), 199-365; Derk Bodde, "China," in *Mythologies of the Ancient World,* New York, Doubleday, 1961; Yang K'uan, *Ku Shih Pien, 7,* 1941; Hsüan Chu, *Chung-kuo Shen-hua Yen-chiu ABC,* Shanghai, Shih-chieh Book Co., 1929.

Part VIII

The Old World: Europe

Ruth Tringham received her Ph.D. from Edinburgh University in 1966 and now is assistant professor of anthropology and Assistant Curator of European Archaeology at the Peabody Museum, Harvard University. She has participated in archaeological expeditions in Czechoslovakia, Russia, and is currently directing a project in Yugoslavia. Her recent book *Hunters, Fishers and Farmers of Eastern Europe 6000-3000 B.C.* (1971) is a long awaited and masterful summary of this area. Her contribution to this volume has not been previously published.

The Concept of "Civilization" in European Archaeology

Ruth Tringham

"Why 'Savage Europe'?" asked a friend who recently witnessed my departure from Charing Cross for the Near East.

"Because," I replied, "the term accurately describes the wild and lawless countries between the Adriatic and Black Seas."

For some mystic reason, however, most Englishmen are less familiar with the geography of the Balkan States than with that of Darkest Africa. This was my case, and I had therefore yet to learn that these same Balkans can boast of cities which are miniature replicas of London and Paris. But these are civilized centres. . . . Moreover, do not the new palatial capitals of Servia and Bulgaria occasionally startle the outer world with political crimes of Mediaeval barbarity?

H. deWindt, Through Savage Europe, *London, 1919*

Thus wrote a participant in West European Civilisation about barbaric Eastern Europe with a degree of patronization which cannot even be equalled by Herodotus in describing the barbarians north of Greece. (Herodotus, *The Histories,* Book IV).

But the sentiment pervades many descriptions, written by people who think themselves civilised, about societies whom they believe are not civilised. This holds true of descriptions of both present and past societies. It is certainly implicit in the works of historians and prehistorians of both the late nineteenth century (when the British Empire was at the height of its power and patronization) and the twentieth century up to the present day. Their studies are imbued with the concept of a dichotomy existing between civilised and non-civilised peoples, expressed in terms of civilised/barbarian, civilised/savage, or civilised/primitive societies. The idea which is more or less explicit is that "civilisation" implies progress or development towards a beneficial goal. "Progress" is a concept which has been closely associated with the laws of social evolution (Morgan, 1877), in which "civilisation" is seen as the ultimate stage of human development.

There have been spasmodic instances of the state of non-civilisation being regarded as the ideal, for example the concept of the Noble Savage, the movement of "back to the land," and more recently "living on this earth." So far, however, these latter movements have had little lasting effect, at least on studies of history and prehistory.

'The idea of progress is, in this modern age, one of the most important ideas by which men live, not least because most hold it unconsciously and therefore unquestioningly' (Pollard, 1971, 13). The concept of the dichotomy of civilised/non-civilised societies is frequently equally unconscious and is also a very powerful factor in the organization of research and syntheses in European archaeology. A large number of syntheses on the prehistory of Europe have been written, by far the most successful and lasting of which have been those which are organised around the themes of progress towards a more civilised world and the contrast between the civilised and non-civilised worlds. One might say that prehistorians like Lubbock, Worsaae, Childe, Piggott, Schuchhardt and G. Clark, to name only a few, used the most powerful models of culture change in prehistoric Europe available. Until very recently, no model of equal dynamism has been offered.

For Sir John Lubbock writing his treatise on *"The Origin of Civilisation"* in 1870, "civilisation" meant West European Civilisation, although he was familiar with "civilisations" in India, East Asia, and the New World. But the underlying reason for his labours, and for those of many subsequent archaeologists, historians, and art historians has been to trace the origins, emergence, rise, development, florescence, and climax of West European Civilisation of which the majority of the writers was a part. In certain cases this aim has been stated explicitly (Clark, K. 1971; Childe, 1936), but in other cases it is implicit in the organisation of their studies (Piggott, 1965).

The two associated basic models which were mentioned above result in the organisation of syntheses of European archaeology into two parts. The first recurring theme is the cultural connection between the Near East and the east Mediterranean basin, and the diffusion of techniques, equipment, and "civilisation" from the Near East to the east and then west Mediterranean. The second theme is to trace the influence of the latter on the cultural development and change among the non-civilised barbarian societies of temperate Europe. (Childe, 1925; 1936; 1942; 1958 ; Schuchhardt, 1926, Clark, 1969; Piggott, 1965; Clark & Piggott, 1965; Nestor, 1970) Thus in every case the Mediterranean "civilisations" of Greece and Italy are seen as acting as a bridge carrying "civilisation" from the Near East to temperate Europe, providing the foundations of European civilisation:

> But once the new economy [urban civilisation] had been established in the
> three primary centres, it spread thence to secondary centres, much like
> Western capitalism spread to colonies and economic dependencies. First on
> the borders of Egypt, Babylonia, and the Indus Valley—in Crete and the
> Greek Islands, Syria, Assyria, Iran and Baluchistan—then further afield, on
> the Greek mainland, the Anatolian plateau, South Russia, we see villages
> converted into cities and self-sufficient food-producers turning to industrial
> specialisation and external trade. And the process is repeated in ever-
> widening circles around each secondary and tertiary centre. (Childe, 1936,
> 169)

Childe indicates that his model for the diffusion of civilisation from the Near East to Europe was the spread of Western capitalism to the colonies, and it is possible to see that he might have been tempted by the lyrical description of this latter phenomenon written by Marx and Engels in the *Communist Manifesto* of 1847:

> The bourgeoisie has created more massive and more colossal productive forces than have all preceding generations together. . . . The need of a constantly expanding market for its products drives the bourgeoisie over the whole sur- face of the globe . . . by the rapid improvement of all instruments of pro- duction, by the vastly easier means of communication [it] draws all, even the most barbarian, nations into civilisation. . . . It compels them to introduce what it calls civilisation into their midst, i.e. to become bourgeois themselves. In one word, it creates a world after its own image.

There is no doubt, however, in the minds of any of the archaeologists that in the prehistoric period, i.e. before the Christian conversion, in temperate Europe, no societies which could be termed "civilised" in the definition of Childe (1950; 1951, 161) or Kluckhohn (1960) existed:

> Meanwhile, in central Europe [Late Bronze Age], a vigorous if barbarian culture had grown up, with a highly competent and technologically ad- venturous tradition in working true bronze. (Clark & Piggott, 1965, 295)

> However squalid and barbarous the material culture with which we are concerned may appear at first sight, it is recognizably the product of societies differing in degree rather than in kind from those of the Iliad and the Odyssey. . . . Agricultural in basic economy, a pattern of farm- steads and villages and rustic princelings' courts. . . . It is a Heroic Society, with all the barbarity and insecurity that such a condition involves, the antithesis of the corporate civic life which out of Oriental seed was now striking new roots in the Aegean. (Clark & Piggott, 1965, 304)

Thus for *prehistoric* archaeologists in Europe, following Childe's definition of "civilisation," as well as that of Morgan, there is no "civilisation" in temperate Europe, only its "foundations" (e.g. Clark, G., 1969, Childe, 1958). The sole representatives of "civilisation" to be found in Europe in prehistory are those of the Mediterranean basin in Greece and Italy.

For many historians and archaeologists the spread of "civilisation" to temperate Europe is associated with the diffusion of Christianity. In addition to the diffusion of a unified religion, Christianity brought along with it two of Kluckhohn's three and Childe's ten criteria of "civilisation": a written language and monumental ceremonial centres. Without the force of the Christian church, the Roman and Classical Greek civilisations were able to have no lasting "civilising" effect on the barbarians of temperate Europe:

> . . . barbarian Europe outside their frontiers was a direct continuation of Bronze Age Europe. . . . In the sequel centralised empires were never permanent enough, and seldom efficient enough to root out fissiparous traditions of local autonomy. (Childe, 1958, 172)

During the late first millennium A.D., the agents of the Christian Church, both Western and Eastern, had succeeded in spreading over most of temperate Europe, even to "the fissiparous traditions of local autonomy," many of the characteristic features of what Sir Kenneth Clark calls Western Civilisation or even just "Civilisation." These include not only the written language and monumental architecture, but also the objects of individual creative genius expressed through various media. As Engels has succinctly put it:

> Civilisation achieved things which gentile [barbaric] society was not even remotely capable. But it achieved them by setting in motion the lowest instincts and passions in man and developing them at the expense of all his other abilities. From its first day to this, sheer greed was the driving spirit of civilisation; wealth, and again wealth and once more wealth, wealth, not of society but of the single scurvy individual—here was its one and final aim. If at the same time the progressive development of science and a repeated flowering of supreme art dropped into its lap, it was only because without them modern wealth could not have completely realized its achievements. (Engels, 1891)

The characteristic features of Western Civilisation are generally thought to have been directly developed from the "civilisations" of Greece and Rome along with a "Hebrew component." For this reason it is thought to be an essential prerequisite of studying Western Civilisation to study not only the "civilisations" of Classical Greece and Rome, the immediate chronological predecessors of Mediaeval Europe, but also *their* predecessors: the Etruscan and Mycenaean-Minoan civilisations, and those of the Ancient Near East.

There are some very striking differences between the methods of studying societies in non-civilised temperate Europe and those used in studying civilised temperate Europe. These differences go beyond those usually discussed with reference to methods of history and archaeology, and the differences concern the various definitions of "civilisation." Archaeologists and anthropologists have frequently been very precise and explicit in their definition of "civilisation" and its symptoms. (Kroeber, 1962; Childe, 1950; 1951; Kluckhohn, 1960; Morgan, 1877). Among all their definitions and symptoms of "civilisation," it is clear that for all of them "civilisation" is one kind of culture, it is a particular kind of set—a very complex set—of behavioural patterns representing the whole known range of activities of a particular society. In this way, archaeologists studying ancient civilisations and prehistoric "foundations of civilisations" investigate not only the artistic and written works of the society, not only its monumental architecture, but also its settlement pattern, its technology, economy, social organization, political organization, trade, and communications systems, etc.

"Civilisation" in the West European Civilisation sense, on the other hand, does not necessarily have the same definition. For many authors writing about this phenomenon, "civilisation" refers to some ethereal superstructure of a society expressed in works of creative genius, intellectual endeavour and so on, which affect our senses with pleasurable emotions. For Sir Kenneth Clark, "civilisation" clearly means something very different from Marx and Engels.

Assuming, for the moment, that "civilisation" is a useful concept, in order to compare the rise and diffusion of civilisation in the Near East, or East Asia, or the New World with that in Early Mediaeval temperate Europe, or in order to trace the development of civilisation in temperate Europe, it would be necessary to take one or both of two alternative steps. Firstly it is possible to consult the few historians and political scientists, for example Marx and Engels and their successors, who are interested in the term "civilisation" and its socio-economic criteria. Secondly, it is possible to consult historians and mediaeval archaeologists who rarely use the concept of "civilisation" but are nevertheless interested in tracing the development of complex urban societies in temperate Europe. (e.g. Burckhart, 1929; de Coulanges, 1864)

This brings us to the question: Is the concept of "civilisation," as defined by V. Gordon Childe, useful in European archaeology? In his definition of "civilisation," Childe suggested at least ten criteria, including urban settlements, written language, state religion with associated monumental public buildings, social stratification, and craft specialisation (Childe, 1950, 1951). It has been shown that many of the cultures regarded as "civilisations" do not have evidence of certain of Childe's criteria (Daniel, 1968). On the other hand, in temperate Europe there are societies which exhibit certain of Childe's criteria and yet are not considered civilisations (except perhaps by the excavators). Examples of these include evidence of written symbols found at Tărtăria in Rumania (Vlassa, 1963; Hood, 1967), monumental architecture at Stonehenge and Malta which could be interpreted as being associated with a "state religion" (Renfrew, 1972, 7), evidence of urban settlements in Bronze Age and Iron Age Europe in association with craft specialisation and social organization (Pittioni, 1962, 225; Moberg, 1962), and evidence of higher mathematics and astronomy in Bronze Age Britain (Hawkins, 1965).

There have been at least three significant results of the employment of the concept of "civilisation" in European archaeology.

Firstly, and most importantly, the classification of the Mediterranean societies of Greece and Italy in the Bronze Age as "civilised" has tended to set them up in contrast to the mass of "uncivilised" or "barbaric" societies of temperate Europe, a contrast which may be entirely false, in which differences between the cultures of the two areas have been exaggerated and similarities and interaction which may have existed have been ignored, or not even investigated.

Secondly, the term "civilisation," with its connotation of progress, encourages unconscious value-judgments in favour of "civilisation," and the idea that "barbarians" or peasants were most likely to adopt those social, economic, and technological innovations which would enable them to approach more closely the state of "civilisation". The cultures of Europe and the Near East have been classified, in some cases more consciously than in others, into "high" and "low" cultures, in which it was assumed that the "high" cultures had more to offer the "low" cultures in terms of innovations than *vice versa*. The result was the exaggeration of the use of the concept of diffusion, so that almost every instance of culture change in "barbarian" temperate Europe was explained as the result of diffusion of innovations from the "high cultures" or "civilisation" of the Near East and the Mediterranean.

Finally, with the investigation of the origin, foundation, and spread of civilisation being in the mainstream, implicitly or explicitly, of much European prehistory, there has been a tendency for "less interesting" or "marginal" areas to receive less attention, less research time, and less financial aid. Thus a settlement with evidence of food-production is "more interesting" to investigate than a contemporary one whose subsistence is based on hunting and fishing, because it is in the direct line of progress towards civilisation (Hawkes, 1939, 70). It even happens that the art history concept of "civilisation" described above filters through into archaeological research programmes, so that a site which produces stone sculptures or large clay figurines is thought more worthy of attention since they provide evidence of the roots of civilisation. A site whose "art material" is not so rich but provides excellent information on subsistence economy is regarded as less spectacular and less worthy of interest.

Closely related to this and the preceding two assumptions is the notion that civilisations or complex societies are more interesting to investigate than simple ones because, for various assumed reasons, the former engage in activities which are not only directly connected with "problems of securing food and shelter":

> In many simple societies the majority of people are closely involved in ensuring adequate food supply; . . a close study of the subsistence basis of such a community . . . tells the archaeologist much of what he wishes to learn about them. For more complex societies this is no longer enough. An understanding of the subsistence base is still indispensable to an understanding of an early civilisation-state, but what distinguishes it from its early formative or neolithic predecessor . . . is dependent rather more on the interactions between human individuals and between human groups than upon those between humans and the natural environment, although these still provide the raw materials and energy resources for the society. In other words many of the crucial developments are *social* ones, and the ecological approach, or a study of the technology, are not in themselves enough. (Renfrew, 1973).

As if the "ecological approach, or a study of technology" provide the only information on "simple" societies! There is evidence enough of complex mechanisms of interpersonal behaviour in living so-called "simple" societies, for example Australian aborigines. It is very difficult to find evidence of such behaviour in the archaeological remains of pre-literate societies of temperate Europe, many archaeologists in Europe would say it is impossible (Hawkes, 1954; Piggott, 1972). But this is not to say that such behaviour did not exist!

The three powerful assumptions described above, which underly so much of European archaeological research, not only syntheses but also specific problem and area studies and even research designs, are the direct result of the employment of the concept of "civilisation" and the civilisation/non-civilisation dichotomy as the basic explanatory model of culture change and "culture contact" in European prehistory and ancient history. The model underlies even the period before the first "emergence" of the earliest Near Eastern civilisations with the explanations of the beginning of agriculture in Europe. But it becomes especially explicit in those works discussing the prehistory of Europe from the end of the second millennium B.C., with the emergence of the earliest civilisations on the south-eastern edge of Europe. The model continues to be prevalent in the explanation of culture change in the late Roman Empire, in the so-called Migration

Period or Dark Ages, and even after the "spread of civilisation" to temperate Europe, with the C16 Mongol invasions of eastern Europe. The themes include especially the ever-useful concept of the "invading barbarian horde," but also trade with and partial civilisation of the "barbarians."

The contrast between the barbarians of temperate Europe and the civilised world of the Mediterranean and the Near East has been particularly clearly stressed in four periods of European prehistory:

1) Disturbances to the civilised world of the Near East and the emerging East Mediterranean civilisation in the late third millennium B.C. caused by "movements of Indo-European speaking pastoralist tribes."

2) Intensified trade interaction between the "barbarian chiefdoms" of Bronze Age temperate Europe and the Minoan-Mycenaean civilisation of the East Mediterranean.

3) The "proto-Celtic" Urnfield and Halstatt cultures of west and central temperate Europe and the Scythian barbarians on the northern borders of the expanding Classical Greek and Etruscan civilisations.

4) The Roman Empire and the "barbarians beyond the frontier."

Quotations and a brief description must suffice to indicate in a short space the wealth and variety of imaginative speculation which have been offered on the relationships and contrast between the civilised and non-civilised worlds in each of these periods.

> The last centuries of the third millennium B.C. were times of stress and trouble for the two great powers of Sumer and Egypt. . . . It is clear that the Near East and the Aegean, by a series of related circumstances whereby barbarian movements were temporarily favoured by the weakened power of the great states, were jolted into an uneasy condition of change and conflict. . . . we can infer from the archaeological evidence that widespread movements of peoples were affecting Europe beyond the Aegean shores, and that some at least of the events of the late third millennium B.C. were connected with peoples speaking languages of the Indo-European language group. (Piggott, 1965, 77-78)

Complicated mechanisms have been suggested by Piggott whereby the barbarian movements against the civilised world indirectly led to the establishment of copper- and bronze-working in Europe immediately after this period, for example "a movement of craftsmen, losing their patrons by civil disruption, escaping from impending violence or carried by capture into alien service" from the troubles of the civilised world to the new pastoralist chieftain patrons of temperate Europe.

The problem becomes complicated by the desire of many archaeologists to equate the evidence of stress and trouble in the Near Eastern civilisations with long distance movement of peoples who can be identified as Indo-European speakers at the end of the third millennium B.C. Many desire to see a similar spread of Indo-European languages, through the agent of moving pastoralist tribes, into Europe at the same time. Thus a parallel dichotomy exists in this period in European prehistory comprising pastoralist-barbarians/agricultural-peasant-barbarians, alongside the pastoralist-barbarian/civilised-world dichotomy. For the explanation of culture change in the end of the third millennium B.C., therefore, the former concept is as important as the latter. But in both, there is an underlying assumption which could be very false, and could, in fact, have distorted all the explanations of culture change in European prehistory in this period. It has been unquestionably assumed (a) that the Indo-Europeans were nomadic pastoralists, and (b) that archaeological evidence of the late third millennium B.C. in temperate Europe, particularly the eastern and northern part, indicates nomadic pastoralist tribes in a state of large-scale movement. (Gimbutas, 1970) "Pastoralism" involves an enormous variety of subsistence mechanisms and population movements. To describe a society as "nomadic pastoralist" means very little, and to base a whole theory of culture change upon this general term means even less (Goodenough, 1970). In fact there is very little positive evidence in the archaeological record of large-scale population movements or pastoralist societies in temperate Europe in this period. Thus the dichotomy between the peasants and the pastoralists, on the one hand, and the pastoralists and the civilised world, on the other, may be exaggerated and in certain cases non-existent.

Whereas speculation on the character of the "barbarism" of the east European "pastoralist nomads" is rather obscure, that on the Bronze Age barbarians of temperate Europe who are contrasted with the Minoan-Mycenaean civilisation is very rich. The basis of much of the inferences can be found in references to Homer's description of his Mycenaean heroes.

> The background of Bronze Age Europe provides a setting for a scene which suddenly takes on a familiar aspect, for we are, in the early second millennium, at the prologue of a play whose main action is set in the world of Homer. (Clark & Piggot, 1965, 304)

> The nobility of the hexameters should not deceive us into thinking that the *Iliad* and the *Odyssey* are other than the poems of a largely barbarian Bronze Age or Early Iron Age Europe. (Piggott, 1965, 126)

The situation of Mycenae, and whether it should or should not be called "civilisation," aggravates the whole problem of the usefulness of the concept of "civilisation" in Europe. Each archaeologist dealing with the subject has found it necessary to take a good deal of effort to justify the use of the term for Mycenae:

> So it is really the wealth of the finds, and the magnificence of their craftsmanship, which has earned the designation "civilisation" for the early Mycenaean period. But clearly, on the operative criteria of Kluckhohn, its use is not merited until the emergence of the palaces and the effective use of writing a couple of centuries later. . . . At present it is difficult to decide, using the criteria defined, at just what date Mycenaean culture became "civilised". (Renfrew, 1972, 49)

> While we should be on our guard against over-rating the degree of sophistication achieved, we should equally beware of placing too wide a gulf between the early Mycenaean world, before literacy and bureaucracy had been acquired from Crete, and the contemporary societies in central or eastern Europe. (Piggott, 1965, 126)

Thus the Mycenaean culture falls short of the standard we have laid down

for civilisation. After all, the little citadels with a cluster of hamlets
outside their walls belong to a different order of magnitude from the
Bronze Age cities of Mesopotamia. . . . For all their specialised craftsmen
and merchants they are not cities. (Childe, 1951, 52)

This surely must be a very clear illustration of a set of archaeologists trying to fight
against the limits which are being imposed on their interpretation by the dogma of
their own typology, in this case the typology of cultures. In spite of the large amount of
archaeological evidence, and the warnings such as those given by Piggott, the unconscious
explanation of culture change in terms of diffusion, stimulus or "influence" from a
"high" culture to a "low" culture takes over. The possibility of looking at Bronze Age
Europe in terms of interacting culture systems or "interaction spheres" is lost, and the
"antithetical relation between civilisation and barbarism" is back:

The commercial system [of Bronze Age Europe] had been called into being
to supply the Aegean market. . . . Once established, the machinery could
profitably be used to supply the demands of metal gear of barbarian societies
living on or near its routes. . . . [The Bronze Age chieftains of central Europe]
concentrated enough wealth to form stimulating markets and as patrons to
encourage craftsmanship, but certainly not enough to promote unaided the
mining developments in the Austrian Alps. . . . On the other hand, the peasant
villages of Central Europe were now large enough and prosperous enough to
constitute effective markets for craft products and metal wares once the
initial difficulty of starting up the extractive and distributive industries had
been overcome by the proximity of the Aegean market. (Childe, 1958, 163-
168)

Very recently, Colin Renfrew has been consistently reacting against the idea of the
Mediterranean civilisations being indirectly or directly responsible for all the technological
innovations and economic growth of Bronze Age temperate Europe. He has attempted to
show in a number of ways that, in southern Britain at least, the social organization and
economic development was enough to be responsible for the high level of metal technology,
and monumental architecture such as Stonehenge, and that even if this society need not
be termed a "civilisation," it was an independently developed culture. (Renfrew, 1968,
1970) His argument loses much of its power, as I have argued elsewhere (Tringham, 1973)
as a result of two factors. On the one hand he stresses the autonomy of the British Bronze
Age to such an extent that there is the danger of an equally exaggerated explanation of
culture change being employed, i.e. one of complete autonomous evolution, with the
cultural activities of the south British Wessex culture acting as closed systems. On the
other hand, the evidence which he cites is frequently not convincing enough to support
his very cogent argument.

And yet his argument for societies in temperate Europe who were independent of
and interacting with the Aegean "civilisations" is a very attractive one. It is worth
noting, in fact, that evidence of such societies is presently much more available from
Early and Middle Bronze Age central Europe, for example the "fortified" upland settlements of the Late Unětice culture, such as Veterov and Madarovce, and of the Otomani
culture (Tringham, 1972).The settlements are as large as those of the Mycenaean "civili-

sation," and may possibly comprise hierarchical networks of settlements, which were almost proto-urban in character. They are closely associated with the exploitation and distribution of metal resources, and the complexity of their technological and economic subsystems hardly differs in degree from that of Mycenae. (Gimbutas, 1965) They lack monumental stone architecture and writing, and have thus fallen on the "lower" side of the barbarian/civilised antithesis.

During the period of the development of the Classical Greek civilisation and the "emergence" of the Etruscan civilisation in Italy in the mid-first millennium B.C., the escalation of the speed and degree of culture change in the Mediterranean Basin becomes very clear. At the same time, a similar escalation of change can be seen in the barbarian societies with the Urnfield and Halstatt Iron Age cultures of central Europe. Many of their settlements clearly show evidence of a hierarchical network, and may be regarded as more or less urban (Moberg, 1962). Escalating increase and change in population density, production economy, and communication and exchange systems have again generally been studied in the context of increasing "contact" with the Mediterranean civilisations. They have rarely been studied in terms of processes of systemic change:

> [By the eighth century B.C.] Europe north of the Alps was beginning to take
> on its familiar aspect as the territory of barbarians outside the bounds of the
> civilised Mediterranean world, and much of its ensuing story is told in terms
> of the commercial and political relationships inherent in such a situation. . . .
> By the early seventh century . . . settlements, fortifications and richly furnished
> graves . . . show us a stratified society in which, on a secure agricultural
> basis, the warrior aristocracy . . . now becomes a demonstrable and insistent
> feature. It is a phase in which contacts with the civilised world become
> numerous. (Clark & Piggott, 1965, 316-318)

East of the "warrior aristocracies" of the Halstatt and La Tène cultures of central Europe, there is evidence of even greater changes in the societies of the S. Russian steppes and forest-steppes. Evidence of horse-riding nomadic pastoralists becomes increasingly common from the sixth century B.C. onwards. On the basis of historical accounts (Herodotus) and archaeological material, the pastoralists, (Cimmerians and then Scythians) are thought to have invaded south Russia from the lower Volga and Kuban area to the east. The same evidence, however, could be interpreted not in terms of population movement, but in terms of mixed farmers undergoing very rapid and marked economic and social change as a result, like the Blackfoot Indians, of the adoption of certain technological innovations including horse-riding, use of iron, and the use of the bow and arrow. There is also evidence, both archaeological and historical, that there were Scythians who were agricultural and lived in substantial settlements. In fact, when Herodotus describes the Scythians he stresses their antithesis to the civilised world much less than certain modern archaeologists referring to the same peoples. One can even find reference to "monumental structures" which are admittedly not built in what might be termed permanent materials:

> It is not their [Scythian] custom to make statues, or to build altars and
> temples, in honour of any god except Ares. . . . In every district, at the

seat of government, Ares has his temple; it is of a peculiar kind, and
consists of an immense heap of brushwood, three furlongs [app. 600 yds.]
each way and somewhat less in height. On top the heap is levelled off square,
like a platform, accessible on one side, but rising sheer on the other three.
(Herodotus, Book IV)

Herodotus then goes on to describe the sacrifices made to the sword which is planted
on top of the platform, in ritual acts vaguely reminiscent of sacrifices carried out in the
temples of the Aztec "civilisation."

Both historical sources and archaeological evidence tend to indicate that the term
"Scythian" refers to a large variety of societies with different cultures—different economic
bases, different settlement patterns, different environmental backgrounds. To follow
Herodotus blindly and call them all "Scythian" belies the fact that there is evidence of
advanced agricultural proto-urban groups as well as nomadic horse-riding pastoralists.

An anecdote of Herodotus' throws interesting light on one possible attitude of the
"barbarians" to the civilised world:

Like the Egyptians, the Scythians are dead-set against foreign ways,
especially against Greek ways. An illustration of this is what happened to
Anacharsis. . . [He] was a great traveller, . . . and was on his way home to
Scythia. . . . Anacharsis made a vow that, if he got home safe and sound,
he would celebrate a night-festival and offer sacrifice [to the Mother of the
Gods] in exactly the same way as he had seen it done at Cyzicus. On his
arrival in Scythia, he entered the Woodland . . . and went through the
ceremony with all the proper rites and observances. . . . He happened to
be noticed by some Scythian or other, who at once went and told Saulius,
the king; Saulius then came in person, and seeing Anacharsis occupied
with these outlandish rites, shot him dead. (Herodotus, Book IV)

In the final period discussed here, the antithesis of the civilised world to the barbarian
world takes a rather different form. There was a deliberate policy on the part of the Roman
Empire to convey the benefits of "civilisation" to the barbarians "beyond the frontier":

The following winter was spent on schemes of the most salutary kind.
To induce a people, hitherto scattered, uncivilised and therefore prone
to fight, to grow pleasurably inured to peace and ease, Agricola gave
private encouragement and official assistance to the building of
temples, public squares and private mansions. . . . He trained the sons
of chiefs in the liberal arts. . . . The result was that in place of distaste
for the Latin language came a passion to command it. In the same way
our National dress came into favour. . . . And so the Britons were
gradually led on to the amenities that make vice agreeable—arcades,
baths, sumptuous banquets. They spoke of such novelties as "civilisation," when really they were only a feature of enslavement.
(Tacitus, *Agricola,* 21)

Thus in a few short sentences Tacitus is able to sum up what the controversy over "civilisation" is all about. For the agents of the Roman Empire, the spread of "civilisation" was

a deliberate policy to maximise control and exploitation of the barbarians, similar to the policy carried out by the agents of the nineteenth century A.D. "bourgeois empires" described by Marx and Engels in the Communist Manifesto (see above). Archaeologists, historians, and art historians have tended to adopt the criteria of "civilisation" employed by the Roman Imperialists, and use them in discussions of the dichotomy of civilisation/barbarism of the Roman and later periods, and some of them, particularly the art historians, have even applied them to the pre-Roman period.

But the criteria used by the agents of the Roman Empire are very different from those suggested, for example, by V. Gordon Childe. The former have to do with comfort and intellectual activity, with acts of creative genius, with pleasures such as "peace and ease," whereas the latter are based on technological economic, and social complexity. And from historical sources and archaeological evidence, it would seem that many of Childe's criteria were present among the "barbarian" societies beyond the Roman Imperial frontier:

> The Roman armies came into contact with many communities in western Europe which can fairly be claimed to have had an urban character. . . . The hilltop strongholds that Caesar and his successors found in Gaul, and later Britain, were described by them as towns—*oppida*—and excavations . . . show that the term in a broad sense is justified. (Hassall, 1972, 857)

The urban character of many settlements in temperate Europe "beyond the frontiers" of the Roman Empire is becoming increasingly accepted by European archaeologists, and a few further suggest that these urban centers were not the result of stimulus or "influence" or "contact" from the towns of the Mediterranean "civilisations," but were the result of a relatively autonomous and quite different process of urban growth, which began, as has already been indicated, as early as the mid-second millennium B.C. (Alexander, 1972, 847):

> The main characteristics which seem to distinguish this from the Mediterranean urbanism . . . might be summarised as follows:
> i) Growth was due to trade and commerce, both local and long-distance, but not apparently related to immigrant trading colonies from more developed societies.
> ii) Strong links with tribal systems but not with particular potentates . . .
> iii) Communal enterprise shows particularly in the elaborate defences of the settlements . . .
> iv) A particularly ingenious and inventive metallurgical tradition whose craftsmen came to be concentrated in the settlements. The crafts are based on strong indigenous traditions.

Many other of Childe's criteria are indicated by the evidence from temperate Europe, and the problem of classification into "barbarian" or "civilised" is stressed by Stuart Piggott:

> In the world of Roman and barbarian in Europe . . . to some extent, we have conditions of technological disparity between innovating and conserving traditions, but this had been narrowed down to restricted limits, with

literacy as the greatest single factor of differentiation. . . . The moral barrier existed in terms of incompatible patterns of culture. (Piggott, 1965, 256)

In fact, Piggott regards this period as a

crisis of antithesis in Europe which we have already seen recurring in other contexts of the remoter past . . . that of the developed and underdeveloped peoples, the innovators and the conservators, presented in its acute form as the division between the civilised and the barbarian worlds of Ancient Europe. (Piggott, 1965, 255)

Until very recently no model of equal power had been offered as an alternative to that described in the pages above for explaining cultural change in prehistoric Europe. To show that the "barbarians" of temperate Europe were as "civilised," or almost as "civilised" as the societies of Mediterranean Europe is not enough. The implication that societies should be "civilised" or "uncivilised" still continues, along with all the inherent distortions for explanation of culture change which this contains. An alternative model should enable the objective comparison of cultures from the point of view, above all, of the *processes* involved in their change, whatever the level of technological, economic, social, or political complexity. Just such an alternative model has very recently been suggested by Colin Renfrew (Renfrew, 1972). His model is based on the application of systems theory to archaeological data, in quite a similar way to that used by the "anthropological archaeologists" (Flannery, 1968). He uses his model to assist in the explanation of those changes in the cultural systems of the Aegean area which led to the emergence and florescence of the "Aegean Civilisation."

It is now possible to make a statement about civilisations which does not seek to define them in terms of a single principal culture trait, or even polythetically, in terms of, for example, two out of three traits. Nor does it appeal to "form" or "culture style". We can see the process of the growth of a civilisation as the gradual creation by man of a larger and more complex environment, not only in the natural field through increasing exploitation of a wider range of resources of the ecosystem, but also in the social and spiritual fields. . . . Civilised man lives in an environment very much of his own creation. . . . All the artefacts which he uses serve as intermediaries between himself and this natural environment and, in creating civilisation, he spins . . . a web of culture so complex and so dense that most of his activities now relate to this artificial environment rather than directly to the fundamentally natural one. (Renfrew, 1972, 11)

His explanation of the emergence of "civilisation," as defined above, is what he has termed the "multiplier effect":

When the multiplier effect comes into operation, and remains in operation, there is sustained and rapid growth, not merely in the scale of the systems of the culture but in their structure. Changes in one area of human experience lead to developments in another. In this way the created environment is enlarged in many dimensions, and itself becomes more complex.

> This is . . . something more complicated than the operation of a simple
> positive feedback, causing growth and amplifying the processes already
> present: it is a feedback with coupled subsystems, favouring innovation.
> (Renfrew, 1972, 39)

He suggests that a "threshold or take-off point" is reached at which instant it is possible for the "multiplier effect" to come into operation. The explanation of how this threshold is reached will, in fact, provide the explanation of the "emergence of civilisation."

> For a "take-off" at least two systems [sub-systems] must be changing and
> mutually influencing their changes. (Renfrew, 1972, 39)

> It is accepted that societies and cultures live in a state of equilibrium. . . .
> For any *significant* [author's italics] change to take place the innovations
> must be linked in a deviation-amplifying mutual causal system: the in-
> novation produces effects which favour the further development of the
> innovation. In some cases the innovation arising in one subsystem has
> marked effects in other subsystems. . . . In such a case, if positive feed-
> back occurs, the multiplier effect can come into operation: coupled
> developments occur in both subsystems, and the innovation is favoured.
> When the structure of the subsystems is such that marked change can
> occur in them (for example when a technological threshold such as the
> invention of metal casting, or the sowing of grain, can be surmounted)
> a cultural take-off is possible. Most or all of the subsystems of the society
> will then undergo marked structural change. (Renfrew, 1972, 43)

Renfrew has applied his model only to the Aegean area, specifically to the problem of explaining the emergence of "civilisation" in the Aegean. In that this is his primary aim he is perpetuating, although I suspect unconsciously, the same civilisation/barbarism dichotomy which, as we have seen, underlies so much of European archaeology. The "take-off point" at which the "multiplier effect" went into operation in the Aegean occurred during the third millennium B.C., at a time in which the societies in the Aegean are by no means classified as "civilisations." For many "anthropological archaeologists," the fact that the "multiplier effect" led to a culture system which has been termed "civilisation" is a less interesting, one might even say less vital, topic than both the processes by which the "take-off point" was reached, and the processes involved in the escalation of speed and degree of cultural change.

The concept of "civilisation" in fact tends to distract from these "processual" thoughts, firstly for the reasons mentioned throughout this article, namely the distortions caused by the dichotomy of the developed and the underdeveloped. Secondly, "civili-sation" is regarded, even by Renfrew, as the end-product of the "multiplier effect," which tends to distract from the fact that processual change continues before, during, and after "civilisation."

Without the overriding power of the concept of "civilisation" as an end-product or an ultimate aim, it would be easier and very interesting, and I would even say essential, to apply a model such as Renfrew's to the study of culture change in prehistoric Europe (and historic Europe) as a whole. It would certainly be possible to recognise the "multiplier effect" in operation in temperate Europe in various periods of prehistory. The scale of change may be smaller in *absolute* terms in some areas (for example Bronze Age Britain) than in others (for example the Aegean). But, relative to the particular cultural system, the change may have been extremely great, for example horse-riding for the Scythians. In treating the cultural systems of Europe as open-ended interrelated sets of interrelated subsystems, undergoing continual processes of change in time and space, it would be possible to understand much more constructively and positively the interrelationships between the Mediterranean basin and temperate Europe. This is indeed a model which may be regarded as a worthy alternative to the very powerful progressive model of culture change in the archaeology of Europe—an alternative to the model which involves "civilisation" as the highest cultural development to be attained by human society.

References

Alexander, J. 1972. The beginnings of urban life in Europe. *in* Ucko, P., Tringham, R., and Dimbleby, G. (Eds.) *Man, Settlement and Urbanism*, 843-850.

Burckhart, J. 1929. *The Civilisation of the Rennaissance*, New York.

Childe, V. G. 1925. *The Dawn of European Civilisation*, London.

———— 1936. *Man Makes Himself*, London.

———— 1942. *What Happened in History*, London.

———— 1950. The Urban Revolution. *Town Planning Review, 21.*

———— 1951. *Social Evolution*, London.

———— 1958. *The Prehistory of European Society*, London.

Clark, G. 1969. *World Prehistory—a new outline*, Cambridge.

Clark, G. and Piggott, S. 1965. *Prehistoric Societies*, London.

Clark, K. 1971. *Civilisation*, London.

DeCoulanges, F. 1955. *The Ancient City*, (originally published 1864).

Daniel, G. 1968. *The First Civilisations*, New York.

Engels, F. 1891. *The Origin of the Family, Private Property and the State*, (Ed. by E. B. Leacock, International Publishers, New York, 1972).

Flannery, K. 1968. Archaeological systems theory and early Mesoamerica, *in* Meggers, B. (Ed.) *Anthropological Archeology in the Americas*, 67-87.

Gimbutas, M. 1965. *The Bronze Age Cultures of Eastern Europe*, The Hague.

———— 1970. Proto-Indo-European Culture *in* Cardona, G., Hoenigswald, H., and Senn A. (Eds.) *Indo-European and Indo-Europeans*, Pennsylvania.

Goodenough, W. 1970. The Evolution of Pastoralism and Indo-European Origins *in* Cardona, G., Hoenigswald H., and Senn A. (Eds.) *Indo European and Indo-Europeans*. Pennsylvania.

Hassall, M. 1972. Roman urbanization in western Europe, *in* Ucko P., Tringham, R., and Dimbleby G. (Eds.), *Man, Settlement and Urbanism*, London, 857-862.

Hawkes, C. 1939. *The prehistoric foundations of Europe*, London.

———— 1954. Archaeological theory and method: some suggestions from the Old World, *American Anthropologist, LVI*, 155-168.

Hawkins, G. 1965. *Stonehenge Decoded*, New York.

Hood, S. 1967. The Tărtăria Tablets, *Antiquity XLI*, 99-113.

Kluckhohn, C. 1960. The Moral Order in the Expanding Society, *in* Kraeling, C. and Adams, R. McC. (Eds.) *City Invincible: an Oriental Institute Symposium,* Chicago.

Kroeber, A. L. 1962. *A Roster of Civilisations and Culture,* Chicago.

Moberg C-A. 1962. Northern Europe *in* Braidwood R. and Willey G. (Eds.) *Courses towards Urban Life,* Chicago, 309-329.

Morgan, L. 1877, *Ancient Society,* (Ed. by Leacock, New York, 1963).

Nestor, I. 1970. Les Grands Problèmes de l'Heritage de l'Époque des Metaux. *Sources Archéologiques de la Civilisation Européenne,* 69-74, Bucuresti.

Piggott, S. 1965. *Ancient Europe,* Edinburgh.

———— 1972. Conclusion, *in* Ucko, P., Tringham, R. and Dimbleby, G. (Eds.), *Man, Settlement and Urbanism,* 947-953.

Pittioni, R. 1962. Southern Middle Europe and Southeast Europe *in* Braidwood R. and Willey, G. (Eds.) *Courses Towards Urban Life,* Chicago.

Pollard, S. 1968. *The Idea of Progress,* London.

Renfrew, A. C. 1968. Wessex without Mycenae, *Ann. Brit. School of Arch. in Athens,* 63 277.

———— 1970. New Configurations in Old World Archaeology, *World Archaeology II,* 199.

———— 1972. *The Emergence of Civilisation,* Cambridge.

———— 1973. Beyond a subsistence economy: the evolution of social organisation in prehistoric Europe. *Reconstruction of Complex Societies,* An International Symposium organised by the Cambridge Seminar, Cambridge, Mass.

Schuchhardt, C. 1926, *Alteuropa,* Berlin and Leipzig.

Tringham, R. 1972. Territorial demarcation of prehistoric settlements, *in* Ucko, P., Tringham R. and Dimbleby, G. (Eds.) *Man, settlement and urbanism,* London, 463.

———— 1973. Comments on Renfrew's paper, *Reconstruction of Complex Societies,* An International symposium organised by the Cambridge Seminar, Cambridge, Mass.

Vlassa, N. 1963. Chronology of the Neolithic of Transilvania in the light of the Tărtăria settlement's stratigraphy, *Dacia VII* 485-494.

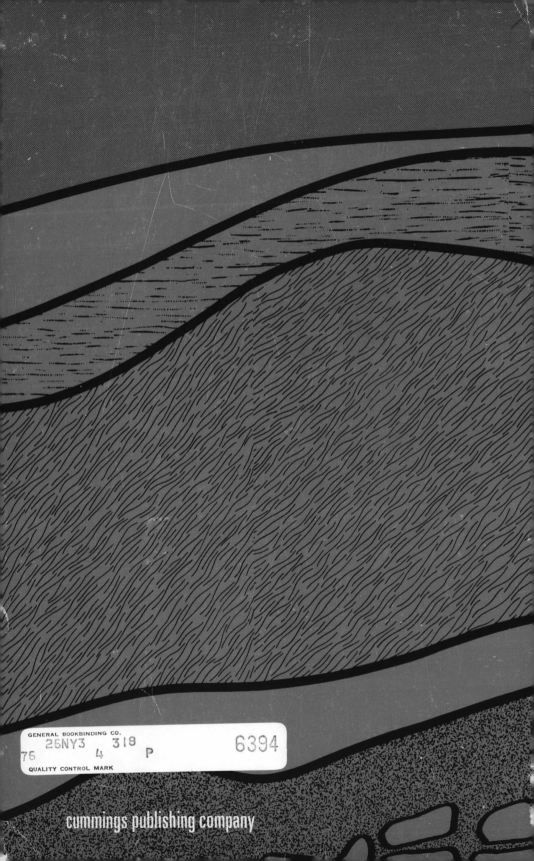

cummings publishing company